Chambers
mini book of facts

Chambers

Chambers

An imprint of Chambers Harrap Publishers Ltd

7 Hopetoun Crescent

Edinburgh

EH7 4AY

© Chambers Harrap Publishers Ltd 2007

This edition published by Chambers Harrap Publishers Ltd 2007

Previously published as *Chambers Super-Mini Book of Facts*

First edition published 1999

Second edition published 2001

Third edition published 2003

Fourth edition published 2005

A CIP catalogue record for this book is available from the British Library.

ISBN: 978 0550 10288 1

Editors: Vicky Aldus and Katie Brooks

Data Management: Ruth O'Donovan

Prepress: Becky Pickard

Publishing Manager: Camilla Rockwood

This book contains information originally assembled for *Chambers Book of Facts* (2007). The editors would like to thank Catherine Gaunt, Edward Gibbes, Hilary Marsden, Michael Munro, Christopher Riches, Marian Sheil, Wendy Smith and Helen Treacy for their contributions to that title.

Designed and typeset by Chambers Harrap Publishers Ltd, Edinburgh

Printed and bound in Italy by Legoprint

CONTENTS

iv

ARTS AND CULTURE

THOUGHT AND BELIEF

SPORTS AND GAMES

ALPHABETICAL CONTENTS

x

ABBREVIATIONS

AD	Anno Domini
admin	administration
Ave	Avenue
BC	Before Christ
c	century
c.	circa
C	Celsius (centigrade)
Chin	Chinese
CIS	Commonwealth of Independent States
cm	centimetre(s)
Co	County
cont.	continued
cu	cubic
cwt	hundredweight
e	estimate
E	East(ern)
eg	for example (*exempli gratia*)
Eng	English
F	Fahrenheit
fl	flourished (*floruit*)
fl oz	fluid ounce(s)
Fr	French
ft	foot (feet)
g	gram(s)
gal	gallons
Ger	German
Gr	Greek
h	hour(s)
ha	hectare(s)
Hung	Hungarian
I(s)	Island(s)
ie	that is (*id est*)
in	inch(es)

Ital	Italian
Jap	Japanese
K	Kelvin
kg	kilogram(s)
kJ	kilojoules
l	litre(s)
L	Lake
Lat	Latin
lb	pound(s)
m	metre(s)
mi	mile(s)
mm	millimetre(s)
Mt	Mount(ain)
Mts	Mountains
N	North(ern)
no.	number
oz	ounce(s)
p(p)	page(s)
pop	population
pt	pint(s)
R	River
Russ	Russian
S	South(ern)
sec	second(s)
Span	Spanish
sq	square
St	Saint
Sta	Santa
Ste	Sainte
Swed	Swedish
TV	television
UT	Unified Team
W	West(ern)
yd	yard(s)

SPACE

Planetary data

| Planet | Distance from Sun (million km) | | Planet year | Planet day (equatorial) | Diameter (equatorial) km |
	Maximum	Minimum			
Mercury	69.4	46.8	88d	58d 16h	4878
Venus	109.0	107.6	224.7d	243d	12104
Earth	152.6	147.4	365.256d	23h 56m	12756
Mars	249.2	207.3	687d	24h 37m 23s	6794
Jupiter	817.4	741.6	11.86y	9h 50m 30s	142800
Saturn	1512	1346	29.46y	10h 14m	120536
Uranus	3011	2740	84.01y	16–28h[1]	51118
Neptune	4543	4466	164.79y	18–20h[1]	49492

y: Earth years   d: Earth days   h: hours   m: minutes   s: seconds   km: kilometres
[1] Different latitudes rotate at different speeds.

Dwarf planets

In 2006, the International Astronomical Union (IAU) created a new category of 'dwarf planets' and reclassified Pluto as such, along with two other celestial bodies. Dwarf planets are objects that orbit the sun and are massive enough to be nearly spherical in shape, but differ from planets as they do not have a clear neighbourhood around their orbit.

Dwarf planet	Region	Diameter	Classification date
Ceres	Asteroid belt	975 × 909km	Aug 2006
Eris	Scattered disc	2400 ± 100km	Aug 2006
Pluto	Kuiper belt	2306 ± 20km	Aug 2006

Sun data

Physical characteristics of the Sun

Diameter	1392530km/864950mi
Volume	1.414×10^{18}km³/3.388×10^{17} cu mi
Mass	1.9891×10^{30}kg/4.385×10^{30} lb

Density (water = 1)

Mean density of entire Sun	1.410g cm⁻³
Interior (centre of Sun)	150g cm⁻³
Surface (photosphere)	10^{-3}g cm⁻³
Chromosphere	10^{-6}g cm⁻³
Low corona	1.7×10^{-16}g cm⁻³

Temperature

Interior (centre)	15 000 000K
Surface (photosphere)	6 050K
Sunspot umbra (typical)	4 240K
Penumbra (typical)	5 680K
Chromosphere	4 300 to 50 000K
Corona	800 000 to 5 000 00K

Rotation (as seen from Earth)

Of solar equator	26.8 days
At solar latitude 30°	28.2 days
At solar latitude 60°	30.8 days

Chemical composition of photosphere

Element	% weight
Hydrogen	73.46
Helium	24.85
Oxygen	0.77
Carbon	0.29
Iron	0.16
Neon	0.12
Nitrogen	0.09
Silicon	0.07
Magnesium	0.05
Sulphur	0.04
Other	0.10

Solar system

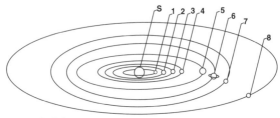

S = Sun
1 = Mercury
2 = Venus
3 = Earth
4 = Mars
5 = Jupiter
6 = Saturn
7 = Uranus
8 = Neptune

Total and annular solar eclipses 2001–20

The eclipse begins in the first country named. In an annular eclipse, part of the Sun remains visible.

Date	Type of eclipse	Visibility path
2001 Jun 21	Total	S Atlantic, S Africa, Madagascar
2001 Dec 14	Annular	Pacific, Central America
2002 Jun 10	Annular	Indonesia, Pacific, Mexico
2002 Dec 4	Total	S Africa, Indian Ocean, Australia
2003 May 31	Annular	Iceland, Greenland
2003 Nov 23	Total	Antarctic
2005 Apr 8	Annular / Total	Pacific, Panama, Venezuela
2005 Oct 3	Annular	Atlantic, Spain, Libya, Indian Ocean
2006 Mar 29	Total	Atlantic, Libya, Turkey, Russia
2006 Sep 22	Annular	Guyana, Atlantic, Indian Ocean
2008 Feb 7	Annular	Antarctic
2008 Aug 1	Total	Arctic, Siberia, China
2009 Jan 26	Annular	S Atlantic, Indian Ocean, Borneo
2009 Jul 22	Total	India, China, Pacific
2010 Jan 15	Annular	Africa, Indian Ocean, China
2010 Jul 11	Total	Pacific, S Chile
2012 May 20–21	Annular	China, N Pacific, N America
2012 Nov 13	Total	N Australia, Pacific
2013 May 9–10	Annular	Australia, Pacific
2013 Nov 3	Total	Atlantic, central Africa, Ethiopia
2015 Mar 20	Total	N Atlantic, Arctic
2016 Mar 9	Total	Indonesia, Pacific
2016 Sep 1	Annular	Atlantic, Africa, Madagascar, Indian Ocean
2017 Feb 26	Annular	Pacific, S America, Atlantic, Africa
2017 Aug 21	Total	Pacific, N America, Atlantic
2019 Jul 2	Total	Pacific, S America
2019 Dec 26	Annular	Middle East, Sri Lanka, Indonesia, Pacific
2020 Jun 21	Annular	Africa, Middle East, China, Pacific
2020 Dec 12	Total	Pacific, S America, Atlantic

Lunar eclipses 2001–20

Date	Type of eclipse	Time of mid-eclipse UT[1]	Where visible
2001 Jan 9	Total	20.22	Europe, Asia, Africa
2001 Jul 5	Partial	14.57	Asia, Australia, Pacific
2003 May 16	Total	03.41	Americas, Europe, Africa
2003 Nov 9	Total	01.20	Americas, Europe, Africa, W Asia
2004 May 4	Total	20.32	Europe, Africa, Asia
2004 Oct 28	Total	03.05	Americas, Europe, Africa
2005 Oct 17	Partial	12.05	E Asia, Pacific, N America
2006 Sep 7	Partial	18.53	Australia, Asia, E Africa

Date	Type of eclipse	Time of mid-eclipse UT[1]	Where visible
2007 Mar 3	Total	23.22	Europe, Asia, Africa
2007 Aug 28	Total	10.39	Australia, Pacific, part of N America
2008 Feb 21	Total	03.27	Americas, Europe, Africa
2008 Aug 16	Partial	21.12	Europe, Africa, W Asia
2009 Dec 31	Partial	19.23	Asia, Africa, Europe
2010 Jun 26	Partial	11.39	Pacific Rim
2010 Dec 21	Total	08.17	N and S America
2011 Jun 15	Total	20.12	Asia, Africa, Europe
2011 Dec 10	Total	14.32	Pacific, Australia, E Asia
2012 Jun 4	Partial	11.03	Pacific, Australasia
2013 Apr 25	Partial	20.09	Asia, Africa, Europe
2014 Apr 14	Total	07.47	N and S America
2014 Oct 8	Total	10.54	Pacific, Australia, W Americas
2015 Apr 4	Partial	12.01	Pacific, Australasia
2015 Sep 28	Total	02.47	Africa, Europe, Americas
2017 Aug 7	Partial	18.21	Asia, Africa, Australia
2018 Jan 31	Total	13.30	Pacific, Australia, Asia
2018 Jul 27	Total	20.22	Asia, Africa, part of Europe
2019 Jan 21	Total	05.12	Americas, part of Europe
2019 Jul 16	Partial	21.31	Asia, Africa, Europe

[1] Universal Time, equivalent to Greenwich Mean Time (GMT).

The lunar 'seas'

Latin name	English name	Latin name	English name
Lacus Mortis	Lake of Death	Mare Serenitatis	Sea of Serenity
Lacus Somniorum	Lake of Dreams	Mare Smythii	Smyth's Sea
Mare Australe	Southern Sea	Mare Spumans	Foaming Sea
Mare Crisium	Sea of Crises	Mare Tranquillitatis	Sea of Tranquillity
Mare Fecunditatis	Sea of Fertility	Mare Undarum	Sea of Waves
Mare Frigoris	Sea of Cold	Mare Vaporum	Sea of Vapours
Mare Humboldtianum	Humboldt's Sea	Oceanus Procellarum	Ocean of Storms
Mare Humorum	Sea of Moisture	Palus Epidemiarum	Marsh of Epidemics
Mare Imbrium	Sea of Showers	Palus Nebularum	Marsh of Mists
Mare Ingenii[1]	Sea of Geniuses	Palus Putredinis	Marsh of Decay
Mare Marginis	Marginal Sea	Palus Somnii	Marsh of Sleep
Mare Moscoviense[1]	Moscow Sea	Sinus Aestuum	Bay of Heats
Mare Nectaris	Sea of Nectar	Sinus Iridum	Bay of Rainbows
Mare Nubium	Sea of Clouds	Sinus Medii	Central Bay
Mare Orientale[1]	Eastern Sea	Sinus Roris	Bay of Dew

[1] On the far side of the Moon.

The constellations

Latin name	English name	Latin name	English name
Andromeda	Andromeda	Lacerta	Lizard
Antlia	Air Pump	Leo	Lion
Apus	Bird of Paradise	Leo Minor	Little Lion
Aquarius	Water Bearer	Lepus	Hare
Aquila	Eagle	Libra	Scales
Ara	Altar	Lupus	Wolf
Aries	Ram	Lynx	Lynx
Auriga	Charioteer	Lyra	Harp
Boötes	Herdsman	Mensa	Table
Caelum	Chisel	Microscopium	Microscope
Camelopardalis	Giraffe	Monoceros	Unicorn
Cancer	Crab	Musca	Fly
Canes Venatici	Hunting Dogs	Norma	Level
Canis Major	Great Dog	Octans	Octant
Canis Minor	Little Dog	Ophiuchus	Serpent Bearer
Capricornus	Sea Goat	Orion	Orion
Carina	Keel	Pavo	Peacock
Cassiopeia	Cassiopeia	Pegasus	Winged Horse
Centaurus	Centaur	Perseus	Perseus
Cepheus	Cepheus	Phoenix	Phoenix
Cetus	Whale	Pictor	Easel
Chamaeleon	Chameleon	Pisces	Fishes
Circinus	Compasses	Piscis Austrinus	Southern Fish
Columba	Dove	Puppis	Ship's Stern
Coma Berenices	Berenice's Hair	Pyxis	Mariner's Compass
Corona Australis	Southern Crown	Reticulum	Net
Corona Borealis	Northern Crown	Sagitta	Arrow
Corvus	Crow	Sagittarius	Archer
Crater	Cup	Scorpius	Scorpion
Crux	Southern Cross	Sculptor	Sculptor
Cygnus	Swan	Scutum	Shield
Delphinus	Dolphin	Serpens	Serpent
Dorado	Swordfish	Sextans	Sextant
Draco	Dragon	Taurus	Bull
Equuleus	Little Horse	Telescopium	Telescope
Eridanus	River Eridanus	Triangulum	Triangle
Fornax	Furnace	Triangulum Australe	Southern Triangle
Gemini	Twins	Tucana	Toucan
Grus	Crane	Ursa Major	Great Bear
Hercules	Hercules	Ursa Minor	Little Bear
Horologium	Clock	Vela	Sails
Hydra	Sea Serpent	Virgo	Virgin
Hydrus	Water Snake	Volans	Flying Fish
Indus	Indian	Vulpecula	Fox

The 20 brightest stars

The apparent brightness of a star is represented by a number called its magnitude. The larger the number, the fainter the star. The faintest stars visible to the naked eye are slightly fainter than magnitude 6. Only about 6,000 of the billions of stars in the sky are visible to the naked eye.

Star name	Distance (light years)	Apparent magnitude	Absolute magnitude
Sirius A	8.7	-1.46	+1.4
Canopus	98	-0.72	-3.1
Arcturus	36	-0.06	-0.3
Rigil Kentaurus	4.2	-0.01	+4.4
Vega	26.5	+0.04	+0.5
Capella	45	+0.05	-0.6
Rigel	900	+0.14	-7.1
Procyon	11.4	+0.37	+2.6
Betelgeuse	520	+0.41	-5.6
Achernar	118	+0.51	-2.3
Hadar	490	+0.63	-5.2
Altair	16.5	+0.76	+2.2
Aldebaran	68	+0.86	-0.7
Spica	220	+0.91	-3.3
Antares	520	+0.92	-5.1
Fomalhaut	22.6	+1.15	+2.0
Pollux	35	+1.16	+1.0
Deneb	1 600	+1.26	-7.1
Beta Crucis	490	+1.28	-4.6
Regulus	84	+1.36	-0.7

The 20 nearest stars

The Sun, the star of our own solar system, is excluded.

Star name	Distance (light years)	Apparent magnitude	Absolute magnitude
Proxima Centauri	4.3	+11.05	+15.5
Alpha Centauri A	4.3	-0.01	+4.4
Alpha Centauri B	4.3	+1.33	+5.7
Barnard's Star	5.9	+9.54	+13.3
Wolf 359	7.6	+13.53	+16.7
Lalande 21185	8.1	+7.50	+10.5
Sirius A	8.6	-1.46	+1.4
Sirius B	8.6	+8.68	+11.6
Luyten 726-8A	8.9	+12.45	+15.3

Star name	Distance (light years)	Apparent magnitude	Absolute magnitude
UV 726-8B	8.9	+12.95	+15.3
Ross 154	9.4	+10.60	+13.3
Ross 248	10.3	+12.29	+14.8
Epsilon Eridani	10.8	+3.73	+6.1
Ross 128	10.8	+11.10	+13.5
Luyten 789-6	10.8	+12.18	+14.6
61 Cygni A	11.1	+5.22	+7.6
61 Cygni B	11.1	+6.03	+8.4
Epsilon Indi	11.2	+4.68	+7.0
Procyon A	11.2	+0.37	+2.7
Procyon B	11.2	+10.70	+13.0

Significant space missions

Launch date	Mission	Nation/ Agency	Event description
1957 Oct 4	Sputnik 1	USSR	First satellite to orbit Earth
1957 Nov 3	Sputnik 2	USSR	First living creature in space; dog (Laika) dies
1958 Feb 1	Explorer 1	USA	Discovered radiation belt (Van Allen)
1959 Jan 2	Luna 1	USSR	Escaped Earth's gravity
1959 Feb 17	Vanguard 2	USA	Took photo of Earth
1959 Sep 12	Luna 2	USSR	Made a lunar impact
1959 Oct 4	Luna 3	USSR	Took photo of far side of Moon
1960 Apr 1	TIROS 1	USA	First weather satellite
1960 Apr 13	Transit 1B	USA	First navigation satellite
1960 Aug 12	ECHO 1	USA	First communications satellite
1960 Aug 19	Sputnik 5	USSR	Two dogs recovered alive
1961 Apr 12	Vostok 1	USSR	First man in space; orbits Earth
1962 Aug 26	Mariner 2	USA	Venus flyby
1963 Jun 16	Vostok 6	USSR	First woman in space; orbits Earth
1964 Jul 28	Ranger VII	USA	Close-up television pictures of the Moon
1964 Nov 28	Mariner 4	USA	Mars flyby pictures
1965 Mar 18	Voshkod 2	USSR	First space walk
1965 Apr 6	Early Bird	USA	Commercial geostationary communications satellite
1965 Nov 16	Venera 3	USSR	Venus impact
1965 Nov 26	A-1 Asterix	France	First French satellite
1965 Dec 15	Gemini 7–A	USA	First manned rendezvous (with Gemini 7)

Launch date	Mission	Nation/Agency	Event description
1966 Jan 31	Luna 9	USSR	Lunar soft landing
1966 Mar 16	Gemini 8	USA	First manned docking
1966 Mar 31	Luna 10	USSR	Lunar orbiter
1966 May 30	Surveyor 1	USA	Lunar soft landing
1966 Aug 10	Lunar Orbiter 1	USA	US lunar orbiter
1967 Oct 22–28	Cosmos 186/188	USSR	Automatic docking
1967 Nov 29	WRESAT	Australia	First Australian satellite
1968 Sep 14	Zond 5	USSR	Animals orbit the Moon
1968 Dec 21	Apollo VIII	USA	First manned orbit of Moon
1969 Jan 14	Soyuz 4	USSR	Transfer of crews
1969 Jan 15	Soyuz 5	USSR	Transfer of crews
1969 Jul 16	Apollo XI	USA	First men on Moon
1970 Feb 11	Oshumi	Japan	First Japanese satellite
1970 Apr 24	Long March	China	First Chinese satellite
1970 Aug 17	Venera 7	USSR	Venus soft landing
1970 Sep 12	Luna 16	USSR	Unmanned sample return
1970 Nov 10	Luna 17	USSR	Unmanned Moon rover
1971 Apr 19	Salyut 1	USSR	First space station launched
1971 May 19	Mars 2	USSR	Mars orbit; first crash landing
1971 May 28	Mars 3	USSR	Mars soft landing
1971 May 30	Mariner 9	USA	Mars orbit
1971 Oct 28	Prospero	UK	First UK satellite
1972 Mar 3	Pioneer 10	USA	Jupiter flyby; crossed Pluto orbit; escaped solar system
1973 Apr 6	Pioneer 11	USA	Jupiter flyby; Saturn flyby
1973 Nov 3	Mariner 10	USA	Venus flyby; three Mercury flybys
1975 Jun 8	Venera 9	USSR	Venus orbit
1975 Jul 15	Apollo/Soyuz	USA/USSR	First manned international mission; craft dock in space
1975 Aug 20	Viking 1	USA	Spacecraft operations on Mars surface
1977 Aug 20	Voyager 2	USA	Jupiter flyby; Saturn flyby; Uranus flyby; Neptune flyby
1977 Sep 5	Voyager 1	USA	Jupiter flyby; Saturn flyby
1978 Aug 12	ISEE-C	USA	Comet intercept
1979 Dec 24	Ariane/CAT	ESA	European launcher
1980 Jul 18	Rohini	India	Indian-launched satellite
1981 Apr 12	STS 1	USA	First space shuttle flight
1981 Nov 12	STS 2	USA	Launch vehicle re-use
1983 Jun 27	Soyuz T9	USSR	Construction in space
1984 Dec 15	Vega 1	USSR	Comet Halley flyby
1985 Jul 2	Giotto	ESA	Close-up of comet Halley
1986	Mir	USSR	Main module of space station launched

Launch date	Mission	Nation/Agency	Event description
1988 Nov 15	Buran	USSR	Unmanned space shuttle
1989 Oct 18	Galileo	USA	Close-up photographs of an asteroid
1990 Jan 24	Muses-A	Japan	Moon orbiter
1990 Apr 5	Pegsat	USA	First airborne launch
1990 Apr 24	Hubble Space Telescope	USA/ESA	Space telescope
1990 Dec 2	Soyuz TM11	USSR	Paying passenger flight
1991 Apr 5	CGRO	USA	Gamma-ray astronomy
1991 May 18	Soyuz TM12	USSR	First Briton (Helen Sharman) in space
1992 Sep 12	STS 47	USA	50th space shuttle flight
1994 Jan 25	Clementine	USA	Lunar/asteroid exploration
1994 May 19	P. 91 (STEP 2)	USA	Explosion scattered space debris
1995 Nov 17	Infrared Space Observatory	ESA	Space observatory
1996 Feb 17	NEAR	USA	Asteroid rendezvous
1996 Nov 7	Mars Global Survey	USA	Mars survey
1996 Dec 4	Mars Pathfinder	USA	Mars surface exploration
1997 Feb 12	Haruka	Japan	Radio astronomy
1997 May 5	Iridium	USA	Communication constellation
1997 Oct 15	Cassini/Huygens	USA	Saturn/Titan study in 2004
1998 Jan 6	Lunar Prospector	USA	Lunar surface investigation
1998 Oct 24	Deep Space 1	USA	Ion propulsion spacecraft
1998 Oct 29	STS 95	USA	John Glenn's return to space
1998 Nov 20	Zarya	USA/Russia/ESA/Canada/Japan	First launch in International Space Station assembly
1998 Dec 11	MCO	USA	Mars climate survey
1999 Jan 3	MPL	USA	Mars surface investigation
1999 Feb 7	Stardust	USA	Capture and analysis of comet particles
1999 Nov 22	Shenzhou	China	First Chinese unmanned spacecraft
2000 Jul 12	Zvezda	USA/Russia/ESA/Canada/Japan	International Space Station command module
2000 Jul 16	Cluster II	ESA	Earth's magnetosphere survey
2000 Aug 9	Cluster II	ESA	Earth's magnetosphere survey
2000 Oct 11	STS 92	USA	100th space shuttle flight
2000 Oct 31	Expedition 1	USA/Russia/ESA/Canada/Japan	First residents of International Space Station
2001 Jan 24	Progress M1	Russia	Brought Mir back to earth
2001 Apr 28	Soyuz TM32	Russia	First space tourist goes to International Space Station

Launch date	Mission	Nation/ Agency	Event description
2003 Jun 2	Mars Express	ESA	Mars surface imaging; survey of Mars atmosphere and sub-surface
2003 Jun 10	Mars Rover Spirit	USA	Mars surface investigation
2003 Jul 7	Mars Rover Opportunity	USA	Mars surface investigation
2003 Oct 15	Shenzhou 5	China	First Chinese manned spacecraft
2004 Mar 2	Rosetta	ESA	Comet orbiter and lander
2004 Jun 21	SpaceShipOne	private	First private spacecraft
2004 Aug 3	Messenger	USA	Mercury orbiter
2005 Jan 12	Deep Impact	USA	First comet impact
2005 Aug 12	Mars Reconnaissance Orbiter	USA	Mars surface imaging
2005 Nov 9	Venus Express	ESA	Venus exploration
2006 Jan 19	New Horizons	USA	Pluto flyby; Jupiter flyby
2006 Sep 18	Expedition 14	USA	International Space Station crew delivery
2006 Oct 25	Solar Terrestrial Relations Observatories (STEREO)	USA	Solar imaging

EARTH

There are no universally agreed estimates of the natural phenomena given in this section. Surveys make use of different criteria for identifying natural boundaries, and use different techniques of measurement. The sizes of continents, oceans, seas, deserts and rivers are particularly subject to variation.

Vital statistics

Age	4 600 000 000 years (accurate to within a very small percentage of possible error)
Area	509 600 000 sq km / 197 000 000 sq mi
Mass	5976×10^{24} kg
Land surface	148 000 000 sq km / 57 000 000 sq mi (c.29% of total area)
Water surface	361 600 000 sq km / 140 000 000 sq mi (c.71% of total area)
Circumference at equator	40 076 km / 24 902 mi
Circumference of meridian	40 000 km / 24 860 mi

Continents

Name	Area sq km	Area sq mi	Percentage of total land mass
Africa	30 293 000	11 696 000	20.2%
Antarctica	13 975 000	5 396 000	9.3%
Asia	44 493 000	17 179 000	29.6%
Europe[1]	10 245 000	3 956 000	6.8%
North America	24 454 000	9 442 000	16.3%
Oceania	8 945 000	3 454 000	6%
South America	17 838 000	6 887 000	11.9%

[1] Including the former western USSR.

Highest mountains

Name	Height[1] m	ft	Location
Everest	8850	29 030	China / Nepal
K2	8610	28 250	Kashmir / Jammu
Kangchenjunga	8590	28 170	India / Nepal
Lhotse	8500	27 890	China / Nepal
Kangchenjunga S Peak	8470	27 800	India / Nepal
Makalu I	8470	27 800	China / Nepal
Kangchenjunga W Peak	8420	27 620	India / Nepal

Name	Height[1] m	ft	Location
Lhotse E Peak	8380	27500	China/Nepal
Dhaulagiri	8170	26810	Nepal
Cho Oyu	8150	26750	China/Nepal
Manaslu	8130	26660	Nepal
Nanga Parbat	8130	26660	Kashmir/Jammu
Annapurna I	8080	26500	Nepal
Gasherbrum I	8070	26470	Kashmir/Jammu
Broad Peak I	8050	26400	Kashmir/Jammu
Gasherbrum II	8030	26360	Kashmir/Jammu
Gosainthan	8010	26290	China
Broad Peak Central	8000	26250	Kashmir/Jammu
Gasherbrum III	7950	26090	Kashmir/Jammu
Annapurna II	7940	26040	Nepal
Nanda Devi	7820	25660	India
Rakaposhi	7790	25560	Kashmir
Kamet	7760	25450	India
Ulugh Muztagh	7720	25340	China (Tibet)
Tirich Mir	7690	25230	Pakistan
Muz Tag Ata	7550	24760	China
Imeni Ismail Samani Peak (Communism Peak)	7490	24590	Tajikistan
Pobedy Peak	7440	24410	China/Kyrgyzstan
Aconcagua	6960	22830	Argentina
Ojos del Salado	6910	22660	Argentina/Chile

[1] Heights are given to the nearest 10m/ft.

Largest deserts

Name/Location	Area[1] sq km	sq mi
Sahara, N Africa	8600000	3320000
Arabian, SW Asia	2330000	900000
Gobi, Mongolia and NE China	1166000	450000
Patagonian, Argentina	673000	260000
Great Victoria, SW Australia	647000	250000
Great Basin, SW USA	492000	190000
Chihuahuan, Mexico	450000	174000
Great Sandy, NW Australia	400000	154000
Sonoran, SW USA	310000	120000
Kyzyl Kum, Kazakhstan	300000	116000
Takla Makan, N China	270000	104000
Kalahari, SW Africa	260000	100000
Kara Kum, Turkmenistan	260000	100000
Kavir, Iran	260000	100000
Nubian, Sudan	260000	100000
Syrian, Saudi Arabia/Jordan/Syria/Iraq	260000	100000

Name/Location	Area[1] sq km	sq mi
Thar, India/Pakistan	200 000	77 000
Ust'-Urt, Kazakhstan	160 000	62 000
Bet-Pak-Dala, S Kazakhstan	155 000	60 000
Simpson, C Australia	145 000	56 000
Dzungaria, China	142 000	55 000
Atacama, Chile	140 000	54 000
Namib, SE Africa	134 000	52 000
Bolson de Mapimi, Mexico	130 000	50 000
Ordos, China	130 000	50 000
Sturt, SE Australia	130 000	50 000
Alashan, China	116 000	45 000

[1] Desert areas are very approximate, because clear physical boundaries may not occur.

Deepest caves

Name/Location	Depth m	ft
Jean Bernard, France	1 494	4 902
Snezhnaya, Georgia	1 340	4 396
Puertas de Illamina, Spain	1 338	4 390
Pierre-Saint-Martin, France	1 321	4 334
Sistema Huautla, Mexico	1 240	4 068
Berger, France	1 198	3 930
Vqerdi, Spain	1 195	3 921
Dachstein-Mammuthöhle, Austria	1 174	3 852
Zitu, Spain	1 139	3 737
Badalona, Spain	1 130	3 707
Batmanhöhle, Austria	1 105	3 625
Schneeloch, Austria	1 101	3 612
G E S Malaga, Spain	1 070	3 510
Lamprechtsofen, Austria	1 024	3 360

Oceans

Name	Area sq km	sq mi	Greatest depth		m	ft
Arctic	14 056 000	5 427 021	(4%)	Molloy Deep	5 680	18 635
Atlantic	76 762 000	29 637 808	(22%)	Puerto Rico Trench	8 648	28 372
Indian	68 556 000	26 469 471	(19%)	Java Trench	7 725	25 344
Pacific	155 557 000	60 060 557	(43%)	Mariana Trench	11 040	36 220
Southern	20 327 000	7 848 254	(6%)	South Sandwich Trench	7 235	23 737

Largest seas

Name/Location	Area[1] sq km	sq mi
Coral Sea	4791000	1850000
Arabian Sea	3863000	1492000
S China (Nan) Sea	3685000	1423000
Caribbean Sea	2718000	1050000
Mediterranean Sea	2516000	971000
Bering Sea	2304000	890000
Bay of Bengal	2172000	839000
Sea of Okhotsk	1590000	614000
Gulf of Mexico	1543000	596000
Gulf of Guinea	1533000	592000
Barents Sea	1405000	542000
Norwegian Sea	1383000	534000
Gulf of Alaska	1327000	512000
Hudson Bay	1232000	476000
Greenland Sea	1205000	465000
Arafura Sea	1037000	400000
Philippine Sea	1036000	400000
Sea of Japan (East Sea)	978000	378000
E Siberian Sea	901000	348000
Kara Sea	883000	341000
E China Sea	664000	256000
Andaman Sea	565000	218000
North Sea	520000	201000
Black Sea	508000	196000
Red Sea	453000	175000
Baltic Sea	414000	160000
Arabian Gulf	239000	92000
St Lawrence Gulf	238000	92000

Oceans are excluded.
[1] Areas are rounded to the nearest 1000 sq km/sq mi.

Largest islands

Name	Area[1] sq km	sq mi
Australia[2]	7692300	2970000
Greenland	2175600	840000
New Guinea	790000	305000
Borneo	737000	285000
Madagascar	587000	226600
Baffin	507000	195800
Sumatra	425000	164100
Honshu (Hondo)	228000	88000
Great Britain	219000	84600
Victoria Island, Canada	217300	83900

Name	Area[1] sq km	sq mi
Ellesmere Island, Canada	196 000	75 700
Celebes	174 000	67 200
South Island, New Zealand	151 000	58 300
Java	129 000	49 800
North Island, New Zealand	114 000	44 000
Cuba	110 900	42 800
Newfoundland	109 000	42 100
Luzon	105 000	40 500
Iceland	103 000	39 800
Mindanao	94 600	36 500
Novaya Zemlya (two islands)	90 600	35 000
Ireland	84 100	32 500
Hokkaido	78 500	30 300
Hispaniola	77 200	29 800
Sakhalin	75 100	29 000
Tierra del Fuego	71 200	27 500

[1] Areas are rounded to the nearest 100 sq km/sq mi.
[2] Sometimes discounted, as a continent.

Major island groups

Name	Country	Sea/Ocean	Constituent islands
Aeolian	Italy	Mediterranean	Alicudi, Basiluzzo, Filicudi, Lipari, Salina, Stromboli, Vulcano
Åland	Finland	Gulf of Bothnia	over 300 islands including Ahvenanmaa, Eckero, Fasta Åland, Lemland, Lumparland, Vardo
Aleutian	USA	Pacific	five island groups: Andreanof, Four Mountains, Fox, Near, Rat
Alexander	Canada	Pacific	Admiralty, Baranof, Chichagof, Dall, Kupreanof, Prince of Wales, Revillagigedo, Wrangell
Andaman	India	Bay of Bengal	over 300 islands including Baratang, Little Andaman, Middle Andaman, N Andaman, Rutland, S Andaman
Antilles, Greater	—	Caribbean	Cuba, Hispaniola, Jamaica, Puerto Rico
Antilles, Lesser	—	Caribbean	three island groups: Leeward, Netherlands Antilles, Windward
Azores	Portugal	Atlantic	nine main islands: Corvo, Faial, Flores, Graciosa, Pico, Santa Maria, São Jorge, São Miguel, Terceira
Bahamas, The	The Bahamas	Atlantic	700 islands including Acklins, Andros, Berry, Cat, Cay, Crooked, Exuma, Grand Bahama, Great Abaco, Inagua, Long, Mayaguana, New Providence, Ragged

Name	Country	Sea/Ocean	Constituent islands
Balearic	Spain	Mediterranean	Cabrera, Formentera, Ibiza, Majorca, Menorca
Bay	Honduras	Caribbean	Guanja, Roatan, Utila
Bismarck Archipelago	Papua New Guinea	Pacific	c.200 islands including Admiralty, Duke of York, Lavonga, Mussau, New Britain, New Hanover, New Ireland, Vitu
Bissagos	Guinea-Bissau	Atlantic	15 islands including Caravela, Formosa, Orango, Roxa
Canadian Arctic Archipelago	Canada	Arctic	main islands: Baffin, Banks, Ellesmere, Victoria
Canary	Spain	Atlantic	main islands: Fuerteventura, Gomera, Graciosa, Gran Canaria, Hierro, Lanzarote, La Palma, Tenerife
Cape Verde	Cape Verde	Atlantic	10 islands divided into Barlaventos (windward) group: Boa Vista, Sal, Santa Luzia, Santo Antão, São Nicolau, São Vicente; and Sotaventos (leeward) group: Brava, Fogo, Maio, São Tiago
Caroline	—	Pacific	c.680 islands including Kusac, Palau, Ponape, Truk, Yap
Chagos Archipelago	UK	Indian	Blenheim Reef, Diego Garcia, Egmont, Great Chagos Bank, Peros Banhos, Salomon, Speakers Bank
Channel	UK	English	Alderney, Jersey, Guernsey, Herm, Sark
Chonos Archipelago	Chile	Pacific	main islands: Benjamin, Chaffers, James, Luz, Melchior, Victoria
Commander	Russia	Bering Sea	Arii Kamen, Bering, Medny, Toporkov
Comoro	Comoros and France (Mayotte)	Mozambique Channel	Anjouan, Grand Comore, Mayotte, Mohéli, Pamanzi
Cook	New Zealand	Pacific	three island groups: High Cook (includes Mangaia, Rarotonga), Low, Northern Cook (includes Palmerston)
Cyclades	Greece	Aegean	c.220 islands including Amorges, Anafi, Andros, Antiparos, Delos, Ios, Kéa, Mikonos, Milos, Naxos, Paros, Kithnos, Sérifos, Tinos, Siros
Denmark	Denmark	Baltic	main islands: Zealand, Falster, Fyn, Lolland, North Jutland, Bornholm
Dodecanese	Greece	Aegean	12 islands including Astipalaia, Kálimnos, Kárpathos, Kásos, Khalki, Kós, Léros, Pátmos, Rodos
Ellice	Tuvalu	Pacific	main islands: Funafuti, Nukefetau, Nukulailai, Nanumea
Falkland	UK	Atlantic	main islands: E Falkland, W Falkland
Faroe	Denmark	Atlantic	18 islands including Stromo, Ostero
Fiji	Fiji	Pacific	main islands: Vanua Levu, Viti Levu

Name	Country	Sea/Ocean	Constituent islands
Franz Josef Land ▶ Zemlya Frantsa-Iosifa			
Frisian, East	Germany and Denmark	North Sea	main islands: Baltrum, Borkum, Juist, Langeoog, Norderney, Spiekeroog, Wangerooge
Frisian, North	Germany and Denmark	North Sea	main islands: (German) Amrum, Föhr, Nordstrand, Pellworm, Sylt; (Danish) Fanø, Mandø, Rømø
Frisian, West	Netherlands	North Sea	main islands: Ameland, Griend, Schiermonnikoog, Texel, Terschelling, Vlieland
Galapagos	Ecuador	Pacific	main islands: Fernandina, Floreana, Isabela, San Cristóbal, Santa Cruz, Santiago
Gilbert	Kiribati	Pacific	main islands: Abaiang, Abemama, Beru, Butaritari, Nonouti, Tabiteuea, Tarawa
Gotland	Sweden	Baltic	main islands: Gotland, Fårö, Karlsö
Greenland	Denmark	N Atlantic/ Arctic	main islands: Greenland, Disko
Hawaiian	USA	Pacific	eight main islands: Hawaii, Kahoolawe, Kauai, Lanai, Maui, Molokai, Niihau, Oahu
Hebrides, Inner	UK	Atlantic	main islands: Coll, Eigg, Iona, Islay, Jura, Mull, Skye, Staffa, Tiree
Hebrides, Outer	UK	Atlantic	Barra, Benbecula, Harris, Lewis, Harris, N Uist, S Uist
Indonesia	Indonesia	Pacific	17 508 islands and islets including Celebes, Java, Kalimantan, Lesser Sundas, Moluccas, New Guinea (Papua), Sumatra
Ionian	Greece	Aegean	main islands: Ithaki, Kefallinia, Kerkira, Lefkada, Levkas, Paxi, Zakinthos
Japan	Japan	Pacific	main islands: Hokkaido, Honshu, Kyushu, Ryuku, Shikoku
Juan Fernández	Chile	Pacific	Más Afuera, Más á Tierra, Santa Clara
Kerguélen	France	Indian	Grande Terre (Kerguélen) and 300 islets
Kuril	Russia	Pacific	56 islands including Iturup, Kunashir, Onekotan, Paramushir, Shiaskhotan, Shikotanto, Shimushir, Shumsu, Urup
Laccadive	India	Arabian Sea	27 islands including Amindivi, Androth, Kavaratti, Laccadive, Minicoy
Line	Kiribati	Pacific	main islands: Christmas, Fanning, Washington
Lofoten	Norway	Norwegian Sea	main islands: Hinnøy, Austvågøy, Moskenes, Vestvågøy

Name	Country	Sea/Ocean	Constituent islands
Madeira	Portugal	Atlantic	Madeira, Desertas, Porto Santo, Selvagens
Malay Archipelago	Indonesia, Malaysia, Philippines	Pacific/Indian	main islands: Borneo, Celebes, Java, Luzon, Mindanao, New Guinea, Sumatra
Maldives	Maldives	Indian	19 clusters, main island: Male
Maltese	Malta	Mediterranean	main islands: Malta, Comino, Gozo, Manoel
Mariana	USA	Pacific	14 islands including Agrihan, Anatahan, Alamagan, Guguan, Pagan, Rota, Saipan, Tinian
Marquesas	France	Pacific	Northern group: Eiao, Hatutu, Motu Iti, Moto Oa, Motu One, Nuku Hiva, Ua Huka, Ua Pu; Southern group: Fatu Hiva, Fatu Huku, Hiva Oa, Moho Tani, Motu Nao, Tahuata, Terihi
Marshall	Marshall Islands	Pacific	main islands: Bikini, Enewetak, Jaluit, Kwajalein, Majuro, Rongelap, Wotho
Mascarene	—	Indian	main islands: Mauritius, Réunion, Rodrigues
Melanesia	—	Pacific	main groups of islands: Bismarck Archipelago, Fiji, Maluku, New Caledonia, Palau, Papua New Guinea, Solomon Islands, Torres Strait, Vanuatu
Micronesia	—	Pacific	main groups of islands: Caroline, Gilbert, Guam, Mariana, Marshall, Nauru
Newfoundland	Canada	Atlantic	Prince Edward, Anticosti
New Hebrides	Vanuatu	Pacific	main islands: Espíritu Santo, Ambrym, Aurora, Éfaté, Épi, Erromanga, Malakula, Pentecôte, Tanna
New Siberian	Russia	Arctic	main islands: Faddeyevsky, Kotelny, Great Lyakhovsky, Little Lyakhovsky
Nicobar	India	Bay of Bengal	main islands: Great Nicobar, Camorta with Nancowry, Car Nicobar, Katchal, Little Nicobar, Teressa
Novaya Zemlya	Russia	Arctic	two main islands: Severny, Yuzhny
Orkney	UK	North Sea	main islands: Mainland, Burray, Hoy, Rousay, Sanday, Shapinsay, South Ronaldsay, Stronsay, Westray
Pelagian	Italy	Mediterranean	Lampedusa, Lampione, Linosa
Philippines	Philippines	Pacific	over 7100 islands and islets; main islands: Bohol, Cebu, Leyte; Luzon, Masbate, Mindanao, Mindoro, Negros, Palawan, Panay, Samar

Name	Country	Sea/Ocean	Constituent islands
Polynesia	—	Pacific	main groups of islands: Cook, Easter, Ellice, French Polynesia, Hawaiian, Line, New Zealand, Phoenix, Pitcairn, Samoa, Society, Tokelau, Tonga, Samoa
Queen Charlotte	Canada	Pacific	main islands: Graham, Moresby
São Tomé and Príncipe	São Tomé and Príncipe	Atlantic	main islands: São Tomé, Príncipe
Scilly	UK	English Channel	c.140 islands including Bryher, St Agnes, St Martin's, St Mary's, Tresco
Severnaya Zemlya	Russia	Arctic	main islands: Bolshevik, Komsomolets, October Revolution, Pioneer, Schmidt
Seychelles	Seychelles	Indian	115 islands including Mahé, Bird, La Digue, Praslin, Silhouette
Shetland	UK	North Sea	over 100 islands including Mainland, Bressay, Fair Isle, Muckle Roe, Trondra, Unst, West Burra, Whalsay, Yell
Society	France	Pacific	two island groups: Windward, Leeward; main island: Tahiti
Solomon	Solomon Islands	Pacific	main islands: Choiseul, Guadalcanal, Malaita, New Georgia, Santa Isabel, Makira (San Cristobal)
South Orkney	UK	Southern	main islands: Coronation, Inaccessible, Laurie, Signy
South Shetland	UK	Southern	main islands: King George, Elephant, Clarence, Gibbs, Nelson, Livingstone, Greenwich, Snow, Deception, Smith
Sri Lanka	Sri Lanka	Indian	main islands: Sri Lanka, Mannar
Taiwan	Taiwan	China Sea/ Pacific	main islands: Taiwan, Lan Hsü, Lü Tao, Quemoy, the Pescadores
Tasmania	Australia	Tasman Sea	main islands: Tasmania, Bruny, Furneaux group, King
Tierra del Fuego	Argentina/ Chile	Pacific	main islands: Tierra del Fuego, Clarence, Dawson, Desolación, Diego Ramírez, Isla de los Estados (Staten), Hoste, Navarino, Santa Inés, Wollaston
Tres Marías	Mexico	Pacific	María Madre, María Magdalena, María Cleofás, San Juanito
Tristan da Cunha	UK	Atlantic	Tristan da Cunha, Gough, Inaccessible, Middle, Nightingale, Stoltenhoff
Tuamotu Archipelago	France	Pacific	island groups: Acteon, Disappointment, Duke of Gloucester, King George, Palliser, Raeffsky
Vesterålen	Norway	Norwegian Sea	main islands: Andøya, Hadseløy, Hinnøy, Langøya

Name	Country	Sea/Ocean	Constituent islands
Virgin	UK and USA	Caribbean	over 90 islands and islets including Anegada, Jost Van Dyke, Tortola, Virgin Gorda (UK) and St Croix, St John, St Thomas (USA)
Zanzibar	Tanzania	Indian	main islands: Zanzibar, Tumbatu, Kwale
Zemlya Frantsa-Iosifa	Russia	Arctic	c.191 islands including Aleksandry, Georga, Greem-Bell, Rudolf, Vilcheka

Largest lakes

	Area[1]	
Name/Location	sq km	sq mi
Caspian Sea, Iran/Russia/Turkmenistan/Kazakhstan/Azerbaijan	371 000	143 240[2]
Superior, USA/Canada	82 260	31 760[3]
Victoria, E Africa	62 940	24 300
Huron, USA/Canada	59 580	23 000[3]
Michigan, USA	58 020	22 400
Tanganyika, E Africa	32 000	12 360
Baikal, Russia	31 500	12 160
Great Bear, Canada	31 330	12 100
Great Slave, Canada	28 570	11 030
Erie, USA/Canada	25 710	9 930[3]
Winnipeg, Canada	24 390	9 420
Malawi/Nyasa, E Africa	22 490	8 680
Ontario, Canada	19 270	7 440[3]
Ladoga, Russia	18 130	7 000
Aral Sea, Uzbekistan/Kazakhstan	17 160	6 626[2]
Balkhash, Kazakhstan	17 000–22 000	6 560–8 490[2]
Maracaibo, Venezuela	13 010	5 020[4]
Patos, Brazil	10 140	3 920[4]
Chad, W Africa	10 000–26 000	3 860–10 040
Onega, Russia	9 800	3 780
Rudolf, E Africa	9 100	3 510
Eyre, Australia	8 800	3 400[4]
Titicaca, Peru/Bolivia	8 300	3 200

The Caspian and Aral Seas, being entirely surrounded by land, are classified as lakes.

[1] Areas are rounded to the nearest 10 sq km/sq mi.
[2] Salt lakes.
[3] Average of areas given by Canada and USA.
[4] Salt lagoons.

Longest rivers

Name	Outflow	Length [1] km	mi
Nile-Kagera-Ruvuvu-Ruvusu-Luvironza	Mediterranean Sea (Egypt)	6690	4160
Amazon-Ucayali-Tambo-Ene-Apurimac	Atlantic Ocean (Brazil)	6570	4080
Mississippi-Missouri-Jefferson-Beaverhead-Red Rock	Gulf of Mexico (USA)	6020	3740
Chang Jiang (Yangtze)	E China Sea (China)	5980	3720
Yenisey-Angara-Selenga-Ider	Kara Sea (Russia)	5870	3650
Amur-Argun-Kerulen	Tartar Strait (Russia)	5780	3590
Ob-Irtysh	Gulf of Ob, Kara Sea (Russia)	5410	3360
Plata-Parana-Grande	Atlantic Ocean (Argentina/Uruguay)	4880	3030
Huang He (Yellow)	Yellow Sea (China)	4840	3010
Congo-Lualaba	S Atlantic Ocean (Angola/Democratic Republic of the Congo)	4630	2880
Lena	Laptev Sea (Russia)	4400	2730
Mackenzie-Slave-Peace-Finlay	Beaufort Sea (Canada)	4240	2630
Mekong	S China Sea (Vietnam)	4180	2600
Niger	Gulf of Guinea (Nigeria)	4100	2550

[1] Lengths are given to the nearest 10km/mi, and include the river plus tributaries comprising the longest watercourse.

Highest waterfalls

Name	Total height m	ft	Greatest single drop m	ft
Angel Falls, Venezuela	979	3212	807	2648
Tugela Falls, South Africa	948	3110	411	1350
Tres Hermanas (Three Sisters), Peru	914	3000	—	—
Olo'upena Falls, Hawaii, USA	900	2953	—	—
Vinnufossen, Norway	860	2822	420	1378
Baläifossen, Norway	850	2788	452	1482
Pu'uka'oku Falls, Hawaii, USA	840	2756	—	—
Browne Falls, New Zealand	836	2744	244	800
Strupenfossen, Norway	820	2690	—	—
Ramnefjellsfossen (Utigardsfossen), Norway	818	2685	600	1968

Major volcanoes

Name	Height m	ft	Last major eruption (year)
Aconcagua (Argentina)	6959	22831	extinct
Kilimanjaro (Tanzania)	5928	19450	extinct
Cotopaxi (Ecuador)	5897	19347	1904
Popocatèpetl (Mexico)	5483	17990	2006

Name	Height m	ft	Last major eruption (year)
Ararat (Turkey)	5137	16853	extinct
Klyuchevskoy (Russia)	4850	15910	2005
Rainier, Mt (USA)	4394	14416	1854
Mauna Loa (Hawaii)	4171	13685	1984
Erebus (Antarctica)	4023	13200	2005
Fuji (Japan)	3776	12388	1707
Etna (Italy)	3239	10625	2004
Paricutín (Mexico)	3188	10460	1952
Lassen Peak (USA)	3186	10453	1921
Nyamuragira (Democratic Republic of the Congo)	3056	10026	2006
Tambora (Sumbawa, Indonesia)	2868	9410	1967
Bezymianny (Russia)	2800	9186	2005
Ruapehu (New Zealand)	2797	9175	2006
St Helens, Mt (USA)	2549	8364	2006
Mayon (Philippines)	2464	8084	2006
Galunggung (Java)	2181	7155	1984
Katmai (Alaska)	2047	6715	1974
Lamington (Papua New Guinea)	1781	5844	1956
Pinatubo, Mt (Philippines)	1759	5770	1992
Hudson (Chile)	1750	5742	1991
Grímsvötn (Iceland)	1725	5658	2004
Hekla (Iceland)	1500	4920	2000
Taal (Philippines)	1448	4752	1977
Pelée, Mt (Martinique)	1397	4584	1932
Unzen (Japan)	1360	4461	1996
El Chichón (Mexico)	1350	4430	1982
Jorullo (Mexico)	1330	4255	1774
Awu (Sangihe Is, Indonesia)	1327	4355	2004
Vesuvius (Italy)	1289	4230	1944
Kilauea (Hawaii)	1250	4100	2006
Soufrière (St Vincent)	1234	4048	1979
Tarawera (New Zealand)	1149	3770	1886
Stromboli (Italy)	931	3055	2006
Soufrière Hills (Montserrat)	914	3000	2006
Krakatoa (Sumatra)	818	2685	2001
Santorini/Thíra (Greece)	566	1857	1950
Vulcano (Italy)	503	1650	1890
Eldfell (Iceland)	279	915	1973
Surtsey (Iceland)	174	570	1967

Major earthquakes

All magnitudes are on the Richter scale. The energy released by earthquakes is measured on the logarithmic Richter scale. Thus:

2 Barely perceptible; 5 Rather strong; 7+ Very strong

Year	Location	Magnitude	Deaths
2006	Kuril Is (Russia)	7.8	0
2006	Hawaii (USA)	6.7	0
2006	Java (Indonesia) [1]	7.7	650+
2006	Java (Indonesia)	6.2	5 500+
2005	Democratic Republic of the Congo	6.8	2
2005	Kithira I (Greece)	6.9	0
2005	Kashmir	7.6	74 500+
2005	Fukoka (Japan)	7.0	1
2005	Sumatra (Indonesia)	8.7	1 300
2004	Indian Ocean	9.3	[2]
2004	Niigata state (N Japan)	6.8	25+
2004	Al Hoceima (NE Morocco)	6.3	560+
2003	Bam (Iran)	6.5	26 000+
2003	N Algeria	6.7	2 200+
2003	Xinjiang Region (China)	6.3	250+
2003	Colima (Mexico)	7.6	21+
2002	Vanuatu	7.2	0
2002	Alaska (USA)	7.9	0
2002	Papua New Guinea	7.6	5+
2002	Qazvin (Iran)	6.0	500+
2002	Hindu Kush (Afghanistan)	6.1	1 800+
2001	Gujarat (India)	6.9	20 000+
2001	El Salvador	7.7	675+
2000	Bengkulu (Sumatra)	7.9	115+
1999	Nantou Province (Taiwan)	7.6	2 400+
1999	Izmit (NW Turkey)	7.4	17 000+
1999	Armenia (Colombia)	6.0	1 100+
1998	Badakhshan Province (Afghanistan)	7.1	5 000+
1998	Rustaq (Afghanistan)	6.1	4 000+
1997	Qayen (E Iran)	7.1	2 400
1997	Ardabil (NW Iran)	5.5	965+
1996	Xinjiang Region (China)	6.9	26
1996	Biak I (Indonesia)	7.9	108
1996	Flores Sea (near Indonesia)	7.9	—
1996	Samar (Philippines)	7.9	—
1996	Lijiang, Yunan Province (China)	7.0	304
1995	Kuril Is (Russia)	7.9	0
1995	Manzanillo (Mexico)	7.6	66
1995	S Mexico	7.3	—
1995	Sakhalin I (E Russia)	7.5	2 000
1995	Kobe (Japan)	7.2	6 300

Year	Location	Magnitude	Deaths
1994	Hokkaido I (Japan) and Kuril Is (Russia) (undersea)	8.2	16+
1994	Bolivia (617km underground)	8.2	5
1994	Paez River Valley (SW Colombia)	6.8	269
1994	Java (Indonesia)	7.7	200
1994	Sumatra I (Indonesia)	7.2	215
1994	Halmahera I (Indonesia)	6.8	7+
1994	Los Angeles, California (USA)	6.8	61
1993	Maharashtra State (India)	6.5	22 000
1993	Guam (Mariana Is)	8.1	—
1993	Okushiri and Hokkaido Is (N Japan)	7.8	185
1993	Papua New Guinea	6.8	60
1992	Maumere, Flores I (Indonesia)	7.5	1 232
1992	Joshua Tree and Yucca Valley, California (USA)	7.4	2
1992	Erzincan (Turkey)	6.8	500
1992	Nusa Tenggara Is (Indonesia)	6.8	2 500
1991	Uttar Pradesh (India)	6.1	1 000
1991	Costa Rica/Panama	7.5	80
1991	Georgia	7.2	100
1991	Afghanistan	6.8	1 000
1991	Pakistan	6.8	300
1990	Cabanatuan City (Philippines)	7.7	1 653
1990	NW Iran	7.5	40 000
1990	N Peru	5.8	200
1990	Romania	6.6	70
1990	Philippines	7.7	1 600
1989	San Francisco (USA)	6.9	100
1988	Armenia	7.0	25 000
1988	SW China	7.6	1 000
1988	Nepal/India	6.9	900
1985	Mexico City (Mexico)	8.1	7 200
1982	N Yemen	6.0	2 800
1980	S Italy	7.2	4 500
1980	El Asnam (Algeria)	7.3	5 000
1978	NE Iran	7.7	25 000
1976	Tangshan (China)	8.2	242 000
1976	Guatemala City (Guatemala)	7.5	22 778
1974	Kashmir (India)	6.3	5 200
1972	Managua (Nicaragua)	6.2	5 000
1972	S Iran	6.9	5 000
1970	Chimbote (Peru)	7.7	66 000
1968	NE Iran	7.4	11 600
1964	Anchorage (USA)	8.5	131
1962	NW Iran	7.1	12 000
1960	Agadir (Morocco)	5.8	12 000
1939	Erzincan (Turkey)	7.9	23 000
1939	Chillan (Chile)	7.8	30 000

Year	Location	Magnitude	Deaths
1935	Quetta (India)	7.5	60 000
1932	Gansu (China)	7.6	70 000
1927	Nan-shan (China)	8.3	200 000
1923	Kwanto (Japan)	8.3	143 000
1920	Gansu (China)	8.6	180 000
1915	Avezzano (Italy)	7.5	30 000
1908	Messina (Italy)	7.5	120 000
1906	Valparaiso (Chile)	8.6	20 000
1906	San Francisco (USA)	8.3	500
1868	Ecuador/Colombia	*	70 000
1783	Calabria (Italy)	*	50 000
1755	Lisbon (Portugal)	*	70 000
1737	Calcutta (India)	*	300 000
1730	Hokkaido (Japan)	*	137 000
1693	Catania (Italy)	*	60 000
1667	Caucasia (Caucasus)	*	80 000
1556	Shensi (China)	*	830 000
1290	Chihli (China)	*	100 000
1268	Silicia (Asia Minor)	*	60 000
856	Corinth (Greece)	*	45 000
526	Antioch (Turkey)	*	250 000

*Magnitude not available
[1] Earthquakes occurred in May and July 2006; the later one is shown first.
[2] Caused the tsunami which killed 225 000+ people in SE Asia.

Earthquake severity measurement

Modified Mercalli (MM) and Richter scales.

MM	Description	Richter
1	instrumental detected only by seismographs	<3
2	feeble just noticeable by some people	3–3.4
3	slight similar to passing of heavy lorries	3.5–4
4	moderate rocking of loose objects	4.1–4.4
5	quite strong felt by most people even when sleeping	4.5–4.8
6	strong trees rock and some structural damage is caused	4.9–5.4
7	very strong walls crack	5.5–6
8	destructive weak buildings collapse	6.1–6.5

MM	Description	Richter
9	ruinous	6.6–7
	houses collapse and ground pipes crack	
10	disastrous	7.1–7.3
	landslides occur, ground cracks and buildings collapse	
11	very disastrous	7.4–8.1
	few buildings remain standing	
12	catastrophic	>8.1
	ground rises and falls in waves	

Geological time scale

Aeon	Era	Period	Epoch	Million years before present
Phanerozoic	Cenozoic	Quaternary	Holocene	0.01–
			Pleistocene	2–0.01
		Tertiary	Pliocene	7–2
			Miocene	25–7
			Oligocene	38–25
			Eocene	54–38
			Palaeocene	65–54
	Mesozoic	Cretaceous		140–65
		Jurassic		210–140
		Triassic	Late	
			Middle	250–210
			Early	
	Palaeozoic	Permian	Late	
			Early	290–250
		Carboniferous	Pennsylvanian	
			Mississippian	360–290
		Devonian		410–360
		Silurian		440–410
		Ordovician		505–440
		Cambrian		580–505
Precambrian	Proterozoic			2500–580
	Archaean			4500–2500

Great ice ages

Precambrian era	Early Proterozoic
Precambrian era	Upper Proterozoic
Palaeozoic era	Upper Carboniferous
Cenozoic era	Pleistocene [1]
	(Last 4 periods of glaciation)
	Günz (Nebraskan or Jerseyan) 520 000–490 000 years ago
	Mindel (Kansan) 430 000–370 000 years ago
	Riss (Illinoian) 130 000–100 000 years ago
	Würm (Wisconsinian and Iowan) 40 000–18 000 years ago

[1] The Pleistocene epoch is synonymous with 'The Ice Age'.

CLIMATE AND ENVIRONMENT

Climatic zones

The earth may be divided into zones, approximating to zones of latitude, such that each zone possesses a distinct type of climate.

The principal zones are:

- **Tropical**   One zone of wet climate near the equator (either constantly wet or monsoonal with wet and dry seasons, tropical savannah with dry winters); the average temperature is not below 18°C;
  - Amazon forest
  - Malaysia
  - S Vietnam
  - India
  - Africa
  - Congo Basin
  - Indonesia
  - SE Asia
  - Australia
- **Subtropical**   Two zones of steppe and desert climate (transition through semi-arid to arid);
  - Sahara
  - Central Asia
  - Mexico
  - Australia
  - Kalahari
- **Mediterranean**   Zones of rainy climate with mild winters; coolest month above 0°C but below 18°C;
  - California
  - South Africa
  - S Europe
  - parts of Chile
  - SW Australia
- **Temperate**   Rainy climate (includes areas of temperate woodland, mountain forests, and plains with no dry season;

influenced by seas – rainfall all year, small temperate changes); average temperature between 3°C and 18°C;
  - Most of Europe
  - Asia
  - NW / NE USA
  - New Zealand
  - Chile
- **Boreal**   Climate with a great range of temperature in the northern hemisphere (in some areas the most humid month is in winter and there is ten times more precipitation than the driest part of winter; in other areas the most humid month is in winter and there is ten times more precipitation than in the driest part of summer); in the coldest period temperatures do not exceed 3°C and in the hottest do not go below 10°C;
  - Prairies of USA
  - parts of South Africa
  - parts of Russia
  - parts of Australia
- **Polar caps**   Snowy climate (tundra and ice-cap) with little or no precipitation. There is permafrost in the tundra and vegetation includes lichen and moss all year, and grass in the summer; the highest annual temperature in the polar region is below 0°C and in the tundra the average temperature is 10°C;
  - Arctic regions of Russia and N America
  - Antarctica

Meteorological extremes

The hottest place is Dallol, Ethiopia, at 34.4°C/93.9°F (annual mean temperature).

The highest recorded temperature in the shade is 58°C/136.4°F at al'Aziziyah, Libya, on 13 September 1922.

The coldest place is Plateau Station, Antarctica, at -56.6°C/-69.8°F (annual mean temperature).

The lowest recorded temperature is -89.2°C/-128.6°F at Vostok, Antarctica, on 21 July 1983.

The driest place is the Atacama desert near Calama, Chile, where no rainfall was recorded in over 400 years to 1972.

The most rain to fall in 24 hours was 1870mm/74in which fell on Cilaos, Réunion, in the Indian Ocean, on 15–16 March 1952.

The wettest place is Mawsynram, Meghalaya State, India, where the annual average rainfall is 11870mm/467in.

The greatest amount of snow to fall in 12 months was 31102mm/1225in, at Paradise, Mt Rainier, in Washington, USA, in 1971–2.

The most rainy days in a year are the c.350 experienced on Mt Waialeale, Kauai, Hawaii, USA.

The least sunshine occurs at the North and South Poles, where the Sun does not rise for 182 days of winter.

The greatest amount of sunshine occurs in Yuma, Arizona, USA: with a mean average of 4055 hours of sun a year (91% of possible hours of sunlight).

The highest recorded surface wind speed is 371.75kph/231mph, at Mt Washington, New Hampshire, USA, on 12 April 1934.

Forest area and rate of change

Deforestation has taken place largely as a result of economic pressures for more agricultural land. Deforestation has serious implications for the environment (as carbon dioxide is released into the atmosphere) and can also cause the degradation of topsoil, increasing the risk of rivers silting up and flooding. Rainforests, which are home to half the world's plant and animal species, are in particular danger. The following data are taken from *State of the World's Forests 2005*, published by the Food and Agricultural Organization (FAO) of the United Nations.

Country/Area	Forest area 2000		Forest cover change 1990–2000	
	Total forest (1000ha)[1]	% of land area	Annual change (1000ha)	Annual rate of change (%)
Africa	649866	21.8	-5262	-0.8
Asia	547796	17.8	-364	-0.1
Europe	1039251	46	881	0.1
North & Central America	549304	25.7	-570	-0.1
Oceania	197623	23.3	-365	-0.2
South America	885618	50.5	-3711	-0.4
World	3869455	29.6	-9391	-0.2

[1] One hectare (ha) = 10000 sq m. To convert ha to sq km, divide by 100; to convert ha to sq mi, multiply by 0.003861.

Tropical rainforest distribution

World temperatures

The maps below show the average world temperatures for January and July.

Temperatures (January)

-40° -20° 0° 10° 20° 30° Celsius

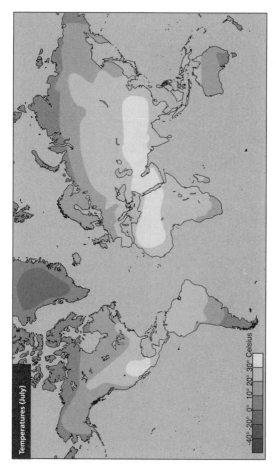

Temperatures (July)

-40° -20° 0° 10° 20° 30° Celsius

World temperature change

Global average near-surface temperature 1850–2006, relative to the average for 1961–90.

Map of shipping forecast areas

* Formerly Finisterre (renamed 2002). Reproduced with data supplied by the Met Office.

Wind force and sea disturbance

Beaufort number	Windspeed			Wind name	Observable wind characteristics	Sea disturbance number	Average wave ht.		Observable sea characteristics
	m/sec	kph	mph				m	ft	
0	1	<1	<1	Calm	Smoke rises vertically	0	0	0	Sea like a mirror
1	1	1–5	1–3	Light air	Wind direction shown by smoke drift, but not by wind vanes	0	0	0	Ripples like scales, without foam crests
2	2	6–11	4–7	Light breeze	Wind felt on face; leaves rustle; vanes moved by wind	1	0.3	0–1	More definite wavelets, but crests do not break
3	4	12–19	8–12	Gentle breeze	Leaves and small twigs in constant motion; wind extends light flag	2	0.3–0.6	1–2	Large wavelets; crests begin to break; scattered white horses
4	7	20–28	13–18	Moderate breeze	Raises dust, loose paper; small branches moved	3	0.6–1.2	2–4	Small waves become longer; fairly frequent white horses
5	10	29–38	19–24	Fresh breeze	Small trees in leaf begin to sway; crested wavelets on inland waters	4	1.2–2.4	4–8	Moderate waves with a more definite long form; many white horses; some spray possible
6	12	39–49	25–31	Strong breeze	Large branches in motion; difficult to use umbrellas; whistling heard in telegraph wires	5	2.4–4	8–13	Large waves form; more extensive white foam crests; some spray probable

Beaufort number	Windspeed			Wind name	Observable wind characteristics	Sea disturbance number	Average wave ht.		Observable sea characteristics
	m/sec	kph	mph				m	ft	
7	15	50–61	32–38	Near gale	Whole trees in motion; inconvenience walking against wind	6	4–6	13–20	Sea heaps up; streaks of white foam blown along
8	18	62–74	39–46	Gale	Breaks twigs off trees; impedes progress	6	4–6	13–20	Moderately high waves of greater length; well-marked streaks of foam
9	20	75–88	47–54	Strong gale	Slight structural damage occurs	6	4–6	13–20	High waves; dense streaks of foam; sea begins to roll; spray affects visibility
10	26	89–102	55–63	Storm	Trees uprooted; considerable damage occurs	7	6–9	20–30	Very high waves with long overhanging crests; dense streaks of foam blown along; generally white appearance of surface; heavy rolling
11	30	103–17	64–72	Violent storm	Widespread damage	8	9–14	30–45	Exceptionally high waves; long white patches of foam; poor visibility; ships lost to view behind waves
12–17	≥30	≥118	≥73	Hurricane		9	14	>45	Air filled with foam and spray; sea completely white; very poor visibility

World Heritage sites

This list is up-to-date to December 2006. It comprises 830 properties selected by UNESCO as being of such outstanding natural, environmental or cultural importance that they merit exceptional international efforts to make them more widely known and to save them from damage and destruction.

- **Afghanistan**
  Bamiyan Valley
  Minaret of Jam
- **Albania**
  Butrint
  Gjirokastra (museum-city)
- **Algeria**
  Algiers (Kasbah)
  Al Qal'a of Beni Hammad
  Djémila (Roman ruins)
  M'Zab Valley
  Tassili N'Ajjer
  Timgad (Roman ruins)
  Tipasa (archaeological site)
- **Andorra**
  Madriu-Perafita-Claror Valley
- **Argentina**
  Córdoba (Jesuit block)
  Cueva de las Manos
  Iguazú National Park
  Ischigualasto/Talampaya Natural Parks
  Jesuit Missions of the Guaranis (shared with Brazil)
  Los Glaciares National Park
  Península Valdés
  Río Pinturas (Cueva de las Manos)
  Quebrada de Humahuaca
- **Armenia**
  Echmiatsin (cathedral, churches) and Zvartnots (archaeological site)
  Geghard monastery and the Upper Azat Valley
  Haghpat and Sanahin monasteries
- **Australia**
  Central Eastern Australian Rainforest Reserves
  Fraser Island
  Great Barrier Reef
  Greater Blue Mountains Area
  Heard and McDonald Islands
  Kakadu National Park
  Lord Howe Island
  Macquarie Island
  Purnululu National Park
  Queensland (wet tropics)

- Riversleigh/Naracoorte (fossil sites)
  Royal Exhibition Building and Carlton Gardens
  Shark Bay
  Tasmanian Wilderness
  Uluru-Kata Tjuta National Park
  Willandra Lakes region
- **Austria**
  Fertő/Neusiedlersee cultural landscape (shared with Hungary)
  Graz (historic centre)
  Hallstatt-Dachstein Salzkammergut cultural landscape
  Salzburg (historic centre)
  Schönbrunn palace and gardens
  Semmering Railway
  Vienna (historic centre)
  Wachau cultural landscape
- **Azerbaijan**
  Baku
- **Bahrain**
  Qal'at al-Bahrain (ancient harbour and capital of Dilmun)
- **Bangladesh**
  Bagerhat (historic mosque city)
  Paharpur (ruins of the Buddhist Vihara)
  Sundarbans (mangrove forest)
- **Belarus**
  Architectural, residential and cultural complex of the Radziwill family at Nesvizh
  Belovezhskaya Pushcha/Białowieża Forest (shared with Poland)
  Mir Castle complex
  Struve Geodetic Arc *
- **Belgium**
  Belfries of Belgium and France (shared with France)
  Bruges (historic centre)
  Flemish Béguinages
  Four lifts on the Canal du Centre, La Louvière and Le Roeulx
  Houses of Victor Horta
  La Grand-Place, Brussels
  Plantin-Moretus house-museum complex

Spiennes (Neolithic flint mines)
Tournai (Notre-Dame Cathedral)
- **Belize**
Barrier Reef Reserve System
- **Benin**
Abomey (royal palaces)
- **Bolivia**
Fuerte de Samaipata
Jesuit Missions of the Chiquitos
Noel Kempff Mercado National Park
Potosi (mining town)
Sucre (historic city)
Tiwanaku
- **Bosnia and Herzegovina**
Mostar (Old Bridge area)
- **Botswana**
Tsodilo
- **Brazil**
Bom Jesus do Congonhas (sanctuary)
Atlantic Forest South-East Reserves
Brasilia
Central Amazon conservation complex
Chapada dos Veadeiros and Emas
National Parks
Diamantina (historic centre)
Discovery Coast Atlantic Forest Reserves
Fernando de Noronha and Atol das
Rocas Reserves
Goiás (historic centre)
Iguaçu National Park
Jesuit Missions of the Guaranis (shared
with Argentina)
Olinda (historic centre)
Ouro Preto (historic town)
Pantanal conservation area
Salvador da Bahia (historic centre)
São Luis (historic centre)
Serra da Capivara National Park
- **Bulgaria**
Boyana Church
Ivanovo rock-hewn churches
Kazanlak (Thracian tomb)
Madara Rider
Nessebar (ancient city)
Pirin National Park
Rila Monastery
Srebarna Nature Reserve
Sveshtari (Thracian tomb)
- **Cambodia**
Angkor

- **Cameroon**
Dja Wildlife Reserve
- **Canada**
Canadian Rocky Mountain Parks
Dinosaur Provincial Park
Gros Morne National Park
Head-Smashed-In Buffalo Jump complex
L'Anse aux Meadows Historic Park
Lunenburg (old town)
Miguasha National Park
Nahanni National Park
Quebec (historic area, old town)
SGaang Gwaii
Tatshenshini-Alsek, Kluane National
Park, Wrangell St Elias National Park
and Reserve, and Glacier Bay National
Park (shared with USA)
Waterton Glacier International Peace
Park (shared with USA)
Wood Buffalo National Park
- **Central African Republic**
Manovo-Gounda St Floris National Park
- **Chile**
Chiloé Churches
Humberstone and Santa Laura saltpetre
works
Rapa Nui National Park (Easter Island)
Sewell mining town
Valparaíso (historic quarter)
- **China**
Beijing and Shenyang: imperial palaces
of the Ming and Qing dynasties
Beijing: Summer Palace (imperial garden)
Beijing: Temple of Heaven (sacrificial
altar)
Chengde (mountain resort and outlying
temples)
Dazu (rock carvings)
Great Wall
Huanglong area
Jiuzhaigou Valley area
Koguryo Kingdom (ancient capital cities
and tombs)
Lhasa (Potala Palace complex)
Lijiang (old town)
Longmen Grottoes
Lushan National Park
Macao (historic centre)
Mausoleum of the first Qin emperor
Ming and Qing dynasties imperial tombs

Mogao caves
Mt Emei scenic area including Leshan
  Giant Buddha scenic area
Mt Huangshan
Mt Qingcheng and Dujiangyan irrigation
  system
Mt Taishan
Mt Wuyi
Ping Yao (ancient city)
Qufu (temple and cemetery of Confucius
  and the K'ung family mansion)
Sichuan giant panda sanctuaries
Suzhou (classical gardens)
Three Parallel Rivers of Yunnan protected
  areas
Wudang mountains (ancient building
  complex)
Wulingyuan area
Xidi and Hongcun (ancient villages)
Yin Xu
Yungang Grottoes
Zhoukoudian (Peking Man site)
■ **Colombia**
Cartagena (port, fortress and
  monuments)
Los Katios National Park
Malpelo Fauna and Flora Sanctuary
San Agustín Archaeological Park
Santa Cruz de Mompox (historic centre)
Tierradentro National Archaeological
  Park
■ **Congo, Democratic Republic of the**
Garamba National Park
Kahuzi-Biega National Park
Okapi Wildlife Reserve
Salonga National Park
Virunga National Park
■ **Costa Rica**
Cocos Island National Park
Guanacaste conservation area
La Amistad National Park (shared with
  Panama)
■ **Côte d'Ivoire**
Comoé National Park
Mt Nimba Nature Reserve (shared with
  Guinea)
Taï National Park
■ **Croatia**
Cathedral of St James, Šbenik
Dubrovnik (old city)

Plitvice Lakes National Park
Poreč (episcopal complex of the
  Euphrasian basilica in the historic centre)
Split (historic centre with Diocletian's
  Palace)
Trogir (historic city)
■ **Cuba**
Alejandro de Humboldt National Park
Cienfuegos (historic centre)
Desembarco del Granma National Park
First coffee plantations in SE Cuba
  (archaeological landscape)
Old Havana and its fortifications
San Pedro de la Roca Castle, Santiago
  de Cuba
Trinidad and the Valley de los Ingenios
Viñales Valley
■ **Cyprus**
Choirokoitia
Paphos (archaeological site)
Troödos (painted churches)
■ **Czech Republic**
Český Krumlov (historic centre)
Holašovice (historical village reservation)
Kroměř (gardens and castle)
Kutná Hora (historic centre) with Church
  of St Barbara and the Cathedral of Our
  Lady at Sedlec
Lednice-Valtice cultural landscape
Litomyšl Castle
Olomouc (Holy Trinity Column)
Pilgrimage church of St John of
  Nepomuk, Zelena Hora
Prague (historic centre)
Telč (historic centre)
Trebič (Jewish quarter and St Procopius
  Basilica)
Tugendhat Villa, Brno
■ **Denmark**
Ilulissat Icefjord
Jelling (mounds, runic stones and
  church)
Kronberg Castle
Roskilde Cathedral
■ **Dominica**
Morne Trois Pitons National Park
■ **Dominican Republic**
Santo Domingo
■ **Ecuador**
Galápagos Islands National Park

Quito (old city)
Sangay National Park
Santa Ana de los Rios de Cuenca
(historic centre)

■ **Egypt**
Abu Mena (Christian ruins)
Abu Simbel to Philae (Nubian
monuments)
Cairo (Islamic district)
Memphis and its necropolis, with the
Pyramid fields from Giza to Dahshur
St Catherine area
Thebes and its necropolis
Wadi Al-Hitan (Whale Valley)

■ **El Salvador**
Joya de Cerén (archaeological site)

■ **Estonia**
Struve Geodetic Arc *
Tallinn (historic centre, old town)

■ **Ethiopia**
Aksum (archaeological site)
Awash Lower Valley
Fasil Ghebbi and Gondar monuments
Harar Jugol (fortified historic town)
Lalibela rock-hewn churches
Omo Lower Valley
Simien National Park
Tiya (carved steles)

■ **Finland**
Kvarken Archipelago/High Coast (shared
with Sweden)
Old Rauma
Petäjävesi Old Church
Sammallahdenmäki (Bronze Age burial
site)
Struve Geodetic Arc *
Suomenlinna (fortress)
Verla groundwood and board mill

■ **France**
Amiens Cathedral
Arc-et-Senans (royal saltworks)
Arles (Roman and Romanesque
monuments)
Avignon (historic centre, papal palace
and bridge)
Belfries of Belgium and France (shared
with Belgium)
Bourges Cathedral
Canal du Midi
Carcassonne (historic fortified city)

Chartres Cathedral
Corsica (Gulf of Girolata, Cape Porto,
Scandola Natural Reserve and Calanche
of Piana)
Fontainebleau (palace and park)
Fontenay (Cistercian abbey)
Le Havre
Loire Valley between Sully-sur-Loire and
Chalonnes
Lyons (historic site)
Mont St Michel and its bay
Nancy (Place Stanislas, Place de la
Carrière and Place d'Alliance)
Orange (Roman theatre and triumphal
arch)
Paris (banks of the Seine)
Pont du Gard (Roman aqueduct)
Provins
Pyrenees, Mt Perdu landscape (shared
with Spain)
Rheims (Cathedral of Notre-Dame, St
Remy Abbey and Palace of Tau)
Routes of Santiago de Compostela
St Emilion (jurisdiction)
St Savin sur Gartempe (abbey church)
Strasbourg (Grande Île)
Versailles (palace and park)
Vezelay (basilica and hill)
Vézère (prehistoric sites and decorated
caves)

■ **The Gambia**
James Island and related sites
Senegambia stone circles (shared with
Senegal)

■ **Georgia**
Bagrati Cathedral and Gelati Monastery
Mtskheta (historic monuments)
Upper Svaneti region

■ **Germany**
Aachen Cathedral
Bamberg
Bauhaus and its sites in Weimar and
Dessau
Bremen (town hall and Roland on the
Marketplace)
Brühl (Augustusburg and Falkenlust
castles)
Cologne Cathedral
Dessau-Wörlitz (Garden Kingdom)
Dresden Elbe Valley

Frontiers of the Roman Empire (shared with UK)
Hildesheim (St Mary's Cathedral and St Michael's Church)
Lorsch (abbey and Altenmünster)
Lübeck (Hanseatic city)
Luther memorials in Eisleben and Wittenberg
Maulbronn monastery complex
Messel Pit (fossil site)
Museum Island, Berlin
Muskauer Park/Park Muzakowski (shared with Poland)
Potsdam and Berlin palaces and parks
Quedlinburg (collegiate church, castle and old town)
Rammelsberg mines and historic town of Goslar
Regensburg with Stadtamhof (old town)
Reichenau (monastic island)
Speyer Cathedral
Stralsund and Wismar (historic centres)
Trier (Roman monuments, cathedral and Liebfrauen church)
Upper Middle Rhine Valley
Völklingen ironworks
Wartburg Castle
Weimar (classical quarter)
Wies (pilgrimage church)
Würzburg Residence
Zollverein Coal Mine (industrial complex), Essen

■ Ghana
Ashante traditional buildings
Forts and castles, Volta, Greater Accra, Central and Western regions

■ Greece
Athens (Acropolis)
Bassae (temple of Apollo Epicurius)
Chorá (historic centre), with the monastery of St John 'the Theologian' and the cave of the Apocalypse on Pátmos
Daphni, Hossios Luckas and Nea Moni of Chios monasteries
Delos
Delphi (archaeological site)
Epidaurus (archaeological site)
Meteora
Mt Athos
Mycenae and Tiryns (archaeological site)

Mystras
Olympia (archaeological site)
Rhodes (medieval city)
Samos (Pythagoreion and Heraion)
Thessalonika (Paleochristian and Byzantine monuments)
Vergina (archaeological site)

■ Guatemala
Antigua Guatemala
Quirigua (archaeological site and ruins)
Tikal National Park

■ Guinea
Mt Nimba Nature Reserve (shared with Côte d'Ivoire)

■ Haiti
National Historic Park (citadel, Sans-Souci, Ramiers)

■ Honduras
Maya ruins of Copan
Río Plátano Biosphere Reserve

■ Hungary
Aggtelek Karst and Slovak Karst caves (shared with Slovakia)
Budapest (banks of the Danube, the Buda Castle quarter and Andrássy Ave)
Fertő/Neusiedlersee cultural landscape (shared with Austria)
Hollókő (traditional village)
Hortobágy National Park
Pannonhalma, Millenary Benedictine Abbey and its natural environment
Pécs (early Christian necropolis, Sophianae)
Tokaj wine region

■ Iceland
Thingvellir National Park

■ India
Agra Fort
Ajanta caves
Bhimbetka rock shelters
Champaner-Pavagadh Archaelogical Park
Chhatrapati Shivaji Terminus (formerly Victoria Terminus)
Elephanta caves
Ellora caves
Fatehpur Sikri (Moghul city)
Goa (churches and convents)
Great Living Chola Temples
Hampi (monuments)
Humayun's Tomb, Delhi

Kaziranga National Park
Keoladeo National Park
Khajuraho (monuments)
Konarak (Sun Temple)
Mahabalipuram (monuments)
Mahabodhi temple complex, Bodh Gaya
Manas Wildlife Sanctuary
Mountain railways
Nanda Devi and Valley of Flowers
  National Parks
Pattadakal (monuments)
Qutb Minar and monuments, Delhi
Sanchi Buddhist monuments
Sundarbans National Park
Taj Mahal

■ Indonesia
Borobudur temple compounds
Komodo National Park
Lorentz National Park
Prambanan temple compounds
Sangiran (early man site)
Sumatra tropical rainforest heritage
Ujung Kulon National Park

■ Iran
Bam
Bisotun
Esfahan (Meidan Emam)
Pasargadae
Persepolis
Soltaniyeh
Takht-e Soleyman
Tchogha Zanbil Ziggurat and complex

■ Iraq
Ashur (Qal'at Sherqat)
Hatra

■ Ireland
Skellig Michael
Valley of the Boyne (archaeological site)

■ Israel
Acre (old city)
Biblical Tels – Megiddo, Hazor, Beer
  Sheba
Incense Route – desert cities in the
  Negev
Jerusalem (old city and its walls)
Masada
Tel-Aviv (White City – the Modern
  Movement)

■ Italy
Aeolian Islands

Agrigento (archaeological area)
Alberobello (the trulli)
Amalfi (the coast)
Aquileia (archaeological area and the
  patriarchal basilica)
Assisi (Basilica of San Francesco and
  other Franciscan sites)
Barumini, Sardinia ('nuraghi' defensive
  towers)
Casale (Villa Romana)
Caserta (18c palace, park, aqueduct of
  Vanvitelli and the San Leucio complex)
Castel del Monte
Cerveteri and Tarquinia (Etruscan
  necropolises)
Cilento and Vallo di Diano National Park
  with archaeological sites of Paestum
  and Velia, and the Certosa di Padula
Crespi d'Adda
Ferrara (Renaissance city) and the Po delta
Florence (historic centre)
Genoa (Strade Nuove and Palazzi dei
  Rolli system)
I Sassi di Matera
Modena (cathedral, Torre Civica and
  Piazza Grande)
Naples (historic centre)
Padua (botanical garden)
Pienza (historic centre)
Pisa (Piazza del Duomo)
Pompeii, with Herculaneum and Torre
  Annunziata archaeological areas
Portovenere, Cinque Terre and the
  islands of Palmaria, Tino and Tinetto
Ravenna, early Christian monuments
  and mosaics
Rome (historic centre)
Sacri Monti of Piedmont and Lombardy
San Gimignano (historic centre)
Santa Maria delle Grazie with *The Last
  Supper* by Leonardo da Vinci, Milan
Siena (historic centre)
Syracuse and Pantalica (necropolis)
Turin residences of royal house of Savoy
Urbino (historic centre)
Valcamonica (rock drawings)
Val di Noto (late Baroque towns)
Val d'Orcia
Venice and its lagoon
Verona (city)

Vicenza (city) and Palladian villas of the Veneto
Villa Adriana, Tivoli
Villa d'Este, Tivoli

■ **Japan**
Ancient Kyoto (Kyoto, Uji and Otsu cities)
Ancient Nara (historic monuments)
Himeji-jo
Hiroshima Peace Memorial (Genbaku Dome)
Horyu-ji (Buddhist monuments)
Itsukushima Shinto shrine
Kii mountain range (sacred sites and pilgrimage routes)
Nikko (shrines and temples)
Ryuku Kingdom (Gusuku sites and related properties)
Shirakami-Sanchi
Shirakawa-go and Gokayama (historic villages)
Shiretoko
Yakushima

■ **Jordan**
Petra
Quseir Amra
Um er-Rasas (Kastrom Mefa'a)

■ **Kazakhstan**
Mausoleum of Khoja Ahmed Yasawi
Tamgaly (petroglyphs)

■ **Kenya**
Mt Kenya National Park and forest
Lake Turkana National Parks
Lamu (old town)

■ **Korea, North**
Koguryo Tombs complex

■ **Korea, South**
Ch'angdokkung Palace complex
Chongmyo Shrine
Gochang, Hwasun and Ganghwa Dolmen sites
Gyeongju historic areas
Haeinsa Temple, including the Tripitaka Koreana woodblocks
Hwasong Fortress
Seokguram Grotto and Bulguksa Temple

■ **Laos**
Luang Prabang
Vat Phou and associated ancient settlements

■ **Latvia**
Riga (historic centre)
Struve Geodetic Arc *

■ **Lebanon**
Anjar (archaeological site)
Baalbek
Byblos
Ouadi Qadisha and the Forest of the Cedars of God
Tyre (archaeological site)

■ **Libya**
Cyrene (archaeological site)
Ghadamès (old town)
Leptis Magna (archaeological site)
Sabratha (archaeological site)
Tadrart Acacus (rock-art sites)

■ **Lithuania**
Curonian Spit (shared with Russia)
Kernave (archaeological site)
Struve Geodetic Arc *
Vilnius (historic centre)

■ **Luxembourg**
City of Luxembourg, old quarters and fortifications

■ **Macedonia**
Ohrid region (natural and cultural heritage)

■ **Madagascar**
Royal Hill of Ambohimanga
Tsingy de Bemaraha Nature Reserve

■ **Malawi**
Chongoni (rock art area)
Lake Malawi National Park

■ **Malaysia**
Gunung Mulu National Park
Kinabalu Park

■ **Mali**
Cliffs of Bandiagara (land of the Dogons)
Djenné (old towns)
Timbuktu
Tomb of Askia

■ **Malta**
Hal Saflieni Hypogeum
Megalithic temples
Valetta (old city)

■ **Mauritania**
Ancient ksour of Ouadane, Chinguetti, Tichitt and Oualata
Banc d'Arguin National Park

■ **Mauritius**
Aapravasi Ghat

- **Mexico**
  Calakmul (ancient Maya city)
  Campeche (historic fortified town)
  Chichen Itza (pre-Hispanic city)
  El Tajin (pre-Hispanic city)
  El Vizcaino Whale Sanctuary
  Franciscan missions in Sierra Gorda of Querétaro
  Guadalajara (Hospicio Cabañas)
  Guanajuato (historic town) and mines
  Gulf of California (islands and protected areas)
  Luis Barragán House and Studio, Mexico City
  Mexico City (historic centre and Xochimilco)
  Morelia (historic centre)
  Oaxaca (historic centre) and Monte Albán (archaeological site)
  Palenque (pre-Hispanic city and national park)
  Paquimé, Casas Grandes (archaeological zone)
  Popocatepetl (16c monasteries)
  Puebla (historic centre)
  Querétaro (historic monuments zone)
  Sian Ka'an (biosphere reserve)
  Sierra de San Francisco (rock paintings)
  Teotihuacán (pre-Hispanic city)
  Tequila (agave landscape and ancient industrial facilities)
  Tlacotalpan (historic monuments zone)
  Uxmal (pre-Hispanic town)
  Xochicalco (archaeological monuments zone)
  Zacatecas (historic centre)
- **Moldova**
  Struve Geodetic Arc *
- **Mongolia**
  Orkhon Valley (cultural landscape)
  Uvs Nuur basin (shared with Russia)
- **Montenegro**
  Durmitor National Park
  Kotor (natural and culturo-historical region)
- **Morocco**
  Aït-Ben-Haddou (fortified village)
  Essaouira (Medina)
  Fez (Medina)
  Marrakesh (Medina)

  Meknes (historic city)
  Portuguese City of Mazagan (El Jadida)
  Tétouan (Medina)
  Volubilis (archaeological site)
- **Mozambique**
  Island of Mozambique
- **Nepal**
  Kathmandu Valley
  Lumbini (birthplace of Lord Buddha)
  Royal Chitwan National Park
  Sagarmatha National Park
- **The Netherlands**
  Amsterdam defence line
  Beemster Polder
  D F Wouda Steam Pumping Station
  Kinderdijk-Elshout (mill network)
  Rietveld Schröder House
  Schokland and its surroundings
  Willemstad (historic area, inner city and harbour), Netherlands Antilles
- **New Zealand**
  Sub-Antarctic Islands
  Te Wahipounamu (SW New Zealand)
  Tongariro National Park
- **Nicaragua**
  Ruins of León Viejo
- **Niger**
  Air and Ténéré Nature Reserves
  'W' National Park
- **Nigeria**
  Osun-Osogbo sacred grove
  Sukur (cultural landscape)
- **Norway**
  Alta (rock drawings)
  Bergen (Bryggen area)
  Røros (mining town)
  Struve Geodetic Arc *
  Urnes Stave Church
  Vega Archipelago
  West Norwegian Fjords (Geirangerfjord and Nærøyfjord)
- **Oman**
  Aflaj irrigation systems
  Arabian Oryx Sanctuary
  Bahla Fort
  Bat, Al-Khutm and Al-Ayn (archaeological sites)
  Land of Frankincense
- **Pakistan**
  Lahore (fort and Shalamar gardens)

Mohenjo Daro (archaeological site)
Rohtas Fort
Takht-i-Bahi (Buddhist ruins) and Sahr-i-Bahlol (city remains)
Taxila (archaeological remains)
Thatta (historical monuments)

■ **Panama**
Coiba National Park and marine protection zone
Darien National Park
La Amistad National Park (shared with Costa Rica)
Panama (archaeological site and historic district)
Portobelo and San Lorenzo fortifications

■ **Paraguay**
Jesuit Missions of La Santísima Trinidad de Paraná and Jesús de Tavarangue

■ **Peru**
Arequipa (historic centre)
Chan Chan (archaeological site)
Chavin (archaeological site)
Cuzco (old city)
Huascarán National Park
Lima (historic centre)
Machu Picchu (historic sanctuary)
Manú National Park
Nasca and Pampas de Jumana (lines and geoglyphs)
Río Abiseo National Park

■ **Philippines**
Baroque churches of the Philippines
Puerto-Princesa Subterranean River National Park
Rice terraces of the Philippine Cordilleras
Tubbataha Reef Marine Park
Vigan (historic town)

■ **Poland**
Auschwitz concentration camp
Belovezhskaya Pushcha/Białowieża Forest (shared with Belarus)
Cracow (historic centre)
Jawor and Swidnica Churches of Peace
Kalwaria Zebrzydowska (Mannerist architectural and park landscape complex, and pilgrimage park)
Malbork (castle of the Teutonic Order)
Muskauer Park/Park Muzakowski (shared with Germany)
Torún (medieval town)

Warsaw (historic centre)
Wieliczka saltmines
Wooden churches of southern Little Poland
Wroclaw Centennial Hall
Zamość (old city)

■ **Portugal**
Alcobaça monastery
Alto Douro wine region
Angra do Heroismo (town centre), Azores
Batalha monastery
Belém Tower and Monastery of the Hieronymites, Lisbon
Côa Valley (rock-art sites)
Évora (historic centre)
Guimarães (historic centre)
Laurisilva (laurel forest), Madeira
Oporto (historic centre)
Pico Island (vineyard culture)
Sintra (cultural landscape)
Tomar (Convent of Christ)

■ **Romania**
Biertan and its fortified church
Dacian fortresses, Orastie Mountains
Danube Delta
Horezu Monastery
Painted churches of northern Moldavia
Sighişoara (historic centre)
Wooden churches of Maramureş

■ **Russian Federation**
Central Sikhote-Alin
Curonian Spit (shared with Lithuania)
Derbent (citadel, ancient city and fortress)
Ferrapontov Monastery
Golden Mountains of Altai
Kamchatka volcanoes
Kazan Kremlin
Kizhi Pogost
Kolomenskoye (Church of the Ascension)
Lake Baikal
Moscow (Kremlin and Red Square)
Novodevichy Convent
Novgorod (historic monuments)
St Petersburg (historic centre)
Sergiev Posad (Trinity Sergius Lavra complex)
Solovetsky Islands
Struve Geodetic Arc *
Uvs Nuur basin (shared with Mongolia)
Virgin Komi forests

Vladimir and Suzdal monuments
Western Caucasus
Wrangel Island Reserve
Yaroslavl (historic centre)

■ **St Kitts and Nevis**
Brimstone Hill Fortress National Park

■ **St Lucia**
Pitons Management Area

■ **Senegal**
Djoudj Bird Sanctuary
Gorée Island
Niokolo-Koba National Park
Saint-Louis Island
Senegambia stone circles (shared with
the Gambia)

■ **Serbia**
Kosovo medieval monuments
Stari Ras and Sopoćani
Studenica Monastery

■ **Seychelles**
Aldabra Atoll
Vallée de Mai Nature Reserve

■ **Slovakia**
Aggtelek Karst and Slovak Karst caves
(shared with Hungary)
Banská Štiavnica and technical
monuments
Bardejov Town Conservation Reserve
Spišský Hrad and cultural monuments
Vlkolínec

■ **Slovenia**
Škocjan caves

■ **Solomon Islands**
East Rennell

■ **South Africa**
Cape Floral Region
Greater St Lucia Wetland Park
Mapungubwe (cultural landscape)
Robben Island
Sterkfontein, Swartkrans, Kromdraai and
environs (fossil hominid sites)
uKhahlamba/Drakensberg Park
Vredefort Dome

■ **Spain**
Alcalá de Henares (university and historic
precinct)
Altamira Cave
Aragon (Mudejar architecture)
Aranjuez (cultural landscape)
Atapuerca (archaeological site)

Ávila (old town) with its Extra-Muros
churches
Barcelona: Palau de la Música Catalana
and Hospital de Sant Pau
Barcelona: works of Antoni Gaudí
Burgos Cathedral
Cáceres (old town)
Córdoba (historic centre)
Cuenca (historic walled town)
Doñana National Park
El Escurial (monastery and site)
Garajonay National Park (Canary Is)
Granada (Alhambra, Generalife and
Albayzín)
Ibiza (biodiversity and culture)
Kingdom of Asturias (its churches) and
monuments of Oviedo
Las Médulas
Lugo (Roman walls)
Mérida
Palmeral of Elche
Poblet Monastery
Pyrenees, Mt Perdu landscape (shared
with France)
Rock art of the Mediterranean Basin on
the Iberian Peninsula
Routes of Santiago de Compostela
Salamanca (old city)
San Cristóbal de La Laguna
San Millán Yuso and Suso monasteries
Santa Maria de Guadalupe (royal
monastery)
Santiago de Compostela (old town)
Segovia (old town and aqueduct)
Seville (cathedral, Alcázar and Archivo
de Indias)
Tárraco (archaeological ensemble)
Toledo (historic city)
Úbeda and Baeza (Renaissance
monumental ensembles)
Valencia, 'La Lonja de la Seda'
Vall de Boi (Catalan Romanesque churches)
Vizcaya Bridge

■ **Sri Lanka**
Anuradhapura (sacred city)
Dambulla (Golden Rock Temple)
Galle (old town and its fortifications)
Kandy (sacred city)
Polonnaruwa (ancient city)
Sigiriya (ancient city)

Sinharaja Forest Reserve
- **Sudan**
  Gebe Barkal and the sites of the
  Napatan region
- **Suriname**
  Central Suriname Nature Reserve
  Paramaribo (historic inner city)
- **Sweden**
  Birka and Hovgården
  Drottningholm Palace and domain
  Engelsberg ironworks
  Falun (mining area of the Great Copper
  Mountain)
  Gammelstad (church village), Luleå
  Karlskrona (naval port)
  Kvarken Archipelago/High Coast (shared
  with Finland)
  Laponian area
  Skogskyrkogården
  Southern Öland (agricultural landscape)
  Struve Geodetic Arc *
  Tanum (rock carvings)
  Varberg Radio Station
  Visby (Hanseatic town)
- **Switzerland**
  Bellinzone (castles, defensive walls and
  ramparts)
  Berne (old city)
  Jungfrau-Aletsch-Bietschhorn
  Monte San Giorgio
  Müstair: Benedictine convent of St John
  St Gall convent
- **Syria**
  Aleppo (ancient city)
  Bosra (ancient city)
  Crac des Chevaliers and Qal'at Salah El-Din
  Damascus (ancient city)
  Palmyra (archaeological site)
- **Tanzania**
  Kilimanjaro National Park
  Kilwa Kisiwani and Songa Mnara ruins
  Kondos (rock art sites)
  Ngorongoro conservation area
  Selous Game Reserve
  Serengeti National Park
  Zanzibar (stone town)
- **Thailand**
  Ayutthaya (historic city)
  Ban Chiang (archaeological site)
  Dong Phayayen-Khao Yai forest complex

Sukhothai (historic city) and associated
  towns
  Thungyai-Huai Kha Khaeng wildlife
  sanctuaries
- **Togo**
  Koutammakou (land of the Batammariba)
- **Tunisia**
  Carthage (archaeological site)
  Dougga/Thugga
  El Djem (amphitheatre)
  Ichkeul National Park
  Kairouan
  Kerkuane (Punic town and necropolis)
  Sousse (Medina)
  Tunis (Medina)
- **Turkey**
  Divriği (Great Mosque and hospital)
  Göreme National Park and rock sites of
  Cappadocia
  Hattusha (Hittite city)
  Hierapolis-Pamukkale
  Istanbul (historic areas)
  Nemrut Dağ (archaeological site)
  Safranbolu (old city)
  Troy (archaeological site)
  Xanthos-Letoon
- **Turkmenistan**
  Ancient Merv (state historical and
  cultural park)
  Kunya-Urgench
- **Uganda**
  Bwindi Impenetrable National Park
  Kasubi (tombs of Buganda Kings)
  Rwenzori Mountains National Park
- **Ukraine**
  L'viv (historic centre)
  St Sophia Cathedral and Kiev-Pechersk
  Lavra, Kiev
  Struve Geodetic Arc *
- **UK**
  Bath (city)
  Blaenavon (industrial landscape)
  Blenheim Palace
  Canterbury Cathedral, St Augustine's
  Abbey and St Martin's Church
  Cornwall and West Devon mining
  landscape
  Derwent Valley Mills
  Dorset and East Devon coast
  Durham castle and cathedral

Edinburgh Old and New Towns
Frontiers of the Roman Empire (shared with Germany)
Giant's Causeway and its coast
Gough and Inaccessible Islands (South Atlantic Ocean)
Greenwich (maritime buildings and park)
Gwynedd castles and towns of King Edward I
Henderson Island (Pacific Ocean)
Ironbridge Gorge
Liverpool (maritime mercantile city)
New Lanark
Orkney (Neolithic areas)
Royal Botanic Gardens, Kew
Saltaire
St George, Bermuda (historic town and fortifications)
St Kilda (island)
Stonehenge, Avebury and related megalithic sites
Studley Royal Park and the ruins of Fountains Abbey
Tower of London
Westminster (palace and abbey) and St Margaret's Church

■ **USA**
Cahokia Mounds historic site
Carlsbad Caverns National Park
Chaco Culture National Historical Park
Everglades National Park
Grand Canyon National Park
Great Smoky Mountains National Park
Hawaii Volcanoes National Park
Independence Hall, Philadelphia
La Fortaleza and San Juan historic site, Puerto Rico
Mammoth Cave National Park
Mesa Verde National Park
Monticello and the University of Virginia in Charlottesville
Olympic National Park
Pueblo de Taos
Redwood National Park
Statue of Liberty

Tatshenshini-Alsek, Kluane National Park, Wrangell St Elias National Park and Reserve, and Glacier Bay National Park (shared with Canada)
Waterton Glacier International Peace Park (shared with Canada)
Yellowstone National Park
Yosemite National Park

■ **Uruguay**
Colonia del Sacramento (historic quarter)

■ **Uzbekistan**
Bukhara (historic centre)
Itchan Kala (historic city)
Samarkand
Shakhrisyabz (historic centre)

● **Vatican City**
Rome properties of the Holy See outside the Vatican City, and San Paolo Fuori le Mura
Vatican City

■ **Venezuela**
Canaima National Park
Coro and its port
Cuidad Universitaria de Caracas

● **Vietnam**
Ha Long Bay
Hoi An (ancient town)
Hué monuments complex
My Son Sanctuary
Phong Nha-Ke Bang National Park

■ **Yemen**
San'a (old city)
Shibam (old walled city)
Zabid (historic town)

■ **Zambia**
Mosi-oa-Tunya/Victoria Falls (shared with Zimbabwe)

■ **Zimbabwe**
Khami Ruins National Monument
Great Zimbabwe National Monument
Mana Pools National Park and Sapi and Chewore safari areas
Matobo Hills
Mosi-oa-Tunya/Victoria Falls (shared with Zambia)

* Struve Geodetic Arc is shared by Belarus, Estonia, Finland, Latvia, Lithuania, Moldova, Norway, Russia, Sweden and Ukraine.

NATURAL HISTORY

Cereals

English name	Species	Area of origin
barley	*Hordeum vulgare*	Middle East
maize (or corn, sweetcorn, Indian corn)	*Zea mays*	C America
millet, bulrush	*Pennisetum americanum*	tropics, warm temperate regions
millet, common	*Panicum miliaceum*	tropics, warm temperate regions
millet, foxtail (or Italian millet)	*Setaria italica*	tropics, warm temperate regions
oats	*Avena sativa*	Mediterranean basin
rice	*Oryza sativa*	Asia
rye	*Secale cereale*	Mediterranean, SW Asia
sorghum (or Kaffir corn)	*Sorghum bicolor*	Africa, Asia
wheat	Genus *Triticum*, 20 species	Mediterranean, W Asia

Edible fruits (temperate and Mediterranean)

English name	Species	Colour	Area of origin
apple	*Malus pumila*	green, yellow, red	temperate regions
apricot	*Prunus armeniaca*	yellow, orange	Asia
bilberry	*Vaccinium myrtillus*	blue, black	Europe, N Asia
blackberry (or bramble)	*Rubus fruticosus*	purple, black	N hemisphere
blackcurrant	*Ribes nigrum*	black	Europe, Asia, Africa
blueberry	*Vaccinium corymbosum*	blue, purple, black	America, Europe
Cape gooseberry ▶ physalis			
cherry (sour)	*Prunus cerasus*	red	temperate regions
cherry (sweet)	*Prunus avium*	purple, red	temperate regions
clementine	*Citrus reticulata*	orange	W Mediterranean
cranberry	*Vaccinium oxycoccus*	red	N America
damson	*Prunus damascena*	purple	temperate regions
date	*Phoenix dactylifera*	yellow, red, brown	Persian Gulf
date-plum ▶ persimmon			
fig	*Ficus carica*	white, black, purple, green	W Asia
gooseberry	*Ribes grossularia*	green, red	Europe

English name	Species	Colour	Area of origin
grape	*Vitis vinifera*	green, purple, black	Asia
grapefruit	*Citrus × paradisi*	yellow	W Indies
greengage	*Prunus italica*	green	temperate regions
kiwi fruit	*Actinidia chinensis*	brown skin, green flesh	China
kumquat	*Fortunella margarita*	orange	China
lemon	*Citrus limon*	yellow	India, S Asia
lime	*Citrus aurantifolia*	green	SE Asia
loganberry	*Rubus loganobaccus*	red	America
loquat	*Eriobotrya japonica*	yellow	China, Japan
lychee	*Litchi chinensis*	reddish-brown skin, white flesh	China
mandarin (or tangerine)	*Citrus reticulata*	orange	China
medlar	*Mespilus germanica*	russet brown	SE Europe, Asia
melon	*Cucumis melo*	green, yellow	Egypt
minneola ▶ tangelo			
mulberry	*Morus nigra*	purple, red	W Asia
nectarine	*Prunus persica nectarina*	orange, red	China
orange	*Citrus sinensis*	orange	China
peach	*Prunus persica var. nectarina*	yellow, red	China
pear	*Pyrus communis*	yellow	Middle East, E Europe
persimmon (or date-plum)	*Diospyros kaki*	yellow, orange	E Asia
physalis (or Cape gooseberry)	*Physalis alkekengi*	yellow	S America
plum	*Prunus domestica*	red, yellow, purple, orange	temperate regions
pomegranate	*Punica granatum*	red, yellow	Persia
pomelo	*Citrus maxima*	yellow	Malaysia
quince	*Cydonia oblonga*	golden	Iran
raspberry	*Rubus idaeus*	red, crimson	N hemisphere
redcurrant	*Ribes rubrum*	red	Europe, Asia, Africa
rhubarb	*Rheum rhaponticum*	red, green, pink	Asia
satsuma	*Citrus reticulata*	orange	Japan
strawberry	*Fragaria ananassa*	red	Europe, Asia
tangelo (or minneola, or ugli)	*Citrus × tangelo*	orange, yellow	N America
tangerine ▶ mandarin			
ugli ▶ tangelo			
watermelon	*Citrullus vulgaris*	green, yellow	Africa
white currant	*Ribes rubrum* cv.	white	W Europe

Edible fruits (tropical)

English name	Species	Colour	Area of origin
acerola	*Malpighia glabra*	yellow, red	S America
avocado	*Persea americana*	green, purple	C America, Mexico
banana	*Musa acuminita*	yellow	India, S Asia
breadfruit	*Artocarpus altilis*	greenish brown, yellow	Malaysia
carambola	*Averrhoa carambola*	yellow, green	S China
cherimoya	*Annona cherimola*	green skin, white flesh	Peru
guava	*Psidium guajava*	green, yellow	S America
mango	*Mangifera indica*	green, yellow, orange, red, purple	S Asia
papaya (or pawpaw)	*Carica papaya*	green, yellow, orange	tropics
passion fruit	*Passiflora edulis*	purple, yellow, brown	S America
pineapple	*Ananas comosus*	green, yellow	S America
sapodilla plum	*Manilkara zapota*	brown	C America
soursop	*Anona muricata*	green	C and S America
tamarind	*Tamarindus indica*	brown	Africa, S Asia

Herbs

Herbs may be used for medicinal, cosmetic or culinary purposes. Any part of those marked * may be poisonous when ingested.

English name	Species	Part of plant used	Area of origin
aconite* (or monkshood or winter aconite)	*Aconitum napellus*	tuber	Europe, NW Asia
agrimony	*Agrimonia eupatoria*	flowers	Europe
alecost (or costmary)	*Balsamita major*	leaves, flowers	E Mediterranean
aloe	*Aloe vera*	leaves	Africa
aniseed	*Pimpinella anisum*	fruits (seed heads)	Asia
basil	*Ocimum basilicum*	leaves, flowering shoots	tropics
borage	*Borago officinalis*	leaves, flowers	Mediterranean
camomile	*Anthemis nobilis*	flowers	Europe, Asia
celandine	*Chelidonium majus*	buds	Europe
celery	*Apium graveolens*	roots, stems, leaves	Europe
chervil	*Anthriscus cerefolium*	leaves	Europe, Asia
chicory	*Cichorium intybus*	leaves, roots	Europe
chives	*Allium schoenoprasum*	leaves	Europe, Asia, N America
coriander	*Coriandrum sativum*	leaves, fruits	N Africa, W Asia

English name	Species	Part of plant used	Area of origin
dandelion	*Taraxacum officinalis*	leaves, roots	Europe
deadly nightshade*	*Atropa belladonna*	root	Europe, Asia
dill	*Anethum graveolens*	leaves, fruits (seeds)	S Europe
elderberry	*Sambucus nigra*	flowers, fruits	Europe
epazote	*Chenopodium ambrosioides*	leaves	C and S America
fennel, Florentine	*Foeniculum vulgare* var. *azoricum*	leaves, stems, fruits (seeds)	Mediterranean
feverfew	*Tanacetum parthenium*	leaves, flowers	SE Europe, W Asia
foxglove*	*Digitalis purpurea*	leaves	Europe
garlic	*Allium sativum*	bulbs	Asia
gentian	*Gentiana lutea*	rhizomes, roots	Europe
ginseng	*Panax pseudo-ginseng*	roots	China
guaiacum	*Guaiacum officinale*	leaves	Caribbean
heart's-ease (or wild pansy)	*Viola tricolor*	flowers	Europe
hemlock*	*Conium maculatum*	all parts	Europe
hemp (or ganja or cannabis or marijuana)	*Cannabis sativa*	leaves, flowers	Asia
henbane*	*Hyoscyamus niger*	leaves, fruits (seeds)	Europe, W Asia, N Africa
henna	*Lawsonia inermis*	leaves	Asia, Africa
horseradish	*Armoracia rusticana*	roots, flowering shoots, leaves	SE Europe, W Asia
hyssop	*Hyssopus officinalis*	leaves, flowers	S Europe
juniper	*Juniperus communis*	fruits (berries), wood	Mediterranean
lavender	*Lavandula vera*	flowers, stems	Mediterranean
leek	*Allium porrum*	stem, leaves	Europe
lemon	*Citrus limon*	fruits	Asia
lemon balm	*Melissa officinalis*	leaves	S Europe
lily of the valley	*Convallaria majalis*	leaves, flowers	Europe, N America
lime	*Tilia cordata*	flowers	Europe
liquorice	*Glycyrrhiza glabra*	roots	Europe
lovage	*Levisticum officinale*	leaves, shoots, stems, roots	W Asia
mandrake*	*Mandragora officinarum*	roots	Himalayas, SE Europe, W Asia
marjoram	*Oreganum majorana*	leaves, shoots, stems	Africa, Mediterranean, Asia
marsh mallow	*Althaea officinalis*	leaves, roots	Europe, Asia

English name	Species	Part of plant used	Area of origin
maté	Ilex paraguariensis	leaves	S America
milfoil ▶ yarrow			
monkshood ▶ aconite			
mugwort	Artemesia vulgaris	leaves	Europe, Asia
myrrh	Commiphora myrrha	resin	Arabia, Africa
myrtle	Myrtus communis	leaves, flower heads, fruits (berries)	Asia, Mediterranean
nasturtium	Tropaeolom majus	leaves, flowers, fruits	Peru
onion	Allium cepa	bulbs	Asia
oregano	Origanum vulgare	leaves, shoots, stems	Mediterranean
parsley	Petroselinum crispum	leaves, stems	Mediterranean
peony	Paeonia officinalis	roots, seeds	Europe, Asia, N America
peppermint	Mentha × piperita	leaves	Europe
poppy, opium*	Papaver somniferum	fruits, seeds	Asia
purslane	Portulaca oleracea	leaves	Europe
rosemary	Rosmarinus officinalis	leaves	Mediterranean
rue	Ruta graveolens	leaves, stems, flowers	Mediterranean
saffron	Crocus sativus	flowers	Asia Minor
sage	Salvia officinalis	leaves	N Mediterranean
sorrel	Rumex acetosa	leaves	Europe
spearmint	Mentha spicata	leaves	Europe
tansy	Tanacetum vulgare	leaves, flowers	Asia
tarragon, French	Artemesia dracunculus	leaves, stems	Asia, E Europe
thyme	Thymus vulgaris	leaves, stems, flowers	Mediterranean
valerian	Valeriana officinalis	rhizomes, roots	Europe, Asia
vervain	Verbena officinalis	leaves, flowers	Europe, Asia, N Africa
watercress	Nasturtium officinale	leaves, shoots, stems	Europe, Asia
witch-hazel	Hamamelis virginiana	leaves, shoots, bark	N America, E Asia
wormwood	Artemesia absinthium	leaves, flowering shoots	Europe
yarrow (or milfoil)	Achillea millefolium	flower heads, leaves	Europe, W Asia

Spices

English name	Species	Part of plant used	Area of origin
allspice	*Pimenta dioica*	fruits	America, W Indies
annatto	*Bixa orellana*	seeds	S America, W Indies
asafoetida	*Ferula assa-foetida*	sap	W Asia
bay	*Laurus nobilis*	leaves	Mediterranean, Asia Minor
caper	*Capparis spinosa*	flower buds	Europe
caraway	*Carum carvi*	seeds	Europe, Asia
cardamom	*Elettaria cardamomum*	seeds	SE Asia
cayenne	*Capsicum annuum*	fruit pods	America, Africa
chilli pepper	*Capsicum frutescens*	fruit pods	America
cinnamon	*Cinnamomum zeylanicum*	bark	India
cloves	*Eugenia caryophyllus*	buds	Moluccas
cocoa	*Theobroma cacoa*	seeds (beans)	S America
coconut	*Cocus nucifera*	fruits	Polynesia
coriander	*Coriandrum sativum*	fruits	S Europe
cumin	*Cuminum cyminum*	fruits (seed heads)	Mediterranean
curry leaf	*Murraya koenigi*	leaves	India
fennel	*Foeniculum vulgare*	fruits	S Europe
fenugreek	*Trigonella foenum-graecum*	seeds	India, S Europe
ginger	*Zingiber officinale*	rhizomes	SE Asia
horseradish	*Armoracia rusticana*	roots	E Europe
mace	*Myristica fragrans*	seeds	Moluccas
mustard, black	*Brassica nigra*	seeds	Europe, Africa, Asia, America
mustard, white	*Sinapis alba*	seeds	Europe, Asia
nutmeg	*Myristica fragrans*	seeds	Indonesia
paprika	*Capsicum annuum*	fruit pods	S America
pepper	*Piper nigrum*	seeds	India
sandalwood	*Santalum album*	heartwood, roots	India, Indonesia, Australia
sassafras	*Sassafras albidum*	root bark	N America
sesame	*Sesamum indicum*	seeds	tropics
soya	*Glycine max*	fruit (beans)	China
tamarind	*Tamarindus indica*	fruits	Africa
turmeric	*Curcuma longa*	rhizomes	SE Asia
vanilla	*Vanilla planifolia*	fruit pods	C America

Vegetables

English name	Species	Part eaten	Area of origin
artichoke, Chinese	*Stachys affinis*	tuber	China
artichoke, globe	*Cynara scolymus*	buds	Mediterranean
artichoke, Jerusalem	*Helianthus tuberosus*	tuber	N America
asparagus	*Asparagus officinalis*	young shoots	Europe, Asia
aubergine (or eggplant)	*Solanum melongena*	fruit	Asia, Africa
avocado	*Persea americana*	fruit	C America
bean sprout	*Vigna radiata*	shoots	China
bean, blackeyed	*Vigna unguiculata*	seeds	India, Iran
bean, borlotti (or Boston bean or pinto bean)	*Phaseolus vulgaris*	seeds	America
bean, broad	*Vicia faba*	seeds and pods	Africa, Europe
bean, flageolet	*Phaseolus vulgaris*	seeds	America
bean, French	*Phaseolus vulgaris*	pods	America
bean, haricot	*Phaseolus vulgaris*	seeds	America
bean, kidney	*Phaseolus vulgaris*	seeds	America
bean, runner	*Phaseolus coccineus*	pods	America
bean, soya	*Glycine max*	seeds	E Asia
beetroot	*Beta vulgaris*	root	Mediterranean
broccoli	*Brassica oleracea*	buds and leaves	Europe
Brussels sprout	*Brassica oleracea* (gemmifera)	buds	N Europe
cabbage	*Brassica oleracea*	leaves	Europe, W Asia
cardoon	*Cynara cardunculus*	inner stalks and flower heads	Mediterranean
carrot	*Daucus carota*	root	Asia
cauliflower	*Brassica oleracea* (botrytis)	flower buds	Middle East
celeriac	*Apium graveolens* var. *rapaceum*	root	Mediterranean
celery	*Apium graveolens* var. *dulce*	stalks	Europe, N Africa, America
chayote (or chocho)	*Sechium edule*	fruit	America
chickpea	*Cicer arietinum*	seeds	W Asia
chicory	*Cichorium intybus*	leaves	Europe, W Asia
chinese leaf	*Brassica pekinensis*	leaf stalks	E Asia, China
chives	*Allium schoenoprasum*	leaves	Europe, N America
courgette (or zucchini)	*Cucurbita pepo*	fruit	S America, Africa

English name	Species	Part eaten	Area of origin
cucumber	*Cucumus sativus*	fruit	S Asia
eggplant ▶ aubergine			
endive	*Cichorium endivia*	leaves	S Europe, E Indies, Africa
fennel, Florentine	*Foeniculum vulgare* var. *dulce*	leaf stalks	Europe
kale (or borecole)	*Brassica oleracea* (acephala)	leaves	Europe
kohlrabi	*Brassica oleracea* (gongylodes)	stems	Europe
laver	*Porphyra leucosticta, P. umbilicalis*	leaves and stems	Europe
leek	*Allium porrum*	leaves and stems	Europe, N Africa
lentil	*Lens culinaris*	seeds	S Asia
lettuce	*Lactuca sativa*	leaves	Middle East
marrow	*Cucurbita pepo*	fruit	America
mooli	*Raphanus sativus*	root	E Africa
mushroom	*Agaricus campestris*	fruiting body	worldwide
okra	*Abelmoschus esculentus*	pods and seeds	Africa
onion	*Allium cepa*	bulb	C Asia
parsnip	*Pastinaca sativa*	root	Europe
pea	*Pisum sativum*	pods and seeds	Asia, Europe
pepper	*Capsicum annuum*	fruit	S America
potato	*Solanum tuberosum*	tuber	S America
pumpkin	*Cucurbita pepo*	fruit	S America
radish	*Raphanus sativus*	root	China, Japan
salsify	*Tragopogon porrifolius*	root	S Europe
sorrel	*Rumex acetosa*	leaves	Europe
spinach	*Spinacea oleracea*	leaves	Asia
squash, winter	*Cucurbita maxima*	fruit	America
squash, summer	*Cucurbita pepo*	fruit	America
swede	*Brassica napus* (napobrassica)	root	Europe
sweet potato	*Ipomoea batatas*	tuber	C America
swiss chard	*Beta vulgaris* subsp. *cicla*	leaves and stems	Europe
tomato	*Lycopersicon esculentum*	fruit	S America
turnip	*Brassica rapa*	root	Middle East
watercress	*Nasturtium officinale*	leaves and stems	Europe, Asia

English name	Species	Part eaten	Area of origin
yam	Genus *Dioscorea*, 60 species	tuber	tropics
zucchini ▶ courgette			

Flowers (bulbs, corms, rhizomes and tubers)

English name	Genus/Family	Colour	Area of origin
acidanthera	*Acidanthera*	white	NE Africa
African lily (or lily-of-the-Nile)	*Agapanthus*	white, purple	S Africa
agapanthus	*Agapanthus*	blue, white	S Africa
allium	*Allium*	blue, lilac, white, rose	Asia, Europe
amaryllis (or belladonna lily)	*Amaryllis*	rose-pink	S Africa, tropical America
anemone	*Anemone*	white, lilac, blue	Mediterranean, Asia, Europe
belladonna lily ▶ amaryllis			
bluebell	*Hyacinthoides*	blue	Europe
camassia	*Camassia*	white, cream, blue, purple	N America
chionodoxa (or glory of the snow)	*Chionodoxa*	blue, white, pink	Greece, Turkey
crinum	*Crinum*	rose-pink, white	S Africa
crocosmia	*Crocosmia*	orange	S Africa
crocus	*Crocus*	purple, rose, yellow, pink, orange	Mediterranean, Asia, Africa
crown imperial	*Fritillaria*	orange	N India
curtonus	*Curtonus*	orange	S Africa
cyclamen	*Cyclamen*	white, pink, red	Asia, Mediterranean
daffodil (or narcissus)	*Narcissus*	white, yellow, orange	Mediterranean, Europe
dogtooth violet ▶ erythronium			
erythronium (or dogtooth violet)	*Erythronium*	purple, pink, white, yellow	Europe, Asia
fritillaria	*Fritillaria*	red, yellow	Europe, Asia, N America
galtonia	*Galtonia*	white	S Africa
gladiolus	*Gladiolus*	purple, yellow	Europe, Asia
glory of the snow ▶ chionodoxa			
harebell	*Campanula*	blue	N temperate regions
hippeastrum	*Hippeastrum*	pink, white, red	tropical America
hyacinth	*Hyacinthus*	blue, white, red	S Europe, Asia
hyacinth, grape	*Muscari*	blue	Europe, Mediterranean

English name	Genus/Family	Colour	Area of origin
hyacinth, wild	*Scilla*	blue, purple, pink, white	Asia, S Europe
iris	*Iris*	purple, white, yellow	N temperate regions
Ithuriel's spear	*Brodiaea*	white, pink, blue	N America
lapeirousia	*Lapeirousia*	red	S Africa
lily	*Lilium*	white, pink, crimson, yellow, orange, red	China, Europe, America
lily-of-the-Nile ▶ African lily			
lily-of-the-valley	*Convallaria*	white	Europe, Asia, America
naked ladies	*Colchicum*	white, pink, purple	Asia, Europe
nerine	*Nerine*	pink, salmon	S Africa
ornithogalum	*Ornithogalum*	white, yellow	S Africa
peacock (or tiger flower)	*Tigridia*	white, orange, red, yellow	Asia
rouge, giant	*Tigridia*	white, yellow, red, lilac	Mexico
snake's-head	*Fritillaria*	purple, white	Europe
snowdrop	*Galanthus*	white	Europe
snowflake	*Leucojum*	white, green	S Europe
solfaterre	*Crocosmia × crocosmiflora*	orange, red	S Africa
Solomon's seal	*Polygonatum*	white	Europe, Asia
squill	*Scilla*	blue, purple	Europe, Asia, S Africa
sternbergia	*Sternbergia*	yellow	Europe
striped squill	*Puschkinia*	bluish-white	Asia
tiger flower ▶ peacock			
tiger lily	*Lilium*	orange	Asia
tulip	*Tulipa*	orange, red, pink, white, crimson, lilac	Europe, Asia
wand flower	*Dierama*	white, pink, mauve, purple	S Africa
winter aconite	*Eranthis*	yellow	Greece, Turkey

Flowers (herbaceous)

English name	Genus/Family	Colour	Area of origin
acanthus	*Acanthus*	white, rose, purple	Europe
African violet	*Saintpaulia*	violet, white, pink	Africa
alum root	*Heuchera*	rose, pink, red	N America
alyssum	*Alyssum*	white, yellow, pink	S Europe
anchusa	*Anchusa*	blue	Asia, S Europe
anemone	*Hepatica*	white, red-pink, blue	Europe, Caucasus
asphodel	*Asphodelus*	white, yellow	S Europe

English name	Genus/Family	Colour	Area of origin
aster	*Aster*	white, blue, purple, pink	Europe, Asia, N America
astilbe	*Astilbe*	white, pink, red	Asia
aubrietia	*Aubrieta*	purple	SE Europe
begonia	*Begonia*	pink	S America, the Pacific
bellflower	*Campanula*	blue, white	N temperate regions
bergamot	*Monarda*	white, pink, red, purple	N America
bistort	*Polygonum*	rose-pink	Japan, Himalayas
bleeding heart	*Dicentra*	pink, white, red	China, Japan, N America
bugbane	*Cimicifuga*	white	N America, Japan
busy lizzie	*Impatiens*	crimson, pink, white	tropics
buttercup	*Ranunculus*	yellow	temperate regions
carnation	*Dianthus*	white, pink, red	temperate regions
catmint	*Nepeta*	blue, mauve	Europe, Asia
celandine, giant	*Ranunculus*	white, copper-orange	Europe
Christmas rose	*Helleborus*	white, pink	Europe
chrysanthemum	*Chrysanthemum*	yellow, white	China
cinquefoil	*Potentilla*	orange, red, yellow	Europe, Asia
columbine (or granny's bonnet)	*Aquilegia*	purple, dark blue, pink, yellow	Europe
cupid's dart	*Catananche*	blue, white	Europe
dahlia	*Dahlia*	red, yellow, white	Mexico
daisy	*Bellis*	white, yellow, pink	Europe
delphinium	*Delphinium*	white, mauve, pink, blue	Europe, N America
echinacea	*Echinacea*	rose-red, purple	N America
edelweiss	*Leontopodium*	yellow, white	Europe, Asia
evening primrose	*Oenothera*	yellow	N America
everlasting flower (or immortelle)	*Helichrysum bracteatum*	yellow	Australia
everlasting flower, pearly	*Anaphalis*	white	N America, Himalayas
fleabane	*Erigeron*	white, pink, blue, violet	Australia
forget-me-not	*Myosotis*	blue	Europe
foxglove	*Digitalis*	white, yellow, pink, red	Europe, Asia
fraxinella	*Dictamnus*	white, mauve	Europe, Asia
gentian	*Gentiana*	blue, yellow, white, red	temperate regions
geranium	*Pelargonium*	scarlet, pink, white	temperate regions, subtropics
geum	*Geum*	orange, red, yellow	S Europe, N America
goat's-beard	*Aruncus*	white	N Europe

English name	Genus/Family	Colour	Area of origin
golden rod	*Solidago*	yellow	Europe
granny's bonnet ▶ columbine			
gypsophila	*Gypsophila*	white, pink	Europe, Asia
Hattie's pincushion (or the melancholy gentleman)	*Astrantia*	white, pink	Europe
heliopsis	*Heliopsis*	orange-yellow	N America
hellebore	*Helleborus*	plum-purple, white	Asia, Greece
herb Christopher	*Actaea*	white	N America
hollyhock	*Alcaea*	white, yellow, pink, red, maroon	Europe, China
hosta	*Hosta*	violet, white	China, Japan
immortelle ▶ everlasting flower			
kaffir lily	*Schizostylis*	red, pink	S Africa
kirengeshoma	*Kirengeshoma*	yellow	Japan
liatris	*Liatris*	heather-purple	N America
lobelia	*Lobelia*	white, red, blue, purple	Africa, N America, Australia
loosestrife	*Lysimachia*	rose-pink, purple	Europe
lotus	*Lotus*	yellow, pink, white	Asia, America
lupin	*Lupinus*	blue, yellow, pink, red	N America
marigold, African (or French marigold)	*Tagetes*	yellow, orange	Mexico
marigold, pot	*Calendula*	orange, apricot, cream	unknown
meadow rue	*Thalictrum*	yellow-white	Europe, Asia
mullein	*Verbascum*	yellow, white, pink, purple	Europe, Asia
nasturtium	*Tropaeolum*	yellow, red, orange	S America, Mexico
orchid	*Orchidaea*	red, purple, white, violet, green, brown, yellow, pink	tropics
ox-eye	*Buphthalmum*	yellow	Europe
pansy	*Viola*	white, yellow	temperate regions
peony	*Paeonia*	white, yellow, pink, red	Asia, Europe
Peruvian lily	*Alstroemeria*	cream, pink, yellow, orange, red	S America
petunia	*Petunia*	blue, violet, purple, white, pink	S America
phlox	*Phlox*	blue, white, purple, red	America
poppy	*Papaver*	red, orange, white, yellow, lilac	N temperate regions

English name	Genus/Family	Colour	Area of origin
primrose	*Primula*	yellow	N temperate regions
primula	*Primula*	white, pink, yellow, blue, purple	N temperate regions
red-hot poker	*Kniphofia*	white, yellow, orange, red	S Africa
salvia	*Salvia*	red, yellow, blue	S America, Europe, Asia
sea holly	*Eryngium*	blue, green-grey, white	Europe, S America
sidalcea	*Sidalcea*	lilac, pink, rose	N America
snapdragon	*Antirrhinum*	white, yellow, pink, red, maroon	Europe, Asia, S America
speedwell	*Veronica*	blue, white	Europe, Asia
spiderwort	*Tradescantia*	white, blue, pink, red, purple	N America
stokesia	*Stokesia*	white, blue, purple	N America
sunflower	*Helianthus*	yellow	N America
sweet pea	*Lathyrus*	purple, pink, white, red	Mediterranean
sweet william	*Dianthus*	white, pink, red, purple	S Europe
thistle, globe	*Echinops*	blue, white-grey	Europe, Asia
thistle, Scotch (or cotton thistle)	*Onopordum*	purple	Europe
violet	*Viola*	mauve, blue	N temperate regions
water chestnut	*Trapa*	white, lilac	Asia
water lily	*Nymphaea*	white, blue, red, yellow	worldwide
wolfsbane	*Aconitum*	blue, white, rose, yellow	Europe, Asia
yarrow	*Achillea*	white, cream	Europe, W Asia

Flowers (shrubs)

English name	Genus / Family	Colour	Area of origin
abelia	*Abelia*	white, rose-purple	Asia, China, Mexico
abutilon	*Abutilon*	lavender-blue	S America
acacia (or mimosa or wattle)	*Acacia*	yellow	Australia, tropical Africa, tropical America
almond, dwarf	*Prunus*	white, crimson, rose-pink	Asia, Europe
ampelopsis	*Ampelopsis*	green (blue-black fruit)	Far East
anthyllis	*Anthyllis*	yellow	Europe
azalea	*Rhododendron*	pink, purple, white, yellow, crimson	N hemisphere
berberis	*Berberis*	yellow, orange	Asia, America, Europe

English name	Genus / Family	Colour	Area of origin
bottlebrush	*Callistemon*	red	Australia
bougainvillea	*Bougainvillea*	lilac, pink, purple, red, orange, white	S America
broom	*Cytisus*	yellow	Europe
buckthorn	*Rhamnus*	red, black	N hemisphere
buddleia	*Buddleja*	purple, yellow, white	China, S America
cactus	*Cactaceae*	red, purple, orange, yellow, white	America
calico bush (or mountain laurel)	*Kalmia*	white, pink	China
camellia	*Camellia*	white, pink, red	Asia
caryopteris	*Caryopteris*	blue, violet	Asia
ceanothus	*Ceanothus*	pink, blue, purple	N America
ceratostigma	*Ceratostigma*	purple-blue	China
Chinese lantern	*Physalis*	orange, red	Japan
cistus	*Cistus*	white, pink	Europe
clematis	*Clematis*	white, purple, violet, blue, pink, yellow	N temperate regions
clerodendron	*Clerodendron*	white, purple-red	China
colquhounia	*Colquhounia*	scarlet, yellow	Himalayas
cornelian cherry	*Cornus*	yellow	Europe
coronilla	*Coronilla*	yellow	S Europe
corylopsis	*Corylopsis*	yellow	China, Japan
cotoneaster	*Cotoneaster*	white (red fruit)	Asia
currant, flowering	*Ribes*	red, white, pink	N America
desfontainia	*Desfontainia*	scarlet-gold	S America
deutzia	*Deutzia*	white, pink	Asia
diplera	*Diplera*	pale pink	China
dogwood	*Cornus*	white	Europe, SW Asia
embothrium	*Embothrium*	scarlet	S America
escallonia	*Escallonia*	white, pink	S America
euchryphia	*Euchryphia*	white	Chile, Australasia
euryops	*Euryops*	yellow	S Africa
fabiana	*Fabiana*	white, mauve	S America
firethorn	*Pyracantha*	white (red, orange, yellow fruits)	China
forsythia	*Forsythia*	yellow	China
frangipani	*Plumeria*	white, pink, yellow	tropical America
fuchsia	*Fuchsia*	red, pink, white	C and S America, New Zealand
gardenia	*Gardenia*	white	tropics
garland flower	*Daphne*	pink, crimson, white, purple	Europe, Asia
garrya	*Garrya*	green	California and Oregon

English name	Genus / Family	Colour	Area of origin
gorse (or furze or whin)	Ulex	yellow	Europe, Britain
hawthorn	Crataegus	white (orange-red berries)	N America, Europe, N Africa
heath, winter-flowering	Erica	white, pink, red	Africa, Europe
heather	Calluna	pink, purple, white	Europe, W Asia
hebe	Hebe	blue-white	New Zealand
helichrysum	Helichrysum	yellow	Australia, S Africa
hibiscus	Hibiscus	pink, mauve, purple, white, red	China, India
honeysuckle	Lonicera	white, yellow, pink, red	temperate regions
hydrangea	Hydrangea	white, pink, blue	Asia, America
hyssop	Hyssopus	bluish-purple	S Europe, W Asia
indigofera	Indigofera	rose-purple	Himalayas
ipomoea (or morning glory)	Ipomoea	white, red, blue	tropical America
japonica	Chaenomeles	white, pink, orange, red, yellow	N Asia
jasmine	Jasminum	white, yellow, red	Asia
Jerusalem sage	Phlomis	yellow	Europe
kerria	Kerria	yellow	China
kolkwitzia	Kolkwitzia	pink	China
laburnum	Laburnum	yellow	Europe, Asia
lavender	Lavandula	purple	Europe
leptospermum	Leptospermum	red, white	Australasia
lespedeza	Lespedeza	rose-purple	China, Japan
leycesteria	Leycesteria	claret	Himalayas
lilac (or syringa)	Syringa	purple, pink, white	Balkans
lion's tail	Leonotis	red	S Africa
magnolia	Magnolia	yellow, white, rose, purple	China, Japan
mahonia	Mahonia	yellow	Japan
malus	Malus	white, pink, red	N America, Asia
menziesa	Menziesa	wine-red	Japan
mimosa ▶ acacia			
mimulus	Mimulus	cream, orange, red	N America
mock orange	Philadelphus	white	Europe, Asia, N America
moltkia	Moltkia	violet-blue	Greece
morning glory ▶ ipomoea			
mother-of-pearl	Symphoricarpus	pink, white, red fruit	N America
mountain ash ▶ rowan			
myrtle	Myrtus	pink, white	Europe

English name	Genus / Family	Colour	Area of origin
oleander	*Nerium*	white, pink, purple, red	Mediterranean
olearia	*Olearia*	white, yellow	New Zealand
oleaster	*Elaeagnus*	yellow	Europe, Asia, N America
osmanthus	*Osmanthus*	white	China
pearl bush	*Exochorda*	white	China
peony	*Paeonia*	pink, red, white, yellow	Europe, Asia, N America
pieris	*Pieris*	white	China
poinsettia	*Euphorbia*	scarlet	Mexico
potentilla	*Potentilla*	yellow, red, orange	Asia
rhododendron	*Rhododendron*	red, purple, pink, white	S Asia
rhus	*Rhus*	foliage grey, purple, red	Europe, N America
ribbon woods	*Hoheria*	white	New Zealand
robinia	*Robinia*	rose-pink	N America
rock rose (or sun rose)	*Helianthemum*	white, yellow, pink, orange, red	Europe
rose	*Rosa*	pink, red, white, cream, yellow	N temperate regions
rosemary	*Rosmarinus*	violet	Europe, Asia
rowan (or mountain ash)	*Sorbus*	white (red, yellow berries)	Europe, Asia
sage, common	*Salvia*	green, white, yellow, reddish purple	S Europe
St John's wort	*Hypericum*	yellow	Europe, Asia
sea buckthorn	*Hippophae*	silver, orange	SW Europe
senecio	*Senecio*	yellow	New Zealand
skimmia	*Skimmia*	white	Japan, China
snowberry	*Symphoricarpos*	pink, white	N America
spiraea	*Spiraea*	white, pink, crimson	China, Japan
stachyurus	*Stachyurus*	pale yellow	China
staphylea	*Staphylea*	rose-pink	Europe, Asia
sun rose ▶ rock rose			
syringa ▶ lilac			
tamarisk	*Tamarix*	pink, white	Europe
thyme	*Thymus*	purple, white, pink	Europe
veronica	*Veronica*	white, pink, lilac, purple	New Zealand
viburnum	*Viburnum*	white, pink	Europe, Asia, Africa
Virginia creeper	*Parthenocissus*	foliage orange, red (blue-black fruits)	N America

wattle ▶ acacia

English name	Genus / Family	Colour	Area of origin
weigela	*Weigela*	pink, red	N China
winter sweet	*Chimonanthus*	yellow	China
wisteria	*Wisteria*	mauve, white, pink	China, Japan
witch-hazel	*Hamamelis*	red, yellow	China, Japan

Trees (Europe and N America)

English name	Species	Deciduous/ Evergreen	Area of origin
alder, common	*Alnus glutinosa*	deciduous	Europe
almond	*Prunus dulcis*	deciduous	W Asia, N Africa
apple	*Malus pumila*	deciduous	Europe, W Africa
ash, common	*Fraxinus excelsior*	deciduous	Europe
aspen	*Populus tremula*	deciduous	Europe
bean tree, Red Indian	*Catalpa bignonioides*	deciduous	America, E Asia
beech, common	*Fagus sylvatica*	deciduous	Europe
beech, copper	*Fagus purpurea* ('Atropunicea')	deciduous	Europe
beech, noble	*Nothofagus obliqua*	deciduous	S America
birch, silver	*Betula pendula*	deciduous	Europe, America, Asia
box	*Buxus sempervirens*	evergreen	Europe, N Africa
Brazil nut	*Bertholletia excelsa*	evergreen	S America
camellia, deciduous	*Stewartia pseudo-camellia*	deciduous	Asia
castor-oil tree, prickly	*Eleutherococcus pictus*	deciduous	tropics
cedar of Lebanon	*Cedrus libani*	evergreen	Asia
cedar, smooth Tasmanian	*Athrotaxis cupressoides*	evergreen	Australia
cedar, white	*Thuja occidentalis*	evergreen	America
cherry, morello (or sour cherry)	*Prunus cerasus*	deciduous	Europe, Asia
cherry, wild (or gean)	*Prunus avium*	deciduous	Europe
chestnut, horse	*Aesculus hippocastanum*	deciduous	Asia, SW Europe
chestnut, sweet (or Spanish chestnut)	*Castanea sativa*	deciduous	Europe, Africa, Asia
crab apple	*Malus sylvestris*	deciduous	Europe, Asia
cypress, Lawson	*Chamaecyparis lawsoniana*	evergreen	America
deodar	*Cedrus deodara*	evergreen	Asia
dogwood, common	*Cornus sanguinea*	deciduous	Europe
elm, Dutch	*Ulmus × hollandica*	deciduous	Europe
elm, English	*Ulmus procera*	deciduous	Europe
elm, wych	*Ulmus glabra*	deciduous	Europe

English name	Species	Deciduous/ Evergreen	Area of origin
fig	Ficus carica	evergreen	Asia
fir, Douglas	Pseudotsuga menziesii	evergreen	America
fir, red	Abies magnifica	evergreen	America
ginkgo	Ginkgo biloba	deciduous	Asia
grapefruit	Citrus × paradisi	evergreen	Asia
gum, blue	Eucalyptus globulus	evergreen	Australia
gum, cider	Eucalyptus gunnii	evergreen	Australia
gum, snow	Eucalyptus panciflora	evergreen	Australia
gutta-percha tree	Eucommia ulmoides	deciduous	China
hawthorn	Crataegus monogyna	deciduous	Europe
hazel, common	Corylus avellana	deciduous	Europe, W Asia, N Africa
hemlock, Western	Tsuga heterophylla	evergreen	America
holly	Ilex aquifolium	evergreen	Europe, N Africa, W Asia
hornbeam	Carpinus betulus	deciduous	Europe, Asia
Joshua-tree	Yucca brevifolia	evergreen	America
Judas-tree	Cercis siliquastrum	deciduous	S Europe, Asia
juniper, common	Juniperus communis	evergreen	Europe, Asia
laburnum, common	Laburnum anagyroides	deciduous	Europe
larch, European	Larix decidua	deciduous	Europe
larch, golden	Pseudolarix kaempferi	deciduous	E Asia
leatherwood	Eucryphia lucida	evergreen	Australia
lemon	Citrus limon	evergreen	Asia
lime	Citrus aurantifolia	evergreen	Asia
lime, small-leafed	Tilia cordata	deciduous	Europe
locust tree	Robinia pseudoacacia	deciduous	America
magnolia (or white laurel)	Magnolia virginiana	evergreen	America
maple, field (or common maple)	Acer campestre	deciduous	Europe
maple, sugar	Acer saccharum	deciduous	America
medlar	Mespilus germanica	deciduous	Europe
mimosa	Acacia dealbata	deciduous	Australia, Europe
mockernut	Carya tomentosa	deciduous	America
monkey puzzle	Araucaria araucana	evergreen	S America
mountain ash ▶ rowan			
mulberry, common	Morus nigra	deciduous	Asia
mulberry, white	Morus alba	deciduous	Asia
myrtle, orange bark	Myrtus apiculata	evergreen	S America
nutmeg, California	Torreya californica	evergreen	America
oak, California live	Quercus agrifolia	deciduous	America
oak, cork	Quercus suber	evergreen	S Europe, N Africa
oak, English (or common oak)	Quercus robur	deciduous	Europe, Asia, Africa

English name	Species	Deciduous/ Evergreen	Area of origin
oak, red	Quercus rubra	deciduous	America
olive	Olea europaea	evergreen	S Europe
orange, sweet	Citrus sinensis	evergreen	Asia
pagoda-tree	Sophora japonica	deciduous	China, Japan
pear	Pyrus communis	deciduous	Europe, W Asia
pine, Austrian	Pinus nigra subsp. nigra	evergreen	Europe, Asia
pine, Corsican	Pinus nigra subsp. laricio	evergreen	Europe
pine, Monterey	Pinus radiata	evergreen	America
pine, Scots	Pinus sylvestris	evergreen	Europe
plane, London	Platanus × hispanica	deciduous	Europe
plane, Oriental	Platanus orientalis	deciduous	SE Europe, Asia
plum	Prunus domestica	deciduous	Europe, Asia
poplar, balsam	Populus balsamifera	deciduous	America, Asia
poplar, black	Populus nigra	deciduous	Europe, Asia
poplar, Lombardy	Populus nigra 'Italica'	deciduous	Europe
poplar, white	Populus alba	deciduous	Europe
quince	Cydonia oblonga	deciduous	Asia
raoul	Nothofagus procera	deciduous	S America
rowan (or mountain ash)	Sorbus aucuparia	deciduous	Europe
sassafras, American	Sassafras albidum	deciduous	America
service tree, true	Sorbus domestica	deciduous	Europe
silver fir, common	Abies alba	evergreen	Europe
spruce, Norway	Picea abies	evergreen	Europe
spruce, sitka	Picea sitchensis	evergreen	America, Europe
strawberry tree	Arbutus unedo	evergreen	Europe
sycamore ('plane')	Acer pseudoplatanus	deciduous	Europe, W Asia
tamarack	Larix laricina	deciduous	N America
tree of heaven	Ailanthus altissima	deciduous	China
tulip tree	Liriodendron tulipifera	deciduous	America
walnut, black	Juglans nigra	deciduous	America
walnut, common	Juglans regia	deciduous	Europe, Asia
whitebeam	Sorbus aria	deciduous	Europe
willow, pussy (or goat willow or sallow willow)	Salix caprea	deciduous	Europe, Asia
willow, weeping	Salix babylonica	deciduous	Asia
willow, white	Salix alba	deciduous	Europe
yew, common	Taxus baccata	evergreen	N temperate regions

Trees (tropical)

Name	Species	Deciduous/ Evergreen	Area of origin
African tulip tree	Spathodea campanulata	evergreen	Africa
almond, tropical	Terminalia catappa	deciduous	Asia

Name	Species	Deciduous/ Evergreen	Area of origin
angel's trumpet	*Brugmansia × candida*	deciduous	S America
autograph tree	*Clusia rosea*	evergreen	Asia
avocado	*Persea americana*	evergreen	C America, Mexico
bamboo	*Schizostachyum glauchifolium*	deciduous	America
banana	*Musa × paradisiaca*	plant dies after fruiting	Asia
banyan	*Ficus benghalensis*	evergreen	Asia
baobab (or dead rat's tree)	*Adansonia digitata*	deciduous	Africa
beach heliotrope	*Argusia argentea*	evergreen	S America
bo tree	*Ficus religiosa*	deciduous	Asia
bombax	*Bombax ceiba*	deciduous	Asia
bottlebrush	*Callistemon citrinus*	evergreen	Australia
breadfruit	*Artocarpus altilis*	evergreen	Asia
brownea	*Brownea macrophylla*	evergreen	C America
calabash	*Crescentia cujete*	evergreen	America
candlenut	*Aleurites moluccana*	evergreen	Asia
cannonball	*Courouptia guianensis*	evergreen	S America
chinaberry (or bead tree)	*Melia azedarach*	deciduous	Asia
Christmas-berry	*Schinus terebinthifolius*	evergreen	America
coconut palm	*Cocus nucifera*	evergreen	Asia
coffee tree	*Coffea liberica*	evergreen	Africa
Cook pine	*Araucaria columnaris*	evergreen	America
coral shower	*Cassia grandis*	deciduous	Asia
coral tree	*Erythrina coralloides*	deciduous	C America
cotton, wild	*Cochlospermum vitifolium*	deciduous	C and S America
crape myrtle	*Lagerstroemia indica*	deciduous	Asia
date palm	*Phoenix dactylifera*	evergreen	Asia and Africa
dragon tree	*Dracaena draco*	evergreen	Africa (Canary Is)
durian	*Durio zibethinus*	evergreen	Asia
ebony	*Diospyros ebenum*	evergreen	Asia
elephant's-ear	*Enderolobium cyclocarpum*	deciduous	S America
flame tree	*Delonix regia*	deciduous	Africa (Madagascar)
gold tree	*Cybistax donnell-smithii*	deciduous	Asia
golden rain	*Koelreuteria paniculata*	deciduous	Asia
golden shower	*Cassia fistula*	deciduous	Asia
guava	*Psidium guajeva*	evergreen	S America
ironwood (or casuarina)	*Casuarina equisetifolia*	deciduous	Australia and Asia
jacaranda	*Jacaranda mimosifolia*	deciduous	S America
jackfruit (or jack)	*Artocarpus heterophyllus*	evergreen	Asia

Name	Species	Deciduous/ Evergreen	Area of origin
kapok tree	Ceiba pentandra	deciduous	Old and New World tropics
koa	Acacia koa	evergreen	Oceania (Hawaii)
lipstick tree	Bixa orellanna	evergreen	America
lychee	Litchi chinensis	evergreen	China
macadamia nut	Macadamia integrifolia	evergreen	Australia
mahogany	Swietenia mahogoni	evergreen	S America
mango	Mangifera indica	evergreen	Asia
mesquite	Prosopis pallida	evergreen	America
monkeypod (or rain tree)	Albizia saman	evergreen	S America
Norfolk Island pine	Araucaria heterophylla	evergreen	Oceania (Norfolk I)
octopus tree	Schefflera actinophylla	evergreen	Australia
ohi' a lehua	Metrosideros collina	evergreen	Oceania (Hawaii)
pandanus (or screw pine)	Pandanus tectorius	evergreen	Oceania
paperbark tree	Melaleuca quinquenervia	evergreen	Australia
powderpuff	Calliandra haematocephala	evergreen	S America
royal palm	Roystonea regia	evergreen	America (Cuba)
sandalwood	Santalum album	deciduous	Asia
sand-box tree	Hura crepitans	deciduous	Americas
sausage tree	Kigelia pinnata	evergreen	Africa
scrambled egg tree	Cassia glauca	evergreen	Americas
Surinam cherry	Eugenia uniflora	evergreen	S America
teak tree	Tectona grandis	evergreen	Asia
tiger's claw	Erythrina variegata	deciduous	Asia
yellow oleander	Thevetia peruviana	evergreen	Americas (W Indies)

Fungi

English name	Species	Colour	Edibility
base toadstool (or ugly toadstool)	Lactarius necator	green, brown	poisonous
beautiful clavaria	Ramaria formosa	yellow, ochre, red, purple	poisonous
beefsteak fungus	Fistulina hepatica	red	edible
blusher	Amanita fubescens	red, brown	poisonous (raw) or edible (cooked)
brain mushroom	Gyromitra esculenta	chestnut, dark brown	poisonous
buckler agaric	Entoloma clypeatum	grey, brown	edible
Caesar's mushroom	Amanita caesarea	red, yellow	edible

English name	Species	Colour	Edibility
chanterelle	*Cantharellus cibarius*	yellow, ochre	excellent
clean mycena	*Mycena pura*	purple	poisonous
clouded agaric	*Lepista nebularis*	grey, brown	poisonous
common deceiver	*Laccaria laccata*	purple, pink, orange	edible
common earthball	*Scleroderma aurantium*	ochre, yellow, brown	poisonous
common grisette	*Amanita vaginita*	grey, yellow	edible
common morel	*Morchella esculenta*	light brown, black	edible
common puffball	*Lycoperdon perlatum*	white, cream, brown	edible
common stinkhorn	*Phallus impudicus*	white, green	inedible
death cap	*Amanita phalloides*	grey, green, yellow, brown	deadly
destroying angel	*Amanita virosa*	white, brown	deadly
dingy agaric	*Tricholoma portentosum*	grey, black, yellow, lilac	edible
dryad's saddle	*Polyporus squamosus*	yellow, brown	edible
fairies' bonnets	*Coprinus disseminatus*	grey, purple	worthless
fairy-ring champignon	*Marasmius oreades*	beige, ochre, red, brown	edible
field mushroom	*Agaricus campestris*	white, brown	excellent
firwood agaric	*Tricholoma auratum*	green, yellow, brown	edible
fly agaric	*Amanita muscaria*	red, orange, white	poisonous
garlic marosmius	*Marosmius scorodonius*	red, brown	edible
gypsy mushroom	*Rozites caperata*	yellow, ochre	edible
hedgehog mushroom	*Hydnum repandum*	white, beige, yellow	edible
honey fungus	*Armillaria mellea*	honey, brown, red	inedible
horn of plenty (or trumpet of the dead)	*Craterellus cornucopiodes*	brown, black	very good
horse mushroom	*Agaricus arvensis*	white, yellow, ochre	very good
Jew's ear fungus	*Auricularia auricula judae*	yellow, brown	edible
larch boletus	*Suillus grevillei*	yellow	edible
liberty cap (or 'magic mushroom')	*Psilocybe semilanceata*	brown	poisonous

English name	Species	Colour	Edibility
lurid boletus	*Boletus luridus*	olive, brown, yellow	poisonous (raw) or edible (cooked)
morel	*Morchella*	brown	good
naked mushroom	*Lepista nuda*	purple, brown	edible
old man of the woods	*Strobilomyces floccopus*	brown, black	edible
orange-peel fungus	*Aleuria aurantia*	orange, red	edible
oyster mushroom	*Pleurotus ostreatus*	brown, black, grey, blue, purple	edible
panther cap (or false blusher)	*Amanita pantherina*	brown, ochre, grey, white	poisonous
parasol mushroom	*Macrolepiota procera*	beige, ochre, brown	excellent
penny-bun fungus	*Boletus edulis*	chestnut brown	excellent
Périgord truffle	*Tuber melanosporum*	black, red-brown	excellent
Piedmont truffle	*Tuber magnatum*	white	edible
purple blewits	*Tricholomopsis rutilans*	yellow, red	edible
saffron milk cap	*Lactorius delicioses*	orange, red	poisonous (raw) or edible (cooked)
St George's mushroom	*Calocybe gambosa*	white, cream	edible
Satan's boletus	*Boletus satanus*	grey	poisonous (raw) or edible (cooked)
scarlet-stemmed boletus	*Boletus calopus*	grey, brown	poisonous
shaggy ink cap (or lawyer's wig)	*Coprinus comatus*	white, ochre	edible
sickener (or emetic russula)	*Russula emetica*	pink, red	poisonous
stinking russula	*Russula foetens*	ochre, brown	poisonous
stout agaric	*Amanita spissa*	grey, brown	edible
strong scented garlic	*Tricholoma saponaceum*	grey, green, brown	poisonous
sulphur tuft (or clustered woodlover)	*Hypholoma fasciculare*	yellow, red, brown	poisonous
summer truffle	*Tuber aestivum*	dark brown	very good
white truffle	*Tuber magnatum*	cream, pale brown	excellent
winter fungus (or velvet shank)	*Flammulina velutipes*	yellow, brown, ochre	edible
wood agaric	*Collybia dryophila*	yellow, brown, rust	edible
wood mushroom	*Agaricus sylvaticus*	grey, red, brown	edible

English name	Species	Colour	Edibility
woolly milk-cap (or griping toadstool)	*Lactarius torminosus*	pink, brown	poisonous
yellow stainer	*Agaricus xanthodermus*	white, yellow, grey	poisonous
yellow-brown boletus (or slippery jack)	*Suillus luteus*	yellow, brown	edible

Mammals

Mammals are the group of animals to which humans belong. They are characterized by the presence of mammary glands in the female which produce milk on which the young can be nourished. They are divided into monotremes or egg-laying mammals; marsupials in which the young are born at an early stage of development and then grow outside the mother's womb, often in a pouch; and placental mammals in which the young are nourished in the womb by the mother's blood and are born at a late stage of development. A crucial aspect of mammals is the fact that their hair and skin glands allow them to regulate their temperatures from within, ie they are endothermic (warm-blooded). This confers on them a greater adaptability to more varied environments than that of reptiles. There are over 4,000 species of mammals, most of which are terrestrial, the exceptions being species of bat which have developed the ability to fly, and cetaceans (including dolphins, porpoises and whales) which lead aquatic existences.

Name	Size (cm)[1]	Distribution	Special features
■ Monotremes			
echidna, long-beaked	45–90	New Guinea	prominent beak
echidna, short-beaked	30–45	Australia, Tasmania and New Guinea	fur covered in protective spines
platypus	45–60	E Australia and Tasmania	duck-like snout
■ Marsupials			
bandicoot	15–56	Australia and New Guinea	highest reproductive rate of all marsupials
kangaroo	to 165	Australia and New Guinea	bounding motion and prominent female pouch
kangaroo, rat	28.4–30	Australia and New Guinea	rabbit-sized version of its larger namesake
koala	78	E Australia	diet consists of eucalyptus leaves; intensive management has significantly revived population numbers
mole, marsupial	13–15	Australia	specializes in burrowing
opossum	7–55	C and S America	known for its dreadful smell

Name	Size (cm)[1]	Distribution	Special features
possum, brushtail	34–70	Australia, New Guinea, Solomon Is and New Zealand	most commonly encountered of all Australian mammals
wallaby ► kangaroo			
wombat	80–115	SE Australia and Tasmania	poor eyesight; keen senses of smell and hearing
■ Placental mammals			
aardvark	105–130	Africa S of the Sahara	long, tubular snout
anteater	16–22	C and S America	elongated snout
antelope, dwarf	45–55	Africa	female larger than male
armadillo	12.5–100	southern N America, C and S America	protective suit of armour
ass	200–210	Africa and Asia	renowned as a beast of burden
baboon and mandrill	56–80	Africa	able to walk over long distances
badger	50–100	Africa, Europe, Asia and N America	European species characterized by black and white markings
bat	15–200 (wingspan)	worldwide except for the Arctic and Antarctic	the only vertebrate, except for birds, capable of sustained flight
bear, black	130–180	N America	more adaptable than grizzly bear
bear, grizzly (or brown bear)	200–280	NW America and former USSR	large in size (up to half a ton)
beaver	80–120	N America, Asia and Europe	constructs dams and lodges in water
beaver, mountain	30–41	Pacific Coast of Canada and USA	land-dwelling and burrowing animal
bison, American	to 380	N America	now exists only in parks and refuges
bison, European	to 290	former USSR	extinct in the wild in 1919, but now re-established in parts of the former USSR
boar	58–210	Europe, Africa and Asia	intelligent and highly adaptable
buffalo, wild water	240–280	SE Asia	adept at moving through its muddy habitat
bushbaby	12–32	Africa and S Asia	highly agile, arboreal
bushbuck	110–145	Africa S of the Sahara	dark brown or chestnut coat with white markings
camel	190–230 (height of hump)	Mongolia	two humps

Name	Size (cm)[1]	Distribution	Special features
capybara	106–134	S America	largest living rodent
cat	20–400	worldwide	acute sense of vision and smell
cattle	180–200	worldwide	long-horned and polled or hornless breeds
chamois	125–135	Europe and Asia	adapted to alpine and subalpine conditions
cheetah	112–135	Africa	fastest of all land animals
chimpanzee	70–85	W and C Africa	most intelligent of the great apes
chinchilla	25	S America	hunted as food and for fur
civet	33–84	Africa and Asia	cat-like carnivore
colugo	33–42	SE Asia	stretched membrane allows it to glide from tree to tree
cougar ▶ puma			
coyote	70–97	N America	unique howling sound
coypu	50	S America	highly aquatic rodent
deer	41–152	N and S America, Europe and Asia	male uses antlers to attack other males during rutting period
dingo	150	Australasia	descendant of the wolf
dog	20–75	worldwide	first animal to be domesticated
dolphin	120–400	worldwide	highly developed social organization and communication systems
dolphin, river	210–260	SE Asia and S America	highly sensitive system of echo location
dormouse	6–19	Europe, Africa, Turkey, Asia and Japan	nocturnal rodent; hibernates in winter
dromedary	190–230 (height of hump)	SW Asia, N Africa and Australia	camel with one hump
duiker	55–72	Africa S of the Sahara	dives into cover when disturbed
eland	250–350	Africa	spiral-horned antelope
elephant, African	600–750	Africa S of the Sahara	largest living land mammal
fox	24–100	N and S America, Europe, Asia and Africa	noted for its cunning and intelligence
gazelle	122–166	Africa	birth peaks coincide with abundance of feeding vegetation during spring
gerbil	6–7.5	Africa and Asia	wide field of vision; low frequency hearing
gerenuk	140–160	Africa	graceful and delicate
gibbon	45–65	SE Asia	swings among trees using arms

Name	Size (cm)[1]	Distribution	Special features
giraffe	380–470	Africa S of the Sahara	mottled coat and long neck
gnu	194–209	Africa	massive head and mane
goat, mountain	to 175	N America	ponderous rock climber
goat, wild	130–140	S Europe, Middle East and Asia	subspecies includes domestic goat
gopher	12–22.5	N America	highly adapted burrower
gorilla	150–170	C Africa	largest living primate
guinea pig	28	S America	tailless rodent
hamster	5.3–10.2	Europe, Middle East, former USSR and China	aggressive towards own species in the wild
hare	40–76	N and S America, Africa, Europe, Asia and Arctic	well-developed ability to run from predators
hare, Patagonian	45	S America	strictly monogamous
hartebeest	195–200	Africa	long face, sloping back
hedgehog	10–15	Europe, Asia and Africa	protective spined back
hippo-potamus	150–345	Africa	barrel-shaped; short stumpy legs
horse	200–210	worldwide in domesticated form; Asia, N and S America and Australia in the wild	historically useful as a beast of burden and means of transport
hyena	85–140	Africa and Asia	scavenger and hunter
ibex	85–143	C Europe, Asia and Africa	large horns; saved from extinction in C Europe
impala	128–142	Africa	fawn and mahogany coat
jackal	65–106	Africa, SE Europe and Asia	unfair reputation as cowardly scavenger
jaguar	112–185	C and S America	only cat in the Americas
jerboa	4–26	N Africa, Turkey, Middle East and C Asia	moves by hopping and jumping with long hind legs
lemming	10–11	N America and Eurasia	Norway lemming is noted for its mass migration
lemur	12–70	Madagascar, Africa	mainly nocturnal and arboreal
lemur, flying ▶ colugo			
leopard	100–190	Africa and Asia	nocturnal hunter
lion	240–300	Africa and Asia	most socially organized of the cat family

Name	Size (cm)[1]	Distribution	Special features
llama	230–400	S America	S American beast of burden
lynx	67–110	Europe and N America	well adapted to snow
macaque	38–70	Asia and N Africa	heavily built; partly terrestrial
marmoset	17.5–40	S America	squirrel-like monkey
marten	30–75	N America, Europe and Asia	one species, the fisher, unique for its ability to penetrate the quilled defences of the porcupine
mole	2.4–7.5	Europe, Asia and N America	almost exclusively subterranean existence
mongoose	24–58	Africa, S Asia and SW Europe	often seen in the tripod position, ie standing up on hind legs and tail
monkey, capuchin	25–63	S America	lives in social groups
mouse ▶ rat			
narwhal	400–500	former USSR, N America and Greenland	distinctive single tusk in the male can reach lengths of up to 300cm
okapi	190–200	C Africa	mixture of giraffe and zebra
orang-utan	150	forests of N Sumatra and Borneo	sparse covering of long red-brown hair
otter	40–123	N and S America, Europe, Asia and Africa	only truly amphibious member of the general weasel family
panda, giant	130–150	China	rare; poor breeder
polar bear	250–300	N polar regions	large; white coat
porcupine (New World)	30–86	N and S America	arboreal; excellent climber
porcupine (Old World)	37–47	Africa and Asia	heavily quilled and spiny body
porpoise	120–150	N temperate zone, W Indo-Pacific, temperate and sub-antarctic waters of S America and Auckland Is	large range of sounds for the purpose of echo location
puma	105–196	N and S America	wide-ranging hunter; includes subspecies cougar
rabbit, European	38–58	Europe, Africa, Australia, New Zealand and S America	burrowing creature; opportunistic animal in widespread environment
raccoon	55	N, S and C America	black-masked face
rat (New World)	5–8	N and S America	highly adaptable

Name	Size (cm)[1]	Distribution	Special features
rat (Old World)	4.5–8.2	Europe, Asia, Africa and Australia	highly adaptable
reedbuck	110–176	Africa	distinctive whistling sounds, leaping movements
rhinoceros	250–400	Africa and tropical Asia	horn grows from snout
seal	117–490	mainly polar, subpolar and temperate seas	graceful swimmer and diver
sheep, American bighorn	168–186	N America	large horns and body similar to an ibex
sheep, barbary	155–165	N Africa	large head and horns up to 84cm in length
sheep, blue	91 (shoulder height)	Asia	blue coat; curved horns
shrew	3.5–4.8	Europe, Asia, Africa, N America and northern S America	generally poor eyesight compensated for by acute senses of smell and hearing
shrew, elephant	10.4–29.4	Africa	long pointed snout
skunk	40–68	N and S America	evil-smelling defence mechanism
sloth, three-toed	56–60	S America	smaller version of the two-toed sloth
sloth, two-toed	58–70	S America	arboreal; nocturnal; slow
springbok	96–115	S Africa	migrates in herds of tens of thousands
springhare	36–43	S Africa	burrowing creature; like a miniature kangaroo
squirrel	6.6–10	N and S America, Europe, Africa and Asia	includes arboreal, burrowing and flying species
tapir	180–250	C and S America and SE Asia	nocturnal mammal with distinctive snout
tarsier	11–14	islands of SE Asia	extraordinary ability to rotate neck
tiger	220–360	India, Manchuria, China and Indonesia	solitary hunter; stalks for prey
vole	10–11	N America, Europe, Asia and the Arctic	population fluctuates in regular patterns or cycles
walrus	250–320	Arctic seas	thick folds of skin; twin tusks
waterbuck	177–235	Africa	shaggy coat; heavy gait

Name	Size (cm)[1]	Distribution	Special features
weasel	15–55	Arctic, N and S America, Europe, Asia and Africa	certain species have been exploited for fur, eg mink, ermine
whale, beaked	400–1280	worldwide	dolphin-like beak
whale, blue	to 3300	Arctic and subtropics	largest living animal
whale, grey	1190–1520	N Pacific	long migration to breed, from the Arctic to the subtropics
whale, humpback	1600	worldwide	highly acrobatic; wide range of sounds
whale, killer	900–1000	worldwide in cool coastal waters	toothed; dorsal fin narrow and vertical
whale, long-finned pilot	600	temperate waters of the N Atlantic	best known for mysterious mass strandings on beaches
whale, sperm	to 2070	widespread in temperate and tropical waters	largest of the toothed whales; prodigious deep sea diver
whale, white (or beluga)	300–500	N Russia, N America and Greenland	white skin; wide range of bodily, facial and vocal expressions
wild cat	50–80	Europe, India and Africa	domestic cat may be descended from the African wild cat
wolf, grey	100–150	N America, Europe, Asia and Middle East	noted for hunting in packs
wolverine	to 83	Arctic and subarctic regions	heavily built; long, dark coat of fur
zebra	215–230	Africa	black and white stripes

[1] Generally, the size given in the table denotes length from head to tip of tail. To convert from cm to inches, multiply by 0.3937.

Mammals – record holders

Largest	The blue whale, up to 33m/110ft long and weighing up to 190 tonnes, is the largest known mammal. The largest existing land mammal is the male African elephant, standing up to 3.7m/12ft at the shoulder and weighing up to 7 tonnes.
Tallest	The giraffe stands up to 5.5m/18ft high.
Smallest	Savi's pygmy shrew has a body length of 3.6–5.3cm/1.4–2.1in and weighs 1.2–2.7g/0.4–0.9oz.
Fastest on land	The cheetah can reach 103kph/64mph, but only in short bursts. The pronghorn can maintain speeds of 50kph/31mph for several kilometres.
Most prolific breeder	A North American meadow vole produced 17 litters in a single year (4–9 babies per litter).

Most widespread	Humans are the most widely distributed mammals, closely followed by the house mouse and brown rat, which have accompanied humans to all parts of the world.

Birds

Birds are warm-blooded, egg-laying, and, in the case of adults, feathered vertebrates of the class Aves; there are approximately 8,600 species classified into 29 Orders and 181 Families. Birds are constructed for flight. The body is streamlined to reduce air resistance, the forelimbs are modified as feathered wings, and the skeletal structure, heart and wing muscles, centre of gravity and lung capacity are all designed for the act of flying. Two exceptions to this are the ratites or flightless birds which have become too large to be capable of sustained flight, eg the ostrich, kiwi and emu, and the penguin which has evolved into a highly aquatic creature. Birds are thought to have evolved from reptiles, their closest living relative being the crocodile.

Name	Size (cm)[1]	Distribution	Special features
■ Flightless birds			
cassowary	150	Australia and New Guinea	claws can be lethal
emu	160–190	Australia	highly mobile, nomadic population
kiwi	35–55	New Zealand	smallest of the Ratitae order; nocturnal
ostrich	275	dry areas of Africa	fastest animal on two legs
rhea	100–150	grasslands of S America	lives in flocks
tinamou	15–49	C and S America	sustains flight over short distances
■ Birds of prey			
buzzard	80	worldwide except Australasia and Malaysia	perches often; kills prey on ground
condor	60–100	the Americas	Andean condor has largest wingspan of any living bird (up to 300cm)
eagle, bald	80–100	N America	white plumage on head and neck
eagle, golden	80–100	N hemisphere	kills with talons
eagle, harpy	90	C America to Argentina	world's largest eagle
eagle, sea	70–120	coastline worldwide	breeds on sea cliffs
falcon	15–60	worldwide	remarkable powers of flight and sight
harrier	50	worldwide	hunts using regular search pattern
kite	52–58	worldwide	most varied group of hawks
osprey	55–58	worldwide	feet adapted for catching fish
owl	12–73	worldwide	acute sight and hearing
owl, barn	30–45	worldwide	feathered legs
secretary bird	100	Africa	walks up to 30km/20mi per day

Name	Size (cm)[1]	Distribution	Special features
sparrowhawk	to 27 (male), to 38 (female)	Eurasia, NW Africa, C and S America	long tail, small round wings
vulture (New World)	60–100	the Americas	lives in colonies
vulture (Old World)	150–270 (wing-span)	worldwide except the Americas	no sense of smell

■ Songbirds

Name	Size (cm)[1]	Distribution	Special features
accentor	14–18	Palaearctic	complex social organization
bird of paradise	12.5–100	New Guinea, Moluccas and Eastern Australia	brilliantly ornate plumage
bowerbird	25–37	Australia and New Guinea	male builds bowers to attract female
bulbul	13–23	Africa, Madagascar, S Asia and the Philippines	beautiful singing voice
bunting	15–20	worldwide	large family including species of sparrow, finch, and cardinals
butcherbird	26–58	Australia, New Guinea and New Zealand	highly aggressive; known as 'bushman's clock'
cowbird	17–54	N and S America	gaping movements of the bill
crow	20–66	worldwide, except New Zealand	with complex social systems
dipper	17–20	Europe, S Asia and W regions of N and S America	strong legs and toes allow mobility to walk under water
drongo	18–38	S Asia and Africa	pugnacious
finch	11–19	Europe, N and S America, Africa, and Asia	strong bill; melodious singing voice
flowerpecker	8–20	SE Asia and Australasia	short tongue specially adapted for feeding on nectar
flycatcher (Old World)	9–27	worldwide except N and S America	tropical species brightly coloured
flycatcher, silky	to 14	N and S America	feeds on the wing
honeycreeper, Hawaiian	10–20	Hawaiian Is	varying bills between species
honeyeater	10–32	Australasia, Pacific Is, Hawaii and S Africa	brush tongue adapted for nectar feeding

Name	Size (cm)[1]	Distribution	Special features
lark	11–19	worldwide	ground-dwelling; elaborate singing displays
leafbird	12–24	S Asia	forest dwellers; ability to mimic sounds of other birds
magpie lark	19–50	Australasia and New Guinea	adapted to urban environment
mockingbird	20–33	N and S America	great ability to mimic sounds
nuthatch	14–20	worldwide except S America and New Zealand	European species can break open nuts
oriole (Old World)	18–30	Europe, Africa, Asia, Philippines, New Guinea and Australia	melodious singing voice
palmchat	18	Hispaniola and W Indies	communal nesting with individual compartments for each nesting pair
robin	13	worldwide except New Zealand	territorial, uses song to deter intruders
shrike	15–35	Africa, N America, Asia and New Guinea	sharply hooked bill
shrike, cuckoo	14–40	Africa, S Asia	peculiar courtship display
shrike, vanga	12–30	Madagascar	some endangered species
sparrow	10–20	African tropics in origin, now worldwide	some species renowned for urban adaptability
starling	16–45	Europe, Asia and Africa	nests in colonies
sunbird	8–16	Africa, SE Asia and Australasia	bright plumage
swallow	12–23	worldwide	strong and agile flight
thrush	12–26	worldwide, except New Zealand	loud and varied singing voice
tit	11–14	N America, Europe, Asia and Africa	nests in holes
treecreeper	12–15	N hemisphere and S Africa	forages on trees for food
treecreeper, Australian	15	Australia and New Guinea	forages for food on tree trunks
vireo	10–17	N and S America	thick and slightly hooked bill
wagtail	14–17	worldwide, although rare in Australia	spectacular song in flight
warbler, American	10–16	N and S America	well developed and often complex songs

Name	Size (cm)¹	Distribution	Special features
wattle-bird	25–53	New Zealand	distinctive fleshy fold of skin at base of bill
waxbill	9–13.5	Africa, SE Asia and Australasia	several species drink by sucking
waxwing	18	W hemisphere	wax-like, red tips on secondary flight feathers
white-eye	12	Africa, SE Asia and Australasia	ring of tiny white feathers around the eyes
wood swallow	15–20	tropical Asia and Australasia	tends to huddle together in small groups in trees
wren	8–15	N and S America, Europe and Asia	nests play ceremonial role in courtship

■ **Waterfowl**

diver ▶ loon

duck	wide range	worldwide	gregarious; migratory
flamingo	90–180	tropics, N America, S Europe	red/pink colour of plumage caused by diet
goose	wide range	N hemisphere	migratory

great northern diver ▶ loon

grebe	22–60	worldwide	highly aquatic
hamerkop	56	Africa S of the Sahara, Madagascar and S Arabia	elaborate nest with entrance tunnel and internal chamber
heron	30–140	worldwide	mainly a wading bird
ibis	50–100	warmer regions of all continents	includes species of spoonbill
loon (or diver)	66–95	high latitudes of the N hemisphere, migrating to temperate zones	highly territorial and aggressive
screamer	69–90	warmer parts of S America	trumpet-like alarm call
shoebill	120	E Africa	large head on a short neck
stork	60–120	S America, Asia, Africa and Australia	long bill and long neck
swan	100–160	worldwide, fresh water, sheltered shores and estuaries	very long neck

■ **Shorebirds**

auk	16–76	cold waters of the N hemisphere	includes varieties of puffin and guillemot
avocet	29–48	worldwide, except high latitudes	particularly graceful walk

Name	Size (cm)[1]	Distribution	Special features
courser	15–25	Africa, S Europe, Asia and Australia	inhabits dry, flat savanna, grassland and river shores
curlew, stone	36–52	Africa, Europe, Asia, Australia and parts of S America	leg joints give alternative name of 'thick knee'
gull	31–76	worldwide, scarce in the tropics	elaborate communication system
jacana	17–53	tropics	ability to walk on floating vegetation gives alternative name of 'lily trotter'
oystercatcher	40–45	tropical and temperate coastlines, except tropical Africa and S Asia	powerful bill for breaking shells; do not eat oysters
phalarope	19–25	high latitudes of the N hemisphere	wading bird; also regularly swims
plover	15–40	worldwide	swift runner; strong flyer
plover, crab	38	coasts of E Africa, India, Persian Gulf, Sri Lanka and Madagascar	single species with mainly white and black plumage
sandpiper	12–60	worldwide	spectacular flight patterns
seedsnipe	17–28	W coast of S America	named after its diet
sheathbill	35–43	subantarctic and E coast of S America	communal and quarrelsome scavenger
skimmer	37–51	tropics and subtropics of N and S America, Africa, and S Asia	uniquely shaped bill aids capture of prey in shallow waters
skua	43–61	mainly high latitudes of the N hemisphere	chases other seabirds until they disgorge their food
snipe, painted	19–24	S America, Africa, S Asia and Australia	spectacular female plumage

■ Seabirds

Name	Size (cm)[1]	Distribution	Special features
albatross	70–140	S hemisphere	noted for its size and power of flight
cormorant (or shag)	50–100	worldwide	marine equivalent of falcons
darter	80–100	tropical, subtropical, temperate regions	distinctive swimming action
frigatebird	70–110	tropical oceans	enormous wings; forces other birds to disgorge their food
fulmar	to 60	N and S oceans	comes to land only to breed
gannet	to 90	worldwide	complex behaviour during mating

Name	Size (cm)[1]	Distribution	Special features
guillemot	38–42	N hemisphere	egg shape adapted to cliff-side dwelling
pelican	140–180	tropics and subtropics	known for its long bill
penguin	40–115	S hemisphere	flightless: wings modified as flippers; highly social
petrel, diving	16–25	S hemisphere	great resemblance to the auk
petrel, storm	12–25	high latitudes of N and S hemispheres	considerable powers of migration
puffin	28–32	N hemisphere	nests in burrows in very large colonies
shag ▶ cormorant			
shearwater	28–91	subantarctic and subtropical zones	many species known for long migrations
tropicbird	25–45	tropical seas	elongated central tail feathers

■ Arboreal birds

Name	Size (cm)[1]	Distribution	Special features
barbet	9–32	tropics, except Australasia	nests in rotten timber or sandbanks
bee-eater	15–38	Africa, Asia and Australia	colourful plumage
cuckoo	15–90	worldwide	some species lay eggs in the nests of other birds
cuckoo-roller	38–43	Madagascar and Comoros Is	diminishing population
honeyguide	10–20	Africa and S Asia	eats the wax of honeycombs
hoopoe	31	Africa, SE Asia and S Europe	distinctive 'hoo hoo' call
hornbill	38–126	tropics of Africa and Australasia	long, heavy bill
jacamar	13–30	tropical America	long, slender bill
kingfisher	10–46	worldwide	colourful plumage
motmot	20–50	tropical America	distinctive long tail feathers
mousebird	30–35	Africa S of the Sahara	crest and long tail
parrot	10–100	mainly tropics of S hemisphere	mainly sedentary; unmelodic voice
pigeon	17–90	worldwide, except high latitudes	distinctive cooing sound
puffbird	14–32	tropical America	stout, puffy appearance
roller	27–38	Africa, Europe, Asia, Australia	courtship display of diving from great heights in a rolling motion
sandgrouse	25–48	Africa, S Europe and S Asia	mainly terrestrial
tody	10–12	Greater Antilles	captures insects from the underside of leaves and twigs
toucan	34–66	S America	bright plumage and immense bill

Name	Size (cm)[1]	Distribution	Special features
trogon	25–35	tropics, except Australasia	colourful, attractive plumage
turaco	35–76	Africa S of the Sahara	loud and resounding call
woodhoopoe	21–43	Africa S of the Sahara	long graduated tail; strongly hooked bill
woodpecker	10–58	worldwide, except Australasia and Antarctica	excavates wood and tree bark for food

■ **Aerial feeders**

Name	Size (cm)[1]	Distribution	Special features
frogmouth	23–53	SE Asia and Australasia	distinctively shaped bill
hummingbird	6–22	N and S America	wings hum when hovering
nightjar	19–29	worldwide	nocturnal
nightjar, owlet-	23–44	Australasia	perches in upright owl-like way
oilbird	53	tropical S America	the only nocturnal fruit-eating bird
potoo	23–51	tropical C and S America	nocturnal bird, known as 'tree-nighthawk'
swift	10–25	worldwide	spends most of life flying
swift, crested	17–33	SE Asia and New Guinea	prominent crest on its head

■ **Passerines[2]**

Name	Size (cm)[1]	Distribution	Special features
antbird	8–36	parts of S America and W Indies	some species follow armies of ants to prey
bellbird	9–45	C and S America	long, metallic-sounding call
broadbill	13–28	tropical Africa and Asia, and the Philippines	colourful broad bill
false sunbird	15	Madagascar	bright blue and emerald wattle develops around the male's eyes during breeding season
flycatcher (New World)	9–27	N and S America	feeds on the wing
flycatcher, tyrant	5–14	N and S America, W Indies and Galapagos Is	spectacular aerial courtship display
gnateater	14	parts of S America	long thin legs; short tail
lyrebird	80–90	SE Australia	extravagant tail which resembles a Greek lyre
manakin	9–15	C and S America	highly elaborate courtship display
ovenbird	to 25	S America	builds substantial nests like mud-ovens
pitta	15–28	Africa, Asia and Australasia	long legs; short tail; colourful plumage

Name	Size (cm)[1]	Distribution	Special features
plantcutter	18–19	western S America	bill is adapted for feeding on fruit and plants
scrub-bird	16–21	E and SW Australia	small terrestrial bird; long graduated tail
tapaculo	8–25	S and C America	movable flap covers the nostril
woodcreeper	20–37	S America and W Indies	stiff tail feathers used as support in climbing trees
wren, New Zealand	8–10	New Zealand	bird family thought to have colonized the islands in the Tertiary Period[3]

■ Gamebirds and cranes

Name	Size	Distribution	Special features
bustard	37–132	Africa, S Europe, Asia and Australia	frequently pauses for observation while walking
coot	14–51	worldwide	loud nocturnal vocal strains
crane	80–150	worldwide, except S America and Antarctica	long legs
curassow	75–112	Southern N America and S America	agility in running along branches before taking flight
finfoot	30–62	tropics of America, and SE Asia	long, slender neck
grouse	30–90	N hemisphere	many species threatened by hunting
guinea fowl	45–60	Africa	virtually unfeathered head and neck
hoatzin	60	tropical S America	musky odour; top-heavy
kagu	56	New Caledonia	sole species; forest dwelling
limpkin	60–70	C and S America	sole species; wailing voice
mesite	25–27	Madagascar	highly terrestrial; sedentary
pheasant	40–235	worldwide	elaborate courtship display
plains wanderer	16	SE Australia	male incubates the eggs and raises the young
quail, button	11–19	Africa, S Asia and Australia	secretive; terrestrial
seriema	75–90	S America	heavily feathered head and crest
sun bittern	46	forest swamps of C and S America	complex markings
trumpeter	43–53	tropical S America	trumpeting call of warning or alarm
turkey	90–110	N America	male exhibits distinctive strutting displays during breeding

[1] Generally, the size given in the table denotes height. To convert cm to inches, multiply by 0.3937.
[2] Any bird of the worldwide order Passeriformes ('perching birds'), which comprises more than half the living species of birds; landbirds.
[3] See Geological time scale page 26.

Birds – record holders

Highest flyer	Ruppell's griffon vulture has been measured at 11 277m (about 7mi) above sea level.
Furthest migrator	The arctic tern travels at least 36 000km/18 641mi each year, flying from the Arctic to the Antarctic and back again.
Fastest flyer	The peregrine falcon can dive through the air at speeds exceeding 322kph/200mph. Species such as red-breasted merganser, eider, canvasback and spur-winged goose can probably reach 90–100kph/56–62mph on rare occasions.
Fastest animal on two legs	The ostrich can maintain a speed of 50kph/31mph for 15 minutes or more, and it may reach up to 72kph/45mph in short bursts, eg when escaping from predators.
Smallest	The bee hummingbird of Cuba is under 6cm/2.4in long and weighs 1.6–1.9g/0.06–0.07oz.
Greatest wingspan	The wandering albatross can reach 3.4m/11ft 1in.
Heaviest flying bird	The kori bustard weighs up to 22kg/49lb; swans weigh about 16kg/35lb.
Deepest diver	The emperor penguin can reach a depth of 483m/1585ft. The great northern diver or loon can dive to about 80m/262ft – deeper than any other flying bird.
Most abundant	Africa's red-billed quelea is the most numerous wild bird, with a population guessed to be in the hundreds of millions. The domestic chicken is the most abundant of all birds, numbering thousands of millions.
Most feathers	The greatest number of feathers counted on a bird was 25 216, on a swan.

Fish

Name	Size (cm)[1]	Range and habitat	Special features
albacore	to 130	tropical, warm temperate	food and sport fish
anchovy	9–12	temperate	important food fish
anglerfish	5–8	tropical, temperate	large jaws
barracuda	30–240	tropical, warm temperate	carnivorous; large teeth
blenny	20–49	temperate, tropical	devoid of scales
bonito	to 90	temperate, warm	food fish; sport fish
bream	41–80	temperate (N Europe)	deep-bodied; food fish
brill	to 70	temperate	flatfish; food fish
butterfly fish	to 15	tropical	brightly coloured
carp	51–61	temperate	important food fish
catfish	90–135	temperate (N America)	important food fish
chub	30–60	temperate (Europe)	popular sport fish
cod	to 120	temperate (N hemisphere)	common cod important food fish
conger eel	274	temperate	upper jaw longer than lower

Name	Size (cm)[1]	Range and habitat	Special features
dab	20–40	temperate (Europe)	flatfish; food fish
dace	15–30	temperate (Europe, former USSR)	sport fish
damselfish	5–15	tropical, temperate	brightly coloured
dogfish	60–100	temperate (Europe)	food fish (sold as rock salmon)
dolphinfish (dorado)	to 200	tropical, warm temperate	prized sport fish; food fish
dory	30–60	temperate	deep-bodied; food fish
eagle ray	to 200	tropical, temperate	fins form 'wings'; young born live
eel	to 50 (male), to 100 (female)	temperate	elongated cylindrical body; important food fish
electric eel	to 240	Orinoco, Amazon basins (S America)	produces powerful electric shocks
electric ray (or torpedo ray)	to 180	tropical, temperate	produces powerful electric shocks
file fish	5–13	tropical, warm temperate	food fish
flounder	to 51	temperate (Europe)	flatfish; locally important food fish
flying fish	25–50	tropical, warm temperate	can jump and glide above water surface
goatfish ▶ red mullet			
goby	1–27	tropical, temperate	pelvic fins form single sucker-like fin
goldfish	to 30	temperate	popular ornamental fish
grenadier ▶ rat-tail			
grey mullet	to 75	tropical, temperate	food fish
grouper	5–370	tropical, warm temperate	prized sport and food fish
gurnard (or sea robin)	to 75	tropical, warm temperate	many produce audible sounds
hake	to 180	temperate	large head and jaws; food fish
halibut	to 250	temperate (Atlantic)	prized food fish
herring	to 40	temperate (N Atlantic, Arctic)	important food fish
lamprey	to 91	temperate (N Atlantic)	primitive jawless fish; food fish
lanternfish	2–15	tropical, temperate	body has numerous light organs
lemon sole	to 66	temperate	flatfish; feeds on polychaete worms; food fish
loach	to 15	temperate (Europe, Asia)	popular aquarium fish
mackerel	to 66	temperate (N Atlantic)	important food fish
manta ray (or devil ray)	120–900 (width)	tropical	fleshy 'horns' at side of head

Name	Size (cm)[1]	Range and habitat	Special features
minnow	to 12	temperate (N Europe, Asia)	locally abundant
monkfish	to 180	temperate (N Atlantic, Mediterranean)	cross between shark and ray in shape
moorish idol	to 22	tropical (Indo-Pacific)	bold black/white stripes with some yellow
moray eel	to 130	temperate, tropical	pointed snout; long, sharp teeth
parrotfish	25–190	tropical	teeth fused to form parrot-like beak
perch	30–50	temperate	food fish; sport fish
pike	to 130	temperate	prized by anglers
pilchard (or sardine)	to 25	temperate (N Atlantic, Mediterranean)	important food fish, often canned
pipefish	15–160	tropical, warm temperate	males of some species carry eggs in brood pouch
plaice	50–90	temperate (Europe)	flatfish; important food fish
puffer	3–25	tropical, warm temperate	body often spiny; food delicacy in Japan
rat-tail (or grenadier)	40–110	temperate, tropical	large head, tapering body
ray	39–113	temperate	front flattened with large pectoral fins
red mullet (or goatfish)	to 40	tropical, temperate	food fish
remora	12–46	tropical, warm temperate	large sucking disc on head
roach	35–53	temperate (Europe, former USSR)	popular sport fish
sailfish	to 360	tropical, warm temperate	long, tall dorsal fin; prized sport fish
salmon	to 150	temperate	prized sport and food fish
sand eel	to 20	temperate (N hemisphere)	very important food for seabirds
sardine ▶ pilchard			
scorpionfish	to 50	tropical, temperate	distinctive fin and body spines
sea bass	60–100	tropical, temperate	food fish; sport fish
sea robin ▶ gurnard			
sea-bream	35–51	tropical, temperate	food fish; sport fish
seahorse	to 15	tropical, warm temperate	horse-like head; swims upright
shark, basking	870–1350	tropical, temperate	second largest living fish
shark, great white	to 630	tropical	fierce; young born, not hatched

Name	Size (cm)[1]	Range and habitat	Special features
shark, hammer-head	360–600	tropical, warm temperate	head flattened into hammer shape
shark, tiger	360–600	tropical, warm temperate	vertical stripes on body; fierce
shark, whale	1020–1800	tropical	largest living fish; feeds on plankton
skate	200–285	temperate	food fish
smelt	20–30	temperate	related to salmon and trout
sole	30–60	tropical, temperate	flatfish; food fish
sprat	13–16	temperate	food fish; called whitebait when small
squirrelfish	12–30	tropical	brightly coloured; nocturnal
stickleback	5–10	temperate (N hemisphere)	male builds nest, guards eggs
stingray	106–140	tropical, temperate	tail whip-like, armed with poison spine(s)
sturgeon	100–500	temperate (N hemisphere)	eggs prized as caviar
sunfish	to 400	tropical, warm temperate	tail fin absent; body almost circular
surgeonfish (or tang)	20–45	tropical, subtropical	spine on sides of tail can be erected for defence
swordfish	200–500	tropical, temperate	upper jaws form flat 'sword'
tang ▶ surgeonfish			
triggerfish	10–60	tropical	dorsal spine can be erected for defence
trout	23–140	temperate	prized food fish
tuna, skipjack	to 100	tropical, temperate	important food fish
tuna, yellow-fin	to 200	tropical, warm temperate	elongated body; important food fish
turbot	50–100	temperate (N Atlantic)	flatfish; prized food fish
wrasse	7–210	tropical, warm temperate	brightly coloured

[1] Generally, the size given in the table denotes length. To convert cm to inches, multiply by 0.3937.

Fish – record holders

Fastest	Over short distances, the sailfish can reach a speed of 109kph/68mph; however, marlins are the fastest over longer distances, and can reach a burst speed of 64–80kph/40–50mph.
Largest	The whale shark (*Rhincodon typus*) is said to reach over 18m/59ft, with the largest on record being 12.65m/41ft 5in, weighing an estimated 21.5 tonnes.

Smallest	The stout infantfish (*Schindleria brevipinguis*), found in Great Barrier Reef coral lagoons in Australia, measures 6.5–8.4mm/0.2–0.3in.
Smallest in British waters	Guillet's goby (*Lebetus guilleti*) reaches a maximum length of 24mm.
Most widespread	The distribution of the bristlemouths of genus *Cyclothone* is worldwide; *Cyclothone microdon* may even be found in the Arctic Ocean.
Most restricted	The devil's hole pupfish (*Cyprinodon diabolis*) inhabits only a small area of water above a rock shelf in a spring-fed pool in Ash Meadows, Nevada, USA.
Deepest dweller	In 1970 a brotulid, *Bassogigas profundissimus*, was recovered from a depth of 8300m/27 231ft, making it the deepest living vertebrate.
Largest fish ever caught on a rod	In 1959 a great white shark measuring 5.13m/16ft 10in and weighing 1208kg/2 664lb was caught off S Australia.
Largest freshwater fish found in Britain and Ireland	Reportedly, in 1815 a pike (*Esox lucius*) was taken from the River Shannon in Ireland weighing 41.7kg/92lb; however, there is evidence of a pike weighing 32.7kg/72lb having been caught on Loch Ken, Scotland, in 1774.
Largest saltwater fish caught by anglers in the UK	In 1933 a tunny weighing 386kg/851lb was caught near Whitby, Yorkshire.
Longest-lived species	Some specimens of the lake sturgeon of N America are thought to be over 80 years old.
Shortest-lived species	Some species of the killifish (*Aplocheilidae* family), which are found in Africa, live for only 8 months in the wild.
Greatest distance covered by a migrating fish	A bluefin tuna was tagged in 1958 off Baja California and caught in 1963 south of Japan; it had covered a distance of 9335km/5800mi.

Amphibians and reptiles

Amphibians are a class of cold-blooded vertebrates including frogs, toads, newts and salamanders. There are approximately 4,000 species. They have a moist, thin skin without scales, and the adults live partly or entirely on land, but can usually only survive in damp habitats. They return to water to lay their eggs, which hatch to form fish-like larvae or tadpoles that breathe by means of gills, but gradually develop lungs as they approach adulthood.

Reptiles are egg-laying vertebrates of the class Reptilia, having evolved from primitive amphibians; there are 6,547 species divided into Squamata (lizards and snakes), Chelonia (tortoises and turtles), Crocodylia (crocodiles and alligators) and Rhynchocephalia (the tuatara).

Most reptiles live on the land, breathe with lungs, and have horny or plated skins. Reptiles require the rays of the sun to maintain their body temperature, ie they are cold-blooded or ectothermic. This confines them to warm, tropical and subtropical regions, but does allow some species to exist in particularly hot desert environments in which mammals and birds would find it impossible to survive.

Extinct species of reptile include the dinosaur and pterodactyl.

Name	Size (cm)[1]	Distribution	Special features
■ Amphibians			
common spadefoot	to 8	C Europe	toad with a pale-coloured tubercle (the spade) on its hind foot
frog, common	to 10	Europe except Mediterranean region and most of Iberia	most widespread European frog
frog, edible	to 12	S and C Europe	often heavily spotted; whitish vocal sacs
frog, goliath	to 81.5	Africa	world's largest frog
frog, leopard	5–13	N America	usually has light-edged dark spots on body
frog, marsh	to 15	SW and E Europe and SE England	extremely aquatic
frog, painted	to 7	Iberia and SW France	usually smooth and yellow-brown, grey or reddish with dark spots
frog, parsley	to 5	W Europe	slender bodied, with a whitish underside
frog, poison-arrow	0.85–1.24	C and S America	smallest known amphibian; skin highly poisonous
hellbender	to 63	America	salamander with wrinkled folds of flesh on body
mudpuppy	18–43	N America	salamander with bright red external gills
natterjack	to 10	SW and C Europe	toad with bright yellow stripe along its back
newt, alpine	to 12	C Europe	dark mottled back and a uniformly orange belly and bluish spotted sides
newt, Bosca's	7–10	Iberian peninsula	similiar to smooth newt without a dorsal crest
newt, marbled	to 15	Iberia and W France	bright yellow or orange stripe on velvety green and black mottled back
newt, palmate	to 9	W Europe	palmate (webbed feet); short filament at end of breeding male's tail
newt, smooth	to 11	Europe	breeding male develops a wavy crest
newt, warty (great crested newt)	to 17	Europe except Iberia and Ireland	bright red, orange or yellow spotted belly and warty skin
salamander, alpine	to 15	C Europe	large glands on back of head
salamander, Chinese giant	114 (average)	China	world's largest amphibian

Name	Size (cm)[1]	Distribution	Special features
salamander, fire	to 25	C and S Europe	large glands on sides of head contain venomous secretion
salamander, goldstriped	15–16	Iberian peninsula	thin with shiny skin
salamander, spectacled	to 11	W Italy	only European salamander with four toes on hind feet
toad, common	to 15	Europe except N Scandinavia, Ireland and some Mediterranean islands	largest European toad; usually brownish or greyish with warty skin
toad, green	to 10	E Europe	distinctive colouring: grey or greenish with darker marbled markings
toad, marine	to 23.8	S America	world's largest toad
toad, midwife	to 5	W Europe	male carries strings of eggs wrapped around hind legs
toad, Surinam	to 20	S America	female incubates eggs on her back
toad, yellow-bellied	to 5	C and S Europe	usually bright yellow or orange, black-blotched belly
treefrog, common	to 5	C and S Europe	usually bright green; often found in trees high above ground
■ Reptiles			
alligator	200–550	S USA, C and S America and E China	although rare, attacks can cause human fatalities; endangered species apart from American alligator
anaconda ▶ boa			
anguid	6–30	N and S America, Europe, Asia and NW Africa	bony-plated scales reach round its underside giving a rigid appearance
boa	200–400	Western N America, S America, Africa, Madagascar, Asia, Fiji, Solomon Is and New Guinea	famous constricting snake; includes species of anaconda
chameleon	2–28	Africa outside the Sahara, Madagascar, Middle East, S Spain, S Arabian peninsula, Sri Lanka, Crete, India and Pakistan	ability to change colour and blend into environment
crocodile	150–750	pantropical and some temperate regions of Africa	distinguished from the alligator by the visible fourth tooth in the lower jaw; several species are endangered

Name	Size (cm)[1]	Distribution	Special features
gecko	1.5–24	N and S America, Africa, S Europe, Asia and Australia	vocalization and ability to climb; able to shed its tail for defence
iguana	to 200	C and S America, Madagascar, Fiji and Tonga	terrestrial and tree-dwelling lizard; able to survive in exceptionally high temperatures
lizard, beaded	33–45	SW USA, W Mexico to Guatemala	possesses a mildly venomous bite
lizard, blind	12–16.5	SE Asia	eyes concealed within the skin
lizard, Bornean earless	to 20	Borneo	no external ear opening; partly aquatic
lizard, chisel-tooth	4–35	Africa, Asia and Australia	named after its distinctive teeth; family includes the flying dragon
lizard, girdle-tailed	5–27.5	Africa S of the Sahara, Madagascar	terrestrial; active by day; adapted to arid environments
lizard, monitor	12–150	Africa, S Asia, Indo-Australian archipelago, Philippines, New Guinea and Australia	consumes its prey whole; includes the Komodo dragon, the largest living lizard, which is capable of killing pigs and small deer
lizard, night	3.5–12	C America	most species active by night
lizard, snake	6.5–31	New Guinea and Australia	snake-like appearance; broad but highly extensible tongue
lizard, wall and sand	4–22	Europe, Africa, Asia and Indo-Australian archipelago	lives in open and sandy environments; terrestrial, active by day
lizard, worm	15–35	subtropical regions of N and S America, Africa, Middle East, Asia and Europe	worm-like, burrowing reptile; some of the species have the rare ability to move backwards and forwards
pipesnake	to 100	S America, SE Asia	tail has brilliantly coloured red underside; feeds on other snakes
python	100–1000	tropical and subtropical Africa, SE Asia, Australia, Mexico and C America	capable of killing humans, especially children, by constriction
skink	2.8–35	tropical and temperate regions	terrestrial, tree-dwelling or burrowing species, including highly adept swimmers
snake, dawn blind	11–30	C and S America	short tail, indistinct head, one or two teeth in the lower jaw
snake, front-fanged	38–560	worldwide in warm regions	highly venomous family with short fangs
snake, harmless	13–350	worldwide	most species unable to produce venomous saliva
snake, shieldtail	20–50	S India and Sri Lanka	tail forms a rough cylindrical shield

Name	Size (cm)[1]	Distribution	Special features
snake, thread	15–90	C and S America, Africa and Asia	small and exceptionally slender burrowing snake
snake, typical blind	15–90	C and S America, Africa S of the Sahara, SE Europe, S Asia, Taiwan and Australia	burrowing snake with tiny, concealed eyes and no teeth on lower jaw
tortoise	10–140	S Europe, Africa, Asia, C and S America	includes smallest species of turtle, the speckled Cape tortoise (10cm), and one of the longest-lived turtles, the spur-thighed tortoise
tuatara	45–61	islands off New Zealand	'third eye' in the top of the head
turtle, Afro-American side-necked	12–90	S America, Africa, Madagascar, Seychelles and Mauritius	seabed-dweller that rarely requires to come to the surface
turtle, American mud and musk	11–27	N and S America	lives mostly in fresh water; glands produce evil-smelling secretion
turtle, Austro-American side-necked	14–48	S America, Australia and New Guinea	includes the peculiar looking matamata, the most adept of the ambush-feeders at the gape and suck technique of capturing prey
turtle, big-headed	20	SE Asia	large head which cannot be retracted
turtle, Central American river	to 65	Vera Cruz, Mexico, Honduras	freshwater creature with well-developed shell
turtle, Mexican musk	to 38	Mexico to Honduras	freshwater creature dwelling in marshes and swamps
turtle, pig-nosed softshell	55 or over	New Guinea and N Australia	specialized swimmer; plateless skin and fleshy, pig-like snout
turtle, pond and river	11.4–80	N and C America, S Europe, N Africa, Asia and Argentina	family ranges from tiny bog turtle (11.4cm) to the largest of the river turtles, the Malaysian giant turtle
turtle, sea	75–213	pantropical, and some subtropical and temperate regions	rapid movement through water contrasts with slow movements on land
turtle, snapping	47–66	N and C America	large-headed, aggressive seabed dweller
turtle, softshell	30–115	N America, Africa, Asia and Indo-Australian archipelago	leathered, plateless skin; noted for its prominent, pointed snout

Name	Size (cm)[1]	Distribution	Special features
viper	25–365	N and S America, Africa, Europe and Asia	venomous family of snakes, including the rattlesnake and the sidewinder
whiptail and racerunner	37–45	N and S Asia	eaten by S American Indians; used in traditional medicines
xenosaur	10–15	Mexico, Guatemala and S China	terrestrial, sedentary and secretive

[1] Generally, the size given in the table denotes length. To convert from cm to inches, multiply by 0.3937.

Invertebrates

Invertebrates are animals with no backbone. Some have no skeleton at all, but many have external skeletons or shells that give them a rigid shape and provide anchorage for their muscles. There are about 30 major groups or phyla of invertebrates although the great majority of species belong to just two phyla – the Mollusca and the Arthropoda. The latter includes the insects, spiders, crustaceans and several other groups, all of which have segmented bodies and jointed legs. The majority of invertebrates are quite small, but examples of the largest – the giant squid – have been recorded as much as 15m/49ft long and may weigh well over a tonne.

For molluscs, lengths given are normally maximum shell lengths, but (b) indicates body length; for spiders, lengths are body lengths, although legs may be much longer; for insects, sizes given are normally body lengths, but (w) indicates wingspan.

Name	Size [1]	Range and habitat	Special features
MOLLUSCS: Phylum Mollusca			
■ Slugs and snails/Gastropoda (c.50 000 species)			
abalone	<30cm	warm seas worldwide	collected for food and for their pearly shells
conch	<33cm	tropical seas	shells used as trumpets
cone shell	<23cm	warm seas worldwide	some species dangerous to humans; beautiful shells much sought after
cowrie	<10cm	warm seas worldwide	shiny, china-like shells were once used as money
limpet, common	<5.5cm	worldwide	conical shell pulled tightly down on rocks when tide is out
limpet, slipper	<6cm	originally N America, now common on coasts of Europe	serious pest in oyster and mussel farms, settling on the shells and cutting off food supplies
periwinkle, common	<2.5cm	N Atlantic and adjacent seas; rocky shores	thick, dull brown shell; the fishmonger's winkle
sea butterfly	<5cm	oceans worldwide; most common in warm waters	swims by flapping wing-like extensions of the foot

Name	Size[1]	Range and habitat	Special features
slug, great grey	<20cm (b)	Europe	common in gardens; mates in mid-air, hanging from a rope of slime
snail, giant African	<15cm	originally Africa, now tropical Asia and Pacific	agricultural pest; lays hard-shelled eggs as big as those of a thrush
snail, great ramshorn	<3cm	Europe; still and slow-moving fresh water	shell forms a flat spiral; body has bright red blood
snail, roman	<5cm	C and S Europe; lime soils	often a pest, but cultivated for food in some areas
whelk	<12cm	N Atlantic and neighbouring seas	collected for human consumption

■ Bivalves/Lamellibranchia (c.8000 species)

Name	Size	Range and habitat	Special features
cockle, common	<5cm	European coasts	important food for fish and wading birds
mussel, common	<11cm	coasts of Europe and eastern North America	farmed on a large scale for human consumption
oyster	<15cm	coasts of Europe and Africa	large numbers farmed for human consumption
piddock	<12cm	coasts of Europe and eastern North America	uses rasp-like shell to bore into soft rocks and wood
razor-shell, pod	<20cm	European coasts	long, straight shell, shaped like a cut-throat razor
scallop, great	<15cm	European coasts; usually below tide level	strongly ribbed, eared shells with one valve flatter than the other

■ Squids and octopuses/Cephalopoda (c.750 species)

Name	Size	Range and habitat	Special features
cuttlefish, common	<30cm	coastal waters of Atlantic and neighbouring seas	flat, oval body can change colour
octopus, blue-ringed	10cm (span)	Australian coasts	only octopus known to have killed people
octopus, common	<3m (span)	Atlantic and Mediterranean coastal waters	not dangerous to people
squid, common	<50cm	Atlantic and Mediterranean coastal waters	deep pink in life, fading to grey after death
squid, giant	<15m	oceans worldwide	main food of the sperm whale

CRUSTACEANS: Phylum Arthropoda

■ Crustacea (c.30 000 species)

Name	Size	Range and habitat	Special features
barnacle, acorn	<1.5cm (diam.)	worldwide	cemented to intertidal rocks
crab, edible	<20cm	eastern N Atlantic and neighbouring seas	widely caught for human consumption
crab, fiddler	<3cm	tropical seashores and mangrove swamps	male has one big, colourful claw

Name	Size [1]	Range and habitat	Special features
crab, hermit	<15cm	worldwide; mainly in coastal waters	soft-bodied crab that uses empty seashells as portable homes
crab, robber	<45cm	islands and coasts of Indian and Pacific oceans	related to hermit crab
crayfish, noble	<15cm	Europe	reared in large numbers for human consumption, especially in France
krill	<5cm	mainly the southern oceans	main food of the baleen whales and many other animals
lobster, common	<70cm	European coasts	now rare in many places through overfishing
lobster, Norway	<25cm	European seas	marketed as scampi
lobster, spiny	<45cm	Mediterranean and Atlantic; rocky coasts	popular food in S Europe; also known as crayfish
prawn, common	<10cm	European coasts; usually stony or rocky shores	scavenger; almost transparent
shrimp, common	<7cm	coasts of Europe and eastern North America	much used for human consumption
water flea	<0.5cm	worldwide; fresh water	major food of small fish
woodlouse	<2.5cm	worldwide	only major group of terrestrial crustaceans; also called 'sowbugs' and 'slaters'

SPIDERS: Phylum Arthropoda
■ Arachnida (c.40 000 species)

bird-eating spider	<10cm	warmer parts of the Americas and southern Africa	often in trees, where they sometimes capture nesting birds; venom not dangerous to humans
black widow	<1.6cm	most warm parts of the world, including S Europe	has caused many human deaths, but bites are now quickly cured with antivenin
bolas spider	<1.5cm	N and S America, Africa and Australasia	catches moths by whirling a single thread of silk
crab spider	<2cm	worldwide	mostly squat, crab-like spiders that lie in wait for prey – often in flowers
funnel-web spider	<5cm	Australia	among the deadliest spiders, inhabit tubular webs
garden spider	<1.2cm	N hemisphere	black to ginger, with a white cross on the back
gladiator spider	<2.5cm	warm regions and some cooler parts of North America and Australia	make sticky webs which they throw at passing prey, usually at night

Name	Size [1]	Range and habitat	Special features
house spider	<2cm	mostly N hemisphere	long-legged; fast-moving; harmless
jumping spider	<1.5cm	worldwide	large-eyed spiders that leap onto their prey; often brilliantly coloured
money spider	<0.6cm	worldwide, but most common in cooler areas of N hemisphere	believed to bring wealth or good fortune
orb-web spider	<3cm	worldwide	makers of the familiar wheel-shaped webs, up to a metre or more in diameter
raft spider	<2.5cm	worldwide	hunting spiders that lurk at the edge of pools or on floating objects
spitting spider	<0.6cm	worldwide; normally only in buildings	catches prey by spitting strands of sticky, venom-coated gum at them
tarantula	<3cm	S Europe	wolf spider whose bite was believed to be curable only by performing a frantic dance – the tarantella; although painful, the bite is not really dangerous
trapdoor spider	<3cm	most warm parts of the world, including S Europe	live in burrows closed by hinged lids of silk and debris
water spider	<1.5cm	Eurasia; in ponds and slow-moving streams	world's only truly aquatic spider, lives in an air-filled, thimble-shaped web fixed to water plants
wolf spider	<3cm	worldwide, but most common in cooler parts of N hemisphere	large-eyed hunting spiders; generally harmless but some of the larger species have dangerous bites
zebra spider	<0.6cm	N hemisphere; often in and around houses	black and white jumping spider, commonly hunts on rocks and walls

INSECTS: Phylum Arthropoda

■ Silverfish/Thysanura (c.370 species)

silverfish	10mm	worldwide	wingless scavenger of starchy foods in houses

■ Mayflies/Ephemeroptera (c.2500 species)

mayfly	16mm	worldwide	flimsy insects with 2 or 3 long 'tails'; adults live only a few hours

■ Damselflies and dragonflies/Odonata (c.5500 species)

dragonfly	<20–130mm	worldwide	long-bodied insects with gauzy wings; most catch insects in mid-air

Name	Size [1]	Range and habitat	Special features

■ Crickets and grasshoppers/Orthoptera (c.17 000 species)

cricket, bush	<150mm	worldwide, apart from coldest areas	like grasshoppers but with very long antennae; several N American species are called katydids
cricket, house	<20mm	worldwide	scavenger in houses and rubbish dumps
locust, desert	85mm	Africa and S Asia	swarms periodically destroy crops in Africa
locust, migratory	<50mm	Africa and S Europe	swarm in Africa, but solitary in Europe

■ Stick insects and leaf insects/Phasmida (c.2500 species, mostly tropical)

insect, leaf	<90mm	SE Asia	very flat, leaf-like, green or brown bodies
insect, stick	<350mm	warm areas, including S Europe	stick-like green or brown bodies with or without wings; often kept as pets

■ Earwigs/Dermaptera (c.1300 species)

earwig	<30mm	originally Africa, now worldwide	slender, brownish insects with prominent pincers at the rear

■ Cockroaches and mantids/Dictyoptera (c.5500 species)

American cockroach	40mm	worldwide	scavenger, living outside (if warm) or in buildings; chestnut brown
praying mantis	<75mm	all warm areas	catches other insects with spiky front legs

■ Termites/Isoptera (over 2000 species)

termite	<22mm	mostly tropical	colonies in mounds of earth, in dead wood or underground; many are timber pests

■ Bugs/Hemiptera (c.70 000 species)

aphid	<5mm	worldwide	sap-sucking insects; many are serious pests
bedbug	5mm	worldwide	bloodsucking; feeds at night
cicada	<40mm (w)	worldwide, mainly in warm climates	males make loud, shrill sounds; young stages live underground
froghopper	6mm	N hemisphere	young stages live in froth, often called cuckoo-spit
pondskater	10mm	N hemisphere	skims across the surface of still water

■ Thrips/Thysanoptera (over 3000 species)

thrips	2.5mm	worldwide	cause much damage; fly in huge numbers in thundery weather

■ Lacewings/Neuroptera (over 6000 species)

antlion	90mm (w)	Eurasia	larvae make small pits in sandy soil and feed on insects that fall into them

Name	Size [1]	Range and habitat	Special features
green lacewing	<50mm	worldwide	predators of aphids and other small insects

■ **Scorpion flies/Mecoptera (c.400 species)**

Name	Size [1]	Range and habitat	Special features
scorpionfly	20mm	worldwide	male abdomen is usually turned up like a scorpion's tail; harmless

■ **Butterflies and moths/Lepidoptera (c.150 000 species)**

Butterflies (c.18 000 species)

Name	Size [1]	Range and habitat	Special features
birdwing butterfly	<300mm (w)	SE Asia and N Australia, tropical forests	include the world's largest butterflies; many are becoming rare through collecting and loss of habitat
cabbage white butterfly	<70mm (w)	Eurasia, N Africa, flowery places	caterpillar is a serious pest of cabbages and other brassicas
fritillary butterfly	<80mm (w)	mostly N hemisphere	mostly orange with black spots above and silvery spots below
monarch butterfly	<100mm (w)	mostly Pacific area and N America	orange with black markings; hibernates in huge swarms in Mexico and southern USA
skipper butterfly	<80mm (w)	worldwide	mostly small brown or orange grassland insects with darting flight
swallowtail butterfly	<120mm (w)	worldwide, but mostly tropical	prominent 'tails' on hindwings; many becoming rare through collecting and loss of habitat

Moths (c. 132 000 species)

Name	Size [1]	Range and habitat	Special features
burnet moth	<40mm (w)	Eurasia and N Africa	protected by foul-tasting body fluids and gaudy black and red colours
clothes moth	<15mm	worldwide	caterpillars damage woollen fabrics; live mainly in buildings
death's-head hawk moth	<135mm (w)	Africa and Eurasia	skull-like pattern on thorax
hummingbird hawk moth	<60mm (w)	Eurasia	produces a loud hum as it hovers
pine processionary moth	<40mm (w)	S and C Europe	larvae feed in long processions at night; forest pest
silk moth	<60mm (w)	native of China; now unknown in the wild	cream-coloured moth bred for the fine silk obtained from its cocoon; all cultured moths flightless
tiger moth	<100mm (w)	worldwide	mostly brightly coloured and hairy, with evil-tasting body fluids

■ **True flies/Diptera (c.90 000 species, a few without wings)**

Name	Size [1]	Range and habitat	Special features
cranefly (or leather-jacket)	<35mm (w)	worldwide	slender, long-legged flies; larvae of many are leatherjackets that damage crop roots
housefly	7mm	worldwide	abundant on farms and rubbish dumps; becoming less common in houses; breeds in dung and other decaying matter and carries germs
hoverfly	<40mm	worldwide	many have amazing hovering ability; adults feed on pollen and nectar; many are black and yellow mimics of bees and wasps
mosquito	<15mm	worldwide	females are bloodsuckers; spread malaria and other diseases
tsetse fly	10mm	tropical Africa	bloodsuckers; spread human sleeping sickness and cattle diseases

■ Fleas/Siphonaptera (c.1800 species)

European flea	3mm	worldwide	wingless, bloodsucking parasites; long hind legs enable them to jump many times their own lengths

■ Bees, wasps and ants/Hymenoptera (over 120000 species)

ant, army	<40mm	tropics	live in mobile colonies, some of over a million ants
ant, honeypot	20mm	deserts across the world	some workers gorge themselves with sugar-rich food and become living food for other ants
ant, weaver	10mm	Old World tropics	nest made from leaves, joined by sticky silk
bee, bumble	<35mm	worldwide, except Australia	plump, hairy bees living in annual colonies; only mated queen survives winter to start new colonies in spring
bee, honey	<20mm	worldwide (probably native of SE Asia)	less hairy than bumble bee; lives in permanent colonies mostly in artificial hives; stores honey for winter
hornet, European	<35mm	Eurasia and now America	large brown and yellow wasp; nests in hollow trees
ichneumon	<50mm	worldwide	parasites; the young grow inside their hosts and gradually kill them
sawfly	<50mm	worldwide	saw-like ovipositor of most females, used to cut slits in plants before laying eggs

Name	Size [1]	Range and habitat	Special features
■ Beetles/Coleoptera (over 350 000 species; front wings usually form casing over body)			
click beetle (or wireworm)	<40mm	worldwide	bullet-shaped; flick into the air to turn over, making a loud click; larvae damage crop roots
Colorado beetle	10mm	N America and now Europe	black and yellow adults and pink grubs both seriously damage potato crops
deathwatch beetle	7mm	N hemisphere	tunnelling larvae do immense damage to old building timbers; adults tap wood as mating call
devil's coach-horse	25mm	Eurasia	also called cocktail because it raises its rear end
furniture beetle (or woodworm)	5mm	worldwide	causes much damage to furniture and building timbers
glow-worm	15mm	Europe	wingless female glows with greenish light to attract males
goliath beetle	<150mm	Africa	world's heaviest beetles, up to 100g; fly well and feed on fruit
grain weevil	3mm	worldwide	destroys all kinds of stored grain
ladybird	10mm	worldwide	aphid-eating habits make them friends of gardeners
scarab beetle	30mm	most warm parts of the world	some form dung into balls and roll it around before burying it; introduced into Australia to deal with sheep and cattle dung
sexton beetle	<25mm	worldwide	often orange and black; beetles work in pairs to bury small dead animals, near which they then lay their eggs
stag beetle	50mm	Eurasia	males have huge antler-like jaws with which they wrestle rivals

woodworm ► furniture beetle

[1] To convert from cm to inches, multiply by 0.3937.

HUMAN LIFE

Main types of vitamin

Vita-min	Chemical name	Deficiency symptoms	Source
■ **Fat-soluble vitamins**			
A	retinol (carotene)	night blindness; rough skin; impaired bone growth	dairy products, egg yolk, fortified margarine, liver, oily fish
D	calciferols (eg cholecalciferol)	osteomalacia (rickets); osteoporosis	egg yolk, liver, oily fish; made on skin in sunlight
E	tocopherols	multiple symptoms follow impaired fat absorption	vegetable oils, nuts, seeds, wheatgerm
K	phytomenadione	haemorrhagic problems	green leafy vegetables, vegetable oils, cereals, beef, liver
■ **Water-soluble vitamins**			
B_1	thiamin	headache, fatigue, muscle wasting; beri-beri; Wernicke–Korsakov's syndrome	pork, fruit, vegetables, dairy products, eggs, whole grains, some fortified breakfast cereals
B_2	riboflavin	skin disorders; light sensitivity; itching; anaemia; associated with cataracts and rheumatoid arthritis	dairy products, eggs, fortified breakfast cereals, rice, mushrooms; destroyed by light
B_3	niacin	pellagra (gastrointestinal problems, skin and neurological symptoms)	milk, eggs, poultry, meats, wheat flour, maize flour
B_5	pantothenic acid	fatigue; gastrointestinal problems; sleep disturbances; neurological disorders	found in virtually all meat and vegetable foods; destroyed in heavily processed food
B_6	pyridoxine	anxiety and depression; weight gain or loss	liver, meats, milk, eggs, fruits, cereals, brown rice, soya beans, whole grains, nuts, leafy vegetables
B_7	biotin	dermatitis; hair loss; conjunctivitis; loss of co-ordination	liver, kidney, egg yolk, dried fruit, yeast extract; made by micro-organisms in large intestine

Vita-min	Chemical name	Deficiency symptoms	Source
B$_9$	folic acid	anaemia; neural tube defects in offspring of folic acid-deficient mothers	liver, green leafy vegetables, some fruits, brown rice, yeast extract; cooking and processing can cause serious losses in food
B$_{12}$	cyanocobalamin	anaemia; neurological disorders	liver, kidney, other meats, fish, eggs, dairy products, some fortified breakfast cereals; none in plants
C	ascorbic acid	scurvy	soft and citrus fruits, green leafy vegetables, potatoes, liver, kidney; losses occur during storage and cooking

Main trace minerals

Mineral	Deficiency symptoms	Source
calcium	osteomalacia (rickets) in children; osteoporosis in adults	milk, cheese, most green leafy vegetables, soya beans, nuts, fortified cereals and flours
chromium	impaired regulation of blood sugar; weight loss; neuropathy	processed meats, whole grains, pulses, spices
copper	anaemia; bone abnormalities	nuts, shellfish, offal
fluoride	tooth decay; possibly osteoporosis	fluoridated drinking water, seafood, tea
iodine	goitre; cretinism in newborn children	shellfish, saltwater fish, seaweed, iodized table salt
iron	anaemia	liver, other meats, dark green leafy vegetables, beans, nuts, dried fruit, whole grains, fortified cereals and flours
magnesium	irregular heartbeat; muscular weakness; fatigue; loss of appetite	green leafy vegetables, nuts, whole grains
manganese	not known in humans	green vegetables, cereals, bread, tea
molybdenum	not known in humans	legumes, leafy vegetables, cauliflower, cereals, nuts
phosphorus	muscular weakness; bone pain; loss of appetite	meats, poultry, fish, dairy products, cereals, bread
potassium	irregular heartbeat; muscular weak-ness; gastrointestinal symptoms	milk, fruits, vegetables, fish, shellfish, meats, liver
selenium	Keshan disease	eggs, fish, offal, brazil nuts, cereals
sodium	low blood pressure, dehydration, muscle cramps (very rare)	table salt, cereals, bread, meat products, processed foods
zinc	impaired growth and development; nerve damage; impaired wound healing; loss of appetite; susceptibility to infection	meat, shellfish, dairy products, whole grains

Infectious diseases and infections

Name	Cause	Transmission	Incubation	Symptoms
AIDS (Acquired Immune Deficiency Syndrome)	human immunodeficiency virus (HIV, retrovirus family)	sexual intercourse, sharing of syringes, blood transfusion	several years	fever, lethargy, weight loss, diarrhoea, lymph node enlargement, viral and fungal infections
amoebiasis	Entamoeba histolytica amoeba	organism in contaminated food	up to several years	fever, diarrhoea, exhaustion, rectal bleeding
anthrax	Bacillus anthracis bacterium	animal hair	1–3 days	small red pimple on hand or face enlarges and discharges pus
appendicitis	usually E. coli bacterium	not transmitted	sudden onset	abdominal pain which moves from left to right after a few hours, nausea
bilharziasis (schistosomiasis)	Schistosoma haematobium (also called Bilharzia), S. mansoni or S. japonicum parasites	certain snails living in calm water	varies with lifespan of parasite	fever, muscle aches, abdominal pain, headaches
bronchiolitis (babies only)	respiratory syncytical virus (RSV; paramyxovirus family)	droplet infection	1–3 days	blocked or runny nose, irritability
brucellosis	Brucella abortus or B. meliteusis bacteria	cattle or goats	3–6 days	fever, drenching sweats, weight loss, muscle and joint pains, confusion and poor memory
bubonic plague	Yersinia pestis bacterium	fleas	3–6 days	fever, muscle aches, headaches, exhaustion, enlarged lymph glands ('buboes')
chickenpox (varicella)	varicella-zoster virus (herpesvirus family)	droplet infection	14–21 days	blister-like eruptions, lethargy, headaches, sore throat
cholera	Vibrio cholerae bacterium	contaminated water	a few hours to 5 days	severe diarrhoea, vomiting

Name	Cause	Transmission	Incubation	Symptoms
common cold (coryza)	rhinoviruses, adenoviruses	droplet infection	1–3 days	blocked or runny nose, sneezing, sore throat, runny eyes
conjunctivitis	viruses; bacteria eg Staphylococcus species; allergy	variable	variable	if viral, watery discharge from eyes; if bacterial, sticky yellow discharge from eyes
dengue fever (break-bone fever)	dengue fever virus (flavivirus family)	mosquito	5–6 days	fever, severe muscle cramps, enlarged lymph nodes
diphtheria	Corynebacterium diphtheriae bacterium	droplet infection	4–6 days	grey exudate across throat; swelling of throat tissues may lead to asphyxiation; toxin secreted by bacteria may seriously damage heart
dysentery	Shigella genus of bacteria	contaminated food or water	variable; can cause death within 48 hours	diarrhoea, with or without bleeding
gastroenteritis	bacteria, viruses and food poisoning	droplet infection of food	variable	varies from nausea to severe fever, vomiting and diarrhoea
German measles (rubella)	rubella virus (togavirus family)	droplet infection	18 days	1–2 days catarrh and sore throat, then red rash, enlargement of lymph nodes
glandular fever (infectious mononucleosis)	Epstein–Barr virus (herpesvirus family)	saliva of infected person	1–6 weeks	sore throat, fever, enlargement of tonsils and lymph nodes, lethargy, depression
gonorrhoea	Neisseria gonorrhoeae bacterium	usually sexually transmitted	2–10 days	in men, burning sensation on urination and discharge from urethra; in women (if any), vaginal discharge
hepatitis	hepatitis A, B or C virus (picornavirus, hepadnavirus and flavivirus families)	contaminated food or water (type A); sexual relations; infected blood (types B and C)	3–6 weeks (type A); up to a few weeks (type B); over 10 years (type C)	often no symptoms, otherwise similar to flu; loss of appetite, tenderness below right ribs, jaundice

Name	Cause	Transmission	Incubation	Symptoms
influenza (flu)	influenza A, B or C virus (orthomyxovirus family)	droplet infection	1–3 days	fever, sweating, muscle aches
kala-azar (leishmaniasis)	parasites of the genus *Leishmania*	sandfly	usually 1–2 months; can be up to 10 years	lymph gland, spleen and liver enlargement
laryngitis	same viruses that cause colds, ie adeno- and rhinoviruses	droplet infection	1–3 days	sore throat, coughing, hoarseness
lassa fever	lassa virus (arenavirus family)	urine	3 weeks	fever, sore throat, muscle aches and pains, haemorrhage into the skin
legionnaire's disease	*Legionella pneumophila* bacterium	water droplets in infected humidifiers, cooling towers; stagnant water in cisterns and shower heads	1–3 days	flu and pneumonia- like symptoms, fever, diarrhoea, mental confusion
leprosy	*Mycobacterium leprae* bacterium	droplet infection; minimally contagious	variable	insensitive white patches on skin, nodules, thickening of and damage to nerves
malaria	*Plasmodium falciparum, P. vivax, P ovale* and *P. malariae* parasites	*Anopheles* mosquito	7–30 days (shortest for *P. falciparum*, longest for *P. malariae*)	severe swinging fever, cold sweats, shivers
Marburg (or green monkey) disease	Marburg virus (filiovirus family)	transmission by unknown animal(s), body fluids	5–9 days	fever, diarrhoea; affects brain, kidneys and lungs
measles	measles virus (paramyxovirus family)	droplet infection	14 days	fever, severe cold symptoms, bloody red rash

Name	Cause	Transmission	Incubation	Symptoms
meningitis	*Streptococcus pneumoniae* or *Neisseria meningitidis* bacteria; viruses eg enteroviruses; fungi eg *Cryptococcus* species	droplet infection	variable	severe headache, stiffness in neck muscles, dislike of the light, nausea, vomiting, confusion
MRSA	methicillin-resistant strains of *Staphylococcus aureus* bacteria	skin-to-skin contact	variable	various, including skin or wound infections or septicaemia
mumps	mumps virus (paramyxovirus family)	droplet infection	18 days	lethargy, fever, pain at the angle of the jaw, swelling of parotid gland(s)
orchitis	bacteria or viruses; if bacterial, urinary infection due to eg gonorrhoea; if viral, due to eg mumps	see cause	variable	painful red and swollen testes, fever, nausea
osteomyelitis	bacteria eg *Staphylococcus* species	infection spreads from eg boil or impetigo	1–10 days	abrupt onset of fever, and pain at site of infected bone (usually tibia)
parotitis	bacteria eg *Staphylococcus aureus*; viruses eg mumps	common in mumps (viral), may follow severe febrile illness or abdominal operation	1–10 days	inflammation of one or both parotid glands
pericarditis	bacteria eg *Staphylococcus* species; viruses eg Coxsackie B	infection follows a chest disease or heart attack	variable	inflamed pericardium (fibrous bag which encloses the heart); tight chest pain
peritonitis	bacteria eg *E. coli* or *Staphylococcus aureus*; chemical irritation	usually appendicitis; perforation of the gut allows escape of barrel contents into peritoneal cavity	1–10 days	severe abdominal pain, vomiting, rigidity, shock

Name	Cause	Transmission	Incubation	Symptoms
pharyngitis	viruses eg adenoviruses; bacteria eg *Streptococcus* species	droplet infection	3–5 days	sore throat, fever, pain on swallowing, enlarged neck glands
pneumonia	viruses eg influenza virus; bacteria eg *Streptococcus pneumoniae*	droplet infection	1–3 weeks	cough, fever, chest pain
poliomyelitis	three strains of polio virus (picornavirus family)	droplet infection and hand to mouth infection from faeces	7–14 days	affects spinal cord and brain; headache, fever, neck and muscle stiffness; may result in meningitis or paralysis
proctitis	sexually transmitted bacterial infections eg gonorrhoea	contact	variable	inflammation of the rectum and anus resulting from thrush, piles or fissures; pain on defecation
psittacosis	*Chlamydis psittaci* bacterium	infected birds (eg parrots)	1–2 weeks	headache, chest pain, fever, nausea
puerperal fever	*Streptococcus* infection within uterine cavity or vagina	follows childbirth	1–10 days	fever; often fatal in past, now rare
pyelitis (or pyelonephritis)	bacteria eg *E. coli*	kidney infection resulting from urinary tract infection	1–10 days	fever, rigor, loin pain, burning on passing urine
rabies	rabies virus (rhabdovirus family)	animal bite	2–6 weeks	headache, sickness, excitability, fear of drinking water, convulsions, coma and death
river blindness (or onchocerciasis)	*Onchocerca volvulus* worm	bites of infected flies of genus *Simulium*	worms mature in 2–4 months, may live 12 years	worms inhabit skin, causing nodules and sometimes blindness

Name	Cause	Transmission	Incubation	Symptoms
salpingitis	Bacteria eg *Neisseria gonorrhoeae* or *Chlamydia trachomatis*	infection of the Fallopian tubes	variable	abdominal pain, fever, irregular periods, vaginal discharge
SARS (Severe Acute Respiratory Syndrome)	SARS virus (coronavirus family)	droplet infection; possibly also direct contact	2–10 days	fever, cough, breathing difficulty
scarlet fever	*Streptococcus pyogenes* bacterium	droplet infection or streptococci-infected milk or ice cream	2–4 days	sudden onset; headache, sore throat, fever, vomiting, red skin rash pain, numbness, blisters
shingles	herpes-zoster virus (also causes chickenpox)	dormant virus in body becomes active following a minor infection	variable	
sinusitis	bacteria eg *Streptococcus pneumoniae*; indirect consequence of allergy or viral infection	droplet infection	1–3 days	fever, sinus pain, nasal discharge
sleeping sickness (or African trypanosomiasis)	1. *Trypanosoma brucei gambiense* or 2. *Tb. rhodesiense*	bites by infected tsetse fly	1. weeks–months; 2. 7–14 days	fever, lymph node enlargement, headache, behavioural change, drowsiness, coma, sometimes death
smallpox	variola major or minor virus	now eradicated worldwide, but was transmitted by direct contact	12 days	fever, rash followed by pustules on face and extremities
syphilis	*Treponema pallidum* bacterium	sexually transmitted: bacteria enter bloodstream through a mucous membrane, usually genital skin	ulcer after 2–6 weeks, skin rash after weeks or months	late syphilis damages brain, heart and main blood vessels, and unborn babies
tetanus	*Clostridium tetani* bacterium	bacteria from soil infect wounds	2 days–4 weeks	muscular spasms cause lockjaw and affect breathing; potentially fatal

Name	Cause	Transmission	Incubation	Symptoms
thrush (or candidiasis)	*Candida albicans* yeast	the yeast is present on skin of most people and multiplies when resistance to infection is low, when hormonal balance is altered, or when taking antibiotics	variable	white spots on tongue and cheeks (oral thrush); irritant vaginal discharge (vaginal thrush); rash in genital area or between folds of skin (one form of 'nappy rash')
tonsillitis	usually same viruses responsible for colds; sometimes bacterial, eg *Streptococcus* species	droplet infection	1–3 days	red inflamed tonsils, sore throat
trachoma	*Chlamydia trachomatis* bacterium	poor hygiene: bacteria infect eye	5 days	conjunctivitis, swelling and scarring in cornea, often leading to blindness
tuberculosis	*Mycobacterium tuberculosis* bacterium	inhalation of bacteria from person with active tuberculosis pneumonia; drinking infected milk	up to several years	cough with bloodstained sputum, weight loss, chest pain
typhoid	*Salmonella typhi* bacterium	contaminated water or food	10–14 days	slow onset of fever, abdominal discomfort, cough, rash, constipation then diarrhoea, delirium, coma; potentially fatal
typhus	species of *Rickettsia* bacteria	bite by infected flea, tick, mite or louse, which carry the bacteria as parasites	7–14 days	fever, rigor, headache, muscular pain, rash
urethritis	viruses eg cytomegalovirus; bacteria eg *Chlamydia trachomatis*	may occur with cystitis or venereal infection	variable	abdominal pain, burning on urination, discharge from genitalia
whooping cough	*Bordetella pertussis* bacterium	droplet infection	7–14 days	severe coughing followed by 'whoop' of respiration
yellow fever	yellow fever virus (flavivirus family)	mosquitoes infected by monkeys	3–6 days	rigor, high fever, bone pain, headache, nausea, jaundice, kidney failure, coma; potentially fatal

Immunization schedule for children up to age 18

Age	Vaccine	How given
2 months	Diphtheria, tetanus, pertussis (whooping cough), polio, *Haemophilus influenzae* type b	Combined injection (DTaP/IPV/Hib)
	Pneumococcal infection	Injection (Pneumococcal conjugate vaccine, PCV)
3 months	Diphtheria, tetanus, pertussis, polio, *Haemophilus influenzae* type b	Combined injection (DTaP/IPV/Hib)
	Meningitis C	Injection (MenC)
4 months	Diphtheria, tetanus, pertussis, polio, *Haemophilis influenzae* type b	Combined injection (DTaP/IPV/Hib)
	Meningitis C	Injection (MenC)
	Pneumococcal infection	Injection (PCV)
Around 12 months	*Haemophilus influenzae* type b, Meningitis C	Combined injection (Hib/MenC)
Around 13 months	Measles, mumps, rubella (German measles)	Combined injection (MMR)
	Pneumococcal infection	Injection (PCV)
3 years 4 months– 5 years	Pneumococcal infection	Injection (PCV)
	Diphtheria, tetanus, pertussis, polio	Combined injection (dTaP/IPV or DTaP/IPV)
	Measles, mumps, rubella	Combined injection (MMR)
13–18 years	Diphtheria, tetanus, polio	Combined injection (Td/IPV)

Immunization for foreign travel

Immunization is recommended for travellers of all ages who are visiting countries where there is a chance of contracting serious or potentially fatal diseases. The information below is included for guidance only; travellers should check which immunizations are required for their particular destination, and whether they require immunization certificates. Malaria prophylaxis may also be recommended for some areas.

Disease	Area where immunization needed	Effective for
Cholera	Certificates of vaccination no longer officially required by any country; vaccine no longer available in the UK. Rarely, unofficial requests are made for evidence of vaccination following an outbreak. Confirmation of non-requirement of vaccination can be obtained if such a request is anticipated.	N/A
Diphtheria	For longer stays in E Europe, S America, Africa, the Middle East, the Indian subcontinent, SE Asia, the Far East.	10 years

Disease	Area where immunization needed	Effective for
Hepatitis A	Generally recommended for the Caribbean, S America, N Africa, the Middle East, sub-Saharan and southern Africa, the Indian subcontinent, SE Asia, the Far East, the Pacific Islands.	5–10 years, if booster given after 6–12 months
Hepatitis B	For longer stays in C and S America, the Caribbean, Africa, the Middle East, the Indian subcontinent, SE Asia, the Far East.	Unknown
Japanese encephalitis	Recommended for eastern Russia, certain parts of Australia and the Pacific Islands, and for longer, rural travel in the Indian subcontinent, SE Asia, the Far East.	1–3 years
Meningococcal meningitis (strains A and C)	Recommended for longer stays in Mongolia and certain parts of S America, sub-Saharan Africa, the Indian subcontinent.	up to 5 years
Meningococcal meningitis (ACWY vaccine)	Pilgrims travelling to Saudi Arabia must have evidence of vaccination.	2 years
Polio	For most areas, if no recent booster received.	10 years
Rabies	Vaccine not recommended as routine but may be advisable for longer, rural travel in SE Asia, the Far East. Also may be advisable for travel to very remote areas of E Europe, C and S America, N Africa, the Middle East.	2–3 years
Tetanus	For all areas, if no recent booster received.	10 years
Tuberculosis	Recommended for longer stays in E Europe, C and S America, the Caribbean, Africa, the Middle East, the Indian subcontinent, SE Asia, the Far East, the Pacific Islands.	over 15 years; only given if skin test is negative and there is no BCG scar
Typhoid fever	Countries with poor hygiene and sanitation. Generally recommended for C America, some countries in S America, most African countries, the Middle East, the Indian subcontinent, SE Asia, the Far East, the Pacific Islands.	3 years
Yellow fever	Many African countries; tropical S American countries. Many countries require evidence of vaccination if arriving from an infected area.	10 years

Energy expenditure

During exercise, the amount of energy consumed depends on the age, sex, size and fitness of the individual, and how vigorous the exercise is. This table shows the approximate energy used up by a person of average size and fitness carrying out certain activities over a one-hour period.

| | Energy used per hour | |
Activity	kcals [1]	kJ [1]
Badminton	340	1428
Climbing stairs	620	2604
Cycling	660	2772
Football	540	2268
Gardening, heavy	420	1764
Gardening, light	270	1134
Golf	270	1134
Gymnastics	420	1764
Hockey	540	2268
Housework	270	1134
Jogging	630	2646
Rugby	540	2268
Squash	600	2520
Standing	120	504
Staying in bed	60	252
Swimming	720	3024
Tennis	480	2016
Walking, brisk	300	1260
Walking, easy	180	756

[1] kcals = kilocalories; kJ = kilojoules.

Average daily energy requirements

| CHILDREN | Energy used per day | |
Age	kcals [1]	kJ [1]
0–3 months	550	2300
3–6 months	760	3200
6–9 months	905	3800
9–12 months	1000	4200
8 years	2095	8800
15 years (female)	2285	9600
15 years (male)	3000	12600

| ADULT FEMALES | Energy used per day | |
Age	kcals [1]	kJ [1]
18–55 years		
Inactive	1900	7980
Active	2150	9030
Very active	2500	10500
Pregnant	2380	10000
Breastfeeding	2690	11300

ADULT FEMALES	Energy used per day	
Age	kcals[1]	kJ[1]
Over 56 years		
Inactive	1700	7140
Active	2000	8400

ADULT MALES	Energy used per day	
Age	kcals[1]	kJ[1]
18–35 years		
Inactive	2500	10500
Active	3000	12600
Very active	3500	14700
36–55 years		
Inactive	2400	10080
Active	2800	11760
Very active	3400	14280
Over 56 years		
Inactive	2200	9240
Active	2500	10500

[1] kcals = kilocalories; kJ = kilojoules.

Measuring your Body Mass Index

Body Mass Index (BMI) can give an indication of obesity. In order to determine your BMI, find out your height in metres and weight in kilograms. To convert height in inches to metres, multiply the number of inches by 0.0254; to convert weight in pounds to kilos, multiply the number of pounds by 0.4536.

$$BMI = \frac{weight\ (kg)}{height\ (m) \times height\ (m)}$$

BMI values:

Less than 18 – underweight

18 to 25 – in the ideal weight range

25 to 30 – overweight

Over 30 – obese; endangering health

Optimum weight according to height

Height in feet and inches

Weight in kilograms

Height in metres

Weight in pounds

Dietary recommendations

- **Dietary recommendations to protect the heart**
  Eat less fat, especially saturated fats, and avoid sugary and processed foods.
  Avoid obesity.
  Eat plenty of fibre-rich foods, including foods containing soluble fibre (eg oats).
  Cut down on salt – too much salt can increase your blood pressure.
  Eat at least 5 portions (400g) of a variety of fruit and vegetables each day.
- **Dietary recommendations to reduce cancer risks**
  Eat foods rich in fibre daily: these help to prevent bowel and colon cancers.
  Eat at least five portions (400g) of a variety of fruit and vegetables each day: these are
  rich in fibre and vitamins.
  Eat less fat. There seems to be a close correlation between fat consumption and breast
  cancer.
  Consume alcohol only in moderation. Excessive alcohol intake has been linked to
  cancers of the bowel, liver, mouth, oesophagus, stomach and throat, especially in
  smokers.
  Eat fewer smoked and salted foods. High consumption of salt-cured meat and fish and
  nitrate-cured meat has been linked to throat and stomach cancers. There is also a link
  between eating pickled foods and stomach cancer.
  Keep body weight at recommended level.
- **Dietary recommendations to lose weight**
  To be healthy, a diet designed to reduce body weight needs to be in tune with the
  body's physiology. An effective diet should promote the loss of fatty, or adipose,
  tissue from the body so that its overall fat content is reduced. To do this successfully,
  the dieter should eat a well-balanced, high-carbohydrate, high-fibre, low-fat diet
  with an energy content of between 1200 and 1500 calories per day, combining this
  with regular exercise. Foods that can be consumed in this kind of low-calorie diet are
  shown (*overleaf*) as Type A and Type B foods; Type C foods should be avoided, and fat-
  containing Type B foods, such as meat, should be eaten in moderation.
- **Dieting tips**
  Reduce alcohol intake to a minimum.
  Avoid convenience foods because many contain 'hidden' fats and sugar.
  Exercise at least three times a week.
  Remove fat from meat, and fatty skin from poultry.
  Avoid frying food – bake, grill, microwave or steam instead.
  Avoid mayonnaise and rich sauces.
  If you overeat, work out why you do it (eg through boredom or depression) and find
  other ways of relieving these feelings.
  Plan meals for the next day the night before, or early in the morning, to avoid impulse
  eating of high-calorie foods.
  Use a smaller plate to make smaller helpings look larger than they really are.
  Eat regularly. Do not miss meals but try to eat 3–5 small meals each day.
  Avoid second helpings.
  Avoid between-meal snacks, except for raw fruit and vegetables if very hungry.
  Eat at a table rather than eg in front of the television, which may encourage you to eat
  more and faster.
  Take more time when eating – chew well.

Type A foods

Vegetarian foods

Cereals (unsweetened)
Fruits – all except avocados
Vegetables – all, including
  potatoes
Vegetable protein, eg tofu
Wholemeal bread

Meat, fish and dairy foods

Chicken and other poultry
  (not duck) with skin
  removed
Cod, haddock and other
  non-oily fish
Mussels and other shellfish
Salmon (if tinned, in brine
  or water)
Tuna (if tinned, in brine or
  water)
Yoghurt (plain, low fat)

Type B foods

Vegetarian foods

Dried fruit
Margarine, mono- or
  polyunsaturated
Nuts
Pasta, especially
  wholewheat
Pulses, such as beans and
  lentils
Rice, especially wholegrain
Vegetable oils

Meat, fish and dairy foods

Beef, lean cuts
Eggs
Lamb, lean cuts
Oily fish such as herring or
  mackerel
Pork, lean cuts
Sardines (if tinned, in brine)

Type C foods

Meat, fish and dairy foods

Bacon
Beef, fatty cuts
Butter
Cheeses, apart from low-fat
Duck
Fish, fried
Ice cream
Lamb, fatty cuts
Mayonnaise
Milk, full cream
Pâté
Pork, fatty cuts
Salami
Sausages

Convenience foods

Biscuits
Burgers
Cakes
Chips
Chocolate
Crisps

SCIENCE, ENGINEERING AND MEASUREMENT

Scientists

Airy, Sir George Biddell (1802–92) English astronomer and geophysicist, born Alnwick. Astronomer Royal (1835–81) who reorganized the Greenwich Observatory. Initiated measurement of Greenwich Mean Time, determined the mass of the Earth from gravity experiments in mines, and carried out extensive work in optics.

Alzheimer, Alois (1864–1915) German psychiatrist and neuropathologist, born Markbreit. Gave full clinical and pathological description of presenile dementia (Alzheimer's disease) (1907).

Ampère, André Marie (1775–1836) French mathematician and physicist, born Lyons. Laid the foundations of the science of electrodynamics. His name is given to the basic SI unit of electric current (ampere, amp).

Archimedes (c.287–212 BC) Greek mathematician, born Syracuse. Discovered formulae for the areas and volumes of plane and solid geometrical figures using methods which anticipated theories of integration to be developed 1800 years later. Also founded the science of hydrostatics; in popular tradition remembered for the cry of 'Eureka' when he discovered the principle of upthrust on a floating body.

Aristotle (384–322 BC) Greek philosopher and scientist, born Stagira. One of the most influential figures in the history of Western thought and scientific tradition. Wrote enormous amounts on biology, zoology, physics and psychology.

Avogadro, Amedeo (1776–1856) Italian physicist, born Turin. Formulated the hypothesis (Avogadro's law) that equal volumes of gas contain equal numbers of molecules, when at the same temperature and pressure.

Babbage, Charles (1791–1871) English mathematician, born Teignmouth. Attempted to build two calculating machines – the 'difference engine', to calculate logarithms and similar functions by repeated addition performed by trains of gearwheels, and the 'analytical engine', to perform much more varied calculations. Babbage is regarded as the pioneer of modern computers.

Bacon, Francis, Viscount St Albans (1561–1626) English statesman and natural philosopher, born London. Creator of scientific induction; stressed the importance of experiment in interpreting nature, giving significant impetus to future scientific investigation.

Barnard, Christiaan Neethling (1922–2001) South African surgeon, born Beaufort West. Performed first successful heart transplant in December 1967 at Groote Schuur Hospital. Although the recipient died 18 days later from pneumonia, a second patient operated on in January 1968 survived for 594 days.

Becquerel, Antoine Henri (1852–1908) French physicist, born Paris. While researching fluorescence (the ability of substances to give off visible light), discovered radioactivity in the form of rays emitted by uranium salts, leading to the beginnings of modern nuclear physics. For this he shared the 1903 Nobel Prize for physics with Marie and Pierre Curie.

Bohr, Niels Henrik David (1885–1962) Danish physicist, born Copenhagen. Greatly extended the theory of atomic structure by explaining the spectrum of hydrogen by means of an atomic model and quantum theory (1913). Awarded the Nobel Prize for physics in 1922. Assisted in atom bomb research in America during World War II.

Boyle, The Hon Robert (1627–91) Irish physicist and chemist, born Munster. One of the first members of the Royal Society. Carried out experiments on air, vacuum, combustion and respiration, and in 1662 arrived at Boyle's law, which states that the pressure and volume of a gas are inversely proportional at constant temperature.

Brahe, Tycho or **Tyge** (1546–1601) Danish astronomer, born Knudstrup, Sweden (then under Danish crown). After seeing the partial solar eclipse of 1569, became obsessed with astronomy. Accurately measured and compiled catalogues of the positions of stars, providing vital information for later astronomers, and recorded unique observations of a new star in Cassiopeia in 1572 (a nova now known as Tycho's star).

Brenner, Sydney (1927–) British molecular biologist, born Germiston, South Africa. With Francis Crick, carried out experiments to determine the nature of the genetic code. Established the nematode (roundworm) *Caenorhabditis elegans* as an important model organism for studying genetics, cell biology and development; for this he shared the 2002 Nobel Prize for physiology or medicine with Robert Horvitz (1947–) and John Sulston (1942–).

Celsius, Anders (1701–44) Swedish astronomer, born Uppsala. Devised the centigrade, or 'Celsius', scale of temperature. Also advocated the introduction of the Gregorian calendar, and made observations of the aurora borealis, or northern lights.

Charles, Jacques-Alexandre-César (1746–1823) French experimental physicist, born Beaugency. Formulated Charles's law, which relates the volume of a gas at constant pressure to its absolute temperature.

Copernicus, Nicolaus (1473–1543) Polish astronomer, born Toruń. Studied mathematics, optics, perspective and canon law before pursuing a varied career involving law, medicine and astronomy. Published a theory in 1543 that the Sun is at the centre of the Universe; this was not initially accepted owing to opposition from the Church, which held that the Universe was Earth-centred.

Crick, Francis Harry Compton (1916–2004) English biologist, born Northampton. Constructed a molecular model of the complex genetic material deoxyribonucleic acid (DNA). Later research on nucleic acids led to far-reaching discoveries concerning the genetic code. Joint winner of the Nobel Prize for physiology or medicine in 1962 with James Watson (1928–).

Curie, Marie (originally **Manya**) née Sklodowska (1867–1934) Polish–French physicist, born Warsaw. Worked on magnetism and radioactivity, isolating radium and polonium. Shared the Nobel Prize for physics in 1903 with her husband, Pierre Curie (1859–1906), and Antoine Henri Becquerel (1852–1908). Became professor of physics at the Sorbonne in 1906; awarded the Nobel Prize for chemistry in 1911. Element 96 is named curium after the Curies.

Curie, Pierre (1859–1906) French chemist and physicist, born Paris. Carried out research on magnetism and radioactivity with his wife, Marie Curie (1867–1934), for which they were jointly awarded the Nobel Prize for physics in 1903, with Antoine Henri Becquerel (1852–1908).

Cuvier, Georges (Léopold Chrétien Frédéric Dagobert) (1769–1832) French anatomist, born Montbéliard. Linked comparative anatomy and palaeontology through studies of animal and fish fossils, and is known as the father of comparative anatomy and palaeontology. Also originated the natural system of animal classification. He opposed the theory of evolution, instead favouring catastrophism (a series of mass extinctions).

Dalton, John (1766–1844) English chemist, born Eaglesfield, near Cockermouth. Researched mixed gases, the force of steam, the elasticity of vapours and deduced the law of partial pressures, or Dalton's law. Also made important contributions in atomic theory.

Darwin, Charles Robert (1809–82) English naturalist, born Shrewsbury. Recommended as naturalist for a scientific survey of South American waters (1831–6) on HMS *Beagle*, during which he made many geological and zoological discoveries that led him to speculate on the origin of species. In 1859 published his theory of evolution in *The Origin of Species by Means of Natural Selection*.

Davy, Sir Humphry (1778–1829) English chemist, born Penzance. Experimented with newly discovered gases, and discovered the anaesthetic effect of nitrous oxide (laughing gas). Discovered the new metals potassium, sodium, barium, strontium, magnesium and calcium. Also investigated volcanic action, devised safety lamps for use in mining and was important in promoting science within industry.

Descartes, René (1596–1650) French philosopher and mathematician, born near Tours. Creator of analytical or co-ordinate geometry, also named after him as Cartesian geometry. Also theorized extensively in physics and physiology, and is regarded as the father of modern philosophy.

Doppler, Christian Johann (1803–53) Austrian physicist, born Salzburg. Published a paper in 1842 describing the Doppler effect, an increase and decrease of wave frequency observed when a wave source and the observer respectively approach or recede from one another.

Ehrlich, Paul (1854–1915) German bacteriologist, born Strehlen (now Strzelin), Silesia. Pioneer in haematology and chemotherapy, he synthesized salvarsan as a treatment for syphilis. Also propounded the side-chain theory in immunology, for which he was joint winner of the 1908 Nobel Prize for physiology or medicine with Ilya Metchnikov (1845–1916).

Einstein, Albert (1879–1955) German–Swiss–US mathematical physicist, born Ulm, Bavaria. Achieved world fame through his special and general theories of relativity (1905 and 1916); also studied gases and discovered the photoelectric effect, for which he was awarded the Nobel Prize for physics in 1921. Element 99 was named einsteinium after him.

Euler, Leonhard (1707–83) Swiss mathematician, born Basel. Published over 800 different books and papers on mathematics, physics and astronomy, introducing many new functions and carrying out important work in calculus. Introduced many important mathematical notations, including e (the base of the natural logarithm) and i (the square root of −1). Also studied motion and celestial mechanics.

Fahrenheit, Gabriel Daniel (1686–1736) German physicist, born Danzig. Devised the alcohol thermometer (1709) and later invented the mercury thermometer (1714). Also devised the temperature scale named after him, and was the first to show that the boiling point of liquids varies at different atmospheric pressures.

Faraday, Michael (1791–1867) English chemist and physicist, born Grenoble. Discovered electromagnetic induction (1831), the laws of electrolysis (1833) and the rotation of polarized light by magnetism (1845). First to isolate benzene and to synthesize chlorocarbons. The unit of electrical capacitance, the farad, is named after him.

Fermi, Enrico (1901–54) Italian–US nuclear physicist, born Rome. Published a statistical method of calculating atomic properties. In 1943 succeeded in splitting the nuclei of uranium atoms to produce artificial radioactive substances; awarded the 1938 Nobel Prize for physics for this work. Constructed the first US nuclear reactor at Chicago (1942). Element 100 was named fermium after him, and a class of subatomic particle is now known as the fermion.

Feynman, Richard Phillips (1918–88) US physicist, born New York City. Made considerable theoretical advances in quantum electrodynamics, for which he was joint winner of the 1965 Nobel Prize for physics with Julian Schwinger (1918–94) and Sin-itiro Tomonaga (1906–79). Involved in building the first atomic bomb during World War II.

Fleming, Sir Alexander (1881–1955) Scottish bacteriologist, born Loudoun, Ayrshire. Was the first to use anti-typhoid vaccines on humans, and pioneered the use of salvarsan to treat syphilis. In 1928 discovered penicillin by chance. For this he was joint winner of the 1945 Nobel Prize for physiology or medicine with Ernst Chain (1906–79) and Sir Howard Florey (1898–1968), who developed large-scale production of the drug.

Foucault, Jean Bernard Léon (1819–68) French physicist, born Paris. Determined the velocity of light using a revolving mirror, and proved that light travels more slowly in water than in air (1850). In 1851, by means of a freely suspended pendulum, he proved that the Earth rotates. In 1852 he constructed the gyroscope and in 1857 the Foucault prism.

Franklin, Rosalind Elsie (1920–58) English X-ray crystallographer, born London. Together with Maurice Wilkins (1916–2004), used X-ray crystallography techniques to obtain data on the structure of DNA. This work was instrumental in allowing James Watson (1928–) and Francis Crick (1916–2004) to deduce the helical structure of DNA. Franklin died before she could be considered for the Nobel Prize later awarded to Watson, Crick and Wilkins.

Galilei, Galileo, known as **Galileo** (1564–1642) Italian astronomer, mathematician and natural philosopher, born Pisa. Inferred the value of a pendulum for exact measurement of time, and proved that all falling bodies, great or small, descend due to gravity at the same rate. Perfected the refracting telescope and pursued astronomical observations that revealed mountains and valleys on the Moon, four satellites of Jupiter, and sunspots. These observations convinced him of the correctness of the Copernican theory that the Earth moves around the Sun. His advocacy of the Copernican theory led to his imprisonment by the Inquisition; he remained under house arrest until his death.

Gay-Lussac, Joseph Louis (1778–1850) French chemist and physicist, born Saint-Léonard. Established the law governing the expansion of gases in relation to their temperature, independently of Jacques Charles. Also formulated the law of combining volumes of gases (Gay-Lussac's law).

Geiger, Hans Wilhelm (1882–1945) German physicist, born Neustadt-an-der-Haart. Investigated beta-ray radioactivity and, with Walther Müller (1905–79), devised a counter to measure it.

Halley, Edmond (1656–1742) English astronomer and mathematician, born London. Studied the solar system and correctly predicted the return (in 1758, 1835 and 1910) of a comet that had been observed in 1583, and is now named after him.

Harvey, William (1578–1657) English physician, born Folkestone. Discovered the circulation of the blood, and proposed that the heart is a muscle that pumps the blood around the body.

Hawking, Stephen William (1942–) English theoretical physicist, born Oxford. Research on relativity led him to study gravitational singularities such as the 'Big Bang', out of which the Universe is thought to have originated, and 'black holes', which result from the death of stars. His book *A Brief History of Time* is a popular account of modern cosmology. Since the 1960s he has suffered from a highly disabling progressive neuromotor disease.

Heisenberg, Werner Karl (1901–76) German theoretical physicist, born Würzburg. Developed quantum mechanics and formulated the principle of indeterminacy (uncertainty principle), for which he was awarded the 1932 Nobel Prize for physics.

Henle, Friedrich Gustav Jakob (1809–85) German anatomist, born Fürth. Discovered the portion of the kidney nephron, known as the loop of Henle, that allows water and salt to be reabsorbed from the urine. Wrote treatises on systematic anatomy.

Herschel, Sir (Frederick) William (1738–1822) German–British astronomer, born Hanover. Made a reflecting telescope (1773–4) with which he discovered the planet Uranus in 1781. Also discovered satellites of Uranus and Saturn, the rotation of Saturn's rings and Saturn's rotation period. Researched binary stars, nebulae and the Milky Way.

Hertz, Heinrich Rudolph (1857–94) German physicist, born Hamburg. Confirmed James Clerk Maxwell's predictions in 1887 by his discovery of invisible electromagnetic waves, of the same fundamental form as light waves. The SI unit of frequency is named hertz after him.

Hooke, Robert (1635–1703) English chemist, physicist and architect, born Freshwater, Isle of Wight. Anticipated the invention of the steam engine, formulated Hooke's Law of the extension and compression of elastic bodies, and anticipated Isaac Newton's inverse square law of gravitation. Constructed the first reflecting telescope and inferred the rotation of Jupiter. Also materially improved or invented the compound microscope, the quadrant and a marine barometer.

Hubble, Edwin Powell (1889–1953) US astronomer, born Marshfield, Missouri. Demonstrated that some nebulae are independent galaxies. In 1929 discovered galaxy 'redshift', the phenomenon whereby distant galaxies are receding from us and the apparent speed of recession of a galaxy is proportional to its distance from us.

Hunt, Sir (Richard) Tim(othy) (1943–) English biologist, born Neston, Cheshire. Made important discoveries regarding the regulation of the cell cycle, allowing more accurate cancer diagnostics. Appointed Principal Scientist at Cancer Research UK's London Institute in 1991. Joint winner of the 2001 Nobel Prize for physiology or medicine with Leland Hartwell (1939–) and Sir Paul Nurse (1949–).

Hutton, James (1726–97) Scottish geologist, born Edinburgh. Pioneered modern geology by proposing the theory of uniformitarianism, emphasizing that the formation of rocks is a continuous process and that the same processes have taken place throughout time.

Huxley, Thomas Henry (1825–95) English biologist, born Ealing. Assistant surgeon on a surveying expedition to the South Seas (1846–50), during which he collected marine invertebrate specimens and carried out comparative anatomical research. Became the foremost scientific supporter of Charles Darwin's theory of evolution. Also studied fossils and later turned to philosophy and theology.

Huygens, Christiaan (1629–93) Dutch physicist, born The Hague. Made the first pendulum clock (1657), based on a suggestion by Galileo (1564–1642), and developed Galileo's doctrine of accelerated motion under gravity. Discovered the rings and fourth satellite of Saturn and the laws of collision of elastic bodies, and first proposed the wave theory of light.

Jeffreys, Sir Alec John (1950–) English molecular biologist, born Oxford. Developed the technique of 'DNA fingerprinting', in which DNA from an individual can be broken down and separated into a unique pattern of fragments.

Jenner, Edward (1749–1823) English physician, born Berkeley. In 1796 made the revolutionary discovery of vaccination by inoculating a child first with cowpox and then with smallpox, and finding that the child failed to develop the disease. Within five years vaccination was being practised in many parts of the world.

Joule, James Prescott (1818–89) English physicist, born Salford. Showed experimentally that heat is a form of energy and established the mechanical equivalent of heat; this became the basis for the theory of conservation of energy. With Lord Kelvin he studied temperatures of gases and formulated the absolute scale of temperature. The joule, a unit of work or energy, is named after him.

Kant, Immanuel (1724–1804) German philosopher, born Königsberg, Prussia (now Kaliningrad, Russia). Researched astronomy and geophysics, and predicted the existence of the planet Uranus before its discovery. His philosophical works had enormous influence.

Katz, Sir Bernard (1911–2003) German–British biophysicist, born Leipzig. Discovered how the neural transmitter acetylcholine is released by neural impulses. Joint winner of the 1970 Nobel Prize for physiology or medicine with Ulf von Euler (1905–83) and Julius Axelrod (1912–2004).

Kelvin, William Thomson, 1st Baron (1824–1907) Irish–Scottish physicist and mathematician, born Belfast. Solved important problems in electrostatics, proposed the absolute, or Kelvin, temperature scale and established the second law of thermodynamics simultaneously with Rudolf Clausius. Also investigated geomagnetism and hydrodynamics, and invented instruments.

Kepler, Johannes (1571–1630) German astronomer, born Württemberg. Formulated laws of planetary motion describing elliptical orbits and forming the starting point of modern astronomy. Also made discoveries in optics, physics and geometry.

Kirchhoff, Gustav Robert (1824–87) German physicist, born Königsberg, Prussia (now Kaliningrad, Russia). Carried out important research in electricity, heat, optics and spectrum analysis. His work led to the discovery of caesium and rubidium (1859).

Kroto, Sir Harold Walter (1939–) English chemist, born Wisbech, Cambridgeshire. Distinguished for his work in detecting unstable molecules, especially those found in space, and the discovery of the C_{60} form of carbon (buckminsterfullerene). Joint winner of the 1996 Nobel Prize for chemistry (with Robert Curl, 1933– , and Richard Smalley, 1943–) for the C_{60} work.

Lamarck, Jean (Baptiste Pierre Antoine de Monet) Chevalier de (1744–1829) French naturalist, born Bazentin. Made the basic distinction between vertebrates and invertebrates. Postulated that species could change over time (transmutation), preparing the way for the Darwinian theory of evolution, although his proposal that acquired characteristics can be inherited by later generations has largely been superseded by natural selection as a mechanism for evolution.

Leibniz, Gottfried Wilhelm (1646–1716) German mathematician and philosopher, born Leipzig. Discovered calculus around the same time as Isaac Newton (1642–1727); also made original contributions in the fields of optics, mechanics, statistics, logic and probability, and laid the foundations of 18c philosophy.

Leishman, Sir William Boog (1865–1926) Scottish bacteriologist, born Glasgow. Discovered an effective vaccine for inoculation against typhoid and was first to discover the parasite (leishmania) of the disease kala-azar (also known as leishmaniasis).

Linnaeus, Carolus (Carl von Linné) (1707–78) Swedish naturalist and physician, born Raceshult. Introduced the modern binomial system of scientific nomenclature for plants and animals.

Lorentz, Hendrik Antoon (1853–1928) Dutch physicist, born Arnhem. Carried out important work in electromagnetism; joint winner of the Nobel Prize for physics in 1902 (with Pieter Zeeman, 1865–1943) for explaining the effect whereby atomic spectral lines are split in the presence of magnetic fields.

Lorenz, Konrad Zacharias (1903–89) Austrian zoologist and ethologist, born Vienna. Regarded as the father of ethology, favouring the study of the instinctive behaviour of animals in the wild. In 1935 published observations on imprinting in young birds by which hatchlings 'learn' to recognize substitute parents, and argued that while aggressive behaviour in humans is inborn, it may be channelled into other forms of activity, whereas in other animals it is purely survival-motivated. Joint winner of the 1973 Nobel Prize for physiology or medicine with Karl von Frisch (1886–1982) and Nikolaas Tinbergen (1907–88).

Lyell, Sir Charles (1797–1875) Scottish geologist, born Kinnordy, Fife. Popularized the principle of uniformitarianism in geology, which proposes that geological changes have been gradual and produced by forces still at work rather than by catastrophic changes. His work significantly influenced Charles Darwin, although Lyell never accepted the theory of evolution by natural selection.

Mach, Ernst (1838–1916) Austrian physicist and philosopher, born Turas, Moravia. Carried out experimental work on projectiles and the flow of gases. His name has been given to the ratio of the speed of an object through a gas to the speed of sound in the same gas (Mach number) and to the angle of a shock wave to the direction of motion (Mach angle).

Maxwell, James Clerk (1831–79) Scottish physicist, born Edinburgh. Produced a mathematical theory of electromagnetism and identified light as electromagnetic radiation. Also suggested that invisible electromagnetic waves could be generated in a laboratory, as later carried out by Hertz. Other research included the kinetic theory of gases, the nature of Saturn's rings, colour perception and colour photography.

Medawar, Sir Peter Brian (1915–87) British zoologist and immunologist, born Rio de Janeiro. Pioneered experiments in skin grafting and the prevention of rejection in transplant operations. Joint winner of the Nobel Prize for physiology or medicine in 1960 with Sir Frank Macfarlane Burnet (1899–1985).

Mendel, Gregor Johann (1822–84) Austrian biologist and botanist, born near Udrau, Silesia. Became an abbot in 1868. Researched inheritance characteristics in plants, leading to the formulation of Mendel's law of segregation and the law of independent assortment. These principles became the basis of modern genetics.

Mendeleyev, Dmitri Ivanovich (1834–1907) Russian chemist, born Tobolsk. Formulated the periodic law and hence devised the periodic table, from which he predicted the existence of several elements that were subsequently discovered. Element 101 was named mendelevium after him.

Michelson, Albert Abraham (1852–1931) German–US physicist, born Strelno (now Strzelno, Poland). Carried out the famous Michelson–Morley experiment confirming the non-existence of 'ether', a result that set Einstein on the road to the theory of relativity. Became the first American scientist to win a Nobel Prize (physics) in 1907.

Milstein, César (1927–2002) British molecular biologist and immunologist, born Bahía Blanca, Argentina. Together with Georges Köhler (1946–95), devised the hybridoma technique for the production of monoclonal antibodies. Milstein and Köhler shared the 1984 Nobel Prize for physiology or medicine with Niels Jerne (1911–94).

Mullis, Kary Banks (1944–) US biochemist, born Lenoir, North Carolina. Developed the 'polymerase chain reaction' (PCR) technique, which allows tiny amounts of DNA to be copied millions of times. This has many analytical uses, including forensics and diagnosis of viral infections. Joint winner of the 1993 Nobel Prize for chemistry with Michael Smith (1932–2000). His more recent work has focused on the chemical manipulation of the immune system.

Napier, John (1550–1619) Scottish mathematician, born Edinburgh. Famous for the invention of logarithms to simplify computation, and for devising a calculating machine using a set of rods, known as 'Napier's Bones'.

Newton, Sir Isaac (1642–1727) English scientist, born Woolsthorpe, Lincolnshire. Formulated his complete theory of gravitation by 1684. Also carried out important work in optics, concluding that the different colours of light making up white light are refracted differently, developed the reflecting telescope, and invented calculus around the same time as Leibniz (1646–1716).

Nurse, Sir Paul M(axime) (1949–) English biologist, born Norwich. Made important discoveries regarding the regulation of the cell cycle, allowing more accurate cancer diagnostics. Appointed Principal Scientist at the London Institute of the Imperial Cancer Research Fund (now part of Cancer Research UK) in 1991. Joint winner of the 2001 Nobel Prize for physiology or medicine with Leland Hartwell (1939–) and Sir Tim Hunt (1943–).

Ohm, Georg Simon (1787–1854) German physicist, born Erlangen. In 1827 published 'Ohm's law', relating voltage, current and resistance in an electrical circuit. The SI unit of electrical resistance (ohm) is named after him.

Pascal, Blaise (1623–62) French mathematician and physicist, born Clermont-Ferrand. Carried out important work in geometry, invented a calculating machine, and demonstrated that air pressure decreases with altitude as previously predicted and developed probability theory. The SI unit of pressure (pascal) and the modern computer programming language, Pascal, are named after him.

Pasteur, Louis (1822–95) French chemist, born Dôle. Father of modern bacteriology. Discovered the possibility of attenuating the virulence of injurious micro-organisms by exposure to air, by variety of culture, or by transmission through various animals, and demonstrated that the attenuated organisms could be used for immunization. From this he developed vaccinations against anthrax and rabies. Introduced pasteurization (moderate heating) to kill disease-producing organisms in wine, milk and other foods. Also discovered that certain molecules can exist in two distinct chiral ('handed') forms.

Pauli, Wolfgang (1900–58) Austrian theoretical physicist, born Vienna. Formulated the exclusion principle (1924), which states that no two electrons can be in the same energy state. This led to important advances in the application of quantum theory to the periodic table of elements. He was awarded the Nobel Prize for physics in 1945.

Pauling, Linus (1901–94) US chemist, born Portland, Oregon. He made important discoveries concerning chemical bonding and complex molecular structures; this led him into work on the chemistry of biological molecules and the chemical basis of hereditary disease. He was awarded the 1954 Nobel Prize for chemistry, and also the 1962 Nobel Peace Prize for his campaigning against nuclear weapons.

Pavlov, Ivan Petrovich (1849–1936) Russian physiologist, born near Ryazan. Studied the physiology of circulation, digestion and 'conditioned' or acquired reflexes, believing the brain's only function is to couple neurones to produce reflexes. Awarded the Nobel Prize for physiology or medicine in 1904.

Perutz, Max Ferdinand (1914–2002) Austrian–British biochemist, born Vienna. Studied the structure of haemoglobin, for which work he was the joint winner of the 1962 Nobel Prize for chemistry with John Kendrew (1917–97).

Planck, Max Karl Ernst (1858–1947) German theoretical physicist, born Kiel. Researched thermodynamics and black-body radiation. This led him to formulate quantum theory (1900), which assumes that energy changes take place in small discrete instalments or quanta. Awarded the Nobel Prize for physics in 1918.

Ptolemy or **Claudius Ptolemaeus** (c.90–168 AD) Egyptian astronomer and geographer, believed born Ptolemaeus Hermion. Corrected and improved the astronomical work of his predecessors to form the Ptolemaic System, described by Plato and Aristotle, with the Earth at the centre of the Universe and heavenly bodies revolving round it; beyond this lay the sphere of the fixed stars. Also compiled geographical catalogues and maps.

Pythagoras (6c BC) Greek mathematician and philosopher, born Samos. Associated with mathematical discoveries involving the chief musical intervals, the relations of numbers and the relations between the lengths of sides of right-angled triangles (Pythagoras's theorem). Profoundly influenced Plato and later astronomers and mathematicians.

Ramón y Cajal, Santiago (1852–1934) Spanish physician and histologist, born Petilla de Aragon. Carried out important work on the brain and nerves, isolated the neuron and discovered how nerve impulses are transmitted to brain cells. Joint winner of the 1906 Nobel Prize for physiology or medicine with Camillo Golgi (1843–1926).

Rayleigh, John William Strutt, 3rd Baron (1842–1919) English physicist, born near Maldon, Essex. Carried out valuable research on vibratory motion, the theory of sound and the wave theory of light. With Sir William Ramsay (1852–1916) discovered argon (1894). Awarded the Nobel Prize for physics in 1904.

Richter, Charles Francis (1900–85) US seismologist, born near Hamilton, Ohio. Devised the scale of earthquake strength that bears his name (1927–35).

Röntgen, Wilhelm Konrad von (1845–1923) German physicist, born Lennep, Prussia. Discovered the electromagnetic rays that he called X-rays (also known as Röntgen rays) in 1895. For his work on X-rays he was joint winner of the Rumford medal in 1896 and winner of the 1901 Nobel Prize for physics. Also carried out important work on the heat conductivity of crystals, the specific heat of gases, and the electromagnetic rotation of polarized light.

Rutherford, Ernest, 1st Baron Rutherford of Nelson (1871–1937) New Zealand–British physicist, born Spring Grove, near Nelson. Made the first successful wireless transmissions over two miles. Discovered the three types of uranium radiations, formulated a theory of atomic disintegration and determined the nature of alpha particles; this led to a new atomic model in which the mass is concentrated in the nucleus. Also discovered that alpha-ray bombardment could produce atomic transformation, and predicted the existence of the neutron. Awarded the Nobel Prize for chemistry in 1908.

Schrödinger, Erwin (1887–1961) Austrian physicist, born Vienna. Originated the study of wave mechanics as part of the quantum theory with the celebrated Schrödinger wave equation, for which he was joint winner of the 1933 Nobel Prize for physics with P A M Dirac (1902–1984). Also made contributions to field theory.

Szent-Györgyi, Albert von Nagyrapolt (1893–1986) Hungarian–US biochemist, born Budapest. Discovered actin, which interacts with myosin and the energy source ATP during muscle contraction. Isolated vitamin C and studied cellular respiration; for this work he was awarded the Nobel Prize for physiology or medicine in 1937.

Thomson, Sir Joseph John (1856–1940) English physicist, born Cheetham Hill, near Manchester. Studied gaseous conductors of electricity and the nature of cathode rays; this led to his discovery of the electron. Also pioneered mass spectrometry and discovered the existence of different isotopes of elements. Awarded the Nobel Prize for physics in 1906.

Thomson, Sir William ▶ Kelvin, 1st Baron

Van de Graaff, Robert Jemison (1901–67) US physicist, born Tuscaloosa, Alabama. Conceived of an improved type of electrostatic generator, in which electric charge could be built up on a hollow metal sphere. Constructed the first model, later to be known as the Van de Graaff generator, which could generate potentials of over a million volts. Developed the generator for use as a particle accelerator for atomic and nuclear physicists. The generator was also adapted to produce high-energy X-rays for cancer treatment and for examination of the interior structure of heavy artillery.

Volta, Alessandro Giuseppe Anastasio, Count (1745–1827) Italian physicist, born Como. Developed an electric battery able to produce a continuous flow of electrical current. Invented the electrophorus (a precursor to the induction motor) and the electroscope (a device for detecting electricity). Also made investigations into heat and gases, and discovered methane. His name is given to the SI unit of electric potential difference, the volt.

Watson, James Dewey (1928–) US biologist, born Chicago. Deduced with Francis Crick the two-stranded helical structure of DNA, for which they shared the 1962 Nobel Prize for physiology or medicine. Later became professor at Harvard and Director of the Cold Spring Harbor Laboratory in New York.

Wilkins, Maurice Hugh Frederick (1916–2004) British physicist, born New Zealand. Together with Rosalind Franklin, used X-ray crystallography techniques to obtain data on the structure of DNA. This work was instrumental in allowing James Watson and Francis Crick to deduce the helical structure of DNA. Shared the 1962 Nobel Prize for physiology or medicine with Watson and Crick.

Young, Thomas (1773–1829) English physicist and physician, born Milverton, Somerset. Carried out experiments involving the generation of interference patterns by splitting beams of light, in support of the wave theory of light. Also made valuable contributions in haemodynamics, insurance and deciphering the inscriptions on the Rosetta Stone.

Nobel Prizes 1980–2006

Nobel Prizes for chemistry, physics and physiology or medicine were first awarded in 1901.

Year	Chemistry	Physics	Physiology/Medicine
1980	Paul Berg, Walter Gilbert, Frederick Sanger	James W Cronin, Val L Fitch	Baruj Benacerraf, George D Snell, Jean Dausset
1981	Kenichi Fukui, Roald Hoffman	Nicolaas Bloembergen, Arthur L Schawlow, Kai M Siegbahn	Roger W Sperry, David H Hubel, Torsten N Wiesel
1982	Sir Aaron Klug	Kenneth G Wilson	Sune K Bergström, Bengt I Samuelsson, Sir John Vane
1983	Henry Taube	Subramanyan Chandrasekhar, William A Fowler	Barbara McClintock
1984	Robert B Merrifield	Carlo Rubbia, Simon van der Meer	Niels K Jerne, Georges J F Köhler, César Milstein
1985	Herbert A Hauptman, Jerome Karle	Klaus von Klitzing	Joseph L Goldstein, Michael S Brown
1986	Dudley R Herschbach, Yuan Tseh Lee, John C Polanyi	Gerd Binnig, Heinrich Rohrer, Ernst Ruska	Stanley Cohen, Rita Levi-Montalcini
1987	Charles J Pedersen, Donald J Cram, Jean-Marie Lehn	J Georg Bednorz, K Alexander Müller	Susumu Tonegawa
1988	Johann Deisenhofer, Robert Huber, Hartmut Michel	Leon M Lederman, Melvin Schwartz, Jack Steinberger	Sir James W Black, Gertrude B Elion, George H Hitchings
1989	Sidney Altman, Thomas R Cech	Hans G Dehmelt, Wolfgang Paul, Norman F Ramsey	J Michael Bishop, Harold E Varmus

Year	Chemistry	Physics	Physiology/Medicine
1990	Elias James Corey	Jerome I Friedman, Henry W Kendall, Richard E Taylor	Joseph E Murray, E Donnall Thomas
1991	Richard R Ernst	Pierre-Gilles de Gennes	Erwin Neher, Bert Sakmann
1992	Rudolph A Marcus	Georges Charpak	Edmond H Fischer, Edwin G Krebs
1993	Kary Banks Mullis, Michael Smith	Russell A Hulse, Joseph H Taylor Jr	Richard J Roberts, Phillip A Sharp
1994	George Olah	Clifford G Shull, Bertram N Brockhouse	Alfred G Gilman, Martin Rodbell
1995	F Sherwood Roland, Mario J Molina, Paul J Crutzen	Martin L Perl, Frederick Reines	Edward B Lewis, Christiane Nüsslein-Volhard, Eric F Wieschaus
1996	Sir Harold W Kroto, Robert F Curl, Jr, Richard E Smalley	David M Lee, Douglas D Osheroff, Robert C Richardson	Peter C Doherty, Rolf M Zinkernagel
1997	Jens C Skou, John E Walker, Paul D Boyer	Steven Chu, William D Phillips, Claude Cohen-Tannoudji	Stanley B Prusiner
1998	Walter Kohn, John A Pople	Robert B Laughlin, Horst L Störmer, Daniel C Tsui	Robert F Furchgott, Louis J Ignarro, Ferid Murad
1999	Ahmed H Zewail	Gerardus 't Hooft, Martinus J G Veltman	Günter Blobel
2000	Alan J Heeger, Alan G MacDiarmid, Hideki Shirakawa	Zhores I Alferov, Herbert Kroemer, Jack S Kilby	Arvid Carlsson, Paul Greengard, Eric Kandel
2001	William S Knowles, Ryoji Noyori, K Barry Sharpless	Eric A Cornell, Wolfgang Ketterle, Carl E Wieman	Leland H Hartwell, R Timothy Hunt, Sir Paul Nurse
2002	John B Fenn, Koichi Tanaka, Kurt Wüthrich	Raymond Davis Jr, Masatoshi Koshiba, Riccardo Giacconi	Sydney Brenner, H Robert Horvitz, John E Sulston
2003	Peter Agre, Roderick MacKinnon	Alexei A Abrikosov, Vitaly L Ginzburg, Anthony J Leggett	Paul C Lauterbur, Sir Peter Mansfield
2004	Aaron Ciechanover, Avram Hershko, Irwin Rose	David J Gross, H David Politzer, Frank Wilczek	Richard Axel, Linda B Buck
2005	Yves Chauvin, Robert H Grubbs, Richard R Schrock	Roy J Glauber, John L Hall, Theodor W Hänsch	Barry J Marshall, J Robin Warren
2006	Roger D Kornberg	John C Mather, George F Smoot	Andrew Z Fire, Craig C Mello

Electromagnetic spectrum

Radiation	Approximate wavelengths	Uses
Radio waves	>10 cm	communications; radio and TV broadcasting
Microwaves	1 mm–10 cm	communications; radar; microwave ovens
Infrared	10^{-3}–7.8×10^{-7} m	night and smoke vision systems; intruder alarms; weather forecasting; missile guidance systems
Visible	7.8×10^{-7}–3×10^{-7} m	human eyesight
Ultraviolet	3×10^{-7}–10^{-8} m	forensic science; medical treatment; sterilization of food, water and equipment
X-rays	10^{-8}–3×10^{-11} m	medical X-ray photographs; material structure analysis
Gamma rays	$<3 \times 10^{-11}$ m	medical imaging; cancer treatment; sterilization of medical equipment and food

Decibel scale

Source	Decibel level (dB)
Breathing	10
Whisper	20
Conversation	50–60
Vacuum cleaner	80
Traffic	60–90
Pneumatic drill	110
Jet aircraft	120
Space vehicle launch	140–170

Mohs' hardness scale

The relative hardness of solids can be expressed using a scale of numbers from 1 to 10, each relating to a mineral (1 representing talc, 10 representing diamond). The method was devised by Friedrich Mohs (1773–1839), a German mineralogist. Sets of hardness pencils are used to test specimens to see what will scratch them; other useful instruments for testing include: fingernail (will stratch a specimen with a hardness of 2.5 or lower), copper coin (3.5 or lower), steel knife (5.5 or lower), and glass (6.0 or lower).

Talc	1
Gypsum	2
Calcite	3
Fluorite	4
Apatite	5
Orthoclase	6
Quartz	7
Topaz	8
Corundum	9
Diamond	10

Periodic table

He 2
helium

B 5	C 6	N 7	O 8	F 9	Ne 10
boron	carbon	nitrogen	oxygen	fluorine	neon

Al 13	Si 14	P 15	S 16	Cl 17	Ar 18
aluminium	silicon	phosphorus	sulphur	chlorine	argon

Ni 28	Cu 29	Zn 30	Ga 31	Ge 32	As 33	Se 34	Br 35	Kr 36
nickel	copper	zinc	gallium	germanium	arsenic	selenium	bromine	krypton

Pd 46	Ag 47	Cd 48	In 49	Sn 50	Sb 51	Te 52	I 53	Xe 54
palladium	silver	cadmium	indium	tin	antimony	tellurium	iodine	xenon

Pt 78	Au 79	Hg 80	Tl 81	Pb 82	Bi 83	Po 84	At 85	Rn 86
platinum	gold	mercury	thallium	lead	bismuth	polonium	astatine	radon

Uun 110	Uuu 111	Uub 112
unununilium	unununium	ununbium

Gd 64	Tb 65	Dy 66	Ho 67	Er 68	Tm 69	Yb 70	Lu 71
gadolinium	terbium	dysprosium	holmium	erbium	thulium	ytterbium	lutetium

Cm 96	Bk 97	Cf 98	Es 99	Fm 100	Md 101	No 102	Lr 103
curium	berkelium	californium	einsteinium	fermium	mendelevium	nobelium	lawrencium

Mathematical signs and symbols

+	plus; positive; underestimate
−	minus; negative; overestimate
±	plus or minus; positive or negative; degree of accuracy
∓	minus or plus; negative or positive
x	multiplies (colloq. 'times') (6 x 4)
·	multiplies (colloq. 'times') (6.4); scalar product of two vectors (A · B)
÷	divided by (6 ÷ 4)
/	divided by; ratio of (6/4)
—	divided by; ratio of ($\frac{6}{4}$)
=	equals
≠, ≠	not equal to
≡	identical with
≢, ≢	not identical with
:	ratio of (6 : 4); scalar product of two tensors (X : Y)
::	proportionally equals (1 : 2 :: 2 : 4)
≈	approximately equal to; equivalent to; similar to
>	greater than
≫	much greater than
≯	not greater than
<	less than
≪	much less than
≮	not less than
⩾, ≧, ≥	equal to or greater than
⩽, ≦, ≤	equal to or less than
∝	directly proportional to
( )	parentheses
[ ]	brackets
{ }	braces
—	vinculum: division ($\overline{a-b}$); chord of circle or length of line ($\overline{AB}$); arithmetic mean ($\overline{X}$)

∞	infinity
→	approaches the limit
√	square root
³√, ⁴√	cube root, fourth root, etc.
!	factorial (4! = 4 x 3 x 2 x 1)
%	per cent
'	prime; minute(s) of arc; foot/feet
"	double prime; second(s) of arc; inch(es)
⌒	arc of circle
°	degree of arc
∠, ∠s	angle(s)
⩝	equiangular
⊥	perpendicular
∥	parallel
○, Ⓢ	circle(s)
△, ⚠	triangle(s)
□	square(s)
▭	rectangle
▱	parallelogram
≅	congruent to
∴	therefore
∵	because
m̲	measured by
△	increment
Σ	summation
Π	product
∫	integral sign
∇	del: differential operator
∩	union
∪	interaction

Inventions

Name	Date	Inventor (nationality)[1]
adding machine (mechanical)	1623	Wilhelm Schickard (Ger)
adhesive (rubber-based glue)	1850	anon
adhesive (epoxy resin)	1958	Certas Co
aeroplane (steam-powered)	1886	Clement Ader (Fr)
aeroplane	1903	Orville and Wilbur Wright (US)
aeroplane (swing-wing)	1954	Barnes Wallis (UK)
aerosol	1926	Erik Rotheim (Nor)
airship (non-rigid)	1851	Henri Giffard (Fr)
airship (rigid)	1900	Graf Ferdinand von Zeppelin (Ger)
ambulance	1792	Jean Dominique Larrey (Fr)
aspirin (introduction into medicine)	1899	Felix Hoffmann (Ger)
atomic bomb	1939–45	Otto Frisch (Aus), Niels Bohr (D), Rudolf Peierls (Ger), Robert Oppenheimer (US) and others
balloon (first manned flight)	1783	Jacques and Joseph Montgolfier (Fr)
barbed wire (first patent)	1867	Lucien B Smith (US)
barbed wire (manufacture)	1874	Joseph Glidden (US)
barbiturates (preparation of barbituric acid)	1863	Adolf von Baeyer (Pruss)
barometer	1643	Evangelista Torricelli (Ital)
battery (electric)	1800	Alessandro Volta (Ital)
bicycle	1839–40	Kirkpatrick MacMillan (UK)
bifocal lens	1780	Benjamin Franklin (US)
blood (artificial oxygen-carrying substitute)	1966	Clark and Gollan (US)
bronze (copper with tin)	c.3700 BC	Pre-dynastic Egypt
bunsen burner	1855	Robert Wilhelm Bunsen (Pruss)
burglar alarm	1858	Edwin T Holmes (US)
cable-car	1866	W Ritter (Ger) or anon (US)
calendar (modern)	525	Dionysius Exiguus (Scythian)
camera (polaroid)	1947	Edwin Land (US)
canning	1810	Nicolas Appert (Fr)
cannon	2c BC	Archimedes (Gr)
car (three-wheeled steam tractor)	1769	Nicolas Cugnot (Fr)
car (internal combustion)	1884	Gottlieb Daimler (Ger)
car (petrol)	1886	Karl Benz (Ger)
car (air-conditioning)	1902	J Wilkinson (US)
car (disc brakes)	1902	Frederick W Lanchester (UK)
car (speedometer)	1902	Thorpe and Salter (US)
carbon fibres	1964	Courtaulds Ltd (UK)
carburettor	1876	Gottlieb Daimler (Ger)
carpet sweeper	1876	Melville Bissell (US)
cash register	1892	William Burroughs (US)
celluloid	1870	John W Hyatt (US)

Name	Date	Inventor (nationality) [1]
cement (Portland)	1824	Joseph Aspdin (UK)
chocolate (solid)	1819	François-Louis Cailler (Swiss)
chocolate (solid, milk)	1875	Daniel Peter (Swiss)
chronometer	1735	John Harrison (UK)
cinema	1895	Auguste and Louis Lumière (Fr)
cinema (wide screen)	1900	Raoul Grimoin-Sanson (Fr)
clock (mechanical)	725	I-Hsing (Chinese)
clock (pendulum)	1657	Christiaan Huygens (NL)
clock (quartz)	1929	Warren Alvin Marrison (US)
coffee (instant)	1937	Nestlé (Swiss)
compact disc	1979	Philips (NL) and Sony (Japanese)
compass (discovery of magnetite)	1c	China
compass (first record of mariner's compass)	1187	Alexander Neckam (UK)
computer (mechanical, fully programmable)	1835	Charles Babbage (UK)
computer (electronic, digital, stored program)	1949	J Presper Eckert, John W Mauchly, John von Neumann (US)
concrete	1c	anon, Rome
concrete (reinforced)	1892	François Hennebique (Fr)
contact lenses	1887	Adolph E Fick (Ger)
contraceptive pill	1950	Gregory Pincus (US)
corrugated iron	1853	Pierre Carpentier (Fr)
credit card	1950	Ralph Scheider (US)
crossword	1913	Arthur Wynne (US) in New York World
crystal (glass)	c.1450	anon, Venice
decompression chamber	1929	Robert H Davis (UK)
dental plate	1817	Anthony A Plantson (US)
dental plate (rubber)	1854	Charles Goodyear (US)
detergents	1916	anon, Germany
diesel engine	1892	Rudolf Diesel (Ger)
dishwasher (automatic)	1889	Mrs W A Cockran (US)
drill (pneumatic)	1861	Germain Sommelier (Fr)
drill (electric, hand)	1895	Wilhelm Fein (Ger)
electric chair	1888	Harold P Brown and E A Kenneally (US)
electric flat iron	1882	Henry W Seeley (US)
electric generator	1831	Michael Faraday (UK)
electric guitar	1931	Adolph Rickenbacker, Barth and Beauchamp (US)
electric heater	1887	W Leigh Burton (US)
electric light bulb	1879	Thomas Alva Edison (US)
electric motor (AC)	1888	Nikola Tesla (US)
electric motor (DC)	1870	Zenobe Gramme (Belg)
electric oven	1889	Bernina Hotel, Switzerland
electrocardiography	1903	Willem Einthoven (NL)
electromagnet	1824	William Sturgeon (UK)

Name	Date	Inventor (nationality)[1]
encyclopedia	c.47 BC	Marcus Terentius Varro (Roman)
endoscope	1827	Pierre Segalas (Fr)
escalator	1892	Jesse W Reno (Fr)
explosives (dynamite)	1866	Alfred Nobel (Swed)
explosives (nitroglycerine)	1847	Ascanio Sobrero (Ital)
extinguisher	1866	François Carlier (Fr)
facsimile machine (fax)	1907	Arthur Korn (Ger)
ferrofluids	1968	Ronald Rosensweig (US)
film (moving outlines)	1874	Jules Janssen (Fr)
	1888	Louis Le Prince (Fr)
	1891	Thomas Alva Edison (US)
film (with soundtrack)	1896	Lee De Forest (US)
forceps (obstetric)	c.1630	Peter Chamberlen (UK)
freeze-drying	1906	Arsene D'Arsonval and Georges Bordas (Fr)
galvanometer	1834	André Marie Ampère (Fr)
gas lighting	1792	William Murdock (UK)
gearbox (automatic)	1910	Hermann Fottinger (Ger)
glass (heat-resistant)	1884	Carl Zeiss (Ger)
glass (stained)	pre-850	Europe
glass (toughened)	1893	Leon Appert (Fr)
glass fibre	1713	René de Réaumur (Fr)
glass fibre (industrial)	1931	Owens Illinois Glass Co (US)
glassware	c.2600 BC	Egypt
glider	1853	George Cayley (UK)
gramophone	1877	Thomas Alva Edison (US)
gun	245 BC	Ctesibius (Gr)
gyrocompass	1911	Elmer A Sperry (US)
heart (artificial)	1937	Vladimir P Demikhov (USSR)
	1982	Robert Jarvik (US)
heat pump	1851	William Thomson, Lord Kelvin (UK)
helicopter	1907	Louis and Jacques Breguet (Fr)
holography	1948	Denis Gabor (Hung/UK)
hovercraft	1955	Christopher Cockerell (UK)
integrated circuit (concept)	1952	Geoffrey Dummer (UK)
interferometry	1802	Thomas Young (UK)
interferometer	1856	J-C Jamin (Fr)
iron (working of)	c.1323 BC	Hittites, Anatolia
jeans	1872	Levi-Strauss (US)
kidney, artificial (haemodialysis machine)	1945	Willem Kolff (NL)
laser	1960	Theodore Maiman (US)
launderette	1934	J F Cantrell (US)
lawnmower	1830	Edwin Beard Budding (UK)
lift (mechanical)	1851	Elisha G Otis (US)
lightning conductor	1752	Benjamin Franklin (US)

Name	Date	Inventor (nationality)[1]
linoleum	1860	Frederick Walton (UK)
lithography	1796	Aloys Senefelder (Bav)
locomotive (railed)	1804	Richard Trevithick (UK)
lock	c.4000 BC	Mesopotamia
loom (power)	1785	Edmund Cartwright (UK)
loudspeaker	1900	Horace Short (UK)
machine gun	1718	James Puckle (UK)
maps	c.2250 BC	Mesopotamia
margarine	1868	Hippolyte Mergé-Mouriès (Fr)
match	1680	Robert Boyle (UK)
match (safety)	1845	Anton von Schrotter (Ger)
microchip	1958	Jack Saint Clair Kilby (US)
microphone	1876	Alexander Graham Bell and Thomas Alva Edison (US)
microprocessor	1971	Marcian E Hoff (US)
microscope	1590	Zacharias Janssen (NL)
microscope (electron)	1933	Max Knoll and Ernst Ruska (Ger)
microscope (scanning tunnelling)	1982	Gerd Binnig and Heinrich Rohrer (Swiss)
microscope (atomic force)	1985	Gerd Binnig and Heinrich Rohrer (Swiss)
microwave oven	1945	Percy Le Baron Spencer (US)
missile (air-to-air)	1943	Herbert Wagner (Ger)
motorcycle	1885	Gottlieb Daimler (Ger)
neon lamp	1910	Georges Claude (Fr)
newspaper	59 BC	Julius Caesar (Roman)
non-stick pan	1954	Marc Grégoir (Fr)
novel (serialized)	1836	Charles Dickens, Chapman and Hall Publishers (UK)
nylon	1937	Wallace H Carothers (US)
optical fibres	c.1955	Navinder S Kapany (Ind)
optical sound recording	1920	Lee De Forest (US)
pacemaker (implantable)	1956	Wilson Greatbach (US)
paint (fluorescent)	1933	Joe and Bob Switzer (US)
paint (acrylic)	1964	Reeves Ltd (UK)
paper	AD 105	Ts'ai Lun (Chinese)
paper clip	1900	Johann Vaaler (Nor)
parachute	c.2c BC	China
parachute (jump)	1797	André-Jacques Garnerin (Fr)
parachute (patent)	1802	André-Jacques Garnerin (Fr)
parchment	2c BC	Eumenes II of Pergamum (reigned 197–159 BC)
parking meter	1932	Carlton C Magee (US)
pasteurization	1863	Louis Pasteur (Fr)
pen (fountain)	1884	Lewis Waterman (US)
pen (ballpoint)	1938	Laszlo Biro (Hung)
pencil	1795	Nicholas Jacques Conté (Fr)
pentium processor	1995	Intel (US)

Name	Date	Inventor (nationality) [1]
phonograph	1877	Thomas Alva Edison (US)
photoelectric cell	1896	Julius Elster and Hans F Geitel (Ger)
photography (colour)	1861	James Clerk Maxwell (UK)
photographic film	1889	George Eastman (US)
photographic lens (for camera obscura)	1812	William H Wollaston (UK)
photography (on metal)	1816	Joseph Nicéphore Niepce (Fr)
photography (on paper)	1838	William Henry Fox Talbot (UK)
phototypesetting	1894	Eugene Porzott (Hung)
pianoforte	1720	Bartolomeo Cristofori (Ital)
plastics	1868	John W Hyatt (US)
pocket calculator	1972	Jack Saint Clair Kilby, James Van Tassell and Jerry D Merryman (US)
porcelain	c.960	China
pressure cooker	1679	Denis Papin (Fr)
printing press (wooden)	c.1450	Johannes Gutenberg (Ger)
printing press (rotary)	1845	Richard Hoe (US)
propeller (boat, hand-operated)	1775	David Bushnell (US)
propeller (ship)	1844	Isambard Kingdom Brunel (UK)
radar (theory)	1900	Nikola Tesla (Croat)
	1922	Guglielmo Marconi (Ital)
radar (application)	c.1930	A Hoyt Taylor and Leo C Young (US)
radio telegraphy (discovery and production of sound waves)	1888	Heinrich Hertz (Ger)
radio (transatlantic)	1901	Guglielmo Marconi (Ital)
rails (iron)	1738	Abraham Darby (UK)
railway (underground)	1843	Charles Pearson (UK)
railway (electric)	1878	Ernst Werner von Siemens (Ger)
rayon	1883	Joseph Swan (UK)
razor (safety)	1895	King Camp Gillette (US)
razor (electric)	1928	Jacob Schick (US)
record (flat disc)	1888	Emil Berliner (Ger)
record (long-playing microgroove)	1948	Peter Goldmark (US)
refrigerator (compressed ether)	1855	James Harrison (US)
refrigerator (absorption)	1857	Ferdinand Carré (Fr)
revolver	1835	Samuel Colt (US)
Richter seismographic scale	1935	Charles Francis Richter (US)
rocket (missile)	1232	Mongols, China
rubber (latex foam)	1929	E A Murphy, W H Chapman and John Dunlop (US)
rubber (butyl)	1937	Robert Thomas and William Sparks, Exxon (US)
rubber (vulcanized)	1939	Charles Goodyear (US)
Rubik cube	1975	Erno Rubik (Hung)
safety pin	1849	Walter Hunt (US)
satellite (artificial)	1957	USSR

Name	Date	Inventor (nationality)[1]
saw	c.4000 BC	Egypt
scanner	1973	Godfrey N Hounsfield (UK)
scotch tape	1930	Richard Drew (UK)
screw	3c BC	Archimedes (Gr)
serotherapy	1890	Emil von Behring (Ger)
sewing machine	1830	Barthelemy Thimonnier (Fr)
ship (metal hull and propeller)	1844	Isambard Kingdom Brunel (UK)
ship (steam)	1775	Jacques C Perier (Fr)
ship (turbine)	1894	Charles Parsons (UK)
silicon chip	1961	Texas Instruments (US)
silk (reeling)	c.2640 BC	Hsi Ling Shi (Chinese)
skin (artificial)	c.1980	John Tanner (US), Bell (US), Neveu (Fr), Ioannis Yannas (Gr), Howard Green (US) and Jacques Thivolet (Fr)
skyscraper	1882	William Le Baron Jenney (US)
slide rule	1621	William Oughtred (UK)
soap	c.2500 BC	Sumer, Babylonia
soda (extraction of)	c.16c BC	Egypt
space shuttle	1981	NASA (US)
spectacles	c.1280	Alessandro della Spina and Salvino degli Armati (Ital)
spinning frame	1768	Richard Arkwright (UK)
spinning jenny	c.1764	James Hargreaves (UK)
spinning mule	1779	Samuel Crompton (UK)
stapler	1868	Charles Henry Gould (UK)
starter motor	1912	Charles F Kettering (US)
steam engine	1698	Thomas Savery (UK)
steam engine (condenser)	1769	James Watt (UK)
steam engine (piston)	1705	Thomas Newcomen (UK)
steel (production)	1854	Henry Bessemer (UK) and William Kelly (US)
steel (stainless)	1913	Henry Brearley (UK)
stethoscope	1816	René Théophile Hyacinthe Laennec (Fr)
stereotype	1725	William Ged (UK)
submarine	c.1620	Cornelis Brebbel or Van Drebbel (NL)
suntan cream	1936	Eugène Schueller (Fr)
suspension bridge	25 BC	China
syringe (scientific)	1646	Blaise Pascal (Fr)
syringe (hypodermic)	c.1835	Charles Gabriel Pravaz (Fr)
table tennis	1890	James Gibb (UK)
tampon	1930	Earl Hass (US)
tank	1916	Ernest Swinton (UK)
telegraph (electric)	1774	Georges Louis Lesage (Swiss)
telegraph (transatlantic cable)	1866	William Thomson, Lord Kelvin (UK)
telegraph code	1837	Samuel F B Morse (US)
telephone (first practical)	1876	Alexander Graham Bell (US)

Name	Date	Inventor (nationality)[1]
telephone (automatic exchange)	1889	Alman B Strowger (US)
telephone, mobile cellular (first commercially available)	1983	Motorola (US)
telescope (refractor)	1608	Hans Lippershey (NL)
telescope (space)	1990	Edwin Hubble (US)
television (mechanical)	1926	John Logie Baird (UK)
television (colour)	1940	Peter Goldmark (US)
tennis	1873	Walter G Wingfield (UK)
thermometer	3c BC	Ctesibius (Gr)
thermometer (mercury)	1714	Gabriel Fahrenheit (Ger)
timeclock	1894	Daniel M Cooper (US)
toaster	1927	Charles Strite (US)
traffic lights	1868	J P Knight (UK)
traffic lights (automatic)	1914	Alfred Benesch (US)
transformer	1831	Michael Faraday (UK)
tranquillizers	1952	Henri Laborit (Fr)
transistor	1948	John Bardeen, Walter Brattain and William Shockley (US)
travel agency	1841	Thomas Cook (UK)
traveller's cheques	1891	American Express Travel Agency (US)
turbojet	1928	Frank Whittle (UK)
typewriter	1829	William Burt (US)
typewriter (electric)	1872	Thomas Alva Edison (US)
tyre (pneumatic, coach)	1845	Robert William Thomson (UK)
tyre (pneumatic, bicycle)	1888	John Boyd Dunlop (UK)
ultrasonography (obstetric)	1958	Ian Donald (UK)
universal joint	c.140 BC	Fang Feng (Chinese)
vacuum cleaner (steam-powered)	1871	Ives W McGaffrey (US)
vacuum cleaner (electric)	1901	Hubert Cecil Booth (UK)
vending machine	1883	Percival Everitt (UK)
ventilator	1858	Théophile Guibal (Fr)
videophone	1927	American Telegraph and Telephone Co
video recorder	1956	Ampex Co (US)
washing machine (electric)	1907	Hurley Machine Co (US)
watch	1462	Bartholomew Manfredi (Ital)
watch (waterproof)	1927	Rolex (Swiss)
wheel	c.3500 BC	Mesopotamia
windmill	c.600	Syria
word processor	1965	IBM (US)
writing (pictography)	c.3000 BC	Egypt
xerography	1938	Chester Carlson (US)
zip fastener	1893	Whitcomb L Judson (US)

[1] Aus: Austrian Bav: Bavarian Belg: Belgian Croat: Croatian D: Danish Fr: French Ger: German Gr: Greek Hung: Hungarian Ind: Indian Ital: Italian NL: Dutch Nor: Norwegian Pruss: Prussian Swed: Swedish

Engineering: bridges

Name	Location	Length (m)[1]	Type
Akashi-Kaikyo	Honshu–Shikoku, Japan	3911	suspension
Alex Fraser (previously called Annacis)	Vancouver, Canada	465	cable-stayed
Ambassador	Detroit, Michigan, USA	564	suspension
Angostura	Ciudad Bolivar, Venezuela	712	suspension
Astoria	Astoria, Oregon, USA	376	truss
Bayonne (Kill van Kull)	New Jersey–Staten Island, USA	504	steel arch
Bendorf	Rhine River, Coblenz, Germany	1030	cement girder
Benjamin Franklin	Philadelphia–Camden, USA	534	suspension
Baishazhou	Wuhan, China	618	cable-stayed
Bosporus	Istanbul, Turkey	1074	suspension
Bosporus II	Istanbul, Turkey	1090	suspension
Bridge of Sighs	Doge's Palace–Pozzi Prison, Venice, Italy	c.5	enclosed arch
Britannia tubular rail	Menai Strait, Wales	420	plate girder
Brooklyn	Brooklyn–Manhattan Island, New York City, USA	486	suspension
Chao Phraya	Bangkok, Thailand	450	cable-stayed
Clifton	Bristol, England	214	suspension
Commodore Barry	Chester, Pennsylvania, USA	501	cantilever
Cooper River	Charleston, S Carolina, USA	488	truss
Delaware River	Chester, Pennsylvania, USA	501	cantilever
Evergreen	Seattle, Washington, USA	longest span 2293	floating pontoon
Forth (rail)	Firth of Forth, South Queensferry, Scotland	1658 (spans 521)	cantilever
Forth Road Bridge (road)	Firth of Forth, South Queensferry, Scotland	1006	suspension
George Washington	Hudson River, New York City, USA	1067	suspension
Gladesville	Sydney, Australia	305	(longest) concrete arch
Golden Gate	San Francisco, California, USA	1280	suspension
Grand Trunk railroad	Niagara Falls, New York, USA	250	suspension
Great Belt (Storebælt) East	Halskov–Kudshoved, Denmark	1624	suspension
Greater New Orleans	Mississippi River, Louisiana, USA	480	cantilever
High Coast	Västernorrland, Sweden	1210	suspension

Name	Location	Length (m)[1]	Type
Howrah (railroad)	Hooghly River, Kolkata, India	457	cantilever
Humber Estuary	Hull–Grimsby, England	1410	suspension
Humen	Humen, China	888	suspension
Jiangsu Yangtze	Jiangsu Province, China	1385	suspension
Kap Shui Mun	Lantau I–Ma Wan I, Hong Kong	430	cable-stayed (double-deck road/rail)
Kincardine	Forth River, Scotland	822 (swing span 111)	movable
Kurushima-Kaikyo II	Oshima–Mashima, Japan	4015	(longest) suspension
Lake Pontchartrain Causeway	Maudeville–Jefferson, Louisiana, USA	3842	twin concrete trestle
Lion's Gate	Vancouver, Canada	473	suspension
London	Southwark–City of London	centre span 46	concrete arch
Lupu	Shanghai, China	550	(longest) steel arch
McCall's Ferry	Susquehanna River, Lancaster, Pennsylvania, USA	110	wooden covered
Mackinac	Michigan, USA	1158	suspension
Meiko Chuo	Tokyo Bay, Japan	590	cable-stayed
Menai Strait	Menai Strait, N Wales	177	suspension
Millau	River Tarn, France	2460 (tallest at 340 m)	suspension
Minami Bisan-Seto	Honshu–Shikoku, Japan	1118	suspension
Nanjing II	Nanjing, China	628	cable-stayed
Nanjing III	Nanjing, China	648	cable-stayed
New River Gorge	Fayetteville, West Virginia, USA	518	steel arch
Nord Sundet	Norway	223	lattice
Normandie	Le Havre, France	856	cable-stayed
Øresund	Flinterenden, Denmark–Malmö, Sweden	7800 (main span 490)	
Plauen	Plauen, Germany	span 90	(longest) masonry arch
Pont d'Avignon	Rhône River, France	c.60	arch
Ponte Infante Dom Henrique	Oporto, Portugal	280	concrete arch
Pontypridd	S Wales	43	single-span arch

Name	Location	Length (m)[1]	Type
Quebec (railroad)	St Lawrence, Canada	549	(largest-span) cantilever
Qingzhou	Fuzhou, China	605	cable-stayed
Rainbow	Canada–USA, Niagara Falls	300	steel arch
Ravenswood	West Virginia, USA	525	cantilever
Rialto	Grand Canal, Venice, Italy	25	single-span arch
Rio-Niteroi	Guanabara Bay, Brazil	1 400 (centre span 300)	box and plate girder
Runyang	Zhenjiang, China	1490	suspension
Salazar	Tagus River, Lisbon, Portugal	1014	suspension
Iron Bridge	Ironbridge Gorge, Shropshire, England	31	(first) cast-iron arch
Severn	Beachley, England	988	suspension
Severn II	Severn Estuary, England	456	cable-stayed
Shibanpo	Chongqing, China	330	concrete girder
Skarnsundet	Norway	530	cable-stayed
Sky Train Bridge (rail)	Vancouver, Canada	340	cable-stayed
Sydney Harbour	Sydney, Australia	503	steel arch
Tacoma Narrows II	Puget Sound, Washington, USA	854	suspension
Tagus II	Lisbon, Portugal	420	cable-stayed
Tatara, Great	Japan	890	cable-stayed
Tay (road)	Dundee, Scotland	2 246	box girder
Thatcher Ferry	Panama Canal, C America	344	arch
Tower	River Thames, London	76	movable
Transbay	San Francisco, California, USA	705	suspension
Trans-Tokyo Bay Highway	Kawasaki–Kisarazu, Japan	590	box girder
Trois-Rivières	St Lawrence River, Quebec, Canada	336	steel arch
Tsing Ma	Tsing Yi I–Ma Wan I, Hong Kong	1377	suspension (double deck)
Vasco da Gama	Tagus Estuary, Lisbon, Portugal	1 800 (main span 820)	cable-stayed/ marine viaduct
Verrazano Narrows	Brooklyn–Staten Island, New York Harbour, USA	1298	suspension
Veterans Memorial	Louisiana, USA	445	cantilever
Victoria Jubilee	St Lawrence River, Montreal, Canada	2742	open steel
Wanxian	Wanzhou, China	420	concrete arch

Name	Location	Length (m)[1]	Type
Wheeling	Wheeling, Virginia, USA	308	suspension
Wushan	Chongqing, China	460	steel arch
Xiling Yangtze	Three Gorges Dam, China	900	suspension
Yokohama Bay (road)	Japan	855	suspension
Zoo	Cologne, Germany	259	steel box girder

[1] To convert m to ft, multiply by 3.2808.
[2] To convert km to mi, multiply by 0.6214.

Engineering: tunnels

Name	Use	Location	Length (km)[1]
Aki	rail	Japan	13
Box	rail	Wiltshire, England	3
Cascade	rail	Washington, USA	13
Channel	rail	Cheriton, England–Sargette, France	50
Chesapeake Bay Bridge-Tunnel	road	USA	28
Chesbrough	water supply	Chicago, USA	3
Cumberland Mountain	underground parking	Cumberland Gap, USA	1.402
Dai-shimizu	rail	Honshu, Japan	22
Delaware Aqueduct	water supply	Catskill Mts, New York, USA	169
Detroit River	rail	Detroit, Michigan, USA–Windsor, Ontario, Canada	2
Eupalinus	water supply	Samos, Greece	1.037
FATIMA (Magerøy)	road	Norway	6.82 (longest undersea road)
Fenguoshan	rail	China–Tibet	1.338 (highest rail tunnel)
Flathead	rail	Washington, USA	13
Fredhällstunneln	road	Stockholm, Sweden	0.210
Fréjus	rail	Modane, France–Bardonecchia, Italy	13
Fucino	drainage	Lake Fucino, Italy	6
Great Apennine	rail	Vernio, Italy	19
Hokuriku	rail	Japan	15
Holland	road	Hudson River, New York City–Jersey City, New Jersey, USA	3
Hoosac	rail	Massachusetts, USA	8
Hsuehshan	road	Taiwan	13

Name	Use	Location	Length (km)[1]
Hyperion	sewer	Los Angeles, California, USA	8
Kanmon	rail	Kanmon Strait, Japan	19
Keijo	rail	Japan	11
Kilsby Ridge	rail	London–Birmingham line, England	2
Laerdal	road	Bergen–Oslo, Norway	24.5 (longest road tunnel)
Languedoc (Canal du Midi)	canal	Malpas, France	0.157
Lierasen	rail	Norway	11
London and Southwark Subway	rail	London, England	11
Lötschberg	rail	Switzerland	15
Mersey	road	River Mersey, Birkenhead–Liverpool, England	4
Moffat	rail	Colorado, USA	10
Mont Blanc	road	France–Italy	12
Mt MacDonald	rail	Canada	15
NEAT (Bern–Lötschberg–Simplon)	rail	Switzerland	38
NEAT (St Gotthard)	rail	Switzerland	57
North Cape	road	Norway	7
Orange-Fish River	irrigation	South Africa	82 (longest irrigation tunnel)
Øresund	road–rail	Copenhagen, Denmark–Malmö, Sweden	3.75 (longest immersed tube)
Owingsburg Landing	canal	Pennsylvania, USA	0.137
Päijänne	water supply	Finland	120
Posilipo	road	Naples–Pozzuoli, Italy	6
Rennsteig	road	Germany	8
Rogers Pass	rail	Calgary–Vancouver, Canada	15
Rogers Pass	road	British Columbia, Canada	35
Rokko	rail	Osaka–Köbe, Japan	16
Seikan	rail	Tsugaru Strait, Honshu–Hokkaido, Japan	54 (longest undersea rail)
Shin-shimizu	rail	Japan	13
Simplon I and II	rail	Brigue, Switzerland–Iselle, Italy	20
St Gotthard	rail	Switzerland	15
St Gotthard	road	Göschenen, Switzerland–Airolo, Italy	16

Name	Use	Location	Length (km) [1]
(First) Thames	pedestrian; rail after 1865	Wapping–Rotherhithe, London, England	0.366
Tower Subway	rail	London, England	0.411
Tronquoy	canal	France	1.099

[1] To convert km to mi, multiply by 0.6214.

Engineering: dams

Name	River, country	Height (m) [1]
Afsluitdijk Sea	Zuider Zee, Netherlands	20 (largest sea dam, length 31 km)
Alberto Lleras	Orinoco, Colombia	243
Aswan High	Nile, Egypt	111
Atatürk	Euphrates, Turkey	184
Bakun	Rajang, Malaysia	204
Chicoasén	Grijalva, Mexico	263
Chivor	Cundinamarca, Colombia	237
Cipasang	Cimanuk, Indonesia	200
Daniel Johnson	Manicouagan, Canada	214
Ertan	Yalong, China	240
Esmeralda	Batá, Colombia	237
Grand Coulee	Columbia (Franklin D Roosevelt Lake), USA	168
Grand Dixence	Dixence, Switzerland	285
Guavio	Guaviare, Colombia	245
Hoover	Colorado (Lake Mead), USA	221
Inguri	Inguri, Georgia	272
Itaipú	Paraná, Paraguay/Brazil border	189; length 8 km (world's largest hydroelectric complex)
Kambaratinsk	Naryn, Kyrgyzstan	255
Katse	Malibamatso, Lesotho	182
Kiev	Dnieper, Ukraine	256
Kishau	Tons, India	253
La Grande 2A	La Grande, Canada	168
Longtan	Hongshui, China	285
Manuel M Torres	Grijalva, Mexico	261
Mauvoisin	Drance de Bagnes, Switzerland	237
Mica	Columbia, Canada	244
New China (Three Gorges)	Chang Jiang (Yangtze), China	175
Nurek	Vakhsh, Tajikistan	310
Oroville	Feather, California, USA	235
Poti	Paraná, Argentina	109 (most massive: vol 238 180 000 m³)
Rogun	Vakhsh, Tajikistan	335 (tallest)

Name	River, country	Height (m)[1]
San Roque	Agno, Philippines	210
Sardar Sarovar	Narmada, India	163
Sayansk	Yenisey, Russia	236
Tehri	Bhagirathi, India	261
Thames Barrier	Thames, England	spans 520 (largest tidal barrier)
Vaiont	Vaiont, Italy	265
Xiaolangdi	Huang He, China	154
Xiaowan	Lancang, China	292

[1] To convert m to ft, multiply by 3.2808.

Engineering: tallest inhabited buildings

Name	Location	Height (m)[1]	Date
Taipei 101	Taipei, Taiwan	508	2003
Petronas I	Kuala Lumpur, Malaysia	452	1996
Petronas II	Kuala Lumpur, Malaysia	452	1996
Sears Tower	Chicago, USA	443	1974
Jin Mao Building	Shanghai, China	420	1998
Two International Finance Centre	Hong Kong, China	415	2003
CITIC Plaza	Guangzhou, China	391	1997
Shun Hing Square	Shenzen, China	348	1996
Empire State Building	New York City, USA	381	1931
Central Plaza	Hong Kong	374	1992

[1] To convert m to ft, multiply by 3.2808.

Numerical equivalents

Arabic	Roman	Greek	Binary numbers
1	I	α′	1
2	II	β′	10
3	III	γ′	11
4	IV	δ′	100
5	V	ε′	101
6	VI	ϛ′	110
7	VII	ζ′	111
8	VIII	η′	1000
9	IX	θ′	1001
10	X	ι′	1010
11	XI	ια′	1011
12	XII	ιβ′	1100
13	XIII	ιγ′	1101
14	XIV	ιδ′	1110
15	XV	ιε′	1111
16	XVI	ιϛ′	10000
17	XVII	ιζ′	10001
18	XVIII	ιη′	10010
19	XIX	ιθ′	10011
20	XX	κ′	10100
30	XXX	λ′	11110
40	XL	μ′	101000
50	L	ν′	110010
60	LX	ξ′	111100
70	LXX	ο′	1000110
80	LXXX	π′	1010000
90	XC	ϟ′	1011010
100	C	ρ′	1100100
200	CC	σ′	11001000
300	CCC	τ′	100101100
400	CD	υ′	110010000
500	D	φ′	111110100
1000	M	͵α	1111101000
5000	V̄	͵ε	1001110001000
10000	X̄	͵ι	10011100010000
100000	C̄	͵ρ	11000011010100000

Fraction	Decimal	Fraction	Decimal	Fraction	Decimal
$\frac{1}{2}$	0.5000	$\frac{8}{9}$	0.8889	$\frac{15}{16}$	0.9375
$\frac{1}{3}$	0.3333	$\frac{1}{10}$	0.1000	$\frac{1}{20}$	0.0500
$\frac{2}{3}$	0.6667	$\frac{3}{10}$	0.3000	$\frac{3}{20}$	0.1500
$\frac{1}{4}$	0.2500	$\frac{7}{10}$	0.7000	$\frac{7}{20}$	0.3500
$\frac{3}{4}$	0.7500	$\frac{9}{10}$	0.9000	$\frac{9}{20}$	0.4500
$\frac{1}{5}$	0.2000	$\frac{1}{11}$	0.0909	$\frac{11}{20}$	0.5500
$\frac{2}{5}$	0.4000	$\frac{2}{11}$	0.1818	$\frac{13}{20}$	0.6500
$\frac{3}{5}$	0.6000	$\frac{3}{11}$	0.2727	$\frac{17}{20}$	0.8500
$\frac{4}{5}$	0.8000	$\frac{4}{11}$	0.3636	$\frac{19}{20}$	0.9500
$\frac{1}{6}$	0.1667	$\frac{5}{11}$	0.4545	$\frac{1}{32}$	0.0312
$\frac{5}{6}$	0.8333	$\frac{6}{11}$	0.5454	$\frac{3}{32}$	0.0937
$\frac{1}{7}$	0.1429	$\frac{7}{11}$	0.6363	$\frac{5}{32}$	0.1562
$\frac{2}{7}$	0.2857	$\frac{8}{11}$	0.7272	$\frac{7}{32}$	0.2187
$\frac{3}{7}$	0.4286	$\frac{9}{11}$	0.8181	$\frac{9}{32}$	0.2812
$\frac{4}{7}$	0.5714	$\frac{10}{11}$	0.9090	$\frac{11}{32}$	0.3437
$\frac{5}{7}$	0.7143	$\frac{1}{12}$	0.0833	$\frac{13}{32}$	0.4062
$\frac{6}{7}$	0.8571	$\frac{5}{12}$	0.4167	$\frac{15}{32}$	0.4687
$\frac{1}{8}$	0.1250	$\frac{7}{12}$	0.5833	$\frac{17}{32}$	0.5312
$\frac{3}{8}$	0.3750	$\frac{11}{12}$	0.9167	$\frac{19}{32}$	0.5937
$\frac{5}{8}$	0.6250	$\frac{1}{16}$	0.0625	$\frac{21}{32}$	0.6562
$\frac{7}{8}$	0.8750	$\frac{3}{16}$	0.1875	$\frac{23}{32}$	0.7187
$\frac{1}{9}$	0.1111	$\frac{5}{16}$	0.3125	$\frac{25}{32}$	0.7812
$\frac{2}{9}$	0.2222	$\frac{7}{16}$	0.4375	$\frac{27}{32}$	0.8437
$\frac{4}{9}$	0.4444	$\frac{9}{16}$	0.5625	$\frac{29}{32}$	0.9062
$\frac{5}{9}$	0.5556	$\frac{11}{16}$	0.6875	$\frac{31}{32}$	0.9687
$\frac{7}{9}$	0.7778	$\frac{13}{16}$	0.8125		

Multiplication table

×	2	3	4	5	6	7	8	9	10	11	12	13	14	15	16	17	18	19	20	21	22	23	24	25
2	4	6	8	10	12	14	16	18	20	22	24	26	28	30	32	34	36	38	40	42	44	46	48	50
3	6	9	12	15	18	21	24	27	30	33	36	39	42	45	48	51	54	57	60	63	66	69	72	75
4	8	12	16	20	24	28	32	36	40	44	48	52	56	60	64	68	72	76	80	84	88	92	96	100
5	10	15	20	25	30	35	40	45	50	55	60	65	70	75	80	85	90	95	100	105	110	115	120	125
6	12	18	24	30	36	42	48	54	60	66	72	78	84	90	96	102	108	114	120	126	132	138	144	150
7	14	21	28	35	42	49	56	63	70	77	84	91	98	105	112	119	126	133	140	147	154	161	168	175
8	16	24	32	40	48	56	64	72	80	88	96	104	112	120	128	136	144	152	160	168	176	184	192	200
9	18	27	36	45	54	63	72	81	90	99	108	117	126	135	144	153	162	171	180	189	198	207	216	225
10	20	30	40	50	60	70	80	90	100	110	120	130	140	150	160	170	180	190	200	210	220	230	240	250
11	22	33	44	55	66	77	88	99	110	121	132	143	154	165	176	187	198	209	220	231	242	253	264	275
12	24	36	48	60	72	84	96	108	120	132	144	156	168	180	192	204	216	228	240	252	264	276	288	300
13	26	39	52	65	78	91	104	117	130	143	156	169	182	195	208	221	234	247	260	273	286	299	312	325
14	28	42	56	70	84	98	112	126	140	154	168	182	196	210	224	238	252	266	280	294	308	322	336	350
15	30	45	60	75	90	105	120	135	150	165	180	195	210	225	240	255	270	285	300	315	330	345	360	375
16	32	48	64	80	96	112	128	144	160	176	192	208	224	240	256	272	288	304	320	336	352	368	384	400
17	34	51	68	85	102	119	136	153	170	187	204	221	238	255	272	289	306	323	340	357	374	391	408	425
18	36	54	72	90	108	126	144	162	180	198	216	234	252	270	288	306	324	342	360	378	396	414	432	450
19	38	57	76	95	114	133	152	171	190	209	228	247	266	285	304	323	342	361	380	399	418	437	456	475
20	40	60	80	100	120	140	160	180	200	220	240	260	280	300	320	340	360	380	400	420	440	460	480	500
21	42	63	84	105	126	147	168	189	210	231	252	273	294	315	336	357	378	399	420	441	462	483	504	525
22	44	66	88	110	132	154	176	198	220	242	264	286	308	330	352	374	396	418	440	462	484	506	528	550
23	46	69	92	115	138	161	184	207	230	253	276	299	322	345	368	391	414	437	460	483	506	529	552	575
24	48	72	96	120	144	168	192	216	240	264	288	312	336	360	384	408	432	456	480	504	528	552	576	600
25	50	75	100	125	150	175	200	225	250	275	300	325	350	375	400	425	450	475	500	525	550	575	600	625

Squares and roots

Number	Square	Cube	Square root	Cube root
1	1	1	1.000	1.000
2	4	8	1.414	1.260
3	9	27	1.732	1.442
4	16	64	2.000	1.587
5	25	125	2.236	1.710
6	36	216	2.449	1.817
7	49	343	2.646	1.913
8	64	512	2.828	2.000
9	81	729	3.000	2.080
10	100	1000	3.162	2.154
11	121	1331	3.317	2.224
12	144	1728	3.464	2.289
13	169	2197	3.606	2.351
14	196	2744	3.742	2.410
15	225	3375	3.873	2.466
16	256	4096	4.000	2.520
17	289	4913	4.123	2.571
18	324	5832	4.243	2.621
19	361	6859	4.359	2.668
20	400	8000	4.472	2.714
25	625	15625	5.000	2.924
30	900	27000	5.477	3.107
40	1600	64000	6.325	3.420
50	2500	125000	7.071	3.684

Common measures

■ Metric units		Imperial equivalent
Length		
	1 millimetre	0.03937 in
10 mm	1 centimetre	0.39 in
10 cm	1 decimetre	3.94 in
100 cm	1 metre	39.37 in
1000 m	1 kilometre	0.62 mile
Area		
	1 square millimetre	0.0016 sq in
	1 square centimetre	0.155 sq in
100 sq cm	1 square decimetre	15.5 sq in
10000 sq cm	1 square metre	10.76 sq ft
10000 sq m	1 hectare	2.47 acres
Volume		
	1 cubic centimetre	0.061 cu in
1000 cu cm	1 cubic decimetre	61.024 cu in
1000 cu dm	1 cubic metre	35.31 cu ft

■ Metric units		Imperial equivalent
		1.308 cu yds
Liquid volume		
	1 litre	1.76 pints
100 litres	1 hectolitre	22 gallons
Weight		
	1 gram	0.035 oz
1 000 g	1 kilogram	2.2046 lb
1 000 kg	1 tonne	0.9842 ton

■ Imperial units		Metric equivalent
Length		
	1 inch	2.54 cm
12 in	1 foot	30.48 cm
3 ft	1 yard	0.9144 m
1 760 yd	1 mile	1.6093 km
Area		
	1 square inch	6.45 sq cm
144 sq in	1 square foot	$0.0929 \, m^2$
9 sq ft	1 square yard	$0.836 \, m^2$
4 840 sq yd	1 acre	0.405 ha
640 acres	1 square mile	259 ha
Volume		
	1 cubic inch	$16.3871 \, cm^3$
1 728 cu in	1 cubic foot	$0.028 \, m^3$
27 cu ft	1 cubic yard	$0.765 \, m^3$
Liquid volume		
	1 pint	0.57 litres
2 pints	1 quart	1.14 litres
4 quarts	1 gallon	4.55 litres
Weight		
	1 ounce	28.3495 g
16 oz	1 pound	0.4536 kg
14 lb	1 stone	6.35 kg
8 stones	1 hundredweight	50.8 kg
20 cwt	1 ton	1.016 tonnes

Conversion factors

■ Imperial to metric

Length			Multiply by
inches	→	millimetres	25.4
inches	→	centimetres	2.54
feet	→	metres	0.3048
yards	→	metres	0.9144
statute miles	→	kilometres	1.6093
nautical miles	→	kilometres	1.852

Area			
square inches	→	square centimetres	6.4516
square feet	→	square metres	0.0929
square yards	→	square metres	0.8361
acres	→	hectares	0.4047
square miles	→	square kilometres	2.5899

Volume			
cubic inches	→	cubic centimetres	16.3871
cubic feet	→	cubic metres	0.0283
cubic yards	→	cubic metres	0.7646

Capacity			
UK fluid ounces	→	litres	0.0284
US fluid ounces	→	litres	0.0296
UK pints	→	litres	0.5682
US pints	→	litres	0.4732
UK gallons	→	litres	4.546
US gallons	→	litres	3.7854

Weight			
ounces (avoirdupois)	→	grams	28.3495
ounces (troy)	→	grams	31.1035
pounds	→	kilograms	0.4536
tons (long)	→	tonnes	1.016

■ Metric to imperial

Length			Multiply by
millimetres	→	inches	0.0394
centimetres	→	inches	0.3937
metres	→	feet	3.2808
metres	→	yards	1.0936
kilometres	→	statute miles	0.6214
kilometres	→	nautical miles	0.54

Area			
square centimetres	→	square inches	0.155
square metres	→	square feet	10.764
square metres	→	square yards	1.196
hectares	→	acres	2.471
square kilometres	→	square miles	0.386

Volume			
cubic centimetres	→	cubic inches	0.061
cubic metres	→	cubic feet	35.315
cubic metres	→	cubic yards	1.308

Capacity			
litres	→	UK fluid ounces	35.1961
litres	→	US fluid ounces	33.8150
litres	→	UK pints	1.7598
litres	→	US pints	2.1134
litres	→	UK gallons	0.2199
litres	→	US gallons	0.2642

Weight			
grams	→	ounces (avoirdupois)	0.0353
grams	→	ounces (troy)	0.0322
kilograms	→	pounds	2.2046
tonnes	→	tons (long)	0.9842

Conversion tables: length

in	cm	cm	in	in	mm	mm	in
$\frac{1}{8}$	0.3	1	0.39	$\frac{1}{8}$	3.2	1	0.04
$\frac{1}{4}$	0.6	2	0.79	$\frac{1}{4}$	6.4	2	0.08
$\frac{3}{8}$	1.0	3	1.18	$\frac{3}{8}$	9.5	3	0.12
$\frac{1}{2}$	1.3	4	1.57	$\frac{1}{2}$	12.7	4	0.16
$\frac{5}{8}$	1.6	5	1.97	$\frac{5}{8}$	15.9	5	0.20
$\frac{3}{4}$	1.9	6	2.36	$\frac{3}{4}$	19.1	10	0.39
$\frac{7}{8}$	2.2	7	2.76	$\frac{7}{8}$	22.2	15	0.59
1	2.5	8	3.15	1	25.4	20	0.79
2	5.1	9	3.54	2	50.8	25	0.98
3	7.6	10	3.94	3	76.2	30	1.18
4	10.2	11	4.33	4	101.6	35	1.38
5	12.7	12	4.72	5	127.0	40	1.57
6	15.2	13	5.12	6	152.4	45	1.77
7	17.8	14	5.51	7	177.8	50	1.97
8	20.3	15	5.91	8	203.2	55	2.17
9	22.9	16	6.30	9	228.6	60	2.36
10	25.4	17	6.69	10	254.0	65	2.56
11	27.9	18	7.09	11	279.4	70	2.76
12	30.5	19	7.48	12	304.8	75	2.95
13	33.0	20	7.87				
14	35.6	21	8.27				
15	38.1	22	8.66				
16	40.6	23	9.06				
17	43.2	24	9.45				
18	45.7	25	9.84				
19	48.3	26	10.24				
20	50.8	27	10.63				
21	53.3	28	11.02				
22	55.9	29	11.42				
23	58.4	30	11.81				
24	61.0	31	12.20				
25	63.5	32	12.60				
26	66.0	33	12.99				
27	68.6	34	13.39				
28	71.1	35	13.78				
29	73.7	40	15.75				
30	76.2	45	17.72				
40	101.6	50	19.66				
50	127.0	55	21.65				
60	152.4	60	23.62				

Exact conversions:
1 in = 2.54 cm   1 cm = 0.3937 in   1 in = 25.4 mm   1 mm = 0.0394 in

ft	m	m	ft	yd	m	m	yd
1	0.3	1	3.3	1	0.9	1	1.1
2	0.6	2	6.6	2	1.8	2	2.2
3	0.9	3	9.8	3	2.7	3	3.3
4	1.2	4	13.1	4	3.7	4	4.4
5	1.5	5	16.4	5	4.6	5	5.5
6	1.8	6	19.7	6	5.5	6	6.6
7	2.1	7	23.0	7	6.4	7	7.7
8	2.4	8	26.2	8	7.3	8	8.7
9	2.7	9	29.5	9	8.2	9	9.8
10	3.0	10	32.8	10	9.1	10	10.9
15	4.6	15	49.2	15	13.7	15	16.4
20	6.1	20	65.5	20	18.3	20	21.9
25	7.6	25	82.0	25	22.9	25	27.3
30	9.1	30	98.4	30	27.4	30	32.8
35	10.7	35	114.8	35	32.0	35	38.3
40	12.2	40	131.2	40	36.6	40	43.7
45	13.7	45	147.6	45	41.1	45	49.2
50	15.2	50	164.0	50	45.7	50	54.7
75	22.9	75	246.1	75	68.6	75	82.0
100	30.5	100	328.1	100	91.4	100	109.4
200	61.0	200	656.2	200	182.9	200	218.7
300	91.4	300	984.3	220	201.2	220	240.6
400	121.9	400	1312.3	300	274.3	300	328.1
500	152.4	500	1640.4	400	365.8	400	437.4
600	182.9	600	1968.5	440	402.3	440	481.2
700	213.4	700	2296.6	500	457.2	500	546.8
800	243.8	800	2624.7	600	548.6	600	656.2
900	274.3	900	2952.8	700	640.1	700	765.5
000	304.8	1000	3280.8	800	731.5	800	874.9
1500	457.2	1500	4921.3	880	804.7	880	962.4
2000	609.6	2000	6561.7	900	823.0	900	984.2
2500	762.0	2500	8202.1	1000	914.4	1000	1093.6
3000	914.4	3000	9842.5	1500	1371.6	1500	1640.4
3500	1066.8	3500	11482.9	2000	1828.8	2000	2187.2
4000	1219.2	4000	13123.4	2500	2286.0	2500	2734.0
5000	1524.0	5000	16404.2	5000	4572.0	5000	5468.1

Exact conversions:
1 ft = 0.3048 m   1 m = 3.2808 ft   1 yd = 0.9144 m   1 m = 1.0936 yd

mi[1]	km	km	mi[1]	mi[1]	km	km	mi[1]
1	1.6	1	0.6	55	88.5	55	34.2
2	3.2	2	1.2	60	96.6	60	37.3
3	4.8	3	1.9	65	104.6	65	40.4
4	6.4	4	2.5	70	112.7	70	43.5
5	8.0	5	3.1	75	120.7	75	46.6
6	9.7	6	3.7	80	128.7	80	49.7
7	11.3	7	4.3	85	136.8	85	52.8
8	12.9	8	5.0	90	144.8	90	55.9
9	14.5	9	5.6	95	152.9	95	59.0
10	16.1	10	6.2	100	160.9	100	62.1
15	24.1	15	9.3	200	321.9	200	124.3
20	32.2	20	12.4	300	482.8	300	186.4
25	40.2	25	15.5	400	643.7	400	248.5
30	48.3	30	18.6	500	804.7	500	310.7
35	56.3	35	21.7	750	1207.0	750	466.0
40	64.4	40	24.9	1000	1609.3	1000	621.4
45	72.4	45	28.0	2500	4023.4	2500	1553.4
50	80.5	50	31.1	5000	8046.7	5000	3106.9

[1] Statute miles
Exact conversions:
1 mi = 1.6093 km   1 km = 0.6214 mi

Conversion tables: area

sq in	sq cm	sq cm	sq in	sq ft	sq m	sq m	sq ft
1	6.45	1	0.16	1	0.09	1	10.8
2	12.90	2	0.31	2	0.19	2	21.5
3	19.35	3	0.47	3	0.28	3	32.3
4	25.81	4	0.62	4	0.37	4	43.1
5	32.26	5	0.78	5	0.46	5	53.8
6	38.71	6	0.93	6	0.56	6	64.6
7	45.16	7	1.09	7	0.65	7	75.3
8	51.61	8	1.24	8	0.74	8	86.1
9	58.06	9	1.40	9	0.84	9	96.9
10	64.52	10	1.55	10	0.93	10	107.6
11	70.97	11	1.71	11	1.02	11	118.4
12	77.42	12	1.86	12	1.11	12	129.2
13	83.87	13	2.02	13	1.21	13	139.9
14	90.32	14	2.17	14	1.30	14	150.7
15	96.77	15	2.33	15	1.39	15	161.5
16	103.23	16	2.48	16	1.49	16	172.2
17	109.68	17	2.64	17	1.58	17	183.0
18	116.13	18	2.79	18	1.67	18	193.8
19	122.58	19	2.95	19	1.77	19	204.5
20	129.03	20	3.10	20	1.86	20	215.3
25	161.29	25	3.88	25	2.32	25	269.1
50	322.58	50	7.75	50	4.65	50	538.2

sq in	sq cm	sq cm	sq in	sq ft	sq m	sq m	sq ft
75	483.87	75	11.63	75	6.97	75	807.3
100	645.16	100	15.50	100	9.29	100	1076.4
125	806.45	125	19.38	250	23.23	250	2691.0
150	967.74	150	23.25	500	46.45	500	5382.0
175	1129.03	175	27.13	750	69.68	750	8072.9
200	1290.32	200	31.00	1000	92.90	1000	10763.9

Exact conversions:
$1 in^2 = 6.4516 cm^2$ $1 cm^2 = 0.155 in^2$ $1 ft^2 = 0.0929 m^2$ $1 m^2 = 10.7639 ft^2$

acres	hectares	hectares	acres	sq mi[1]	sq km	sq km	sq mi[1]
1	0.40	1	2.5	1	2.6	1	0.39
2	0.81	2	4.9	2	5.2	2	0.77
3	1.21	3	7.4	3	7.8	3	1.16
4	1.62	4	9.9	4	10.4	4	1.54
5	2.02	5	12.4	5	12.9	5	1.93
6	2.43	6	14.8	6	15.5	6	2.32
7	2.83	7	17.3	7	18.1	7	2.70
8	3.24	8	19.8	8	20.7	8	3.09
9	3.64	9	22.2	9	23.3	9	3.47
10	4.05	10	24.7	10	25.9	10	3.86
11	4.45	11	27.2	20	51.8	20	7.72
12	4.86	12	29.7	21	54.4	21	8.11
13	5.26	13	32.1	22	57.0	22	8.49
14	5.67	14	34.6	23	59.6	23	8.88
15	6.07	15	37.1	24	62.2	24	9.27
16	6.47	16	39.5	25	64.7	25	9.65
17	6.88	17	42.0	30	77.7	30	11.58
18	7.28	18	44.5	40	103.6	40	15.44
19	7.69	19	46.9	50	129.5	50	19.31
20	8.09	20	49.4	100	259.0	100	38.61
25	10.12	25	61.8	200	518.0	200	77.22
50	20.23	50	123.6	300	777.0	300	115.83
75	30.35	75	185.3	400	1036.0	400	154.44
100	40.47	100	247.1	500	1295.0	500	193.05
250	101.17	250	617.8	600	1554.0	600	231.66
500	202.34	500	1235.5	700	1813.0	700	270.27
750	303.51	750	1853.3	800	2072.0	800	308.88
1000	404.69	1000	2471.0	900	2331.0	900	347.49
1500	607.03	1500	3706.6	1000	2590.0	1000	386.10
2000	809.37	2000	4942.1	1500	3885.0	1500	579.15
2500	1011.72	2500	6177.6	2000	5180.0	2000	772.20

[1] Statute miles
Exact conversions:
1 acre = 0.4047 hectares   1 hectare = 2.471 acres   1 sq mi = 2.5899 sq km   1 sq km = 0.3861 sq mi

Conversion tables: volume

cu in	cu cm	cu cm	cu in	cu ft	cu m	cu m	cu ft
1	16.39	1	0.06	1	0.03	1	35.3
2	32.77	2	0.12	2	0.06	2	70.6
3	49.16	3	0.18	3	0.08	3	105.9
4	65.55	4	0.24	4	0.11	4	141.3
5	81.93	5	0.30	5	0.14	5	176.6
6	93.32	6	0.37	6	0.17	6	211.9
7	114.71	7	0.43	7	0.20	7	247.2
8	131.10	8	0.49	8	0.23	8	282.5
9	147.48	9	0.55	9	0.25	9	317.8
10	163.87	10	0.61	10	0.28	10	353.1
15	245.81	15	0.92	15	0.42	15	529.7
20	327.74	20	1.22	20	0.57	20	706.3
50	819.35	50	3.05	50	1.41	50	1 765.7
100	1 638.71	100	6.10	100	2.83	100	3 531.5

cu yd	cu m	cu m	cu yd
1	0.76	1	1.31
2	1.53	2	2.62
3	2.29	3	3.92
4	3.06	4	5.23
5	3.82	5	6.54
6	4.59	6	7.85
7	5.35	7	9.16
8	6.12	8	10.46
9	6.88	9	11.77
10	7.65	10	13.08
15	11.47	15	19.62
20	15.29	20	26.16
50	38.23	50	65.40
100	76.46	100	130.80

Exact conversions:
$1 \, in^3 = 16.3871 \, cm^3$
$1 \, ft^3 = 0.0283 \, m^3$
$1 \, yd^3 = 0.7646 \, m^3$
$1 \, cm^3 = 0.0610 \, in^3$
$1 \, m^3 = 35.3147 \, ft^3$
$1 \, m^3 = 1.3080 \, yd^3$

Conversion tables: capacity

■ Liquid measures

UK fluid ounces	litres		US fluid ounces	litres
1	0.0284		1	0.0296
2	0.0568		2	0.0592
3	0.0852		3	0.0888
4	0.114		4	0.118
5	0.142		5	0.148
6	0.170		6	0.178
7	0.199		7	0.207
8	0.227		8	0.237
9	0.256		9	0.266
10	0.284		10	0.296
11	0.312		11	0.326
12	0.341		12	0.355
13	0.369		13	0.385
14	0.397		14	0.414
15	0.426		15	0.444
20	0.568		20	0.592
50	1.42		50	1.48
100	2.84		100	2.96

litres	UK fluid ounces	US fluid ounces
1	35.2	33.8
2	70.4	67.6
3	105.6	101.4
4	140.8	135.3
5	176.0	169.1
6	211.2	202.9
7	246.4	236.7
8	281.6	270.5
9	316.8	304.3
10	352.0	338.1
11	387.2	372.0
12	422.4	405.8
13	457.5	439.6
14	492.7	473.4
15	527.9	507.2
20	703.9	676.3
50	1759.8	1690.7
100	3519.6	3381.5

Exact conversions:
1 UK fl oz = 0.0284 l   1 US fl oz = 0.0296 l   1 l = 35.1961 UK fl oz   1 l = 33.8140 US fl oz

UK pints	litres		US pints	litres
1	0.57		1	0.47
2	1.14		2	0.95
3	1.70		3	1.42
4	2.27		4	1.89
5	2.84		5	2.37
6	3.41		6	2.84
7	3.98		7	3.31
8	4.55		8	3.78
9	5.11		9	4.26
10	5.68		10	4.73
11	6.25		11	5.20
12	6.82		12	5.68
13	7.38		13	6.15
14	7.95		14	6.62
15	8.52		15	7.10
20	11.36		20	9.46
50	28.41		50	23.66
100	56.82		100	47.32

litres	UK pints	US pints
1	1.76	2.11
2	3.52	4.23
3	5.28	6.34
4	7.04	8.45
5	8.80	10.57
6	10.56	12.68
7	12.32	14.79
8	14.08	16.91
9	15.84	19.02
10	17.60	21.13
11	19.36	23.25
12	21.12	25.36
13	22.88	27.47
14	24.64	29.59
15	26.40	31.70
20	35.20	42.27
50	87.99	105.67
100	175.98	211.34

Exact conversions:
1 UK pt = 0.5682 l   1 US pt = 0.4732 l   1 l = 1.7598 UK pt/2.1134 US pt   1 UK pt = 1.20 US pt
1 US pt = 0.83 UK pt   1 US cup = 8 fl oz

UK gallons	litres	US gallons	litres
1	4.55	1	3.78
2	9.09	2	7.57
3	13.64	3	11.36
4	18.18	4	15.14
5	22.73	5	18.93
6	27.28	6	22.71
7	31.82	7	26.50
8	36.37	8	30.28
9	40.91	9	34.07
10	45.46	10	37.85
11	50.01	11	41.64
12	54.55	12	45.42
13	59.10	13	49.21
14	63.64	14	52.99
15	68.19	15	56.78
20	90.92	20	75.71
25	113.65	25	94.63
50	227.30	50	189.27
75	340.96	75	283.90
100	454.61	100	378.54

litres	UK gallons	US gallons
1	0.22	0.26
2	0.44	0.53
3	0.66	0.79
4	0.88	1.06
5	1.10	1.32
6	1.32	1.58
7	1.54	1.85
8	1.76	2.11
9	1.98	2.38
10	2.20	2.64
11	2.42	2.91
12	2.64	3.17
13	2.86	3.43
14	3.08	3.70
15	3.30	3.96
20	4.40	5.28
25	5.50	6.60
50	11.00	13.20
75	16.50	19.81
100	22.00	26.42

Exact conversions:
1 UK gal = 4.546 l   1 US gal = 3.785 4 l   1 l = 0.220 UK gal/ 0.2642 US gal

UK gallons	US gallons		US gallons	UK gallons
1	1.2		1	0.8
2	2.4		2	1.7
3	3.6		3	2.5
4	4.8		4	3.3
5	6.0		5	4.2
6	7.2		6	5.0
7	8.4		7	5.8
8	9.6		8	6.7
9	10.8		9	7.5
10	12.0		10	8.3
11	13.2		11	9.2
12	14.4		12	10.0
13	15.6		13	10.8
14	16.8		14	11.7
15	18.0		15	12.5
20	24.0		20	16.6
25	30.0		25	20.8
50	60.0		50	41.6

Exact conversions
1 UK gal = 1.200929 US gal   1 US gal = 0.832688 UK gal

■ **Dry capacity measures**

UK bushels	cu m	litres		US bushels	cu m	litres
1	0.037	36.4		1	0.035	35.2
2	0.074	72.7		2	0.071	70.5
3	0.111	109.1		3	0.106	105.7
4	0.148	145.5		4	0.141	140.9
5	0.184	181.8		5	0.175	176.2
10	0.369	363.7		10	0.353	352.4

Exact conversions:
1 UK bushel = 0.0369 m³   1 US bushel = 0.9353 m³   1 UK bushel = 36.3677 l
1 US bushel = 35.2381 l

cu m	UK bushels	US bushels		litres	UK bushels	US bushels
1	27.5	28.4		1	0.027	0.028
2	55.0	56.7		2	0.055	0.057
3	82.5	85.1		3	0.082	0.085
4	110.0	113.0		4	0.110	0.114
5	137.0	142.0		5	0.137	0.142
10	275.0	284.0		10	0.275	0.284

Exact conversions:
$1 m^3 = 27.4962$ UK bu $1 l = 0.0275$ UK bu $1 m^3 = 28.3776$ US bu $1 l = 0.0284$ US bu

UK pecks	litres		US pecks	litres		litres	UK pecks	US pecks
1	9.1		1	8.8		1	0.110	0.113
2	18.2		2	17.6		2	0.220	0.226
3	27.3		3	26.4		3	0.330	0.339
4	36.4		4	35.2		4	0.440	0.454
5	45.5		5	44.0		5	0.550	0.567
10	90.9		10	88.1		10	1.100	1.135

Exact conversions:
1 UK pk = 9.0919 l   1 US pk = 8.8095 l   1 l = 0.1100 UK pk = 0.1135 US pk

US quarts	cu cm	litres		US pints	cu cm	litres
1	1101	1.1		1	551	0.55
2	2202	2.2		2	1101	1.10
3	3304	3.3		3	1652	1.65
4	4405	4.4		4	2202	2.20
5	5506	5.5		5	2753	2.75
10	11012	11.0		10	5506	5.51

Exact conversions:
1 US qt $= 1101.2209 cm^3$ 1 US pt $= 550.6105 cm^3$ 1 US qt = 1.1012 l   1 US pt = 0.5506 l

Conversion tables: weight

ounces[1]	grams	grams	ounces[1]	pounds	kilo-grams	kilo-grams	pounds
1	28.3	1	0.04	1	0.45	1	2.2
2	56.7	2	0.07	2	0.91	2	4.4
3	85.0	3	0.11	3	1.36	3	6.6
4	113.4	4	0.14	4	1.81	4	8.8
5	141.7	5	0.18	5	2.27	5	11.0
6	170.1	6	0.21	6	2.72	6	13.2
7	198.4	7	0.25	7	3.18	7	15.4
8	226.8	8	0.28	8	3.63	8	17.6
9	255.1	9	0.32	9	4.08	9	19.8
10	283.5	10	0.35	10	4.54	10	22.0
11	311.7	20	0.71	11	4.99	11	24.3
12	340.2	30	1.06	12	5.44	12	26.5
13	368.5	40	1.41	13	5.90	13	28.7
14	396.9	50	1.76	14	6.35	14	30.9
15	425.2	60	2.12	15	6.80	15	33.1
16	453.6	70	2.47	16	7.26	16	35.3
		80	2.82	17	7.71	17	37.5
		90	3.18	18	8.16	18	39.7
		100	3.53	19	8.62	19	41.9
				20	9.07	20	44.1
				25	11.34	25	55.1
				30	13.61	30	66.1
				35	15.88	35	77.2
				40	18.14	40	88.2
				45	20.41	45	99.2
				50	22.68	50	110.2
				60	27.24	60	132.3
				70	31.78	70	154.4
				80	36.32	80	176.4
				90	40.86	90	198.5
				100	45.36	100	220.5
				200	90.72	200	440.9
				250	113.40	250	551.2
				500	226.80	500	1 102.3
				750	340.19	750	1 653.5
				1 000	453.59	1 000	2 204.6

[1] avoirdupois

Exact conversions:

1 oz (avdp) = 28.3495 g   1 g = 0.0353 oz (avdp)   1 lb = 0.454 kg   1 kg = 2.205 lb

UK tons[1]	US tons[2]	US tons[2]	UK tons[1]	UK tons[1]	tonnes[3]	US tons[2]	tonnes[3]
1	1.12	1	0.89	1	1.02	1	0.91
2	2.24	2	1.79	2	2.03	2	1.81
3	3.36	3	2.68	3	3.05	3	2.72
4	4.48	4	3.57	4	4.06	4	3.63
5	5.6	5	4.46	5	5.08	5	4.54
10	11.2	10	8.93	10	10.16	10	9.07
15	16.8	15	13.39	15	15.24	15	13.61
20	22.4	20	17.86	20	20.32	20	18.14
50	56	50	44.64	50	50.80	50	45.36
75	84	75	66.96	75	76.20	75	68.04
100	112	100	89.29	100	101.60	100	90.72

tonnes[3]	UK tons[1]	US tons[2]
1	0.98	1.10
2	1.97	2.20
3	2.95	3.30
4	3.94	4.40
5	4.92	5.50
10	9.84	11.02
15	14.76	16.53
20	19.68	22.05
50	49.21	55.11
75	73.82	82.67
100	98.42	110.23

[1] UK (long) ton = 2 240 lb
[2] US (short) ton = 2 000 lb
[3] metric tonne = 1 000 kg
Exact conversions:
1 UK ton = 1.1199 US tons   1 US ton = 0.8929 UK ton   1 UK ton = 1.0160 tonnes
1 US ton = 0.9072 tonne   1 tonne = 0.9842 UK ton   1 tonne = 1.1023 US tons

UK cwt[1]	US cwt[2]	US cwt[2]	UK cwt[1]	UK cwt[1]	kg	US cwt[2]	kg
1	1.12	1	0.89	1	50.8	1	45.4
2	2.24	2	1.79	2	102	2	90.7
3	3.36	3	2.68	3	152	3	136
4	4.48	4	3.57	4	203	4	181
5	5.6	5	4.46	5	254	5	227
10	11.2	10	8.93	10	508	10	454
15	16.8	15	13.39	15	762	15	680
20	22.4	20	17.86	20	1016	20	907
50	56	50	44.64	50	2540	50	2268
75	84	75	66.96	75	3810	75	3402
100	112	100	89.29	100	5080	100	4536

kg	UK cwt[1]	US cwt[2]
1	0.0197	0.022
2	0.039	0.044
3	0.059	0.066
4	0.079	0.088
5	0.098	0.11
10	0.197	0.22
15	0.295	0.33
20	0.394	0.44
50	0.985	1.10
75	1.477	1.65
100	1.970	2.20

[1] UK (long) hundredweight = 112 lb
[2] US (short) hundredweight = 100 lb
Exact conversions:
1 UK cwt = 1.1199 US cwt   1 US cwt = 0.8929 UK cwt   1 UK cwt = 50.8023 kg
1 US cwt = 45.3592 kg   1 kg = 0.0197 UK cwt = 0.0220 US cwt

stones	pounds	stones	pounds	stones	kilograms
1	14	11	154	1	6.35
2	28	12	168	2	12.70
3	42	13	182	3	19.05
4	56	14	196	4	25.40
5	70	15	210	5	31.75
6	84	16	224	6	38.10
7	98	17	238	7	44.45
8	112	18	252	8	50.80
9	126	19	266	9	57.15
10	140	20	280	10	63.50

Exact conversions:
1 st = 14 lb   1 lb = 0.07 st   1 st = 6.350 kg   1 kg = 0.1575 st

Temperature conversion

To convert	To	Equation
°Fahrenheit	°Celsius	−32, ×5, ÷9
°Fahrenheit	°Rankine	+459.67
°Fahrenheit	°Réaumur	−32, ×4, ÷9
°Celsius	°Fahrenheit	×9, ÷5, +32
°Celsius	Kelvin	+273.15
°Celsius	°Réaumur	×4, ÷5
Kelvin	°Celsius	−273.15
°Rankine	°Fahrenheit	−459.67
°Réaumur	°Fahrenheit	×9, ÷4, +32
°Réaumur	°Celsius	×5, ÷4

Carry out operations in sequence.

Degrees Fahrenheit (°F) → Degrees Celsius (Centigrade) (°C)

°F →	°C	°F →	°C	°F →	°C	°F →	°C	°F →	°C
1	−17.2	33	0.5	65	18.3	97	36.1	158	70.0
2	−16.7	34	1.1	66	18.9	98	36.7	160	71.1
3	−16.1	35	1.7	67	19.4	99	37.2	162	72.2
4	−15.5	36	2.2	68	20.0	100	37.8	164	73.3
5	−15.0	37	2.8	69	20.5	102	38.9	166	74.4
6	−14.4	38	3.3	70	21.1	104	40.0	168	75.5
7	−13.9	39	3.9	71	21.7	106	41.1	170	76.7
8	−13.3	40	4.4	72	22.2	108	42.2	172	77.8
9	−12.8	41	5.0	73	22.8	110	43.3	174	78.9
10	−12.2	42	5.5	74	23.3	112	44.4	176	80.0
11	−11.6	43	6.1	75	23.9	114	45.5	178	81.1
12	−11.1	44	6.7	76	24.4	116	46.7	180	82.2
13	−10.5	45	7.2	77	25.0	118	47.8	182	83.3
14	−10.0	46	7.8	78	25.5	120	48.9	184	84.4
15	−9.4	47	8.3	79	26.1	122	50.0	186	85.5
16	−8.9	48	8.9	80	26.7	124	51.1	188	86.7
17	−8.3	49	9.4	81	27.2	126	52.2	190	87.8
18	−7.8	50	10.0	82	27.8	128	53.3	192	88.8
19	−7.2	51	10.5	83	28.3	130	54.4	194	90.0
20	−6.7	52	11.1	84	28.9	132	55.5	196	91.1
21	−6.1	53	11.7	85	29.4	134	56.7	198	92.2
22	−5.5	54	12.2	86	30.0	136	57.8	200	93.3
23	−5.0	55	12.8	87	30.5	138	58.9	202	94.4
24	−4.4	56	13.3	88	31.1	140	60.0	204	95.5
25	−3.9	57	13.9	89	31.7	142	61.1	206	96.7
26	−3.3	58	14.4	90	32.2	144	62.2	208	97.8
27	−2.8	59	15.0	91	32.8	146	63.3	210	98.9
28	−2.2	60	15.5	92	33.3	148	64.4	212	100.0
29	−1.7	61	16.1	93	33.9	150	65.5		
30	−1.1	62	16.7	94	34.4	152	66.7		
31	−0.5	63	17.2	95	35.0	154	67.8		
32	0	64	17.8	96	35.5	156	68.9		

Degrees Celsius (Centigrade) (°C) →Degrees Fahrenheit (°F)

°C →	°F	°C →	°F	°C →	°F
1	33.8	35	95.0	69	156.2
2	35.6	36	96.8	70	158.0
3	37.4	37	98.6	71	159.8
4	39.2	38	100.4	72	161.6
5	41.0	39	102.2	73	163.4
6	42.8	40	104.0	74	165.2
7	44.6	41	105.8	75	167.0
8	46.4	42	107.6	76	168.8
9	48.2	43	109.4	77	170.6
10	50.0	44	111.2	78	172.4
11	51.8	45	113.0	79	174.2
12	53.6	46	114.8	80	176.0
13	55.4	47	116.6	81	177.8
14	57.2	48	118.4	82	179.6
15	59.0	49	120.2	83	181.4
16	60.8	50	122.0	84	183.2
17	62.6	51	123.8	85	185.0
18	64.4	52	125.6	86	186.8
19	66.2	53	127.4	87	188.6
20	68.0	54	129.2	88	190.4
21	69.8	55	131.0	89	192.2
22	71.6	56	132.8	90	194.0
23	73.4	57	134.6	91	195.8
24	75.2	58	136.4	92	197.6
25	77.0	59	138.2	93	199.4
26	78.8	60	140.0	94	201.2
27	80.6	61	141.8	95	203.0
28	82.4	62	143.6	96	204.8
29	84.2	63	145.4	97	206.6
30	86.0	64	147.2	98	208.4
31	87.8	65	149.0	99	210.2
32	89.6	66	150.8	100	212.0
33	91.4	67	152.6		
34	93.2	68	154.4		

HISTORY

Journeys of exploration

More is known about exploration that originated in Europe than anywhere else. This table comprises mainly European explorers; 'discovers' is used to indicate the first recorded visit by a European.

Date	Name and exploration
490 BC	**Hanno** makes a voyage round part of the coast of Africa
325 BC	**Alexander the Great** leads his fleet along the N Indian coast and up the Persian Gulf
AD 84	**Agricola** and his fleet circumnavigate Britain
c.985	**Erik the Red** explores Greenland's coast and founds settlements there
1003	**Leif Ericsson** voyages to N America and discovers 'Vinland' (possibly Nova Scotia)
1405–33	**Admiral Zheng He** and his fleets of Chinese junks explore the Indian Ocean, reaching the African coast
1418	**João Gonçalves Zarco** discovers Madeira (dispatched by Henry the Navigator)
1434	**Gil Eanes** sails round Cape Bojador (dispatched by Henry the Navigator)
1446	**Dinís Dias** discovers Cape Verde and the Senegal River (dispatched by Henry the Navigator)
1488	**Bartolomeu Dias** sails round the Cape of Storms (Cape of Good Hope)
1492	**Christopher Columbus** discovers the New World
1493	**Christopher Columbus** discovers Puerto Rico, Antigua and Jamaica
1497	**John Cabot** explores the coast of Newfoundland
1497	**Vasco da Gama** voyages round the Cape of Good Hope
1498	**Vasco da Gama** explores the coast of Mozambique, and discovers a sea route to India
1498	**Christopher Columbus** discovers Trinidad and Venezuela
1499	**Amerigo Vespucci** discovers the mouth of the River Amazon
1500	**Pedro Alvares Cabral** discovers Brazil
1500	**Diogo Dias** discovers Madagascar
1500	**Gaspar Corte Real** explores the east coast of Greenland and Labrador
1501	**Amerigo Vespucci** explores the S American coast
1502	**Christopher Columbus** explores Honduras and Panama
1513	**Vasco Núñez de Balboa** crosses the Panama Isthmus to discover the Pacific Ocean
1520	**Ferdinand Magellan** discovers the Straits of Magellan
1521	**Ferdinand Magellan** discovers the Philippines
1524	**Giovanni da Verrazano** discovers New York Bay and the Hudson River
1526	**Sebastian Cabot** explores the Rio de la Plata

Date	Name and exploration
1534	Jacques Cartier explores the Gulf of St Lawrence
1535	Jacques Cartier navigates the St Lawrence River
1536	Pedro de Mendoza founds Buenos Aires and explores the Parana and Paraguay rivers
1539	Hernando de Soto explores Florida
1540	García López de Cárdenas discovers the Grand Canyon
1580	Francis Drake completes his circumnavigation of the globe
1585	John Davis discovers the Davis Strait on an expedition to Greenland
1595	Walter Raleigh explores the Orinoco River
1610	Henry Hudson discovers Hudson's Bay
1616	William Baffin discovers Baffin Bay during his search for the NW Passage
1617	Walter Raleigh begins an expedition to Guiana
1642	Abel Janszoon Tasman discovers Van Diemen's Land (Tasmania) and New Zealand
1678	Robert Cavelier de la Salle explores the Great Lakes of Canada
1682	Robert Cavelier de la Salle follows the course of the Mississippi River to the Gulf of Mexico
1692	Ijsbrand Iders explores the Gobi Desert
1736	Anders Celsius undertakes an expedition to Lapland
1761	Carsten Niebuhr undertakes an expedition to Arabia
1766	Louis de Bougainville makes a voyage of discovery in the Pacific, and names the Navigator Is
1769	James Cook names the Society Is; charts coasts of New Zealand and E Australia
1770	James Cook lands at Botany Bay, Australia
1772	James Bruce explores Abyssinia and the confluence of the Blue Nile and White Nile
1774	James Cook makes discoveries and rediscoveries in the Pacific, and discovers and names S Georgia and the S Sandwich Is
1778	James Cook discovers the Hawaiian group and surveys the N American coast as far as the Bering Strait
1787	Horace Saussure makes the first ascent of Mont Blanc
1790	George Vancouver explores the coast of NW America
1795	Mungo Park explores the course of the Niger
1804–6	Meriwether Lewis and William Clark follow the Missouri and Columbia rivers to the Pacific
1818	John Ross attempts to discover the NW Passage
1819	John Barrow enters the Barrow Straits in the N Arctic
1823	Walter Oudney discovers Lake Chad in C Africa
1841	David Livingstone discovers Lake Ngami
1845	John Franklin attempts to discover the NW Passage
1854	Richard Burton and John Speke explore the interior of Somaliland
1855	David Livingstone discovers the Victoria Falls on the Zambesi River
1858	Richard Burton and John Speke discover Lake Tanganyika
1860	Robert Burke and William Wills mount the first expedition to cross the interior of Australia, south to north

Date	Name and exploration
1872–6	The British Challenger expedition explores the ocean floor, mapping depths, taking core samples and discovering 4417 new species
1875	Henry Morton Stanley traces the Congo to the Atlantic
1888	Fridtjof Nansen crosses Greenland
1893	Fridtjof Nansen attempts to reach the N Pole
1905	Roald Amundsen sails through the NW Passage
1909	Robert Peary reaches the N Pole
1911	Roald Amundsen reaches the S Pole
1912	Robert Scott reaches the S Pole
1914	Ernest Shackleton leads an expedition to the Antarctic
1953	Edmund Hillary and Tenzing Norgay make the first ascent of Mt Everest
1961	Yuri Gagarin becomes the first man in space
1969	Neil Armstrong and Buzz Aldrin make the first landing on the moon

Ancient Egyptian dynasties

Date BC	Dynasty	Period
c.3100–2890	I	Early Dynastic Period
c.2890–2686	II	(First use of stone in building.)
c.2686–2613	III	Old Kingdom
c.2613–2494	IV	(The age of the great pyramid builders. Longest reign in
c.2494–2345	V	history: Pepi II, 90 years.)
c.2345–2181	VI	
c.2181–2173	VII	First Intermediate Period
c.2173–2160	VIII	(Social order upset; few monuments built.)
c.2160–2130	IX	
c.2130–2040	X	
c.2133–1991	XI	
1991–1786	XII	Middle Kingdom
1786–1633	XIII	(Golden age of art and craftsmanship.)
1786–c.1603	XIV	Second Intermediate Period
1674–1567	XV	(Country divided into principalities.)
c.1684–1567	XVI	
c.1660–1567	XVII	
1567–1320	XVIII	New Kingdom
1320–1200	XIX	(Began with colonial expansion, ended in divided rule.)
1200–1085	XX	
1085–945	XXI	Third Intermediate Period
945–745	XXII	(Revival of prosperity and restoration of cults.)
745–718	XXIII	
718–715	XXIV	

Date BC	Dynasty	Period
715–668	XXV	
664–525	XXVI	**Late Period**
525–404	XXVII	(Completion of Nile–Red Sea canal. Alexander the Great
404–399	XXVIII	reached Alexandria in 332 BC.)
399–380	XXIX	
380–343	XXX	
343–332	XXXI	

Chinese dynasties

Regnal dates	Name
c.22c–18c BC	Xia Dynasty
c.18c–12c BC	Shang or Yin Dynasty
c.1122/1066–771 BC	Western Chou Dynasty
771–256 BC	Eastern Chou Dynasty
403–222 BC	Warring States Period
222–206 BC	Qin (Ch'in) Dynasty
206 BC–AD 9	Western ('Former') Han Dynasty
AD 8–23	Interregnum (Wang Mang)
AD 25–220	Eastern Han Dynasty
AD 220–80	Three Kingdoms Period
AD 266–317	Western Jin (Chin) Dynasty
AD 317–420	Eastern Jin (Chin) Dynasty
AD 420–589	Southern Dynasties
581–618	Sui Dynasty
618–907	Tang Dynasty
907–60	Five Dynasties and Ten Kingdoms Period
960–1279	Song (Sung) Dynasty
1122–1234	Jin (Jurchen) Dynasty
1279–1368	Yuan (Mongol) Dynasty
1368–1644	Ming Dynasty
1644–1911	Qing (Manchu) Dynasty

Japanese emperors

The first 14 emperors (to Chuai) are regarded as legendary, and the regnal dates for the 15th to the 28th emperor (Senka), taken from the early Japanese chronicle, 'Nihon shoki', are not considered to be authentic.

The reign of an emperor is known by a name that is not necessarily the emperor's personal name.

Regnal dates	Name	Regnal dates	Name
660–585 BC	Jimmu	475–393 BC	Kosho
581–549 BC	Suizei	392–291 BC	Koan
549–511 BC	Annei	290–215 BC	Korei
510–477 BC	Itoku	214–158 BC	Kogen

Regnal dates	Name
158–98 BC	Kaika
97–30 BC	Sujin
29 BC–AD 70	Suinin
AD 71–130	Keiko
AD 131–90	Seimu
AD 192–200	Chuai
AD 270–310	Ojin
AD 313–99	Nintoku
AD 400–5	Richu
AD 406–10	Hanzei
AD 412–53	Ingyo
AD 453–6	Anko
AD 456–79	Yuryaku
AD 480–4	Seinei
AD 485–7	Kenzo
AD 488–98	Ninken
AD 498–506	Buretsu
507–31	Keitai
531–5	Ankan
535–9	Senka
539–71	Kimmei
572–85	Bidatsu
585–7	Yomei
587–92	Sushun
592–628	Suiko (Empress)
629–41	Jomei
642–5	Kogyoku (Empress)[1]
645–54	Kotoku
655–61	Saimei (Empress)[1]
662–71	Tenji
671–2	Kobun
673–86	Temmu
686–97	Jito (Empress)
697–707	Mommu
707–15	Gemmei (Empress)
715–24	Gensho (Empress)
724–49	Shomu
749–58	Koken (Empress)[2]
758–64	Junnin
764–70	Shotoku (Empress)[2]
770–81	Konin
781–806	Kammu
806–9	Heizei
809–23	Saga
823–33	Junna
833–50	Nimmyo

Regnal dates	Name
850–8	Montoku
858–76	Seiwa
876–84	Yozei
884–7	Koko
887–97	Uda
897–930	Daigo
930–46	Suzaku
946–67	Murakami
967–9	Reizei
969–84	En-yu
984–6	Kazan
986–1011	Ichijo
1011–16	Sanjo
1016–36	Go-Ichijo
1036–45	Go-Suzaku
1045–68	Go-Reizei
1068–72	Go-Sanjo
1072–86	Shirakawa
1086–1107	Horikawa
1107–23	Toba
1123–41	Sutoku
1141–55	Konoe
1155–8	Go-Shirakawa
1158–65	Nijo
1165–8	Rokujo
1168–80	Takakura
1180–3	Antoku
1183–98	Go-Toba
1198–1210	Tsuchimikado
1210–21	Juntoku
1221	Chukyo
1221–32	Go-Horikawa
1232–42	Shijo
1242–6	Go-Saga
1246–59	Go-Fukakusa
1259–74	Kameyama
1274–87	Go-Uda
1287–98	Fushimi
1298–1301	Go-Fushimi
1301–8	Go-Nijo
1308–18	Hanazono
1318–39	Go-Daigo
1339–68	Go-Murakami
1368–83	Chokei
1383–92	Go-Kameyama

Regnal dates	Name	Regnal dates	Name
■ *Northern Court*		1643–54	Go-Komyo
		1654–63	Go-Sai
1331–3	Kogon	1663–87	Reigen
1336–48	Komyo	1687–1709	Higashiyama
1348–51	Suko	1709–35	Nakamikado
1352–71	Go-Kogon	1735–47	Sakuramachi
1371–82	Go-Enyu	1747–62	Momozono
1382–1412	Go-Komatsu	1762–70	Go-Sakuramachi
1412–28	Shoko		(Empress)
1428–64	Go-Hanazono	1770–9	Go-Momozono
1464–1500	Go-Tsuchimikado	1779–1817	Kokaku
1500–26	Go-Kashiwabara	1817–46	Ninko
1526–57	Go-Nara	1846–66	Komei
1557–86	Ogimachi	1867–1912	Meiji
1586–1611	Go-Yozei	1912–26	Taisho
1611–29	Go-Mizuno-o	1926–89	Showa
1629–43	Meisho (Empress)	1989–	Heisei

[1] Same empress although reigns have different names.
[2] Same empress although reigns have different names.

Roman emperors

Dates of emperors overlap where there are periods of joint rule (eg Marcus Aurelius and Lucius Verus) and where the government of the empire divides between east and west.

Regnal dates	Name	Regnal dates	Name
27 BC–AD 14	Augustus (Caesar Augustus)	AD 193–211	Septemius Severus
		AD 198–217	Caracalla
AD 14–37	Tiberius	AD 209–12	Geta
AD 37–41	Caligula (Gaius Caesar)	AD 217–18	Macrinus
		AD 218–22	Elagabalus
AD 41–54	Claudius	AD 222–35	Alexander Severus
AD 54–68	Nero	AD 235–38	Maximin
AD 68–9	Galba	AD 238	Gordian I
AD 69	Otho	AD 238	Gordian II
AD 69	Vitellius	AD 238	Maximus
AD 69–79	Vespasian	AD 238	Balbinus
AD 79–81	Titus	AD 238–44	Gordian III
AD 81–96	Domitian	AD 244–9	Philip
AD 96–8	Nerva	AD 249–51	Decius
AD 98–117	Trajan	AD 251	Hostilian
AD 117–138	Hadrian	AD 251–3	Gallus
AD 138–161	Antoninus Pius	AD 253	Aemilian
AD 161–180	Marcus Aurelius	AD 253–60	Valerian
AD 161–9	Lucius Verus	AD 253–68	Gallienus
AD 176–192	Commodus	AD 268–9	Claudius II (the Goth)
AD 193	Pertinax	AD 269–70	Quintillus
AD 193	Didius Julianus	AD 270–5	Aurelian

Regnal dates	Name	Regnal dates	Name
AD 275–6	Tacitus	AD 375–83	Gratian (West)
AD 276	Florian	AD 375–92	Valentinian II (West)
AD 276–82	Probus	AD 379–95	Theodosius I
AD 282–3	Carus	AD 395–408	Arcadius (East)
AD 283–5	Carinus	AD 395–423	Honorius (West)
AD 283–4	Numerian	AD 408–50	Theodosius II (East)
AD 284–305	Diocletian (East)	AD 421–3	Constantius III (West)
AD 286–305	Maximian (West)	AD 423–55	Valentinian III (West)
AD 305–11	Galerius (East)	AD 450–7	Marcian (East)
AD 305–6	Constantius I	AD 455	Petronius Maximus (West)
AD 306–7	Severus (West)		
AD 306–12	Maxentius	AD 455–6	Avitus (West)
AD 306–37	Constantine I	AD 457–74	Leo I (East)
AD 308–24	Licinius (East)	AD 457–61	Majorian (West)
AD 337–40	Constantine II	AD 461–7	Libius Severus (West)
AD 337–50	Constans I	AD 467–72	Anthemius (West)
AD 337–61	Constantius II	AD 472–3	Olybrius (West)
AD 350–1	Magnentius	AD 474–80	Julius Nepos (West)
AD 360–3	Julian	AD 474	Leo II (East)
AD 364–75	Valentinian I (West)	AD 474–91	Zeno (East)
AD 364–78	Valens (East)	AD 475–6	Romulus Augustus (West)
AD 365–6	Procopius (East)		

Mughal emperors

The second Mughal emperor, Humayun, lost his throne in 1540, became a fugitive, and did not regain his title until 1555.

Regnal dates	Name	Regnal dates	Name
1526–30	Babur	1719	Rafid-ud-Darajat
1530–56	Humayun	1719	Rafi-ud-Daulat
1556–1605	Akbar I (the Great)	1719	Neku-siyar
1605–27	Jahangir	1719	Ibrahim
1627–58	Shah Jahan	1719–48	Muhammad Shah
1658–1707	Aurangzeb (Alamgir)	1748–54	Ahmad Shah
1707–12	Bahadur Shah I (Shah Alam I)	1754–9	Alamgir II
		1759–1806	Shah Alam II
1712–13	Jahandar Shah	1806–37	Akbar II
1713–19	Farruk-siyar	1837–57	Bahadur Shah II

European monarchs

Austria

The head of the German branch of the Habsburg Dynasty held the (elective) title of Holy Roman Emperor with few interruptions from medieval times until 1804, when the title 'Emperor of Austria' was adopted.

Regnal dates	Name
Habsburg Dynasty	
1440–93	Frederick III
1493–1519	Maximilian I
1519–58	Charles V
1558–64	Ferdinand I
1564–76	Maximilian II
1576–1612	Rudolf II
1612–19	Matthias
1619–37	Ferdinand II
1637–57	Ferdinand III
1658–1705	Leopold I
1705–11	Joseph I
1711–40	Charles VI
1740–2	*Interregnum*
1742–5	Charles VII
1745–65	Francis I
1765–90	Joseph II
1790–2	Leopold II
1792–1835	Francis II
1835–48	Ferdinand I
1848–1916	Francis Joseph
1916–18	Charles I

Belgium

Belgium became an independent kingdom in 1831. A national congress elected Prince Leopold of Saxe-Coburg as king.

Regnal dates	Name
1831–65	Léopold I
1865–1909	Léopold II
1909–34	Albert I
1934–51	Leopold III
1951–93	Baudouin
1993–	Albert II

Denmark

Regnal dates	Name
1448–81	Christian I
1481–1513	John
1513–23	Christian II
1523–34	Frederick I
1534–59	Christian III
1559–88	Frederick II
1588–1648	Christian IV
1648–70	Frederick III
1670–99	Christian V
1699–1730	Frederick IV
1730–46	Christian VI
1746–66	Frederick V
1766–1808	Christian VII
1808–39	Frederick VI
1839–48	Christian VIII
1848–63	Frederick VII
1863–1906	Christian IX
1906–12	Frederick VIII
1912–47	Christian X
1947–72	Frederick IX
1972–	Margrethe II

England

Regnal dates	Name
■ *West Saxon Kings*	
802–39	Egbert
839–58	Æthelwulf
858–60	Æthelbald
860–5	Æthelbert
866–71	Æthelred
871–99	Alfred
899–924	Edward (the Elder)
924–39	Athelstan
939–46	Edmund
946–55	Edred
955–9	Edwy
959–75	Edgar
975–8	Edward (the Martyr)
978–1016	Æthelred (the Unready)
1016	Edmund (Ironside)
■ *Danish Kings*	
1016–35	Knut (Canute)

Regnal dates	Name
1035–7	Harold *Regent*
1037–40	Harold I (Harefoot)
1040–2	Hardaknut
1042–66	Edward (the Confessor)
1066	Harold II

■ *House of Normandy*

1066–87	William I (the Conqueror)
1087–1100	William II (Rufus)
1100–35	Henry I

■ *House of Blois*

1135–54	Stephen

■ *House of Plantagenet*

1154–89	Henry II
1189–99	Richard I (Cœur de Lion)
1199–1216	John
1216–72	Henry III
1272–1307	Edward I
1307–27	Edward II
1327–77	Edward III
1377–99	Richard II

■ *House of Lancaster*

1399–1413	Henry IV
1413–22	Henry V
1422–61	Henry VI

■ *House of York*

1461–70	Edward IV

■ *House of Lancaster*

1470–1	Henry VI

■ *House of York*

1471–83	Edward IV
1483	Edward V
1483–5	Richard III

■ *House of Tudor*

1485–1509	Henry VII
1509–47	Henry VIII
1547–53	Edward VI
1553–8	Mary I
1558–1603	Elizabeth I

Finland

Finland was under Swedish control from the 13c until it was ceded to Russia in 1809 by the Treaty of Friedrichsham. Russian rulers then assumed the title of Grand Duke of Finland. In 1917 it became an independent monarchy. However in November 1918, after initially accepting the throne the previous month, Landgrave Frederick Charles of Hesse, the brother-in-law of the German Emperor William II, withdrew his acceptance because of the Armistice and the ensuing abdication of William II. The previous regent remained in power until a republic was declared in July 1919.

Regnal dates	Name
1918	Dr Pehr Evind Svinhufvud *Regent*
1918	Landgrave Frederick Charles of Hesse (withdrew acceptance)
1918–19	Dr Pehr Evind Svinhufvud

France

France became a republic in 1793, and an empire in 1804 under Napoleon Bonaparte. The monarchy was restored in 1814 and then once more dissolved in 1848.

Regnal dates	Name

■ *House of Capet*

987–996	Hugh Capet
996–1031	Robert II
1031–60	Henry I
1060–1108	Philip I
1108–37	Louis VI
1137–80	Louis VII
1180–1223	Philip II Augustus
1223–6	Louis VIII
1226–70	Louis IX
1270–85	Philip III
1285–1314	Philip IV
1314–16	Louis X
1316	John I
1316–22	Philip V
1322–8	Charles IV

■ *House of Valois*

Regnal dates	Name
1328–50	Philip VI
1350–64	John II
1364–80	Charles V
1380–1422	Charles VI
1422–61	Charles VII
1461–83	Louis XI
1483–98	Charles VIII
1498–1515	Louis XII
1515–47	Francis I
1547–59	Henry II
1559–60	Francis II
1560–74	Charles IX
1574–89	Henry III

■ *House of Bourbon*

Regnal dates	Name
1589–1610	Henry IV (of Navarre)
1610–43	Louis XIII
1643–1715	Louis XIV
1715–74	Louis XV
1774–93	Louis XVI
1793–1814	*Republican and Bonapartist regimes*
1814–24	Louis XVIII
1824–30	Charles X
1830–48	Louis-Philippe

Germany

Modern Germany was united under Prussia in 1871; it became a republic (1919) after World War I and the abdication of William II in 1918.

Regnal dates	Name
1871–88	William I
1888	Frederick
1888–1918	William II

Greece

In 1832 the Greek National Assembly elected Otto of Bavaria as King of modern Greece. In 1917 Constantine I abdicated the throne in favour of his son Alexander. In 1920 a plebiscite voted for his return. In 1922 he again abdicated. In 1923 the monarchy was deposed and a republic was proclaimed in 1924. In 1935 a plebiscite restored the monarchy until in 1967 a military junta staged a coup. The monarchy was formally abolished in 1973; Greece became a republic again in 1975.

Regnal dates	Name
1832–62	Otto of Bavaria
1863–1913	George I (of Denmark)
1913–17	Constantine I
1917–20	Alexander
1920–2	Constantine I
1922–3	George II
1924–35	*Republic*
1935–47	George II
1947–64	Paul
1964–7	Constantine II

Italy

Modern Italy became a united kingdom in 1861; it became a republic in 1946.

Regnal dates	Name
1861–78	Victor Emmanuel II
1878–1900	Humbert I
1900–46	Victor Emmanuel III
1946	Humbert II

Luxembourg

The Duchy of Luxembourg formally separated from the Netherlands in 1890.

Regnal dates	Name
1890–1905	Adolf of Nassau
1905–12	William
1912–19	Marie Adélaïde
1919–64	Charlotte
1964–2000	John
2000–	Henry

The Netherlands

The House of Orange were hereditary Stadholders and Captains-General of the Netherlands until the French Revolutionary Wars, taking the title 'King of the United Provinces of the Netherlands' after the post-Napoleonic settlement reunited the southern and northern provinces.

Regnal dates	Name
1572–84	William the Silent
1584–1625	Maurice
1625–47	Frederick Henry
1647–50	William II

Regnal dates	Name
1672–1702	William III
1747–51	William IV
1751–95	William V
1794–1813	*French Revolutionary and Bonapartist regimes*
1813–40	William I
1840–9	William II
1849–90	William III
1890–1948	Wilhelmina
1948–80	Juliana
1980–	Beatrix

Portugal

The Count of Portugal assumed the title 'King of Portugal' in 1139. From 1383 to 1385 the Portuguese throne was the subject of a dispute between John of Castile and John of Aviz. In 1826 Peter IV (I of Brazil) renounced his right to the Portuguese throne in order to remain in Brazil. His abdication was contingent upon his successor and daughter, Maria II, marrying her uncle, Miguel. In 1828 Miguel usurped the throne on his own behalf. In 1834 Miguel was deposed and Maria II was restored to the throne. In 1910 Manuel II was deposed and Portugal became a republic.

Regnal dates	Name
1112–85	Alfonso I
1185–1211	Sancho I
1211–23	Alfonso II
1223–45	Sancho II
1245–79	Alfonso III
1279–1325	Diniz
1325–57	Alfonso IV
1357–67	Peter I
1367–83	Ferdinand

■ *House of Avis*

1385–1433	John I
1433–8	Edward
1438–81	Alfonso V
1481–95	John II
1495–1521	Manuel I
1521–57	John III

Regnal dates	Name
1557–78	Sebastian

■ *House of Habsburg*

1580–98	Philip I (II of Spain)
1598–1621	Philip II (III of Spain)
1621–40	Philip III (IV of Spain)

■ *House of Braganza*

1640–56	John IV
1656–83	Alfonso VI
1683–1706	Peter II
1706–50	John V
1750–77	Joseph
1777–1816	Maria I
1777–86	Peter III (King Consort)
1816–26	John VI
1826	Peter IV (Emperor of Brazil, as Peter I, 1822–31)
1826–8	Maria II
1828–34	Miguel
1834–53	Maria II
1853–61	Peter V (Emperor of Brazil, as Peter II, 1831–89)
1861–89	Luis
1889–1908	Charles
1908–10	Manuel II

Russia

In 1610 Vasili Shuisky was deposed as Tsar and the throne remained vacant until the election of Michael Romanov in 1613. In 1682 a condition of the succession was that the two step-brothers, Ivan V and Peter I (the Great) should jointly be proclaimed as Tsars. In 1917 the empire was overthrown and Tsar Nicholas II was forced to abdicate.

Regnal dates	Name
1283–1303	Daniel
1303–25	Yuri
1325–41	Ivan I
1341–53	Simeon
1353–9	Ivan II
1359–89	Dimitri Donskoi
1389–1425	Vasili I

Regnal dates	Name
1425–62	Vasili II
1462–1505	Ivan III (the Great)
1505–33	Vasili III
1533–84	Ivan IV (the Terrible)
1584–98	Feodor I
1598–1605	Boris Godunov
1605	Feodor II
1605–6	Dimitri II
1606–10	Vasili IV Shuisky

■ *House of Romanov*

1613–45	Michael
1645–76	Alexei
1676–82	Feodor III
1682–96	Ivan V
1682–1725	Peter I (the Great)
1725–7	Catherine I
1727–30	Peter II
1730–40	Anne
1740–1	Ivan VI
1741–62	Elizabeth
1762	Peter III
1762–96	Catherine II (the Great)
1796–1801	Paul
1801–25	Alexander I
1825–55	Nicholas I
1855–81	Alexander II
1881–94	Alexander III
1894–1917	Nicholas II

Scotland

When the Athol line died out in 1290, the crown was awarded to John Balliol by adjudication of Edward I of England; Edward declared John Balliol to have forfeited the throne for contumacy in 1296 and took the government of Scotland into his own hands. In 1332 Edward Balliol, son of John Balliol, was crowned King of Scots; he was expelled a few months later but was restored and reigned 1333–6.

Regnal dates	Name
1005–34	Malcolm II

■ *House of Athol*

1034–40	Duncan I
1040–57	Macbeth

Regnal dates	Name
1057–8	Lulach
1058–93	Malcolm III
1093–4	Donald III (Donald Bane)
1094	Duncan II
1094–7	Donald III (Donald Bane)
1097–1107	Edgar
1107–24	Alexander I
1124–53	David I
1153–65	Malcolm IV
1165–1214	William I
1214–49	Alexander II
1249–86	Alexander III
1286–90	Margaret
1290–2	*Interregnum*

■ *House of Balliol*

1292–96	John Balliol
1296–1306	*Interregnum*

■ *House of Bruce*

1306–29	Robert I (the Bruce)
1329–71	David II

■ *House of Stewart*

1371–90	Robert II
1390–1406	Robert III
1406–37	James I
1437–60	James II
1460–88	James III
1488–1513	James IV
1513–42	James V
1542–67	Mary, Queen of Scots
1567–1625	James VI[1]

[1] In 1603, James VI succeeded Elizabeth I on the English throne (Union of the Crowns) and united the thrones of Scotland and England.

Spain

Philip V abdicated in favour of Luis in 1724, but returned to the throne in the same year following Luis' death. After the French invasion of Spain in 1808, Napoleon set up Joseph Bonaparte as king. In 1814 Ferdinand was restored to the crown. In 1868 a revolution deposed Isabella II. In 1870 Amadeus of Savoy was elected as king. In 1873 he resigned the throne and a temporary republic was formed. In 1874 Alfonso XII restored the Bourbon dynasty to the throne. In 1931 Alfonso XIII was deposed and a republican constitution was proclaimed. From 1939 Franco ruled Spain under a dictatorship until his death in 1975 and the restoration of King Juan Carlos.

Regnal dates	Name
■ *House of Habsburg*	
1516–56	Charles I (Emperor Charles V)
1556–98	Philip II
1598–1621	Philip III
1621–65	Philip IV
1665–1700	Charles II
■ *House of Bourbon*	
1700–24	Philip V
1724	Luis
1724–46	Philip V
1746–59	Ferdinand VI
1759–88	Charles III
1788–1808	Charles IV
1808	Ferdinand VII
1808–14	*Bonapartist regime*
1814–33	Ferdinand VII
1833–68	Isabella II
1870–3	Amadeus of Savoy
1873–4	*First Republic*
1874–85	Alfonso XII
1886–1931	Alfonso XIII
1931–75	*Second Republic and Franco dictatorship*
1975–	Juan Carlos

Sweden

Sigismund, a Catholic, was driven from the throne by the Protestant nobility, led by his uncle, who became regent before accepting the crown in 1604. On Christina's abdication in 1654, she nominated her cousin as heir. In 1720, Ulrika Eleonora abdicated in favour of her husband, Frederick of Hesse, who died without heirs, when the throne passed to Adolf Frederick, whose succession was imposed by Russia as a term of an armistice. The childless Charles XIII was succeeded by the French

marshal Jean Baptiste Jules Bernadotte, selected as heir by the Diet in 1810.

Regnal dates	Name
■ *House of Vasa*	
1523–60	Gustav I
1560–8	Erik XIV
1568–92	John III
1592–9	Sigismund
1599–1604	*Regency*
1604–11	Charles IX
1611–32	Gustav II Adolf
1632–54	Christina
■ *House of Zweibrucken*	
1654–60	Charles X Gustav
1660–97	Charles XI
1697–1718	Charles XII
1718–20	Ulrika Eleonora
■ *House of Hesse*	
1720–51	Fredrick
■ *House of Oldenburg-Holstein-Gottorp*	
1751–71	Adolf Fredrick
1771–92	Gustav III
1792–1809	Gustav IV Adolf
1809–18	Charles XIII
■ *House of Bernadotte*	
1818–44	Charles XIV John
1844–59	Oscar I
1859–72	Charles XV
1872–1907	Oscar II
1907–50	Gustav V
1950–73	Gustav VI Adolf
1973–	Carl XVI Gustav

United Kingdom

Regnal dates	Name
■ *House of Stuart*	
1603–25	James I (VI of Scotland)
1625–49	Charles I
■ *Commonwealth and Protectorate*	
1649–53	*Council of State*
1653–8	Oliver Cromwell *Lord Protector*
1658–9	Richard Cromwell *Lord Protector*

Regnal dates	Name
■ *House of Stuart (restored)*	
1660–85	Charles II
1685–8	James II (VII of Scotland)
1689–94	William III (*jointly with Mary II*)
1694–1702	William III (*alone*)
1702–14	Anne
■ *House of Hanover*	
1714–27	George I
1727–60	George II
1760–1820	George III
1820–30	George IV
1830–7	William IV
1837–1901	Victoria
■ *House of Saxe-Coburg-Gotha*	
1901–10	Edward VII

Regnal dates	Name
■ *House of Windsor*	
1910–36	George V
1936	Edward VIII
1936–52	George VI
1952–	Elizabeth II

Roman Kings

The founding of Rome by Romulus is a Roman literary tradition.

Regnal dates	Name
753–715 BC	Romulus
715–673 BC	Numa Pompilius
673–642 BC	Tullus Hostilius
642–616 BC	Ancus Marcius
616–578 BC	Tarquinius Priscus
578–534 BC	Servius Tullius
534–509 BC	Tarquinius Superbus

Emperors of the Holy Roman Empire

Regnal dates	Name	Regnal dates	Name
800–14	Charles I (Charlemagne)	1081–93	Hermann [24]
		1093–1101	Conrad [24]
814–40	Louis I (the Pious)	1106–25	Henry V
840–3	*Civil war*	1125–37	Lothair II
843–55	Lothair I	1138–52	Conrad III [4]
855–75	Louis II	1152–90	Frederick I (Barbarossa)
875–7	Charles II (the Bald)	1190–7	Henry VI
877–81	*Interregnum*	1198–1214	Otto IV
881–7	Charles III (the Fat)	1198–1208	Philip [24]
887–91	*Interregnum*	1215–50	Frederick II
891–4	Guido of Spoleto	1246–7	Henry Raspe [24]
892–8	Lambert of Spoleto [1]	1247–56	William of Holland [24]
896–9	Arnulf [2]	1250–4	Conrad IV [4]
901–5	Louis III	1254–73	*Great Interregnum*
905–24	Berengar	1257–72	Richard [24]
911–18	Conrad I [24]	1257–75	Alfonso (Alfonso X of Castile) [24]
919–36	Henry I (the Fowler) [4]		
936–73	Otto I (the Great)	1273–91	Rudolf I [4]
973–83	Otto II	1292–8	Adolf [4]
983–1002	Otto III	1298–1308	Albert I [4]
1002–24	Henry II (the Saint)	1308–13	Henry VII
1024–39	Conrad II	1314–26	Frederick (III) [34]
1039–56	Henry III (the Black)	1314–46	Louis IV
1056–1106	Henry IV	1346–78	Charles IV
1077–80	Rudolf [24]	1378–1400	Wenceslas [4]

Regnal dates	Name	Regnal dates	Name
1400–10	Rupert[4]	1637–57	Ferdinand III[4]
1410–37	Sigismund	1658–1705	Leopold I[4]
1438–9	Albert II[4]	1705–11	Joseph I[4]
1440–93	Frederick III	1711–40	Charles VI[4]
1493–1519	Maximilian I[4]	1740–2	*Interregnum*
1519–56	Charles V[4]	1742–5	Charles VII[4]
1556–64	Ferdinand I[4]	1745–65	Francis I[4]
1564–76	Maximilian II[4]	1765–90	Joseph II[4]
1576–1612	Rudolf II[4]	1790–2	Leopold II[4]
1612–19	Matthias[4]	1792–1806	Francis II[4]
1619–37	Ferdinand II[4]		

[1] Co-emperor

[2] Rival

[3] Co-regent

[4] Ruler not crowned at Rome; therefore, strictly speaking, only King of Germany

Popes

Antipopes (those who claimed to be pope in opposition to those canonically chosen) are given in square brackets.

All dates are AD.

until c.64	Peter	259–68	Dionysius
c.64–c.76	Linus	269–74	Felix I
c.76–c.90	Anacletus	275–83	Eutychianus
c.90–c.99	Clement I	283–96	Caius
c.99–c.105	Evaristus	296–304	Marcellinus
c.105–c.117	Alexander I	308–9	Marcellus I
c.117–c.127	Sixtus I	310	Eusebius
c.127–c.137	Telesphorus	311–14	Miltiades
c.137–c.140	Hyginus	314–35	Sylvester I
c.140–c.154	Pius I	336	Mark
c.154–c.166	Anicetus	337–52	Julius I
c.166–c.175	Soter	352–66	Liberius
175–89	Eleutherius	[355–65	Felix (II)]
189–98	Victor I	366–84	Damasus I
198–217	Zephyrinus	[366–7	Ursinus]
217–22	Callistus I	384–99	Siricius
[217–c.235	Hippolytus]	399–401	Anastasius I
222–30	Urban I	402–17	Innocent I
230–5	Pontian	417–18	Zosimus
235–6	Anterus	418–22	Boniface I
236–50	Fabian	[418–19	Eulalius]
251–3	Cornelius	422–32	Celestine I
[251–c.258	Novatian]	432–40	Sixtus III
253–4	Lucius I	440–61	Leo I
254–7	Stephen I	461–8	Hilarius
257–8	Sixtus II	468–83	Simplicius

483–92	Felix III (II)	741–52	Zacharias
492–6	Gelasius I	752	Stephen II (*not consecrated*)
496–8	Anastasius II		
498–514	Symmachus	752–7	Stephen II (III)
[498, 501–5	Laurentius]	757–67	Paul I
514–23	Hormisdas	[767–9	Constantine (II)]
523–6	John I	[768	Philip]
526–30	Felix IV (III)	768–72	Stephen III (IV)
530–2	Boniface II	772–95	Adrian I
[530	Dioscorus]	795–816	Leo III
533–5	John II	816–17	Stephen IV (V)
535–6	Agapetus I	817–24	Paschal I
536–7	Silverius	824–7	Eugenius II
537–55	Vigilius	827	Valentine
556–61	Pelagius I	827–44	Gregory IV
561–74	John III	[844	John]
575–9	Benedict I	844–7	Sergius II
579–90	Pelagius II	847–55	Leo IV
590–604	Gregory I	855–8	Benedict III
604–6	Sabinianus	[855	Anastasius (III)]
607	Boniface III	858–67	Nicholas I
608–15	Boniface IV	867–72	Adrian II
615–18	Deusdedit *or* Adeodatus I	872–82	John VIII
619–25	Boniface V	882–4	Marinus I
625–38	Honorius I	884–5	Adrian III
640	Severinus	885–91	Stephen V (VI)
640–2	John IV	891–6	Formosus
642–9	Theodore I	896	Boniface VI
649–55	Martin I	896–7	Stephen VI (VII)
654–7	Eugenius I[1]	897	Romanus
657–72	Vitalian	897	Theodore II
672–6	Adeodatus II	898–900	John IX
676–8	Donus	900–3	Benedict IV
678–81	Agatho	903	Leo V
682–3	Leo II	[903–4	Christopher]
684–5	Benedict II	904–11	Sergius III
685–6	John V	911–13	Anastasius III
686–7	Conon	913–14	Lando
[687	Theodore]	914–28	John X
[687–92	Paschal]	928	Leo VI
687–701	Sergius I	928–31	Stephen VII (VIII)
701–5	John VI	931–5	John XI
705–7	John VII	936–9	Leo VII
708	Sisinnius	939–42	Stephen VIII (IX)
708–15	Constantine	942–6	Marinus II
715–31	Gregory II	946–55	Agapetus II
731–41	Gregory III	955–64	John XII

[963–5	Leo (VIII)]
964–6	Benedict V
965–72	John XIII
973–4	Benedict VI
[974, 984–5	Boniface (VII)]
974–83	Benedict VII
983–4	John XIV
985–96	John XV
996–9	Gregory V
[997–8	John (XVI)]
999–1003	Sylvester II
1003	John XVII
1004–9	John XVIII
1009–12	Sergius IV
1012–24	Benedict VIII
[1012	Gregory (VI)]
1024–32	John XIX
1032–44	Benedict IX
1045	Sylvester III
1045	Benedict IX (second pontificate)
1045–6	Gregory VI
1046–7	Clement II
1047–8	Benedict IX (third pontificate)
1048	Damasus II
1048–54	Leo IX
1055–7	Victor II
1057–8	Stephen IX (X)
[1058–9	Benedict (X)]
1059–61	Nicholas II
1061–73	Alexander II
[1061–72	Honorius (II)]
1073–85	Gregory VII
[1080, 1084–1100	Clement (III)]
1086–7	Victor III
1088–99	Urban II
1099–1118	Paschal II
[1100–2	Theodoric]
[1102	Albert]
[1105–11	Sylvester (IV)]
1118–19	Gelasius II
[1118–21	Gregory (VIII)]
1119–24	Callistus II
1124–30	Honorius II
[1124	Celestine (II)]
1130–43	Innocent II
[1130–8	Anacletus (II)]
[1138	Victor (IV)][2]
1143–4	Celestine II
1144–5	Lucius II
1145–53	Eugenius III
1153–4	Anastasius IV
1154–9	Adrian IV
1159–81	Alexander III
[1159–64	Victor (IV)][2]
[1164–8	Paschal (III)]
[1168–78	Callistus (III)]
[1179–80	Innocent (III)]
1181–5	Lucius III
1185–7	Urban III
1187	Gregory VIII
1187–91	Clement III
1191–8	Celestine III
1198–1216	Innocent III
1216–27	Honorius III
1227–41	Gregory IX
1241	Celestine IV
1243–54	Innocent IV
1254–61	Alexander IV
1261–4	Urban IV
1265–8	Clement IV
1271–6	Gregory X
1276	Innocent V
1276	Adrian V
1276–7	John XXI[3]
1277–80	Nicholas III
1281–5	Martin IV
1285–7	Honorius IV
1288–92	Nicholas IV
1294	Celestine V
1294–1303	Boniface VIII
1303–4	Benedict XI
1305–14	Clement V
1316–34	John XXII
[1328–30	Nicholas (V)]
1334–42	Benedict XII
1342–52	Clement VI
1352–62	Innocent VI
1362–70	Urban V
1370–8	Gregory XI
1378–89	Urban VI
[1378–94	Clement (VII)]
1389–1404	Boniface IX

[1394–1423	Benedict (XIII)]	1605	Leo XI
1404–6	Innocent VII	1605–21	Paul V
1406–15	Gregory XII	1621–3	Gregory XV
[1409–10	Alexander (V)]	1623–44	Urban VIII
[1410–15	John (XXIII)]	1644–55	Innocent X
1417–31	Martin V	1655–67	Alexander VII
[1423–9	Clement (VIII)]	1667–9	Clement IX
[1425–30	Benedict (XIV)]	1670–6	Clement X
1431–47	Eugenius IV	1676–89	Innocent XI
[1439–49	Felix (V)]	1689–91	Alexander VIII
1447–55	Nicholas V	1691–1700	Innocent XII
1455–8	Callistus III	1700–21	Clement XI
1458–64	Pius II	1721–4	Innocent XIII
1464–71	Paul II	1724–30	Benedict XIII
1471–84	Sixtus IV	1730–40	Clement XII
1484–92	Innocent VIII	1740–58	Benedict XIV
1492–1503	Alexander VI	1758–69	Clement XIII
1503	Pius III	1769–74	Clement XIV
1503–13	Julius II	1775–99	Pius VI
1513–21	Leo X	1800–23	Pius VII
1522–3	Adrian VI	1823–9	Leo XII
1523–34	Clement VII	1829–30	Pius VIII
1534–49	Paul III	1831–46	Gregory XVI
1550–5	Julius III	1846–78	Pius IX
1555	Marcellus II	1878–1903	Leo XIII
1555–9	Paul IV	1903–14	Pius X
1559–65	Pius IV	1914–22	Benedict XV
1566–72	Pius V	1922–39	Pius XI
1572–85	Gregory XIII	1939–58	Pius XII
1585–90	Sixtus V	1958–63	John XXIII
1590	Urban VII	1963–78	Paul VI
1590–1	Gregory XIV	1978	John Paul I
1591	Innocent IX	1978–2005	John Paul II
1592–1605	Clement VIII	2005–	Benedict XVI

[1] Elected during the banishment of Martin I.
[2] Different individuals.
[3] There was no John XX.

Political leaders 1905–2007

Countries and organizations are listed alphabetically, with former or alternative names given in parentheses. Rulers are named chronologically since 1905 or (for new nations) since independence. For some major English-speaking nations, relevant details are also given of pre–20c rulers, along with a note of any political affiliation. The list does not distinguish successive terms of office by a single ruler. Listings complete to end of April 2007.

There is no universally agreed way of transliterating proper names in non-Roman alphabets; variations from the spellings given are therefore to be expected, especially in the case of Arabic rulers. Minor variations in the titles adopted by heads of state, or in the name of an administration, are not given; these occur most notably in countries under military rule.

Australia

Head of State: British monarch, represented by Governor-General

Prime Minister

1904–5	George Houston Reid *Free*
1905–8	Alfred Deakin *Prot*
1908–9	Andrew Fisher *Lab*
1909–10	Alfred Deakin *Fusion*
1910–13	Andrew Fisher *Lab*
1913–14	Joseph Cook *Lib*
1914–15	Andrew Fisher *Lab*
1915–17	William Morris Hughes *Nat Lab*
1917–23	William Morris Hughes *Nat*
1923–9	Stanley Melbourne Bruce *Nat*
1929–32	James Henry Scullin *Lab*
1932–9	Joseph Aloysius Lyons *Un*
1939	Earle Christmas Page *Co*
1939–41	Robert Gordon Menzies *Un*
1941	Arthur William Fadden *Co*
1941–5	John Joseph Curtin *Lab*
1945	Francis Michael Forde *Lab*
1945–9	Joseph Benedict Chifley *Lab*
1949–66	Robert Gordon Menzies *Lib*
1966–7	Harold Edward Holt *Lib*
1967–8	John McEwen *Co*
1968–71	John Grey Gorton *Lib*
1971–2	William McMahon *Lib*
1972–5	Edward Gough Whitlam *Lab*
1975–83	John Malcolm Fraser *Lib*
1983–91	Robert James Lee Hawke *Lab*
1991–6	Paul Keating *Lab*
1996–	John Howard *Lib*

Co = Country   Con = Conservative
Free = Free Trade   Lab = Labor
Lib = Liberal   Nat = Nationalist
Nat Lab = National Labor
Prot = Protectionist   Un = United

Austria

President

1918–20	Karl Sätz
1920–8	Michael Hainisch
1928–38	Wilhelm Miklas
1938–45	*German rule*
1945–50	Karl Renner
1950–7	Theodor Körner
1957–65	Adolf Schärf
1965–74	Franz Jonas
1974–86	Rudolf Kirchsläger
1986–92	Kurt Waldheim
1992–2004	Thomas Klestil
2004–	Heinz Fischer

Chancellor

1918–20	Karl Renner
1920–1	Michael Mayr
1921–2	Johann Schober
1922	Walter Breisky
1922	Johann Schober
1922–4	Ignaz Seipel
1924–6	Rudolph Ramek
1926–9	Ignaz Seipel
1929–30	Ernst Streeruwitz
1930	Johann Schober
1930	Carl Vaugoin
1930–1	Otto Ender
1931–2	Karl Buresch
1932–4	Engelbert Dollfuss
1934–8	Kurt von Schuschnigg
1938–45	*German rule*
1945	Karl Renner
1945–53	Leopold Figl
1953–61	Julius Raab
1961–4	Alfons Gorbach
1964–70	Josef Klaus
1970–83	Bruno Kreisky
1983–6	Fred Sinowatz
1986–97	Franz Vranitzky
1997–2000	Viktor Klima
2000–7	Wolfgang Schüssel
2007–	Alfred Gusenbauer

Belgium

Monarch

1831–65	Léopold I
1865–1909	Léopold II
1909–34	Albert I
1934–44	Léopold III
1944–50	Prince Charles *Regent*
1950–93	Baudouin I *Regent 1950–1*
1993–	Albert II

Prime Minister

1899–1907	Paul de Smet de Nayer
1907–8	Jules de Trooz
1908–11	Frans Schollaert
1911–18	Charles de Broqueville
1918	Gerhard Cooreman
1918–20	Léon Delacroix
1920–1	Henri Carton de Wiart
1921–5	Georges Theunis
1925	Alois van de Vyvere
1925–6	Prosper Poullet
1926–31	Henri Jaspar
1931–2	Jules Renkin
1932–4	Charles de Broqueville
1934–5	Georges Theunis
1935–7	Paul van Zeeland
1937–8	Paul Émile Janson
1938–9	Paul Spaak
1939–45	Hubert Pierlot
1945–6	Achille van Acker
1946	Paul Spaak
1946	Achille van Acker
1946–7	Camille Huysmans
1947–9	Paul Spaak
1949–50	Gaston Eyskens
1950	Jean Pierre Duvieusart
1950–2	Joseph Pholien
1952–4	Jean van Houtte
1954–8	Achille van Acker
1958–61	Gaston Eyskens
1961–5	Théodore Lefèvre
1965–6	Pierre Harmel
1966–8	Paul Vanden Boeynants
1968–72	Gaston Eyskens
1973–4	Edmond Leburton
1974–8	Léo Tindemans
1978	Paul Vanden Boeynants
1979–81	Wilfried Martens
1981	Marc Eyskens
1981–91	Wilfried Martens
1992–9	Jean-Luc Dehaene
1999–	Guy Verhofstadt

Canada

Head of State: British monarch, represented by Governor General

Prime Minister

1896–1911	Wilfrid Laurier *Lib*
1911–20	Robert Borden *Con/Un*
1920–1	Arthur Meighen *Un/Con*
1921–6	William Lyon Mackenzie King *Lib*
1926	Arthur Meighen *Con*
1926–30	William Lyon Mackenzie King *Lib*
1930–5	Richard Bedford Bennett *Con*
1935–48	William Lyon Mackenzie King *Lib*
1948–57	Louis St Laurent *Lib*
1957–63	John George Diefenbaker *Con*
1963–8	Lester Bowles Pearson *Lib*
1968–79	Pierre Elliott Trudeau *Lib*
1979–80	Joseph Clark *Con*
1980–4	Pierre Elliott Trudeau *Lib*
1984	John Turner *Lib*
1984–93	Brian Mulroney *Con*
1993	Kim Campbell *Con*
1993–2004	Jean Chrétien *Lib*
2004–6	Paul Martin *Lib*
2006–	Stephen Harper *Con*

Con = Conservative   Lib = Liberal
Un = Unionist

China

■ Qing (Ch'ing) dynasty
Emperor

| 1875–1908 | Guangxu (Kuang-hsü) |
| 1908–12 | Xuantong (Hsüan-t'ung) |

Prime Minister

1903–11	Prince Qing (Ch'ing)
1912	Lu Zhengxiang (Lu Cheng-hsiang)
1912	Yuan Shikai (Yüan Shih-k'ai)

■ **Republic of China**

President

1912	Sun Yat-sen (Sun Yixian) *Provisional*
1912–16	Yuan Shikai (Yüan Shih-k'ai)
1916–17	Li Yuanhong (Li Yüan-hung)
1917–18	Feng Guozhang (Feng Kuo-chang)
1918–22	Xu Shichang (Hsü Shih-ch'ang)
1921–5	Sun Yat-sen *Canton Administration*
1922–3	Li Yuanhong
1923–4	Cao Kun (Ts'ao K'un)
1924–6	Duan Qirui (Tuan Ch'i-jui)
1926–7	*Civil Disorder*
1927–8	Zhang Zuolin (Chang Tso-lin)
1928–31	Chiang K'ai-shek (Jiang Jieshi)
1931–2	Cheng Minxu (Ch'eng Ming-hsü) *Acting*
1932–43	Lin Sen (Lin Sen)
1940–4	Wang Jingwei (Wang Ching-wei) *In Japanese-occupied territory*
1943–9	Chiang K'ai-shek
1945–9	*Civil War*
1949	Li Zongren (Li Tsung-jen)

Premier

1912	Tang Shaoyi (T'ang Shao-i)
1912–13	Zhao Bingjun (Chao Ping-chün)
1912–13	Xiong Xiling (Hsiung Hsi-ling)
1914	Sun Baoyi (Sun Pao-chi)
1915–16	*no Premier*
1916–17	Duan Qirui (Tuan Ch'i-jui)
1917–18	Wang Shizhen (Wang Shih-chen)
1918	Duan Qirui
1918–19	Qian Nengxun (Ch'ien Neng-hsün)
1919	Gong Xinzhan (Kung Hsin-chan)
1919–20	Jin Yunpeng (Chin Yün-p'eng)
1920	Sa Zhenbing (Sa Chen-ping)
1920–1	Jun Yunpeng
1921–2	Liang Shiyi (Liang Shih-i)
1922	Zhou Ziqi (Chow Tzu-ch'i) *Acting*
1922	Yan Huiqing (Yen Hui-ch'ing)
1922	Wang Chonghui (Wang Ch'ung-hui)
1922–3	Wang Daxie (Wang Ta-hsieh)
1923	Zhang Shaozeng (Chang Shao-ts'eng)
1923–4	Gao Lingwei (Kao Ling-wei)
1924	Sun Baoyi (Sun Pao-ch'i)
1924	Gu Weijun (Ku Wei-chün) *Acting*
1924	Yan Huiqing
1924–5	Huang Fu (Huang Fu) *Acting*
1925	Duan Qirui
1925–6	Xu Shiying (Hsü Shih-ying)
1926	Jia Deyao (Chia Te-yao)
1926	Hu Weide (Hu Wei-te)
1926	Yan Huiqing
1926	Du Xigui (Tu Hsi-kuei)
1926–7	Gu Weijun
1927	*Civil Disorder*

President of the Executive Council

1928–30	Tan Yankai (T'an Yen-k'ai)
1930	T V Soong (Sung Tzu-wen) *Acting*
1930	Wang Jingwei (Wang Ching-wei)
1930–1	Chiang K'ai-shek
1931–2	Sun Fo (Sun Fo)
1932–5	Wang Jingwei
1935–7	Chiang K'ai-shek
1937–8	Wang Chonghui (Wang Ch'ung-hui) *Acting*
1938–9	Kong Xiangxi (K'ung Hsiang-hsi)
1939–44	Chiang K'ai-shek

1944–7	T V Soong
1945–9	*Civil War*
1948	Wang Wenhao (Wong Wen-hao)
1948–9	Sun Fo
1949	He Yingqin (Ho Ying-ch'in)
1949	Yan Xishan (Yen Hsi-shan)

■ People's Republic of China
President

1949–59	Mao Zedong (Mao Tse-tung)
1959–68	Liu Shaoqi (Liu Shao-ch'i)
1968–75	Dong Biwu (Tung Pi-wu)
1975–6	Zhu De (Chu Te)
1976–8	Sung Qingling (Sung Ch'ing-ling)
1978–83	Ye Jianying (Yeh Chien-ying)
1983–8	Li Xiannian (Li Hsien-nien)
1988–93	Yang Shangkun (Yang Shang-k'un)
1993–2003	Jiang Zemin (Chiang Tse-min)
2003–	Hu Jintao

Prime Minister

1949–76	Zhou Enlai (Chou En-lai)
1976–80	Hua Guofeng (Huo Kuo-feng)
1980–7	Zhao Ziyang (Chao Tzu-yang)
1987–98	Li Peng (Li P'eng)
1998–2003	Zhu Rongji
2003–	Wen Jiabao

Communist Party
Chairman

1935–76	Mao Zedong
1976–81	Hua Guofeng
1981–2	Hu Yaobang (Hu Yao-pang)

General Secretary

1982–7	Hu Yaobang
1987–9	Zhao Ziyang
1989–2002	Jiang Zemin
2002–	Hu Jintao

Commonwealth
Secretary-General

1965–75	Arnold Smith *Canada*
1975–90	Shridath Ramphal *Guyana*
1990–2000	Emeka Anyaoku *Nigeria*
2000–	Donald C McKinnon *New Zealand*

Denmark
Monarch

1863–1906	Christian IX
1906–12	Frederick VIII
1912–47	Christian X
1947–72	Frederick IX
1972–	Margrethe II

Prime Minister

1901–5	J H Deuntzer
1905–8	J C Christensen
1908–9	Niels Neergaard
1909	Ludvig Holstein-Ledreborg
1909–10	C Th Zahle
1910–13	Klaus Berntsen
1913–20	C Th Zahle
1920	Otto Liebe
1920	M P FrIls
1920–4	Niels Neergaard
1924–6	Thorvald Stauning
1926–9	Thomas Madsen-Mygdal
1929–42	Thorvald Stauning
1942	Wilhelm Buhl
1942–3	Erik Scavenius
1943–5	*No government*
1945	Wilhelm Buhl
1945–7	Knud Kristensen
1947–50	Hans Hedtoft
1950–3	Erik Eriksen
1953–5	Hans Hedtoft
1955–60	Hans Christian Hansen
1960–2	Viggo Kampmann
1962–8	Jens Otto Krag
1968–71	Hilmar Baunsgaard
1971–2	Jens Otto Krag
1972–3	Anker Jørgensen
1973–5	Poul Hartling
1975–82	Anker Jørgensen
1982–93	Poul Schlüter

1993–2001	Poul Nyrup Rasmussen
2001–	Anders Fogh Rasmussen

European Commission

President

1967–70	Jean Rey *Belgium*
1970–2	Franco Malfatti *Italy*
1972–3	Sicco Mansholt *Netherlands*
1973–7	François-Xavier Ortoli *France*
1977–81	Roy Jenkins *UK*
1981–5	Gaston Thorn *Luxembourg*
1985–95	Jacques Delors *France*
1995–9	Jacques Santer *Luxembourg*
1999–2004	Romano Prodi *Italy*
2004–	José Manuel Barroso *Portugal*

Finland

President

1919–25	Kaarlo Juho Ståhlberg
1925–31	Lauri Kristian Relander
1931–7	Pehr Evind Svinhufvud
1937–40	Kyösti Kallio
1940–4	Risto Ryti
1944–6	Carl Gustaf Mannerheim
1946–56	Juho Kusti Paasikivi
1956–81	Urho Kekkonen
1982–94	Mauno Koivisto
1994–2000	Martti Ahtisaari
2000–	Tarja Halonen

Prime Minister

1917–18	Pehr Evind Svinhufvud
1918	Juho Kusti Paasikivi
1918–19	Lauri Johannes Ingman
1919	Kaarlo Castrén
1919–20	Juho Vennola
1920–1	Rafael Erich
1921–2	Juho Vennola
1922	Aino Kaarlo Cajander
1922–4	Kyösti Kallio
1924	Aino Kaarlo Cajander
1924–5	Lauri Johannes Ingman
1925	Antti Agaton Tulenheimo

1925–6	Kyösti Kallio
1926–7	Väinö Tanner
1927–8	Juho Emil Sunila
1928–9	Oskari Mantere
1929–30	Kyösti Kallio
1930–1	Pehr Evind Svinhufvud
1931–2	Juhu Emil Sunila
1932–6	Toivo Kivimäki
1936–7	Kyösti Kallio
1937–9	Aino Kaarlo Cajander
1939–41	Risto Ryti
1941–3	Johann Rangell
1943–4	Edwin Linkomies
1944	Andreas Hackzell
1944	Urho Jonas Castrén
1944–5	Juho Kusti Paasikivi
1946–8	Mauno Pekkala
1948–50	Karl August Fagerholm
1950–3	Urho Kekkonen
1953–4	Sakari Tuomioja
1954	Ralf Törngren
1954–6	Urho Kekkonen
1956–7	Karl August Fagerholm
1957	Väinö Johannes Sukselainen
1957–8	Rainer von Fieandt
1958	Reino Ilsakki Kuuskoski
1958–9	Karl August Fagerholm
1959–61	Väinö Johannes Sukselainen
1961–2	Martti Miettunen
1962–3	Ahti Karjalainen
1963–4	Reino Ragnar Lehto
1964–6	Johannes Virolainen
1966–8	Rafael Paasio
1968–70	Mauno Koivisto
1970	Teuvo Ensio Aura
1970–1	Ahti Karjalainen
1971–2	Teuvo Ensio Aura
1972	Rafael Paasio
1972–5	Kalevi Sorsa
1975	Keijo Antero Liinamaa
1975–7	Martti Miettunen
1977–9	Kalevi Sorsa
1979–82	Mauno Koivisto
1982–7	Kalevi Sorsa
1987–91	Harri Holkeri
1991–5	Esko Aho

1995–2003	Paavo Lipponen
2003	Anneli Jääteenmaki
2003–	Matti Vanhanen

France

President
■ Third Republic
1899–1906	Emile Loubet
1906–13	Armand Fallières
1913–20	Raymond Poincaré
1920	Paul Deschanel
1920–4	Alexandre Millerand
1924–31	Gaston Doumergue
1931–2	Paul Doumer
1932–40	Albert Lebrun

■ Fourth Republic
| 1947–54 | Vincent Auriol |
| 1954–8 | René Coty |

■ Fifth Republic
1958–69	Charles de Gaulle
1969–74	Georges Pompidou
1974–81	Valéry Giscard d'Estaing
1981–95	François Mitterrand
1995–2007	Jacques Chirac
2007–	Nicolas Sarkozy

Prime Minister
■ Third Republic
1902–5	Emile Combes
1905–6	Maurice Rouvier
1906	Jean Sarrien
1906–9	Georges Clemenceau
1909–11	Aristide Briand
1911	Ernest Monis
1911–12	Joseph Caillaux
1912–13	Raymond Poincaré
1913	Aristide Briand
1913	Jean Louis Barthou
1913–14	Gaston Doumergue
1914	Alexandre Ribot
1914–15	René Viviani
1915–17	Aristide Briand
1917	Alexandre Ribot
1917	Paul Painlevé
1917–20	Georges Clemenceau
1920	Alexandre Millerand

1920–1	Georges Leygues
1921–2	Aristide Briand
1922–4	Raymond Poincaré
1924	Frédéric François-Marsal
1924–5	Édouard Herriot
1925	Paul Painlevé
1925–6	Aristide Briand
1926	Édouard Herriot
1926–9	Raymond Poincaré
1929	Aristide Briand
1929–30	André Tardieu
1930	Camille Chautemps
1930	André Tardieu
1930–1	Théodore Steeg
1931–2	Pierre Laval
1932	André Tardieu
1932	Édouard Herriot
1932–3	Joseph Paul-Boncour
1933	Édouard Daladier
1933	Albert Sarrault
1933–4	Camille Chautemps
1934	Édouard Daladier
1934	Gaston Doumergue
1934–5	Pierre-Étienne Flandin
1935	Fernand Bouisson
1935–6	Pierre Laval
1936	Albert Sarrault
1936–7	Léon Blum
1937–8	Camille Chautemps
1938	Léon Blum
1938–40	Édouard Daladier
1940	Paul Reynaud
1940	Philippe Pétain

■ Vichy Government
| 1940–4 | Philippe Pétain |

■ Provisional Government of the French Republic
1944–6	Charles de Gaulle
1946	Félix Gouin
1946	Georges Bidault

■ Fourth Republic
1946–7	Léon Blum
1947	Paul Ramadier
1947–8	Robert Schuman
1948	André Marie

1948	Robert Schuman
1948–9	Henri Queuille
1949–50	Georges Bidault
1950	Henri Queuille
1950–1	René Pleven
1951	Henri Queuille
1951–2	René Pleven
1952	Edgar Faure
1952–3	Antoine Pinay
1953	René Mayer
1953–4	Joseph Laniel
1954–5	Pierre Mendès-France
1955–6	Edgar Faure
1956–7	Guy Mollet
1957	Maurice Bourgès-Maunoury
1957–8	Félix Gaillard
1958	Pierre Pflimlin
1958–9	Charles de Gaulle

■ Fifth Republic

1959–62	Michel Debré
1962–8	Georges Pompidou
1968–9	Maurice Couve de Murville
1969–72	Jacques Chaban Delmas
1972–4	Pierre Mesmer
1974–6	Jacques Chirac
1976–81	Raymond Barre
1981–4	Pierre Mauroy
1984–6	Laurent Fabius
1986–8	Jacques Chirac
1988–91	Michel Rocard
1991–2	Édith Cresson
1992–3	Pierre Bérégovoy
1993–5	Édouard Balladur
1995–7	Alain Juppé
1997–2002	Lionel Jospin
2002–5	Jean-Pierre Raffarin
2005–2007	Dominique de Villepin
2007–	François Fillon

Germany

■ German Empire

Emperor

1888–1918	William II *abdicated* 1918

Chancellor

1909–17	Theobald von Bethmann Hollweg
1917	Georg Michaelis
1917–18	Georg Graf von Hertling
1918	Prince Max von Baden
1918	Friedrich Ebert

■ German Republic

President

1919–25	Friedrich Ebert
1925–34	Paul von Hindenburg

Reich Chancellor

1919	Philipp Scheidemann
1919–20	Gustav Bauer
1920	Hermann Müller
1920–1	Konstantin Fehrenbach
1921–2	Karl Joseph Wirth
1922–3	Wilhelm Cuno
1923	Gustav Stresemann
1923–4	Wilhelm Marx
1925–6	Hans Luther
1926–8	Wilhelm Marx
1928–30	Hermann Müller
1930–2	Heinrich Brüning
1932	Franz von Papen
1932–3	Kurt von Sleicher
1933	Adolf Hitler

Chancellor and Führer

1933–45	Adolf Hitler (*Führer from 1934*)
1945	Karl Dönitz

■ German Democratic Republic (East Germany)

President

1949–60	Wilhelm Pieck

Chairman of the Council of State

1960–73	Walter Ernst Karl Ulbricht
1973–6	Willi Stoph
1976–89	Erich Honecker
1989	Egon Krenz
1989–90	Gregor Gysi *General Secretary as Chairman*

Premier

1949–64	Otto Grotewohl

1964–73	Willi Stoph
1973–6	Horst Sindermann
1976–89	Willi Stoph
1989–90	Hans Modrow
1990	Lothar de Maizière

■ **German Federal Republic (West Germany)**
President

1949–59	Theodor Heuss
1959–69	Heinrich Lübke
1969–74	Gustav Heinemann
1974–9	Walter Scheel
1979–84	Karl Carstens
1984–90	Richard von Weizsäcker

Chancellor

1949–63	Konrad Adenauer
1963–6	Ludwig Erhard
1966–9	Kurt Georg Kiesinger
1969–74	Willy Brandt
1974–82	Helmut Schmidt
1982–90	Helmut Kohl

■ **Germany**
President

1990–4	Richard von Weizsäcker
1994–9	Roman Herzog
1999–2004	Johannes Rau
2004–	Horst Köhler

Chancellor

1990–8	Helmut Kohl
1998–2005	Gerhard Schröder
2005–	Angela Merkel

Greece

■ **Kingdom of Greece**
Monarch

1863–1913	George I
1913–17	Constantine I
1917–20	Alexander
1920–2	Constantine I
1922–3	George II
1923–4	Paul Koundouriotis *Regent*

■ **Republic**
President

| 1924–6 | Paul Koundouriotis |

1926	Theodore Pangalos
1926–9	Paul Koundouriotis
1929–35	Alexander T Zaïmis

■ **Kingdom of Greece**
Monarch

1935	George Kondylis *Regent*
1935–47	George II
1947–64	Paul
1964–7	Constantine II
1967–73	*Military Junta*
1973	George Papadopoulos *Regent*

■ **New Republic**
President

1973	George Papadopoulos
1973–4	Phaedon Gizikis
1974–5	Michael Stasinopoulos
1975–80	Constantine Tsatsos
1980–5	Constantine Karamanlis
1985–90	Christos Sartzetakis
1990–5	Constantine Karamanlis
1995–2005	Constantine Stephanopoulos
2005–	Karolos Papoulias

Prime Minister

1904–5	Theodore Deligiannis
1905	Demetrius G Rallis
1905–9	George Theotokis
1909	Demetrius G Rallis
1909–10	Kyriakoulis P Mavromichalis
1910	Stephen N Dragoumis
1910–15	Eleftherios K Venizelos
1915	Demetrius P Gounaris
1915	Eleftherios K Venizelos
1915	Alexander T Zaïmis
1915–16	Stephen Skouloudis
1916	Alexander T Zaïmis
1916	Nicholas P Kalogeropoulos
1916–17	Spyridon Lambros
1917	Alexander T Zaïmis
1917–20	Eleftherios K Venizelos
1920–1	Demetrius G Rallis
1921	Nicholas P Kalogeropoulos
1921–2	Demetrius P Gounaris

1922	Nicholas Stratos
1922	Peter E Protopapadakis
1922	Nicholas Triandaphyllakos
1922	Sortirios Krokidas
1922	Alexander T Zaïmis
1922–3	Stylianos Gonatas
1924	Eleftherios K Venizelos
1924	George Kaphandaris
1924	Alexander Papanastasiou
1924	Themistocles Sophoulis
1924–5	Andreas Michalakopoulos
1925–6	Alexander N Chatzikyriakos
1926	Theodore Pangalos
1926	Athanasius Eftaxias
1926	George Kondylis
1926–8	Alexander T Zaïmis
1928–32	Eleftherios K Venizelos
1932	Alexander Papanastasiou
1932	Eleftherios K Venizelos
1932–3	Panagiotis Tsaldaris
1933	Eleftherios K Venizelos
1933	Nicholas Plastiras
1933	Alexander Othonaos
1933–5	Panagiotis Tsaldaris
1935	George Kondylis
1935–6	Constantine Demertzis
1936–41	John Metaxas
1941	Alexander Koryzis
1941	*Chairman of Ministers* George II
1941	*German Occupation* (Emmanuel Tsouderos)
1941–2	George Tsolakoglou
1942–3	Constantine Logothetopoulos
1943–4	John Rallis

Government in exile

1941–4	Emmanuel Tsouderos
1944	Sophocles Venizelos
1944–5	George Papandreou

Post-war

1945	Nicholas Plastiras
1945	Peter Voulgaris
1945	Damaskinos, Archbishop of Athens

1945	Panagiotis Kanellopoulos
1945–6	Themistocles Sophoulis
1946	Panagiotis Politzas
1946–7	Constantine Tsaldaris
1947	Demetrius Maximos
1947	Constantine Tsaldaris
1947–9	Themistocles Sophoulis
1949–50	Alexander Diomedes
1950	John Theotokis
1950	Sophocles Venizelos
1950	Nicholas Plastiras
1950–1	Sophocles Venizelos
1951	Nicholas Plastiras
1952	Demetrius Kiusopoulos
1952–5	Alexander Papagos
1955	Stephen C Stefanopoulos
1955–8	Constantine Karamanlis
1958	Constantine Georgakopoulos
1958–61	Constantine Karamanlis
1961	Constantine Dovas
1961–3	Constantine Karamanlis
1963	Panagiotis Pipinellis
1963	Stylianos Mavromichalis
1963	George Papandreou
1963–4	John Parskevopoulos
1964–5	George Papandreou
1965	George Athanasiadis-Novas
1965	Elias Tsirimokos
1965–6	Stephen C Stefanopoulos
1966–7	John Paraskevopoulos
1967	Panagiotis Kanellopoulos
1967–74	*Military Junta*
1967	Constantine Kollias
1967–73	George Papadopoulos
1973	Spyridon Markezinis
1973–4	Adamantios Androutsopoulos
1974–80	Constantine Karamanlis
1980–1	George Rallis
1981–9	Andreas Papandreou
1989	Tzannis Tzannetakis
1989–90	Xenofon Zolotas
1990–3	Constantine Mitsotakis
1993–6	Andreas Papandreou
1996–2004	Costas Simitis
2004–	Costas Karamanlis

India

President

1950–62	Rajendra Prasad
1962–7	Sarvepalli Radhakrishnan
1967–9	Zakir Husain
1969	Varahagiri Venkatagiri *Acting*
1969	Mohammed Hidayatullah *Acting*
1969–74	Varahagiri Venkatagiri
1974–7	Fakhruddin Ali Ahmed
1977	B D Jatti *Acting*
1977–82	Neelam Sanjiva Reddy
1982–7	Giani Zail Singh
1987–92	Ramaswami Venkataraman
1992–7	Shankar Dayal Sharma
1997–2002	Kocheril Raman Narayanan
2002–	A P J Abdul Kalam

Prime Minister

1947–64	Jawaharlal Nehru
1964	Gulzari Lal Nanda *Acting*
1964–6	Lal Bahadur Shastri
1966	Gulzari Lal Nanda *Acting*
1966–77	Indira Gandhi
1977–9	Morarji Desai
1979–80	Charan Singh
1980–4	Indira Gandhi
1984–9	Rajiv Gandhi
1989–90	Vishwanath Pratap Singh
1990–1	Chandra Shekhar
1991–6	P V Narasimha Rao
1996	Atal Behari Vajpayee
1996–7	H D Deve Gowda
1997	Inder Kumar Gujral
1998–2004	Atal Behari Vajpayee
2004–	Manmohan Singh

Ireland

Head of State until 1937: British monarch, represented by a Governor-General

President

1937–8	*Presidential Commission*
1938–45	Douglas Hyde
1945–59	Sean Thomas O'Kelly
1959–73	Éamon de Valera
1973–4	Erskine H Childers
1974–6	Carroll Daly
1976–90	Patrick J Hillery
1990–7	Mary Robinson
1997–	Mary McAleese

Prime Minister

1919–21	Éamon de Valera
1922	Arthur Griffiths
1922–32	William Cosgrave
1932–48	Éamon de Valera
1948–51	John Aloysius Costello
1951–4	Éamon de Valera
1954–7	John Aloysius Costello
1957–9	Éamon de Valera
1959–66	Sean Lemass
1966–73	John Lynch
1973–7	Liam Cosgrave
1977–9	John Lynch
1979–82	Charles Haughey
1982–7	Garrett Fitzgerald
1987–92	Charles Haughey
1992–4	Albert Reynolds
1994–7	John Bruton
1997–	Bertie Ahern

Italy

■ **Kingdom of Italy**

Monarch

1900–46	Victor Emmanuel III
1946	Humbert II

■ **Italian Republic**

President

1946–8	Enrico de Nicola
1948–55	Luigi Einaudi
1955–62	Giovanni Gronchi
1962–4	Antonio Segni
1964–71	Giuseppe Saragat
1971–8	Giovanni Leone
1978–85	Alessandro Pertini
1985–92	Francesco Cossiga
1992–9	Oscar Luigi Scalfaro
1999–2006	Carlo Azeglio Ciampi
2006–	Giorgio Napolitano

Prime Minister

1903–5	Giovanni Giolitti
1905–6	Alessandro Fortis
1906	Sydney Sonnino
1906–9	Giovanni Giolitti
1909–10	Sydney Sonnino
1910–11	Luigi Luzzatti
1911–14	Giovanni Giolitti
1914–16	Antonio Salandra
1916–17	Paolo Boselli
1917–19	Vittorio Emmanuele Orlando
1919–20	Francesco Saverio Nitti
1920–1	Giovanni Giolitti
1921–2	Ivanoe Bonomi
1922	Luigi Facta
1922–43	Benito Mussolini
1943–4	Pietro Badoglio
1944–5	Ivanoe Bonomi
1945	Ferrucio Parri
1945–53	Alcide de Gasperi
1953–4	Giuseppe Pella
1954	Amintore Fanfani
1954–5	Mario Scelba
1955–7	Antonio Segni
1957–8	Adone Zoli
1958–9	Amintore Fanfani
1959–60	Antonio Segni
1960	Fernando Tambroni
1960–3	Amintore Fanfani
1963	Giovanni Leone
1963–8	Aldo Moro
1968	Giovanni Leone
1968–70	Mariano Rumor
1970–2	Emilio Colombo
1972–4	Giulio Andreotti
1974–6	Aldo Moro
1976–8	Giulio Andreotti
1979–80	Francisco Cossiga
1980–1	Arnaldo Forlani
1981–2	Giovanni Spadolini
1982–3	Amintore Fanfani
1983–7	Bettino Craxi
1987	Amintore Fanfani
1987–8	Giovanni Goria
1988–9	Ciriaco de Mita
1989–92	Giulio Andreotti
1992–3	Giuliano Amato
1993–4	Carlo Azeglio Ciampi
1994	Silvio Berlusconi
1995–6	Lamberto Dini
1996–8	Romano Prodi
1998–2000	Massimo D'Alema
2000–1	Giuliano Amato
2001–6	Silvio Berlusconi
2006–	Romano Prodi

Japan

Monarch (Emperor)

1867–1912	Mutsuhito (Meiji Era)
1912–26	Yoshihito (Taisho Era)
1926–89	Hirohito (Showa Era)
1989–	Akihito (Heisei Era)

Prime Minister

1901–6	Taro Katsura
1906–8	Kimmochi Saionji
1908–11	Taro Katsura
1911–12	Kimmochi Saionji
1912–13	Taro Katsura
1913–14	Gonnohyoe Yamamoto
1914–16	Shigenobu Okuma
1916–18	Masatake Terauchi
1918–21	Takashi Hara
1921–2	Korekiyo Takahashi
1922–3	Tomosaburo Kato
1923–4	Gonnohyoe Yamamoto
1924	Keigo Kiyoura
1924–6	Takaaki Kato
1926–7	Reijiro Wakatsuki
1927–9	Giichi Tanaka
1929–31	Osachi Hamaguchi
1931	Reijiro Wakatsuki
1931–2	Tsuyoshi Inukai
1932–4	Makoto Saito
1934–6	Keisuke Okada
1936–7	Koki Hirota
1937	Senjuro Hayashi
1937–9	Fumimaro Konoe
1939	Kiichiro Hiranuma
1939–40	Nobuyuki Abe
1940	Mitsumasa Yonai
1940–1	Fumimaro Konoe
1941–4	Hideki Tojo
1944–5	Kuniaki Koiso

1945	Kantaro Suzuki
1945	Naruhiko Higashikuni
1945–6	Kijuro Shidehara
1946–7	Shigeru Yoshida
1947–8	Tetsu Katayama
1948	Hitoshi Ashida
1948–54	Shigeru Yoshida
1954–6	Ichiro Hatoyama
1956–7	Tanzan Ishibashi
1957–60	Nobusuke Kishi
1960–4	Hayato Ikeda
1964–72	Eisaku Sato
1972–4	Kakuei Tanaka
1974–6	Takeo Miki
1976–8	Takeo Fukuda
1978–80	Masayoshi Ohira
1980–2	Zenko Suzuki
1982–7	Yasuhiro Nakasone
1987–9	Noburu Takeshita
1989	Sasuke Uno
1989–91	Toshiki Kaifu
1991–93	Kiichi Miyazawa
1993	Morihiro Hosokawa
1994	Tsutoma Hata
1994–6	Tomiichi Murayama
1996–8	Ryutaro Hashimoto
1998–2000	Keizo Obuchi
2000	Mikio Aoki *Acting*
2000–1	Yoshiro Mori
2001–6	Junichiro Koizumi
2006–	Shinzo Abe

Liechtenstein

Prince

1858–1929	Johann II
1929–38	Franz von Paula
1938–89	Franz Josef II
1989–	Hans Adam II

Prime Minister

1928–45	Franz Josef Hoop
1945–62	Alexander Friek
1962–70	Gérard Batliner
1970–4	Alfred J Hilbe
1974–8	Walter Kieber
1978–93	Hans Brunhart
1993	Markus Büchel
1994–2001	Mario Frick

| 2001– | Otmar Hasler |

Luxembourg

Grand Duke/Duchess

1905–12	William IV
1912–19	Marie Adelaide
1919–64	Charlotte (*in exile 1940–4*)
1964–2000	John
2000–	Henry

Prime Minister

1889–1915	Paul Eyschen
1915	Mathias Mongenast
1915–16	Hubert Loutsch
1916–17	Victor Thorn
1917–18	Léon Kaufmann
1918–25	Emil Reuter
1925–6	Pierre Prum
1926–37	Joseph Bech
1937–53	Pierre Dupong (*in exile 1940–4*)
1953–8	Joseph Bech
1958	Pierre Frieden
1959–69	Pierre Werner
1969–79	Gaston Thorn
1979–84	Pierre Werner
1984–95	Jacques Santer
1995–	Jean-Claude Juncker

The Netherlands

Monarch

1890–1948	Wilhelmina
1948–80	Juliana
1980–	Beatrix

Prime Minister

1901–5	Abraham Kuyper
1905–8	Theodoor H de Meester
1908–13	Theodorus Heemskerk
1913–18	Pieter W A Cort van der Linden
1918–25	Charles J M Ruys de Beerenbrouck
1925–6	Hendrikus Colijn
1926	Dirk J de Geer
1926–33	Charles J M Ruys de Beerenbrouck

1933–9	Hendrikus Colijn
1939–40	Dirk J de Geer
1940–5	Pieter S Gerbrandy (*in exile*)
1945–6	Willem Schemerhorn/ Willem Drees
1946–8	Louis J M Beel
1948–51	Willem Drees/Josephus R H van Schaik
1951–8	Willem Drees
1958–9	Louis J M Beel
1959–63	Jan E de Quay
1963–5	Victor G M Marijnen
1965–6	Joseph M L T Cals
1966–7	Jelle Zijlstra
1967–71	Petrus J S de Jong
1971–3	Barend W Biesheuvel
1973–7	Joop M Den Uyl
1977–82	Andreas A M van Agt
1982–94	Ruud F M Lubbers
1994–2002	Wim Kok
2002–	Jan Peter Balkenende

New Zealand

Head of State: British monarch, represented by Governor-General

Prime Minister

1893–1906	Richard John Seddon *Lib*
1906	William Hall-Jones *Lib*
1906–12	Joseph George Ward *Lib/Nat*
1912	Thomas Mackenzie *Nat*
1912–25	William Ferguson Massey *Ref*
1925	Francis Henry Dillon Bell *Ref*
1925–8	Joseph Gordon Coates *Ref*
1928–30	Joseph George Ward *Lib/Nat*
1930–5	George William Forbes *Un*
1935–40	Michael Joseph Savage *Lab*
1940–9	Peter Fraser *Lab*
1949–57	Sidney George Holland *Nat*
1957	Keith Jacka Holyoake *Nat*
1957–60	Walter Nash *Lab*

1960–72	Keith Jacka Holyoake *Nat*
1972	John Ross Marshall *Nat*
1972–4	Norman Eric Kirk *Lab*
1974–5	Wallace Edward Rowling *Lab*
1975–84	Robert David Muldoon *Nat*
1984–89	David Russell Lange *Lab*
1989–90	Geoffrey Palmer *Lab*
1990	Mike Moore *Lab*
1990–7	James Bolger *Nat*
1997–9	Jenny Shipley *Nat*
1999–	Helen Clark *Lab*

Lab = Labour　Lib = Liberal
Nat = National　Ref = Reform　Un = United

Norway

Union with Sweden dissolved on independence in 1905

Monarch

1905–57	Haakon VII
1957–91	Olav V
1991–	Harald V

Prime Minister

1903–5	George Francis Hagerup
1905–7	Christian Michelsen
1907–8	Jørgen Løvland
1908–10	Gunnar Knudsen
1910–12	Wollert Konow
1912–13	Jens Bratlie
1913–20	Gunnar Knudsen
1920–1	Otto Bahr Halvorsen
1921–3	Otto Albert Blehr
1923	Otto Bahr Halvorsen
1923–4	Abraham Berge
1924–6	Johan Ludwig Mowinckel
1926–8	Ivar Lykke
1928	Christopher Hornsrud
1928–31	Johan Ludwig Mowinckel
1931–2	Peder L Kolstad
1932–3	Jens Hundseid
1933–5	Johan Ludwig Mowinckel
1935–45	Johan Nygaardsvold
1945–51	Einar Gerhardsen

1951–5	Oscar Torp
1955–63	Einar Gerhardsen
1963	John Lyng
1963–5	Einar Gerhardsen
1965–71	Per Borten
1971–2	Trygve Bratteli
1972–3	Lars Korvald
1973–6	Trygve Bratteli
1976–81	Odvar Nordli
1981	Gro Harlem Brundtland
1981–6	Kåre Willoch
1986–9	Gro Harlem Brundtland
1989–90	Jan P Syse
1990–6	Gro Harlem Brundtland
1996–7	Thorbjørn Jagland
1997–2000	Kjell Magne Bondevik
2000–1	Jens Stoltenberg
2001–5	Kjell Magne Bondevik
2005–	Jens Stoltenberg

Portugal

President

■ First Republic

1910–11	Teófilo Braga
1911–15	Manuel José de Arriaga
1915	Teófilo Braga
1915–17	Bernardino Machado
1917–18	Sidónio Pais
1918–19	João do Canto e Castro
1919–23	António José de Almeida
1923–5	Manuel Teixeira Gomes
1925–6	Bernardino Machado

■ New State

1926	*Military Junta* (José Mendes Cabeçadas)
1926	*Military Junta* (Manuel de Oliveira Gomes da Costa)
1926–51	António Oscar Fragoso Carmona
1951–8	Francisco Craveiro Lopes
1958–74	Américo de Deus Tomás

■ Second Republic

| 1974 | *Military Junta* (António Spínola) |
| 1974–6 | *Military Junta* (Francisco da Costa Gomes) |

■ Third Republic

1976–86	António dos Santos Ramalho Eanes
1986–96	Mário Soares
1996–2006	Jorge Sampaio
2006–	Aníbal Cavaço Silva

Prime Minister

1932–68	António de Oliveira Salazar
1968–74	Marcelo Caetano
1974	Adelino da Palma Carlos
1974–5	Vasco Gonçalves
1975–6	José Pinheiro de Azevedo
1976–8	Mário Soares
1978	Alfredo Nobre da Costa
1978–9	Carlos Alberto de Mota Pinto
1979	Maria de Lurdes Pintasilgo
1980–1	Francisco de Sá Carneiro
1981–3	Francisco Pinto Balsemão
1983–5	Mário Soares
1985–95	Aníbal Cavaço Silva
1995–2001	António Guterres
2002–4	José Manuel Durão Barroso
2004–5	Pedro Santana Lopes
2005–	José Sócrates

Russia

Monarch (Tsar)
| 1894–1917 | Nicholas II |

For 1917–91 ▶ USSR.
President
| 1991–9 | Boris Yeltsin |
| 2000– | Vladimir Putin |

Prime Minister
1991–2	Boris Yeltsin
1992	Yegor Gaidar *Acting*
1992–8	Viktor Chernomyrdin
1998	Sergei Kiriyenko
1998	Viktor Chernomyrdin *Acting*
1998–9	Yevgeny Primakov
1999	Sergei Stepashin

1999–2000	Vladimir Putin
2000–4	Mikhail Kasyanov
2004	Viktor Khristenko
2004–	Mikhael Fradkov

Spain

Monarch

1886–1931	Alfonso XIII

■ Second Republic
President

1931	Niceto Alcalá Zamora y Torres
1931	Manuel Azaña y Díez
1931–6	Niceto Alcalá Zamora y Torres
1936	Diego Martínez Barrio *Acting*

■ Civil War

1936–9	Manuel Azaña y Díez
1936–9	Miguel Cabanellas Ferrer

Prime Minister

1904–5	Marcelo de Azcárraga y Palmero
1905	Raimundo Fernández Villaverde
1905	Eugenio Montero Ríos
1905–6	Segismundo Moret y Prendergast
1906	José López Domínguez
1906	Segismundo Moret y Prendergast
1906–7	Antonio Aguilař y Correa
1907–9	Antonio Maura y Montaner
1909–10	Segismundo Moret y Prendergast
1910–12	José Canalejas y Méndez
1912	Álvaro Figueroa y Torres
1912–13	Manuel García Prieto
1913–15	Eduardo Dato y Iradier
1915–17	Álvaro Figueroa y Torres
1917	Manuel García Prieto
1917	Eduardo Dato y Iradier
1917–18	Manuel García Prieto
1918	Antonio Maura y Montaner

1918	Manuel García Prieto
1918–19	Álvaro Figueroa y Torres
1919	Antonio Maura y Montaner
1919	Joaquín Sánchez de Toca
1919–20	Manuel Allendesalazar
1920–1	Eduardo Dato y Iradier
1921	Gabino Bugallal Araujo *Acting*
1921	Manuel Allendesalazar
1921–2	Antonio Maura y Montaner
1922	José Sánchez Guerra y Martínez
1922–3	Manuel García Prieto
1923–30	Miguel Primo de Rivera y Oraneja
1930–1	Dámaso Berenguer y Fusté
1931	Juan Bautista Aznar-Cabañas
1931	Niceto Alcalá Zamora y Torres
1931–3	Manuel Azaña y Díez
1933	Alejandro Lerroux y García
1933	Diego Martínez Barrio
1933–4	Alejandro Lerroux y García
1934	Ricardo Samper Ibáñez
1934–5	Alejandro Lerroux y García
1935	Joaquín Chapaprieta y Terragosa
1935–6	Manuel Portela Valladares
1936	Manuel Azaña y Díez
1936	Santiago Casares Quiroga
1936	Diego Martínez Barrio
1936	José Giral y Pereyra
1936–7	Francisco Largo Caballero
1937–9	Juan Negrín

■ Nationalist Government
Head of State

1936–75	Francisco Franco Bahamonde

Chairman of the Council of Ministers
1939–73	Francisco Franco Bahamonde

■ **Kingdom of Spain (from 1975)**

Monarch
1975–	Juan Carlos I

Prime Minister
1973	Torcuato Fernández Miranda y Hevía *Acting*
1973–6	Carlos Arias Navarro
1976–81	Adolfo Suárez
1981–2	Calvo Sotelo
1982–96	Felipe González
1996–2004	José María Aznar
2004–	José Luis Rodríguez Zapatero

Sweden

Monarch
1872–1907	Oscar II
1907–50	Gustav V
1950–73	Gustav VI Adolf
1973–	Carl XVI Gustaf

Prime Minister
1902–5	Erik Gustaf Boström
1905	Johan Ramstedt
1905	Christian Lundeberg
1905–6	Karl Staaf
1906–11	Arvid Lindman
1911–14	Karl Staaf
1914–17	Hjalmar Hammarskjöld
1917	Carl Swartz
1917–20	Nils Edén
1920	Hjalmar Branting
1920–1	Louis de Geer
1921	Oscar von Sydow
1921–3	Hjalmar Branting
1923–4	Ernst Trygger
1924–5	Hjalmar Branting
1925–6	Rickard Sandler
1926–8	Carl Gustaf Ekman
1928–30	Arvid Lindman
1930–2	Carl Gustaf Ekman
1932	Felix Hamrin
1932–6	Per Albin Hansson
1936	Axel Pehrsson-Branstorp
1936–46	Per Albin Hansson
1946–69	Tage Erlander
1969–76	Olof Palme
1976–8	Thorbjörn Fälldin
1978–9	Ola Ullsten
1979–82	Thorbjörn Fälldin
1982–6	Olof Palme
1986–91	Ingvar Carlsson
1991–4	Carl Bildt
1994–6	Ingvar Carlsson
1996–2006	Göran Persson
2006–	Fredrik Reinfeldt

Switzerland

President (annually rotating post)
1905	Marc-Emile Ruchet
1906	Ludwig Forrer
1907	Eduard Müller
1908	Ernst Brenner
1909	Adolf Deucher
1910	Robert Comtesse
1911	Marc-Emile Ruchet
1912	Ludwig Forrer
1913	Eduard Müller
1914	Arthur Hoffmann
1915	Giuseppe Motta
1916	Camille Decoppet
1917	Edmund Schulthess
1918	Felix Calonder
1919	Gustave Ador
1920	Giuseppe Motta
1921	Edmund Schulthess
1922	Robert Haab
1923	Karl Scheurer
1924	Ernest Chuard
1925	Jean-Marie Musy
1926	Heinrich Häberlin
1927	Giuseppe Motta
1928	Edmund Schulthess
1929	Robert Haab
1930	Jean-Marie Musy
1931	Heinrich Häberlin
1932	Giuseppe Motta
1933	Edmund Schulthess
1934	Marcel Pilet-Golaz
1935	Rudolf Minger
1936	Albert Meyer

1937	Giuseppe Motta
1938	Johannes Baumann
1939	Philipp Etter
1940	Marcel Pilet-Golaz
1941	Ernst Wetter
1942	Philipp Etter
1943	Enrico Celio
1944	Walter Stampfli
1945	Eduard von Steiger
1946	Karl Kobelt
1947	Philipp Etter
1948	Enrico Celio
1949	Ernst Nobs
1950	Max Petitpierre
1951	Eduard von Steiger
1952	Karl Kobelt
1953	Philipp Etter
1954	Rodolphe Rubattel
1955	Max Petitpierre
1956	Markus Feldmann
1957	Hans Streuli
1958	Thomas Holenstein
1959	Paul Chaudet
1960	Max Petitpierre
1961	Friedrich Wahlen
1962	Paul Chaudet
1963	Willy Spühler
1964	Ludwig von Moos
1965	Hans Peter Tschudi
1966	Hans Schaffner
1967	Roger Bonvin
1968	Willy Spühler
1969	Ludwig von Moos
1970	Hans Peter Tschudi
1971	Rudolf Gnägi
1972	Nello Celio
1973	Roger Bonvin
1974	Ernst Brugger
1975	Pierre Graber
1976	Rudolf Gnägi
1977	Kurt Furgler
1978	Willi Ritschard
1979	Hans Hürlimann
1980	Georges-André Chevallaz
1981	Kurt Furgler
1982	Fritz Honegger
1983	Pierre Aubert

1984	Leon Schlumpf
1985	Kurt Furgler
1986	Alphons Egli
1987	Pierre Aubert
1988	Otto Stich
1989	Jean-Pascal Delamuraz
1990	Arnold Koller
1991	Flavio Cotti
1992	René Felber
1993	Adolf Ogi
1994	Otto Stich
1995	Kaspar Villiger
1996	Jean-Pascal Delamuraz
1997	Arnold Koller
1998	Flavio Cotti
1999	Ruth Dreifuss
2000	Adolf Ogi
2001	Moritz Leuenberger
2002	Kaspar Villinger
2003	Pascal Couchepin
2004	Joseph Deiss
2005	Samuel Schmid
2006	Moritz Leuenberger
2007	Micheline Calmy-Rey

United Kingdom

Prime Minister

1721–42	Robert Walpole *Whig*
1742–3	Earl of Wilmington (Spencer Compton) *Whig*
1743–54	Henry Pelham *Whig*
1754–6	Duke of Newcastle (Thomas Pelham-Holles) *Whig*
1756–7	Duke of Devonshire (William Cavendish) *Whig*
1757–62	Duke of Newcastle *Whig*
1762–3	Earl of Bute (John Stuart) *Tory*
1763–5	George Grenville *Whig*
1765–6	Marquess of Rockingham (Charles Watson Wentworth) *Whig*
1766–70	Duke of Grafton (Augustus Henry Fitzroy) *Whig*

1770–82	Lord North (Frederick North) *Tory*
1782	Marquess of Rockingham *Whig*
1782–3	Earl of Shelburne (William Petty-Fitzmaurice) *Whig*
1783	Duke of Portland (William Henry Cavendish) *Coal*
1783–1801	William Pitt *Tory*
1801–4	Henry Addington *Tory*
1804–6	William Pitt *Tory*
1806–7	Lord Grenville (William Wyndham) *Whig*
1807–9	Duke of Portland *Tory*
1809–12	Spencer Perceval *Tory*
1812–27	Earl of Liverpool (Robert Banks Jenkinson) *Tory*
1827	George Canning *Tory*
1827–8	Viscount Goderich (Frederick John Robinson) *Tory*
1828–30	Duke of Wellington (Arthur Wellesley) *Tory*
1830–4	Earl Grey (Charles Grey) *Whig*
1834	Viscount Melbourne (William Lamb) *Whig*
1834–5	Robert Peel *Con*
1835–41	Viscount Melbourne *Whig*
1841–6	Robert Peel *Con*
1846–52	Lord John Russell *Lib*
1852	Earl of Derby (Edward George Smith Stanley) *Con*
1852–5	Lord Aberdeen (George Hamilton-Gordon) *Peelite*
1855–8	Viscount Palmerston (Henry John Temple) *Lib*
1858–9	Earl of Derby *Con*
1859–65	Viscount Palmerston *Lib*
1865–6	Lord John Russell *Lib*
1866–8	Earl of Derby *Con*
1868	Benjamin Disraeli *Con*
1868–74	William Ewart Gladstone *Lib*
1874–80	Benjamin Disraeli *Con*
1880–5	William Ewart Gladstone *Lib*
1885–6	Marquess of Salisbury (Robert Gascoyne-Cecil) *Con*
1886	William Ewart Gladstone *Lib*
1886–92	Marquess of Salisbury *Con*
1892–4	William Ewart Gladstone *Lib*
1894–5	Earl of Rosebery (Archibald Philip Primrose) *Lib*
1895–1902	Marquess of Salisbury *Con*
1902–5	Arthur James Balfour *Con*
1905–8	Henry Campbell-Bannerman *Lib*
1908–15	Herbert Henry Asquith *Lib*
1915–16	Herbert Henry Asquith *Coal*
1916–22	David Lloyd George *Coal*
1922–3	Andrew Bonar Law *Con*
1923–4	Stanley Baldwin *Con*
1924	James Ramsay MacDonald *Lab*
1924–9	Stanley Baldwin *Con*
1929–31	James Ramsay MacDonald *Lab*
1931–5	James Ramsay MacDonald *Nat*
1935–7	Stanley Baldwin *Nat*
1937–40	Neville Chamberlain *Nat*
1940–5	Winston Churchill *Coal*
1945–51	Clement Attlee *Lab*
1951–5	Winston Churchill *Con*
1955–7	Anthony Eden *Con*
1957–63	Harold Macmillan *Con*
1963–4	Alec Douglas-Home *Con*
1964–70	Harold Wilson *Lab*
1970–4	Edward Heath *Con*
1974–6	Harold Wilson *Lab*
1976–9	James Callaghan *Lab*
1979–90	Margaret Thatcher *Con*
1990–7	John Major *Con*
1997–2007	Anthony Blair *Lab*
2007–	Gordon Brown *Lab*

Coal = Coalition   Con = Conservative
Lab = Labour   Lib = Liberal   Nat = Nationalist

United Nations

Secretary-General
1946–53	Trygve Lie *Norway*
1953–61	Dag Hammarskjöld *Sweden*
1962–71	U Thant *Burma*
1972–81	Kurt Waldheim *Austria*
1982–91	Javier Pérez de Cuéllar *Peru*
1992–6	Boutros Boutros-Ghali *Egypt*
1997–2006	Kofi Annan *Ghana*
2006–	Ban Ki-moon *South Korea*

United States of America

President
(Vice President in parentheses)

1789–97	George Washington (1st) (John Adams)
1797–1801	John Adams (2nd) *Fed* (Thomas Jefferson)
1801–9	Thomas Jefferson (3rd) *Dem-Rep* (Aaron Burr, 1801–5) (George Clinton, 1805–9)
1809–17	James Madison (4th) *Dem-Rep* (George Clinton, 1809–12) *no Vice President 1812–13* (Elbridge Gerry, 1813–14) *no Vice President 1814–17*
1817–25	James Monroe (5th) *Dem-Rep* (Daniel D Tompkins)
1825–9	John Quincy Adams (6th) *Dem-Rep* (John C Calhoun)
1829–37	Andrew Jackson (7th) *Dem* (John C Calhoun, 1829–32) *no Vice President 1832–3* (Martin van Buren, 1833–7)
1837–41	Martin van Buren (8th) *Dem* (Richard M Johnson)
1841	William Henry Harrison (9th) *Whig* (John Tyler)
1841–5	John Tyler (10th) *Whig no Vice President*
1845–9	James Knox Polk (11th) *Dem* (George M Dallas)
1849–50	Zachary Taylor (12th) *Whig* (Millard Fillmore)
1850–3	Millard Fillmore (13th) *Whig no Vice President*
1853–7	Franklin Pierce (14th) *Dem* (William R King, 1853) *no Vice President 1853–7*
1857–61	James Buchanan (15th) *Dem* (John C Breckinridge)
1861–5	Abraham Lincoln (16th) *Rep* (Hannibal Hamlin, 1861–5) (Andrew Johnson, 1865)
1865–9	Andrew Johnson (17th) *Dem-Nat no Vice President*
1869–77	Ulysses Simpson Grant (18th) *Rep* (Schuyler Colfax, 1869–73) (Henry Wilson, 1873–5) *no Vice President 1875–7*
1877–81	Rutherford Birchard Hayes (19th) *Rep* (William A Wheeler)
1881	James Abram Garfield (20th) *Rep* (Chester A Arthur)
1881–5	Chester Alan Arthur (21st) *Rep no Vice President*
1885–9	Grover Cleveland (22nd) *Dem* (Thomas A Hendricks, 1885) *no Vice President 1885–9*
1889–93	Benjamin Harrison (23rd) *Rep* (Levi P Morton)
1893–7	Grover Cleveland (24th) *Dem* (Adlai E Stevenson)
1897–1901	William McKinley (25th) *Rep* (Garrat A Hobart, 1897–9) *no Vice President 1899–1901* (Theodore Roosevelt, 1901)

1901–9	Theodore Roosevelt (26th) *Rep no Vice President 1901–5* (Charles W Fairbanks, 1905–9)
1909–13	William Howard Taft (27th) *Rep* (James S Sherman, 1909–12) *no Vice President 1912–13*
1913–21	Woodrow Wilson (28th) *Dem* (Thomas R Marshall)
1921–3	Warren Gamaliel Harding (29th) *Rep* (Calvin Coolidge)
1923–9	Calvin Coolidge (30th) *Rep no Vice President 1923–5* (Charles G Dawes, 1925–9)
1929–33	Herbert Clark Hoover (31st) *Rep* (Charles Curtis)
1933–45	Franklin Delano Roosevelt (32nd) *Dem* (John N Garner, 1933–41) (Henry A Wallace, 1941–5) (Harry S Truman, 1945)
1945–53	Harry S Truman (33rd) *Dem no Vice President 1945–9* (Alben W Barkley, 1949–53)
1953–61	Dwight David Eisenhower (34th) *Rep* (Richard M Nixon)
1961–3	John Fitzgerald Kennedy (35th) *Dem* (Lyndon B Johnson)
1963–9	Lyndon Baines Johnson (36th) *Dem no Vice President 1963–5* (Hubert H Humphrey, 1965–9)
1969–74	Richard Milhous Nixon (37th) *Rep* (Spiro T Agnew, 1969–73) *no Vice President 1973, Oct–Dec* (Gerald R Ford, 1973–4)

1974–7	Gerald Rudolph Ford (38th) *Rep no Vice President 1974, Aug–Dec* (Nelson A Rockefeller, 1974–7)
1977–81	Jimmy Carter (39th) *Dem* (Walter F Mondale)
1981–9	Ronald Wilson Reagan (40th) *Rep* (George H W Bush)
1989–93	George Herbert Walker Bush (41st) *Rep* (J Danforth Quayle)
1993–2001	William Jefferson Blythe IV Clinton (42nd) *Dem* (Albert Gore)
2001–	George Walker Bush (43rd) *Rep* (Richard B Cheney)

Dem = Democrat   Fed = Federalist
Nat = National Union   Rep = Republican

USSR (Union of Soviet Socialist Republics)

No longer in existence, but included for reference.

President

1917	Leo Kamenev
1917–19	Yakov Sverlov
1919–46	Mikhail Kalinin
1946–53	Nikolai Shvernik
1953–60	Klimentiy Voroshilov
1960–4	Leonid Brezhnev
1964–5	Anastas Mikoyan
1965–77	Nikolai Podgorny
1977–82	Leonid Brezhnev
1982–3	Vasily Kuznetsov *Acting*
1983–4	Yuri Andropov
1984	Vasily Kuznetsov *Acting*
1984–5	Konstantin Chernenko
1985	Vasily Kuznetsov *Acting*
1985–8	Andrei Gromyko
1988–90	Mikhail Gorbachev

Executive President

1990–91	Mikhail Gorbachev
1991	Gennady Yanayev *Acting*
1991	Mikhail Gorbachev

Chairman (Prime Minister)

Council of Ministers

1917	Georgy Lvov
1917	Aleksandr Kerensky

Council of People's Commissars

1917–24	Vladimir Ilyich Lenin
1924–30	Aleksei Rykov
1930–41	Vyacheslav Molotov
1941–53	Josef Stalin

Council of Ministers

1953–5	Georgiy Malenkov
1955–8	Nikolai Bulganin
1958–64	Nikita Khrushchev

1964–80	Alexei Kosygin
1980–5	Nikolai Tikhonov
1985–90	Nikolai Ryzhkov
1990–1	Yuri Maslyukov *Acting*
1991	Valentin Pavlov
1991	Ivan Silayev *Acting*

General Secretary

1922–53	Josef Stalin
1953	Georgiy Malenkov
1953–64	Nikita Khrushchev
1964–82	Leonid Brezhnev
1982–4	Yuri Andropov
1984–5	Konstantin Chernenko
1985–91	Mikhail Gorbachev

ARTS AND CULTURE

Novelists

Selected works are listed.

Achebe, Chinua (originally **Albert Chinualumogu**) (1930–) Nigerian novelist, born Ogidi; *Things Fall Apart* (1958), *Anthills of the Savannah* (1987).

Ackroyd, Peter (1949–) English novelist, poet, critic, born London; *Notes for a New Culture* (1976), *The Last Testament of Oscar Wilde* (1983), *Hawksmoor* (1985), *Chatterton* (1987), *First Light* (1989), *English Music* (1992), *Milton in America* (1996), *London: The Biography* (2002), *Shakespeare* (2005).

Adams, Douglas (Noël) (1952–2001) English novelist, short-story writer, born Cambridge; *The Hitch Hiker's Guide to the Galaxy* (1979), *Life, the Universe and Everything* (1982), *Mostly Harmless* (1992).

Adams, Richard (George) (1920–) English novelist, short-story writer, born Newbury, Berkshire; *Watership Down* (1972), *Shardik* (1974), *The Girl in a Swing* (1980), *The Day Gone By* (autobiography) (1990).

Aldiss, Brian (Wilson) (1925–) English novelist, poet, short-story writer, playwright, critic, born Dereham, Norfolk; *Helliconia Spring* (1982), *Helliconia Summer* (1983), *Helliconia Winter* (1985), *Forgotten Life* (1988), *Dracula Unbound* (1991), *Remembrance Day* (1993), *Jocasta* (2004).

Amis, Sir Kingsley (William) (1922–95) English novelist, poet, born London; *Lucky Jim* (1954), *That Uncertain Feeling* (1955), *Jake's Thing* (1978), *The Old Devils* (1986, Booker Prize).

Amis, Martin (Louis) (1949–) English novelist, short-story writer, born Oxford; *The Rachel Papers* (1973), *Money* (1984), *London Fields* (1989), *Time's Arrow* (1991), *The Information* (1995), *Experience* (2000), *Yellow Dog* (2003), *House of Meetings* (2006).

Angelou, Maya (Marguerite Annie) (née **Johnson**) (1928–) US novelist, poet, playwright, born St Louis, Missouri; *I Know Why the Caged Bird Sings* (1970), *All God's Children Need Travelling Shoes* (1986), *Wouldn't Take Nothing for My Journey Now* (1993), *Even the Stars Look Lonesome* (1998), *A Song Flung up to Heaven* (2002).

Archer, Jeffrey (Howard) **Archer, Baron** (1940–) English novelist, short-story writer, born London; *Not a Penny More, Not a Penny Less* (1975), *Kane and Abel* (1979), *First Among Equals* (1984), *Honour Among Thieves* (1993), *The Fourth Estate* (1996), *False Impressions* (2006).

Asimov, Isaac (1920–92) US novelist, short-story writer, born Petrovichi, Russia; *I Robot* (1950), *Foundation* (1951), *The Disappearing Man and Other Stories* (1985), *Nightfall* (1990).

Atwood, Margaret (Eleanor) (1939–) Canadian novelist, poet, short-story writer, born Ottawa; *The Handmaid's Tale* (1985), *Cat's Eye* (1988), *The Robber Bride* (1993), *The Blind Assassin* (2000, Booker Prize), *Oryx and Crake* (2003), *The Penelopiad* (2005).

Austen, Jane (1775–1817) English novelist, born Steventon, Hampshire; *Sense and Sensibility* (1811), *Pride and Prejudice* (1813), *Mansfield Park* (1814), *Emma* (1816), *Persuasion* (1818).

Bainbridge, Dame Beryl (Margaret) (1934–) English novelist, born Liverpool; *The Dressmaker* (1973), *Injury Time* (1977), *An Awfully Big Adventure* (1989), *Every Man for Himself* (1996), *Master Georgie* (1998), *According to Queeney* (2001).

Ballard, J(ames) G(raham) (1930–) English novelist, born Shanghai, China; *The Drowned World* (1962), *The Terminal Beach* (1964), *Empire of the Sun* (1984), *The Kindness of Women* (1991), *Super-Cannes* (2000), *Kingdom Come* (2006).

Balzac, Honoré de (1799–1850) French novelist, born Tours; *Comédie humaine* (1827–47), *Illusions perdues* (1837–43).

Banks, Iain M(enzies) (1954–) Scottish novelist, born Dunfermline; *The Wasp Factory* (1984), *The Bridge* (1986), *The Crow Road* (1992), *Whit* (1995), *Excession* (1996), *A Song of Stone* (1997), *Dead Air* (2002), *The Steep Approach to Garbadale* (2007).

Banville, John (1945–) Irish novelist, born Wexford; *Birchwood* (1973), *Dr Copernicus* (1976), *Kepler* (1981), *Book of Evidence* (1989), *The Untouchables* (1997), *The Sea* (2005, Man Booker Prize).

Barker, Pat (Patricia Margaret) (1943–) English novelist, short-story writer, born Thornaby-on-Tees; *Union Street* (1982), *Blow Your House Down* (1984), *The Century's Daughter* (1986), *The Man Who Wasn't There* (1989), *Regeneration* (1991), *The Eye in the Door* (1993), *The Ghost Road* (1995, Booker Prize), *Border Crossing* (2001), *Double Vision* (2003).

Barnes, Julian (Patrick) (1946–) English novelist, born Leicester; *Metroland* (1980), *Flaubert's Parrot* (1984), *Staring at the Sun* (1986), *A History of the World in 10½ Chapters* (1989), *Love, Etc* (1992), *Something to Declare* (2002), *Arthur and George* (2005).

Bates, H(erbert) E(rnest) (1905–74) English novelist, short-story writer, born Rushden, Northamptonshire; *Fair Stood the Wind for France* (1944), *The Jacaranda Tree* (1949), *Love for Lydia* (1952), *The Darling Buds of May* (1958).

Behn, Aphra (1640–89) English novelist, playwright, born Wye, Kent; *The Rover* (play) (1678), *Oroonoko* (1688).

Bellow, Saul (1915–2005) American novelist, born Quebec, Canada; *Henderson the Rain King* (1959), *Herzog* (1964), *Humboldt's Gift* (1975, Pulitzer Prize 1976) *The Dean's December* (1982), *The Actual* (1997), *Ravelstein* (2000); Nobel Prize for literature 1976.

Bennett, (Enoch) Arnold (1867–1931) English novelist, born Hanley, Staffordshire; *Anna of the Five Towns* (1902), *The Old Wives' Tale* (1908), *Clayhanger* series (1910–18).

Berger, John (Peter) (1926–) English novelist, playwright, born London; *A Painter of Our Time* (1958), *A Fortunate Man* (non-fiction) (1967), *G* (1972, Booker Prize), *To the Wedding* (1995), *Photocopies* (1996), *Here is Where We Meet* (2005).

Binchy, Maeve (1940–) Irish novelist, short-story writer, born Dublin; *Light a Penny Candle* (1982), *Echoes* (1985), *Firefly Summer* (1987), *Circle of Friends* (1990), *Copper Beech* (1992), *The Glass Lake* (1994), *Tara Road* (1998), *Whitethorn Woods* (2006).

Blackmore, R(ichard) D(odderidge) (1825–1900) English novelist, born Longworth, Berkshire; *Lorna Doone* (1869).

Bleasdale, Alan (1946–) English novelist, playwright, born Liverpool; *Scully* (1975), *The Boys from the Blackstuff* (TV series) (1982), *Are You Lonesome Tonight?* (musical) (1985), *GBH* (TV series) (1991), *Jake's Progress* (TV series) (1995).

Böll, Heinrich (1917–85) German novelist, born Cologne; *And Never Said a Solitary Word* (1953), *The Unguarded House* (1954), *The Bread of Our Early Years* (1955); Nobel Prize for literature 1972.

Borges, Jorge Luis (1899–1986) Argentinian poet, short-story writer, born Buenos Aires; *Ficciones* (1944), *El Aleph* (1949), *Labyrinths* (1962).

Boyd, William (Andrew Murray) (1952–) Scottish novelist, short-story writer, born Accra, Ghana; *A Good Man in Africa* (1981), *An Ice-Cream War* (1982), *Brazzaville Beach* (1990), *The Blue Afternoon* (1993), *The Destiny of Nathalie X* (stories) (1995), *Nat Tate: An American Artist* (1998), *Armadillo* (1998), *Fascination* (2004), *Restless* (2006).

Bradbury, Sir Malcolm (Stanley) (1932–2000) English novelist, born Sheffield; *Eating People is Wrong* (1959), *The History Man* (1975), *Dr Criminale* (1992).

Bradbury, Ray(mond) (Douglas) (1920–) US novelist, short-story writer, born Waukegan, Illinois; *The Martian Chronicles* (short stories) (1950), *Fahrenheit 451* (1953), *Something Wicked this Way Comes* (1962), *A Graveyard for Lunatics* (1990), *Farewell Summer* (2006).

Bradford, Barbara Taylor (1933–) English novelist, born Leeds; *A Woman of Substance* (1979), *Hold the Dream* (1985), *Love in Another Town* (1995), *Just Rewards* (2003).

Brittain, Vera (Mary) (1893–1970) English novelist, poet, born Newcastle-under-Lyme, Staffordshire; *Testament of Youth* (1933), *Testament of Friendship* (1940), *Testament of Experience* (1957) (all autobiographies).

Brontë, Anne (1820–49) English novelist, poet, born Thornton, Yorkshire; *Agnes Grey* (1847), *The Tenant of Wildfell Hall* (1848).

Brontë, Charlotte (1816–55) English novelist, poet, born Thornton, Yorkshire; *Jane Eyre* (1847), *Shirley* (1849), *Villette* (1853).

Brontë, Emily (1818–48) English novelist, poet, born Thornton, Yorkshire; *Wuthering Heights* (1847).

Brookner, Anita (1928–) English novelist, born London; *Hotel du Lac* (1984, Booker Prize), *Family and Friends* (1985), *Brief Lives* (1990), *Altered States* (1996), *Visitors* (1997), *Leaving Home* (2005).

Buchan, John (1875–1940) Scottish novelist, poet, born Perth; *The Thirty-Nine Steps* (1915), *Greenmantle* (1916), *Sir Walter Scott* (biography) (1932).

Buck, Pearl (née Sydenstricker) (1892–1973) US novelist, born Hillsboro, West Virginia; *The Good Earth* (1931), *Pavilion of Women* (1946); Nobel Prize for literature 1938.

Bunyan, John (1628–88) English novelist, born Elstow, near Bedford; *Pilgrim's Progress* (1678).

Burgess, Anthony (pseudonym of John Anthony Burgess Wilson) (1917–93) English novelist, born Manchester; *A Clockwork Orange* (1962), *The Malayan Trilogy* (1972), *Earthly Powers* (1980), *Kingdom of the Wicked* (1985), *Any Old Iron* (1989).

Burney, Fanny (Frances, later Mme d'Arblay) (1752–1840) English novelist, born King's Lynn; *Evelina* (1778), *Cecilia* (1782).

Burroughs, Edgar Rice (1875–1950) US novelist, born Chicago; *Tarzan of the Apes* (1914), *The Land that Time Forgot* (1924).

Burroughs, William S(eward) (1914–97) US novelist, born St Louis, Missouri; *The Naked Lunch* (1959), *The Soft Machine* (1961), *The Wild Boys* (1971), *Exterminator!* (1974), *My Education: A Book of Dreams* (1995).

Byatt, Dame A(ntonia) S(usan) (1936–) English novelist, born Sheffield; *The Shadow of a Sun* (1964), *The Virgin in the Garden* (1978), *Possession* (1990, Booker Prize), *Babel Tower* (1996), *Elementals: Stories of Fire and Ice* (short stories) (1998), *The Biographer's Tale* (2000).

Calvino, Italo (1923–87) Italian novelist, short-story writer, born Santiago de Las Vegas, Cuba; *Invisible Cities* (1972), *The Castle of Crossed Destinies* (1969), *If on a Winter's Night a Traveller* (1979).

Camus, Albert (1913–60) French novelist, playwright, born Mondovi, Algeria; *The Outsider* (1942), *The Plague* (1948), *The Fall* (1957); Nobel Prize for literature 1957.

Canetti, Elias (1905–94) Bulgarian novelist, born Ruse, Bulgaria; *Auto da Fé* (1935, trans 1946), *Crowds and Power* (1960, trans 1962); Nobel Prize for literature 1981.

Capote, Truman (1924–84) US playwright, novelist, short-story writer, born New Orleans; *Other Voices, Other Rooms* (1948), *Breakfast at Tiffany's* (1958).

Carey, Peter (Philip) (1943–) Australian novelist, short-story writer, born Bacchus Marsh, Victoria; *Illywhacker* (1985), *Oscar and Lucinda* (1988, Booker Prize), *True History of the Kelly Gang* (2001, Booker Prize), *Theft, A Love Story* (2006).

Carr, Philippa ▶ Holt, Victoria

Cather, Willa (Silbert) (1876–1947) US novelist, poet, born near Winchester, Virginia; *O Pioneers!* (1913), *My Antonia* (1918), *One of Ours* (1922), *The Professor's House* (1925), *My Mortal Enemy* (1926), *Death Comes for the Archbishop* (1927), *Sapphira and the Slave Girl* (1940).

Cela, Camilo José (1916–2002) Spanish novelist, born Iria Flavia; *La familia de Pascual Duarte* (1942), *La Colmena* (1951), *Mazurca para dos muertos* (1984); Nobel Prize for literature 1989.

Cervantes (Saavedra), Miguel de (1547–1616) Spanish novelist and poet, born Alcala de Henares; *La Galatea* (1585), *Don Quixote* (1605–15).

Chandler, Raymond (1888–1959) US novelist, born Chicago; *The Big Sleep* (1939), *Farewell, My Lovely* (1940), *The High Window* (1942), *The Lady in the Lake* (1943), *The Long Goodbye* (1953).

Chatwin, Bruce (1940–89) English novelist, born Sheffield; *In Patagonia* (1977), *The Viceroy of Ouidah* (1980), *On The Black Hill* (1982), *The Songlines* (1987), *Utz* (1988).

Chesterton, G(ilbert) K(eith) (1874–1936) English novelist, poet, born London; *The Napoleon of Notting Hill* (1904), *The Innocence of Father Brown* (1911).

Christie, Dame Agatha (Mary Clarissa) (née Miller) (1890–1976) English novelist, born Torquay, Devon; *Murder on the Orient Express* (1934), *Death on the Nile* (1937), *A Murder is Announced* (1950), *Curtain* (1975).

Clarke, Sir Arthur C(harles) (1917–) English novelist, short-story writer, born Minehead, Somerset; *Childhood's End* (1953), *2001: A Space Odyssey* (1968), *The Fountains of Paradise* (1979), *The Garden of Rama* (1991), *The Hammer of God* (1993).

Clavell, James (du Maresq) (1922–94) US novelist, playwright, born England; *King Rat* (1962), *Tai-Pan* (1966), *Shogun* (1975).

Coetzee, J(ohn) M(ichael) (1940–) South African novelist, born Cape Town; *Life and Times of Michael K* (1983, Booker Prize), *Disgrace* (1999, Booker Prize), *Slow Man* (2006); Nobel Prize for literature 2003.

Colette, Sidonie Gabrielle (1873–1954) French novelist, born Saint-Sauveur-en-Puisaye,

Burgundy; *Claudine à l'école* (1900), *Chéri* (1920), *La Fin de Chéri* (1926), *Gigi* (1943).

Collins, (William) Wilkie (1824–89) English novelist, born London; *The Woman in White* (1860), *No Name* (1862), *Armadale* (1866), *The Moonstone* (1868).

Condon, Richard (Thomas) (1915–96) US novelist, born New York City; *The Manchurian Candidate* (1959), *Winter Kills* (1974), *Prizzi's Honor* (1982).

Conrad, Joseph (originally Jozef Teodor Konrad Nalecz Korzeniowski) (1857–1924) Anglo-Polish novelist, short-story writer, born Berdichev, Poland (now Ukraine); *Lord Jim* (1900), *Heart of Darkness* (1902), *Nostromo* (1904), *The Secret Agent* (1907), *Chance* (1914).

Cookson, Dame Catherine (Ann) (1906–98) English novelist, born Tyne Dock, County Durham; *Tilly Trotter* (1956), *The Glass Virgin* (1969), *The Black Candle* (1989).

Dahl, Roald (1916–90) Welsh children's writer, short-story writer, playwright, born Llandaff, Glamorgan; *Over to You* (1946), *Someone Like You* (1954), *Kiss, Kiss* (1960) (all short stories), *James and the Giant Peach* (1961), *Charlie and the Chocolate Factory* (1964), *You Only Live Twice* (screenplay) (1967), *Matilda* (1988).

Davies, (William) Robertson (1913–95) Canadian novelist, playwright, born Thamesville, Ontario; *The Rebel Angels* (1981), *The Deptford Trilogy* (1970–5), *What's Bred in the Bone* (1985).

de Beauvoir, Simone (1908–86) French novelist, born Paris; *The Second Sex* (1949, trans 1953), *Les Mandarins* (1954), *Memoirs of a Dutiful Daughter* (1959).

Defoe, Daniel (1660–1731) English novelist, born Stoke Newington, London; *Robinson Crusoe* (1719), *Moll Flanders* (1722), *A Journal of the Plague Year* (1722).

Deighton, Len (Leonard Cyril) (1929–) English novelist, born London; *The Ipcress File* (1962), *Funeral in Berlin* (1964), *Spy Hook* (1988), *Spy Line* (1989), *Spy Sinker* (1990), *Faith* (1994), *Hope* (1995), *Charity* (1996).

de Quincey, Thomas (1785–1859) English novelist, born Manchester; *Confessions of an English Opium Eater* (1822).

Desai, Anita (née Mazumbar) (1937–) Indian novelist, short-story writer, born Mussoorie; *Cry, The Peacock* (1963), *Clear Light of Day* (1980), *In Custody* (1984), *Baumgartner's Bombay* (1987), *Journey to Ithaca* (1995), *Fasting, Feasting* (1999).

Dickens, Charles (1812–70) English novelist, born Landport, Portsmouth; *Oliver Twist* (1837–9), *David Copperfield* (1849–50), *Bleak House* (1852–3), *Great Expectations* (1860–1).

Dos Passos, John Roderigo (1896–1970) US novelist, born Chicago; *Manhattan Transfer* (1925), *USA* (1930–6).

Dostoevsky, Fyodor Mikhailovich (1821–81) Russian novelist, born Moscow; *Notes from the Underground* (1864), *Crime and Punishment* (1866), *The Brothers Karamazov* (1880).

Doyle, Sir Arthur Conan (1859–1930) Scottish novelist, short-story writer, born Edinburgh; *The Memoirs of Sherlock Holmes* (1894), *The Hound of the Baskervilles* (1902), *The Lost World* (1912).

Doyle, Roddy (1958–) Irish novelist, born Dublin; *The Commitments* (1987), *Paddy Clarke, Ha Ha Ha* (1993, Booker Prize), *The Woman Who Walked into Doors* (1996), *A Star Called Henry* (1999), *Paula Spencer* (2006).

Drabble, Margaret (1939–) English novelist, short-story writer, born Sheffield; *The*

Millstone (1965), *The Ice Age* (1977), *The Gates of Ivory* (1991), *The Witch of Exmoor* (1996), *The Red Queen* (2004).

Duffy, Maureen (Patricia) (1933–) English novelist, playwright, born Worthing, Sussex; *That's How It Was* (1962), *The Microcosm* (1966), *The Paradox Players* (1967), *Occam's Razor* (1993), *Alchemy* (2004).

Dumas, Alexandre (in full **Alexandre Dumas Davy de la Pailleterie**), known as **Dumas père** (1802–70) French novelist, playwright, born Villers-Cotterêts, Aisne; *The Three Musketeers* (1844–5).

Dumas, Alexandre, known as **Dumas fils** (1824–95) French novelist, playwright, born Paris; *La Dame aux camélias* (1848).

du Maurier, Dame Daphne (1907–89) English novelist, born London; *Jamaica Inn* (1936), *Rebecca* (1938), *Frenchman's Creek* (1942), *My Cousin Rachel* (1951).

Durrell, Gerald Malcolm (1925–95) English writer, born Jamshedpur, India; *The Overloaded Ark* (1953), *My Family and Other Animals* (1956).

Durrell, Lawrence George (1912–90) English novelist, poet, born Julundur, India; *The Alexandria Quartet* (1957–60).

Eco, Umberto (1932–) Italian novelist, born Alessandria, Piedmont; *The Name of the Rose* (1980), *Foucault's Pendulum* (1989), *The Island of the Day Before* (1995), *Baudolino* (2002), *The Mysterious Flame of Queen Loana* (2005).

Eliot, George (originally **Mary Ann**, later **Marian Evans**) (1819–80) English novelist, born Arbury, Warwickshire; *Adam Bede* (1858), *The Mill on the Floss* (1860), *Middlemarch* (1871–2), *Daniel Deronda* (1874–6).

Faulkner, William Harrison (1897–1962) US novelist, born near Oxford, Mississippi; *Sartoris* (1929), *The Sound and the Fury* (1929), *Absalom, Absalom!* (1936); Nobel Prize for literature 1949.

Fielding, Henry (1707–54) English novelist, born Sharpham Park, near Glastonbury, Somerset; *Joseph Andrews* (1742), *Tom Jones* (1749).

Fitzgerald, F(rancis) Scott (Key) (1896–1940) US novelist, short-story writer, born St Paul, Minnesota; *The Beautiful and the Damned* (1922), *The Great Gatsby* (1925), *Tender is the Night* (1934).

Fitzgerald, Penelope (Mary) (née **Knox**) (1916–2000) English novelist, born Lincoln; *The Bookshop* (1978), *Offshore* (1979, Booker Prize), *The Gate of Angels* (1990), *The Blue Flower* (1995).

Flaubert, Gustave (1821–80) French novelist, born Rouen; *Madame Bovary* (1857), *Salammbô* (1862).

Fleming, Ian (Lancaster) (1908–64) English novelist, born London; author of the 'James Bond' novels, eg *Casino Royale* (1953), *From Russia with Love* (1957), *Dr No* (1958), *Goldfinger* (1959), *The Man with the Golden Gun* (1965).

Ford, Richard (1944–) US novelist, born Jackson, Mississippi; *A Piece of My Heart* (1976), *The Sportswriter* (1986), *Independence Day* (1995, Pulitzer Prize 1996), *Lay of the Land* (2006).

Forester, C(ecil) S(cott) (1899–1966) British novelist, born Cairo, Egypt; *Payment Deferred* (1926), *The African Queen* (1935), *The Happy Return* (1937).

Forster, E(dward) M(organ) (1879–1970) English novelist, short-story writer, born London; *A Room with a View* (1908), *Howards End* (1910), *A Passage to India* (1922–4).

Forsyth, Frederick (1938–) English novelist, short-story writer, born Ashford, Kent; *The Day of the Jackal* (1971), *The Odessa File* (1972), *The Fourth Protocol* (1984), *The Fist of God* (1993), *The Afghan* (2006).

Fowles, John (Robert) (1926–2005) English novelist, born Leigh-on-Sea, Essex; *The Collector* (1963), *The Magus* (1965, revised 1977), *The French Lieutenant's Woman* (1969), *The Ebony Tower* (1974), *The Tree* (1979).

Frame, Janet Paterson (1924–2004) New Zealand novelist, short-story writer, born Dunedin; *The Lagoon: Stories* (1951), *Scented Gardens for the Blind* (1963), *Living in the Maniototo* (1979), *The Carpathians* (1988); *To the Island* (autobiography) (1982), *An Angel at My Table* (1984), *The Envoy from Mirror City* (1985).

Francis, Dick (Richard Stanley) (1920–) English novelist, born Tenby, Pembrokeshire; *Dead Cert* (1962), *Slay-Ride* (1973), *The Edge* (1988), *Comeback* (1991), *To The Hilt* (1996), *10 lb Penalty* (1997), *Under Orders* (2006).

Fraser, Lady Antonia (née Pakenham) (1932–) English novelist, biographer, born London; *Mary, Queen of Scots* (1969), *Quiet as a Nun* (1977), *A Splash of Red* (1981), *Have a Nice Death* (1983), *Political Death* (1994), *Love and Louis XIV* (2001).

French, Marilyn (1929–) US novelist, born New York City; *The Women's Room* (1977), *The Bleeding Heart* (1980), *Her Mother's Daughter* (1987), *The War Against Women* (1992), *In the Name of Friendship* (2006).

Galsworthy, John (1867–1933) English novelist, playwright, born Coombe, Surrey; *The Man of Property* (1906), *The Forsyte Saga* (1906–31); Nobel Prize for literature 1932.

García Márquez, Gabriel (1928–) Colombian novelist, born Aracataca; *One Hundred Years of Solitude* (1970), *Chronicle of a Death Foretold* (1982), *Love in the Time of Cholera* (1985), *The General in His Labyrinth* (1991), *Of Love and Other Demons* (1995); Nobel Prize for literature 1982.

Gaskell, Mrs Elizabeth (Cleghorn) (née Stevenson) (1810–65) English novelist, born Chelsea, London; *Mary Barton* (1848), *Cranford* (1853), *North and South* (1855), *Sylvia's Lovers* (1863).

Gibbon, Lewis Grassic (pseudonym of James Leslie Mitchell) (1901–35) Scottish novelist, born near Auchterless, Aberdeenshire; trilogy *Sunset Song* (1932), *Cloud Howe* (1933), *Grey Granite* (1934).

Gibbons, Stella (Dorothea) (1902–89) English novelist, born London; *Cold Comfort Farm* (1933).

Gide, André (Paul Guillaume) (1860–1951) French novelist, born Paris; *The Immoralist* (1902), *The Vatican Cellars* (1914).

Godden, (Margaret) **Rumer** (1907–98) English novelist, poet, children's author, born Eastbourne, Sussex; *Black Narcissus* (1939), *Breakfast with the Nikolides* (1942), *The Greengage Summer* (1958), *Coromandel Sea Change* (1991), *Pippa Passes* (1994).

Godwin, William (1756–1836) English novelist, born Wisbech, Cambridgeshire; *Caleb Williams* (1794), *Mandeville* (1817).

Goethe, Johann Wolfgang von (1749–1832) German novelist, poet, born Frankfurt am Main; *The Sorrows of Young Werther* (1774).

Gogol, Nikolai Vasilievich (1809–52) Russian novelist, short-story writer, playwright, born Sorochinstsi, Poltava; *The Overcoat* (1835), *Diary of a Madman* (1835), *Dead Souls* (1842).

Golding, (Sir) William (Gerald) (1911–93) English novelist, born St Columb Minor, Cornwall; *Lord of the Flies* (1954), *The Inheritors* (1955), *Pincher Martin* (1956), *The Spire* (1964), *Darkness Visible* (1979), *Rites of Passage* (1980, Booker Prize), *The Paper Men* (1984), *Close Quarter* (1987), *Fire Down Below* (1989); Nobel Prize for literature 1983.

Goldsmith, Oliver (1728–74) Anglo-Irish playwright, novelist, poet, born Pallasmore, County Longford; *The Vicar of Wakefield* (1766).

Gordimer, Nadine (1923–) South African novelist, short-story writer, born Springs, Transvaal; *Occasion for Loving* (1963), *A Guest of Honour* (1971), *The Conservationist* (1974, Booker Prize), *A Sport of Nature* (1987), *None to Accompany Me* (1994), *Get a Life* (2005); Nobel Prize for literature 1991.

Gorky, Maxim (pseudonym of Aleksei Maksimovich Peshkov) (1868–1936) Russian novelist, short-story writer, born Nizhni Novgorod (New Gorky); *The Mother* (1906–7), *Childhood* (1913), *The Life of Klim Samgin* (1925–36).

Grass, Günter (Wilhelm) (1927–) German novelist, born Danzig; *The Tin Drum* (1962), *A Broad Field* (1995), *My Century* (1999), *Crabwalk* (2003); Nobel Prize for literature 1999.

Graves, Robert (Ranke) (1895–1985) English novelist, poet, born London; *I Claudius* (1934), *Claudius the God* (1934).

Gray, Alasdair (James) (1934–) Scottish novelist, short-story writer, poet, born Glasgow; *Lanark* (1981), *Unlikely Stories, Mostly* (stories) (1983), *Janine* (1984), *Poor Things* (1992, Whitbread Novel Award), *A History Maker* (1994).

Greene, (Henry) Graham (1904–91) English novelist, playwright, born Berkhamsted, Hertfordshire; *Brighton Rock* (1938), *The Power and the Glory* (1940), *The Third Man* (1950), *The Honorary Consul* (1973).

Haggard, Sir (Henry) Rider (1856–1925) English novelist, born Bradenham Hall, Norfolk; *King Solomon's Mines* (1885), *She* (1887), *Allan Quatermain* (1887).

Hailey, Arthur (1920–2004) Canadian novelist, playwright, born Luton, Bedfordshire; *Flight into Danger* (1958), *Airport* (1968), *The Evening News* (1990), *Detective* (1997).

Hammett, (Samuel) Dashiell (1894–1961) US novelist, born St Mary's County, Maryland; *Red Harvest* (1929), *The Maltese Falcon* (1930), *The Glass Key* (1931), *The Thin Man* (1934).

Hardy, Thomas (1840–1928) English novelist, poet, born Higher Bockhampton, Dorset; *Far from the Madding Crowd* (1874), *The Mayor of Casterbridge* (1886), *Tess of the D'Urbervilles* (1891), *Jude the Obscure* (1895).

Hartley, L(eslie) P(oles) (1895–1972) English novelist, short-story writer, born near Peterborough; *The Shrimp and the Anemone* (1944), *The Go-Between* (1953), *The Hireling* (1957).

Hawthorne, Nathaniel (1804–64) US novelist, short-story writer, born Salem, Massachusetts; *The Scarlet Letter* (1850), *The House of the Seven Gables* (1851).

Heller, Joseph (1923–99) US novelist, born Brooklyn, New York City; *Catch-22* (1961), *Something Happened* (1974), *Closing Time* (1994).

Hemingway, Ernest (Millar) (1899–1961) US novelist, short-story writer, born Oak Park (Chicago), Illinois; *A Farewell to Arms* (1929), *For Whom the Bell Tolls* (1940), *The Old Man and the Sea* (1952); Nobel Prize for literature 1954.

Hesse, Hermann (1877–1962) German novelist, born Calw, Württemberg; *Rosshalde* (1914), *Steppenwolf* (1927), *The Glass Bead Game* (1943); Nobel Prize for literature 1946.

Heyer, Georgette (1902–74) English novelist, born London; *The Black Moth* (1929), *Footsteps in the Dark* (1932), *Regency Buck* (1935), *The Corinthian* (1940), *The Grand Sophy* (1950), *Bath Tangle* (1955), *The Nonesuch* (1962), *Frederica* (1965).

Highsmith, (Mary) Patricia (1921–95) US novelist, short-story writer, born Fort Worth, Texas; *Strangers on a Train* (1950), *The Talented Mr Ripley* (1956), *Ripley's Game* (1974).

Hilton, James (1900–54) English novelist, born Leigh, Lancashire; *Lost Horizon* (1933), *Goodbye Mr Chips* (1934).

Hines, (Melvin) Barry (1939–) English novelist, playwright, born Barnsley, Yorkshire; *A Kestrel for a Knave* (1968), *The Gamekeeper* (1975), *The Heart of It* (1994), *Elvis over England* (1998).

Hoban, Russell (Conwell) (1925–) US novelist, playwright, children's writer, born Lansdale, Pennsylvania; *Turtle Diary* (1975), *Riddley Walker* (1980), *Pilgermann* (1983), *Come Dance with Me* (2005).

Hogg, James, 'the Ettrick Shepherd' (1770–1835) Scottish novelist, poet, born Ettrick, Selkirkshire; *Confessions of a Justified Sinner* (1824).

Holt, Victoria (pseudonym of **Eleanor Alice Burford Hibbert**) (1906–93) English novelist, born London, also wrote as Philippa Carr, Jean Plaidy; *Catherine de' Medici* (1969, as JP), *Will You Love Me in September* (1981, as PC), *The Captive* (1989, as VH).

Hughes, Thomas (1822–96) English novelist, born Uffington, Berkshire; *Tom Brown's Schooldays* (1857).

Hugo, Victor (Marie) (1802–85) French novelist, dramatist, poet, born Besançon; *Notre Dame de Paris* (1831), *Les Misérables* (1862).

Hulme, Keri (Ann Ruhi) (1947–) New Zealand novelist, born Christchurch; *The Bone People* (1983, Booker Prize 1985), *Stonefish* (2004).

Hunter, Evan (originally **Salvatore A Lambino**) (1926–2005) US novelist, playwright, short-story writer, born New York City; *The Blackboard Jungle* (1954), *Strangers When We Meet* (1958), *The Paper Dragon* (1966), *Last Summer* (1968), *Privileged Conversation* (1996); also writes as Ed McBain.

Hurston, Zora Neale (1903–60) US novelist, born Eatonville, Florida; *Their Eyes Were Watching God* (1937), *Moses, Man of the Mountain* (1939).

Huxley, Aldous (Leonard) (1894–1963) English novelist, born Godalming, Surrey; *Brave New World* (1932), *Eyeless in Gaza* (1936), *Island* (1962).

Innes, (Ralph) Hammond (1913–98) English novelist, playwright, born Horsham, Sussex; *The Trojan Horse* (1940), *Atlantic Fury* (1962), *Isvik* (1991), *Delta Connection* (1996).

Irving, John (Winslow) (1942–) US novelist, short-story writer, born Exeter, New Hampshire; *The World According to Garp* (1978), *The Hotel New Hampshire* (1981), *A Prayer for Owen Meany* (1988), *A Son of the Circus* (1994), *Until I Find You* (2005).

Isherwood, Christopher (William Bradshaw) (1904–86) Anglo-US novelist, born Disley, Cheshire; *Mr Norris Changes Trains* (1935), *Goodbye to Berlin* (1939), *Down There on a Visit* (1962).

Ishiguro, Kazuo (1954–) British novelist, short-story writer, born Nagasaki, Japan; *The Remains of the Day* (1989, Booker Prize), *The Unconsoled* (1995), *When We Were Orphans* (2000), *Never Let Me Go* (2005).

James, Henry (1843–1916) US novelist, born New York City; *Portrait of a Lady* (1881),

The Bostonians (1886), *The Turn of the Screw* (1889), *The Awkward Age* (1899), *The Ambassadors* (1903).

James, P(hylis) D(orothy) (1920–) English novelist, born Oxford; *Cover Her Face* (1962), *Taste for Death* (1986), *Devices and Desires* (1989), *Original Sin* (1994), *The Lighthouse* (2005).

Jelinek, Elfriede (1946–) Austrian novelist, poet, playwright, born Mürzzuschlag, Styria; *Wonderful Times, Wonderful Times* (1990), *The Piano Teacher* (1988), *Lust* (1992), *Greed* (2006); Nobel Prize for literature 2004.

Jhabvala, Ruth Prawer (1927–) British novelist, born Cologne, Germany; *Heat and Dust* (1975, Booker Prize), *In Search of Love and Beauty* (1983), *Poet and Dancer* (1993), *The Householder* (2001).

Jong, Erica (née **Mann**) (1942–) US novelist, poet, born New York City; *Fear of Flying* (1973), *Fear of Fifty* (1994), *Sappho's Leap* (2003).

Joyce, James (Augustine Aloysius) (1882–1941) Irish novelist, poet, born Dublin; *Dubliners* (1914), *A Portrait of the Artist as a Young Man* (1914–15), *Ulysses* (1922), *Finnegans Wake* (1939).

Kafka, Franz (1883–1924) Austrian novelist, short-story writer, born Prague; *Metamorphosis* (1916), *The Trial* (1925), *The Castle* (1926), *America* (1927).

Kazantzakis, Nikos (1883–1957) Greek novelist, poet, playwright, born Heraklion, Crete; *Zorba the Greek* (1946).

Kelman, James (Alexander) (1946–) Scottish novelist, short-story writer, playwright, born Glasgow; *The Busconductor Hines* (1984), *A Chancer* (1985), *Greyhound for Breakfast* (stories) (1987), *A Disaffection* (1989), *How late it was, how late* (1994, Booker Prize), *Translated Accounts* (2001).

Keneally, Thomas (Michael) (1935–) Australian novelist, short-story writer, playwright, born Sydney; *Bring Larks and Heroes* (1967), *Three Cheers for the Paraclete* (1968), *The Survivor* (1969), *Schindler's Ark* (1982, Booker Prize), *Woman of the Inner Sea* (1992), *The Tyrant's Word* (2004).

Kerouac, Jack (Jean-Louis) (1922–69) US novelist, born Lowell, Massachusetts; *On the Road* (1957), *The Dharma Bums* (1958).

Kesey, Ken (Elton) (1935–2001) US novelist, short-story writer, born La Junta, Colorado; *One Flew Over the Cuckoo's Nest* (1962), *Demon Box* (stories) (1987), *Sailor Song* (1992), *Last Go Round* (1994).

King, Stephen (Edwin) (1947–) US novelist, short-story writer, born Portland, Maine; *Carrie* (1974), *The Shining* (1977), *Christine* (1983), *Pet Sematary* (1983), *Misery* (1988), *Four Past Midnight* (1990), *The Plant* (Internet novel) (2000), *Lisey's Story* (2006).

Kingsley, Charles (1819–75) English novelist, born Holne vicarage, Dartmoor; *Westward Ho!* (1855), *The Water-Babies* (1863), *Hereward the Wake* (1866).

Kipling, Rudyard (1865–1936) English novelist, poet, short-story writer, born Bombay (now Mumbai), India; *Barrack-room Ballads* (1892), *The Jungle Book* (1894), *Kim* (1901), *Just So Stories* (1902); Nobel Prize for literature 1907.

Kundera, Milan (1929–) French novelist, born Brno, Czechoslovakia (now Czech Republic); *Life is Elsewhere* (1973), *The Farewell Party* (1976), *The Unbearable Lightness of Being* (1984), *Immortality* (1991), *Testaments Betrayed* (1995), *Ignorance* (2002).

Laclos, Pierre (Ambroise François) **Choderlos de** (1741–1803) French novelist, born Amiens; *Les Liaisons Dangereuses* (Dangerous Liaisons) (1782).

La Fayette, Marie Madeleine Pioche de Lavergne, Comtesse de (1634–93) French novelist, born Paris; *Zaïde* (1670), *La Princesse de Clèves* (1678).

Lampedusa, Giuseppe Tomasi di (1896–1957) Italian novelist, born Palermo, Sicily; *Il Gattopardo* (The Leopard) (1958).

Lawrence, D(avid) H(erbert) (1885–1930) English novelist, poet, short-story writer, born Eastwood, Nottinghamshire; *Sons and Lovers* (1913), *The Rainbow* (1915), *Women in Love* (1920), *Lady Chatterley's Lover* (1928).

Le Carré, John (pseudonym of David John Moore Cornwell) (1931–) English novelist, born Poole, Dorset; *Tinker, Tailor, Soldier, Spy* (1974), *The Honourable Schoolboy* (1977), *Smiley's People* (1980), *The Little Drummer Girl* (1983), *A Perfect Spy* (1986), *The Russia House* (1989), *The Secret Pilgrim* (1991), *Our Game* (1995), *The Tailor of Panama* (1996), *The Mission Song* (2006).

Lee, (Nelle) Harper (1926–) US novelist, born Monroeville, Alabama; *To Kill a Mockingbird* (1960, Pulitzer Prize 1961).

Lee, Laurie (1914–97) English novelist, poet, born Slad, Gloucestershire; *Cider with Rosie* (1959), *As I Walked Out One Midsummer Morning* (1969).

Le Fanu, (Joseph) Sheridan (1814–73) Irish novelist, short-story writer, born Dublin; *Uncle Silas* (1864), *In a Glass Darkly* (1872).

Le Guin, Ursula K(roeber) (1929–) US novelist, poet, short-story writer, born Berkeley, California; *Rocannon's World* (1966), *The Left Hand of Darkness* (1969), *Searoad* (1991), *Fish Soup* (1992), *Unlocking the Air and Other Stories* (1996), *The Telling* (2000).

Lessing, Doris (May) (née Tayler) (1919–) Rhodesian novelist, short-story writer, born Kermanshah, Iran; *The Grass is Singing* (1950), *The Golden Notebook* (1962), *Canopus in Argos Archives* (1979–83), *The Good Terrorist* (1985), *The Grandmothers* (2003).

Levi, Primo (1919–87) Italian novelist, born Turin; *If this is a Man* (1947), *The Periodic Table* (1984).

Lewis, C(live) S(taples) (1898–1963) Irish novelist, literary scholar and religious writer, born Belfast; trilogy *Out of the Silent Planet* (1938), *Perelandra* (1939), *That Hideous Strength* (1945); *The Screwtape Letters* (1940), *The Chronicles of Narnia* (1950–6), *Mere Christianity* (collected broadcast talks) (1952).

Lewis, (Harry) Sinclair (1885–1951) US novelist, born Sauk Center, Minnesota; *Main Street* (1920), *Babbitt* (1922), *Martin Arrowsmith* (1925), *Elmer Gantry* (1927); Nobel Prize for literature 1930.

Lively, Penelope (Margaret) (née Low) (1933–) English novelist, born Cairo, Egypt; *The Road to Lichfield* (1977), *Moon Tiger* (1987, Booker Prize), *City of the Mind* (1991), *Heat Wave* (1996), *Making it Up* (2005).

Lodge, David (John) (1935–) English novelist, born London; *The British Museum is Falling Down* (1965), *Changing Places* (1975), *Small World* (1984), *Nice Work* (1988), *Paradise News* (1991), *Therapy* (1995), *Thinks…* (2001), *Author, Author* (2004).

London, Jack (John) Griffith (1876–1916) US novelist, born San Francisco; *Call of the Wild* (1903), *White Fang* (1907), *Martin Eden* (1909).

Lurie, Alison (1926–) US novelist, born Chicago; *Love and Friendship* (1962), *The War Between the Tates* (1974), *Foreign Affairs* (1984, Pulitzer Prize 1985), *Women and Ghosts* (short stories) (1994), *The Last Resort* (1998).

Macaulay, Dame (Emilie) Rose (1881–1958) English novelist, born Rugby, Warwickshire;

Dangerous Ages (1921), *The World, My Wilderness* (1950), *The Towers of Trebizond* (1956).

McEwan, Ian (Russell) (1948–) English novelist, short-story writer, playwright, born Aldershot, Hampshire; *The Cement Garden* (1978), *The Child in Time* (1987), *The Innocent* (1990), *Amsterdam* (1998, Booker Prize), *Atonement* (2001), *Saturday* (2005).

MacKenzie, Sir (Edward Montague) **Compton** (1883–1972) English novelist, born West Hartlepool, Cleveland; *Whisky Galore* (1942).

MacLean, Alistair (1922–87) Scottish novelist, born Glasgow; *The Guns of Navarone* (1957), *Ice Station Zebra* (1963), *Where Eagles Dare* (1967), *Force Ten from Navarone* (1968).

Mahfouz, Naguib (1911–2006) Egyptian novelist, born Cairo; *The Cairo Trilogy* (1956–7), *The Thief and the Dogs* (1961), *Adrift on the Nile* (1966), *God's World* (1973), *Arabian Nights and Days* (1995); Nobel Prize for literature 1988.

Mailer, Norman (Kingsley) (1923–) US novelist, born Long Branch, New Jersey; *The Naked and the Dead* (1948), *Barbary Shore* (1951), *An American Dream* (1965), *Armies of the Night* (1968, Pulitzer Prize 1969), *The Executioner's Song* (1979, Pulitzer Prize 1980), *Oswald's Tale* (1995).

Mann, Thomas (1875–1955) German novelist, born Lübeck; *Death in Venice* (1912), *The Magic Mountain* (1924), *Buddenbrooks* (1901); Nobel Prize for literature 1929.

Mansfield, Katherine (pseudonym of **Katherine Mansfield Beauchamp**) (1888–1923) New Zealand short-story writer, born Wellington; *Prelude* (1918), *Bliss and Other Stories* (1920), *The Garden Party and Other Stories* (1922).

Marsh, Ngaio (1899–1982) New Zealand novelist, born Christchurch; *Death in a White Tie* (1958), *A Grave Mistake* (1978).

Martel, Yann (1963–) Canadian novelist, born Salamanca, Spain; *Self* (1996), *Life of Pi* (2002, Man Booker Prize), *We Ate the Children Last* (2004).

Maugham, (William) **Somerset** (1874–1965) English novelist, born Paris; *Of Human Bondage* (1915), *The Moon and Sixpence* (1919), *The Razor's Edge* (1945).

Maupassant, Guy de (1850–93) French short-story writer, novelist, born Miromesnil; *Claire de Lune* (1884), *Bel Ami* (1885).

Mauriac, François (1885–1970) French novelist, born Bordeaux; *Le Baiser au Lépreux* (1922); Nobel Prize for literature 1952.

Melville, Herman (1819–1909) US novelist, poet, born New York City; *Moby Dick* (1851).

Meredith, George (1828–1909) English novelist, poet, born Portsmouth; *The Egoist* (1879), *Diana of the Crossways* (1885).

Michener, James A(lbert) (1907–97) US novelist, short-story writer, born New York City; *Tales of the South Pacific* (1947, Pulitzer Prize 1948), *Hawaii* (1959), *Chesapeake* (1978), *Miracle in Seville* (1995).

Miller, Henry Valentine (1891–1980) US novelist, born New York City; *Tropic of Cancer* (1934), *Tropic of Capricorn* (1938), *The Rosy Crucifixion Trilogy* (1949–60).

Mishima, Yukio (pseudonym of **Hiraoka Kimitake**) (1925–70) Japanese novelist, born Tokyo; *Confessions of a Mask* (1960), *The Temple of the Golden Pavilion* (1959), *The Sea of Fertility* (1969–71).

Mitchell, Margaret (1900–49) US novelist, born Atlanta, Georgia; *Gone with the Wind* (1936).

Mitford, Nancy (1904–73) English novelist, born London; *Love in a Cold Climate* (1949), *Don't Tell Alfred* (1960).

Mo, Timothy (Peter) (1950–) British novelist, born Hong Kong; *The Monkey King* (1978), *Sour Sweet* (1982), *An Insular Possession* (1986), *The Redundancy of Courage* (1991), *Brownout on Breadfruit Boulevard* (1995), *Renegade or Halo2* (1999).

Monsarrat, Nicholas (John Turney) (1910–79) English novelist, born Liverpool; *The Cruel Sea* (1951), *The Story of Esther Costello* (1953).

Morrison, Toni (Chloe Anthony) (née Wofford) (1931–) US novelist, born Lorain, Ohio; *The Bluest Eye* (1970), *Sula* (1973), *Song of Solomon* (1977), *Tar Baby* (1981), *Beloved* (1987, Pulitzer Prize 1988), *Jazz* (1992), *Paradise* (1998), *Love* (2003); Nobel Prize for literature 1993.

Mortimer, Sir John (Clifford) (1923–) English novelist, short-story writer, playwright, born London; *A Cat Among the Pigeons* (1964), *Rumpole of the Bailey* (1978), *Paradise Postponed* (1985), *Under the Hammer* (1994), *Scales of Justice* (2005).

Murdoch, Dame (Jean) Iris (1919–99) Irish novelist, philosopher, born Dublin; *The Bell* (1958), *The Sea, The Sea* (1978, Booker Prize), *The Philosopher's Pupil* (1983), *The Green Knight* (1993).

Nabokov, Vladimir Vladimirovich (1899–1977) Russian–US novelist, poet, born St Petersburg; *Lolita* (1955), *Look at the Harlequins!* (1974).

Naipaul, Sir V(idiadhar) **S**(urajprasad) (1932–) Trinidadian novelist, born Chaguanas; *A House for Mr Biswas* (1961), *In a Free State* (1971, Booker Prize), *A Bend in the River* (1979), *A Way in the World* (1994), *Magic Seeds* (2004); Nobel Prize for literature 2001.

O'Brien, Edna (1932–) Irish novelist, short-story writer, born Tuamgraney, County Clare; *The Country Girls* (1960), *August is a Wicked Month* (1964), *A Pagan Place* (1971), *Lantern Slides* (stories) (1990), *Time and Tide* (1992), *Wild Decembers* (1999).

Oë, Kenzaburo (1935–) Japanese novelist, born Uchiko, Shikoku; *A Personal Matter* (1968), *The Silent Cry* (1974), *Hiroshima Notes* (1981), *Somersault* (2003); Nobel Prize for literature 1994.

Okri, Ben (1959–) Nigerian novelist, born Minna; *The Famished Road* (1991, Booker Prize), *Dangerous Love* (1996), *In Arcadia* (2002).

Ondaatje, (Philip) **Michael** (1943–) Canadian novelist, poet, born Ceylon (now Sri Lanka); *Coming Through Slaughter* (1976), *In the Skin of a Lion* (1987), *The English Patient* (1991, Booker Prize 1992), *Anil's Ghost* (2000).

Orwell, George (pseudonym of Eric Arthur Blair) (1903–50) English novelist, born Bengal, India; *Down and Out in Paris and London* (1933), *The Road to Wigan Pier* (1937), *Animal Farm* (1945), *Nineteen Eighty-Four* (1949).

Pasternak, Boris (Leonidovich) (1890–1960) Russian novelist, born Moscow; *Doctor Zhivago* (1957); Nobel Prize for literature 1958.

Paton, Allan (Stewart) (1903–88) South African novelist, short-story writer, born Pietermaritzburg, Natal; *Cry, the Beloved Country* (1948).

Peake, Mervyn (Laurence) (1911–68) English novelist, poet, born Kuling, China; *Titus Groan* (1946), *Gormenghast* (1950), *Titus Alone* (1959).

Plaidy, Jean ► Holt, Victoria

Poe, Edgar Allan (1809–49) US short-story writer, poet, born Boston, Massachusetts; *Tales of the Grotesque and Arabesque* (eg 'The Fall of the House of Usher') (1840), *The Pit and the Pendulum* (1843).

Porter, Katherine Anne (Maria Veronica Callista Russell) (1890–1980) US novelist, short-story writer, born Indian Creek, Texas; *Pale Horse, Pale Rider* (1939), *Ship of Fools* (1962).

Powell, Anthony (Dymoke) (1905–2000) English novelist, born London; *A Dance to the Music of Time* (1951–75), *The Fisher King* (1986).

Powys, John Cowper (1872–1963) English novelist, born Shirley, Derbyshire; *Wolf Solent* (1929), *Owen Glendower* (1940).

Pratchett, Terry (1948–) English novelist, born Beaconsfield, Buckinghamshire; *The Colour of Magic* (1983), *Only You Can Save Mankind* (1992), *Carpe Jugulum* (1998), *Watersmith* (2006).

Priestley, J(ohn) B(oynton) (1894–1984) English novelist, playwright, born Bradford, Yorkshire; *The Good Companions* (1929), *Angel Pavement* (1930).

Pritchett, Sir V(ictor) S(awdon) (1900–97) English novelist, short-story writer, playwright, born Ipswich, Suffolk; *Nothing like Leather* (1935), *Dead Man Leading* (1937), *Mr Beluncle* (1951), *The Key to My Heart* (1963), *Man of Letters* (essays) (1985).

Proulx, E Annie (1935–) US novelist, short-story writer, born Norwich, Connecticut; *Postcards* (1993), *The Shipping News* (1993, Pulitzer Prize 1994), *That Old Ace in the Hole* (2002), *Bad Dirt* (2004).

Proust, Marcel (1871–1922) French novelist, born Paris; *Remembrance of Things Past* (1913–27).

Puzo, Mario (1920–99) US novelist, born New York City; *The Godfather* (1969), *The Last Don* (1996), *Omerta* (2000).

Pynchon, Thomas (1937–) US novelist, born Long Island, New York; *V* (1963), *Gravity's Rainbow* (1973), *Vineland* (1990), *Mason & Dixon* (1997), *Against the Day* (2006).

Queen, Ellery (pseudonym of **Patrick Dannay** (1905–82) and his cousin **Manfred B Lee** (1905–71)) US novelists and short-story writers, both born Brooklyn, New York City; *The French Powder Mystery* (1930), *The Tragedy of X* (1940), *The Glass Village* (1954).

Rankin, Ian (James) (1960–) Scottish novelist, born Fife; *The Flood* (1985), *Knots and Crosses* (1987), *Black and Blue* (1997), *Resurrection Men* (2002), *The Naming of the Dead* (2006).

Remarque, Erich Maria (1898–1970) German novelist, born Osnabrück; *All Quiet on the Western Front* (1929), *The Road Back* (1931), *The Black Obelisk* (1957).

Rendell, Ruth (Barbara), **Baroness** (1930–) English novelist, born London, also writes as Barbara Vine; *A Judgement in Stone* (1977), *The Killing Doll* (1980), *Heartstones* (1987), *The Water's Lovely* (2006); as Barbara Vine: *The House of Stairs* (1989), *Blood Doctor* (2002).

Richardson, Samuel (1689–1761) English novelist, born near Derby; *Pamela* (1740), *Clarissa* (1747–8), *Sir Charles Grandison* (1753–4).

Robbins, Harold (pseudonym of **Francis Kane**) (1916–97) US novelist, born Hell's Kitchen, New York City; *Never Love a Stranger* (1948), *A Stone for Danny Fisher* (1951), *The Carpetbaggers* (1961), *The Betsy* (1971), *Tycoon* (1996).

Roth, Philip Milton (1933–) US novelist, short-story writer, born Newark, New Jersey; *Goodbye Columbus* (1959), *Portnoy's Complaint* (1969), *The Great American Novel* (1973), *My Life as a Man* (1974), *Patrimony* (1991), *American Pastoral* (1997, Pulitzer Prize 1998), *The Plot Against America* (2004).

Rushdie, (Ahmed) Salman (1947–) British novelist, short-story writer, born Bombay (now Mumbai), India; *Midnight's Children* (1981, Booker Prize), *Shame* (1983), *The Satanic Verses* (1988), *Haroun and the Sea of Stories* (1990), *The Moor's Last Sigh* (1995), *Shalimar the Clown* (2005).

Sackville-West, Vita (Victoria May) (1892–1962) English poet, novelist, short-story writer, born Knole, Kent; *The Edwardians* (1930), *All Passion Spent* (1931).

Sade, Donatien Alphonse François, Comte de, (known as **Marquis**) (1740–1814) French novelist, born Paris; *Les 120 Journées de Sodome* (1784), *Justine* (1791), *La Philosophie dans le boudoir* (1793), *Juliette* (1798), *Les Crimes de l'amour* (1800).

Saki (pseudonym of **Hector Hugh Munro**) (1870–1916) British novelist, short-story writer, born Akyab, Burma (now Myanmar); *The Chronicles of Clovis* (1912), *The Unbearable Bassington* (1912).

Salinger, J(erome) D(avid) (1919–) US novelist, born New York; *The Catcher in the Rye* (1951), *Franny and Zooey* (1961), *Hapworth 16, 1924* (1997).

Sartre, Jean-Paul (1905–80) French novelist, playwright, born Paris; *Nausea* (1949), *The Roads to Freedom* (1945–7); Nobel Prize for literature 1964.

Sayers, Dorothy L(eigh) (1893–1957) English novelist, short-story writer, born Oxford; *Lord Peter Views the Body* (1928), *Gaudy Night* (1935).

Scott, Sir Walter (1771–1832) Scottish novelist, poet, born Edinburgh; *Waverley* (1814), *Rob Roy* (1817), *The Heart of Midlothian* (1818), *The Bride of Lammermoor* (1819), *Ivanhoe* (1820).

Sharpe, Tom (Thomas Ridley) (1928–) English novelist, born London; *Riotous Assembly* (1971), *Porterhouse Blue* (1973), *Blott on the Landscape* (1975), *Wilt* (1976), *Grantchester Grind* (1995), *The Midden* (1996).

Shelley, Mary (Wollstonecraft) (née **Godwin**) (1797–1851) English novelist, born London; *Frankenstein* (1818), *The Last Man* (1826), *Perkin Warbeck* (1830).

Shields, Carol (Ann) (née **Warner**) (1935–2003) Canadian novelist, born Illinois, USA; *Small Ceremonies* (1976), *Happenstance* (1980), *Swann: A Mystery* (1987), *The Republic of Love* (1992), *The Stone Diaries* (1993, Pulitzer Prize 1995), *Larry's Party* (1997, Orange Prize 1998), *Dressing Up for the Carnival* (2000).

Sholokhov, Mikhail Alexandrovich (1905–84) Russian novelist, born near Veshenskayal; *And Quiet Flows the Don* (1928–40), *The Upturned Soil* (1940); Nobel Prize for literature 1965.

Shute, Nevil (pseudonym of **Nevil Shute Norway**) (1899–1960) Anglo-Australian novelist, born Ealing, London; *The Pied Piper* (1942), *A Town Like Alice* (1950), *On the Beach* (1957).

Sillitoe, Alan (1928–) English novelist, poet, short-story writer, born Nottingham; *Saturday Night and Sunday Morning* (1958), *The Loneliness of the Long Distance Runner* (1959), *The Broken Chariot* (1998).

Simenon, Georges (1903–89) French writer, born Liège, Belgium; almost 100 novels featuring Jules Maigret, and 400 other novels: *The Death of Monsieur Gallet* (1932), *The Crime of Inspector Maigret* (1933).

Simon, Claude (Henri Eugène) (1913–2005) French novelist, born Tananarive, Madagascar; *The Wind* (1959), *The Flanders Road* (1962), *Triptych* (1977); Nobel Prize for literature 1985.

Smith, Alexander McCall (1948–) Scottish novelist and children's writer, born

Zimbabwe; *No. 1 Ladies' Detective Agency* (1998), *Tears of the Giraffe* (2000), *The Sunday Philosophy Club* (2004), *Blue Shoes and Happiness* (2006).

Smith, Zadie (1975–) English novelist, born London; *White Teeth* (2000), *The Autograph Man* (2002), *On Beauty* (2005).

Smollett, Tobias George (1721–71) Scottish novelist, born Dalquharn, Dunbartonshire; *Roderick Random* (1748), *The Adventures of Peregrine Pickle* (1751), *The Expedition of Humphrey Clinker* (1771).

Snow, C(harles) P(ercy) (1905–80) English novelist, born Leicester; *Strangers and Brothers* (1940–70).

Solzhenitsyn, Aleksandr Isayevich (1918–) Russian novelist, born Kislovodsk, Caucasus; *One Day in the Life of Ivan Denisovich* (1963), *Cancer Ward* (1968), *The First Circle* (1969), *The Gulag Archipelago 1918–56* (3 vols 1974–8); Nobel Prize for literature 1970.

Spark, Dame Muriel (Sarah) (née **Camberg**) (1918–2006) Scottish novelist, short-story writer, poet, born Edinburgh; *The Ballad of Peckham Rye* (1960), *The Prime of Miss Jean Brodie* (1961), *The Girls of Slender Means* (1963), *The Mandelbaum Gate* (1965), *A Far Cry from Kensington* (1988), *Reality and Dreams* (1996), *Aiding and Abetting* (2000).

Stein, Gertrude (1874–1946) US novelist, short-story writer, born Allegheny, Pennsylvania; *Three Lives* (1909), *Tender Buttons* (1914).

Steinbeck, John Ernest (1902–68) US novelist, born Salinas, California; *Of Mice and Men* (1937), *The Grapes of Wrath* (1939), *Cannery Row* (1945), *East of Eden* (1952); Nobel Prize for literature 1962.

Stendhal (pseudonym of **Henri Marie Beyle**) (1788–1842) French novelist, born Grenoble; *Le Rouge et le noir* (1830), *La Chartreuse de Parme* (1839).

Sterne, Lawrence (1713–68) Irish novelist, born Clonmel, Tipperary; *Tristram Shandy* (1759–67), *A Sentimental Journey* (1768).

Stevenson, Robert Louis (Balfour) (1850–94) Scottish novelist, short-story writer, poet, born Edinburgh; *Travels with a Donkey* (1879), *Treasure Island* (1883), *Kidnapped* (1886), *The Strange Case of Dr Jekyll and Mr Hyde* (1886), *Weir of Hermiston* (1896).

Stewart, Mary (Florence Elinor) (1916–) English novelist, born Sunderland; *This Rough Magic* (1964), *The Last Enchantment* (1979), *The Prince and the Pilgrim* (1995).

Stoker, Bram (Abraham) (1847–1912) Irish novelist, short-story writer, born Dublin; *Dracula* (1897).

Storey, David (Malcolm) (1933–) English novelist, playwright, born Wakefield, Yorkshire; *This Sporting Life* (1960), *Radcliffe* (1963), *Saville* (1976, Booker Prize), *A Prodigal Child* (1982), *Thin-Ice Skater* (2004).

Stowe, Harriet (Elizabeth) Beecher (1811–96) US novelist, born Litchfield, Connecticut; *Uncle Tom's Cabin* (1852).

Styron, William (Clark) (1925–2006) US novelist, born Newport News, Virginia; *The Confessions of Nat Turner* (1967, Pulitzer Prize 1968), *Sophie's Choice* (1979), *A Tidewater Morning* (1993).

Swift, Graham (Colin) (1949–) English novelist, born London; *The Sweet Shop Owner* (1980), *Waterland* (1983), *Out of This World* (1988), *Ever After* (1992), *Last Orders* (1996, Booker Prize), *The Light of Day* (2003).

Swift, Jonathan (1667–1745) Irish novelist, poet, born Dublin; *A Tale of a Tub* (1704), *Gulliver's Travels* (1726).

Tennant, Emma (Christina) (1937–) English novelist, born London; *Hotel de Dream* (1978), *Alice Fell* (1980), *Pemberley* (1993), *Elinor and Marianne* (1996), *The Amazing Marriage* (2006).

Thackeray, William Makepeace (1811–63) English novelist, born Calcutta (now Kolkata), India; *Vanity Fair* (1847–8), *Pendennis* (1848–50).

Theroux, Paul (Edward) (1941–) US novelist, short-story writer, travel writer, born Medford, Massachusetts; *The Mosquito Coast* (1981), *The Kingdom by the Sea* (travel) (1983), *Riding the Iron Rooster* (travel) (1988), *My Secret History* (1989), *My Other Life* (1996), *Blinding Light* (2006).

Thomas, D(onald) M(ichael) (1935–) English novelist, poet, born Redruth, Cornwall; *The White Hotel* (1981); *Ararat* (1983), *Swallow* (1984), *Sphinx* (1986), *Summit* (1987), *Lying Together* (1990), *Eating Pavlova* (1994), *Charlotte* (2000).

Tolkien, J(ohn) R(onald) R(euel) (1892–1973) English novelist, born Bloemfontein, South Africa; *The Hobbit* (1937), *The Lord of the Rings* (1954–5).

Tolstoy, Count Leo Nikolayevich (1828–1910) Russian novelist, born Yasnaya Polyana, Central Russia; *War and Peace* (1863–9), *Anna Karenina* (1873–7), *Resurrection* (1899).

Tranter, Nigel Godwin (1909–99) Scottish novelist, born Glasgow; over 100 novels including *The Steps to the Empty Throne* (1969), *The Path of the Hero King* (1970), *The Price of the King's Peace* (1971), *Honours Even* (1995).

Trevor, William (properly **William Trevor Cox**) (1928–) Irish novelist, short-story writer, born Mitchelstown, County Cork; *Fools of Fortune* (1983), *The Silence in the Garden* (1988), *Two Lives* (1991), *Felicia's Journey* (1994), *The Story of Lucy Gault* (2002).

Trollope, Anthony (1815–82) English novelist, born London; *Barchester Towers* (1857), *Can You Forgive Her?* (1864), *The Way We Live Now* (1875).

Trollope, Joanna (1943–) English novelist, born Gloucestershire; *Eliza Stanhope* (1978), *The Choir* (1988), *A Village Affair* (1989), *The Rector's Wife* (1991), *Second Honeymoon* (2006).

Turgenev, Ivan Sergeevich (1818–83) Russian novelist, born province of Oryel; *Sportsman's Sketches* (1952), *Fathers and Children* (1862).

Twain, Mark (pseudonym of **Samuel Langhorne Clemens**) (1835–1910) US novelist, born Florida, Missouri; *The Celebrated Jumping Frog of Calaveras County* (1865), *The Adventures of Tom Sawyer* (1876), *The Prince and the Pauper* (1882), *The Adventures of Huckleberry Finn* (1884), *A Connecticut Yankee in King Arthur's Court* (1889).

Updike, John (Hoyer) (1932–) US novelist, short-story writer, born Shillington, Pennsylvania; *Rabbit, Run* (1960), *Pigeon Feathers and Other Stories* (1962), *Rabbit is Rich* (1981, Pulitzer Prize 1982), *The Witches of Eastwick* (1984), *Rabbit at Rest* (1990, Pulitzer Prize 1991), *Terrorist* (2006).

Uris, Leon (Marcus) (1924–2003) US novelist, born Baltimore, Maryland; *Battle Cry* (1953), *Exodus* (1958), *The Haj* (1984), *Redemption* (1995).

Van der Post, Sir Laurens (Jan) (1906–96) South African novelist, playwright, born Philippolis; *Flamingo Feather* (1955), *Journey into Russia* (1964), *A Far-Off Place* (1974).

Vargas Llosa, Mario (1936–) Peruvian novelist, born Arequipa; *The Time of the Hero* (1962), *The Green House* (1966), *Aunt Julia and the Scriptwriter* (1977), *The War at the End of the World* (1981), *The Feast of the Goat* (2000).

Verne, Jules (1828–1905) French novelist, born Nantes; *Voyage to the Centre of the Earth* (1864), *Twenty Thousand Leagues under the Sea* (1870).

Vidal, Gore (Eugene Luther, Jr) (1925–) US novelist, short-story writer, playwright, born West Point, New York; *Williwaw* (1946), *The City and the Pillar* (1948), *The Judgement of Paris* (1952), *Myra Breckenridge* (1968), *Creation* (1981), *Lincoln* (1984), *Empire* (1987), *Hollywood* (1989), *The Golden Age* (2000).

Vine, Barbara ▶ Rendell, Ruth

Voltaire, François-Marie Arouet de (1694–1778) French novelist, poet, born Paris; *Zadig* (1747), *Candide* (1759).

Vonnegut, Kurt, Jr (1922–2007) US novelist, short-story writer, born Indianapolis, Indiana; *Cat's Cradle* (1963), *Slaughterhouse-Five* (1969), *Hocus Pocus* (1990), *Timequake* (1997).

Wain, John (Barrington) (1925–94) English novelist, poet, short-story writer, playwright, born Stoke-on-Trent, Staffordshire; *Hurry on Down* (1953), *The Young Visitors* (1965), *Where the Rivers Meet* (1988).

Walker, Alice (Malsenior) (1944–) US novelist, short-story writer, born Eatonville, Georgia; *The Third Life of Grange Copeland* (1970), *Meridian* (1976), *The Color Purple* (1982, Pulitzer Prize 1983), *Now is the Time to Open Your Heart* (2004).

Walpole, Horace (1717–97) English novelist, poet, born London; *Letter from Xotto to his Friend Lien Chi at Pekin* (1757), *Anecdotes of Painting in England* (1761–71), *The Castle of Otranto* (1764), *The Mysterious Mother* (1768), *Historic Doubts on the Life and Reign of King Richard the Third* (1768).

Waterhouse, Keith (Spencer) (1929–) English novelist, playwright, born Leeds, Yorkshire; *Billy Liar* (1959), *Office Life* (1978), *Bimbo* (1990), *Unsweet Charity* (1992), *Palace Pier* (2005).

Waugh, Evelyn (Arthur St John) (1903–66) English novelist, born Hampstead, London; *Decline and Fall* (1928), *A Handful of Dust* (1934), *Brideshead Revisited* (1945).

Weldon, Fay (originally Franklin Birkinshaw) (1931–) English novelist, born Alvechurch, Worcestershire; *Down Among the Women* (1971), *Female Friends* (1975), *Life and Loves of a She-Devil* (1983), *Worst Fears* (1996), *Mantrapped* (2004).

Wells, H(erbert) G(eorge) (1866–1946) English novelist, born Bromley, Kent; *The Time Machine* (1895), *The War of the Worlds* (1898), *The History of Mr Polly* (1910).

Welsh, Irvine (1958–) Scottish novelist, born Edinburgh; *Trainspotting* (1993), *Filth* (1998), *Porno* (2002), *The Bedroom Secrets of the Master Chefs* (2006).

Welty, Eudora (1909–2001) US novelist, short-story writer, born Jackson, Mississippi; *A Curtain of Green* (1941), *The Robber Bridegroom* (1944), *The Golden Apples* (1949), *The Ponder Heart* (1954), *The Optimist's Daughter* (1972, Pulitzer Prize 1973), *A Writer's Eye: Collected Book Reviews* (1994).

Wesley, Mary (pseudonym of Mary Aline Siepmann) (née Farmar) (1912–2002) English novelist, born Englefield Green, Berkshire; *The Camomile Lawn* (1984), *A Sensible Life* (1990), *Part of the Furniture* (1997).

Wharton, Edith (Newbold) (1862–1937) US novelist, short-story writer, born New York; *The House of Mirth* (1905), *Ethan Frome* (1911), *The Age of Innocence* (1920).

White, Patrick Victor Martindale (1912–90) Australian novelist, playwright, short-story writer, born London; *Voss* (1957), *The Vivisector* (1970), *A Fringe of Leaves* (1976); Nobel Prize for literature 1973.

Wilde, Oscar (Fingal O'Flahertie Wills) (1854–1900) Irish novelist, short-story writer, playwright, poet, born Dublin; *The Happy Prince and Other Tales* (1888), *The Picture of Dorian Gray* (1890).

Wilder, Thornton (Niven) (1897–1976) US novelist, playwright, born Madison, Wisconsin; *The Bridge of San Luis Rey* (1927), *The Woman of Andros* (1930), *Heaven's My Destination* (1935).

Winterson, Jeanette (1959–) English novelist, born Manchester; *Oranges Are Not the Only Fruit* (1985), *The Passion* (1987), *Sexing the Cherry* (1989), *Gut Symmetries* (1997), *Lighthouse Keeping* (2004).

Wodehouse, Sir P(elham) G(renville) (1881–1975) English novelist, short-story writer, born Guildford, Surrey; *The Inimitable Jeeves* (1923), *Carry on, Jeeves* (1925).

Wolfe, Thomas Clayton (1900–38) US novelist, born Asheville, North Carolina; *Look Homeward, Angel* (1929), *Of Time and the River* (1935), *From Death to Morning* (1935).

Wolfe, Tom (Thomas Kennerly) (1931–) US novelist, journalist, born Richmond, Virginia; *The Kandy-Kolored Tangerine-Flake Streamline Baby* (1965), *The Electric Kool-Aid Acid Test* (1968), *The Right Stuff* (1979), *The Bonfire of the Vanities* (1st novel) (1988), *A Man in Full* (1998), *I Am Charlotte Simmons* (2004).

Woolf, (Adeline) Virginia (1882–1941) English novelist, born London; *Mrs Dalloway* (1925), *To The Lighthouse* (1927), *Orlando* (1928), *A Room of One's Own* (1929), *The Waves* (1931).

Wouk, Herman (1915–) US novelist, playwright, born New York City; *The Caine Mutiny* (1951, Pulitzer Prize 1952), *The Winds of War* (1971), *War and Remembrance* (1978), *Inside, Outside* (1985), *The Hope* (1993), *The Glory* (1994).

Wyndham, John (pseudonym of John Wyndham Parkes Lucas Beynon Harris) (1903–69) English novelist, born Knowle, Warwickshire; *The Day of the Triffids* (1951), *The Kraken Wakes* (1953), *The Chrysalids* (1955), *The Midwich Cuckoos* (1957), *The Trouble with Lichen* (1960), *Consider Her Ways* (1961) (short stories), *Chocky* (1968).

Yerby, Frank (Garvin) (1916–91) US novelist, born Augusta, Georgia; *The Golden Hawk* (1948), *The Dahomean* (1971), *A Darkness at Ingraham's Crest* (1979).

Yourcenar, Marguerite (pseudonym of Marguerite de Crayencour) (1903–87) French novelist, poet, born Brussels; *Memoirs of Hadrian* (1941).

Zola, Émile (1840–1902) French novelist, born Paris; *Thérèse Raquin* (1867), *Les Rougon-Macquart* (1871–93), *Germinal* (1885).

Literary prizes 1990–2006

■ Booker Prize (UK)

1990	A S Byatt, *Possession*
1991	Ben Okri, *The Famished Road*
1992	Michael Ondaatje, *The English Patient;* Barry Unsworth, *Sacred Hunger*
1993	Roddy Doyle, *Paddy Clarke, Ha Ha Ha*
1994	James Kelman, *How late it was, how late*
1995	Pat Barker, *The Ghost Road*
1996	Graham Swift, *Last Orders*
1997	Arundhati Roy, *The God of Small Things*
1998	Ian McEwan, *Amsterdam*
1999	J M Coetzee, *Disgrace*
2000	Margaret Atwood, *The Blind Assassin*
2001	Peter Carey, *True History of the Kelly Gang*
2002	Yann Martel, *Life of Pi*

2003	D B C Pierre, *Vernon God Little*
2004	Alan Hollinghurst, *The Line of Beauty*
2005	John Banville, *The Sea*
2006	Kiran Desai, *The Inheritance of Loss*

■ Orange Prize for Fiction (women writers)

1998	Carol Shields, *Larry's Party*
1999	Suzanne Berne, *A Crime in the Neighborhood*
2000	Linda Grant, *When I Lived in Modern Times*
2001	Kate Grenville, *The Idea of Perfection*
2002	Ann Patchett, *Bel Canto*
2003	Valerie Martin, *Property*
2004	Andrea Levy, *Small Island*
2005	Lionel Shriver, *We Need to Talk About Kevin*
2006	Zadie Smith, *On Beauty*

■ Prix Goncourt (France)

1990	Jean Rouaud, *Les Champs d'Honneur*
1991	Pierre Combescot, *Les Filles du Calvaire*
1992	Patrick Chamoiseau, *Texaco*
1993	Amin Maalouf, *Le Rocher de Tanios*
1994	Didier van Cauwelaert, *Un Aller simple*
1995	Andréï Makine, *Le Testament français*
1996	Pascale Roze, *Le Chasseur Zéro*
1997	Patrick Rambaud, *La Bataille*
1998	Paule Constant, *Confidence pour confidence*
1999	Jean Echenoz, *Je m'en vais*
2000	Jean-Jacques Schuhl, *Ingrid Caven*
2001	Jean-Christophe Rufin, *Rouge Brésil*
2002	Pascal Quignard, *Les ombres errantes*
2003	Jacques-Pierre Amette, *La maîtresse de Brecht*
2004	Laurent Gaudé, *Le soleil des Scorta*
2005	François Weyergans, *Trois jours chez ma mère*
2006	Jonathan Littel, *Les Bienveillantes*

■ Pulitzer Prize in Letters: Fiction (USA)

1990	Oscar Hijuelos, *The Mambo Kings Play Songs of Love*
1991	John Updike, *Rabbit at Rest*
1992	Jane Smiley, *A Thousand Acres*
1993	Robert Olen Butler, *A Good Scent From A Strange Mountain*
1994	E Annie Proulx, *The Shipping News*
1995	Carol Shields, *The Stone Diaries*
1996	Richard Ford, *Independence Day*
1997	Steven Millhauser, *Martin Dressler: The Tale of an American Dreamer*
1998	Philip Roth, *American Pastoral*
1999	Michael Cunningham, *The Hours*
2000	Jhumpa Lahiri, *Interpreter of Maladies*

■ **Pulitzer Prize in Letters: Fiction (USA)**

2001	Michael Chabon, *The Amazing Adventures of Kavalier & Clay*
2002	Richard Russo, *Empire Falls*
2003	Jeffrey Eugenides, *Middlesex*
2004	Edward P Jones, *The Known World*
2005	Marilynne Robinson, *Gilead*
2006	Geraldine Brooks, *March*

Poets

Selected volumes of poetry are listed.

Abse, Dannie (Daniel) (1923–   ) Welsh, born Cardiff; *After Every Green Thing* (1948), *Tenants of the House* (1957), *There Was a Young Man from Cardiff* (1991), *Arcadia, One Mile* (1998), *Running Late* (2006).

Adcock, (Kareen) Fleur (1934–   ) New Zealander, born Auckland; *The Eye of the Hurricane* (1964), *In Focus* (1977), *The Incident Book* (1986), *Poems 1960–2000* (2000).

Aiken, Conrad (Potter) (1889–1973) American, born Georgia; *Earth Triumphant* (1914), *Preludes for Memnon* (1931).

Akhmatova, Anna (pseudonym of **Anna Andreevna Gorenko**) (1889–1966) Russian, born Odessa; *Evening* (1912), *Poem without a Hero* (1940–62), *Requiem* (1963).

Angelou, Maya (Marguerite Annie) (née **Johnson**) (1928–   ) American, born St Louis, Missouri; *And Still I Rise* (1978), *I Shall Not Be Moved* (1990), *The Complete Collected Poems of Maya Angelou* (1995).

Apollinaire, Guillaume (pseudonym of **Wilhelm Apollinaris de Kostrowitzky**) (1880–1918) French, born Rome; *Alcools* (1913), *Calligrammes* (1918).

Ariosto, Ludovico (1474–1535) Italian, born Reggio; *Orlando Furioso* (1532).

Auden, W(ystan) H(ugh) (1907–73) British, naturalized US citizen, born York; *Another Time* (1940), *The Sea and the Mirror* (1944), *The Age of Anxiety* (1947).

Baudelaire, Charles (Pierre) (1821–67) French, born Paris; *Les Fleurs du mal* (1857).

Beer, Patricia (1919–99) English, born Exmouth, Devon; *The Loss of the Magyar* (1959), *The Lie of the Land* (1983), *Friend of Heraclitus* (1993).

Belloc, (Joseph) Hillaire (Pierre) (1870–1953) British, born St Cloud, France; *Cautionary Tales* (1907), *Sonnets and Verse* (1923).

Berryman, John (1914–72) American, born McAlester, Oklahoma; *Homage to Mistress Bradsheet* (1966), *Dream Songs* (1969).

Betjeman, Sir John (1906–84) English, born Highgate, London; *Mount Zion* (1931), *New Bats in Old Belfries* (1945), *A Nip in the Air* (1972).

Bishop, Elizabeth (1911–79) American, born Worcester, Massachusetts; *North and South* (1946), *Geography III* (1978).

Blake, William (1757–1827) English, born London; *The Marriage of Heaven and Hell* (1793), *The Visions of the Daughters of Albion* (1793), *Songs of Innocence and Experience* (1794), *Vala*, or *The Four Zoas* (1800), *Milton* (1810).

Blunden, Edmund (Charles) (1896–1974) English, born Yalding, Kent; *The Waggoner and Other Poems* (1920).

Brodsky, Joseph (originally **Iosif Aleksandrovich Brodsky**) (1940–96) Russian–American, born Leningrad (now St Petersburg); *Longer and Shorter Poems* (1965), *To Urania: Selected Poems 1965–1985* (1988); Nobel Prize for literature 1987.

Brooke, Rupert (Chawner) (1887–1915) English, born Rugby; *Poems* (1911); *1914 and Other Poems* (1915), *New Numbers* (1915).

Brooks, Gwendolyn (Elizabeth) (1917–2000) American, born Topeka, Kansas; *A Street in Bronzeville* (1945), *Annie Allen* (1949, Pulitzer Prize 1950), *In The Mecca* (1968), *Blacks* (1987).

Browning, Elizabeth Barrett (née Barrett) (1806–61) English, born Coxhoe Hall, near Durham; *Sonnets from the Portuguese* (1850), *Aurora Leigh* (1855).

Browning, Robert (1812–89) English, born Camberwell, London; *Bells and Pomegranates* (1841–6), *Men and Women* (1855), *The Ring and the Book* (1868–9).

Burns, Robert (1759–96) Scottish, born Alloway, Ayr; *Poems, Chiefly in the Scottish Dialect* (1786), *Tam o'Shanter* (1790).

Byron, George Gordon, 6th Baron (1788–1824) English, born London; *Hours of Idleness* (1807), *Childe Harolde's Pilgrimage* (1817), *Don Juan* (1819–24).

Catullus, Gaius Valerius (c.84–c.54 BC) Roman, born Verona; lyric poet, over 100 poems survive.

Causley, Charles (1917–2003) English, born Launceston, Cornwall; *Union St* (1957), *Johnny Alleluia* (1961), *Underneath the Water* (1968), *All Day Saturday* (1994), *Collected Poems for Children* (1996).

Chaucer, Geoffrey (c.1343–1400) English, born London; *Book of the Duchess* (1370), *Troilus and Cressida* (c.1385), *The Canterbury Tales* (1387–1400).

Clampitt, Amy (1920–94) American, born Iowa; *The Kingfisher* (1983), *Archaic Figure* (1987), *Westward* (1990).

Clare, John (1773–1864) English, born Helpstone, Northamptonshire; *Poems Descriptive of Rural Life* (1820), *The Shepherd's Calendar* (1827).

Coleridge, Samuel Taylor (1772–1834) English, born Ottery St Mary, Devon; *Poems on Various Subjects* (1796), 'Kubla Khan' (1797), 'The Rime of the Ancient Mariner' (1798), *Christabel and Other Poems* (1816), *Sibylline Leaves* (1817).

Cowper, William (1731–1800) English, born Great Berkhampstead, Hertfordshire; *The Task* (1785).

Crabbe, George (1754–1823) English, born Aldeburgh, Suffolk; *The Village* (1783).

cummings, e(dward) e(stlin) (1894–1962) American, born Cambridge, Massachusetts; *Tulips and Chimneys* (1923), *XLI Poems* (1925), *is 5* (1926).

Dante Alighieri (1265–1321) Italian, born Florence; *Vita Nuova* (1294), *Divine Comedy* (1321).

Day-Lewis, Cecil (1904–72) Irish, born Ballintubbert, Laois; *Overtures to Death* (1938), *The Aeneid of Virgil* (1952).

de la Mare, Walter (1873–1956) English, born Charleston, Kent; *The Listeners* (1912), *The Burning Glass and Other Poems* (1945).

Dickinson, Emily (Elizabeth) (1830–86) American, born Amherst, Massachusetts; only seven poems published in her lifetime; posthumous publications, eg *Poems* (1890).

Donne, John (c.1572–1631) English, born London; *Satires & Elegies* (1590s), *Holy Sonnets* (1610–11), *Songs and Sonnets*; most verse published posthumously.

Doolittle, Hilda (known as H D) (1886–1961) American, born Bethlehem, Pennsylvania; *Sea Garden* (1916), *The Walls Do Not Fall* (1944), *Helen in Egypt* (1961).

Dryden, John (1631–1700) English, born Adwinckle All Saints, Northamptonshire; *Astrea Redux* (1660), *Absalom and Achitophel* (1681), *'Mac Flecknoe'* (1684).

Duffy, Carol Ann (1955–) Scottish, born Glasgow; *Standing Female Nude* (1985), *Mean Time* (1993), *The World's Wife* (1999), *Rapture* (2005).

Dunbar, William (c.1460–c.1520) Scottish, birthplace probably E Lothian; *'The Thrissill and the Rois'* (1503), *'Lament for the Makaris'* (c.1507).

Dunn, Douglas (Eaglesham) (1942–) Scottish, born Inchinnan, Renfrewshire; *Love or Nothing* (1974), *Elegies* (1985), *Dante's Drum-kit* (1993), *The Year's Afternoon* (2000).

Dutton, Geoffrey (Piers Henry) (1922–98) Australian, born Kapunda; *Antipodes in Shoes* (1958), *Poems, Soft and Loud* (1968), *A Body of Words* (1977), *New and Selected Poems* (1993).

Eliot, T(homas) S(tearns) (1888–1965) American (British citizen 1927), born St Louis, Missouri; *Prufrock and Other Observations* (1917), *The Waste Land* (1922), *Ash Wednesday* (1930), *Four Quartets* (1944).

Éluard, Paul (pseudonym of Eugène Grindel) (1895–1952) French, born Saint-Denis; *La Vie immédiate* (1934), *Poésie et vérité* (1942).

Emerson, Ralph Waldo (1803–84) American, born Boston, Massachusetts; poems published posthumously in *Complete Works* (1903–4).

Empson, Sir William (1906–84) English, born Yokefleet, E Yorkshire; *Poems* (1935), *The Gathering Storm* (1940).

Fanthorpe, U(rsula) A(skham) (1929–) English poet, born Kent; *Side Effects* (1978), *Safe as Houses* (1995), *Consequences* (2000), *Queuing for the Sun* (2003).

Fitzgerald, Edward (1809–83) English, born near Woodbridge, Suffolk; translator of *The Rubaiyat of Omar Khayyam* (1859).

Frost, Robert (Lee) (1874–1963) American, born San Francisco; *North of Boston* (1914), *Mountain Interval* (1916), *New Hampshire* (1923), *In the Clearing* (1962).

Ginsberg, Allen (1926–97) American, born Newark, New Jersey; *Howl and Other Poems* (1956), *Empty Mirror* (1961), *The Fall of America* (1973).

Graves, Robert (Ranke) (1895–1985) English, born London; *Fairies and Fusiliers* (1917).

Gray, Thomas (1716–71) English, born London; *'Elegy Written in a Country Churchyard'* (1751), *Pindaric Odes* (1757).

Gunn, Thom(son William) (1929–2004) English, born Gravesend, Kent; *The Sense of Movement* (1957), *Touch* (1967), *Jack Straw's Castle* (1976), *The Passages of Joy* (1982), *The Man with Night Sweats* (1992), *Boss Cupid* (2000).

Heaney, Seamus (Justin) (1939–) Northern Irish, born Castledawson, County Derry; *Death of a Naturalist* (1966), *Door into the Dark* (1969), *Field Work* (1979), *Seeing Things* (1991), *Spirit Level* (1995), *Beowulf: A New Translation* (2000), *District and Circle* (2006); Nobel Prize for literature 1995.

Henri, Adrian (Maurice) (1932–2000) English, born Birkenhead; *The Mersey Sound: Penguin Modern Poets 10* (with Roger McGough and Brian Patten) (1967), *Tonight at Noon* (1968), *From the Loveless Motel* (1980), *Wish You Were Here* (1990), *Not Fade Away* (1994), *Robocat* (1998).

Henryson, Robert (c.1430–1506) Scottish, birthplace unknown; *Testament of Cresseid*, *Morall Fables of Esope the Phrygian*.

Herbert, George (1593–1633) English, born Montgomery, Wales; *The Temple* (1633).

Herrick, Robert (1591–1674) English, born London; *Hesperides* (1648).

Hill, Geoffrey (William) (1932–) English, born Bromsgrove, Worcestershire; *King Log* (1968), *Mercian Hymns* (1971), *Tenebrae* (1978), *Canaan* (1996), *Without Title* (2006).

Hodgson, Ralph (Edwin) (1871–1962) English, born Yorkshire; *Poems* (1917), *The Skylark and Other Poems* (1958).

Homer (10c–8c BC) Greek, birthplace and existence disputed; he is credited with the writing or writing down of *The Iliad* and *The Odyssey*.

Hopkins, Gerard Manley (1844–89) English, born Stratford, London; 'The Wreck of the Deutschland' (1876), posthumously published *Poems* (1918).

Horace, Quintus Horatius Flaccus (65–8 BC) Roman, born Venusia, Apulia; *Epodes* (30 BC), *Odes* (23–13 BC).

Housman, A(lfred) E(dward) (1859–1936) English, born Flockbury, Worcestershire; *A Shropshire Lad* (1896), *Last Poems* (1922).

Hughes, Ted (1930–98) English, born Mytholmroyd, Yorkshire; *The Hawk in the Rain* (1957), *Lupercal* (1960), *Wodwo* (1967), *Crow* (1970), *Cave Birds* (1975), *Season Songs* (1976), *Gaudete* (1977), *Moortown* (1979), *Wolfwatching* (1989), *Birthday Letters* (1998).

Jennings, Elizabeth (Joan) (1926–2001) English, born Boston, Lincolnshire; *Poems* (1953), *The Mind Has Mountains* (1966), *The Animals' Arrival* (1969), *Relationships* (1972), *Praises* (1998).

Johnson, Samuel (1709–84) English, born Lichfield, Staffordshire; *The Vanity of Human Wishes* (1749).

Kavanagh, Patrick (1905–67) Irish, born Inniskeen; *Ploughman and Other Poems* (1936), *The Great Hunger* (1942).

Keats, John (1795–1821) English, born London; *Endymion* (1818), *Lamia and Other Poems* (1820).

Keyes, Sidney (Arthur Kilworth) (1922–43) English, born Dartford, Kent; *The Iron Laurel* (1942), *The Cruel Solstice* (1943).

La Fontaine, Jean de (1621–95) French, born Château-Thierry, Champagne; *Contes et nouvelles en vers* (1665), *Fables choisies mises en vers* (1668).

Langland or Langley, William (c.1332–c.1400) English, birthplace uncertain, possibly Ledbury, Herefordshire; *Piers Plowman* (1362–99).

Larkin, Philip (Arthur) (1922–85) English, born Coventry; *The North Ship* (1945), *The Whitsun Weddings* (1964), *High Windows* (1974).

Lear, Edward (1812–88) English, born London; *Book of Nonsense* (1846).

Longfellow, Henry (Wadsworth) (1807–82) American, born Portland, Maine; *Voices of the Night* (1839), *Ballads and Other Poems* (1842), *Hiawatha* (1855).

Lowell, Amy (Laurence) (1874–1925) American, born Brookline, Massachusetts; *A Dome of Many-Colored Glass* (1912), *Legends* (1921).

Lowell, Robert (Traill Spence, Jr) (1917–77) American, born Boston, Massachusetts; *Lord Weary's Castle* (1946), *Life Studies* (1959), *Prometheus Bound* (1967).

Macaulay, Thomas (Babington) (1800–59) English, born Rothey Temple, Leicestershire; *The Lays of Ancient Rome* (1842).

MacCaig, Norman (Alexander) (1910–96) Scottish, born Edinburgh; *Far Cry* (1943), *Riding Lights* (1955), *A Round of Applause* (1962), *A Man in My Position* (1969), *Voice-Over* (1988).

MacDiarmid, Hugh (pseudonym of **Christopher Murray Grieve**) (1892–1978) Scottish, born Langholm, Dumfriesshire; *A Drunk Man Looks at the Thistle* (1926).

McGough, Roger (1937–) English, born Liverpool; *The Mersey Sound: Penguin Modern Poets 10* (with Adrian Henri and Brian Patten) (1967), *Gig* (1973), *Waving at Trains* (1982), *An Imaginary Menagerie* (1988), *The Spotted Unicorn* (1998), *The Way Things Are* (1999), *Everyday Eclipses* (2002).

MacLean, Sorley (Gaelic Somhairle Macgill-Eain) (1911–96) Scottish, born Isle of Raasay, off Skye; *Reothairt is Contraigh* (Spring Tide and Neap Tide) (1977).

MacNeice, (Frederick) **Louis** (1907–63) Irish, born Belfast; *Blind Fireworks* (1929), *Solstices* (1961).

Mallarmé, Stéphane (1842–98) French, born Paris; *L'Après-midi d'un faune* (1876), *Poésies* (1899).

Marvell, Andrew (1621–78) English, born Winestead, near Hull; *Miscellaneous Poems by Andrew Marvell, Esq.* (1681).

Masefield, John (Edward) (1878–1967) English, born Ledbury, Herefordshire; *Salt-Water Ballads* (1902).

Millay, Edna St Vincent (1892–1950) American, born Rockland, Maine; *A Few Figs from Thistles* (1920), *The Ballad of Harp-Weaver* (1922).

Milton, John (1608–74) English, born London; *Lycidas* (1637), *Paradise Lost* (1667), *Samson Agonistes* (1671).

Moore, Marianne (Craig) (1887–1972) American, born Kirkwood, Missouri; *The Pangolin and Other Verse* (1936).

Motion, Andrew (1952–) English, born London; *The Pleasure Steamers* (1978), *Love in a Life* (1991), *Salt Water* (1997), *Public Property* (2002).

Muir, Edwin (1887–1959) Scottish, born Deerness, Orkney; *First Poems* (1925), *Chorus of the Newly Dead* (1926), *Variations on a Time Theme* (1934), *The Labyrinth* (1949), *New Poems* (1949–51).

Nash, (Frederick) **Ogden** (1902–71) American, born Rye, New York; *Free Wheeling* (1931).

Ovid (in full **Publius Ovidius Naso**) (43 BC–c.17 AD) Roman, born Sulmo; *Amores* (c.16 BC), *Metamorphoses, Ars Amatoria*.

Owen, Wilfred (Edward Salter) (1893–1918) English, born Oswestry, Shropshire; most poems published posthumously, 1920, by Siegfried Sassoon; *'Dulce et decorum est'*.

Patten, Brian (1946–) English, born Liverpool; *The Mersey Sound: Penguin Modern Poets 10* (with Adrian Henri and Roger McGough) (1967), *Notes to the Hurrying Man* (1969), *Grinning Jack* (1990), *Armada* (1996), *The Blue and Green Ark* (1999).

Paz, Octavio (1914–98) Mexican, born Mexico City; *Sun Stone* (1963), *The Bow and the Lyre* (1973), *Collected Poems 1958–87* (1987), *Glimpses of India* (1995); Nobel Prize for literature 1990.

Petrarch (in full **Francesco Petrarca**) (1304–74) Italian, born Arezzo; *Canzoniere, Trionfi.*

Plath, Sylvia (1932–63) American, born Boston, Massachusetts; *The Colossus and Other Poems* (1960), *Ariel* (1965), *Crossing the Water* (1971).

Pope, Alexander (1688–1744) English, born London; *An Essay on Criticism* (1711), *The Rape of the Lock* (1712), *The Dunciad* (1728–42), *Essay on Man* (1733–4).

Porter, Peter (Neville Frederick) (1929–) Australian, born Brisbane; *Poems, Ancient and Modern* (1964), *English Subtitles* (1981), *The Automatic Oracle* (1987), *Millennial Fables* (1994), *Max is Missing* (2001), *Afterburner* (2004).

Pound, Ezra (Weston Loomis) (1885–1972) American, born Haile, Idaho; *The Cantos* (1917, 1948, 1959).

Pushkin, Aleksandr (Sergeyevich) (1799–1837) Russian, born Moscow; *Eugene Onegin* (1828), *Ruslan and Lyudmilla* (1820).

Raine, Kathleen (Jessie) (1908–2003) English, born London; *Stone and Flower* (1943), *The Hollow Hill* (1965), *Living with Mystery* (1992).

Rich, Adrienne (Cecile) (1929–) American, born Baltimore, Maryland; *The Diamond Cutters* (1955), *Snapshots of a Daughter-in-Law* (1963), *The Will to Change* (1971), *Dark Fields of the Republic* (1995), *The School Among the Ruins* (2004).

Riding, Laura (née **Reichenfeld**) (1901–91) American, born New York; *The Close Chaplet* (1926).

Rilke, Rainer Maria (1875–1926) Austrian, born Prague; *Die Sonette an Orpheus* (1923), *Duino Elegies* (1939).

Rimbaud, (Jean Nicholas) **Arthur** (1854–91) French, born Charleville, Ardennes; *Le Bateau ivre* (1871), *Les Illuminations* (1886).

Rochester, John Wilmot, Earl of (1647–80) English, born Ditchley, Oxfordshire; *A Satyre Against Mankind* (1675).

Roethke, Theodore Huebner (1908–63) American, born Saginaw, Michigan; *Open House* (1941), *The Lost Son and Other Poems* (1948).

Rosenberg, Isaac (1890–1918) English, born Bristol; *Night and Day* (1912), *Youth* (1915), *Poems* (1922).

Saint-John Perse (pseudonym of **Marie René Auguste Alexis Saint-Léger Léger**) (1887–1975) French, born St Léger des Feuilles; *Anabase* (1924), *Exil* (1942), *Chroniques* (1960); Nobel Prize for literature 1960.

Sassoon, Siegfried (Lorraine) (1886–1967) English, born Brenchley, Kent; *Counter-Attack and Other Poems* (1917), *The Road to Ruin* (1933).

Schwarz, Delmore (1913–66) American, born New York City; *In Dreams Begin Responsibilities* (1938), *Vaudeville for a Princess and Other Poems* (1950).

Seifert, Jaroslav (1901–86) Czech, born Prague; *City of Tears* (1921), *All Love* (1923), *A Helmet of Earth* (1945); Nobel Prize for literature 1984.

Shelley, Percy Bysshe (1792–1822) English, born Field Place, Horsham, Sussex; *Alastor* (1816), *The Revolt of Islam* (1818), *Julian and Maddalo* (1818), *The Triumph of Life* (1822).

Sidney, Sir Philip (1554–86) English, born Penshurst, Kent; *Arcadia* (1580), *Astrophel and Stella* (1591).

Sitwell, Dame Edith (Louisa) (1887–1964) English, born Scarborough; *Façade* (1922), *Colonel Fantock* (1926).

Smart, Christopher (1722–71) English, born Shipbourne, Kent; *Jubilate Agno* (first published 1939).

Smith, Stevie (pseudonym of **Florence Margaret Smith**) (1902–71) English, born Hull; *Not Waving but Drowning: Poems* (1957).

Spender, Sir Stephen (Harold) (1909–95) English, born London; *Poems* (1933).

Spenser, Edmund (1552–99) English, born London; *The Shepheardes Calender* (1579), *The Faerie Queene* (1590, 1596).

Stevens, Wallace (1879–1955) American, born Reading, Pennsylvania; *Harmonium* (1923), *Transport to Summer* (1947).

Swinburne, Algernon Charles (1837–1909) English, born London; *Poems and Ballads* (1866), *Songs before Sunrise* (1871), *Tristram of Lyonesse* (1882).

Szymborska, Wislawa (1923–) Polish, born Kórnik; *A Large Number* (1976), *People on the Bridge* (1986), *View with a Grain of Sand* (1996), *Poems New and Collected 1957–1997* (1998), *Miracle Fair* (2001), *Monologue of a Dog* (2005); Nobel Prize for literature 1996.

Tennyson, Alfred, Lord (1809–92) English, born Somersby, Lincolnshire; *Poems* (1832) (eg 'The Lotus-Eaters' and 'The Lady of Shalott'), *The Princess* (1847), *In Memoriam* (1850), *Idylls of the King* (1859), *Maud* (1885).

Thomas, Dylan (Marlais) (1914–53) Welsh, born Swansea; *Twenty-five Poems* (1936), *Deaths and Entrances* (1946), *In Country Sleep and Other Poems* (1952).

Thomas, (Philip) Edward (1878–1917) English, born London; *Six Poems* (1916), *Last Poems* (1918).

Thomas, R(onald) S(tuart) (1913–2000) Welsh, born Cardiff; *Stones of the Field* (1947), *Song at the Year's Turning* (1955), *The Bread of Truth* (1963), *Between Here and Now* (1981), *Counterpoint* (1990), *No Truce with the Furies* (1995).

Thomson, James (1700–48) Scottish, born Ednam, Roxburghshire; *The Seasons* (1730), *The Castle of Indolence* (1748).

Verlaine, Paul (1844–96) French, born Metz; *Fêtes galantes* (1869), *Sagesse* (1881).

Virgil (in full **Publius Vergilius Maro**) (70–19 BC) Roman, born near Mantua; *Eclogues* (37 BC), *Georgics* (29 BC), *The Aeneid* (19 BC).

Walcott, Derek Alton (1930–) West Indian, born St Lucia; *Castaway* (1965), *Fortunate Traveller* (1982), *The Bounty* (1997), *Tiepolo's Hound* (2000), *The Prodigal* (2005); Nobel Prize for literature 1992.

Webb, Francis Charles (1925–73) Australian, born Adelaide; *A Drum for Ben Boyd* (1948), *The Ghost of the Cock* (1964).

Whitman, Walt (1819–92) American, born West Hills, Long Island, New York; *Leaves of Grass* (1855–89).

Wordsworth, William (1770–1850) English, born Cockermouth; *Lyrical Ballads* (with S T Coleridge, 1798), *The Prelude* (1799, 1805, 1850), *The Excursion* (1814).

Wright, Judith (Arundell) (1915–2000) Australian, born Armidale, New South Wales; *The Moving Image* (1946), *Birds* (1962), *Alive* (1973), *The Cry for the Dead* (1981), *Collected Poems 1942–1985* (1994).

Wyatt, Sir Thomas (1503–42) English, born Allington Castle, Kent; poems first published in *Tottel's Miscellany* (1557).

Yeats, W(illiam) B(utler) (1865–1939) Irish, born Sandymount, County Dublin; *The Wanderings of Oisin and Other Poems* (1889), *The Wind Among the Reeds* (1894), *The Wild Swans at Coole* (1917), *Michael Robartes and the Dancer* (1921), *The Winding Stair and Other Poems* (1933); Nobel Prize for literature 1923.

Zephaniah, Benjamin (Obadiah Iqbal) (1958–) English poet and writer, born Birmingham; *Pen Rhythm* (1980), *The Dread Affair* (1985), *Too Black, Too Strong* (2001), *We are Britain* (2002).

Poets laureate

1617	Ben Jonson [1]
1638	Sir William Davenant [1]
1668	John Dryden
1689	Thomas Shadwell
1692	Nahum Tate
1715	Nicholas Rowe
1718	Laurence Eusden
1730	Colley Cibber
1757	William Whitehead
1785	Thomas Warton
1790	Henry Pye
1813	Robert Southey
1843	William Wordsworth
1850	Alfred, Lord Tennyson
1896	Alfred Austin
1913	Robert Bridges
1930	John Masefield
1968	Cecil Day-Lewis
1972	Sir John Betjeman
1984	Ted Hughes
1999	Andrew Motion

[1] The post was not officially established until 1668.

Playwrights

Selected plays are listed.

Aeschylus (c.525–c.456 BC) Athenian; *The Oresteia* trilogy (*Agamemnon, Choephoroe, Eumenides*) (458 BC), *Prometheus Bound, Seven Against Thebes*.

Albee, Edward Franklin, III (1928–) American, born Washington, DC; *The American Dream* (1960), *Who's Afraid of Virginia Woolf?* (1962), *A Delicate Balance* (1966, Pulitzer Prize 1967), *Seascape* (1974, Pulitzer Prize 1975), *Three Tall Women* (1991, Pulitzer Prize 1994), *The Goat* (2000).

Anouilh, Jean (1910–87) French, born Bordeaux; *Antigone* (1944), *Médée* (1946), *L'Alouette* (1953), *Beckett, or the Honour of God* (1960).

Aristophanes (c.448–c.385 BC) Athenian; *The Acharnians* (425 BC), *The Knights* (424 BC), *The Clouds* (423 BC), *The Wasps* (422 BC), *The Birds* (414 BC), *Lysistrata* (411 BC), *The Frogs* (405 BC).

Ayckbourn, Sir Alan (1939–) English, born London; *Absurd Person Singular* (1973), *Absent Friends* (1975), *Joking Apart* (1979), *Way Upstream* (1982), *Woman in Mind*

(1985), *Henceforward* (1987), *Wildest Dreams* (1991), *Communicating Doors* (1994), *The Champion of Paribanou* (1998), *The Boy Who Fell Into a Book* (2000), *If I Were You* (2006).

Beaumont, Sir Francis (1584–1616) English, born Grace-Dieu, Leicestershire, and **John Fletcher** (1579–1625) *Philaster* (1609), *The Maid's Tragedy* (1610).

Beckett, Samuel (Barclay) (1906–89) Irish, born Foxrock, near Dublin; *Waiting for Godot* (1955), *Endgame* (1958), *Krapp's Last Tape* (1958), *Happy Days* (1961), *Not I* (1973); Nobel Prize for literature 1969.

Behan, Brendan (Francis) (1923–64) Irish, born Dublin; *The Quare Fellow* (1956), *The Hostage* (1958).

Bennett, Alan (1934–) English, born Leeds; *Beyond the Fringe* (1960), *Forty Years On* (1968), *The Old Country* (1977), *An Englishman Abroad* (1983, television), *Talking Heads* (1988, television monologues), *Madness of George III* (1991), *The History Boys* (2004).

Bond, (Thomas) Edward (1934–) English, born North London; *Early Morning* (1967), *Lear* (1971), *Summer* (1982), *The War Plays* (1985), *Olly's Prison* (1992), *Coffee* (1995), *Eleven Vests* (1997), *The Crime of the 21st Century* (2001).

Brecht, (Eugen) Bertolt (Friedrich) (1898–1956) German, born Augsburg; *Threepenny Opera* (libretto 1928), *Galileo* (1938–9), *Mutter Courage und ihre Kinder* (Mother Courage and Her Children) (1941), *Der Gute Mensch von Setzuan* (The Good Woman of Setzuan) (1943), *Der Kaukasische Kreidekreis* (The Caucasian Chalk Circle) (1949).

Brieux, Eugène (1858–1932) French, born Paris; *Les Trois Filles de M Dupont* (1897), *The Red Robe* (1900).

Chapman, George (c.1559–1634) English, born near Hitchin, Hertfordshire; *Bussy D'Ambois* (1607).

Chekhov, Anton Pavlovich (1860–1904) Russian, born Taganrog; *The Seagull* (1895), *Uncle Vanya* (1900), *Three Sisters* (1901), *The Cherry Orchard* (1904).

Congreve, William (1670–1729) English, born Bardsey, near Leeds; *Love for Love* (1695), *The Way of the World* (1700).

Corneille, Pierre (1606–84) French, born Rouen; *Le Cid* (1636), *Horace* (1639), *Polyeucte* (1640).

Coward, Sir Noël Peirce (1899–1973) English, born Teddington, Middlesex; *Hay Fever* (1925), *Private Lives* (1933), *Blithe Spirit* (1941).

Dekker, Thomas (c.1570–1632) English, born London; *The Whore of Babylon* (1606).

Dryden, John (1631–1700) English, born Aldwinkle; *The Indian Queen* (1664), *Marriage à la Mode* (1672), *All for Love* (1678), *Amphitryon* (1690).

Eliot, T(homas) S(tearns) (1888–1965) American, naturalized British, born St Louis, Missouri; *Murder in the Cathedral* (1935), *The Family Reunion* (1939), *The Cocktail Party* (1950).

Esson, (Thomas) Louis (Buvelot) (1879–1943) Australian, born Edinburgh; *The Drovers* (1920), *Andeganora* (1937).

Euripides (c.480–406 BC) Athenian; *Medea* (431 BC), *Electra* (413 BC), *The Bacchae* (407 BC).

Fletcher, John (1579–1625) English, born Rye, Sussex; *The Faithful Shepherdess* (1610), *A Wife for a Month* (1624).

Fo, Dario (1926–) Italian, born Lombardy; *Mistero Buffo* (1969), *Accidental Death of an*

Anarchist (1970), *Can't Pay! Won't Pay!* (1974), *The Pope and the Witch* (1989), *The Devil in Drag* (1997); Nobel Prize for literature 1997.

Ford, John (1586–c.1640) English, born Devon; *'Tis Pity She's a Whore* (1633), *Perkin Warbeck* (1634).

Galsworthy, John (1867–1933) English, born Coombe, Surrey; *Strife* (1909), *Justice* (1910); Nobel Prize for literature 1932.

Genet, Jean (1910–86) French, born Paris; *The Maids* (1948), *The Balcony* (1956), *The Screens* (1961).

Giraudoux, (Hippolyte) Jean (1882–1944) French, born Bellac; *Judith* (1931), *Ondine* (1939).

Goethe, Johann Wolfgang von (1749–1832) German, born Frankfurt am Main; *Faust* (1808, 1832).

Gogol, Nikolai (Vasilievich) (1809–52) Russian, born Ukraine; *The Inspector General* (1836).

Goldsmith, Oliver (1728–74) Irish, born Pallas, County Longford; *She Stoops to Conquer* (1773).

Greene, Robert (1558–92) English, born Norwich; *Orlando Furioso* (1594), *James the Fourth* (1598).

Hare, Sir David (1947–) English, born London; *Slag* (1970), *Plenty* (1978), *Pravda* (1985, with Howard Brenton), *The Secret Rapture* (1988), *Amy's View* (1997), *Stuff Happens* (2005).

Hauptmann, Gerhart Johann Robert (1862–1946) German, born Obersalzbrunn, Silesia; *Before Sunrise* (1889), *The Weavers* (1892); Nobel Prize for literature 1912.

Hebbel, (Christian) Friedrich (1813–63) German, born Wesselburen, Dithmarschen; *Judith* (1841), *Maria Magdalena* (1844).

Hewett, Dorothy (Coade) (1923–2002) Australian, born Wickepin, West Australia; *The Chapel Perilous* (1972), *This Old Man Comes Rolling Home* (1976), *Golden Valley* (1984), *Nowhere* (2001).

Heywood, Thomas (c.1574–1641) English, born Lincolnshire; *A Woman Killed with Kindness* (1603), *The Fair Maid of the West* (1631), *The English Traveller* (1633).

Hibberd, Jack (1940–) Australian, born Warracknabeal, Victoria; *Dimboola* (1969), *White with Wire Wheels* (1967), *A Stretch of the Imagination* (1971), *Squibs* (1984), *The Prodigal Son* (1997).

Howard, Sidney (Coe) (1891–1939) American, born Oakland, California; *They Knew What They Wanted* (1924), *The Silver Cord* (1926).

Ibsen, Henrik (1828–1906) Norwegian, born Skien; *Peer Gynt* (1867), *A Doll's House* (1879), *The Pillars of Society* (1880), *The Wild Duck* (1884), *Hedda Gabler* (1890), *The Master Builder* (1892).

Inge, William Motter (1913–73) American, born Kansas; *Picnic* (1953), *Where's Daddy?* (1966).

Ionesco, Eugène (1912–94) French, born Romania; *The Bald Prima Donna* (1948), *The Picture* (1958), *Le Rhinocéros* (1960).

Jonson, Ben(jamin) (c.1572–1637) English, born Westminster, London; *Every Man in His Humour* (1598), *Sejanus* (1603), *Volpone* (1606), *The Alchemist* (1610), *Bartholomew Fair* (1614).

Kaiser, Georg (1878–1945) German, born Magdeburg; *The Burghers of Calais* (1914), *Gas* (1920).

Kane, Sarah (1971–99) English, born Essex; *Blasted* (1995), *Phaedra's Love* (1996), *Cleansed* (1998), *Crave* (1998), *4.48 Psychosis* (1999)

Kushner, Tony (1956–) American, born New York City; *Yes, Yes, No, No* (1985), *Angels in America* (1992, Pulitzer Prize 1993), *Slavs!* (1995), *Henry Box Brown* (1997), *Homebody/Kabul* (2001).

Kyd, Thomas (1558–94) English, born London; *The Spanish Tragedy* (1587).

Lawler, Ray(mond Evenor) (1922–) Australian, born Melbourne; *The Summer of the Seventeenth Doll* (1955), *The Man Who Shot the Albatross* (1970), *Kid Stakes* (1975), *Other Times* (1976), *Godsend* (1982).

Lochhead, Liz (1947–) Scottish, born Motherwell; *Blood and Ice* (1982), *Mary Queen of Scots Got Her Head Chopped Off* (1987), *Misery Guts* (2002).

Lorca, Federico García (1899–1936) Spanish, born Fuente Vaqueros; *Blood Wedding* (1933), *The House of Bernarda Alba* (1945).

Maeterlinck, Maurice, Count (1862–1949) Belgian, born Ghent; *La Princesse Maleine* (1889), *Pélleas et Mélisande* (1892), *The Blue Bird* (1909).

Mamet, David Alan (1947–) American, born Chicago; *Sexual Perversity in Chicago* (1974), *Duck Variations* (1974), *American Buffalo* (1975), *Edmond* (1982), *Glengarry Glen Ross* (1984, Pulitzer Prize), *Oleanna* (1992), *Death Defying Acts* (1996), *Wag the Dog* (screenplay) (1997), *Romance* (2005).

Marlowe, Christopher (1564–93) English, born Canterbury; *Tamburlaine the Great* (in two parts, 1587), *Dr Faustus* (1588), *The Jew of Malta* (c.1589), *Edward II* (1592).

Marston, John (1576–1634) English, born Wardington, Oxfordshire; *Antonio's Revenge* (1602), *The Malcontent* (1604).

Miller, Arthur (1915–2005) American, born New York City; *All My Sons* (1947), *Death of a Salesman* (1949), *The Crucible* (1952), *A View from the Bridge* (1955), *The Misfits* (1961), *After the Fall* (1964), *The Creation of the World and Other Business* (1972), *Playing for Time* (1981), *Danger: Memory!* (1987), *The Ride Down Mount Morgan* (1991), *The Last Yankee* (1994), *Broken Glass* (1994), *Homely Girl* (1995), *Mr Peter's Connections* (1998).

Molière (pseudonym of **Jean-Baptiste Poquelin**) (1622–73) French, born Paris; *Le Bourgeois Gentilhomme* (The Bourgeois Gentleman) (1660), *Tartuffe* (1664), *Le Misanthrope* (The Misanthropist) (1666), *Le Malade Imaginaire* (The Hypochondriac) (1673).

O'Casey, Sean (originally **John Casey**) (1880–1964) Irish, born Dublin; *Juno and the Paycock* (1924), *The Plough and the Stars* (1926).

O'Neill, Eugene Gladstone (1888–1953) American, born New York City; *Beyond the Horizon* (1920), *Desire under the Elms* (1924), *Mourning Becomes Electra* (1931), *Long Day's Journey into Night* (1941), *The Iceman Cometh* (1946); Nobel Prize for literature 1936.

Orton, Joe (John Kingsley) (1933–67) English, born Leicester; *Entertaining Mr Sloane* (1964), *Loot* (1965), *What the Butler Saw* (1969).

Osborne, John (James) (1929–94) Welsh, born Fulham, London; *Look Back in Anger* (1956), *The Entertainer* (1957), *Inadmissible Evidence* (1965), *The Hotel in Amsterdam* (1968), *West of Suez* (1971), *Almost a Vision* (1976), *Déjà Vu* (1989).

Otway, Thomas (1652–85) English, born Milland, Sussex; *Don Carlos* (1676), *The Orphan* (1680), *Venice Preserv'd* (1682).

Patrick, John (1905–95) American, born Louisville, Kentucky; *The Teahouse of the August Moon* (1953).

Pinter, Harold (1930–) English, born East London; *The Birthday Party* (1957), *The Caretaker* (1959), *The Homecoming* (1964), *Landscape* (1967), *Old Times* (1970), *No Man's Land* (1975), *Betrayal* (1978), *A Kind of Alaska* (1982), *Party Time* (1991), *Ashes to Ashes* (1996), *Celebration* (1999), *Remembrance of Things Past* (2000); Nobel Prize for literature 2005.

Pirandello, Luigi (1867–1936) Italian, born near Agrigento, Sicily; *Six Characters in Search of an Author* (1921), *Henry IV* (1922); Nobel Prize for literature 1934.

Plautus, Titus Maccius (c.250–184 BC) Roman; *Menachmi, Miles Gloriosus.*

Potter, Dennis (Christopher George) (1935–94) English, born Forest of Dean; *Vote, Vote, Vote for Nigel Barton* (1965), *Pennies from Heaven* (1978), *The Singing Detective* (1986), *Lipstick on Your Collar* (1993), *Karaoke* (1994).

Racine, Jean (1639–99) French, born near Soissons; *Andromaque* (1667), *Phèdre* (1677), *Bajazet* (1672), *Esther* (1689).

Rattigan, Sir Terence (1911–77) English, born London; *French without Tears* (1936), *The Winslow Boy* (1946), *The Browning Version* (1948), *Separate Tables* (1954).

Romeril, John (1945–) Australian, born Melbourne; *Chicago, Chicago* (1970), *I Don't Know Who to Feel Sorry For* (1969), *The Kelly Dance* (1984), *Love Suicides* (1997), *Miss Tanaka* (2002).

Russell, Willy (William) (1947–) English, born Whiston, Merseyside; *Educating Rita* (1979), *Blood Brothers* (1983), *Shirley Valentine* (1986).

Sackville, Thomas (1553–1608) English, born Buckhurst, Sussex; *Gorboduc* (1592).

Sartre, Jean-Paul (1905–80) French, born Paris; *The Flies* (1943), *Huis Clos* (1945), *The Condemned of Altona* (1961).

Schiller, Johann Christoph Friedrich von (1759–1805) German, born Marbach; *The Robbers* (1781), *Wallenstein* (1799), *Maria Stuart* (1800).

Seneca, Lucius Annaeus (c.4 BC–AD 65) Roman, born Cordoba; *Hercules, Medea, Thyestes.*

Seymour, Alan (1927–) Australian, born Perth; *Swamp Creatures* (1957), *The One Day of the Year* (1960), *Donny Johnson* (1965).

Shaffer, Sir Peter (Levin) (1926–) English, born Liverpool; *The Royal Hunt of the Sun* (1964), *Equus* (1973), *Amadeus* (1979), *Yonadab* (1985), *The Gift of the Gorgon* (1992).

Shakespeare, William ▶ Plays of Shakespeare (over)

Shaw, George Bernard (1856–1950) Irish, born Dublin; *Arms and the Man* (1894), *Man and Superman* (1903), *Pygmalion* (1913), *Saint Joan* (1924); Nobel Prize for literature 1925.

Shepard, Sam (originally **Samuel Shepard Rogers**) (1943–) American, born Fort Sheridan, Illinois; *La Turista* (1967), *The Tooth of Crime* (1972), *Buried Child* (1978, Pulitzer Prize), *True West* (1979), *Fool for Love* (1983), *A Lie of the Mind* (1985), *Simpatico* (1993), *Eyes for Consuela* (1998), *God of Hell* (2004).

Sheridan, Richard Brinsley (1751–1816) Irish, born Dublin; *The Rivals* (1775), *The School for Scandal* (1777), *The Critic* (1779).

Sherwood, Robert (Emmet) (1896–1955) American, born New Rochelle, New York; *Idiot's Delight* (1936), *Abe Lincoln in Illinois* (1938), *There Shall Be No Night* (1940).

Sophocles (496–406 BC) Athenian, born Colonus; *Antigone, Oedipus Rex, Oedipus at Colonus*.

Soyinka, Wole (in full **Akinwande Oluwole Soyinka**) (1934–) Nigerian, born Abeokuta, West Nigeria; *The Swamp Dwellers* (1958), *The Strong Breed* (1962), *The Road* (1964), *The Bacchae of Euripides* (1973), *Opera Wonyosi* (1978), *From Zia, with Love* (1991), *The Beatification of Area Boy* (1995), *King Baabu* (2001); Nobel Prize for literature 1986.

Stoppard, Sir Tom (Thomas Straussler) (1937–) English, born Czechoslovakia (now Czech Republic); *Rosencrantz and Guildenstern are Dead* (1966), *The Real Inspector Hound* (1968), *Travesties* (1974), *Every Good Boy Deserves Favour* (1978), *Rough Crossing* (1984), *Arcadia* (1993), *Indian Ink* (1995), *Shakespeare in Love* (screenplay) (1998), *Coast of Utopia* (trilogy) (2002), *Rock'n'Roll* (2006).

Strindberg, (Johan) **August** (1849–1912) Swedish, born Stockholm; *Master Olof* (1877), *Miss Julie* (1888), *The Dance of Death* (1901).

Synge, (Edmund) **J**(ohn) **M**(illington) (1871–1909) Irish, born near Dublin; *The Well of Saints* (1905), *The Playboy of the Western World* (1907).

Webster, John (c.1578–c.1632) English, born London; *The White Devil* (1612), *The Duchess of Malfi* (1614).

Wilde, Oscar (Fingal O'Flahertie Wills) (1854–1900) Irish, born Dublin; *Lady Windermere's Fan* (1892), *The Importance of Being Earnest* (1895).

Wilder, Thornton (Niven) (1897–1975) American, born Wisconsin; *Our Town* (1938), *The Merchant of Yonkers* (1938), *The Skin of Our Teeth* (1942), *The Matchmaker* (1954, later a musical *Hello, Dolly!*, 1964).

Williams, Tennessee (originally **Thomas Lanier Williams**) (1911–83) American, born Mississippi; *The Glass Menagerie* (1944), *A Streetcar Named Desire* (1947), *Cat on a Hot Tin Roof* (1955), *Sweet Bird of Youth* (1959).

Williamson, David Keith (1942–) Australian, born Melbourne; *The Removalists* (1971), *The Club* (1977), *Sons of Cain* (1985), *Money & Friends* (1991), *Up For Grabs* (2000), *Influence* (2005).

Plays of Shakespeare

William Shakespeare (1564–1616), English playwright and poet, born Stratford-upon-Avon.

Title	Date	Category
The Two Gentlemen of Verona	1590–1	comedy
Henry VI Part One	1592	history
Henry VI Part Two	1592	history
Henry VI Part Three	1592	history
Titus Andronicus	1592	tragedy
Richard III	1592–3	history
The Taming of the Shrew	1593	comedy
The Comedy of Errors	1594	comedy
Love's Labour's Lost	1594–5	comedy
Richard II	1595	history
Romeo and Juliet	1595	tragedy

Title	Date	Category
A Midsummer Night's Dream	1595	comedy
King John	1596	history
The Merchant of Venice	1596–7	comedy
Henry IV Part One	1596–7	history
The Merry Wives of Windsor	1597–8	comedy
Henry IV Part Two	1597–8	history
Much Ado About Nothing	1598	dark comedy
Henry V	1598–9	history
Julius Caesar	1599	tragedy
Hamlet, Prince of Denmark	1600–1	tragedy
As You Like It	1599–1600	comedy
Twelfth Night, or What You Will	1601	comedy
Troilus and Cressida	1602	tragedy
Measure for Measure	1603	dark comedy
Othello	1603–4	tragedy
All's Well That Ends Well	1604–5	dark comedy
Timon of Athens	1605	romantic drama
The Tragedy of King Lear	1605–6	tragedy
Macbeth	1606	tragedy
Antony and Cleopatra	1606	tragedy
Pericles	1607	romance
Coriolanus	1608	tragedy
The Winter's Tale	1609	romance
Cymbeline	1610	comedy
The Tempest	1611	comedy
Henry VIII	1613	history

Film and TV actors

Selected films and television productions are listed. Original and full names of actors are given in parentheses.

Allen, Woody (Allen Stewart Konigsberg) (1935–) American, born Brooklyn, New York City; *What's New, Pussycat?* (1965), *Casino Royale* (1967), *Bananas* (1971), *Play it Again Sam* (1972), *Sleeper* (1973), *Annie Hall* (1977), *Manhattan* (1979), *Hannah and Her Sisters* (1986), *New York Stories* (1989), *Crimes and Misdemeanors* (1989), *Shadows and Fog* (1992), *Husbands and Wives* (1992), *Manhattan Murder Mystery* (1993), *Mighty Aphrodite* (1995), *Anna Oz* (1996), *Deconstructing Harry* (1997), *The Curse of the Jade Scorpion* (2001).

Andrews, Dame Julie (Julia Elizabeth Wells) (1935–) British, born Walton-on-Thames, Surrey; *Mary Poppins* (1964), *The Sound of Music* (1965), *Torn Curtain* (1966), *Thoroughly Modern Millie* (1967), *Star!* (1968), *SOB* (1981), *Victor/Victoria* (1982), *The Man Who Loved Women* (1983), *Tchin Tchin* (1990), *Relative Values* (2000), *The Princess Diaries* (2001), *The Princess Diaries 2* (2004).

Astaire, Fred (Frederick Austerlitz) (1899–1987) American, born Omaha, Nebraska; *Flying Down to Rio* (1933), *The Gay Divorcee* (1934), *Top Hat* (1935), *Funny Face* (1957), *It Takes a Thief* (TV 1965–9), *Finian's Rainbow* (1968).

Atkinson, Rowan (1955–) British, born Newcastle upon Tyne; *The Black Adder* (TV

1984), *Blackadder II* (TV 1985), *Blackadder III* (TV 1986), *Blackadder Goes Forth* (TV 1989), *The Tall Guy* (1989), *The Witches* (1990), *Mr Bean* (TV 1990–4), *Bean: The Ultimate Disaster Movie* (1997), *Johnny English* (2003), *Keeping Mum* (2005).

Attenborough, Richard Samuel Attenborough, Baron (1923–) British, born Cambridge; *In Which We Serve* (1942), *The Man Within* (1942), *Brighton Rock* (1947), *The Guinea Pig* (1949), *The Great Escape* (1963), *Brannigan* (1975), *Jurassic Park* (1993), *Miracle on 34th Street* (1994), *E=MC²* (1995), *The Lost World: Jurassic Park* (1997), *Elizabeth* (1998), *Puckoon* (2002).

Bacall, Lauren (Betty Joan Perske) (1924–) American, born New York City; *To Have and Have Not* (1944), *The Big Sleep* (1946), *How to Marry a Millionaire* (1953), *The Fan* (1981), *Mr North* (1988), *Misery* (1990), *Prêt-à-Porter* (1994), *The Mirror Has Two Faces* (1996).

Bardot, Brigitte (Camille Javal) (1934–) French, born Paris; *And God Created Woman* (1956), *En Cas de Malheur* (1958), *Viva Maria!* (1965).

Barrymore, Drew (1975–) American, born Los Angeles; *ET* (1982), *Firestarter* (1984), *Irreconcilable Differences* (1984), *Cat's Eye* (1984), *Poison Ivy* (1992), *Batman Forever* (1995), *Never Been Kissed* (1999), *Charlie's Angels* (2000), *Riding in Cars with Boys* (2001), *Confessions of a Dangerous Mind* (2002), *50 First Dates* (2004), *Fever Pitch* (2005).

Basinger, Kim (1953–) American, born Athens, Georgia; *From Here to Eternity* (TV 1980), *Hard Country* (1981), *Never Say Never Again* (1983), *The Natural* (1984), *9½ Weeks* (1985), *Blind Date* (1987), *Batman* (1989), *My Stepmother is an Alien* (1989), *The Marrying Man* (1990), *Wayne's World 2* (1993), *Prêt-à-Porter* (1994), *Kansas City* (1996), *LA Confidential* (1997), *8 Mile* (2002), *Even Money* (2006).

Bates, Alan (1934–2003) British, born Allestree, Derbyshire; *A Kind of Loving* (1962), *Whistle Down the Wind* (1962), *Zorba the Greek* (1965), *Far from the Madding Crowd* (1967), *Women in Love* (1969), *The Rose* (1979), *A Prayer for the Dying* (1987), *We Think the World of You* (1988), *Hamlet* (1990), *Grotesque* (1995), *Gosford Park* (2001).

Beatty, Warren (Henry Warren Beaty) (1937–) American, born Richmond, Virginia; *Splendor in the Grass* (1961), *The Roman Spring of Mrs Stone* (1961), *All Fall Down* (1962), *Bonnie and Clyde* (1967), *The Parallax View* (1974), *Shampoo* (1975), *Heaven Can Wait* (1978), *Reds* (1981), *Ishtar* (1987), *Dick Tracy* (1990), *Bugsy* (1991), *Love Affair* (1994), *Bulworth* (1998), *Town and Country* (2001).

Bergman, Ingrid (1915–82) Swedish, born Stockholm; *Intermezzo* (1939), *Dr Jekyll and Mr Hyde* (1941), *Casablanca* (1943), *For Whom the Bell Tolls* (1943), *Gaslight* (1943), *Spellbound* (1945), *Anastasia* (1946), *Notorious* (1946), *Stromboli* (1950), *Indiscreet* (1958), *Cactus Flower* (1969), *Murder on the Orient Express* (1974), *Autumn Sonata* (1978).

Berry, Halle (Maria) (1966–) American, born Cleveland, Ohio; *Boomerang* (1992), *The Flintstones* (1994), *Introducing Dorothy Dandridge* (TV 1999), *X-Men* trilogy (2000–6), *Monster's Ball* (2001), *Die Another Day* (2002), *Catwoman* (2004), *Their Eyes Were Watching God* (TV 2005).

Blanchett, Cate (Catherine Elise Blanchett) (1969–) Australian, born Melbourne; *Oscar and Lucinda* (1997), *Elizabeth* (1998), *The Talented Mr Ripley* (1999), *Bandits* (2001), *Charlotte Gray* (2001), *The Shipping News* (2001), *Lord of the Rings* trilogy (2001–3), *The Missing* (2003), *The Aviator* (2004), *Little Fish* (2005), *Babel* (2006), *Notes on a Scandal* (2006).

Bogarde, Sir Dirk (Derek Niven Van Den Bogaerde) (1921–99) Anglo-Dutch, born

Hampstead, London; *A Tale of Two Cities* (1958), *Victim* (1961), *The Servant* (1963), *Darling* (1965), *Death in Venice* (1971), *Providence* (1977), *Daddy Nostalgie (These Foolish Things)* (1990).

Bogart, Humphrey (De Forest) (1899–1957) American, born New York City; *Broadway's Like That* (1930), *The Petrified Forest* (1936), *High Sierra* (1941), *The Maltese Falcon* (1941), *Casablanca* (1942), *To Have and Have Not* (1944), *The Big Sleep* (1946), *The Treasure of the Sierra Madre* (1947), *The African Queen* (1952), *The Barefoot Contessa* (1954), *The Caine Mutiny* (1954).

Bonham-Carter, Helena (1966–) British, born London; *Lady Jane* (1985), *A Room with a View* (1985), *Hamlet* (1990), *Where Angels Fear to Tread* (1991), *Howards End* (1992), *Frankenstein* (1994), *Twelfth Night* (1996), *Wings of the Dove* (1997), *Fight Club* (1999), *Planet of the Apes* (2001), *Harry Potter and the Order of the Phoenix* (2007).

Branagh, Kenneth (1960–) British, born Belfast; *High Season* (1987), *A Month in the Country* (1988), *Henry V* (1989), *Dead Again* (1991), *Peter's Friends* (1992), *Much Ado About Nothing* (1993), *Frankenstein* (1994), *Othello* (1995), *Hamlet* (1996), *Love's Labour's Lost* (2000), *Rabbit-Proof Fence* (2002), *Harry Potter and the Chamber of Secrets* (2002), *Conspiracy* (TV 2002), *Warm Springs* (TV 2005).

Brando, Marlon (1924–2004) American, born Omaha, Nebraska; *A Streetcar Named Desire* (1951), *Viva Zapata* (1952), *Julius Caesar* (1953), *The Wild One* (1953), *On the Waterfront* (1954), *Guys and Dolls* (1955), *The Teahouse of the August Moon* (1956), *One-Eyed Jacks* (1961), *Mutiny on the Bounty* (1962), *The Chase* (1966), *The Godfather* (1972), *Last Tango in Paris* (1972), *Superman* (1978), *Apocalypse Now* (1979), *A Dry White Season* (1988), *The Freshman* (1990), *Don Juan de Marco* (1995).

Bronson, Charles (Charles Buchinski) (1920–2003) American, born Ehrenfield, Pennsylvania; *Drumbeat* (1954), *Vera Cruz* (1954), *The Magnificent Seven* (1960), *This Property is Condemned* (1966), *The Dirty Dozen* (1967), *Chato's Land* (1972), *The Mechanic* (1972), *The Valachi Papers* (1972), *Death Wish* (1974), *Hard Times* (1975), *Telefon* (1977), *Death Wish II* (1982), *Death Wish III* (1985), *Death Wish IV* (1987), *Murphy's Law* (1987), *Messenger of Death* (1988), *Kinjite: Forbidden Subjects* (1989), *The Indian Runner* (1991), *Death Wish V* (1993).

Brynner, Yul (1915–85) Swiss–Russian, naturalized American, born Sakhalin, Siberia; *The King and I* (1956), *The Brothers Karamazov* (1958), *The Magnificent Seven* (1960), *Return of the Seven* (1966).

Bullock, Sandra (Annette) (1964–) American, born Arlington, Virginia; *Demolition Man* (1993), *Speed* (1994), *While You Were Sleeping* (1995), *Forces of Nature* (1999), *Miss Congeniality* (2000), *Murder by Numbers* (2002), *Crash* (2004), *The Lake House* (2006).

Burton, Richard (Richard Walter Jenkins) (1925–84) Welsh, born Pontrhydfen, S Wales: *My Cousin Rachel* (1952), *Alexander the Great* (1956), *Look Back in Anger* (1959), *Cleopatra* (1962), *The Night of the Iguana* (1964), *The Spy Who Came in from the Cold* (1965), *Who's Afraid of Virginia Woolf?* (1966), *The Taming of the Shrew* (1967), *Where Eagles Dare* (1969), *Equus* (1977), *Exorcist II: The Heretic* (1977), *Absolution* (1979), *1984* (1984).

Cagney, James (Francis Jr) (1899–1986) American, born New York City; *Public Enemy* (1931), *Lady Killer* (1933), *A Midsummer Night's Dream* (1935), *The Roaring Twenties* (1939), *Yankee Doodle Dandy* (1942), *White Heat* (1949), *Love Me or Leave Me* (1955), *Mister Roberts* (1955), *One, Two, Three* (1961), *Ragtime* (1981).

Caine, Sir Michael (Maurice Micklewhite) (1933–) British, born London; *Zulu* (1963),

The Ipcress File (1965), *Alfie* (1966), *The Italian Job* (1969), *Sleuth* (1972), *The Man Who Would Be King* (1975), *The Eagle Has Landed* (1976), *California Suite* (1978), *Dressed to Kill* (1980), *Death Trap* (1983), *Educating Rita* (1983), *Hannah and Her Sisters* (1986), *The Whistle Blower* (1987), *Bullseye* (1990), *Shock to the System* (1990), *Mr Destiny* (1990), *Noises Off* (1992), *Blue Ice* (1992), *Blood and Wine* (1996), *Little Voice* (1998), *The Cider House Rules* (1999), *The Quiet American* (2002), *The Prestige* (2006).

Chaplin, Charlie (Sir Charles Spencer) (1889–1977) British, born London; *The Champion* (1915), *The Tramp* (1915), *Easy Street* (1917), *A Dog's Life* (1918), *Shoulder Arms* (1918), *The Kid* (1921), *The Idle Class* (1921), *The Gold Rush* (1925), *City Lights* (1931), *Modern Times* (1936), *The Great Dictator* (1940), *Limelight* (1952), *A King in New York* (1957).

Christie, Julie (1941–) British, born Chukua, Assam, India; *The Fast Lady* (1963), *Billy Liar* (1963), *Doctor Zhivago* (1965), *Darling* (1965), *Fahrenheit 451* (1966), *Far from the Madding Crowd* (1967), *The Go-Between* (1971), *Don't Look Now* (1974), *Shampoo* (1975), *Heaven Can Wait* (1978), *Heat and Dust* (1982), *Power* (1985), *The Gold Diggers* (1988), *Dragon Heart* (1996), *Hamlet* (1996), *Afterglow* (1997), *Finding Neverland* (2004).

Cleese, John (Marwood) (1939–) British, born Weston-super-Mare; *The Frost Report* (TV 1966), *At Last the 1948 Show* (TV 1967), *Monty Python's Flying Circus* (TV 1969–74), *Monty Python and the Holy Grail* (1974), *Fawlty Towers* (TV 1975, 1979), *Life of Brian* (1979), *The Meaning of Life* (1983), *Clockwise* (1985), *A Fish Called Wanda* (1988), *Fierce Creatures* (1996), *The World is Not Enough* (1999), *Harry Potter and the Philosopher's Stone* (2001), *Harry Potter and the Chamber of Secrets* (2002), *Die Another Day* (2002).

Clift, (Edward) **Montgomery** (1920–66) American, born Omaha, Nebraska; *Red River* (1946), *The Search* (1948), *A Place in the Sun* (1951), *From Here to Eternity* (1953), *Suddenly Last Summer* (1959), *Freud* (1962).

Clooney, George (Timothy) (1961–) American, born Lexington, Kentucky; *ER* (TV 1994–2000), *From Dusk to Dawn* (1996), *O Brother, Where Art Thou* (2000), *The Perfect Storm* (2000), *Ocean's Eleven* (2001), *Confessions of a Dangerous Mind* (2002), *Ocean's Twelve* (2004), *Syriana* (2005), *Good Night and Good Luck* (2005).

Close, Glenn (1947–) American, born Greenwich, Connecticut; *The World According to Garp* (1982), *The Big Chill* (1983), *The Natural* (1984), *Jagged Edge* (1985), *Maxie* (1985), *Fatal Attraction* (1987), *Dangerous Liaisons* (1988), *Reversal of Fortune* (1990), *Hamlet* (1990), *Meeting Venus* (1991), *Hook* (1991), *The Paper* (1994), *Mary Reilly* (1996), *101 Dalmatians* (1996), *Mars Attacks!* (1996), *Cookie's Fortune* (1999), *The Lion in Winter* (TV 2003).

Connery, Sir Sean (Thomas Connery) (1930–) British, born Edinburgh; *Dr No* (1963), *Marnie* (1964), *From Russia With Love* (1964), *Goldfinger* (1965), *Thunderball* (1965), *A Fine Madness* (1966), *You Only Live Twice* (1967), *The Molly Maguires* (1969), *The Anderson Tapes* (1970), *Diamonds are Forever* (1971), *The Offence* (1972), *Zardoz* (1973), *Murder on the Orient Express* (1974), *The Man Who Would Be King* (1975), *Robin and Marian* (1976), *Meteor* (1979), *Outland* (1981), *Time Bandits* (1981), *Never Say Never Again* (1983), *Highlander* (1985), *The Name of the Rose* (1986), *The Untouchables* (1987), *The Presidio* (1988), *Indiana Jones and the Last Crusade* (1989), *The Hunt for Red October* (1990), *The Russia House* (1990), *Highlander II: The Quickening* (1991), *Medicine Man* (1991), *Rising Sun* (1992), *Dreadnought* (1992), *Broken Dreams* (1992), *First Knight* (1995), *The Rock* (1996), *Entrapment* (1999), *Sir Billi the Vet* (2006).

Cooper, Gary (Frank J Cooper) (1901–61) American, born Helena, Montana; *The Winning of Barbara Worth* (1926), *The Virginian* (1929), *A Farewell to Arms* (1932), *City Streets*

(1932), *The Lives of a Bengal Lancer* (1935), *Sergeant York* (1941), *For Whom the Bell Tolls* (1943), *The Fountainhead* (1949), *High Noon* (1952), *Friendly Persuasion* (1956).

Costner, Kevin (1955–) American, born Los Angeles; *American Flyers* (1984), *Silverado* (1985), *The Untouchables* (1987), *No Way Out* (1987), *Bull Durham* (1988), *Field of Dreams* (1989), *Revenge* (1990), *Dances with Wolves* (1990), *Robin Hood: Prince of Thieves* (1991), *JFK* (1991), *The Bodyguard* (1992), *A Perfect World* (1993), *The War* (1994), *Waterworld* (1995), *Tin Cup* (1996), *Message in a Bottle* (1999), *The Upside of Anger* (2005).

Crawford, Joan (Lucille Le Sueur) (1906–77) American, born San Antonio, Texas; *Our Dancing Daughters* (1928), *Our Blushing Brides* (1933), *Dancing Lady* (1933), *The Women* (1939), *Mildred Pierce* (1945), *Possessed* (1947), *What Ever Happened to Baby Jane?* (1962), *Trog* (1970).

Crosby, Bing (Harry Lillis Crosby) (1903–77) American, born Tacoma, Washington; *King of Jazz* (1930), *Mississippi* (1935), *Anything Goes* (1936), *Road to Singapore* (1940), *Road to Zanzibar* (1941), *Holiday Inn* (1942), *Road to Morocco* (1942), *Going My Way* (1944), *The Bells of St Mary's* (1945), *Blue Skies* (1946), *A Connecticut Yankee in King Arthur's Court* (1949), *White Christmas* (1954), *The Country Girl* (1954), *High Society* (1956), *Road to Hong Kong* (1962).

Crowe, Russell (Ira) (1964–) New Zealander, born Wellington; *Romper Stomper* (1992), *LA Confidential* (1997), *The Insider* (1999), *Gladiator* (2000), *A Beautiful Mind* (2001), *Master and Commander* (2003), *Cinderella Man* (2005).

Cruise, Tom (Tom Cruise Mapother IV) (1962–) American, born Syracuse, New York; *The Outsiders* (1983), *Legend* (1984), *Top Gun* (1985), *The Color of Money* (1986), *Cocktail* (1988), *Rain Man* (1988), *Born on the Fourth of July* (1989), *Days of Thunder* (1990), *Far and Away* (1992), *A Few Good Men* (1992), *The Firm* (1993), *Interview with the Vampire* (1994), *Mission: Impossible* (1996), *Jerry Maguire* (1996), *Eyes Wide Shut* (1999), *Mission: Impossible 2* (2000), *Vanilla Sky* (2001), *Minority Report* (2002), *Collateral* (2004), *Mission Impossible 3* (2006).

Cruz, Penélope (Penélope Cruz Sánchez) (1974–) Spanish, born Madrid; *Belle Epoque* (1992), *All About My Mother* (1999), *All the Pretty Horses* (2000), *Vanilla Sky* (2001), *Captain Corelli's Mandolin* (2001), *Blow* (2001), *Non ti muovere* (2004), *Sahara* (2005), *Volver* (2006).

Curtis, Tony (Bernard Schwartz) (1925–) American, born New York City; *Houdini* (1953), *Trapeze* (1956), *The Vikings* (1958), *Some Like it Hot* (1959), *Spartacus* (1960), *The Boston Strangler* (1968), *The Persuaders* (TV 1971–2).

Cushing, Peter (1913–94) British, born Kenley, Surrey; *The Man in the Iron Mask* (1939), *Hamlet* (1948), *1984* (TV 1955), *The Curse of Frankenstein* (1957), *Dracula* (1958), *The Mummy* (1959), *The Hound of the Baskervilles* (1959), *Cash on Demand* (1963), *Dr Who and the Daleks* (1965), *Sherlock Holmes* (TV 1968), *Tales from the Crypt* (1972), *Horror Express* (1972), *Star Wars* (1977), *Biggles* (1988).

Dafoe, Willem (1955–) American, born Appleton, Wisconsin; *Platoon* (1986), *The Last Temptation of Christ* (1988), *Mississippi Burning* (1988), *Triumph of the Spirit* (1989), *Wild At Heart* (1990), *Flight of the Intruder* (1990), *Light Sleeper* (1992), *Body of Evidence* (1992), *Tom and Viv* (1994), *Clear and Present Danger* (1994), *The English Patient* (1996), *Bullfighter* (2001), *eXistenZ* (1999), *Spider-Man* (2002).

Damon, Matt (Matthew Paige Damon) (1970–) American, born Cambridge, Massachusetts; *Good Will Hunting* (1997), *Saving Private Ryan* (1998), *The Talented*

Mr Ripley (1999), *All the Pretty Horses* (2000), *Ocean's Eleven* (2001), *Confessions of a Dangerous Mind* (2002), *The Bourne Supremacy* (2004), *Ocean's Twelve* (2004), *The Departed* (2006).

Davis, Bette (Ruth Elizabeth) (1908–89) American, born Lowell, Massachusetts; *Bad Sister* (1931), *Dangerous* (1935), *Jezebel* (1938), *The Great Lie* (1941), *All About Eve* (1950), *What Ever Happened to Baby Jane?* (1962), *Strangers* (TV 1979), *The Whales of August* (1987).

Day, Doris (Doris von Kappelhoff) (1924–) American, born Cincinnati, Ohio; *Romance on the High Seas* (1948), *Storm Warning* (1950), *Calamity Jane* (1953), *Young at Heart* (1954), *Love Me or Leave Me* (1955), *The Pajama Game* (1957), *Pillow Talk* (1959), *That Touch of Mink* (1962), *With Six You Get Egg Roll* (1968), *The Doris Day Show* (TV 1968–73).

Day-Lewis, Daniel (1958–) Irish, born London; *Gandhi* (1982), *My Beautiful Laundrette* (1985), *Room with a View* (1985), *The Unbearable Lightness of Being* (1988), *Stars and Bars* (1988), *Nanou* (1988), *My Left Foot* (1989), *The Last of the Mohicans* (1992), *The Age of Innocence* (1993), *In the Name of the Father* (1993), *The Crucible* (1996), *The Boxer* (1998), *Gangs of New York* (2002).

Dean, James (Byron) (1931–55) American, born Fairmount, Indiana; *East of Eden* (1955), *Rebel without a Cause* (1955), *Giant* (1956).

De Havilland, Olivia (1916–) British, born Tokyo, Japan; *A Midsummer Night's Dream* (1935), *The Adventures of Robin Hood* (1938), *Gone with the Wind* (1939), *The Dark Mirror* (1946), *To Each His Own* (1946), *The Heiress* (1949), *My Cousin Rachel* (1952).

Dench, Dame Judi (Judith Olivia Dench) (1934–) British, born York; *A Fine Romance* (TV 1981–4), *A Room With a View* (1985), *84 Charing Cross Road* (1987), *A Handful of Dust* (1988), *Henry V* (1989), *Behaving Badly* (TV 1989), *Jack and Sarah* (1995), *GoldenEye* (1995), *Hamlet* (1996), *Mrs Brown* (1997), *Tomorrow Never Dies* (1997), *Shakespeare in Love* (1998), *Tea with Mussolini* (1999), *The World Is Not Enough* (1999), *Chocolat* (2000), *Iris* (2001), *The Shipping News* (2001), *Die Another Day* (2002), *Mrs Henderson Presents* (2005), *Casino Royale* (2006).

Deneuve, Catherine (Catherine Dorleac) (1943–) French, born Paris; *Les Parapluies de Cherbourg* (1964), *Repulsion* (1965), *Belle de Jour* (1967), *Tristana* (1970), *The Hunger* (1983), *Indochine* (1991), *Les Voleurs* (1996), *Dancer in the Dark* (2000), *8 Women* (2002), *Palais Royale* (2005).

De Niro, Robert (1943–) American, born New York City; *Mean Streets* (1973), *The Godfather, Part II* (1974), *1900* (1976), *Taxi Driver* (1976), *The Deer Hunter* (1978), *Raging Bull* (1980), *King of Comedy* (1982), *Brazil* (1985), *Angel Heart* (1987), *The Untouchables* (1987), *Midnight Run* (1988), *Jacknife* (1989), *Stanley & Iris* (1989), *We're No Angels* (1990), *Goodfellas* (1990), *Awakenings* (1990), *Backdraft* (1991), *Cape Fear* (1991), *The Mistress* (1992), *Mad Dog and Glory* (1992), *Night and The City* (1992), *This Boy's Life* (1992), *Frankenstein* (1994), *Casino* (1995), *Heat* (1995), *Sleepers* (1996), *Jackie Brown* (1998), *Ronin* (1998), *Analyze This* (1999), *Meet the Parents* (2000), *Analyze That* (2002).

Depardieu, Gérard (1948–) French, born Châteauroux; *Get Out Your Handkerchiefs* (1977), *The Last Metro* (1980), *The Return of Martin Guerre* (1981), *Danton* (1982), *The Moon in the Gutter* (1983), *Police* (1985), *Jean de Florette* (1986), *Streets of Departure* (1986), *Under the Sun of Satan* (1987), *The Woman Next Door* (1987), *Cyrano de Bergerac* (1990), *Green Card* (1990), *Uranus* (1991), *Merci la Vie* (1991), *Mon Père, Ce Héros* (1991), *Tous les Matins du Monde* (1991), *Christopher Columbus* (1992), *Germinal*

(1992), *Le Colonel Chabert* (1994), *Les Anges Gardiens* (1995), *Unhook the Stars* (1996), *Hamlet* (1996), *The Man in the Iron Mask* (1998), *The Closet* (2001).

Depp, Johnny (1963–) American, born Owensboro, Kentucky; *Nightmare on Elm Street* (1984), *Platoon* (1986), *Cry Baby* (1990), *Edward Scissorhands* (1990), *What's Eating Gilbert Grape?* (1993), *Ed Wood* (1994), *Fear and Loathing in Las Vegas* (1998), *Sleepy Hollow* (1999), *Blow* (2001), *Pirates of the Caribbean* trilogy (2003–7), *Finding Neverland* (2004), *The Libertine* (2004), *Charlie and the Chocolate Factory* (2005).

DeVito, Danny (1944–) American, born Neptune, New Jersey; *One Flew Over the Cuckoo's Nest* (1975), *Taxi* (TV 1978–82), *Romancing the Stone* (1983), *Terms of Endearment* (1984), *The Jewel of the Nile* (1985), *Ruthless People* (1986), *Tin Men* (1987), *Throw Momma from the Train* (1987), *Twins* (1988), *War of the Roses* (1989), *Batman Returns* (1992), *Renaissance Man* (1994), *Junior* (1994), *Get Shorty* (1995), *Matilda* (1996), *LA Confidential* (1997), *Man on the Moon* (1999).

Diaz, Cameron (Michelle) (1972–) American, born San Diego, California; *The Mask* (1994), *My Best Friend's Wedding* (1997), *There's Something About Mary* (1998), *Any Given Sunday* (1999), *Being John Malkovich* (1999), *Charlie's Angels* (2000), *Shrek* (2001), *Vanilla Sky* (2001), *Gangs of New York* (2002), *The Holiday* (2006).

Dietrich, Marlene (Maria Magdalena von Losch) (1901–92) German–American, born Berlin; *The Blue Angel* (1930), *Morocco* (1930), *Blond Venus* (1932), *Shanghai Express* (1932), *The Scarlet Empress* (1934), *The Devil is a Woman* (1935), *Desire* (1936), *Destry Rides Again* (1939), *A Foreign Affair* (1948), *Rancho Notorious* (1952), *Judgement at Nuremberg* (1961).

Douglas, Kirk (Issur Danielovitch Demsky) (1916–) American, born Amsterdam, New York; *The Strange Love of Martha Ivers* (1946), *Lust for Life* (1956), *Gunfight at the OK Corral* (1957), *Paths of Glory* (1957), *The Vikings* (1958), *Spartacus* (1960), *The Man from Snowy River* (1982), *Oscar* (1991), *Greedy* (1994), *Diamonds* (1999).

Douglas, Michael (1944–) American, born New Brunswick, New Jersey; *The Streets of San Francisco* (TV 1972–5), *The China Syndrome* (1980), *The Star Chamber* (1983), *Romancing the Stone* (1984), *The Jewel of the Nile* (1985), *Fatal Attraction* (1987), *Wall Street* (1987), *Black Rain* (1989), *War of the Roses* (1989), *Shining Through* (1991), *Basic Instinct* (1992), *Falling Down* (1993), *Disclosure* (1994), *The Ghost in the Darkness* (1996), *The Game* (1997), *A Perfect Murder* (1998), *Traffic* (2000), *Wonder Boys* (2000), *The Sentinel* (2006).

Dreyfuss, Richard (1947–) American, born Brooklyn, New York City; *American Graffiti* (1973), *Jaws* (1975), *Close Encounters of the Third Kind* (1977), *The Goodbye Girl* (1977), *Whose Life is it Anyway?* (1981), *Down and Out in Beverly Hills* (1986), *Stakeout* (1987), *Tin Men* (1987), *Always* (1989), *The Proud and the Free* (1991), *What About Bob?* (1991), *Prisoners of Honor* (1991), *Rosencrantz and Guildernstern are Dead* (1991), *Lost in Yonkers* (1993), *Another Stakeout* (1993), *The American President* (1995), *Trigger Happy* (1996).

Dunaway, (Dorothy) Faye (1941–) American, born Bascom, Florida; *Bonnie and Clyde* (1967), *Little Big Man* (1970), *The Getaway* (1972), *Chinatown* (1974), *The Towering Inferno* (1974), *Network* (1976), *The Eyes of Laura Mars* (1978), *The Champ* (1979), *Mommie Dearest* (1981), *Barfly* (1987), *Midnight Crossing* (1988), *Burning Secret* (1988), *The Handmaid's Tale* (1990), *Scorchers* (1991), *Silhouette* (TV 1991), *Three Weeks in Jerusalem* (1991), *American Dreamers* (1992), *Don Juan de Marco* (1995), *Albino Alligator* (1996), *The Thomas Crown Affair* (1999).

Eastwood, Clint (1930–) American, born San Francisco, California; *Rawhide* (TV

1958–65), *A Fistful of Dollars* (1964), *For a Few Dollars More* (1965), *The Good, The Bad, and the Ugly* (1966), *Coogan's Bluff* (1968), *Paint Your Wagon* (1969), *Where Eagles Dare* (1969), *Play Misty for Me* (1971), *Dirty Harry* (1972), *High Plains Drifter* (1973), *Magnum Force* (1973), *The Enforcer* (1976), *Every Which Way But Loose* (1978), *Escape from Alcatraz* (1979), *Honky Tonk Man* (1982), *Sudden Impact* (1983), *Heartbreak Ridge* (1986), *The Dead Pool* (1989), *The Rookie* (1990), *Unforgiven* (1992), *In the Line of Fire* (1993), *A Perfect World* (1993), *The Bridges of Madison County* (1995), *Absolute Power* (1997), *True Crime* (1999), *Mystic River* (2003), *Million Dollar Baby* (2004).

Fairbanks, Douglas, Jr (1909–2000) American, born New York City; *Catherine the Great* (1934), *The Prisoner of Zenda* (1937), *Sinbad the Sailor* (1947).

Fairbanks, Douglas, Sr (Douglas Elton Ullman) (1883–1939) American, born Denver, Colorado; *The Mark of Zorro* (1920), *The Three Musketeers* (1921), *Robin Hood* (1922), *The Thief of Baghdad* (1924), *The Black Pirate* (1926).

Fields, W C (William Claude Dukenfield) (1879–1946) American, born Philadelphia, Pennsylvania; *Pool Sharks* (1915), *International House* (1933), *It's a Gift* (1934), *The Old Fashioned Way* (1934), *David Copperfield* (1935), *My Little Chickadee* (1940), *The Bank Dick* (1940), *Never Give a Sucker an Even Break* (1941).

Fiennes, Ralph (Nathaniel) (1962–) British, born Ipswich, Suffolk; *Wuthering Heights* (1992), *Schindler's List* (1993), *Quiz Show* (1994), *The English Patient* (1996), *Oscar and Lucinda* (1998), *The End of the Affair* (1999), *Red Dragon* (2002), *The Constant Gardener* (2005).

Finney, Albert (1936–) British, born Salford, Lancashire; *The Entertainer* (1960), *Saturday Night and Sunday Morning* (1960), *Tom Jones* (1963), *Charlie Bubbles* (1968), *Murder on the Orient Express* (1974), *Shoot the Moon* (1981), *Annie* (1982), *The Dresser* (1983), *Under the Volcano* (1984), *The Green Man* (TV 1990), *Miller's Crossing* (1990), *The Playboys* (1992), *Karaoke* (TV 1996), *Washington Square* (1997), *Erin Brockovich* (2000), *Traffic* (2000), *Big Fish* (2003).

Flynn, Errol (1909–59) Australian–American, born Hobart, Tasmania; *In the Wake of the Bounty* (1933), *Captain Blood* (1935), *The Charge of the Light Brigade* (1936), *The Adventures of Robin Hood* (1938), *The Sea Hawk* (1940), *The Sun Also Rises* (1957).

Fonda, Henry (James) (1905–82) American, born Grand Island, Nebraska; *The Moon's Our Home* (1936), *A Farmer Takes A Wife* (1938), *Young Mr Lincoln* (1939), *The Grapes of Wrath* (1940), *The Lady Eve* (1941), *The Oxbow Incident* (1943), *My Darling Clementine* (1946), *Twelve Angry Men* (1957), *Stage Struck* (1957), *Fail Safe* (1964), *The Boston Strangler* (1968), *On Golden Pond* (1981).

Fonda, Jane (Seymour) (1937–) American, born New York City; *Walk on the Wild Side* (1961), *Barbarella* (1968), *They Shoot Horses Don't They?* (1969), *Klute* (1971), *Julia* (1977), *Coming Home* (1978), *The Electric Horseman* (1979), *The China Syndrome* (1980), *Nine to Five* (1981), *On Golden Pond* (1981), *The Morning After* (1986), *Old Gringo* (1989), *Stanley and Iris* (1989), *Monster in Law* (2005).

Ford, Harrison (1942–) American, born Chicago; *American Graffiti* (1973), *Star Wars* (1977), *Heroes* (1977), *Force 10 from Navarone* (1978), *The Frisco Kid* (1979), *Hanover Street* (1979), *Apocalypse Now* (1979), *The Empire Strikes Back* (1980), *Raiders of the Lost Ark* (1981), *Blade Runner* (1982), *Return of the Jedi* (1983), *Indiana Jones and the Temple of Doom* (1984), *Witness* (1985), *Mosquito Coast* (1986), *Frantic* (1988), *Working Girl* (1988), *Indiana Jones and the Last Crusade* (1989), *Presumed Innocent* (1990), *Regarding Henry* (1991), *Patriot Games* (1992), *The Fugitive* (1993), *Clear and Present Danger* (1994), *The Devil's Own* (1996), *Random Hearts* (1999), *What Lies Beneath* (2000), *K-19: The Widowmaker* (2002).

Foster, Jodie (Alicia Christian Foster) (1962–) American, born Los Angeles, California; *Alice Doesn't Live Here Anymore* (1974), *Bugsy Malone* (1976), *Taxi Driver* (1976), *The Little Girl Who Lives Down the Lane* (1976), *Candleshoe* (1977), *Freaky Friday* (1977), *Siesta* (1987), *The Accused* (1988), *5 Corners* (1988), *Stealing Home* (1988), *Catchfire* (1990), *Silence of the Lambs* (1991), *Little Man Tate* (1991), *Shadows and Fog* (1992), *Sommersby* (1993), *Maverick* (1994), *Nell* (1994), *Contact* (1997), *Anna and the King* (1999), *Panic Room* (2002), *Flightplan* (2005).

Fox, Michael J (1961–) Canadian, born Edmonton, Alberta; *Letters from Frank* (TV 1979), *Family Ties* (TV 1982–9), *Poison Ivy* (TV 1985), *Back to the Future* (1985), *Teenwolf* (1985), *The Secret of My Success* (1987), *Bright Lights Big City* (1988), *Casualties of War* (1989), *Back to the Future II* (1989), *Back to the Future III* (1990), *The Hard Way* (1991), *Doc Hollywood* (1991), *For Love or Money* (1993), *Life with Mikey* (1993), *Don't Drink the Water* (TV 1994), *The American President* (1995), *Blue in the Face* (1995), *Mars Attacks!* (1996), *Spin City* (TV 1996–2001).

Fry, Stephen (John) (1957–) English, born London; *A Handful of Dust* (1988), *A Fish Called Wanda* (1988), *A Bit of Fry and Laurie* (TV 1989–95), *Jeeves and Wooster* (TV 1990–3), *Peter's Friends* (1992), *Cold Comfort Farm* (TV 1995), *Wilde* (1997), *Gosford Park* (2001), *A Cock and Bull Story* (2005).

Gable, Clark (William) (1901–60) American, born Cadiz, Ohio; *Red Dust* (1932), *It Happened One Night* (1934), *Mutiny on the Bounty* (1935), *San Francisco* (1936), *Gone with the Wind* (1939), *The Hucksters* (1947), *Mogambo* (1953), *Never Let Me Go* (1953), *Teacher's Pet* (1958), *The Misfits* (1961).

Gambon, Sir Michael (1940–) Irish, born Dublin; *Turtle Diary* (1985), *The Singing Detective* (TV 1986), *Paris by Night* (1989), *The Cook, The Thief, His Wife and Her Lover* (1989), *The Wings of the Dove* (1997), *Sleepy Hollow* (1999), *Gosford Park* (2001), *Harry Potter* series (2004–), *Amazing Grace* (2006).

Garbo, Greta (Greta Lovisa Gustafsson) (1905–90) Swedish–American, born Stockholm; *Flesh and the Devil* (1927), *Anna Christie* (1930), *Grand Hotel* (1932), *Queen Christina* (1933), *Anna Karenina* (1935), *Camille* (1936), *Ninotchka* (1939).

Gardner, Ava (Lucy Johnson) (1922–90) American, born Smithfield, North Carolina; *The Killers* (1946), *The Hucksters* (1947), *Show Boat* (1951), *Pandora and the Flying Dutchman* (1951), *The Snows of Kilimanjaro* (1952), *Mogambo* (1953), *The Barefoot Contessa* (1954), *The Sun Also Rises* (1957), *The Night of the Iguana* (1964).

Garland, Judy (Frances Gumm) (1922–69) American, born Grand Rapids, Minnesota; *The Wizard of Oz* (1939), *Babes in Arms* (1939), *For Me and My Gal* (1942), *Meet Me in St Louis* (1944), *Ziegfeld Follies* (1946), *The Clock* (1945), *Easter Parade* (1948), *Summer Stock* (1950), *A Star is Born* (1954).

Gere, Richard (1949–) American, born Philadelphia, Pennsylvania; *American Gigolo* (1980), *An Officer and a Gentleman* (1982), *Breathless* (1983), *The Cotton Club* (1984), *No Mercy* (1986), *Internal Affairs* (1990), *Pretty Woman* (1990), *Final Analysis* (1992), *Sommersby* (1993), *First Knight* (1995), *Primal Fear* (1996), *The Jackal* (1997), *Runaway Bride* (1999), *Dr T and the Women* (2000), *The Mothman Prophecies* (2002), *Chicago* (2002).

Gibson, Mel (1956–) American–Australian, born Peekskill, New York; *Tim* (1979), *Mad Max* (1979), *Gallipoli* (1981), *Mad Max 2: The Road Warrior* (1982), *The Year of Living Dangerously* (1982), *Mad Max Beyond Thunderdome* (1985), *Lethal Weapon* (1987), *Tequila Sunrise* (1988), *Lethal Weapon 2* (1989), *Bird on a Wire* (1990), *Air America* (1990), *Hamlet* (1990), *Lethal Weapon 3* (1992), *Forever Young* (1992), *The Man Without*

A Face (1993), *Braveheart* (1995), *Ransom* (1996), *Conspiracy Theory* (1997), *The Patriot* (2000), *What Women Want* (2000), *Signs* (2002).

Gielgud, Sir John (Arthur) (1904–2000) British, born London; also stage; *Julius Caesar* (1953), *The Charge of the Light Brigade* (1968), *Oh What a Lovely War* (1969), *Murder on the Orient Express* (1974), *Providence* (1977), *Brideshead Revisited* (TV 1981), *Arthur* (1981), *Gandhi* (1982), *The Whistle Blower* (1987), *Loser Takes All* (1989), *Prospero's Books* (1991), *First Knight* (1995), *Haunted* (1995), *Hamlet* (1996), *Elizabeth* (1999).

Gish, Lillian (Diana) (Lillian de Guiche) (1893–1993) American, born Springfield, Ohio; *An Unseen Enemy* (1912), *Birth of a Nation* (1915), *Intolerance* (1916), *Broken Blossoms* (1919), *Way Down East* (1920), *Duel in the Sun* (1946), *Night of the Hunter* (1955), *The Whales of August* (1987).

Glover, Danny (1947–) American, born San Francisco, California; *Silverado* (1985), *Witness* (1985), *Lethal Weapon* (1987), *Bat 21* (1988), *Lethal Weapon 2* (1989), *Predator 2* (1990), *Lethal Weapon 3* (1992), *The Saint of Fort Washington* (1993), *Bopha!* (1993), *Lethal Weapon 4* (1998), *The Patriot* (2000), *The Royal Tenenbaums* (2001).

Goldberg, Whoopi (Caryn Johnson) (1949–) American, born Manhattan, New York City; *The Color Purple* (1985), *Burglar* (1985), *Jumping Jack Flash* (1986), *Clara's Heart* (1988), *The Telephone* (1988), *Ghost* (1990), *Soapdish* (1991), *Sister Act* (1992), *Change of Heart* (1992), *The Player* (1992), *Made in America* (1993), *Sister Act 2: Back in the Habit* (1993), *Corrina Corrina* (1994), *Star Trek: Generations* (1994), *Girl Interrupted* (1999).

Goldblum, Jeff (1952–) American, born Pittsburgh, Pennsylvania; *California Split* (1974), *Death Wish* (1974), *Nashville* (1975), *Invasion of the Body Snatchers* (1978), *Escape from Athena* (1979), *The Big Chill* (1983), *Silverado* (1985), *The Fly* (1985), *Vibes* (1988), *The Tall Guy* (1989), *Earth Girls Are Easy* (1989), *Mister Frost* (1990), *The Player* (1992), *Fathers and Sons* (1992), *Jurassic Park* (1993), *Nine Months* (1995), *Independence Day* (1996), *The Lost World: Jurassic Park* (1997, *Cats and Dogs* (2001).

Granger, Stewart (James Lablanche Stewart) (1913–93) British, born London; *The Man in Grey* (1943), *Waterloo Road* (1944), *Love Story* (1944), *Caesar and Cleopatra* (1945), *Captain Boycott* (1947), *King Solomon's Mines* (1950), *Scaramouche* (1952), *The Prisoner of Zenda* (1952), *Beau Brummell* (1954), *The Wild Geese* (1977).

Grant, Cary (Archibald Alexander Leach) (1904–86) Anglo-American, born Bristol, England; *This is the Night* (1932), *The Awful Truth* (1937), *Bringing Up Baby* (1938), *His Girl Friday* (1940), *Arsenic and Old Lace* (1944), *Notorious* (1946), *To Catch a Thief* (1953), *North by Northwest* (1959).

Griffiths, Richard (1947–) English, born Thornaby-on-Tees; *It Shouldn't Happen to a Vet* (1975), *Pie in the Sky* (TV 1994–7), *Harry Potter* series (2001–), *The History Boys* (play, 2004; film, 2006).

Guinness, Sir Alec (1914–2000) British, born London; *Oliver Twist* (1948), *Kind Hearts and Coronets* (1949), *The Lavender Hill Mob* (1951), *The Man in the White Suit* (1951), *The Card* (1952), *Father Brown* (1954), *The Ladykillers* (1955), *The Bridge on the River Kwai* (1957), *The Horse's Mouth* (1958), *Our Man in Havana* (1960), *Tunes of Glory* (1962), *Lawrence of Arabia* (1962), *Doctor Zhivago* (1966), *Star Wars* (1977), *Tinker, Tailor, Soldier, Spy* (TV 1979), *Smiley's People* (TV 1981), *Return of the Jedi* (1983), *A Passage to India* (1984), *Little Dorrit* (1987), *A Handful of Dust* (1988), *Kafka* (1991).

Hackman, Gene (1931–) American, born San Bernardino, California; *Bonnie and Clyde* (1967), *I Never Sang for My Father* (1969), *French Connection* (1971), *The Poseidon Adventure* (1972), *Young Frankenstein* (1974), *French Connection II* (1975), *A Bridge Too*

Far (1977), *Superman* (1978), *Superman II* (1981), *Target* (1985), *Superman IV* (1987), *Bat 21* (1988), *Full Moon in Blue Water* (1988), *Split Decisions* (1988), *Mississippi Burning* (1989), *The Package* (1989), *Loose Cannons* (1990), *Postcards from the Edge* (1990), *Narrow Margin* (1990), *Class Action* (1990), *Company Business* (1991), *Unforgiven* (1992), *The Firm* (1993), *Geronimo: An American Legend* (1993), *Get Shorty* (1995), *The Birdcage* (1996), *The Chamber* (1996), *Extreme Measures* (1996), *Absolute Power* (1997), *Enemy of the State* (1999), *The Royal Tenenbaums* (2001).

Hanks, Tom (1956–) American, born Oakland, California; *Bachelor Party* (1983), *Splash!* (1984), *Dragnet* (1987), *Big* (1988), *Punchline* (1988), *The 'Burbs* (1989), *Turner and Hooch* (1990), *Bonfire of the Vanities* (1991), *A League of Their Own* (1992), *Benny and Joon* (1992), *Sleepless in Seattle* (1993), *Philadelphia* (1993), *Forrest Gump* (1994), *Apollo 13* (1995), *That Thing You Do* (1996), *Saving Private Ryan* (1998), *You've Got Mail* (1998), *The Green Mile* (1999), *Cast Away* (2000), *Road to Perdition* (2002), *The Da Vinci Code* (2006).

Hardy, Oliver (Norvell Hardy Junior) (1892–1957) American, born near Atlanta, Georgia; *Putting Pants on Philip* (1927), *The Battle of the Century* (1927), *Two Tars* (1928), *The Perfect Day* (1929), *Laughing Gravy* (1931), *The Music Box* (1932), *Babes in Toyland* (1934), *Bonnie Scotland* (1935), *Way Out West* (1937), *The Flying Deuces* (1939), *Atoll K* (1950).

Harlow, Jean (Harlean Carpentier) (1911–37) American, born Kansas City, Missouri; *Red Dust* (1932), *Hell's Angels* (1930), *Platinum Blonde* (1931), *Red-Headed Woman* (1932), *Bombshell* (1933), *Dinner at 8* (1933), *Libelled Lady* (1936).

Harris, Richard (1930–2002) Irish, born County Limerick; *The Guns of Navarone* (1961), *Mutiny on the Bounty* (1962), *This Sporting Life* (1963), *Camelot* (1967), *A Man Called Horse* (1969), *Cromwell* (1970), *The Cassandra Crossing* (1977), *Orca – Killer Whale* (1977), *The Wild Geese* (1978), *The Field* (1990), *Gladiator* (2000), *Harry Potter and the Philosopher's Stone* (2001), *Harry Potter and the Chamber of Secrets* (2002).

Hayworth, Rita (Margarita Carmen Cansino) (1918–87) American, born New York City; *Only Angels Have Wings* (1939), *The Lady in Question* (1940), *The Strawberry Blonde* (1940), *Blood and Sand* (1941), *You'll Never Get Rich* (1941), *Cover Girl* (1944), *Gilda* (1946), *The Lady from Shanghai* (1948), *Separate Tables* (1958).

Hepburn, Audrey (Audrey Kathleen Ruston) (1929–93) Anglo-Dutch, born Brussels, Belgium; *Roman Holiday* (1953), *War and Peace* (1956), *Funny Face* (1957), *The Nun's Story* (1959), *Breakfast at Tiffany's* (1961), *My Fair Lady* (1964), *How to Steal a Million* (1966), *Wait Until Dark* (1967), *Robin and Marian* (1976), *Always* (1989).

Hepburn, Katharine (1907–2003) American, born Hartford, Connecticut; *A Bill of Divorcement* (1932), *Morning Glory* (1933), *Stage Door* (1937), *Bringing Up Baby* (1938), *Holiday* (1938), *The Philadelphia Story* (1940), *Woman of the Year* (1942), *Adam's Rib* (1949), *The African Queen* (1951), *Long Day's Journey into Night* (1962), *Guess Who's Coming to Dinner* (1967), *Suddenly Last Summer* (1968), *The Lion in Winter* (1968), *Rooster Cogburn* (1975), *On Golden Pond* (1981), *Love Affair* (1994).

Heston, Charlton (John Charlton Carter) (1923–) American, born Evanston, Illinois; *Arrowhead* (1953), *The Ten Commandments* (1956), *Touch of Evil* (1958), *Ben-Hur* (1959), *El Cid* (1961), *The Greatest Story Ever Told* (1965), *The War Lord* (1965), *Khartoum* (1966), *Planet of the Apes* (1968), *Will Penny* (1968), *Earthquake* (1973), *Airport* (1975), *The Four Musketeers* (1975), *Almost an Angel* (1990), *Wayne's World 2* (1993), *Tombstone* (1993), *Hamlet* (1996), *Any Given Sunday* (1999).

Hoffman, Dustin (1937–) American, born Los Angeles; *The Graduate* (1967), *Midnight Cowboy* (1969), *Little Big Man* (1970), *Papillon* (1973), *Lenny* (1974), *Marathon Man*

(1976), *All the President's Men* (1976), *Kramer vs Kramer* (1979), *Tootsie* (1982), *Death of a Salesman* (TV 1984), *Rain Man* (1988), *Dick Tracy* (1990), *Hook* (1991), *Hero* (1992), *Outbreak* (1995), *Sleepers* (1996), *Wag The Dog* (1997), *Sphere* (1998), *Finding Neverland* (2004), *Perfume* (2006).

Holden, William (William Franklin Beedle, Jr) (1918–82) American, born O'Fallon, Illinois; *Golden Boy* (1939), *Rachel and the Stranger* (1948), *Sunset Boulevard* (1950), *Born Yesterday* (1950), *Stalag 17* (1953), *Love is a Many-Splendored Thing* (1955), *Picnic* (1955), *The Bridge on the River Kwai* (1957), *Casino Royale* (1967), *The Wild Bunch* (1969), *The Towering Inferno* (1974), *Network* (1976), *Damien: Omen II* (1978), *Escape to Athena* (1979), *The Earthling* (1980), *SOB* (1981), *When Time Ran Out* (1981).

Holm, Sir Ian (Ian Holm Cuthbert) (1931–) English, born Goodmayes, Essex; *The Bofors Gun* (1968), *The Lost Boys* (TV 1978), *Chariots of Fire* (1981), *Henry V* (1989), *The Madness of King George* (1994), *The Sweet Hereafter* (1997), *King Lear* (TV 1998), *The Lord of the Rings: The Fellowship of the Ring* (2001).

Hope, Bob (Leslie Townes Hope) (1903–2003) Anglo-American, born Eltham, London; *Thanks for the Memory* (1938), *The Cat and the Canary* (1939), *Road to Singapore* (1940), *The Ghost Breakers* (1940), *Road to Zanzibar* (1941), *My Favorite Blonde* (1942), *Road to Morocco* (1942), *The Paleface* (1948), *Fancy Pants* (1950), *The Facts of Life* (1960), *Road to Hong Kong* (1961), *How to Commit Marriage* (1969).

Hopkins, Sir Anthony (1937–) Welsh–American, born Port Talbot, Wales; *The Lion in Winter* (1968), *When Eight Bells Toll* (1971), *War and Peace* (TV 1972), *Magic* (1978), *The Elephant Man* (1980), *The Bounty* (1983), *84 Charing Cross Road* (1986), *Desperate Hours* (1991), *Silence of the Lambs* (1991), *Spotswood* (1991), *Howards End* (1992), *Charlie* (1992), *The Innocent* (1992), *Dracula* (1992), *The Remains of the Day* (1993), *Shadowlands* (1993), *The Road to Wellville* (1994), *Legends of the Fall* (1994), *Nixon* (1995), *Surviving Picasso* (1996), *Amistad* (1997), *Meet Joe Black* (1998), *Hannibal* (2001), *Red Dragon* (2002), *Bobby* (2006).

Hopper, Dennis (1936–) American, born Dodge City, Kansas; *Rebel Without a Cause* (1955), *Giant* (1956), *Cool Hand Luke* (1967), *Easy Rider* (1969), *Apocalypse Now* (1979), *Blue Velvet* (1986), *River's Edge* (1986), *Blood Red* (1990), *Catchfire* (1990), *Paris Trout* (1991), *The Indian Runner* (1991), *Money Men* (1992), *True Romance* (1993), *Speed* (1994), *Basquiat* (1996), *10th and Wolf* (2006).

Hoskins, Bob (Robert William) (1942–) British, born Bury St Edmunds, Suffolk; *Pennies from Heaven* (TV 1978), *The Long Good Friday* (1980), *The Honorary Consul* (1983), *The Cotton Club* (1984), *Brazil* (1985), *Mona Lisa* (1986), *A Prayer for the Dying* (1987), *Who Framed Roger Rabbit* (1988), *Heart Condition* (1990), *Mermaids* (1990), *Shattered* (1991), *Hook* (1991), *The Inner Circle* (1992), *Rainbow* (1995), *Nixon* (1995), *The Secret Agent* (1996), *Parting Shots* (1998), *Last Orders* (2001), *Mrs Henderson Presents* (2005).

Howard, Trevor (Wallace) (1916–88) British, born Cliftonville, Kent; *The Way Ahead* (1944), *Brief Encounter* (1946), *Green for Danger* (1946), *The Third Man* (1949), *The Heart of the Matter* (1953), *The Key* (1958), *Sons and Lovers* (1960), *Mutiny on the Bounty* (1962), *The Charge of the Light Brigade* (1968), *Ryan's Daughter* (1970), *The Night Visitor* (1971), *Catholics* (TV 1973), *Conduct Unbecoming* (1975), *Meteor* (1979), *Staying On* (TV 1980), *Gandhi* (1982), *White Mischief* (1987), *The Unholy* (1988).

Hudson, Rock (Roy Scherer, Jr) (1925–85) American, born Winnetka, Illinois; *Magnificent Obsession* (1954), *Giant* (1956), *Written on the Wind* (1956), *The Tarnished Angel* (1957), *Pillow Talk* (1959), *Send Me No Flowers* (1964), *Seconds* (1966), *Darling Lili* (1969),

McMillan and Wife (TV 1971–5), *McMillan* (TV 1976), *Embryo* (1976), *The Martian Chronicles* (TV 1980), *Dynasty* (TV 1985).

Hurt, John (1940–) British, born Chesterfield, Derbyshire; *A Man for All Seasons* (1966), *10 Rillington Place* (1971), *The Naked Civil Servant* (TV 1975), *Midnight Express* (1978), *Alien* (1979), *The Elephant Man* (1980), *History of the World Part One* (1981), *Champions* (1983), *1984* (1984), *Spaceballs* (1987), *White Mischief* (1987), *Scandal* (1989), *Frankenstein Unbound* (1990), *King Ralph* (1991), *Rob Roy* (1995), *Darkening* (1996), *Captain Corelli's Mandolin* (2001), *The Proposition* (2005).

Hurt, William (1950–) American, born Washington, DC; *Altered States* (1981), *The Janitor* (1981), *Body Heat* (1981), *Kiss of the Spider Woman* (1985), *Children of a Lesser God* (1986), *Broadcast News* (1987), *The Accidental Tourist* (1989), *Love You to Death* (1990), *Alice* (1990), *The Doctor* (1991), *The Plague* (1992), *Second Best* (1994), *Smoke* (1995), *Jane Eyre* (1995), *Michael* (1996), *Lost in Space* (1998), *Artificial Intelligence: AI* (2001), *A History of Violence* (2005).

Huston, Anjelica (1951–) American, born Los Angeles; *The Last Tycoon* (1976), *Frances* (1982), *This is Spinal Tap* (1984), *Prizzi's Honor* (1985), *The Dead* (1987), *Gardens of Stone* (1987), *A Handful of Dust* (1988), *Mr North* (1988), *The Witches* (1990), *The Grifters* (1990), *The Addams Family* (1991), *Bitter Moon* (1992), *Addams Family Values* (1993), *Manhattan Murder Mystery* (1994), *The Crossing Guard* (1995), *Agnes Browne* (1999), *The Royal Tenenbaums* (2001), *Iron Jawed Angels* (TV 2004).

Irons, Jeremy (1948–) British, born Cowes; *The French Lieutenant's Woman* (1981), *Brideshead Revisited* (TV 1981), *Swann in Love* (1984), *The Mission* (1985), *Dead Ringers* (1988), *Reversal of Fortune* (1990), *Kafka* (1991), *Waterland* (1992), *Damage* (1992), *M Butterfly* (1992), *Die Hard with a Vengeance* (1995), *Stealing Beauty* (1996), *Lolita* (1996), *The Fourth Angel* (2001), *Elizabeth I* (TV 2005).

Jackson, Glenda (1936–) British, born Liverpool; *Women in Love* (1969), *Sunday, Bloody Sunday* (1971), *Mary Queen of Scots* (1971), *Elizabeth R* (TV 1971), *A Touch of Class* (1972), *Hedda* (1975), *Stevie* (1978), *Turtle Diary* (1985), *Business as Usual* (1987), *Salome's Last Dance* (1988), *The Rainbow* (1989), *Doombeach* (1990).

Jacobi, Sir Derek (1938–) British, born Leytonstone, London; *The Odessa File* (1964), *I Claudius* (TV 1976), *Burgess and MacLean* (TV 1977), *Mr Pye* (TV 1986), *Little Dorrit* (1987), *The Fool* (1990), *Hamlet* (1996), *Gladiator* (2000), *Gosford Park* (2001).

Johansson, Scarlett (1984–) American, born New York City; *The Horse Whisperer* (1998), *An American Rhapsody* (2000), *Ghost World* (2001), *Girl with a Pearl Earring* (2003), *Lost in Translation* (2003), *A Love Song for Bobby Long* (2004), *Match Point* (2005), *Scoop* (2006), *The Prestige* (2006).

Jolie, Angelina (Angelina Jolie Voight) (1975–) American, born Los Angeles, California; *George Wallace* (TV 1997), *Gia* (TV 1998), *The Bone Collector* (1999), *Girl, Interrupted* (1999), *Gone in Sixty Seconds* (2000), *Lara Croft, Tomb Raider* (2001), *Mr and Mrs Smith* (2005).

Karloff, Boris (William Henry Pratt) (1887–1969) Anglo-American, born London; *Frankenstein* (1931), *The Mask of Fu Manchu* (1931), *The Lost Patrol* (1934), *The Raven* (1935), *The Bride of Frankenstein* (1935), *The Body Snatcher* (1945).

Keaton, Buster (Joseph Francis Keaton) (1895–1966) American, born Piqua, Kansas; *Our Hospitality* (1923), *The Navigator* (1924), *The General* (1927), *San Diego I Love You* (1944), *Sunset Boulevard* (1950), *Limelight* (1952), *It's a Mad, Mad, Mad, Mad World* (1963).

Keaton, Diane (Diane Hall) (1946–) American, born Los Angeles, California; *The Godfather* (1972), *The Godfather, Part II* (1974), *Sleeper* (1973), *Annie Hall* (1977),

Manhattan (1979), *Reds* (1981), *Shoot the Moon* (1982), *Mrs Soffel* (1984), *Baby Boom* (1987), *The Good Mother* (1988), *The Godfather, Part III* (1990), *Success* (1991), *Father of the Bride* (1991), *Manhattan Murder Mystery* (1993), *Father of the Bride II* (1995), *The First Wives Club* (1996), *Marvin's Room* (1996), *The Other Sister* (1999), *Something's Gotta Give* (2003).

Keitel, Harvey (1939–   ) American, born Brooklyn, New York City; *Mean Streets* (1973), *Taxi Driver* (1976), *Bad Timing* (1980), *The Men's Club* (1986), *The Last Temptation of Christ* (1988), *The January Man* (1989), *Bugsy* (1991), *Thelma and Louise* (1991), *Reservoir Dogs* (1992), *The Bad Lieutenant* (1992), *Sister Act* (1992), *The Piano* (1993), *Pulp Fiction* (1994), *Smoke* (1995), *Clockers* (1995), *Blue in the Face* (1995), *Get Shorty* (1995), *Head Above Water* (1996), *Copland* (1997), *Holy Smoke* (1999), *Red Dragon* (2002), *The Shadow Dancer* (2005).

Kelly, Gene (Eugene Curran Kelly) (1912–96) American, born Pittsburgh, Pennsylvania; *For Me and My Girl* (1942), *Cover Girl* (1944), *Anchors Aweigh* (1945), *Ziegfeld Follies* (1946), *The Pirate* (1948), *The Three Musketeers* (1948), *Take Me Out to the Ball Game* (1949), *On the Town* (1949), *Summer Stock* (1950), *An American in Paris* (1951), *Singin' in the Rain* (1952), *Brigadoon* (1954), *Invitation to the Dance* (1956), *Les Girls* (1957), *Marjorie Morningstar* (1958), *Inherit the Word* (1960), *Sins* (TV 1987).

Kelly, Grace (Patricia) (1928–82) American, born Philadelphia, Pennsylvania; *High Noon* (1952), *Mogambo* (1953), *Dial M for Murder* (1954), *Rear Window* (1954), *The Country Girl* (1954), *To Catch a Thief* (1955), *High Society* (1956).

Kennedy, George (1925–   ) American, born New York City; *Charade* (1963), *The Flight of the Phoenix* (1967), *The Dirty Dozen* (1967), *Cool Hand Luke* (1967), *Sarge* (TV 1971), *Thunderbolt and Lightfoot* (1974), *Earthquake* (1974), *The Blue Knight* (TV 1975–6), *The Eiger Sanction* (1977), *Death on the Nile* (1979), *Bolero* (1984), *Delta Force* (1985), *Creepshow 2* (1987), *Dallas* (TV 1988–91), *Naked Gun* (1989), *Naked Gun $2\frac{1}{2}$: The Smell of Fear* (1991), *Naked Gun $33\frac{1}{3}$: The Final Insult* (1994).

Kerr, Deborah (Deborah Jane Kerr-Trimmer) (1921–   ) British, born Helensburgh, Scotland; *Major Barbara* (1940), *Love on the Dole* (1941), *The Life and Death of Colonel Blimp* (1943), *Perfect Strangers* (1945), *I See a Dark Stranger* (1946), *Black Narcissus* (1947), *From Here to Eternity* (1953), *The King and I* (1956), *Tea and Sympathy* (1956), *An Affair to Remember* (1957), *Separate Tables* (1958), *The Sundowners* (1960), *The Innocents* (1961), *The Night of the Iguana* (1964), *Casino Royale* (1967), *Prudence and the Pill* (1968), *The Assam Garden* (1985).

Kidman, Nicole (1967–   ) Australian–American, born Honolulu, Hawaii; *Days of Thunder* (1990), *To Die For* (1995), *The Portrait of a Lady* (1996), *Practical Magic* (1998), *Eyes Wide Shut* (1999), *Moulin Rouge!* (2001), *The Others* (2001), *The Hours* (2002), *Dogville* (2003), *Cold Mountain* (2003), *Birth* (2004), *Fur* (2006).

Kingsley, Sir Ben (Krishna Banji) (1943–   ) Anglo-Indian, born Snaiton, Yorkshire; *Gandhi* (1982), *Betrayal* (1982), *Turtle Diary* (1985), *Testimony* (1987), *Pascali's Island* (1988), *Without a Clue* (1988), *Slipstream* (1989), *Bugsy* (1992), *Sneakers* (1992), *Schindler's List* (1993), *Death and the Maiden* (1994), *Species* (1996), *Parting Shots* (1998), *Sexy Beast* (2000), *House of Sand and Fog* (2003).

Lancaster, Burt (Stephen Burton) (1913–94) American, born New York City; *Brute Force* (1947), *The Flame and the Arrow* (1950), *Come Back Little Sheba* (1953), *From Here to Eternity* (1953), *Vera Cruz* (1954), *Gunfight at the OK Corral* (1957), *Elmer Gantry* (1960), *Birdman of Alcatraz* (1962), *The Professionals* (1966), *The Swimmer* (1967), *1900* (1976), *Atlantic City* (1980), *Local Hero* (1983), *Rocket Gibraltar* (1988), *Field of Dreams* (1988).

Lansbury, Angela (Brigid) (1925–) American, born London; *National Velvet* (1944), *Gaslight* (1944), *The Picture of Dorian Gray* (1945), *The Private Affairs of Bel Ami* (1947), *The Three Musketeers* (1948), *The Reluctant Debutante* (1958), *The Long Hot Summer* (1958), *The Dark at the Top of the Stairs* (1960), *The Manchurian Candidate* (1962), *The Greatest Story Ever Told* (1965), *Bedknobs and Broomsticks* (1971), *Death on the Nile* (1978), *The Lady Vanishes* (1979), *Lace* (TV 1984), *The Company of Wolves* (1984), *Murder She Wrote* (TV 1984–96).

Laughton, Charles (1899–1962) British, born Scarborough; *The Sign of the Cross* (1932), *The Private Life of Henry VIII* (1932), *The Barretts of Wimpole Street* (1934), *Ruggles of Red Gap* (1935), *Mutiny on the Bounty* (1935), *Les Misérables* (1935), *Rembrandt* (1936), *The Hunchback of Notre Dame* (1939), *Hobson's Choice* (1954), *Witness for the Prosecution* (1957), *Advise and Consent* (1962).

Laurel, Stan (Arthur Stanley Jefferson) (1890–1965) Anglo-American, born Ulverston, Lancashire (now Cumbria); *Nuts in May* (1917), *Monsieur Don't Care* (1925); for films with Hardy ▶ Hardy, Oliver.

Law, Jude (1972–) British, born London; *Wilde* (1997), *The Wisdom of Crocodiles* (1998), *Onegin* (1999), *The Talented Mr Ripley* (1999), *Artificial Intelligence: AI* (2001), *Road to Perdition* (2002), *Cold Mountain* (2003), *Closer* (2004), *The Aviator* (2004).

Lee, Bruce (Lee Jun Fan) (1940–73) American–Chinese, born San Francisco, California; *The Big Boss* (1971), *Fist of Fury* (1972), *Way of the Dragon* (1972), *Enter the Dragon* (1973), *Game of Death* (1978).

Lee, Christopher (1922–) British, born London; *The Curse of Frankenstein* (1956), *Dracula* (1958), *The Man Who Could Cheat Death* (1959), *The Mummy* (1959), *The Face of Fu Manchu* (1965), *Rasputin the Mad Monk* (1965), *Horror Express* (1972), *The Three Musketeers* (1973), *The Man With the Golden Gun* (1974), *Return from Witch Mountain* (1976), *Howling II* (1985), *The Land of Faraway* (1988), *Gremlins 2: The New Batch* (1990), *Police Academy 7: Mission to Moscow* (1994), *The Knot* (1996), *Ivanhoe* (TV 1997), *Sleepy Hollow* (1999), *The Lord of the Rings: The Fellowship of the Ring* (2001), *Star Wars: Attack of the Clones* (2002), *The Lord of the Rings: The Two Towers* (2002), *Star Wars: Revenge of the Sith* (2005).

Leigh, Vivien (Vivian Hartley) (1913–67) British, born Darjeeling, India; *Dark Journey* (1937), *A Yank at Oxford* (1938), *Gone with the Wind* (1939), *Lady Hamilton* (1941), *Caesar and Cleopatra* (1945), *Anna Karenina* (1948), *A Streetcar Named Desire* (1951), *The Roman Spring of Mrs Stone* (1961), *Ship of Fools* (1965).

Lemmon, Jack (John Uhler Lemmon III) (1925–2001) American, born Boston, Massachusetts; *It Should Happen to You* (1953), *Mister Roberts* (1955), *Some Like It Hot* (1959), *The Apartment* (1960), *Irma La Douce* (1963), *The Great Race* (1965), *The Odd Couple* (1968), *The Prisoner of Second Avenue* (1975), *The China Syndrome* (1979), *Missing* (1982), *Dad* (1990), *JFK* (1991), *The Player* (1992), *Glengarry Glen Ross* (1992), *Short Cuts* (1993), *The Grass Harp* (1993), *Hamlet* (1996), *The Odd Couple II* (1998).

Lewis, Jerry (Joseph Levitch) (1926–) American, born Newark, New Jersey; *My Friend Irma* (1949), *The Bellboy* (1960), *Cinderfella* (1960), *The Nutty Professor* (1963), *It's a Mad, Mad, Mad, Mad World* (1963), *The Family Jewels* (1965), *King of Comedy* (1983), *Smorgasbord* (1983), *Cookie* (1988), *Funny Bones* (1995).

Lloyd, Harold (Clayton) (1893–1971) American, born Burchard, Nebraska; *High and Dizzy* (1920), *Grandma's Boy* (1922), *Safety Last* (1923), *Why Worry?* (1923), *The Freshman* (1925), *The Kid Brother* (1927), *Feet First* (1930), *Movie Crazy* (1932).

Loren, Sophia (Sofia Scicolone) (1934–) Italian, born Rome; *Woman of the River* (1955), *Boy on a Dolphin* (1957), *The Key* (1958), *El Cid* (1961), *Two Women* (1961), *The Millionairess* (1961), *Marriage Italian Style* (1964), *Cinderella Italian Style* (1967), *A Special Day* (1977), *Prêt-à-Porter* (1994), *Grumpier Old Men* (1995), *Between Strangers* (2002).

Lugosi, Bela (Bela Ferenc Denzso Blasko) (1882–1956) Hungarian–American, born Lugos (now Romania); *Dracula* (1930), *The Murders in the Rue Morgue* (1931), *White Zombie* (1932), *International House* (1933), *The Black Cat* (1934), *Son of Frankenstein* (1939), *Abbott and Costello Meet Frankenstein* (1948), *Plan 9 from Outer Space* (1956).

McGregor, Ewan (1971–) British, born Crieff; *Lipstick on Your Collar* (TV 1993), *Shallow Grave* (1994), *Blue Juice* (1995), *The Pillow Book* (1995), *Emma* (1995), *Trainspotting* (1996), *Brassed Off* (1996), *A Life Less Ordinary* (1997), *Little Voice* (1998), *Star Wars: The Phantom Menace* (1999), *Moulin Rouge!* (2001), *Star Wars: Attack of the Clones* (2002), *Down with Love* (2003), *Big Fish* (2003), *Young Adam* (2003), *Miss Potter* (2006).

McKellen, Sir Ian (1939–) English, born Burnley; *Amadeus* (play, 1981, Tony Award), *Walter* (TV 1982), *Richard III* (1995), *Rasputin* (TV 1996), *Gods and Monsters* (1998), *X Men* trilogy (2000–6), *Lord of the Rings* trilogy (2001–3).

MacLaine, Shirley (Shirley Beaty) (1934–) American, born Richmond, Virginia; *The Trouble with Harry* (1955), *Ask any Girl* (1959), *The Apartment* (1959), *Irma La Douce* (1963), *Sweet Charity* (1968), *Terms of Endearment* (1983), *Madame Sousatzka* (1988), *Postcards from the Edge* (1990), *Defending Your Life* (1991), *Used People* (1992), *Guarding Tess* (1994), *The Evening Star* (1996), *Bruno* (2000), *In Her Shoes* (2005).

McQueen, Steve (Terence Steven McQueen) (1930–80) American, born Slater, Missouri; *Wanted Dead or Alive* (TV 1958), *The Blob* (1958), *The Magnificent Seven* (1960), *The Great Escape* (1963), *Love with the Proper Stranger* (1963), *The Cincinnatti Kid* (1965), *Bullitt* (1968), *Le Mans* (1971), *Getaway* (1972), *Papillon* (1973), *The Towering Inferno* (1974), *An Enemy of the People* (1977).

Malkovich, John (1953–) American, born Christopher, Illinois; *The Killing Fields* (1984), *Places in the Heart* (1984), *Empire of the Sun* (1987), *Miles from Home* (1988), *Dangerous Liaisons* (1988), *Crazy People* (1990), *The Sheltering Sky* (1990), *Of Mice and Men* (1992), *In the Line of Fire* (1993), *Mary Reilly* (1996), *Being John Malkovich* (1999), *Je rentre à la maison* (2001), *Ripley's Game* (2002), *Klimt* (2006).

Martin, Steve (1945–) American, born Waco, Texas; *Sgt Pepper's Lonely Hearts Club Band* (1978), *The Jerk* (1979), *Muppet Movie* (1979), *Pennies from Heaven* (1981), *Dead Men Don't Wear Plaid* (1982), *The Man With Two Brains* (1983), *The Lonely Guy* (1984), *All of Me* (1984), *The Three Amigos* (1986), *The Little Shop of Horrors* (1986), *Planes, Trains and Automobiles* (1987), *Roxanne* (1987), *Dirty, Rotten Scoundrels* (1989), *Parenthood* (1989), *My Blue Heaven* (1990), *LA Story* (1991), *Father of the Bride* (1991), *Housesitter* (1992), *A Simple Twist of Faith* (1994), *Sgt Bilko* (1995), *Bowfinger* (1999), *Shopgirl* (2005).

Marvin, Lee (1924–87) American, born New York City; *The Wild One* (1954), *Attack* (1957), *The Killers* (1964), *Cat Ballou* (1965), *The Dirty Dozen* (1967), *Paint Your Wagon* (1969), *Gorky Park* (1983), *Dirty Dozen 2: The Next Mission* (TV 1985).

Marx Brothers, The: Chico (Leonard Marx) (1887–1961); **Harpo** (Adolph Marx) (1888–1964); **Groucho** (Julius Henry Marx) (1890–1977); **Zeppo** (Herbert Marx) (1901–79) all American, born New York City; (joint) *The Cocoanuts* (1929), *Monkey Business* (1931), *Horse Feathers* (1932), *Duck Soup* (1933), *A Night at the Opera* (1935), *A Day at the Races* (1937), *A Night in Casablanca* (1946).

Mason, James (1909–84) British, born Huddersfield; *I Met a Murderer* (1939), *The Night Has Eyes* (1942), *The Man in Grey* (1943), *Fanny by Gaslight* (1944), *The Seventh Veil* (1945), *The Wicked Lady* (1946), *Odd Man Out* (1946), *Pandora and the Flying Dutchman* (1951), *The Desert Fox* (1951), *Five Fingers* (1952), *The Prisoner of Zenda* (1952), *Julius Caesar* (1953), *20000 Leagues Under the Sea* (1954), *A Star is Born* (1954), *Journey to the Center of the Earth* (1959), *Lolita* (1962), *The Pumpkin Eater* (1964), *Georgy Girl* (1966), *The Blue Max* (1966), *The Deadly Affair* (1967), *Voyage of the Damned* (1976), *Heaven Can Wait* (1978), *The Boys from Brazil* (1978), *Murder by Decree* (1979), *Evil Under the Sun* (1982), *The Verdict* (1982), *Yellowbeard* (1983), *The Shooting Party* (1984).

Mastroianni, Marcello (1924–96) Italian, born Fontana Liri, near Frosinone; *I Miserabili* (1947), *White Nights* (1957), *La Dolce Vita* (1959), *Divorce Italian Style* (1962), *Yesterday, Today and Tomorrow* (1963), *8½* (1963), *Casanova* (1970), *Diamonds for Breakfast* (1968), *Ginger and Fred* (1985), *Black Eyes* (1987), *The Two Lives of Mattia Pascal* (1988), *Traffic Jam* (1988), *Used People* (1992), *Prêt-à-Porter* (1994), *Beyond the Clouds* (1996).

Matthau, Walter (Walter John Matthow) (1920–2000) American, born New York City; *A Face in the Crowd* (1957), *King Creole* (1958), *Charade* (1963), *Mirage* (1965), *The Fortune Cookie* (1966), *A Guide to the Married Man* (1967), *The Odd Couple* (1968), *Hello Dolly* (1969), *Cactus Flower* (1969), *Kotch* (1971), *Earthquake* (1974), *The Taking of Pelham One Two Three* (1974), *Hopscotch* (1980), *Pirates* (1986), *The Couch Trip* (1988), *JFK* (1991), *Grumpy Old Men* (1993), *Grumpier Old Men* (1995), *Out to Sea* (1997).

Mature, Victor (1913–99) American, born Louisville, Kentucky; *One Million BC* (1940), *My Darling Clementine* (1946), *Kiss of Death* (1947), *Samson and Delilah* (1949), *The Robe* (1953), *The Egyptian* (1954), *Safari* (1956), *The Long Haul* (1957), *After the Fox* (1966).

Midler, Bette (1945–) American, born Honolulu, Hawaii; *The Rose* (1979), *Down and Out in Beverly Hills* (1986), *Ruthless People* (1986), *Outrageous Fortune* (1987), *Beaches* (1988), *Big Business* (1988), *Stella* (1989), *For the Boys* (1991), *Hocus Pocus* (1993), *Gypsy* (1993), *Get Shorty* (1995), *The First Wives Club* (1996), *Bette* (TV 2000), *The Stepford Wives* (2004).

Mills, Hayley (1946–) British, born London; *Tiger Bay* (1959), *Pollyanna* (1960), *The Parent Trap* (1961), *Whistle Down the Wind* (1961), *The Moonspinners* (1965), *Forbush and the Penguins* (1971), *Deadly Strangers* (1974), *After Midnight* (1989).

Mills, Sir John (Lewis Ernest Watts) (1908–2005) British, born Felixstowe, Suffolk; *Those Were the Days* (1934), *Cottage to Let* (1941), *In Which We Serve* (1942), *Waterloo Road* (1944), *The Way to the Stars* (1945), *Great Expectations* (1946), *The October Man* (1947), *Scott of the Antarctic* (1948), *The History of Mr Polly* (1949), *The Rocking Horse Winner* (1950), *The Colditz Story* (1954), *Hobson's Choice* (1954), *Town on Trial* (1957), *Tiger Bay* (1959), *Swiss Family Robinson* (1959), *Tunes of Glory* (1960), *Ryan's Daughter* (1970), *Lady Caroline Lamb* (1972), *The Big Sleep* (1978), *The 39 Steps* (1978), *Quatermass* (TV 1979), *Young at Heart* (TV 1980–1), *Gandhi* (1982), *Sahara* (1983), *Who's That Girl?* (1987), *Hamlet* (1996).

Minnelli, Liza (1946–) American, born Los Angeles; *Cabaret* (1972), *New York New York* (1977), *Arthur* (1981), *Stepping Out* (1991).

Mirren, Helen (Ilyena Lydia Mironov) (1945–) British, born London; *Miss Julie* (1973), *Excalibur* (1981), *Cal* (1984), *2010* (1985), *Heavenly Pursuits* (1985), *White Nights* (1986), *Mosquito Coast* (1986), *Pascali's Island* (1988), *The Cook, the Thief, His Wife and Her Lover* (1989), *The Comfort of Strangers* (1990), *Where Angels Fear to Tread* (1991), *Prime Suspect* (TV 1991–2006), *The Hawk* (1993), *The Madness of King George* (1994), *Gosford Park* (2001), *Calendar Girls* (2003), *Elizabeth I* (TV 2005), *The Queen* (2006).

Mitchum, Robert (1917–97) American, born Bridgeport, Connecticut; *The Story of GI Joe* (1945), *Pursued* (1947), *Crossfire* (1947), *Out of the Past* (1947), *The Big Steal* (1949), *Night of the Hunter* (1955), *Home from the Hill* (1960), *The Sundowners* (1960), *Cape Fear* (1962), *The List of Adrian Messenger* (1963), *Ryan's Daughter* (1970), *Farewell My Lovely* (1975), *The Big Sleep* (1978), *The Winds of War* (TV 1983), *War and Remembrance* (TV 1987), *Mr North* (1988), *Scrooged* (1988), *Cape Fear* (1991), *Tombstone* (1993), *Backfire* (1994).

Monroe, Marilyn (Norma Jean Mortenson or Baker) (1926–62) American, born Los Angeles; *How to Marry a Millionaire* (1953), *Gentlemen Prefer Blondes* (1953), *The Seven Year Itch* (1955), *Bus Stop* (1956), *Some Like It Hot* (1959), *The Misfits* (1960).

Montand, Yves (Ivo Levi) (1921–91) French, born Monsumagno, Italy; *The Wages of Fear* (1953), *Let's Make Love* (1962), *Jean de Florette* (1986), *Manon des Sources* (1986).

Moore, Demi (Demi Guines) (1962–) American, born Roswell, New Mexico; *St Elmo's Fire* (1986), *About Last Night* (1987), *We're No Angels* (1990), *Ghost* (1990), *The Butcher's Wife* (1991), *A Few Good Men* (1992), *Indecent Proposal* (1993), *Disclosure* (1994), *The Scarlet Letter* (1995), *Striptease* (1996), *GI Jane* (1997), *Deconstructing Harry* (1997), *Passion of Mind* (2000), *Bobby* (2006).

Moore, Roger (George) (1927–) British, born London; *Ivanhoe* (TV 1957), *The Saint* (TV 1963–8), *The Persuaders* (TV 1971–2), *Live and Let Die* (1973), *The Man with the Golden Gun* (1974), *Shout at the Devil* (1976), *The Spy Who Loved Me* (1977), *The Wild Geese* (1978), *Escape to Athena* (1979), *Moonraker* (1979), *For Your Eyes Only* (1981), *The Cannonball Run* (1981), *Octopussy* (1983), *A View to a Kill* (1985), *The Quest* (1996).

Moreau, Jeanne (1928–) French, born Paris; *Les Amants* (1958), *Ascenseur Pour L'Échafaud* (1957), *Jules et Jim* (1961), *Eva* (1962), *The Trial* (1963), *Journal d'une Femme de Chambre* (1964), *Viva Maria* (1965), *Nikita* (1990), *La Vieille Qui Marchait Dans La Mer* (1991), *Ever After* (1998).

Murphy, Eddie (1961–) American, born Brooklyn, New York City; *48 Hours* (1982), *Trading Places* (1983), *Beverly Hills Cop* (1985), *The Golden Child* (1986), *Beverly Hills Cop II* (1987), *Coming to America* (1988), *Harlem Nights* (1989), *Another 48 Hours* (1990), *Boomerang* (1992), *Distinguished Gentleman* (1992), *Beverly Hills Cop III* (1994), *The Nutty Professor* (1995), *Doctor Dolittle* (1998), *Bowfinger* (1999), *Nutty Professor II: The Klumps* (2000), *Shrek* (2001).

Murray, Bill (1950–) American, born Evanston, Illinois; *Meatballs* (1977), *Caddyshack* (1980), *Stripes* (1981), *Tootsie* (1982), *Ghostbusters* (1984), *Razor's Edge* (1984), *Little Shop of Horrors* (1986), *Scrooged* (1988), *Ghostbusters II* (1989), *What About Bob?* (1991), *Mad Dog and Glory* (1992), *Groundhog Day* (1993), *Ed Wood* (1994), *Kingpin* (1996), *Cradle Will Rock* (1999), *The Royal Tenenbaums* (2001), *Lost in Translation* (2003), *The Life Aquatic with Steve Zissou* (2004), *Broken Flowers* (2005).

Neeson, Liam (1952–) British, born Ballymena, Northern Ireland; *Excalibur* (1981), *Suspect* (1987), *Satisfaction* (1988), *High Spirits* (1988), *The Good Mother* (1988), *The Dead Pool* (1988), *The Big Man* (1990), *Dark Man* (1990), *Husbands and Wives* (1992), *Schindler's List* (1993), *Nell* (1994), *Rob Roy* (1995), *Michael Collins* (1996), *Star Wars: The Phantom Menace* (1999), *Star Wars: Attack of the Clones* (2002), *K-19: The Widowmaker* (2002), *Kinsey* (2004).

Newman, Paul (1925–) American, born Cleveland, Ohio; *Somebody Up There Likes Me* (1956), *The Long Hot Summer* (1958), *The Hustler* (1961), *Hud* (1963), *The Prize* (1963), *Cool Hand Luke* (1967), *Butch Cassidy and the Sundance Kid* (1969), *Judge Roy Bean* (1972), *The Sting* (1973), *Absence of Malice* (1981), *The Verdict* (1982), *The Color* *of Money* (1986), *Blaze* (1990), *Mr and Mrs Bridge* (1990), *The Hudsucker Proxy* (1994), *Nobody's Fool* (1994), *Twilight* (1998), *Road to Perdition* (2002).

Nicholson, Jack (1937–) American, born Neptune, New Jersey; *The Little Shop of Horrors* (1960), *Easy Rider* (1969), *Five Easy Pieces* (1970), *Carnal Knowledge* (1971), *The Last Detail* (1974), *Chinatown* (1974), *One Flew Over the Cuckoo's Nest* (1975), *Tommy* (1975), *The Shining* (1980), *The Postman Always Rings Twice* (1981), *Reds* (1981), *Terms of Endearment* (1983), *Prizzi's Honor* (1985), *The Witches of Eastwick* (1987), *Batman* (1989), *The Death of Napoleon* (1991), *Man Trouble* (1992), *A Few Good Men* (1992), *Hoffa* (1992), *Wolf* (1994), *The Crossing Guard* (1995), *Blood and Wine* (1996), *Mars Attacks!* (1996), *As Good as it Gets* (1997), *About Schmidt* (2002), *The Departed* (2006).

Niven, David (James David Graham Niven) (1910–83) British, born London; *The Prisoner of Zenda* (1937), *Wuthering Heights* (1939), *Bachelor Mother* (1939), *Raffles* (1940), *The Way Ahead* (1944), *A Matter of Life and Death* (1946), *Carrington VC* (1955), *Around the World in Eighty Days* (1956), *Separate Tables* (1958), *The Guns of Navarone* (1961), *The Pink Panther* (1964), *Casino Royale* (1967), *Candleshoe* (1977), *Death on the Nile* (1978), *Escape to Athena* (1979), *Trail of the Pink Panther* (1982), *Curse of the Pink Panther* (1982).

Nolte, Nick (1941–) American, born Omaha, Nebraska; *Rich Man Poor Man* (TV 1976), *Cannery Row* (1982), *48 Hours* (1982), *Down and Out in Beverly Hills* (1986), *Weeds* (1987), *New York Stories* (1989), *Three Fugitives* (1989), *Another 48 Hours* (1990), *Cape Fear* (1991), *Prince of Tides* (1991), *The Player* (1992), *Lorenzo's Oil* (1992), *Blue Chips* (1993), *I Love Trouble* (1994), *Jefferson in Paris* (1995), *Nightwatch* (1996), *The Thin Red Line* (1998), *The Beautiful Country* (2004), *Hotel Rwanda* (2004).

Oldman, Gary (1959–) British, born New Cross, South London; *Sid and Nancy* (1986), *Prick Up Your Ears* (1987), *Track 29* (1988), *Rosencrantz and Guildenstern are Dead* (1990), *JFK* (1991), *Bram Stoker's Dracula* (1992), *True Romance* (1993), *Leon* (1994), *The Scarlet Letter* (1995), *The Fifth Element* (1997), *Lost in Space* (1998), *Hannibal* (2001), *Harry Potter series* (2004–).

Olivier, Sir Laurence (1907–89) British, born Dorking; *The Divorce of Lady X* (1938), *Wuthering Heights* (1939), *Rebecca* (1940), *Pride and Prejudice* (1940), *Henry V* (1944), *Hamlet* (1948), *Richard III* (1956), *The Prince and the Showgirl* (1958), *The Devil's Disciple* (1959), *The Entertainer* (1960), *Sleuth* (1972), *Marathon Man* (1976), *A Bridge Too Far* (1977), *Brideshead Revisited* (TV 1981), *A Voyage Round My Father* (TV 1982), *The Last Days of Pompeii* (TV 1984), *The Jigsaw Man* (1984), *The Bounty* (1984), *A Talent for Murder* (TV 1986), *War Requiem* (1988).

O'Toole, Peter (Seamus) (1932–) Irish, born Connemara; *Lawrence of Arabia* (1962), *How to Steal a Million* (1966), *The Lion in Winter* (1968), *Goodbye Mr Chips* (1969), *The Ruling Class* (1972), *The Stunt Man* (1980), *My Favourite Year* (1982), *The Last Emperor* (1987), *High Spirits* (1988), *Wings of Fame* (1989), *Isabelle Eberhardt* (1990), *King Ralph* (1991), *Worlds Apart* (1992), *Phantoms* (1998), *Venus* (2006).

Pacino, Al (Alfredo Pacino) (1940–) American, born New York City; *The Godfather* (1972), *The Godfather, Part II* (1974), *Dog Day Afternoon* (1975), *Scarface* (1983), *Revolution* (1985), *Sea of Love* (1990), *Dick Tracy* (1990), *The Godfather, Part III* (1990), *Frankie and Johnny* (1991), *Glengarry Glen Ross* (1992), *Scent of a Woman* (1992), *Damon* (1992), *Carlito's Way* (1993), *Heat* (1995), *Donnie Brasco* (1997), *The Insider* (1999), *Insomnia* (2002), *Angels in America* (TV 2003).

Paltrow, Gwyneth (1972–) American, born Los Angeles, California; *Jefferson in Paris* (1995), *Emma* (1996), *Sliding Doors* (1998), *Shakespeare in Love* (1998), *The Talented Mr Ripley* (1999), *The Royal Tenenbaums* (2001), *Possession* (2002), *Proof* (2005).

Peck, Gregory (Eldred) (1916–2003) American, born La Jolla, California; *The Keys to the Kingdom* (1944), *Spellbound* (1945), *Duel in the Sun* (1946), *Gentleman's Agreement* (1947), *The Macomber Affair* (1947), *The Paradine Case* (1947), *Twelve O'Clock High* (1949), *The Gunfighter* (1950), *Captain Horatio Hornblower* (1951), *The Million Pound Note* (1954), *The Purple Plain* (1955), *The Man in the Gray Flannel Suit* (1956), *The Big Country* (1958), *The Guns of Navarone* (1961), *Cape Fear* (1962), *To Kill a Mockingbird* (1962), *The Omen* (1976), *Old Gringo* (1989), *Other People's Money* (1991), *Cape Fear* (1991).

Penn, Sean (1960–) American, born Burbank, California; *Fast Times at Ridgemont High* (1982), *Racing with the Moon* (1984), *The Falcon and the Snowman* (1985), *At Close Range* (1986), *Shanghai Surprise* (1986), *Colors* (1988), *Casualties of War* (1989), *We're No Angels* (1989), *State of Grace* (1990), *Carlito's Way* (1993), *Dead Man Walking* (1995), *The Thin Red Line* (1998), *I Am Sam* (2001), *Mystic River* (2003), *21grams* (2003), *All the King's Men* (2006).

Phoenix, River (1970–93) American, born Madras, Oregon; *Mosquito Coast* (1986), *Running on Empty* (1988), *Little Nikita* (1988), *Indiana Jones and the Last Crusade* (1989), *I Love You to Death* (1990), *Dogfight* (1991), *My Own Private Idaho* (1991), *Sneakers* (1992), *The Thing Called Love* (1993).

Pickup, Ronald (Alfred) (1940–) British, born Chester; *Day of the Jackal* (1973), *The Thirty-Nine Steps* (1978), *Nijinski* (1980), *Never Say Never Again* (1983), *Fortunes of War* (TV 1987), *Testimony* (1987), *Bring Me the Head of Mavis Davis* (1998).

Pitt, Brad (William Bradley Pitt) (1963–) American, born Shawnee, Oklahoma; *Thelma and Louise* (1991), *A River Runs Through It* (1992), *Kalifornia* (1993), *True Romance* (1993), *Interview with the Vampire* (1994), *Legends of the Fall* (1994), *Seven* (1995), *Twelve Monkeys* (1995), *Sleepers* (1996), *Seven Years in Tibet* (1997), *Fight Club* (1999), *The Mexican* (2001), *Ocean's Eleven* (2001), *Troy* (2004), *Ocean's Twelve* (2004), *Mr and Mrs Smith* (2005), *Babel* (2006).

Pleasence, Donald (1919–95) British, born Worksop; *Robin Hood* (TV 1955–7), *Battle of the Sexes* (1959), *Dr Crippen* (1962), *The Great Escape* (1963), *The Caretaker* (1964), *Cul-de-Sac* (1966), *Fantastic Voyage* (1966), *You Only Live Twice* (1967), *Escape to Witch Mountain* (1975), *The Eagle Has Landed* (1977), *Oh God* (1977), *Telefon* (1977), *Halloween* (1978), *Sgt Pepper's Lonely Hearts Club Band* (1979), *Escape from New York* (1981), *Halloween 4* (1988), *Hanna's War* (1988), *Ground Zero* (1988), *Halloween 5* (1989), *Ten Little Indians* (1989), *Shadows and Fog* (1992), *Halloween 6* (1995).

Poitier, Sidney (1927–) American, born Miami, Florida; *No Way Out* (1950), *Cry, the Beloved Country* (1952), *The Blackboard Jungle* (1955), *The Defiant Ones* (1958), *Porgy and Bess* (1959), *Lilies of the Field* (1963), *To Sir with Love* (1967), *In the Heat of the Night* (1967), *Guess Who's Coming to Dinner* (1967), *Little Nikita* (1988), *Shoot to Kill* (1988), *Separate But Equal* (TV 1991), *Sneakers* (1992), *To Sir with Love II* (1996), *The Jackal* (1997).

Price, Vincent (1911–93) American, born St Louis, Missouri; *Tower of London* (1940), *Dragonwyck* (1946), *His Kind of Woman* (1941), *House of Wax* (1953), *The Story of Mankind* (1957), *The Fly* (1958), *The Fall of the House of Usher* (1961), *The Raven* (1963), *The Tomb of Ligeia* (1964), *City Under the Sea* (1965), *House of a Thousand Dolls* (1967), *The House of Long Shadows* (1983), *Dead Heat* (1988), *Edward Scissorhands* (1991).

Quinn, Anthony (Rudolph Oaxaca) (1915–2001) Irish–American, born Chihuahua, Mexico; *Viva Zapata* (1952), *La Strada* (1954), *Lust for Life* (1956), *The Guns of Navarone* (1961), *Zorba the Greek* (1964), *The Shoes of the Fisherman* (1968), *Revenge* (1989), *Ghosts Can't Do It* (1990), *Jungle Fever* (1991), *Mobsters* (1991), *Last Action Hero* (1993).

Rathbone, Basil (Philip St John) (1892–1967) British, born Johannesburg, South Africa; *David Copperfield* (1935), *Anna Karenina* (1935), *Captain Blood* (1935), *Romeo and Juliet* (1936), *The Adventures of Robin Hood* (1938), *The Hound of the Baskervilles* (1939), *The Adventures of Sherlock Holmes* (1939), *Spider Woman* (1944), *Heartbeat* (1946), *The Court Jester* (1956).

Redford, (Charles) Robert (1937–) American, born Santa Monica, California; *Barefoot in the Park* (1967), *Butch Cassidy and the Sundance Kid* (1969), *The Candidate* (1972), *The Great Gatsby* (1973), *The Sting* (1973), *The Way We Were* (1973), *All the President's Men* (1976), *The Natural* (1984), *Out of Africa* (1985), *Legal Eagles* (1986), *Havana* (1990), *Sneakers* (1992), *Indecent Proposal* (1993), *Up Close and Personal* (1995), *The Horse Whisperer* (1998).

Redgrave, Sir Michael (Scudamore) (1908–85) British, born Bristol; *The Lady Vanishes* (1938), *The Way to the Stars* (1945), *The Browning Version* (1951), *The Importance of Being Earnest* (1952), *The Dam Busters* (1955), *The Quiet American* (1958), *The Innocents* (1961), *Nicholas and Alexandra* (1971).

Redgrave, Vanessa (1937–) British, born London; *Morgan!* (1965), *Blow-Up* (1966), *Camelot* (1967), *Mary, Queen of Scots* (1971), *Julia* (1977), *Playing for Time* (TV 1980), *The Bostonians* (1984), *Wetherby* (1985), *Three Sovereigns for Sarah* (TV 1985), *Prick Up Your Ears* (1987), *Consuming Passions* (1988), *What Ever Happened to Baby Jane?* (1991), *Howards End* (1992), *Little Odessa* (1994), *Mission: Impossible* (1996), *Deep Impact* (1998), *Girl, Interrupted* (1999), *The Gathering Storm* (TV 2003), *Venus* (2006).

Reed, Oliver (Robert Oliver Reed) (1938–99) British, born Wimbledon, London; *The Damned* (1962), *The Jokers* (1966), *Women in Love* (1969), *The Brood* (1980), *Condorman* (1981), *Castaway* (1987), *Gor* (1988), *Return of the Musketeers* (1989), *The Pit and the Pendulum* (1991), *Severed Ties* (1992), *Funny Bones* (1995), *Gladiator* (2000).

Reeve, Christopher (1952–2004) American, born New York City; *Superman* (1978), *Superman II* (1980), *Somewhere in Time* (1980), *Monsignor* (1982), *Death Trap* (1982), *Superman III* (1983), *The Bostonians* (1984), *Superman IV* (1987), *Switching Channels* (1988), *Noises Off* (1992), *The Remains of the Day* (1993), *Morning Glory* (1993), *Speechless* (1994), *Village of the Damned* (1995), *Rear Window* (1998).

Reeves, Keanu (1964–) American, born Beirut, Lebanon; *River's Edge* (1986), *The Night Before* (1988), *Dangerous Liaisons* (1988), *Bill and Ted's Excellent Adventure* (1989), *Parenthood* (1989), *Love You to Death* (1990), *Bill and Ted's Bogus Journey* (1991), *My Own Private Idaho* (1991), *Dracula* (1992), *Much Ado About Nothing* (1993), *Little Buddha* (1993), *Speed* (1994), *Even Cowgirls Get the Blues* (1994), *A Walk in the Clouds* (1995), *Feeling Minnesota* (1995), *The Matrix* (1999), *Hard Ball* (2001), *The Matrix Reloaded* (2003), *The Lake House* (2006).

Reynolds, Burt (1936–) American, born Waycross, Georgia; *Gunsmoke* (TV 1965–7), *Deliverance* (1972), *Nickelodeon* (1976), *Smokey and the Bandit* (1978), *Hooper* (1978), *Starting Over* (1979), *Smokey and the Bandit II* (1980), *The Cannonball Run* (1981), *Sharkey's Machine* (1981), *The Best Little Whorehouse in Texas* (1982), *Stroker Ace* (1983), *The Man Who Loved Women* (1983), *City Heat* (1984), *Switching Channels* (1988), *Breaking In* (1989), *Evening Shade* (TV 1990–4), *Modern Love* (1990), *Cop-and-a-Half* (1992), *The Player* (1992), *The Maddening* (1995), *Striptease* (1996), *Trigger Happy* (1996), *Boogie Nights* (1997), *Driven* (2001).

Richardson, Sir Ralph (1902–83) British, born Cheltenham; *Bulldog Jack* (1935), *Q Planes* (1939), *The Four Feathers* (1939), *Anna Karenina* (1948), *The Fallen Idol* (1948), *The Heiress* (1949), *Richard III* (1956), *Oscar Wilde* (1960), *Long Day's Journey into Night*

(1962), *Dr Zhivago* (1966), *The Wrong Box* (1967), *A Doll's House* (1973), *The Man in the Iron Mask* (1977), *Time Bandits* (1980), *Dragonslayer* (1981), *Greystoke* (1984).

Robbins, Tim (Timothy Francis) (1958–) American, born New York City; *Bull Durham* (1988), *Cadillac Man* (1990), *Jacob's Ladder* (1990), *The Player* (1992), *Bob Roberts* (1992), *Short Cuts* (1993), *The Hudsucker Proxy* (1994), *The Shawshank Redemption* (1994), *Nothing to Lose* (1996), *Arlington Road* (1999), *High Fidelity* (2000), *Mystic River* (2003).

Roberts, Julia (1967–) American, born Smyrna, Georgia; *Mystic Pizza* (1988), *Steel Magnolias* (1989), *Flatliners* (1990), *Pretty Woman* (1990), *Sleeping with the Enemy* (1991), *Hook* (1991), *The Player* (1992), *The Pelican Brief* (1993), *I Love Trouble* (1994), *Prêt-à-Porter* (1994), *Michael Collins* (1996), *My Best Friend's Wedding* (1997), *Notting Hill* (1999), *Runaway Bride* (1999), *Erin Brockovich* (2000), *The Mexican* (2001), *Ocean's Eleven* (2001), *Confessions of a Dangerous Mind* (2002), *Closer* (2004), *Ocean's Twelve* (2004).

Robinson, Edward G (Emanuel Goldenberg) (1893–1973) American, born Bucharest, Romania; *Little Caesar* (1930), *Five Star Final* (1931), *The Whole Town's Talking* (1935), *The Last Gangster* (1937), *A Slight Case of Murder* (1938), *The Amazing Dr Clitterhouse* (1938), *Dr Ehrlich's Magic Bullet* (1940), *Brother Orchid* (1940), *The Sea Wolf* (1941), *Double Indemnity* (1944), *The Woman in the Window* (1944), *Scarlet Street* (1945), *All My Sons* (1948), *Key Largo* (1948), *House of Strangers* (1949), *Two Weeks in Another Town* (1962), *The Cincinnati Kid* (1965), *Soylent Green* (1973).

Rogers, Ginger (Virginia Katherine McMath) (1911–95) American, born Independence, Missouri; *Young Man of Manhattan* (1930), *42nd Street* (1933), *Flying Down to Rio* (1933), *The Gay Divorcee* (1934), *Top Hat* (1935), *Follow the Fleet* (1936), *Stage Door* (1937), *Bachelor Mother* (1939), *Kitty Foyle* (1940), *Roxie Hart* (1942), *Lady in the Dark* (1944).

Rooney, Mickey (Joe Yule, Jr) (1920–) American, born Brooklyn, New York City; *A Midsummer Night's Dream* (1935), *Ah Wilderness* (1935), *A Family Affair* (1937), *Judge Hardy's Children* (1938), *Boys' Town* (1938), *Babes in Arms* (1939), *The Human Comedy* (1943), *National Velvet* (1944), *Summer Holiday* (1948), *The Bold and the Brave* (1956), *Breakfast at Tiffany's* (1961), *It's a Mad, Mad, Mad, Mad World* (1963), *Leave 'Em Laughing* (TV 1980), *Bill* (TV 1981), *Erik the Viking* (1989), *Home for Christmas* (TV 1990), *The Toy Maker* (1991), *The Legend of Wolf Mountain* (1992), *That's Entertainment! III* (1994), *Heidi* (1996), *The First of May* (1999).

Rutherford, Dame Margaret (1892–1972) British, born London; *Blithe Spirit* (1945), *The Happiest Days of Your Life* (1950), *The Importance of Being Earnest* (1952), *The Smallest Show on Earth* (1957), *Murder She Said* (1961), *The VIPs* (1963), *Murder Most Foul* (1964), *Murder Ahoy* (1964).

Ryder, Winona (Winona Laura Horowitz) (1971–) American, born Winona, Michigan; *Beetlejuice* (1988), *1969* (1988), *Heathers* (1989), *Great Balls of Fire* (1989), *Mermaids* (1990), *Night on Earth* (1992), *Dracula* (1992), *The Age of Innocence* (1993), *Reality Bites* (1994), *Little Women* (1994), *How to Make an American Quilt* (1995), *The Crucible* (1996), *Alien: Resurrection* (1997), *Girl, Interrupted* (1999), *Mr Deeds* (2002).

Sarandon, Susan (Susan Abigail Tomalin) (1946–) American, born New York City; *Dragonfly* (1981), *Atlantic City* (1981), *The Hunger* (1983), *The Witches of Eastwick* (1987), *Bull Durham* (1988), *A Dry White Season* (1989), *White Palace* (1991), *Thelma and Louise* (1991), *Light Sleeper* (1991), *Lorenzo's Oil* (1992), *The Client* (1994), *Little Women* (1994), *Dead Man Walking* (1995), *Stepmom* (1998), *Irresistible* (2006).

Schwarzenegger, Arnold (1947–) American, born Thal, near Graz, Austria; *Conan the Barbarian* (1982), *Conan the Destroyer* (1984), *The Terminator* (1984), *Red Sonja* (1985), *Predator* (1987), *The Running Man* (1987), *Twins* (1988), *Red Heat* (1989), *Total Recall* (1990), *Kindergarten Cop* (1990), *Terminator 2: Judgement Day* (1991), *The Last Action Hero* (1993), *True Lies* (1994), *Junior* (1994), *Eraser* (1996), *Batman and Robin* (1997), *Collateral Damage* (2002), *Terminator 3: Rise of the Machines* (2003).

Scott, George C (1927–99) American, born Wise, Virginia; *Anatomy of a Murder* (1959), *The Hustler* (1962), *The List of Adrian Messenger* (1963), *Dr Strangelove* (1963), *Patton* (1970), *The Hospital* (1972), *Fear on Trial* (TV 1976), *The Changeling* (1980), *Taps* (1981), *Oliver Twist* (1982), *Firestarter* (1984), *A Christmas Carol* (TV 1984), *The Last Days of Patton* (TV 1986), *The Exorcist III* (1990), *Malice* (1993), *Family Rescue* (TV 1996).

Selleck, Tom (1945–) American, born Detroit, Michigan; *Coma* (1977), *Magnum* (TV 1981–9), *High Road to China* (1983), *Lassiter* (1984), *Runaway* (1984), *Three Men and a Baby* (1988), *Three Men and a Little Lady* (1990), *Christopher Columbus: The Discovery* (1992), *Mr Baseball* (1992), *Open Season* (1994), *The Love Letter* (1999).

Sellers, Peter (1925–80) British, born Southsea; *The Smallest Show on Earth* (1957), *The Ladykillers* (1959), *I'm Alright Jack* (1959), *Only Two Can Play* (1962), *Lolita* (1962), *Dr Strangelove* (1963), *The Pink Panther* (1963), *A Shot in the Dark* (1964), *Return of the Pink Panther* (1975), *The Pink Panther Strikes Again* (1976), *Revenge of the Pink Panther* (1978), *Being There* (1979).

Shatner, William (1931–) Canadian, born Montreal, Quebec; *Star Trek* (TV 1966–8), *Horror at 37 000 Feet* (TV 1974), *Big Bad Mama* (1974), *Star Trek: The Motion Picture* (1979), *The Kidnapping of the President* (1980), *Star Trek II: The Wrath of Khan* (1982), *T J Hooker* (TV 1982–6), *Star Trek III: The Search for Spock* (1984), *Star Trek IV: The Voyage Home* (1987), *Star Trek V: The Final Frontier* (1989), *Star Trek VI: The Undiscovered Country* (1991), *Star Trek: Generations* (1994), *Miss Congeniality* (2000), *Boston Legal* (TV 2004–6).

Sheen, Martin (Ramon Estevez) (1940–) American, born Dayton, Ohio; *Catch-22* (1970), *Badlands* (1973), *The Execution of Private Slovik* (TV 1974), *The Little Girl Who Lives Down the Lane* (1976), *Apocalypse Now* (1979), *Gandhi* (1982), *That Championship Season* (1982), *The Dead Zone* (1983), *Firestarter* (1984), *Wall Street* (1987), *Siesta* (1987), *Da* (1988), *Judgement in Berlin* (1988), *Stockade* (1990), *JFK* (1991), *Gettysburg* (1993), *Finnegan's Wake* (1993), *Hot Shots! Part Deux* (1993), *A Hundred and One Nights* (1994), *The American President* (1995), *The West Wing* (TV 1999–2006), *Bobby* (2006).

Sher, Sir Antony (1949–) South African, born Cape Town, South Africa; *Richard III* (play, 1985, Olivier Award), *Stanley* (play, 1997, Olivier Award), *Mrs Brown* (1997), *Shakespeare in Love* (1998), *Primo* (2005).

Sim, Alastair (1900–76) British, born Edinburgh; *Inspector Hornleigh* (1939), *Green for Danger* (1946), *The Happiest Days of Your Life* (1950), *Scrooge* (1951), *Laughter in Paradise* (1951), *The Belles of St Trinians* (1954).

Sinatra, Frank (Francis Albert Sinatra) (1915–98) American, born Hoboken, New Jersey; *Anchors Aweigh* (1945), *On the Town* (1949), *From Here to Eternity* (1953), *The Man With the Golden Gun* (1955), *Pal Joey* (1957), *The Manchurian Candidate* (1962), *The Detective* (1963).

Smith, Dame Maggie (1934–) British, born Ilford, Essex; *The VIPs* (1963), *The Pumpkin Eater* (1964), *The Prime of Miss Jean Brodie* (1969), *Travels with My Aunt* (1972), *California Suite* (1978), *A Private Function* (1984), *A Room With a View* (1985), *The Lonely Passion of Judith Hearne* (1987), *Hook* (1991), *Sister Act* (1992), *The Secret Garden* (1993),

Sister Act 2: Back in the Habit (1993), *Richard III* (1995), *The First Wives Club* (1996), *Washington Square* (1997), *Tea with Mussolini* (1999), *Gosford Park* (2001), *Harry Potter* series (2001–), *Ladies in Lavender* (2004).

Smith, Will (Willard Christopher Smith Jr) (1968–) American, born Philadelphia, Pennsylvania; *The Fresh Prince of Bel-Air* (TV 1990–96), *Six Degrees of Separation* (1993), *Bad Boys* (1995), *Independence Day* (1996), *Men in Black* (1997), *Enemy of the State* (1998), *Ali* (2001), *Men in Black II* (2002), *Hitch* (2005).

Spacek, Sissy (Mary Elizabeth Spacek) (1949–) American, born Quitman, Texas; *Badlands* (1973), *Carrie* (1976), *The Coal Miner's Daughter* (1981), *Missing* (1982), *The River* (1984), *Crimes of the Heart* (1986), *In the Bedroom* (2001), *Nine Lives* (2005).

Stallone, Sylvester (1946–) American, born New York City; *Rocky* (1976), *Paradise Alley* (1978), *Rocky II* (1979), *Nighthawks* (1981), *First Blood* (1981), *Rocky III* (1981), *Rambo* (1985), *Rocky IV* (1985), *Rambo II* (1986), *Over the Top* (1987), *Rambo III* (1988), *Lock Up* (1989), *Tango and Cash* (1990), *Rocky V* (1990), *Oscar* (1991), *Stop, Or My Mom Will Shoot* (1992), *Bartholomew vs Neff* (1992), *Cliffhanger* (1992), *Demolition Man* (1993), *The Specialist* (1994), *Judge Dredd* (1995), *Daylight* (1996), *Copland* (1997), *Get Carter* (2000), *Rocky Balboa* (2006).

Stanwyck, Barbara (Ruby Stevens) (1907–90) American, born Brooklyn, New York City; *Broadway Nights* (1927), *Miracle Woman* (1931), *Night Nurse* (1931), *The Bitter Tea of General Yen* (1933), *Baby Face* (1933), *Annie Oakley* (1935), *Stella Dallas* (1937), *Union Pacific* (1939), *The Lady Eve* (1941), *Meet John Doe* (1941), *Ball of Fire* (1941), *Double Indemnity* (1944), *The Strange Love of Martha Ivers* (1946), *Sorry Wrong Number* (1948), *The Furies* (1950), *Executive Suite* (1954), *Walk on the Wild Side* (1962), *The Big Valley* (TV 1965–9), *The Thorn Birds* (TV 1983).

Staunton, Imelda (Mary Philomena Bernadette) (1956–) English , born London; *Much Ado About Nothing* (1993), *Shakespeare in Love* (1998), *Rat* (2000), *Vera Drake* (2004).

Stewart, James (Maitland) (1908–97) American, born Indiana, Pennsylvania; *Seventh Heaven* (1937), *You Can't Take It With You* (1938), *Mr Smith Goes to Washington* (1939), *Destry Rides Again* (1939), *The Shop around the Corner* (1940), *The Philadelphia Story* (1940), *It's a Wonderful Life* (1946), *Harvey* (1950), *Broken Arrow* (1950), *The Glenn Miller Story* (1954), *Rear Window* (1954), *The Man from Laramie* (1955), *Vertigo* (1958), *Anatomy of a Murder* (1959), *Mr Hobbs Takes a Vacation* (1962), *Shenandoah* (1965), *The Big Sleep* (1978), *North and South II* (TV 1986).

Stoltz, Eric (1961–) American, born Whittier, California; *Fast Times at Ridgemont High* (1982), *Mask* (1985), *Some Kind of Wonderful* (1987), *Sister Sister* (1988), *Haunted Summer* (1988), *Fly II* (1989), *Memphis Belle* (1990), *The Waterdance* (1992), *Bodies Rest and Motion* (1993), *Killing Zoë* (1993), *Pulp Fiction* (1994), *Little Women* (1994), *Rob Roy* (1995), *The Rules of Attraction* (2002).

Stone, Sharon (1958–) American, born Meadville, Pennsylvania; *Deadly Blessing* (1981), *Action Jackson* (1987), *Total Recall* (1990), *He Said She Said* (1991), *Basic Instinct* (1992), *Diary of a Hitman* (1992), *Sliver* (1993), *Last Action Hero* (1993), *Intersection* (1994), *Casino* (1995), *Diabolique* (1996), *The Mighty* (1998), *Gloria* (1999), *Basic Instinct 2* (2006).

Streep, Meryl (Mary Louise Streep) (1949–) American, born Summit, New Jersey; *Julia* (1977), *The Deer Hunter* (1978), *Kramer vs Kramer* (1979), *Manhattan* (1979), *The French Lieutenant's Woman* (1981), *Sophie's Choice* (1982), *Silkwood* (1983), *Plenty* (1985), *Out of Africa* (1985), *Ironweed* (1987), *A Cry in the Dark* (1988), *Evil Angels* (1988), *She-Devil* (1989), *Postcards from the Edge* (1990), *Death Becomes Her* (1992), *The River Wild*

(1994), *The Bridges of Madison County* (1995), *Music of the Heart* (1999), *Adaptation* (2002), *The Hours* (2002), *The Manchurian Candidate* (2004), *The Devil Wears Prada* (2006), *A Prairie Home Companion* (2006).

Sutherland, Donald (1935–   ) Canadian, born St John, New Brunswick; *The Dirty Dozen* (1967), *M*A*S*H* (1970), *Klute* (1971), *Casanova* (1976), *1900* (1976), *The Eagle Has Landed* (1977), *Animal House* (1978), *Invasion of the Body Snatchers* (1978), *Ordinary People* (1980), *A Dry White Season* (1989), *Backdraft* (1991), *Buffy the Vampire Slayer* (1992), *Benefit of the Doubt* (1993), *The Poet* (1996), *Instinct* (1999), *Space Cowboys* (2000), *Pride and Prejudice* (2005).

Swank, Hilary (Ann) (1974–   ) American, born Lincoln, Nebraska; *Buffy the Vampire Slayer* (1992), *Boys Don't Cry* (1999), *Insomnia* (2002), *Million Dollar Baby* (2004), *Iron Jawed Angels* (TV 2004), *The Black Dahlia* (2006).

Sydow, Max (Carl Adolf) **von** (1929–   ) Swedish, born Lund; *The Seventh Seal* (1956), *The Face* (1959), *The Greatest Story Ever Told* (1965), *Hawaii* (1966), *Through a Glass Darkly* (1966), *Hour of the Wolf* (1967), *The Emigrants* (1972), *The Exorcist* (1973), *Exorcist II: The Heretic* (1977), *Flash Gordon* (1980), *Never Say Never Again* (1983), *Hannah and Her Sisters* (1986), *Pelle, the Conqueror* (1988), *Awakenings* (1990), *Dr Grassler* (1990), *The Father* (1990), *The Ox* (1991), *The Touch* (1992), *Needful Things* (1993), *Judge Dredd* (1995), *Snow Falling on Cedars* (1999), *Minority Report* (2002).

Taylor, Dame Elizabeth (Rosemond) (1932–   ) British, born London; *National Velvet* (1944), *Little Women* (1949), *The Father of the Bride* (1950), *A Place in the Sun* (1951), *Giant* (1956), *Raintree Country* (1957), *Cat on a Hot Tin Roof* (1958), *Butterfield 8* (1960), *Cleopatra* (1963), *Who's Afraid of Virginia Woolf?* (1966), *Reflections in a Golden Eye* (1967), *The Taming of the Shrew* (1967), *Suddenly Last Summer* (1968), *A Little Night Music* (1977), *The Mirror Crack'd* (1981), *Malice in Wonderland* (TV 1985), *Poker Alice* (TV 1986), *Young Toscanini* (1988), *Sweet Bird of Youth* (TV 1989), *Faithful* (1992), *The Flintstones* (1994).

Temple, Shirley (1928–   ) American, born Santa Monica, California; *Little Miss Marker* (1934), *Curly Top* (1935), *Dimples* (1936), *Heidi* (1937), *The Little Princess* (1939).

Theron, Charlize (1975–   ) South African, born Benoni, Gauteng; *The Devil's Advocate* (1997), *Mighty Joe Young* (1998), *The Cider House Rules* (1999), *Monster* (2003), *The Life and Death of Peter Sellers* (2004), *North Country* (2005).

Thompson, Emma (1959–   ) British, born London; *Tutti Frutti* (TV 1987), *Fortunes of War* (TV 1987), *Henry V* (1989), *Dead Again* (1989), *Howards End* (1992), *Much Ado About Nothing* (1993), *The Remains of the Day* (1993), *In the Name of the Father* (1993), *Junior* (1994), *Carrington* (1995), *Sense and Sensibility* (1995), *Primary Colors* (1998), *Love Actually* (2003), *Angels in America* (TV 2003), *Nanny McPhee* (2005), *Stranger than Fiction* (2006).

Thurman, Uma (Karuna) (1970–   ) American, born Boston, Massachusetts; *Dangerous Liaisons* (1988), *Pulp Fiction* (1994), *A Month by the Lake* (1995), *Hysterical Blindness* (TV 2002), *Kill Bill: Vol 1* (2003), *Kill Bill: Vol 2* (2004), *The Producers* (2005), *Be Cool* (2005).

Tracy, Spencer (1900–67) American, born Milwaukee, Wisconsin; *Twenty Thousand Years in Sing Sing* (1932), *The Power and the Glory* (1933), *A Man's Castle* (1933), *Fury* (1936), *San Francisco* (1936), *Libeled Lady* (1936), *Captains Courageous* (1937), *Boys' Town* (1938), *Stanley and Livingstone* (1939), *Northwest Passage* (1939), *Edison the Man* (1940), *Dr Jekyll and Mr Hyde* (1941), *Woman of the Year* (1942), *The Seventh Cross* (1944), *State of the Union* (1948), *Adam's Rib* (1949), *Father of the Bride* (1950), *Bad Day at Black Rock* (1955), *The Last Hurrah* (1958), *Inherit the Wind* (1960), *Judgement* *at Nuremberg* (1961), *It's a Mad, Mad, Mad, Mad World* (1963), *Guess Who's Coming to Dinner* (1967).

Travolta, John (1954–   ) American, born Englewood, New Jersey; *Welcome Back Kotter* (TV 1975–8), *Carrie* (1976), *Saturday Night Fever* (1977), *Grease* (1978), *Blow Out* (1981), *Staying Alive* (1983), *Two of a Kind* (1984), *Perfect* (1985), *Look Who's Talking* (1989), *Look Who's Talking Too* (1991), *Chains of Gold* (1991), *Pulp Fiction* (1994), *White Man's Burden* (1995), *Get Shorty* (1995), *Broken Arrow* (1996), *Phenomenon* (1996), *Michael* (1996), *The Thin Red Line* (1998), *Swordfish* (2001).

Turner, Kathleen (1954–   ) American, born Springfield, Missouri; *The Doctors* (TV 1977–8), *Body Heat* (1981), *The Man With Two Brains* (1983), *Romancing the Stone* (1984), *Crimes of Passion* (1984), *The Jewel of the Nile* (1985), *Prizzi's Honor* (1985), *Peggy Sue Got Married* (1986), *Switching Channels* (1988), *Julia and Julia* (1988), *The Accidental Tourist* (1988), *War of the Roses* (1989), *V I Warshawski* (1991), *House of Cards* (1992), *Serial Mom* (1994), *Moonlight and Valentino* (1995), *The Virgin Suicides* (1999).

Ustinov, Sir Peter (Alexander) (1921–2004) British, born London; *Private Angelo* (1949), *Hotel Sahara* (1951), *Quo Vadis* (1951), *Beau Brummell* (1954), *The Sundowners* (1960), *Spartacus* (1960), *Romanoff and Juliet* (1961), *Topkapi* (1964), *Logan's Run* (1976), *Death on the Nile* (1978), *Evil Under the Sun* (1982), *Appointment with Death* (1988), *Lorenzo's Oil* (1992), *Stiff Upper Lips* (1997), *The Bachelor* (1999).

Valentino, Rudolph (Rodolpho Alphonso Guglielmi di Valentina d'Antonguolla) (1895–1926) Italian–American, born Castellaneta, Italy; *The Four Horsemen of the Apocalypse* (1921), *The Sheikh* (1921), *Blood and Sand* (1922), *The Young Rajah* (1922), *Monsieur Beaucaire* (1924), *The Eagle* (1925), *The Son of the Sheikh* (1926).

Van Damme, Jean-Claude (1961–   ) Belgian, born Brussels; *No Retreat No Surrender* (1985), *Kickboxer* (1989), *Universal Soldier* (1992), *Nowhere to Run* (1993), *Last Action Hero* (1993), *Timecop* (1994), *Streetfighter* (1994), *The Quest* (1996), *Legionnaire* (1998), *Derailed* (2002).

Walken, Christopher (1943–   ) American, born Astoria, New York; *Annie Hall* (1977), *The Deer Hunter* (1978), *The Dogs of War* (1981), *Pennies from Heaven* (1981), *The Dead Zone* (1983), *Brainstorm* (1983), *A View to a Kill* (1984), *At Close Range* (1986), *The Milagro Beanfield War* (1987), *Biloxi Blues* (1988), *Puss in Boots* (1988), *The Comfort of Strangers* (1990), *Batman Returns* (1992), *True Romance* (1993), *Wayne's World 2* (1993), *Pulp Fiction* (1994), *Things to Do in Denver When You're Dead* (1995), *Darkening* (1996), *Sleepy Hollow* (1999), *Catch Me If You Can* (2002).

Washington, Denzel (1954–   ) American, born Mt Vernon, New York; *St Elsewhere* (TV 1982–9), *Cry Freedom* (1987), *Queen and Country* (1988), *Glory* (1989), *Mo' Better Blues* (1990), *Mississippi Masala* (1991), *Ricochet* (1991), *Malcolm X* (1992), *Philadelphia* (1993), *The Pelican Brief* (1993), *Much Ado About Nothing* (1993), *Devil in a Blue Dress* (1995), *Crimson Tide* (1995), *Courage Under Fire* (1996), *The Preacher's Wife* (1996), *Training Day* (2001), *John Q* (2002), *Antwone Fisher* (2002), *Inside Man* (2006).

Wayne, John (Marion Michael Morrison) (1907–79) American, born Winterset, Iowa; *The Big Trail* (1930), *Stagecoach* (1939), *The Long Voyage Home* (1940), *Red River* (1948), *She Wore a Yellow Ribbon* (1949), *Sands of Iwo Jima* (1949), *The Quiet Man* (1952), *The High and the Mighty* (1954), *The Searchers* (1956), *Rio Bravo* (1959), *The Alamo* (1960), *True Grit* (1969), *The Shootist* (1976).

Weaver, Sigourney (Susan Weaver) (1949–   ) American, born New York City; *Alien* (1979), *The Janitor* (1981), *The Year of Living Dangerously* (1982), *Ghostbusters* (1984), *Aliens* (1986), *Gorillas in the Mist* (1988), *Working Girl* (1988), *Ghostbusters II* (1989),

Alien 3 (1992), *1492* (1992), *Dave* (1993), *Death and The Maiden* (1994), *Copycat* (1995), *Ice Storm* (1996), *Alien: Resurrection* (1997), *Galaxy Quest* (1999), *Holes* (2003), *Imaginary Heroes* (2004).

Welles, Orson (1915–85) American, born Kenosha, Wisconsin; *Citizen Kane* (1941), *Journey into Fear* (1942), *The Stranger* (1945), *The Lady from Shanghai* (1947), *The Third Man* (1949), *The Trial* (1962), *Touch of Evil* (1965), *A Man For All Seasons* (1966), *Casino Royale* (1967), *Voyage of the Damned* (1976), *History of the World Part One* (1981).

West, Mae (1892–1980) American, born Brooklyn, New York City; *She Done Him Wrong* (1933), *I'm No Angel* (1933), *My Little Chickadee* (1939), *Myra Breckenridge* (1970).

Williams, Robin (1952–) American, born Chicago; *Mork and Mindy* (TV 1978–82), *Popeye* (1980), *The World According to Garp* (1982), *Good Morning Vietnam* (1987), *Dead Poets Society* (1989), *Cadillac Man* (1990), *Awakenings* (1990), *Dead Again* (1991), *The Fisher King* (1991), *Hook* (1991), *Toys* (1992), *Ferngully* (1992), *Being Human* (1992), *Mrs Doubtfire* (1993), *Jumanji* (1995), *Hamlet* (1996), *Father's Day* (1997), *Good Will Hunting* (1997), *Bicentennial Man* (1999), *One Hour Photo* (2002), *Insomnia* (2002).

Willis, Bruce (1955–) American, born Idar-Oberstein, West Germany; *Moonlighting* (TV 1985–9), *Blind Date* (1987), *Die Hard* (1988), *Sunset* (1988), *In Country* (1989), *Die Hard 2: Die Harder* (1990), *Bonfire of the Vanities* (1991), *Hudson Hawk* (1991), *Billy Bathgate* (1991), *The Last Boy Scout* (1991), *Death Becomes Her* (1992), *Striking Distance* (1993), *Pulp Fiction* (1994), *Nobody's Fool* (1994), *Die Hard with a Vengeance* (1995), *Twelve Monkeys* (1995), *The Fifth Element* (1996), *The Jackal* (1997), *The Sixth Sense* (1999), *Hart's War* (2002), *Lucky Number Slevin* (2006).

Winslet, Kate (Elizabeth) (1975–) English, born Reading; *Heavenly Creatures* (1994), *Sense and Sensibility* (1995), *Hamlet* (1996), *Titanic* (1997), *Quills* (2000), *Iris* (2002), *Eternal Sunshine of the Spotless Mind* (2004), *Finding Neverland* (2004), *Little Children* (2006).

Wisdom, Sir Norman (1915–) British, born London; *Trouble in Store* (1955), *Man of the Moment* (1955), *Just My Luck* (1958), *There was a Crooked Man* (1960), *On the Beat* (1962), *A Stitch in Time* (1963), *Sandwich Man* (1966), *The Night They Raided Minsky's* (1968), *What's Good for the Goose* (1969), *Five Children and It* (2004).

Witherspoon, Reese (Laura Jeanne Reese Witherspoon) (1976–) American, born New Orleans, Louisiana; *Freeway* (1996), *Pleasantville* (1998), *Cruel Intentions* (1999), *Election* (1999), *Legally Blonde* (2001), *Sweet Home Alabama* (2002), *Walk the Line* (2005).

Wood, Natalie (Natalia Nikolaevna Zakharenko) (1938–81) American, born San Francisco, California; *Miracle on 34th Street* (1947), *The Ghost and Mrs Muir* (1947), *Rebel Without a Cause* (1955), *The Searchers* (1956), *Marjorie Morningstar* (1958), *All The Fine Young Cannibals* (1959), *Splendor in the Grass* (1961), *West Side Story* (1961), *Love with the Proper Stranger* (1964), *The Great Race* (1965), *This Property is Condemned* (1966), *Bob and Carol and Ted and Alice* (1969), *From Here to Eternity* (TV 1979), *Meteor* (1979), *Brainstorm* (1983).

Woodward, Joanne (1930–) American, born Thomasville, Georgia; *Three Faces of Eve* (1957), *No Down Payment* (1957), *The Long Hot Summer* (1958), *The Stripper* (1963), *A Big Hand for the Little Lady* (1966), *Rachel, Rachel* (1968), *Summer Wishes, Winter Dreams* (1973), *The Glass Menagerie* (1987), *Mr and Mrs Bridge* (1990), *Philadelphia* (1993), *Breathing Lessons* (TV 1994).

Zellweger, René (1969–) American, born Katy, Texas; *Jerry Maguire* (1996), *Nurse Betty*

(2000), *Bridget Jones's Diary* (2001), *Chicago* (2002), *Cold Mountain* (2003), *Bridget Jones: The Edge of Reason* (2004), *Miss Potter* (2006).

Zeta-Jones, Catherine (1969–) British, born Swansea; *The Darling Buds of May* (TV 1991), *The Mask of Zorro* (1998), *Entrapment* (1999), *Traffic* (2000), *High Fidelity* (2000), *Chicago* (2002), *Intolerable Cruelty* (2003), *Ocean's Twelve* (2004).

Film directors

Selected films are listed.

Aldrich, Robert (1918–83) American, born Cranston, Rhode Island; *Apache* (1954), *Vera Cruz* (1954), *Kiss Me Deadly* (1955), *Attack!* (1957), *What Ever Happened to Baby Jane?* (1962), *The Dirty Dozen* (1967).

Allen, Woody (Allen Stewart Konigsberg) (1935–) American, born Brooklyn, New York City; *What's Up, Tiger Lily?* (1966), *Bananas* (1971), *Everything You Wanted to Know About Sex, But Were Afraid to Ask* (1972), *Play it Again, Sam* (1972), *Sleeper* (1973), *Love and Death* (1975), *Annie Hall* (1977), *Interiors* (1978), *Manhattan* (1979), *A Midsummer Night's Sex Comedy* (1982), *Hannah and Her Sisters* (1986), *Radio Days* (1987), *Crimes and Misdemeanors* (1990), *Alice* (1991), *Shadows and Fog* (1992), *Husbands and Wives* (1992), *Manhattan Murder Mystery* (1993), *Bullets Over Broadway* (1994), *Mighty Aphrodite* (1996), *Anna Oz* (1996), *Deconstructing Harry* (1997), *Celebrity* (1998), *Sweet and Lowdown* (1999), *The Curse of the Jade Scorpion* (2001), *Melinda and Melinda* (2004), *Match Point* (2005), *Scoop* (2006).

Almodóvar, Pedro (1949–) Spanish, born Calzada de Calatrava; *Women on the Verge of a Nervous Breakdown* (1988), *Tie Me Up! Tie Me Down!* (1990), *High Heels* (1991), *Kika* (1993), *Live Flesh* (1997), *All About My Mother* (1999), *Talk to Her* (2002), *Volver* (2006).

Altman, Robert (1925–2006) American, born Kansas City, Missouri; *The James Dean Story* (1957), *M*A*S*H* (1970), *McCabe and Mrs Miller* (1971), *The Long Goodbye* (1973), *Nashville* (1975), *Popeye* (1980), *Come Back to the 5 & Dime Jimmy Dean Jimmy Dean* (1982), *Fool for Love* (1985), *Aria* (1987), *Vincent and Theo* (1990), *The Player* (1992), *Short Cuts* (1993), *Prêt-à-Porter* (1994), *Kansas City* (1996), *The Gingerbread Man* (1998), *Cookie's Fortune* (1999), *Gosford Park* (2001), *A Prairie House Companion* (2006).

Antonioni, Michelangelo (1912–) Italian, born Ferrara; *L'Avventura* (1959), *La Notte* (1960), *L'Eclisse* (1962), *Blow-Up* (1966), *The Passenger* (1975), *Beyond the Clouds* (1995), *Eros* (2004).

Attenborough, Richard Samuel Attenborough, Baron (1923–) British, born Cambridge; *Oh! What a Lovely War* (1968), *A Bridge Too Far* (1977), *Gandhi* (1982), *A Chorus Line* (1985), *Cry Freedom* (1987), *Chaplin* (1992), *Shadowlands* (1993), *In Love and War* (1996), *Grey Owl* (1998).

Bergman, (Ernst) Ingmar (1918–) Swedish, born Uppsala; *Crisis* (1945), *Prison* (1948), *Sawdust and Tinsel* (1953), *The Face* (1955), *Smiles of a Summer Night* (1955), *The Seventh Seal* (1957), *Wild Strawberries* (1957), *The Virgin Spring* (1959), *Through a Glass Darkly* (1961), *The Silence* (1963), *Shame* (1968), *Cries and Whispers* (1972), *The Magic Flute* (1974), *Autumn Sonata* (1978), *Fanny and Alexander* (1983).

Bertolucci, Bernardo (1940–) Italian, born Parma; *Love and Anger* (1969), *The Conformist* (1970), *Last Tango in Paris* (1972), *1900* (1976), *The Last Emperor* (1987), *The Sheltering Sky* (1990), *Little Buddha* (1993), *Stealing Beauty* (1996), *Besieged* (1998), *The Dreamers* (2003).

Besson, Luc (1959–) French, born Paris; *The Last Battle* (1983), *Subway* (1985), *The Big*

Blue (1988), *Nikita* (1990), *Leon* (1994), *The Fifth Element* (1997), *The Messenger: The Story of Joan of Arc* (1999).

Bogdanovich, Peter (1939–) American, born Kingston, New York; *Targets* (1967), *The Last Picture Show* (1971), *Paper Moon* (1973), *What's Up, Doc?* (1972), *Nickelodeon* (1976), *Mask* (1985), *Illegally Yours* (1987), *Texasville* (1990), *Noises Off* (1992), *The Thing Called Love* (1993), *The Cat's Meow* (2001).

Boorman, John (1933–) English, born Epsom, Surrey; *Point Blank* (1967), *Hell in the Pacific* (1969), *Deliverance* (1972), *Zardoz* (1974), *Excalibur* (1981), *The Emerald Forest* (1984), *Hope and Glory* (1987), *Where the Heart Is* (1990), *Beyond Rangoon* (1995), *The Tailor of Panama* (2001), *The Tiger's Tail* (2006).

Bresson, Robert (1901–99) French, born Bromont-Lamothe; *Les Dames du Bois de Boulogne* (1946), *Journal d'un Curé de Campagne* (1950), *Pickpocket* (1959), *Au hasard, Balthazar* (1966), *Une Femme douce* (1969), *L'Argent* (1983).

Brooks, Mel (Melvin Kaminski) (1926–) American, born Brooklyn, New York City; *The Producers* (1966), *Blazing Saddles* (1974), *Young Frankenstein* (1974), *High Anxiety* (1978), *History of the World Part One* (1981), *Spaceballs* (1987), *Life Stinks* (1991), *Robin Hood: Men in Tights* (1993), *Dracula: Dead and Loving It* (1995).

Buñuel, Luis (1900–83) Spanish, born Calanda; *Un Chien Andalou* (with Salvador Dalí) (1928), *L'Âge d'Or* (1930), *Los Olvidados* (1950), *Robinson Crusoe* (1952), *El* (1953), *Nazarín* (1958), *Viridiana* (1961), *The Exterminating Angel* (1962), *Belle de Jour* (1967), *The Discreet Charm of the Bourgeoisie* (1972), *The Phantom of Liberty* (1974), *That Obscure Object of Desire* (1977).

Burton, Tim (1958–) American, born Burbank, California; *Beetlejuice* (1988), *Batman* (1989), *Edward Scissorhands* (1990), *Batman Returns* (1992), *Ed Wood* (1994), *Mars Attacks!* (1996), *Sleepy Hollow* (1999), *Planet of the Apes* (2001), *Big Fish* (2003), *Corpse Bride* (2005), *Sweeney Todd* (2007).

Capra, Frank (1897–1991) Italian–American, born Bisacquino, Sicily; *Platinum Blonde* (1932), *American Madness* (1932), *Lady for a Day* (1933), *It Happened One Night* (1934), *Mr Deeds Goes to Town* (1936), *Lost Horizon* (1937), *You Can't Take It With You* (1938), *Mr Smith Goes to Washington* (1939), *Meet John Doe* (1941), *Arsenic and Old Lace* (1944), *It's a Wonderful Life* (1946).

Carné, Marcel (1909–96) French, born Batignolles, Paris; *Quai des Brumes* (1938), *Le Jour se lève* (1939), *Les Enfants du Paradis* (1944).

Carpenter, John (1948–) American, born Carthage, New York; *Dark Star* (1974), *Assault on Precinct 13* (1976), *Halloween* (1978), *The Fog* (1979), *Escape from New York* (1981), *The Thing* (1982), *Christine* (1983), *Starman* (1984), *Big Trouble in Little China* (1986), *Prince of Darkness* (1987), *Memoirs of an Invisible Man* (1992), *Escape From LA* (1996), *Vampires* (1998).

Clair, René (René Lucien Chomette) (1891–1981) French, born Paris; *An Italian Straw Hat* (1927), *Sous Les Toits de Paris* (1929), *Le Million* (1931), *À Nous la liberté* (1931), *I Married a Witch* (1942), *It Happened Tomorrow* (1944), *And Then There Were None* (1945), *Les Belles de Nuit* (1952), *Porte des Lila* (1956), *Tout l'or du Monde* (1961).

Cocteau, Jean (1889–1963) French, born Maisons-Lafitte; *Le Sang d'un poète* (1930), *La Belle et La Bête* (1946), *Orphée* (1950), *Le Testament d'Orphée* (1959).

Coen, Ethan (1957–) and **Joel** (1954–) American, both born St Louis Park, Minnesota; *Blood Simple* (1984), *Raising Arizona* (1987), *Miller's Crossing* (1990), *Barton Fink* (1991), *The Hudsucker Proxy* (1994), *Fargo* (1995), *The Big Lebowski* (1998), *O Brother, Where*

Art Thou? (2000), *The Man Who Wasn't There* (2001), *Intolerable Cruelty* (2003), *The Ladykillers* (2004).

Coppola, Francis Ford (1939–) American, born Detroit, Michigan; *The Godfather* (1972), *The Godfather, Part II* (1974), *Apocalypse Now* (1979), *One from the Heart* (1982), *The Outsiders* (1983), *Rumble Fish* (1983), *The Cotton Club* (1984), *Peggy Sue Got Married* (1987), *Gardens of Stone* (1987), *Tucker: The Man and His Dream* (1988), *The Godfather, Part III* (1991), *Dracula* (1992), *The Rainmaker* (1997).

Corman, Roger (1926–) American, born Detroit, Michigan; *Not of This Earth* (1957), *Bucket of Blood* (1959), *Fall of the House of Usher* (1960), *The Little Shop of Horrors* (1960), *The Intruder* (1962), *The Raven* (1963), *The Man with the X-ray Eyes* (1963), *The Masque of the Red Death* (1964), *The Tomb of Ligeia* (1964), *Frankenstein Unbound* (1990), *The Pit and the Pendulum* (1990).

Cronenberg, David (1943–) Canadian, born Toronto, Ontario; *Shivers* (1976), *Rabid* (1977), *The Brood* (1978), *Scanners* (1980), *Videodrome* (1983), *The Dead Zone* (1983), *The Fly* (1985), *Dead Ringers* (1988), *Naked Lunch* (1991), *M Butterfly* (1992), *Crash* (1996), *eXistenZ* (1999), *Spider* (2002), *A History of Violence* (2005).

Curtiz, Michael (Mihály Kertész) (1888–1962) American–Hungarian, born Budapest, Hungary; *Noah's Ark* (1929), *Mammy* (1930), *Doctor X* (1932), *The Mystery of the Wax Museum* (1933), *British Agent* (1934), *Black Fury* (1935), *Captain Blood* (1935), *Charge of the Light Brigade* (1936), *The Adventures of Robin Hood* (1938), *Angels with Dirty Faces* (1938), *The Sea Hawk* (1940), *The Sea Wolf* (1941), *Yankee Doodle Dandy* (1942), *Casablanca* (1943), *Mildred Pierce* (1945), *White Christmas* (1954), *We're No Angels* (1955), *King Creole* (1958).

De Mille, Cecil B(lount) (1881–1959) American, born Ashfield, Massachusetts; *Male and Female* (1919), *King of Kings* (1927), *The Ten Commandments* (1923–56), *The Greatest Show on Earth* (1952).

Demme, Jonathan (1944–) American, born Long Island, New York; *Citizens Band* (1977), *Swing Shift* (1984), *Swimming to Cambodia* (1987), *The Silence of the Lambs* (1991), *Philadelphia* (1993), *Beloved* (1998), *The Manchurian Candidate* (2004).

De Palma, Brian (1940–) American, born Newark, New Jersey; *Greetings* (1968), *Carrie* (1976), *The Fury* (1978), *Dressed to Kill* (1980), *Blow Out* (1981), *Scarface* (1983), *Body Double* (1984), *The Untouchables* (1987), *Casualties of War* (1989), *Bonfire of the Vanities* (1990), *Carlito's Way* (1993), *Mission: Impossible* (1996), *Mission to Mars* (2000), *The Black Dahlia* (2006).

Donner, Richard (1930–) American, born New York City; *The Omen* (1976), *Superman* (1978), *Inside Moves* (1980), *The Final Conflict* (1981), *Ladyhawke* (1984), *The Goonies* (1985), *Lethal Weapon* (1987), *Scrooged* (1988), *Lethal Weapon 2* (1989), *Lethal Weapon 3* (1992), *Maverick* (1994), *Conspiracy Theory* (1997), *Lethal Weapon 4* (1998), *16 Blocks* (2006).

Eastwood, Clint (1930–) American, born San Francisco, California; *Play Misty for Me* (1971), *The Outlaw Josey Wales* (1976), *Pale Rider* (1985), *Birdy* (1988), *Unforgiven* (1992), *The Bridges of Madison County* (1995), *Absolute Power* (1997), *True Crime* (1999), *Space Cowboys* (2000), *Mystic River* (2003), *Million Dollar Baby* (2004), *Flags of Our Fathers* (2006), *Letters from Iwo Jima* (2006).

Eisenstein, Sergei Mikhailovich (1898–1948) Russian, born Riga; *Stride* (1924), *Battleship Potemkin* (1925), *Alexander Nevsky* (1938), *Ten Days that Shook the World* (1928), *The Magic Seed* (1941), *Ivan the Terrible* (1942–6).

Fassbinder, Rainer Werner (1946–82) German, born Bad Wörishofen; *Satan's Brew* (1976), *The Marriage of Maria Braun* (1979).

Fellini, Federico (1920–93) Italian, born Rimini; *I Vitelloni* (1953), *La Strada* (1954), *La Dolce Vita* (1960), *8½* (1963), *Satyricon* (1969), *Fellini's Rome* (1972), *Casanova* (1976), *Orchestra Rehearsal* (1979), *City of Women* (1981), *The Ship Sails On* (1983), *Ginger and Fred* (1986).

Fleming, Victor (1883–1949) American, born Pasadena, California; *Mantrap* (1926), *The Virginian* (1929), *The Wet Parade* (1932), *Red Dust* (1932), *Treasure Island* (1934), *Test Pilot* (1938), *Gone with the Wind* (1939), *The Wizard of Oz* (1939), *Dr Jekyll and Mr Hyde* (1941), *A Guy Named Joe* (1943).

Ford, John (1895–73) American, born Cape Elizabeth, Maine; *The Tornado* (1917), *The Iron Horse* (1924), *Arrowsmith* (1931), *The Informer* (1935), *Stagecoach* (1939), *Young Mr Lincoln* (1939), *The Grapes of Wrath* (1940), *My Darling Clementine* (1946), *The Quiet Man* (1952), *The Searchers* (1956), *The Man Who Shot Liberty Valance* (1962).

Forman, Miloš (1932–   ) Czech, born Kaslov; *Taking Off* (1971), *One Flew Over the Cuckoo's Nest* (1975), *Amadeus* (1984), *The People vs Larry Flynt* (1996), *Man on the Moon* (1999), *Goya's Ghosts* (2006).

Frears, Stephen (1941–   ) British, born Leicester; *The Hit* (1984), *My Beautiful Laundrette* (1985), *Prick Up Your Ears* (1987), *Sammy and Rosie Get Laid* (1987), *Dangerous Liaisons* (1988), *The Grifters* (1990), *The Snapper* (1993), *Mary Reilly* (1995), *High Fidelity* (2000), *Dirty Pretty Things* (2002), *Mrs Henderson Presents* (2005), *The Queen* (2006).

Friedkin, William (1935–   ) American, born Chicago; *The French Connection* (1971), *The Exorcist* (1973), *The Guardian* (1990), *Rules of Engagement* (2000), *Bug* (2006).

Gilliam, Terry (1940–   ) American, born Minneapolis, Minnesota; *Jabberwocky* (1977), *Time Bandits* (1980), *Brazil* (1985), *The Adventures of Baron Munchausen* (1988), *The Fisher King* (1991), *Twelve Monkeys* (1995), *Fear and Loathing in Las Vegas* (1998), *The Brothers Grimm* (2005), *Tideland* (2005).

Godard, Jean-Luc (1930–   ) French, born Paris; *À Bout de Souffle* (1960), *Alphaville* (1965), *Le Plus Vieux Métier du Monde* (1967), *Sauve Qui Peut La Vie* (1980), *Hail Mary* (1985), *Nouvelle Vague* (1990), *The Old Place* (1998), *Notre Musique* (2004).

Greenaway, Peter (1942–   ) British, born Newport, Gwent; *The Draughtsman's Contract* (1982), *The Belly of an Architect* (1987), *Drowning by Numbers* (1988), *The Cook, The Thief, His Wife and Her Lover* (1989), *Prospero's Books* (1991), *The Baby of Macon* (1993), *The Pillow Book* (1995), *8½ Women* (1999).

Griffith, D(avid) W(ark) (1875–1948) American, born La Grange, Kentucky; *Judith of Bethulia* (1913), *The Birth of a Nation* (1915), *Intolerance* (1916), *Hearts of the World* (1918), *Broken Blossoms* (1919), *Orphans of the Storm* (1922).

Hawks, Howard Winchester (1896–1977) American, born Goshen, Indiana; *The Dawn Patrol* (1930), *Scarface* (1932), *Twentieth Century* (1934), *Barbary Coast* (1935), *Bringing Up Baby* (1938), *His Girl Friday* (1940), *To Have and Have Not* (1944), *The Big Sleep* (1946), *Red River* (1948), *Gentlemen Prefer Blondes* (1953), *Rio Bravo* (1959).

Hill, George Roy (1921–2002) American, born Minneapolis, Minnesota; *The World of Henry Orient* (1964), *Thoroughly Modern Millie* (1967), *Butch Cassidy and the Sundance Kid* (1969), *Slaughterhouse 5* (1972), *The Sting* (1973), *The World According to Garp* (1982), *Funny Farm* (1988).

Hitchcock, Sir Alfred Joseph (1899–1980) British, born Leytonstone, London; *The Lodger*

(1926), *Blackmail* (1929), *Murder* (1930), *The Thirty-Nine Steps* (1935), *The Lady Vanishes* (1938), *Rebecca* (1940), *Spellbound* (1945), *Notorious* (1946), *The Paradine Case* (1947), *Strangers on a Train* (1951), *Rear Window* (1954), *Dial M for Murder* (1955), *Vertigo* (1958), *North by Northwest* (1959), *Psycho* (1960), *The Birds* (1963), *Marnie* (1964), *Frenzy* (1972), *Alfred Hitchcock Presents* (TV 1955–61).

Huston, John Marcellus (1906–87) Irish–American, born Nevada, Missouri; *Murders in the Rue Morgue* (1932), *Juarez* (1939), *High Sierra* (1941), *The Maltese Falcon* (1941), *Key Largo* (1948), *The Treasure of the Sierra Madre* (1948), *The Asphalt Jungle* (1950), *The African Queen* (1951), *Moulin Rouge* (1952), *The Misfits* (1960), *Freud* (1962), *Night of the Iguana* (1964), *Casino Royale* (1967), *Fat City* (1972), *The Man Who Would Be King* (1975), *Annie* (1982), *Prizzi's Honor* (1985), *The Dead* (1987).

Ivory, James Francis (1928–) American, born Berkeley, California; *Shakespeare Wallah* (1965), *Heat and Dust* (1982), *The Bostonians* (1984), *A Room with a View* (1985), *Maurice* (1987), *Mr and Mrs Bridge* (1990), *Howards End* (1992), *The Remains of the Day* (1993), *Jefferson in Paris* (1995), *Surviving Picasso* (1996), *The Golden Bowl* (2000), *The White Countess* (2005).

Jarman, (Michael) Derek (1942–94) British, born Northwood, Middlesex; *Sebastiane* (1976), *Jubilee* (1977), *The Tempest* (1979), *Caravaggio* (1985), *The Last of England* (1987), *The Garden* (1990), *Edward II* (1991), *Wittgenstein* (1993).

Jackson, Peter (1961–) New Zealander, born Pukerua Bay, North Island; *Heavenly Creatures* (1994), *The Lord of the Rings* trilogy (2001–3), *King Kong* (2005).

Jordan, Neil (1950–) Irish, born Sligo; *Angel* (1982), *The Company of Wolves* (1984), *Mona Lisa* (1986), *High Spirits* (1988), *The Crying Game* (1992), *Interview with the Vampire* (1994), *Michael Collins* (1996), *The Butcher Boy* (1997), *The End of the Affair* (1999), *The Good Thief* (2002), *Breakfast on Pluto* (2005).

Kasdan, Lawrence (1949–) American, born Miami Beach, Florida; *Body Heat* (1981), *The Big Chill* (1983), *Silverado* (1985), *The Accidental Tourist* (1989), *Love You to Death* (1990), *Wyatt Earp* (1994), *French Kiss* (1995), *Mumford* (1999), *Dreamcatcher* (2003).

Kaufman, Philip (1936–) American, born Chicago; *Invasion of the Body Snatchers* (1978), *The Wanderers* (1979), *The Right Stuff* (1983), *The Unbearable Lightness of Being* (1988), *Henry and June* (1990), *Quills* (2000), *Twisted* (2004).

Kazan, Elia (Elia Kazanjoglou) (1909–2003) American, born Istanbul, Turkey; *Boomerang* (1947), *Gentleman's Agreement* (1947), *Pink* (1949), *A Streetcar Named Desire* (1951), *Viva Zapata* (1952), *On the Waterfront* (1954), *East of Eden* (1955), *Baby Doll* (1956), *A Face in the Crowd* (1957), *Splendor in the Grass* (1962), *America, America* (1963), *The Arrangement* (1969), *The Visitors* (1972), *The Last Tycoon* (1976).

Kieslowski, Krzystof (1941–96) Polish, born Warsaw; *Camera Buff* (1979), *A Short Film About Killing* (1988), *The Double Life of Veronique* (1991), *Three Colours: Blue* (1993), *White* (1993), *Red* (1994).

Kubrick, Stanley (1928–99) American, born The Bronx, New York City; *The Killing* (1956), *Paths of Glory* (1957), *Spartacus* (1960), *Lolita* (1962), *Dr Strangelove* (1964), *2001: A Space Odyssey* (1968), *A Clockwork Orange* (1971), *Barry Lyndon* (1975), *The Shining* (1980), *Full Metal Jacket* (1987), *Eyes Wide Shut* (1999).

Kurosawa, Akira (1910–98) Japanese, born Tokyo; *Rashomon* (1950), *The Idiot* (1951), *Living* (1952), *The Seven Samurai* (1954), *Throne of Blood* (1957), *The Lower Depths* (1957), *The Hidden Fortress* (1958), *Dersu Uzala* (1975), *The Shadow Warrior* (1981), *Ran* (1985), *Dreams* (1990), *Rhapsody in August* (1991).

Landis, John (1950–) American, born Chicago; *Schlock* (1971), *Kentucky Fried Movie* (1977), *Animal House* (1978), *The Blues Brothers* (1980), *An American Werewolf in London* (1981), *Twilight Zone* (1983), *Trading Places* (1983), *Into the Night* (1985), *Spies Like Us* (1985), *The Three Amigos* (1986), *Coming to America* (1988), *Oscar* (1991), *Innocent Blood* (1992), *Beverly Hills Cop III* (1994), *Blues Brothers 2000* (1998).

Lang, Fritz (1890–1976) German, born Vienna, Austria; *Destiny* (1921), *Dr Mabuse the Gambler* (1922), *Siegfried* (1923), *Metropolis* (1926), *Spies* (1927), *M* (1931), *The Testament of Dr Mabuse* (1932), *You Only Live Once* (1937), *The Return of Frank James* (1940), *The Woman in the Window* (1944), *The Big Heat* (1953), *Beyond a Reasonable Doubt* (1956), *While the City Sleeps* (1955).

Lean, Sir David (1908–91) British, born Croydon; *Pygmalion* (1938), *In Which We Serve* (1942), *Blithe Spirit* (1945), *Brief Encounter* (1946), *Great Expectations* (1946), *The Sound Barrier* (1952), *Hobson's Choice* (1954), *Summer Madness* (1955), *Bridge on the River Kwai* (1957), *Lawrence of Arabia* (1962), *Doctor Zhivago* (1965), *Ryan's Daughter* (1970), *A Passage to India* (1984).

Lee, Ang (1954–) Chinese, born Pingtung, Taiwan; *Sense and Sensibility* (1995), *The Ice Storm* (1997), *Crouching Tiger, Hidden Dragon* (2000), *Hulk* (2003), *Brokeback Mountain* (2005).

Lee, Spike (Shelton Jackson Lee) (1957–) American, born Atlanta, Georgia; *She's Gotta Have It* (1986), *School Daze* (1988), *Do the Right Thing* (1989), *Mo' Better Blues* (1990), *Jungle Fever* (1991), *Malcolm X* (1992), *Crooklyn* (1994), *Girl 6* (1996), *He Got Game* (1998), *Summer of Sam* (1999), *25th Hour* (2002), *Inside Man* (2006), *When the Levees Broke* (2006).

Leigh, Mike (1943–) British, born Salford; *Bleak Moments* (1971), *Nuts in May* (1976), *Abigail's Party* (1977), *High Hopes* (1988), *Life is Sweet* (1990), *Naked* (1993), *Secrets and Lies* (1996), *Career Girls* (1997), *Topsy-Turvy* (1999), *All or Nothing* (2002), *Vera Drake* (2004).

Leone, Sergio (1922–89) Italian, born Rome; *A Fistful of Dollars* (1964), *For a Few Dollars More* (1965), *The Good the Bad and the Ugly* (1967), *Once upon a Time in the West* (1969), *A Fistful of Dynamite* (1972), *Once upon a Time in America* (1984).

Levinson, Barry (1942–) American, born Baltimore, Maryland; *Diner* (1982), *The Natural* (1984), *The Young Sherlock Holmes* (1985), *Tin Men* (1987), *Good Morning Vietnam* (1987), *Rain Man* (1988), *Avalon* (1990), *Bugsy* (1991), *Toys* (1992), *Disclosure* (1994), *Sleepers* (1996), *Wag the Dog* (1997), *Sphere* (1998), *Bandits* (2001).

Lucas, George (1944–) American, born Modesto, California; *THX–1138: 4EB/Electronic Labyrinth* (1965), *American Graffiti* (1973), *Star Wars* (1977), *Star Wars: The Phantom Menace* (1999), *Attack of the Clones* (2002), *Revenge of the Sith* (2005).

Lumet, Sidney (1924–) American, born Philadelphia, Pennsylvania; *The Pawnbroker* (1965), *Serpico* (1974), *Dog Day Afternoon* (1975), *Network* (1976), *The Verdict* (1982), *Night Falls on Manhattan* (1994), *Gloria* (1999), *Find Me Guilty* (2005).

Lynch, David K (1946–) American, born Missoula, Montana; *Eraserhead* (1976), *The Elephant Man* (1980), *Dune* (1984), *Blue Velvet* (1986), *Wild at Heart* (1990), *Twin Peaks* (TV 1990–1), *Twin Peaks: Fire Walk With Me* (1992), *Lost Highway* (1997), *Mulholland Drive* (2001), *Inland Empire* (2006).

McBride, Jim (1941–) American, born New York City; *Breathless* (1983), *The Big Easy* (1986), *Great Balls of Fire* (1989), *The Wrong Man* (1992), *The Informant* (1997).

Mankiewicz, Joseph Leo (1909–93) American, born Wilkes-Barre, Pennsylvania; *All*

About Eve (1950), *The Barefoot Contessa* (1954), *Guys and Dolls* (1954), *Suddenly Last Summer* (1959), *Sleuth* (1972).

Miller, George (1945–) Australian, born Brisbane; *Mad Max* (1979), *Mad Max 2: The Road Warrior* (1982), *Mad Max Beyond Thunderdome* (1985), *The Witches of Eastwick* (1987), *Lorenzo's Oil* (1992), *Babe: Pig in the City* (1998), *Happy Feet* (2006).

Miller, Jonathan Wolfe (1934–) British, born London; *The Magic Flute* (1986), *The Tempest* (1988).

Minnelli, Vincente (1913–86) American, born Chicago; *Ziegfeld Follies* (1946), *An American in Paris* (1951), *Lust for Life* (1956), *Gigi* (1958).

Nichols, Mike (Michael Igor Peschkowsky) (1931–) American–German, born Berlin, Germany; *Who's Afraid of Virginia Woolf?* (1966), *The Graduate* (1967), *Catch-22* (1970), *Working Girl* (1988), *Postcards from the Edge* (1990), *Wolf* (1994), *The Birdcage* (1996), *Primary Colors* (1998), *Closer* (2004).

Olivier, Laurence Kerr Olivier, Baron (1907–89) British, born Dorking, Surrey; *Henry V* (1944), *Hamlet* (1948), *Richard III* (1956), *The Prince and the Showgirl* (1958), *The Entertainer* (1960).

Parker, Alan (1944–) British, born London; *Bugsy Malone* (1976), *Midnight Express* (1978), *Fame* (1980), *Shoot the Moon* (1981), *Pink Floyd: The Wall* (1982), *Angel Heart* (1987), *Mississippi Burning* (1988), *Come See the Paradise* (1990), *The Commitments* (1991), *Evita* (1996), *Angela's Ashes* (1999), *The Life of David Gale* (2003).

Pasolini, Pier Paolo (1922–75) Italian, born Bologna; *Accatone!* (1961), *The Gospel According to St Matthew* (1964), *Oedipus Rex* (1967), *Medea* (1970).

Peckinpah, Sam (1925–84) American, born Fresno, California; *The Deadly Companions* (1961), *Major Dundee* (1965), *The Wild Bunch* (1969), *Straw Dogs* (1971), *Bring Me the Head of Alfredo Garcia* (1974), *Cross of Iron* (1977).

Polanski, Roman (1933–) Polish, born Paris; *Knife in the Water* (1962), *Repulsion* (1965), *Cul-de-Sac* (1966), *Rosemary's Baby* (1968), *Macbeth* (1971), *Chinatown* (1974), *Tess* (1979), *Pirates* (1985), *Frantic* (1988), *Bitter Moon* (1992), *Death and the Maiden* (1994), *The Ninth Gate* (1999), *The Pianist* (2002), *Oliver Twist* (2005).

Pollack, Sydney (1934–) American, born South Bend, Indiana; *They Shoot Horses Don't They?* (1969), *The Electric Horseman* (1979), *Absence of Malice* (1981), *Tootsie* (1982), *Out of Africa* (1985), *Havana* (1990), *The Firm* (1993), *Random Hearts* (1999), *The Interpeter* (2005).

Powell, Michael Latham (1905–90) British, born Bekesbourne, near Canterbury; with **Emeric Pressburger** (1902–88) Hungarian–British, born Miskolc, Hungary; *The Spy in Black* (1939), *The Thief of Baghdad* (1940), *The Life and Death of Colonel Blimp* (1943), *Black Narcissus* (1946), *A Matter of Life and Death* (1946), *The Red Shoes* (1948).

Redford, (Charles) Robert (1936–) American, born Santa Monica, California; *Ordinary People* (1980), *The Milagro Beanfield War* (1987), *A River Runs Through It* (1992), *Quiz Show* (1994), *The Horse Whisperer* (1998), *The Legend of Bagger Vance* (2000).

Reed, Sir Carol (1906–76) British, born London; *The Young Mr Pitt* (1942), *The Way Ahead* (1944), *The Fallen Idol* (1948), *The Third Man* (1949), *An Outcast of the Islands* (1952), *The Man Between* (1953), *Our Man in Havana* (1959), *Oliver!* (1968).

Reiner, Carl (1922–) American, born The Bronx, New York City; *Oh God* (1977), *The Jerk* (1979), *Dead Men Don't Wear Plaid* (1982), *The Man with Two Brains* (1983), *Summer School* (1987), *That Old Feeling* (1997).

Reiner, Rob (1947–) American, born The Bronx, New York City; *This is Spinal Tap* (1984), *Stand by Me* (1987), *The Princess Bride* (1988), *When Harry Met Sally ...* (1989), *Misery* (1990), *A Few Good Men* (1992), *North* (1994), *The American President* (1995), *The Story of Us* (1999), *Rumour Has It* (2005).

Renoir, Jean (1894–1979) French, born Paris; *Une Partie de Campagne* (1936), *La Règle du Jeu* (1939), *The Southerner* (1945).

Robbins, Tim (Timothy Francis) (1958–) American, born West Covina, California; *No Small Affair* (1984), *Bob Roberts* (1992), *Dead Man Walking* (1995), *Cradle Will Rock* (1999).

Roeg, Nicolas Jack (1928–) British, born London; *Performance* (1970), *Walkabout* (1971), *Don't Look Now* (1973), *The Man Who Fell to Earth* (1976), *Bad Timing* (1979), *Eureka* (1983), *Insignificance* (1985), *Castaway* (1986), *Black Widow* (1988), *Track 29* (1988), *The Witches* (1990), *Heart of Darkness* (1994), *Two Deaths* (1995).

Rossellini, Roberto (1906–77) Italian, born Rome; *The White Ship* (1940), *Rome, Open City* (1945), *Paisan* (1946), *Germany, Year Zero* (1947), *Stromboli* (1950), *Voyage to Italy* (1953), *General Della Rovera* (1959).

Russell, Ken (Henry Kenneth Alfred Russell) (1927–) British, born Southampton; *Women in Love* (1969), *The Devils* (1971), *Crimes of Passion* (1984), *Gothic* (1987), *Lair of the White Worm* (1989), *The Rainbow* (1989), *Whore* (1991), *Tales of Erotica* (1996), *Trapped Ashes* (2006).

Schlesinger, John Richard (1926–2003) British, born London; *A Kind of Loving* (1962), *Billy Liar!* (1963), *Midnight Cowboy* (1969), *Sunday, Bloody Sunday* (1971), *Marathon Man* (1976), *Honky Tonk Freeway* (1981), *An Englishman Abroad* (TV 1982), *Madame Sousatzka* (1988), *Pacific Heights* (1990), *The Innocent* (1993), *The Next Best Thing* (2000).

Scorsese, Martin (1942–) American, born Queens, New York; *Mean Streets* (1973), *Alice Doesn't Live Here Any More* (1974), *Taxi Driver* (1976), *Raging Bull* (1980), *King of Comedy* (1982), *After Hours* (1985), *The Color of Money* (1986), *The Last Temptation of Christ* (1988), *GoodFellas* (1990), *Cape Fear* (1991), *The Age of Innocence* (1992), *Casino* (1995), *Kundun* (1997), *Gangs of New York* (2002), *The Aviator* (2004), *The Departed* (2006).

Scott, Sir Ridley (1937–) British, born South Shields; *Alien* (1979), *Blade Runner* (1982), *Black Rain* (1989), *Thelma and Louise* (1991), *1492* (1992), *G I Jane* (1997), *Gladiator* (2000), *Hannibal* (2001), *Black Hawk Down* (2001), *Matchstick Men* (2003), *A Good Year* (2006).

Siegel, Don (1912–91) American, born Chicago; *Riot in Cell Block 11* (1954), *Invasion of the Body Snatchers* (1956), *Baby Face Nelson* (1957), *Coogan's Bluff* (1968), *Two Mules for Sister Sara* (1969), *Dirty Harry* (1971), *Charley Varrick* (1973), *The Shootist* (1976), *Telefon* (1977), *Escape from Alcatraz* (1979).

Soderbergh, Steven (1963–) American, born Atlanta, Georgia; *sex, lies and videotape* (1989), *King of the Hill* (1993), *Erin Brockovich* (2000), *Traffic* (2000), *Ocean's Eleven* (2001), *Solaris* (2002), *Ocean's Twelve* (2004).

Spielberg, Steven (1946–) American, born Cincinnati, Ohio; *Duel* (TV 1972), *Sugarland Express* (1973), *Jaws* (1975), *Close Encounters of the Third Kind* (1977), *Raiders of the Lost Ark* (1981), *ET* (1982), *Twilight Zone* (1983), *The Color Purple* (1985), *Indiana Jones and the Temple of Doom* (1984), *Empire of the Sun* (1987), *Indiana Jones and the Last Crusade* (1989), *Hook* (1992), *Jurassic Park* (1993), *Schindler's List* (1993), *The Lost World:*

Jurassic Park (1997), *Amistad* (1997), *Saving Private Ryan* (1998), *Minority Report* (2002), *Munich* (2005).

Stone, Oliver (1946–) American, born New York City; *Platoon* (1987), *Wall Street* (1987), *Born on the Fourth of July* (1989), *The Doors* (1991), *JFK* (1991), *Heaven and Earth* (1993), *Natural Born Killers* (1994), *Nixon* (1995), *Any Given Sunday* (1999), *World Trade Center* (2006).

Tarantino, Quentin (1963–) American, born Knoxville, Tennessee; *Reservoir Dogs* (1993), *Pulp Fiction* (1994), *Jackie Brown* (1997), *Kill Bill: Vol 1* (2003), *Kill Bill: Vol 2* (2004).

Tati, Jacques (Jacques Tatischeff) (1908–82) French, born Le Pecq; *Jour de fête* (1947), *Monsieur Hulot's Holiday* (1952), *Mon Oncle* (1958), *Playtime* (1968), *Traffic* (1981).

Tavernier, Bertrand (1941–) French, born Lyons; *L'Horloger de Saint-Paul* (1973), *La Mort en direct* (1979), *Dimanche à la Campagne* (1984), *La Vie et rien d'autre* (1989), *Daddy Nostalgie* ('These Foolish Things') (1990), *L 627* (1992), *Capitaine Conan* (1996), *It All Starts Today* (1999), *Safe Conduct* (2002), *Holy Lola* (2004).

Truffaut, François (1932–84) French, born Paris; *Jules et Jim* (1961), *The Bride Wore Black* (1967), *Baisers volés* (1968), *L'Enfant Sauvage* (1969), *Day for Night* (1973), *The Last Metro* (1980).

Visconti, Luchino (Count Don Luchino Visconti Di Morone) (1906–76) Italian, born Milan; *The Leopard* (1963), *Ossessione* (1942), *The Damned* (1969), *Death in Venice* (1971).

Weir, Peter (1944–) Australian, born Sydney; *The Cars That Ate Paris* (1974), *Picnic at Hanging Rock* (1975), *Gallipoli* (1981), *The Year of Living Dangerously* (1982), *Witness* (1985), *Mosquito Coast* (1986), *Dead Poets Society* (1989), *Green Card* (1990), *Fearless* (1993), *The Truman Show* (1998), *Master and Commander* (2004).

Welles, (George) Orson (1915–85) American, born Kenosha, Wisconsin; *Citizen Kane* (1941), *The Magnificent Ambersons* (1942), *Jane Eyre* (1943), *Macbeth* (1948), *Othello* (1951), *Touch of Evil* (1958), *The Trial* (1962), *Chimes at Midnight* (1966).

Wenders, Wim (1945–) German, born Düsseldorf; *Summer in the City* (1970), *Alice in the Cities* (1974), *Kings of the Road* (1976), *Paris, Texas* (1984), *Wings of Desire* (1987), *Until the End of the World* (1991), *Faraway, So Close* (1993), *Beyond the Clouds* (co-director 1995), *The End of Violence* (1997), *Buena Vista Social Club* (1999), *The Million Dollar Hotel* (2000), *Don't Come Knocking* (2005).

Wilder, Billy (1906–2002) Austrian–American, born Sucha, Austria; *Double Indemnity* (1944), *The Lost Weekend* (1945), *Sunset Boulevard* (1950), *The Seven Year Itch* (1955), *Some Like It Hot* (1959), *The Apartment* (1960), *Avanti!* (1972).

Wise, Robert (1914–2005) American, born Winchester, Indiana; *The Body Snatcher* (1945), *The Day the Earth Stood Still* (1951), *West Side Story* (1961), *The Sound of Music* (1965), *Star Trek: The Motion Picture* (1979).

Wyler, William (1902–1981) German–American, born Mulhouse, Alsace; *The Little Foxes* (1941), *Mrs Miniver* (1942), *The Best Years of Our Lives* (1946), *Friendly Persuasion* (1956), *Ben-Hur* (1959), *Funny Girl* (1968).

Zeffirelli, Franco (Gianfranco Corsi) (1922–) Italian, born Florence; *The Taming of the Shrew* (1966), *Romeo and Juliet* (1968), *Brother Sun, Sister Moon* (1973), *Jesus of Nazareth* (TV 1977), *The Champ* (1979), *Endless Love* (1981), *La Traviata* (1982), *Otello* (1986), *Hamlet* (1990), *Jane Eyre* (TV 1995), *Tea with Mussolini* (1999), *Callas Forever* (2002).

Zemeckis, Robert (1952–) American, born Chicago; *I Wanna Hold Your Hand* (1978), *Romancing The Stone* (1984), *Back to the Future* (1985), *Who Framed Roger Rabbit?* (1988), *Back to the Future II* (1989), *Back to the Future III* (1990), *Death Becomes Her* (1992), *Forrest Gump* (1994), *Contact* (1997), *What Lies Beneath* (2000), *Cast Away* (2000), *The Polar Express* (2004).

Zinnemann, Fred (1907–97) Austrian–American, born Vienna, Austria; *High Noon* (1952), *From Here to Eternity* (1953), *A Man for All Seasons* (1966), *Five Days One Summer* (1982).

Motion picture Academy Awards 1980–2006

Awarded by the Academy of Motion Picture Arts and Sciences; popularly known as Oscars.

Year	Best film (director)	Best actor	Best actress
1980	*Ordinary People* (Robert Redford)	Robert De Niro *Raging Bull*	Sissy Spacek *Coal Miner's Daughter*
1981	*Chariots of Fire* (Hugh Hudson)	Henry Fonda *On Golden Pond*	Katharine Hepburn *On Golden Pond*
1982	*Gandhi* (Richard Attenborough)	Ben Kingsley *Gandhi*	Meryl Streep *Sophie's Choice*
1983	*Terms of Endearment* (James L Brooks)	Robert Duvall *Tender Mercies*	Shirley MacLaine *Terms of Endearment*
1984	*Amadeus* (Miloš Forman)	F Murray Abraham *Amadeus*	Sally Field *Places in the Heart*
1985	*Out of Africa* (Sydney Pollack)	William Hurt *Kiss of the Spider Woman*	Geraldine Page *The Trip to Bountiful*
1986	*Platoon* (Oliver Stone)	Paul Newman *The Color of Money*	Marlee Matlin *Children of a Lesser God*
1987	*The Last Emperor* (Bernardo Bertolucci)	Michael Douglas *Wall Street*	Cher *Moonstruck*
1988	*Rain Man* (Barry Levinson)	Dustin Hoffman *Rain Man*	Jodie Foster *The Accused*
1989	*Driving Miss Daisy* (Bruce Beresford)	Daniel Day-Lewis *My Left Foot*	Jessica Tandy *Driving Miss Daisy*
1990	*Dances with Wolves* (Kevin Costner)	Jeremy Irons *Reversal of Fortune*	Kathy Bates *Misery*
1991	*The Silence of the Lambs* (Jonathan Demme)	Anthony Hopkins *The Silence of the Lambs*	Jodie Foster *The Silence of the Lambs*
1992	*Unforgiven* (Clint Eastwood)	Al Pacino *Scent of a Woman*	Emma Thompson *Howards End*
1993	*Schindler's List* (Steven Spielberg)	Tom Hanks *Philadelphia*	Holly Hunter *The Piano*
1994	*Forrest Gump* (Robert Zemeckis)	Tom Hanks *Forrest Gump*	Jessica Lange *Blue Sky*
1995	*Braveheart* (Mel Gibson)	Nicolas Cage *Leaving Las Vegas*	Susan Sarandon *Dead Man Walking*
1996	*The English Patient* (Anthony Minghella)	Geoffrey Rush *Shine*	Frances McDormand *Fargo*
1997	*Titanic* (James Cameron)	Jack Nicholson *As Good as it Gets*	Helen Hunt *As Good as it Gets*

Year	Best film (director)	Best actor	Best actress
1998	*Shakespeare in Love* (Guy Madden)	Roberto Benigni *Life is Beautiful*	Gwyneth Paltrow *Shakespeare in Love*
1999	*American Beauty* (Sam Mendes)	Kevin Spacey *American Beauty*	Hilary Swank *Boys Don't Cry*
2000	*Gladiator* (Ridley Scott)	Russell Crowe *Gladiator*	Julia Roberts *Erin Brockovich*
2001	*A Beautiful Mind* (Ron Howard)	Denzel Washington *Training Day*	Halle Berry *Monster's Ball*
2002	*Chicago* (Rob Marshall)	Adrien Brody *The Pianist*	Nicole Kidman *The Hours*
2003	*The Lord of the Rings: The Return of the King* (Peter Jackson)	Sean Penn *Mystic River*	Charlize Theron *Monster*
2004	*Million Dollar Baby* (Clint Eastwood)	Jamie Foxx *Ray*	Hilary Swank *Million Dollar Baby*
2005	*Crash* (Paul Higgins)	Philip Seymour Hoffman *Capote*	Reese Witherspoon *Walk the Line*
2006	*The Departed* (Martin Scorsese)	Forest Whitaker *The Last King of Scotland*	Helen Mirren *The Queen*

Composers

Selected works are listed.

Albéniz, Isaac (1860–1909) Spanish, born Camprodón, Catalonia; works include operas and works for piano based on Spanish folk music (eg *Iberia*).

Arnold, Sir Malcolm Henry (1921–2006) English, born Northampton; works include concertos, ballets, operas, vocal, choral, chamber and orchestral music (eg *Tam O'Shanter*) and film scores (eg *Bridge over the River Kwai*).

Bach, Johann Sebastian (1685–1750) German, born Eisenach; prolific composer, works include over 190 cantatas and oratorios, concertos, chamber music, keyboard music, and orchestral works (eg *Toccata and Fugue in D minor*, *The Well-tempered Clavier*, *Six Brandenburg Concertos*, *St Matthew Passion*, *Mass in B minor*, *Goldberg Variations*, *The Musical Offering*, *The Art of Fugue*).

Bartók, Béla (1881–1945) Hungarian, born Nagyszentmiklós; works include six string quartets, *Sonata for 2 pianos and percussion*, concertos (for piano, violin, viola and notably the *Concerto for Orchestra*), opera (*Duke Bluebeard's Castle*), two ballets (*The Wooden Prince*, *The Miraculous Mandarin*), songs, choruses, folksong arrangements.

Beethoven, Ludwig van (1770–1827) German, born Bonn; works include 33 piano sonatas (eg the 'Pathétique', 'Moonlight', *Waldstein*, *Appassionata*), nine symphonies (eg *Eroica*, 'Pastoral', *Choral Symphony No.9*), string quartets, concertos, *Lebewohl* and the opera *Fidelio*.

Berg, Alban (1885–1935) Austrian, born Vienna; works include songs (*Four Songs*), operas (*Wozzeck*, *Lulu*, unfinished), a violin concerto and a string quartet (*Lyric Suite*).

Berio, Luciano (1925–2003) Italian, born Oneglia; works include compositions using tapes and electronic music (eg *Mutazioni*, *Omaggio a James Joyce*), works for solo instruments (*Sequenzas*), stage works (eg *Laborintus II*, *Opera*) and symphonies (*Sinfonia*).

Berlioz, (Louis) Hector (1803–69) French, born Côte St André, near Grenoble; works include the overture *Le carnival romain*, the cantata *La Damnation de Faust*, symphonies (eg *Symphonie Fantastique, Romeo et Juliette*) and operas (eg *Béatrice et Bénédict, Les Troyens*).

Bernstein, Leonard (1918–90) American, born Laurence, Massachusetts; works include ballets (*Jeremiah, The Age of Anxiety, Kaddish*), symphonies (eg *Fancy Free, The Dybbuk*), and musicals, (eg *Candide, West Side Story, On The Town, Songfest, Halil*).

Birtwistle, Sir Harrison (1934–) English, born Accrington, Lancashire; works include operas (eg *The Mask of Orpheus*), 'dramatic pastorals' (eg *Down by the Greenwood Side*) and orchestral pieces (eg *The Triumph of Time*).

Bizet, Georges (1838–75) French, born Paris; works include opera (eg *Carmen, Les Pêcheurs de Perles, La Jolie Fille de Perth*), incidental music to Daudet's play *L'Arlésienne* and a symphony.

Boulez, Pierre (1925–) French, born Montbrison; works include three piano sonatas, and works for piano and flute (eg *Sonatine*).

Brahms, Johannes (1833–97) German, born Hamburg; works include songs, four symphonies, two piano concertos, choral work (eg *German Requiem*), orchestral work (eg *Variations on a Theme of Haydn*), programme work (eg *Tragic Overture*), also the *Academic Festival Overture* and *Hungarian Dances*.

Britten, (Edward) Benjamin, Baron Britten of Aldeburgh (1913–76) English, born Lowestoft; composer of orchestral works, choral symphonic works, operas (eg *Peter Grimes, The Turn of the Screw*), song cycles (eg *Our Hunting Fathers, On This Island* (text by W H Auden)).

Bruckner, Anton (1824–96) Austrian, born Ansfelden; works include nine symphonies, a string quartet, choral-orchestral Masses and other church music (eg *Te Deum*).

Cage, John (1912–92) American, born Los Angeles; works include unorthodox modern compositions, eg *Sonatas and Interludes for the Prepared Piano*.

Carter, Elliott Cook, Jr (1908–) American, born New York City; works include quartets, symphonies, concertos, songs and chamber music.

Chabrier, Emmanuel (1841–94) French, born Ambert; works include operas (*Gwendoline, Le Roi malgré lui, Briséis*) and an orchestral rhapsody (*España*).

Chopin, Frédéric François (1810–49) Polish, born Zelazowa Wola, near Warsaw; wrote almost exclusively for piano – nocturnes, polonaises, mazurkas, preludes, concertos and a funeral march.

Copland, Aaron (1900–90) American, born Brooklyn, New York City; ballets (eg *Billy The Kid, Appalachian Spring*), film scores (eg *Our Town, The Heiress*), symphonies (eg *Symphonie Ode, Connotations, Clarinet Concerto*).

Corelli, Arcangelo (1653–1713) Italian, born Fusignano, near Bologna; works include twelve concertos (eg *Concerto for Christmas Night*), and solo and trio sonatas for violin.

Couperin, François (1668–1733) French, born Paris; works include chamber music, four books containing 240 harpsichord pieces, motets and other church music.

Debussy, Claude Achille (1862–1918) French, born St Germaine-en-Laye, near Paris; songs (eg the cantata *L'Enfant prodigue*), opera (*Pelléas et Mélisande*), orchestral works (eg *Prélude à l'après-midi d'un faune, La Mer*), chamber and piano music (eg *Feux d'artifice, La Cathédrale engloutie*).

Delius, Frederick (1862–1934) English (of German Scandinavian descent), born Bradford; works include songs (eg *A Song of Summer, Idyll, Songs of Farewell*), concertos, operas (eg *Koanga, A Village Romeo and Juliet*), chamber music and orchestral variations (eg *Appalachia, Sea Drift, A Mass of Life*).

Dukas, Paul (1865–1935) French, born Paris; works include a symphonic poem (*L'Apprenti sorcier*) and opera (*Ariane et Barbe-bleue*).

Dutilleux, Henri (1916–) French, born Angers; works include a piano sonata, two symphonies, a violin concerto, a string quartet (*Ainsi la nuit*), compositions for two pianos and other orchestral works. Awarded Prix de Rome 1938.

Dvořák, Antonin Leopold (1841–1904) Czech, born near Prague; works include songs, concertos, choral (eg *Hymnus*) and chamber music, symphonies (notably *From the New World*), operas (eg *Rusalka, Armida, Slavonic Dances*).

Elgar, Sir Edward (William) (1857–1934) English, born Broadheath, near Worcester; works include chamber music, two symphonies, oratorios (eg *The Dream of Gerontius, The Apostles, The Kingdom*), and the orchestral work *Enigma Variations*.

Fauré, Gabriel Urbain (1845–1924) French, born Pamiers; works include songs (eg *Après un rêve*), chamber music, choral music (eg the *Requiem*), operas and orchestral music (eg *Masques et bergamasques*).

Franck, César Auguste (1822–90) naturalized French, born Liège, Belgium; works include tone-poems, (eg *Les Béatitudes*), sonatas for violin and piano, *Symphony in D minor* and *Variations symphoniques* for piano and orchestra.

Gershwin, George (1898–1937) American, born Brooklyn, New York City; Broadway musicals (eg *Lady Be Good, Of Thee I Sing*), symphonies, songs (notably 'I Got Rhythm', 'The Man I Love'), operas (eg *Porgy and Bess*), and concert works (eg *Rhapsody in Blue, Concerto in F, An American in Paris*).

Glass, Philip (1937–) American, born Baltimore, Maryland; works include stage pieces (eg *Einstein on the Beach*), film scores (eg *Hamburger Hill*) and the opera *Orphee*.

Gluck, Christoph (Willibald) (1714–87) Austro-German, born Erasbach, Bavaria; operas include *Orfeo ed Euridice, Iphigénie en Auilide, Alceste, Paride ed Elena, Iphigénie en Tauride*.

Grainger, Percy Aldridge (1882–1961) Australian, born Melbourne; works include songs, piano and chamber music (eg *Molly on the Shore, Mock Morris, Shepherd's Hey*).

Grieg, Edvard Hagerup (1843–1907) Norwegian, born Bergen; works include songs, a piano concerto, orchestral suites, violin sonatas, choral music, and incidental music for *Peer Gynt* and *Sigurd Jorsalfar*.

Handel, George Frideric (1685–1759) naturalized English, born Halle, Saxony; prolific output including over 27 operas (eg *Almira, Rinaldo*), 20 oratorios (eg the *Messiah, Saul, Israel in Egypt, Samson, Jephthah*), orchestral suites (eg the *Water Music* and *Music for the Royal Fireworks*), organ concertos and chamber music.

Haydn, (Franz) Joseph (1732–1809) Austrian, born Rohrau, Lower Austria; prolific output including 104 symphonies (eg the 'Salomon' or 'London' Symphonies), string quartets and oratorios (notably *The Creation, The Seasons*).

Holst, Gustav Theodore (originally von Holst) (1874–1934) English of Swedish origin, born Cheltenham; works include choral and piano music, operas (eg *The Perfect Fool, At the Boar's Head*), orchestral suites (eg *The Planets, St Paul's Suite for Strings*), choral music (eg *The Hymn of Jesus, Ode to Death*), and *Concerto for Two Violins*.

Honegger, Arthur (1892–1955) French, born Le Havre; works include five symphonies and dramatic oratorios (*King David, Joan of Arc at the Stake*).

Ireland, John Nicholson (1879–1962) English, born Bowden, Cheshire; works include sonatas (eg *Violin Sonata in A*), piano music, songs (eg 'Sea Fever'), the rhapsody *Mai-dun* and orchestral works (eg *The Forgotten Rite*, *These Things Shall Be*).

Ives, Charles (1874–1954) American, born Danbury, Connecticut; works include five symphonies, chamber music (eg *Concord Sonata*) and many songs.

Janáček, Leoš (1854–1928) Czech, born Hukvaldy, Moravia; works include chamber, orchestral and choral music (eg the song cycle *The Diary of One Who Has Vanished*), operas (eg *Janufa*, *The Cunning Little Vixen*, *The Excursions of Mr Brouček*, *From the House of the Dead*), two string quartets and a mass.

Ligeti, György Sándor (1923–2006) Hungarian, born Dicsöszentmárton; works include orchestral compositions (eg *Apparitions*, *Lontano*, *Double Concerto*), choral works (eg *Requiem*) and music for harpsichord, organ, and wind and string ensembles.

Liszt, Franz (1811–86) Hungarian, born Raiding; 400 original compositions including symphonic poems, piano music and masses (eg *The Legend of St Elizabeth*, *Christus*).

Lloyd Webber, Andrew, Baron Lloyd-Webber (1948–) English, born London; works include *Joseph and the Amazing Technicolor Dreamcoat*, *Jesus Christ Superstar*, *Evita* (lyrics Tim Rice), *Cats* (libretto T S Eliot), *Phantom of the Opera*, *Aspects of Love*, *Whistle Down the Wind* and *The Woman in White*.

Mahler, Gustav (1860–1911) Austrian, born Kalist, Bohemia; works include ten symphonies, songs, the cantata *Das klagende Lied*, and the song-symphony *Das Lied von der Erde* (The Song of the Earth).

Maxwell Davies, Sir Peter (1934–) English, born Manchester; works include operas (eg *Taverner*), songs (eg *Eight Songs for a Mad King*), symphonies, concertos and chamber ensembles. Appointed Master of the Queen's Music in 2004.

Mendelssohn, (Jacob Ludwig) Felix (1809–47) German, born Hamburg; prolific output, including concerto overtures (eg *Fingal's Cave*, *A Midsummer Night's Dream*, *Hebrides*), symphonies (*Symphony in C minor*, *Scottish*, *Italian*), quartets, operas and oratorios (eg *Elijah*).

Messiaen, Olivier Eugène Prosper Charles (1908–92) French, born Avignon; works include compositions for piano (*Vingt regards sur l'enfant Jésus*, *Catalogue d'oiseaux*), the symphony *Turangalila*, an oratorio (*La Transfiguration de Notre Seigneur Jésus-Christ*) and an opera (*St François d'Assisi*).

Milhaud, Darius (1892–1974) French, born Aix-en-Provence; works include several operas, incidental music for plays, ballets (eg the jazz ballet *La Création du monde*), symphonies and orchestral, choral and chamber works.

Monteverdi, Claudio (Giovanni Antonio) (1567–1643) Italian, born Cremona; works include masses (eg *Mass* and *Vespers* of the Virgin), cantatas and operas (eg *Orfeo*, *Il Ritorno d'Ulisse*, *L'Incoronazione di Poppea*).

Mozart, (Johann Chrysostom) Wolfgang Amadeus (1756–91) Austrian, born Salzburg; 600 compositions including symphonies (eg 'Jupiter', *Linz*, *Prague*), concertos, string quartets, sonatas, operas (eg *Marriage of Figaro*, *Don Giovanni*, *Così fan tutte*) and the Singspiels, *Die Entführung aus dem Serail*, *Die Zauberflöte*.

Mussorgsky, Modeste (1839–81) Russian, born Karevo; works include operas (eg *Boris Godunov*), song cycles and instrumental works (eg *Pictures from an Exhibition*, *Night on the Bare Mountain*).

Nielsen, Carl August (1865–1931) Danish, born Furen; works include operas (eg *Saul and*

David, *Masquerade*), symphonies (eg 'The Four Temperaments'), string quartets, choral and piano music.

Orff, Carl (1895–1982) German, born Munich; works include the scenic cantata *Carmina Burana* and the operatic pieces *Antigone*, *Oedipus* and *Prometheus*.

Palestrina, Giovanni Pierluigi da (c.1525–1594) Italian, born Palestrina, near Rome; works include chamber music and the organ work *Commotion*, masses, choral music (eg *Song of Songs*), madrigals.

Parry, Sir (Charles) **Hubert** (Hastings) (1848–1918) English, born Bournemouth, Hampshire; works include three oratorios, an opera, five symphonies, and many other pieces. Best-known work is the unison chorus *Jerusalem*.

Penderecki, Krzysztof (1933–) Polish, born Debica; works include compositions for strings (eg *Trenofiarom Hiroszimy*), operas (eg *Die schwarze Maske*) and concertos (eg *Flute Concerto*).

Poulenc, Francis (1899–1963) French, born Paris; works include much chamber music and the ballet *Les Biches*. Best known for his considerable output of songs, such as *Fêtes Galantes*.

Prokofiev, Sergei (1891–1953) Russian, born Sontsovka, Ukraine; works include eleven operas (eg *The Gambler*, *The Love for Three Oranges*, *The Fiery Angels*, *Semyon Kotko*, *Betrothal in a Monastery*, *War and Peace*, *The Story of a Real Man*), ballets (eg *Romeo and Juliet*, *Cinderella*), concertos, sonatas, cantatas (eg *We are Seven*, *Hail to Stalin*), film scores (eg *Alexander Nevsky*), and the 'children's piece' *Peter and the Wolf*.

Puccini, Giacomo (Antonio Domenico Michele Secondo Maria) (1858–1924) Italian, born Lucca; 12 operas (eg *Manon Lescaut*, *La Bohème*, *Tosca*, *Madama Butterfly*, *Turandot*).

Purcell, Henry (1659–95) English, born London; works include songs (eg 'Nymphs and Shepherds', 'Arise, ye Subterranean Winds'), sonatas, string fantasies, church music and opera (eg *Dido and Aeneas*).

Rachmaninov, Sergei Vasilyevich (1873–1943) Russian, born Nizhny Novgorod; works include operas, three symphonies, four piano concertos (eg *Prelude in C Sharp Minor*), the tone-poem *The Isle of the Dead*, and *Rhapsody on a Theme of Paganini* for piano and orchestra.

Rameau, Jean Philippe (1683–1764) French, born Dijon; works include over 30 ballets and operas (eg *Hippolyte et Aricie*, *Castor et Pollux*) and harpsichord pieces.

Ravel, Maurice (1875–1937) French, born Ciboure; works include piano compositions (eg *Sonatina*, *Miroirs*, *Ma Mère L'Oye*, *Gaspard de la nuit*), string quartets, operas (eg *L'Heure espagnol*, *L'Enfant et les sortilèges*), ballets (eg *Daphnis and Chloé*), the 'choreographic poem' *La Valse* and the miniature ballet *Boléro*.

Rimsky-Korsakov, Nikolai Andreyevich (1844–1908) Russian, born Tikhvin, Novgorod; works include orchestral music (eg the symphonic suite *Sheherazade*, *Capriccio Espagnol*, *Easter Festival*) and 15 operas (eg *Sadko*, *The Snow Maiden*, *The Tsar Sultan*, *The Invisible City of Kitesh*, *The Golden Cockerel*).

Rossini, Gioacchino Antonio (1792–1868) Italian, born Pesaro; works include many operas (eg *Il Barbiere de Seviglia*, *Otela*, *Guillaume Tell*) and a number of vocal and piano pieces.

Roussel, Albert (1869–1937) French, born Tourcoing; works include four symphonies, numerous choral works (eg *Évocations*), ballets (eg *Bacchus and Ariane*, *Le Festin de l'araignée*) and an opera (*Padmâvati*).

Saint-Saëns, (Charles) Camille (1835–1921) French, born Paris; works include four symphonic poems (eg *Danse macabre*), piano (*Le Rouet d'Omphale*, *Phaëton*, *La Jeunesse* *d'Hercule*), violin and cello concertos, symphonies, the opera *Samson et Dalila*, church music (eg *Messe solennelle*), and *Carnival des animaux* for two pianos and orchestra.

Satie, Erik Alfred Leslie (1866–1925) French, born Honfleur; works include ballets (eg *Parade*), lyric dramas and whimsical pieces.

Scarlatti, (Giuseppe) Domenico (1685–1757) Italian, born Naples; works include over 600 harpsichord sonatas.

Schönberg, Arnold (1874–1951) naturalized American, born Vienna, Austria; works include chamber music (eg *Chamber Symphony*), concertos (eg *Piano Concerto*) and symphonic poems (eg *Pelleas and Melisande*), the choral-orchestral *Gurrelieder*, string quartets, the oratorio *Die Jacobsiter*, and opera (*Von Heute auf Morgen*, *Moses und Aaron*).

Schubert, Franz Peter (1797–1828) Austrian, born Vienna; prolific output, works include symphonies, piano sonatas, string quartets and songs (eg *Gretchen am Spinnrade*, *Erlkönig*, *Die schöne Müllerin*, *Winterreise*, *Who is Sylvia?*, *Hark, Hark the Lark*, *Schwanengesang*).

Schumann, Robert Alexander (1810–56) German, born Zwickau, Saxony; works include piano music (eg *Fantasiestücke*), songs (eg 'The Fool's Song' in *Twelfth Night*, the Chamisso songs *Frauenliebe und Leben* or 'Woman's Love and Life'), chamber music, and four symphonies (eg the *Rhenish*).

Scriabin, Alexander (1872–1915) Russian, born Moscow; works include a piano concerto, three symphonies, two tone-poems (eg *Poem of Ecstasy*), ten sonatas, studies and preludes.

Shostakovich, Dmitri (1906–75) Russian, born St Petersburg; works include 15 symphonies, operas (eg *The Nose*, *Lady Macbeth of Mtensk*), concertos, string quartets and film music.

Sibelius, Jean (1865–1957) Finnish, born Tavastehus; works include symphonic poems (eg *Swan of Tuonela*, *En Saga*), songs, a violin concerto and seven symphonies.

Stanford, Sir Charles Villiers (1852–1924) Irish, born Dublin; works include oratorios (eg *The Three Holy Children*), choral pieces (eg *Magnificat*, *Songs of the Sea*), organ preludes, operas, chamber and orchestral music.

Stockhausen, Karlheinz (1928–) German, born Mödrath, near Cologne; works include orchestral music (eg *Gruppen*), choral and instrumental compositions.

Strauss, Johann (the Younger) (1825–99) Austrian, born Vienna; works include over 400 waltzes (eg *The Blue Danube*, *Wine, Women, and Song*, *Perpetuum Mobile*, *Artist's Life*, *Tales from the Vienna Woods*, *Voices from Spring*, *The Emperor*), and operettas (eg *Die Fledermaus*, *A Night in Venice*).

Strauss, Richard (1864–1949) German, born Munich; works include symphonic poems (eg *Don Juan*, *Till Eulenspiegels lustige Streiche*, *Also Sprach Zarathustra*, *Tod und Verklärung* ('Death and Transfiguration'), *Don Quixote*, *Ein Heldenleben*) and operas (eg *Der Rosenkavalier*, *Ariadne auf Naxos*, *Capriccio*).

Stravinsky, Igor (1882–1971) Russian, born Oranienbaum, near St Petersburg (naturalized French, then American); works include operas (eg *The Rake's Progress*), oratorios (eg *Oedipus Rex*, *Symphony of Psalms*), concertos, ballets (eg *The Firebird*, *The Rite of Spring*, *Petrushka*, *Pulcinella*, *Apollo Musogetes*, *The Card Game*, *Orpheus*, *Agon*), and a musical play *Elegy for JFK* for voice and clarinets.

Tavener, Sir John (Kenneth) (1944–) English, born London; works include the cantata *The Whale*, the choral-orchestral work *Ultimos ritos*, the sacred opera *Thérèse*, as well as pieces such as *The Protecting Veil* for cello and strings, and *The Repentant Thief* for clarinet, percussion and strings.

Tchaikovsky, Piotr Ilyich (1840–93) Russian, born Kamsko-Votkinsk; works include ten operas (eg *Eugene Onegin, The Queen of Spades*), a violin concerto, six symphonies, two piano concertos, three ballets (*The Nutcracker, Swan Lake, The Sleeping Beauty*) and tone-poems (eg *Romeo and Juliet, Italian Capriccio*).

Telemann, George Philipp (1681–1767) German, born Magdeburg; prolific composer, works include 600 overtures, 40 operas, 200 concertos, sonatas, suites, and overtures (eg *Der Tag des Gerichts, Die Tageszeiten*).

Tippett, Sir Michael Kemp (1905–98) English, born London; works include operas (eg *The Midsummer Marriage, King Priam, The Knot Garden, The Ice Break*), concertos, symphonies, cantatas and oratorios (eg *A Child of Our Time, The Vision of St Augustine*).

Varèse, Edgard (1883–1965) American, born Paris; works are almost entirely orchestral (eg *Metal, Ionization, Hyperprism*).

Vaughan Williams, Ralph (1872–1958) English, born Down Ampney, Gloucestershire; works include songs, symphonies (eg *London Symphony, Pastoral Symphony*), choral-orchestral works (eg *Sea Symphony, Magnificat*), operas (eg *Hugh the Drover, The Pilgrim's Progress*), a ballet *Job*, and film music (eg *Scott of the Antarctic*).

Verdi, Giuseppe (1813–1901) Italian, born le Roncole, near Busseto; works include church music (eg *Requiem*) and operas (eg *Oberto, Nabucco, Rigoletto, Il Trovatore, La Traviata, Un Ballo in Maschera, La Forza del Destino, Aïda, Otello, Falstaff*).

Vivaldi, Antonio (1678–1741) Italian, born Venice; prolific output, works include over 400 concertos (eg *L'Estro Armonico, The Four Seasons*), 40 operas and an oratorio, *Juditha Triumphans*.

Wagner, (Wilhelm) Richard (1813–83) German, born Leipzig; operas include *Lohengrin, Rienzi*, the *Ring* cycle (*Das Rheingold, Die Walküre, Siegfried, Götterdämmerung*), *Die Meistersinger, Tristan und Isolde, Parsifal*.

Walton, Sir William Turner (1902–83) English, born Oldham; works include concertos, operas (*Troilus and Cressida, The Bear*), a cantata (*Belshazzar's Feast*), ballet music for *The Wise Virgins*, a song-cycle (*Anon in Love*) and film music.

Weber, Carl Maria Friedrich von (1786–1826) German, born Eutin, near Lübeck; works include operas (eg *Oberon, Euryanthe, Silvana*), concertos, symphonies, sonatas, scenas, cantatas (eg *Kampf und Sieg*) and songs.

Webern, Anton Friedrich Wilhelm von (1883–1945) Austrian, born Vienna; works include a symphony, three cantatas, *Four Pieces for Violin and Pianoforte, Five Pieces for Orchestra*, and a concerto for nine instruments and songs.

Weill, Kurt (1900–50) German composer, born Dessau; works include songspiel (eg *Mahagonny*), operas (eg *Threepenny Opera, Rise and Fall of the City of Mahagonny*), ballet (eg *The Seven Deadly Sins*), musical comedy and light opera (eg *Lady in the Dark, Street Scene, Lost in the Stars*).

Whitehead, Gillian (1941–) New Zealand, born Whangerei; works include compostitions for choir and chamber orchestra (eg *Inner Harbour*), for soprano and instrumental ensemble (eg *Hotspur*), for opera (eg *Eleanor of Aquitaine*) and for strings (eg *Pakuru*).

Layout of an orchestra

Artists

Selected paintings are listed.

Altdorfer, Albrecht (c.1480–1538) German, born Regensburg; *Danube Landscape* (1520), *Alexander's Victory* (1529).

Andrea del Sarto (properly Andrea d'Agnolo di Francesco) (1486–1530) Italian, born Florence; *Miracles of S Filippo Benizzi* (1509–10), *Madonna del Saeco* (1525).

Angelico, Fra (real name Guido di Pietro) (c.1400–55) Italian, born Vicchio, Tuscany; *Coronation of the Virgin* (1430–5), *San Marco altarpiece* (c.1440).

Auerbach, Frank (1931–) Anglo-German, born Berlin; *Mornington Crescent* (1967), *Jake* (1990), *Ruth* (2000).

Bacon, Francis (1909–92) British, born Dublin; *Three Figures at the Base of a Crucifixion* (1945), *Two Figures with a Monkey* (1973), *Triptych Inspired by the Oresteia of Aeschylus* (1981).

Beardsley, Aubrey (Vincent) (1872–98) British, born Brighton; illustrations to Malory's *Morte d'Arthur* (1893), Wilde's *Salome* (1894).

Bell, Vanessa (1879–1961) British, born Kensington, London; *Still Life on Corner of a Mantlepiece* (1914).

Bellini, Gentile (c.1429–1507) Italian, born Venice; *Procession of the Relic of the True Cross* (1496), *Miracle at Ponte di Lorenzo* (1500).

Blackadder, Elizabeth (1931–   ) British, born Falkirk; *Interior with Self-Portrait* (1972), *White Anemones* (1983), *Texas Flame* (1986), *Still Life with Pagoda* (1998), *Irises* (2004).

Blake, Sir Peter (1932–   ) British, born Dartford, Kent; *On the Balcony* (1955–7), design for the Beatles' album *Sergeant Pepper's Lonely Hearts Club Band* (1967), *The Meeting* (1981).

Blake, William (1757–1827) British, born London; illustrations for his own *Songs of Innocence and Experience* (1794), *Newton* (1795), illustrations for the *Book of Job* (1826).

Böcklin, Arnold (1827–1901) Swiss, born Basel; *Pan in the Reeds* (1857), *The Island of the Dead* (1880).

Bomberg, David (1890–1957) British, born Birmingham; *In the Hold* (1913–14), *The Mud Bath* (1913–14).

Bonnard, Pierre (1867–1947) French, born Paris; *Young Woman in Lamplight* (1900), *Dining Room in the Country* (1913), *Seascape of the Mediterranean* (1941).

Bosch, Hieronymus (real name Jerome van Aken) (c.1450–1516) Dutch, born 's-Hertogenbosch, Brabant; *The Temptation of St Anthony*, *The Garden of Earthly Delights* (work undated).

Botticelli, Sandro (originally Alessandro di Mariano Filepei) (1444–1510) Italian, born Florence; *Primavera* (c.1478), *The Birth of Venus* (c.1485), *Mystic Nativity* (1500).

Boucher, François (1703–70) French, born Paris; *Reclining Girl* (1751), *The Rising* and *The Setting of the Sun* (1753).

Braque, Georges (1882–1963) French, born Argenteuil-sur-Seine; *Still Life with Violin* (1910), *The Portuguese* (1911), *Blue Wash-Basin* (1942).

Brueghel, Pieter (the Elder) (c.1525–69) Dutch, born Bruegel, near Breda; *Road to Calvary* (1564), *Massacre of the Innocents* (c.1566), *The Blind Leading the Blind* (1568), *The Peasant Wedding* (1568), *The Peasant Dance* (1568).

Burne-Jones, Sir Edward (Coley) (1833–98) British, born Birmingham; *The Beguiling of Merlin* (1874), *The Arming of Perseus* (1877), *King Cophetua and the Beggar Maid* (1880–4).

Burra, Edward (1905–76) British, born London; *Dancing Skeletons* (1934), *Soldiers* (1942), *Scene in Harlem (Simply Heavenly)* (1952).

Canaletto (properly **Giovanni Antonio Canal**) (1697–1768) Italian, born Venice; *Stone Mason's Yard* (c.1730).

Caravaggio (properly **Michelangelo Merisi da Caravaggio**) (1573–1610) Italian, born Caravaggio, near Burgamo; *The Supper at Emmaus* (c.1598–1600), *Martyrdom of St Matthew* (1599–1600), *The Death of the Virgin* (1605–6).

Cassatt, Mary (1844–1926) American, born Pittsburgh, Pennsylvania; *The Blue Room* (1878), *Lady at the Tea Table* (1885), *Morning Toilette* (1886), *The Tramway* (1891), *The Bath* (1892).

Cézanne, Paul (1839–1906) French, born Aix-en-Provence; *The Black Marble Clock* (c.1869–70), *Maison du Pendu* (c.1873), *Bathing Women* (1900–5), *Le Jardinier* (1906).

Chagall, Marc (1887–1985) Russian–French, born Vitebsk; *The Musician* (1912–13), *Bouquet of Flying Lovers* (1947).

Chicago, Judy (originally **Judy Gerowitz**) (1939–) American, born Chicago; *The Dinner Party* (1974–9), *Holocaust Project* (1985–93).

Chirico, Giorgio de (1888–1978) Italian, born Volos, Greece; *Portrait of Guillaume Apollinaire* (1914), *The Jewish Angel* (1916), *The Return of Ulysses* (1968).

Christo (originally **Christo Javacheff**) (1935–) American, born Gabovra, Bulgaria, and **Jean-Claude** (originally **Jean-Claude de Guillebon**) (1935–) American, born Casablanca, Morocco; *Surrounded Islands* (1980–3), *Wrapped Reichstag* (1995).

Cimabue (originally **Bencivieni di Pepo**) (c.1240–c.1302) Italian, born Florence; *Crucifix* (date unknown), *Saint John the Evangelist* (1302).

Claude Lorraine (in full **Claude Le Lorrain**) (real name **Claude Gêllée**) (1600–82) French, born near Nancy; *The Mill* (1631), *The Embarkation of St Ursula* (1641), *Ascanius Shooting the Stag of Silvia* (1682).

Constable, John (1776–1837) British, born East Bergholt, Suffolk; *A Country Lane* (c.1810), *The White Horse* (1819), *The Hay Wain* (1821), *Stonehenge* (1835).

Corot, Jean Baptiste Camille (1796–1875) French, born Paris; *Bridge at Narni* (1827), *Souvenir de Marcoussis* (1869), *Woman Reading in a Landscape* (1869).

Correggio (properly **Antonio Allegri da Correggio**) (c.1494–1534) Italian, born Correggio; *The Agony in the Garden* (c.1528).

Courbet, (Jean Désiré) **Gustave** (1819–77) French, born Ornans; *The After-Dinner at Ornans* (1848–9), *The Bathers* (1853), *The Painter's Studio* (1855), *The Stormy Sea* (1869).

Cranach, Lucas (the Elder) (1472–1553) German, born Kronach, near Bamberg; *The Crucifixion* (1503), *The Fountain of Youth* (1550).

Dalí, Salvador (Felipe Jacinto) (1904–89) Spanish, born Figueras, Gerona; *The Persistence of Memory* (1931), *The Transformation of Narcissus* (1934), *Christ of St John of the Cross* (1951).

Daumier, Honoré (1808–78) French, born Marseilles; many caricatures and lithographs; *The Legislative Paunch* (1834), *The Third Class Carriage* (1840s), paintings on the theme of *Don Quixote*.

David, Jacques Louis (1748–1825) French, born Paris; *Death of Socrates* (1788), *The Death of Marat* (1793), *The Rape of the Sabines* (1799), *Madame Récamier* (1800).

Davis, Stuart (1894–1964) American, born Philadelphia; *The President* (1917), *House and Street* (1931), *Visa* (1951), *Premiere* (1957).

Degas, (Hilaire Germain) **Edgar** (1834–1917) French, born Paris; *Cotton-brokers Office* (1873), *L'Absinthe* (1875–6), *Little Fourteen-year-old Dancer* (sculpture) (1881), *Dancer at the Bar* (c.1900).

de Kooning, Willem (1904–97) American, born Rotterdam, the Netherlands; *Woman I–V* (1952–3), *Montauk Highway* (1958), *Pastorale* (1963).

Delacroix, (Ferdinand Victor) **Eugène** (1798–1863) French, born St-Maurice-Charenton; *Dante and Virgil in Hell* (1822), *Liberty Guiding the People* (1831), *Jacob and the Angel* (1853–61).

Derain, André Louis (1880–1954) French, born Chatou; *Mountains at Collioure* (1905), *Westminster Bridge* (1907), *The Bagpiper* (1910–11).

Dix, Otto (1891–1969) German, born Gera-Unternhaus; *The Match Seller* (1920), *The War* (1924).

Doré, (Louis Auguste) **Gustave** (1832–83) French, born Strasbourg; Illustrations to Dante's *Inferno* (1861), Milton's *Paradise Lost* (1866).

Duccio di Buoninsegna (c.1260–c.1320) Italian; *Maestà* (Siena Cathedral altarpiece) (1308–11).

Duchamp, (Henri Robert) **Marcel** (1887–1968) French–American, born Blainville, Normandy; *Nude Descending a Staircase* (1912), *The Bride Stripped Bare by Her Bachelors, Even* (1915–23).

Dufy, Raoul (1877–1953) French, born Le Havre; *Posters at Trouville* (1906), illustrations to Guillaume Apollinaire's *Bestiary* (1911), *Riders in the Wood* (1931).

Dürer, Albrecht (1471–1528) German, born Nuremberg; *Adam and Eve* (1507), *Adoration of the Magi* (1504), *Adoration of the Trinity* (1511).

Eardley, Joan (1921–63) British, born Warnham, Sussex; *Winter Sea IV* (1958), *Two Children* (1962).

Emin, Tracey (1964–) English, born London; *Everyone I Have Ever Slept With* (1995), *My Bed* (1998).

Ernst, M(aximillian) (1891–1976) German–American–French, born Brühl, near Cologne, Germany; *Europe After the Rain* (1940–2), *The Elephant Célèbes* (1921), *Moonmad* (1944) (sculpture), *The King Playing with the Queen* (1959) (sculpture).

Escher, M(aurits) C(ornelis) (1898–1972) Dutch, born Leeuwarden; *Day and Night* (1938), *Convex and Concave* (1955).

Eyck, Jan van (c.1389–1441) Dutch, born Maaseyck, near Maastricht; *The Adoration of the Holy Lamb* (Ghent altarpiece) (1432), *Man in a Red Turban* (1433), *Arnolfni Marriage Portrait* (1434), *Madonna by the Fountain* (1439).

Fini, Léonor (1908–96) Italian–Argentinian, born Buenos Aires; *The End of the World* (1944).

Fragonard, Jean Honoré (1732–1806) French, born Grasse; *Coroesus Sacrificing Himself to Save Callirhoe* (1765), *The Swing* (c.1766), four canvases for Mme du Barry entitled *The Progress of Love* (1771–3).

Freud, Lucian (1922–) German–British, born Berlin; *Woman with a Daffodil* (1945), *Interior in Paddington* (1951), *Hotel Room* (1953–4), *Reflection* (1985).

Friedrich, Caspar David (1774–1840) German, born Pomerania; *The Cross in the Mountains* (1807–8).

Fuseli, Henri (originally **Johann Heinrich Füssli**) (1741–1825) Anglo-Swiss, born Zurich; *The Nightmare* (1781), *Appearance of the Ghost* (1796).

Gainsborough, Thomas (1727–88) British, born Sudbury, Suffolk; *Peasant Girl Gathering Sticks* (1782), *The Watering Place* (1777).

Gauguin, (Eugène Henri) Paul (1848–1903) French, born Paris; *The Vision After the Sermon* (1888), *Still Life with Three Puppies* (1888), *The White Horse* (1898), *Women of Tahiti* (1891), *Tahitian Landscape* (1891), *Where Do We Come From? What Are We? Where Are We Going?* (1897–8), *Golden Bodies* (1901).

Géricault, Théodore (1791–1824) French, born Rouen; *Officer of Light Horse* (c.1812), *Raft of the Medusa* (1819).

Ghirlandaio, Domenico (properly **Domenico di Tommaso Bigordi**) (1449–94) Italian, born Florence; *Virgin of Mercy* (1472), *St Jerome* (1480), *Nativity* (1485).

Giorgione (da Castelfranco) or **Giorgio Barbarelli** (c.1478–1511) Italian, born Castelfranco; *The Tempest* (c.1508), *Three Philosophers* (c.1508), *Portrait of a Man* (1510).

Giotto (in full **Giotto di Bondone**) (c.1266–1337) Italian, born near Florence; frescoes in *Arena Chapel*, Padua (1304–12), *Ognissanti Madonna* (1311–12).

Goes, Hugo van der (c.1440–82) Dutch, born probably Ghent; *Portinari Altarpiece* (1475).

Gorky, Arshile (originally **Vosdanig Manoog Adoian**) (1905–48) American, born Khorkom Vari, Turkish Armenia; *The Artist and His Mother* (c.1926–36), series *Image in Xhorkam* (from 1936), *The Liver is the Cock's Comb* (1944), *The Betrothal II* (1947).

Goya (y Lucientes), Francisco (José) de (1746–1828) Spanish, born Fuendetotos; *Family of Charles IV* (1799), *Los Desastres de la Guerra* (1810–14), *Black Paintings* (1820s).

Greco, El (properly **Domenico Theotocopoulos**) (1541–1614) Greek, born Candia, Crete; *Lady in Fur Wrap* (c.1577–8), *El Espolio* ('The Disrobing of Christ') (1577–9), *The Saviour of the World* (1600), *Portrait of Brother Hortensio Felix Paravicino* (1609), *Toledo Landscape* (c.1610).

Grünewald, Matthias (originally **Mathis Nithardt** or **Gothardt**) (c.1480–1528) German, born probably Würzburg; *Isenheim Altarpiece* (1515).

Hals, Frans (c.1580–1666) Dutch, born Antwerp; *The Laughing Cavalier* (1624), *Banquet of the Company of St Adrian* (1627), *Gypsy Girl* (c.1628–30), *Man in a Slouch Hat* (c.1660–6).

Hamilton, Richard (1922–) British, born London; *Hommage à Chrysler Corp* (1952), *Just what is it that makes today's homes so different, so appealing?* (1956), *Study of Hugh Gaitskell as a Famous Monster of Film Land* (1964), *The Citizen* (1981–3).

Hilliard, Nicholas (c.1547–1619) British, born Exeter; miniature of *Queen Elizabeth I* (1572), *Henry Wriothesley* (1594).

Hirst, Damien (1965–) British, born Bristol; *The Physical Impossibilty of Death in the Mind of Someone Living* (1991), *The Asthmatic Escaped* (1991), *Mother and Child, Divided* (1993).

Hockney, David (1937–) British, born Bradford, Yorkshire; *We Two Boys Together Clinging* (1961), *The Rake's Progress* (1963), *A Bigger Splash* (1967), *Invented Man Revealing a Still Life* (1975), *Dancer* (1980).

Hodgkin, Sir Howard (1932–) English, born London; *Dinner at Smith Square* (1975–9), *Goodbye to the Bay of Naples* (1980–2), *Dirty Mirror* (2000).

Hogarth, William (1697–1764) British, born Smithfield, London; *Before and After* (1731), *A Rake's Progress* (1733–5).

Hokusai, Katsushika (1760–1849) Japanese, born Tokyo; *Tametomo and the Demon* (1811), *Mangwa* (1814–19), *Hundred Views of Mount Fuji* (1835).

Holbein, Hans (the Younger) (1497–1543) German, born Augsburg; *Bonifacius Amerbach* (1519), *Solothurn Madonna* (1522), *Anne of Cleves* (1539).

Hundertwasser, Friedensreich (Friedrich Stowasser) (1928–2000) Austrian, born Vienna; *Many Transparent Heads* (1949–50), *The End of Greece* (1963), *The Court of Sulaiman* (1967).

Hunt, (William) Holman (1827–1910) British, born London; *Our English Coasts* (1852), *Claudio and Isabella* (1853), *The Light of the World* (1854), *Isabella and the Pot of Basil* (1867).

Ingres, Jean August Dominique (1780–1867) French, born Montauban; *Gilbert* (1805), *La Source* (1807–59), *Bather* (1808), *Turkish Bath* (1863).

John, Augustus (Edwin) (1878–1961) British, born Tenby; *The Smiling Woman* (1908), *Portrait of a Lady in Black* (1917).

John, Gwen (1876–1939) British, born Haverfordwest, Pembrokeshire; *Girl with Bare Shoulders* (1909–10).

Johns, Jasper (1930–) American, born Allendale, South Carolina, *Flag* (1954–5), *Beer Cans* (1961) (sculpture), *Seasons* (1985).

Kandinsky, Wassily (1866–1944) Russian–French, born Moscow; *Kossacks* (1910–11), *Swinging* (1925), *Two Green Points* (1935), *Sky Blue* (1940).

Kiefer, Anselm (1945–) German, born Donaueschingen, Baden; *Occupations* (1969), *Parsifal III* (1973), *Innenraum* (1982), *Lilith* (1989).

Kirchner, Ernst Ludwig (1880–1938) German, born Aschaffenburg; *Recumbent Blue Nude with Straw Hat* (1908–9), *The Drinker* (1915), *Die Amselfluh* (1923).

Kitaj, R(onald) B(rooks) (1932–) American, born Cleveland, Ohio; *The Ohio Gang* (1964), *If Not, Not* (1975–6).

Klee, Paul (1879–1940) Swiss, born Münchenbuchsee, near Berne; *Der Vollmond* (1919), *Rosegarden* (1920), *Twittering Machine* (1922), *A Tiny Tale of a Tiny Dwarf* (1925), *Fire in the Evening* (1929).

Klimt, Gustav (1862–1918) Austrian, born Baumgarten, near Vienna; *Music* (1895), *The Kiss* (1907–8), *Judith II (Salome)* (1909).

Kline, Franz Joseph (1910–62) American, born Wilkes-Barre, Pennsylvania; *Orange and Black Wall* (1959), *Chief* (1950), *Mahoning* (1956).

Kokoschka, Oskar (1886–1980) Anglo-Austrian, born Pöchlarn; *The Dreaming Boys* (1908).

Kupka, Frantisek (1871–1957) Czech, born in Opocno, East Bohemia; *Girl with a Ball* (1908), *Amorpha: Fugue in Two Colours* (1912), *Working Steel* (1921–9).

Landseer, Sir Edwin (Henry) (1803–73) British, born London; *The Old Shepherd's Chief Mourner* (1837), *The Monarch of the Glen* (1850).

La Tour, Georges (Dumesnil) de (1593–1652) French, born Vic-sur-Seille, Lorraine; *St Jerome Reading* (1620s), *The Denial of St Peter* (1650).

Léger, Fernand (1881–1955) French, born Argentan; *Contrast of Forms* (1913), *Black Profile* (1928), *The Great Parade* (1954).

Lely, Sir Peter (originally Pietar van der Faes) (1618–80) Anglo-Dutch, born Soest, Westphalia; *The Windsor Beauties* (1668), *Admirals* series (1666–7).

Leonardo da Vinci (in full Leonardo di Ser Piero da Vinci) (1452–1519) Italian, born Vinci; *The Last Supper* (1495–7), *Madonna and Child with St Anne* (begun 1503), *Mona Lisa* (1500–6), *The Virgin of the Rocks* (c.1508).

Lichtenstein, Roy (1923–97) American, born New York City; *Whaam!* (1963), *As I Opened Fire* (1964).

Lippi, Fra Filippo, called Lippo (c.1406–69) Italian, born Florence; *Tarquinia Madonna* (1437), *Barbadori Altarpiece* (begun 1437).

Lochner, Stefan (c.1400–51) German, born Meersburg am Bodensee; *The Adoration of the Magi* (c.1448), triptych in Cologne Cathedral.

Lowry, L(aurence) S(tephen) (1887–1976) English, born Manchester; *Salford Street Scene* (1928), *Coming from the Mill* (1930), *Industrial Landscape* (1955).

Macke, August (1887–1914) German, born Meschede; *Greeting* (1912), *The Zoo* (1912), *Girls Under Trees* (1914).

Magritte, René (François Ghislain) (1898–1967) Belgian, born Lessines, Hainault; *The Menaced Assassin* (1926), *Loving Perspective* (1935), *Presence of Mind* (1960).

Manet, Édouard (1832–83) French, born Paris; *Le Déjeuner sur l'herbe* (1863), *La Brioche* (1870), *A Bar at the Folies-Bergères* (1882).

Mantegna, Andrea (1431–1506) Italian, born Vicenza; *Madonna of Victory* (altarpiece), *San Zeno Altarpiece* (1457–9), *Triumphs of Caesar* (c.1486–94).

Martini or Memmi, Simone (c.1284–1344) Italian, born Siena; *S Caterina Polyptych* (1319), *Annunciation* (1333).

Masaccio (real name Tommaso di Giovanni di Simone Guidi) (1401–28) Italian, born Castel San Giovanni in Val d'Arno; *polyptych* for the *Carmelite Church* in Pisa (1426), frescoes in *Sta Maria del Carmine*, Florence (1424–7).

Masson, André (Aimé René) (1896–1987) French, born Balgny, Oise; *Massacres* (1933), *The Labyrinth* (1939).

Matisse, Henri (Emile Benoît) (1869–1954) French, born Le Cateau-Cambrésis; *La Desserte* (1908), *Notre Dame* (1914), *The Large Red Studio* (1948), *L'Escargot* (1953).

Michelangelo (in full Michelangelo di Lodovico Buonarroti) (1475–1564) Italian, born Caprese, Tuscany; *The Pietà* (1497) (sculpture), *David* (1501–4) (sculpture), *Madonna* (c.1502), ceiling of the *Sistine Chapel*, Rome (1508–12), *The Last Judgement* (begun 1537).

Millais, Sir John Everett (1829–96) British, born Southampton; *Ophelia* (1851–2), *The Bridesmaid* (1851), *Tennyson* (1881), *Bubbles* (1886).

Millet, Jean-François (1814–75) French, born Grouchy; *Sower* (1850), *The Gleaners* (1857).

Miró, Joán (1893–1983) Spanish, born Montroig; *Catalan Landscape* (1923–4), *Maternity* (1924).

Modigliani, Amedeo (1884–1920) Italian, born Leghorn (Livorno), Tuscany; *The Jewess* (1908), *Moise Kisling* (1915), *Reclining Nude* (c.1919), *Jeanne Hébuterne* (1919).

Mondrian, Piet (properly **Pieter Cornelis Mondriaan**) (1872–1944) Dutch, born Amersfoort; *Still Life with Gingerpot II* (1911), *Composition with Red, Black, Blue, Yellow, and Grey* (1920), *Broadway Boogie-Woogie* (1942–3).

Monet, Claude (1840–1926) French, born Paris; *Impression: Sunrise* (1872), *Haystacks* (1890–1), *Rouen Cathedral* (1892–5), *Waterlilies* (1899 onwards).

Moreau, Gustave (1826–98) French, born Paris; *Oedipus and the Sphinx* (1864), *Apparition* (1876), *Jupiter and Semele* (1889–95).

Morisot, Berthe (Marie Pauline) (1841–95) French, born Bourges; *The Harbour at Cherbourg* (1874), *In the Dining Room* (1886).

Morris, William (1834–96) British, born Walthamstow, London; *Queen Guinevere* (1858).

Motherwell, Robert (Burns) (1915–91) American, born Aberdeen, Washington; *Gauloises* (1967), *Opens* (1968–72).

Munch, Edvard (1863–1944) Norwegian, born Löten; *The Scream* (1893), *Mother and Daughter* (c.1897), *Self-Portrait between the Clock and the Bed* (1940–2).

Nash, Paul (1899–1946) British, born London; *We Are Making a New World* (1918), *Menin Road* (1919).

Newman, Barnett (1905–70) American, born New York; *The Moment* (1946), *Onement I* (1948), *Vir Heroicus Sublimis* (1950–1).

Nicholson, Ben (1894–1982) British, born Denham, London; *White Relief* (1935), *November 11, 1947* (1947).

Nicholson, Winifred (1893–1981) British, born Oxford; *Honeysuckle and Sweet Peas* (1950), *The Copper and Capari* (1967), *The Gate to the Isles* (1980).

Nolde, Emil (pseudonym of Emil Hansen) (1867–1956) German, born Nolde; *The Missionary* (1912), *Candle Dancers* (1912).

Oliver, Isaac (c.1560–1617) Anglo-French, born Rouen; *Self-Portrait* (c.1590), *Henry, Prince of Wales* (c.1612).

Palmer, Samuel (1805–81) British, born London; *Repose of the Holy Family* (1824), *The Magic Apple Tree* (1830), *Opening of the Fold* (1880).

Parmigiano or **Parmigianino** (properly **Girolamo Francesco Maria Mazzola**) (1503–40) Italian, born Parma; frescoes in *S Giovanni Evangelista*, Parma (c.1522), *Self-Portrait in a Convex Mirror* (1524), *Vision of St Jerome* (1526–7), *Madonna Altarpiece*, Bologna (c.1528–30), *The Madonna of the Long Neck* (c.1535).

Pasmore, (Edwin John) **Victor** (1908–98) British, born Chelsham, Surrey; *The Evening Star* (1945–7), *Black Symphony – the Pistol Shot* (1977).

Peploe, S(amuel) J(ohn) (1871–1935) British, born Edinburgh; one of the 'Scottish colourists'; *Boats of Royan* (1910).

Perugino (properly **Pietro di Cristoforo Vannucci**) (c.1450–1523) Italian, born Città della Pieve, Umbria; *Christ Giving the Keys to Peter* (fresco in the Sistine Chapel) (c.1483).

Pevsner, Antoine (1886–1962) French, born Orël, Russia; *Torso* (1924–6), *Development Column* (1942).

Picabia, Francis (Marie) (1879–1953) French, born Paris; *I See Again in Memory My Dear Undine* (1913), *The Kiss* (1924).

Picasso, Pablo (Ruiz) (1881–1973) Spanish, born Malaga; *Mother and Child* (1921), *Three Dances* (1925), *Guernica* (1937), *The Charnel House* (1945), *The Artist and His Model* (1968).

Piero della Francesca (c.1420–92) Italian, born Borgo san Sepolcro; *Madonna of the Misericordia* (1445–8), *Resurrection* (c.1450).

Piper, John (1903–92) British, born Epsom; *Windsor Castle* watercolours (1941–2), *Council Chamber, House of Commons* (1941); also stage designs and illustrated publications.

Pissarro, Camille (Jacob) (1830–1903) French, born St Thomas, West Indies; *Landscape at Chaponval* (1880), *The Boieldieu Bridge at Rouen* (1896), *Boulevard Montmartre* (1897).

Pollock, (Paul) Jackson (1912–56) American, born Cody, Wyoming; *Guardians of the Secret* (1943), *No 14* (1948).

Pontormo, Jacopo da (1494–1552) Italian; frescoes eg of the *Passion* (1522–5), *Deposition* (c.1525).

Poussin, Nicolas (1594–1665) French, born Les Andelys, Normandy; *The Adoration of the Golden Calf* (1624), *Inspiration of the Poet* (c.1628), *Seven Sacraments* (1644–8), *Self-Portrait* (1650).

Raeburn, Sir Henry (1756–1823) British, born Edinburgh; *Rev Robert Walker Skating* (1784, although the attribution is now in doubt), *Isabella McLeod, Mrs James Gregory* (c.1798).

Ramsay, Allan (1713–84) British, born Edinburgh; *The Artist's Wife* (1754–5).

Raphael (properly Raffaello Santi or Sanzio) (1483–1520) Italian, born Urbino; *Assumption of the Virgin* (1504), *Madonna of the Meadow* (1505–6), *Transfiguration* (1518–20).

Redon, Odilon (1840–1916) French, born Bordeaux; *Woman with Outstretched Arms* (c.1910–14).

Redpath, Anne (1895–1965) British, born Galashiels; *Pinks* (1947).

Rembrandt (properly Rembrandt Harmenszoon van Rijn) (1606–69) Dutch, born Leiden; *Anatomy Lesson of Dr Tulp* (1632), *Blinding of Samson* (1636), *The Night Watch* (1642), *The Conspiracy of Claudius* (1661–2).

Renoir, (Jean Pierre) Auguste (1841–1919) French, born Limoges; *Woman in Blue* (1874), *Woman Reading* (1876), *The Bathers* (1887).

Reynolds, Sir Joshua (1723–92) British, born Plympton Earls, near Plymouth; *Portrait of Miss Bowles with Her Dog* (1775), *Master Henry Hoare* (1788).

Riley, Bridget (Louise) (1931–) British, born London; *Pink Landscapes* (1959–60), *Zig-Zag* (1961), *Fall* (1963), *Apprehend* (1970).

Rosa, Salvator (1615–73) Italian, born Arenella, near Naples; *Self-Portrait with a Skull* (1656), *Humana Fragilitas* (c.1657).

Rossetti, Dante Gabriel (1828–82) British, born London; *Beata Beatrix* (1849–50), *Ecce Ancilla Domini!* (1850), *Astarte Syriaca* (1877).

Rothko, Mark (originally Marcus Rothkovitch (1903–70) Latvian–American, born Dvinsk; *The Omen of the Eagle* (1942), *Red on Maroon* (1959).

Rousseau, Henri (Julien Félix), known as Le Douanier (1844–1910) French, born Laval; *Monsieur et Madame Stevene* (1884), *Sleeping Gipsy* (1897), *Portrait of Joseph Brunner* (1909).

Rubens, Sir Peter Paul (1577–1640) Flemish, born Siegen, Westphalia; *Marchesa Brigida Spinola-Doria* (1606), *Hélène Fourment with Two of Her Children* (c.1637).

Sargent, John Singer (1856–1925) American, born Florence; *Madame X* (1884), *Lady Agnew* (1893), *Gassel* (1918).

Schiele, Egon (1890–1918) Austrian, born Tulln; *Autumn Tree* (1909), *Pregnant Woman and Death* (1911), *Edith Seated* (1917–18).

Schnabel, Julian (1951–   ) American, born New York City; *The Unexpected Death of Blinky Palermo in the Tropics* (1981), *Humanity Asleep* (1982).

Seurat, Georges (Pierre) (1859–91) French, born Paris; *Bathers at Asnières* (1884), *Sunday on the Island of La Grande Jatte* (1885–6), *Le Cirque* (1891).

Sickert, Walter (Richard) (1860–1942) British, born Munich; *La Hollandaise* (1905–6), *Ennui* (c.1914).

Sisley, Alfred (1839–99) French, born Paris; *Avenue of Chestnut Trees near La Celle Saint-Cloud* (1868), *Mosley Weir, Hampton Court* (1874).

Spencer, Sir Stanley (1891–1959) British, born Cookham-on-Thames, Berkshire; *The Resurrection* (1927), *The Leg of Mutton Nude* (1937).

Steen, Jan (Havicksz) (1627–79) Dutch, born Leiden; *A Woman at Her Toilet* (1663), *The World Upside Down* (1663).

Stubbs, George (1724–1806) British, born Liverpool; *James Stanley* (1755), *Anatomy of the Horse* (1766), *Hambletonian, Rubbing Down* (1799).

Sutherland, Graham (Vivian) (1903–80) British, born London; *Entrance to a Lane* (1939), *Crucifixion* (1946), *A Bestiary and some Correspondences* (1968).

Tanguy, Yves (1900–55) French–American, born Paris; *He Did What He Wanted* (1927), *The Invisibles* (1951).

Tatlin, Vladimir Yevgrafovich (1885–1953) Russian, born Moscow; painted reliefs, relief constructions, corner reliefs (all 1914 onwards); design for *Monument to the Third International* (1920).

Tintoretto (properly Jacopo Robusti) (1518–94) Italian, born probably Venice; *The Miracle of the Slave* (1548), *St George and the Dragon* (c.1558), *The Golden Calf* (c.1560).

Titian (properly Tiziano Vecchelio) (c.1488–1576) Italian, born Pieve di Cadore; *The Assumption of the Virgin* (1516–18), *Bacchus and Ariadne* (1522–3), *Pesaro Madonna* (1519–26), *Crowning with Thorns* (c.1570).

Toulouse-Lautrec, Henri (Marie Raymond de) (1864–1901) French, born Albi; *The Jockey* (1899), *At the Moulin Rouge* (1895), *The Modiste* (1900).

Turner, Joseph Mallord William (1775–1851) British, born London; *Frosty Morning* (1813), *The Shipwreck* (1805), *Crossing the Brook* (1815), *The Fighting Téméraire* (1839), *Rain, Steam and Speed* (1844).

Uccello, Paolo (originally Paolo di Dono) (c.1396–1475) Italian, born Pratovecchio; *The Flood* (c.1445), *The Rout of San Romano* (1454–7).

Utamaro, Kitagawa (1753–1806) Japanese, born Edo (modern Tokyo); *Ohisa* (c.1788), *The Twelve Hours of the Green Houses* (c.1795).

Van Dyck, Sir Anthony (1599–1641) Flemish, born Antwerp; *Marchesa Elena Grimaldi* (c.1625), *The Deposition* (1634–5), *Le Roi à la chasse* (c.1638).

Van Gogh, Vincent (Willem) (1853–90) Dutch, born Groot-Zundert, near Breda; *The Potato Eaters* (1885), *Self-Portrait with Bandaged Ear* (1888), *The Harvest* (1888), *The Sunflowers* (1888), *Starry Night* (1889), *Cornfields with Flight of Birds* (1890).

Velázquez, Diego (Rodríguez de Silva y) (1599–1660) Spanish, born Seville; *The Immaculate Conception* (c.1618), *The Waterseller of Seville* (c.1620), *The Surrender of Breda* (1634–5), *Pope Innocent X* (1650), *Las Meninas* (c.1656).

Vermeer, Jan (Johannes) (1632–75) Dutch, born Delft; *A Lady with a Gentleman at the Virginals* (c.1665), *The Astronomer* (1668), *Christ in the House of Mary and Martha* (date unknown), *The Lacemaker* (date unknown).

Veronese (pseudonym of **Paolo Caliari**) (1528–88) Italian, born Verona; *The Feast in the House of Levi* (1573), *Marriage at Cana* (1573), *Triumph of Venice* (c.1585).

Verrocchio, Andrea del (properly **Andrea di Francesco di Michele di Cioni**) (c.1435–c.1488) Italian, born Florence; *Baptism of Christ* (c.1470), *David* (c.1475) (sculpture).

Vlaminck, Maurice de (1876–1958) French, born Paris; *The Red Trees* (1906), *Tugboat at Chatou* (1906).

Warhol, Andy (originally **Andrew Warhola**) (1928–87) American, born McKeesport, Pennsylvania; *Marilyn* (1962), *Electric Chair* (1963).

Watteau, (Jean) Antoine (1684–1721) French, born Valenciennes; *The Pilgrimage to the Island of Cythera* (1717), *L'Enseigne de Gersaint* (1721).

Whistler, James (Abbott) McNeill (1834–1903) American, born Lowell, Massachusetts; *The Artist's Mother* (1871), *Nocturne in Blue and Silver: Old Battersea Bridge* (1872–5), *Falling Rocket* (1875).

Wilkie, Sir David (1785–1841) British, born Cults, Fife; *The Village Politicians* (1806), *Chelsea Pensioners Reading the Waterloo Despatch* (1822).

Wood, Grant (1891–1942) American, born Iowa; *American Gothic* (1930), *Spring Turning* (1936).

Wright, Joseph (of Derby) (1734–97) British, born Derby; *Experiment with an Air Pump* (1766), *The Alchemist in Search of the Philosopher's Stone Discovers Phosphorus* (1795).

Wyeth, Andrew (Newell) (1917–   ) American, born Chadds Ford, Pennsylvania; *Christina's World* (1948).

Sculptors

Selected works are listed.

Andre, Carl (1935–   ) American, born Quincy, Massachusetts; *144 Magnesium Square* (1969), *Twelfth Copper Corner* (1975), *Bloody Angle* (1985), *Armadillo* (1998).

Armitage, Kenneth (1916–2002) British, born Leeds; *People in the Wind* (1950), *Sprawling Woman* (1958), *Figure and Clouds* (1972), *Richmond Oak* (1985–90).

Arp, Hans (Jean) (1887–1966) French, born Strasbourg; *Eggboard* (1922), *Kore* (1958).

Barlach, Ernst (1870–1938) German, born Wedel; *Moeller-Jarke Tomb* (1901), *Have Pity!* (1919).

Bernini, Gian Lorenzo (1598–1680) Italian, born Naples; *Neptune and Triton* (1620), *David* (1623), *Ecstasy of St Theresa* (1640s), *Fountain of the Four Rivers* (1648–51).

Bologna, Giovanni da (also called **Giambologna**) (1529–1608) French, born Douai; *Mercury* (1564–5), *Rape of the Sabines* (1579–83).

Bourgeois, Louise (1911–) American, born Paris; *Labyrinthine Tower* (1963), *Destruction of the Father* (1974), *Spiders* (1995).

Brancusi, Constantin (1876–1957) Romanian–French, born Hobitza, Gorj; *The Kiss* (1909), *Torso of a Young Man* (1922).

Calder, Alexander (1898–1976) American, born Philadelphia, Pennsylvania; *Stabiles and Mobiles* (1932), *A Universe* (1934).

Canova, Antonio (1757–1822) Italian, born Possagno; *Theseus* (1782), *Cupid and Psyche* (1787), *Pauline Borghese as Venus* (1805–7).

Caro, Sir Anthony (1924–) British, born London; *Sailing Tonight* (1971–4), *Veduggio Sound* (1973), *Ledge Piece* (1978), *Night Movements* (1987–90).

Cellini, Benvenuto (1500–71) Italian, born Florence; salt cellar of *Neptune and Ceres* (1543), *Cosimo de' Medici* (1545–7), *Perseus with the Head of Medusa* (1564).

Deacon, Richard (1949–) British, born Bangor, Wales; *Double Talk* (1987), *Never Mind* (1993), *Show and Tell* (1993), *Just Us* (2000).

Donatello (originally **Donato di Niccolò di Betto Bardi**) (c.1386–1466) Italian, born Florence; *St Mark* (1411–12), *St George Killing the Dragon* (c.1417), *Feast of Herod* (1423–37), *David* (c. 1440), *Judith and Holofernes* (1460).

Epstein, Sir Jacob (1880–1959) Anglo-American, born New York City; *Rima* (1925), *Genesis* (1930), *Ecce Homo* (1934–5), *Adam* (1939), *Christ in Majesty* (Llandaff Cathedral), *St Michael and the Devil* (on the façade of Coventry Cathedral) (1958–9).

Frink, Dame Elisabeth (1930–93) British, born Thurlow, Suffolk; *Horse Lying Down* (1975), *Running Man* (1985), *Seated Man* (1986).

Gabo, Naum (originally **Naum Neemia Pevsner**) (1890–1977) American, born Bryansk, Russia; *Kinetic Construction* (1920), *No.1* (1943).

Gaudier-Brzeska, Henri (1891–1915) French, born St Jean de Braye, near Orléans; *Red stone dancer* (1913).

Ghiberti, Lorenzo (c.1378–1455) Italian, born in or near Florence; *St John the Baptist* (1412–15), *St Matthew* (1419–22), *The Gates of Paradise* (1425–52).

Giacometti, Alberto (1901–66) Swiss, born Bogonova, near Stampa; *Head* (c.1928), *Woman with Her Throat Cut* (1932).

Goldsworthy, Andy (1956–) British, born Cheshire; *Hazel Stick Throws* (1980), *Slate Cone* (1988), *The Wall* (1988–9), *Arch at Goodwood* (2002).

González, Julio (1876–1942) Spanish, born Barcelona; *Angel* (1933), *Woman Combing Her Hair* (1936), *Cactus People* (1930–40).

Gormley, Antony (1950–) English, born London; *Natural Selection* (1981), *Angel of the North* (1997), *Another Place* (1997), *Event Horizon* (2007).

Hepworth, Dame (Jocelyn) Barbara (1903–75) British, born Wakefield, Yorkshire; *Figure of a Woman* (1929–30), *Large and Small Forms* (1945), *Single Form* (1963).

Leonardo da Vinci (in full **Leonardo de Ser Piero da Vinci**) (1452–1519) Italian, born Vinci; *St John the Baptist*.

Kapoor, Anish (1954–) Indian, born Mumbai; *1000 Names* (1989–90), *Marsyas* (2002), *Cloud Gate* (2004).

Michelangelo (in full **Michelangelo di Lodovico Buonarotti**) (1475–1564) Italian, born Caprese, Tuscany; *Cupid* (1495), *Bacchus* (1496), *Pieta* (1497), *David* (c.1500).

Moore, Henry (Spencer) (1898–1986) British, born Castleford, Yorkshire; *Recumbent Figure* (1938), *Fallen Warrior* (1956–7).

Oldenburg, Claes Thure (1929–   ) American, born Stockholm, Sweden; *Giant Clothespin* (1975), *The Course of the Knife* (1985), *Match Cover* (1992).

Paolozzi, Sir Eduardo Luigi (1924–2005) British, born Leith, Edinburgh; *Krokodeel* (c.1956–7), *Japanese War God* (1958), *Medea* (1964), *Piscator* (1981), *Manuscript of Monte Cassino*, Edinburgh (1991), *Daedalus* (1993), *London to Paris* (2000).

Pheidias (c.490–c.417BC) Greek, born Athens; *Athena Promachos* (460–450BC), marble sculptures of the *Parthenon* (447–432BC).

Pisano, Andrea (c.1270–1349) Italian, born Pontedera; bronze doors of the *Baptistry* of Florence (1330–6).

Pisano, Giovanni (c.1248–c.1320) Italian, born Pisa; *Fontana Maggiore*, Perugia (1278), *Duomo pulpit*, Pisa (1302–10).

Pisano, Nicola (c.1225–c.1284) Italian, birthplace unknown; *Baptistry* at Pisa (1260).

Praxiteles (5c BC) Greek, born probably Athens; *Hermes Carrying the Boy Dionysus* (date unknown).

Robbia, Luca della (in full **Luca di Simone di Marco della Robbia**) (c.1400–1482) Italian, born Florence; *Cantoria* (1432–7).

Rodin, (François) **Auguste** (René) (1840–1917) French, born Paris; *The Age of Bronze* (1875–6), *The Gates of Hell* (1880–1917), *The Burghers of Calais* (1884), *The Kiss* (1901–4), *The Thinker* (1904).

Schwitters, Kurt (1887–1948) German, born Hannover; *Merzbau* (1920–43).

Tinguely, Jean (1925–91) Swiss, born Fribourg; *Baluba No 3* (1959), *Métamécanique No 9* (1959), *Homage to New York* (1960), *EOSX* (1967).

Whiteread, Rachel (1963–   ) British, born London; *Torso* (1991), *House* (1993), *Orange Bath* (1996), *Embankment* (2005).

Architects

Selected works are listed.

Aalto, (Hugo) **Alvar** (Henrik) (1898–1976) Finnish, born Kuortane; *Convalescent Home*, Paimio, near Turku (1929–30), *Town Hall*, Saynatsab (1950–2), *Finlandia Concert Hall*, Helsinki (1971).

Adam, Robert (1728–92) Scottish, born Kirkcaldy; *Adelphi*, London (1769–71, demolished 1936), *General Register House* (begun 1774), *Charlotte Square* (1791), *University of Edinburgh, Old College* (1789–94), all Edinburgh; *Culzean Castle*, Ayrshire (1772–92).

Adam, William (1689–1748) Scottish, born Maryburgh; *Hopetoun House*, near Edinburgh (1721).

Alberti, Leon Battista (1404–72) Italian, born Genoa; façade of the *Palazzo Recellai*, Florence (1460), *San Andrea*, Mantua (1470).

Anthemias of Tralles (dates unknown) Greek, born Tralles, Lydia; *Hagia Sophia*, Constantinople (now Istanbul) (532–7).

Apollodorus of Damascus (dates unknown) Greek, born Syria; *Trajan's Forum*, Rome, *The Baths of Trajan*, Rome.

Arnolfo di Cambio (1232–1302) Italian, born Colle di Val d'Elsa, Tuscany; *Florence Cathedral* (1299–1310).

Asplund, Erik Gunnar (1885–1940) Swedish, born Stockholm; *Stockholm City Library* (1924–7), *Law Courts*, Gothenburg (1934–7).

Baker, Sir Herbert (1862–1946) English, born Kent; *Groote Schuur*, near Cape Town (1892–1902), *Union Government Buildings*, Pretoria (1907).

Barry, Sir Charles (1795–1860) English, born London; *Royal Institution of the Arts*, Manchester (1824), *Houses of Parliament*, London (opened 1852).

Behrens, Peter (1868–1940) German, born Hamburg; *Turbine Assembly Works*, Berlin (1909), *German Embassy*, St Petersburg (1912).

Berlage, Hendrick Petrus (1856–1934) Dutch, born Amsterdam; *Amsterdam Bourse* (1903), *Holland House*, London (1914), *Gemeente Museum*, The Hague (1934).

Bernini, Gian Lorenzo (1598–1680) Italian, born Naples; *St Peter's Baldacchino* (1625), *Cornaro Chapel* in the Church of Santa Maria della Vittoria (1645–52), both Rome.

Borromini, Francesco (1599–1667) Italian, born Bissone, on Lake Lugano; *S Carlo alle Quattro Fontane* (1637–41), *S Ivo della Sapienza* (1642–61), both Rome.

Boullée, Étienne-Louis (1728–99) French, born Paris; *Hôtel de Brunoy*, Paris (1772), *Monument to Isaac Newton* (never built) (1794).

Bramante, Donato (originally **Donato di Pascuccio d'Antonio**) (1444–1514) Italian, born near Urbino; *San Maria presso S Satiro*, Milan (begun 1482), *Tempietto of S Pietro*, Rome (1502).

Breuer, Marcel Lajos (1902–81) Hungarian–American, born Pécs, Hungary; *UNESCO Building*, Paris (1953–8).

Brosse, Salomon de (1565–1626) French, born Verneuil-sur-Oise; *Luxembourg Palace*, Paris (1615–20), *Louis XIII's Hunting Lodge*, Versailles (1624–6).

Brunelleschi, Filippo (1377–1446) Italian, born Florence; *San Lorenzo*, Florence (begun 1418), *Dome of Florence Cathedral* (begun 1420), *Ospedale degli Innocenti*, Florence (1419).

Bryce, David (1803–76) Scottish, born Edinburgh; *Fettes College* (1863–9), *former Royal Infirmary* (begun 1870), both Edinburgh.

Burnham, David Hudson (1846–1912) American, born Henderson, New York; *Reliance Building*, Chicago (1890–5), *Monadnock Building*, Chicago (1890–1), *Selfridge Building*, London (1908).

Burton, Decimus (1800–81) English, born London; *Regent's Park Colosseum* (1823), *Arch at Hyde Park Corner* (1825), both London.

Butterfield, William (1814–1900) English, born London; *Keble College*, Oxford (1866–86), *St Augustine's College*, Canterbury (1844–73), *All Saints'*, Margaret Street, London (1849–59).

Calatrava, Santiago (1951–) Spanish, born Valencia; *Puente del Alamillo*, Seville (1992), *Milwaukee Art Museum*, Milwaukee (2001), *Turning Torso*, Malmo (2005).

Campen, Jacob van (1595–1657) Dutch, born Haarlem; *Maurithuis*, The Hague (1633), *Amsterdam Theatre* (1637), *Amsterdam Town Hall* (1647–55).

Candela, Felix (1910–97) Spanish–Mexican, born Madrid; *Sports Palace* for Olympic Games, Mexico City (1968).

Chambers, Sir William (1726–96) Scottish, born Stockholm; *Somerset House* (1776), pagoda in *Kew Gardens* (1757), both London.

Chermayeff, Serge (1900–96) American, born the Caucasus Mountains, Russia; *De La Warr Pavilion*, Bexhill (1933–5).

Churriguera, Don José (1650–1725) Spanish, born Salamanca; *Salamanca Cathedral* (1692–4).

Coates, Wells Wintemute (1895–1958) English, born Tokyo; *BBC Studios* (1932), *EKCO Laboratories* (1936), *Cinema*, Festival of Great Britain Exhibition (1951).

Cockerell, Charles Robert (1788–1863) English, born London; *Fitzwilliam Museum*, Cambridge (1837–40), *Taylorian Institute*, Oxford (1841–5).

Cortona, Pietro Berrettini da (1596–1669) Italian, born Cortona; *Villa Sacchetti*, Castel Fusano (1626–7), *San Firenze*, Florence (1645).

Cuvilliés, François de (1695–1768) Bavarian, born Belgium; *Amelienburg Pavilion* at Schloss Nymphenburg, near Munich (1734–9), *Residenztheater*, Munich (1750–3).

Dance, George (the Elder) (1700–68) English, born London; *Mansion House*, London (1739).

Dance, George (the Younger) (1741–1825) English, born London; rebuilt *Newgate Prison* (1770–83).

Delorme, Philibert (c.1510–70) French, born Lyons; *Châteaux of Anet, Meudon, Saint Germain-en-Laye* (1547–55), *Tuileries* (1565–70).

Doesburg, Theo van (originally Christian Emil Marie Kupper) (1883–1931) Dutch, born Utrecht; *L'Art Nouveau Shop*, Paris (1896), *Keller und Reiner Art Gallery*, Berlin (1898).

Doshi, Balkrishna Vithaldas (1927–) Indian, born Poona; *City Hall*, Toronto (1958), *Indian Institute of Management*, Ahmedabad (1951–7).

Dudok, Willem Marinus (1884–1974) Dutch, born Amsterdam; *Hilversum Town Hall* (1928–30), *Bijenkorf Department Store*, Rotterdam (1929).

Engel, Johann Carl Ludwig (1778–1840) Finnish, born Berlin; layout of Helsinki (1818–26).

Erickson, Arthur Charles (1924–) Canadian, born Vancouver; *Simon Fraser University Buildings*, British Columbia (1963), *Lethbridge University*, Alberta (1971).

Fischer von Erlach, Johann Bernard (1656–1723) Austrian, born Graz; *Karlskirche*, Vienna (1716), *Hofbibliotek*, Vienna (1723), *Kollegienkirche*, Salzburg (1707).

Foster, Norman Foster, Baron (1935–) English, born Manchester; *Willis Faber Dumas Building*, Ipswich (1975), *Sainsbury Centre*, University of East Anglia (1978), *Hong Kong and Shanghai Bank*, Hong Kong (1979–85), *Hong Kong Airport*, Hong Kong (1992–8), *Millau Viaduct*, Millau, France (1993–2004), *Supreme Court*, Singapore (2000–2004), *Beijing Airport*, China (2003–8).

Francesco di Giorgio (1439–1501/2) Italian, born Siena; *Church of San Bernardino all'Osservanza*, Siena (1474–84), *Palazzo Ducale*, Gubbio (1476–82).

Gabriel, Ange-Jacques (1698–1782) French, born Paris; *Pavillon de Pompadour*, Fontainebleau (begun 1749), Paris; layout of *Place de la Concorde*, Paris (1753), *Petit Trianon*, Versailles (1761–8).

Garnier, Tony (Antoine) (1869–1948) French, born Lyons; *Grange Blanche Hospital*, Lyons (1911–27), *Stadium*, Lyons (1913–18), *Hôtel de Ville*, Boulogne-Bilancourt (1931–3).

Gaudí (i Cornet), **Antoni** (1852–1926) Spanish, born Reus, Tarragona; *Casa Vicens* (1878–80), *Sagrada Familia* (1884 onwards), *Casa Batlló* (1904–17), *Casa Milá* (1905–9), all Barcelona.

Gehry, Frank (1929–) US–Canadian, born Toronto; *Los Angeles Children's Museum* (1979), *Dancing House*, Prague (1996), *Guggenheim Museum*, Bilbao (1997), *Maggie's Centre*, Dundee (2003).

Gibbs, James (1682–1754) Scottish, born Aberdeen; *St-Martin-in-the-Fields*, London (1722–6), *King's College Fellows' Building*, Cambridge (1724–49).

Gilbert, Cass (1859–1934) American, born Zanesville, Ohio; *Woolworth Building*, New York City (1913).

Gilly, Friedrich (1772–1800) German, born Berlin; *Funerary Precinct and Temple* to Frederick II, the Great of Prussia (1796), *Prussian National Theatre*, Berlin (1798).

Giotto (in full **Giotto di Bondone**) (c.1266–1337) Italian, born Vespignano, near Florence; *Campanile*, Florence Cathedral (from 1334).

Giulio Romano (properly **Giulio Pippi de' Gianuzzi**) (c.1492–1546) Italian, born Rome; *Palazzo del Tè*, Mantua (1526), *Church of S Petronio* façade, Bologna (1546).

Greenway, Francis Howard (1777–1837) Anglo-Australian, born Bristol; *Macquarie Lighthouse*, Sydney Harbour (1818), *St James' Church*, Sydney (1824).

Gropius, Walter (1883–1969) German–American, born Berlin; *Fagus Shoe Factory*, Alfeld (1911), *The Bauhaus*, Dessau (1925), both Germany; *Harvard University Graduate Centre* (1950), Massachusetts.

Guarini, Guarino (originally **Camillo**) (1624–83) Italian, born Modena; *San Lorenzo* church, Turin (1668–80), *Capella della SS Sindone* church, Turin (1668), *Palazzo Carignano*, Racconigi (1679).

Hadid, Zaha (1950–) Iraqi–British, born Baghdad; *Vitra Fire Station*, Weil am Rhein (1994), *BMW Central Building*, Leipzig (2005), *Maggie's Centre*, Kirkcaldy (2006).

Haussmann, Georges Eugène (1809–91) French, born Paris; layout of *Bois de Boulogne*, *Bois de Vincennes*, Paris (1853–70).

Hawksmoor, Nicholas (1661–1736) English, born Nottinghamshire; *St Mary Woolnoth Church* (1716–24), *St George's*, Bloomsbury (1716–30), both London.

Hildebrandt, Johann Lukas von (1668–1745) Austrian, born Genoa; *Lower and Upper Belvedere*, Vienna, (1714–15, 1720–3).

Hoffmann, Josef (1870–1956) Austrian, born Pirnitz; *Purkersdorf Sanatorium* (1903–5), *Stoclet House*, Brussels (1905–11).

Holland, Henry (1746–1806) English, born London; *Carlton House*, London (1783–96), *Brighton Pavilion* (1787).

Itkinos and **Callicrates** (dates and places of birth unknown), Greek; *The Parthenon*, Athens (447/6–438 BC).

Jacobsen, Arne (1902–71) Danish, born Copenhagen; *Town Hall of Aarhus* (with Erik Moller, 1938–42), *Town Hall of Rodovre* (1955–6), *SAS Tower*, Copenhagen (1960), all Denmark; *St Catherine's College*, Oxford (1959).

Jefferson, Thomas (1743–1826) American, born Shadwell, Virginia; *Monticello*, Albemarle County (1769), *Virginia State Capitol* (1796).

Johnson, Philip Cortelyou (1906–2005) American, born Cleveland, Ohio; *Seagram Building*, New York City (1945), *Glass House*, New Canaan, Connecticut (1949–50), *Amon Carter Museum of Western Art*, Texas (1961), *New York State Theater*, Lincoln Center (1964).

Jones, Inigo (1573–1652) English, born London; *The Queen's House*, Greenwich (1616–18, 1629–35), *Banqueting House*, Whitehall, London (1619–22).

Kahn, Louis Isadore (1901–74) American architect, born Osel (now Saaremaa), Estonia; *City Tower Municipal Building*, Philadelphia (1952–7), *Richards Medical Research Building*, Pennsylvania (1957–61).

Labrouste, (Pierre François) Henri (1801–75) French, born Paris; *Bibliothèque Sainte Geneviève* (1838–50), *Bibliothèque Nationale* reading room (1860–7), both Paris.

Lasdun, Sir Denys Louis (1914–2001) English, born London; *Royal College of Musicians* (1958–64), *National Theatre* (1965–76), both London.

Le Corbusier (pseudonym of **Charles Édouard Jeanneret**) (1887–1965) French, born La Chaux-de-Fonds, Switzerland; *Salvation Army Hostel*, Paris (begun 1929), *Chapel of Ronchamp*, near Belfort (1950–4), *Chandigarh*, Punjab (1951–6), *Museum of Modern Art*, Tokyo (1957).

Ledoux, Claude Nicolas (1736–1806) French, born Dormans, Champagne; *Château*, *Louveciennes* (1771–3), *Theatre*, Besançon (1771–3).

Leonardo da Vinci (in full **Leonardo di Ser Pietro da Vinci**) (1452–1519) Italian, born Vinci; *Mariolo de Guiscardi House*, Milan (1497), *La Veruca Fortress*, near Pisa (1504), *Villa Melzi*, Vaprio, Milan (1513).

Lescot, Pierre (c.1510–78) French, born Paris; screen of *St Germain l'Auxerrois* (1541–4), rebuilt one wing of the *Louvre*, Paris (1546).

Lethaby, William Richard (1857–1931) English, born Barnstaple; *Avon Tyrell*, Hampshire (1891–2), *Eagle Insurance Buildings*, Birmingham (1899–1900).

Le Vau or **Levau, Louis** (1612–70) French, born Paris; *Hôtel Lambert*, Paris (1640–4), part of *Palace of Versailles* (from 1661), *Collège des Quatre Nations*, Paris (1661).

Libeskind, Daniel (1946–) Polish-American, born Łódź; *Jewish Museum*, Berlin (1999), *Imperial War Museum North*, Manchester (2002).

Loos, Adolf (1870–1933) Austrian, born Bruno, Moravia; *Steiner House*, Vienna (1910).

Lorimer, Sir Robert Stodart (1864–1929) Scottish, born Edinburgh; *Thistle Chapel, St Giles*, Edinburgh (1909–11), *Scottish National War Memorial*, Edinburgh Castle (1923–8).

Lutyens, Sir Edwin Landseer (1869–1944) English, born London; *Cenotaph*, Whitehall, London (1919–20), *Liverpool Roman Catholic Cathedral* (unfinished) (1929–c.1941), *Viceroy's House*, New Delhi (1921–5).

Mackintosh, Charles Rennie (1868–1928) Scottish, born Glasgow; *Glasgow School of Art* (1897–9), *Hill House*, Helensburgh (1902–3).

Mackmurdo, Arthur Heygate (1851–1942) English, born London; *Gordon Institute for Boys*, St Helens (1890).

Maderna or **Maderno, Carlo** (1556–1629) Italian, born Capalago; *S Susanna* (1597–1603), façade of *St Peter's* (1606–12), *Palazzo Barberini* (1628–38), all Rome.

Mansard or **Mansart**, **François** (1598–1666) French, born Paris; *Sainte-Marie de la Visitation*, Paris (1632), north wing of *Château de Blois* (1635).

Mansard or **Mansart**, **Jules Hardouin** (1645–1708) French, born Paris; *Grand Trianon*, *Palace of Versailles* (1678–89).

Mendelsohn, **Eric** (1887–1953) German, born Allenstein; *De La Warr Pavilion*, Bexhill (1933–5), *Anglo-Palestine Bank*, Jerusalem (1938).

Michelozzo di Bartolommeo (1396–1472) Italian, born Florence; *Villa Medici*, Fiesole (1458–61), *San Marco*, Florence (begun 1437).

Mies van der Rohe, **Ludwig** (1886–1969) German–American, born Aachen; *Seagram Building*, New York City (1956–8), *Public Library*, Washington (1967).

Miralles, **Enric** (1955–2000) Spanish, born Catalonia; *Santa Caterina Market*, Barcelona (2001), *Scottish Parliament Building*, Edinburgh (2002).

Moore, **Charles Willard** (1925–93) American, born Benton Harbor, Michigan; *Sea Ranch Condominium Estate*, Glendale, California (1965), *Kresge College*, Santa Cruz, California (1974), *Piazza d'Italia*, New Orleans (1975–8), *Civic Center*, Beverly Hills, California (1990).

Nash, **John** (1752–1835) English, born London; layout of *Regent's Park* and *Regent Street*, London (1811 onwards), *Brighton Pavilion* (1815).

Nervi, **Pier Luigi** (1891–1979) Italian, born Sondrio; *Berta Stadium*, Florence (1930–2), *Olympic Stadia*, Rome (1960), *San Francisco Cathedral* (1970).

Neumann, **(Johann) Balthasar** (1687–1753) German, born Eger; *Würzburg Palace* (1730–43), *Schloss Bruchsal* (1738–53).

Niemeyer, **Oscar** (1907–) Brazilian, born Rio de Janeiro; *Church of St Francis of Assisi*, Belo Horizonte, Brazil (1942–4), *Niemeyer House*, Rio de Janeiro (1953), *Museum of Contemporary Art*, Niteroi, Brazil (1996).

Oud, **Jacobus Johann Pieter** (1890–1963) Dutch, born Purmerend; *Alida Hartog-Ond House*, Purmerend (1906), *Café de Unie*, Rotterdam (1924), *Convention Centre*, The Hague (1957–63).

Palladio, **Andrea** (1508–80) Italian, born Padua; *Godi-Porto* (villa at Lonedo) (1540), *La Malcontenta* (villa near Padua) (1560), *San Giorgio Maggiore*, Venice (begun 1566).

Paxton, **Sir Joseph** (1801–65) English, born Milton-Bryant, near Woburn; building for *Great Exhibition* of 1851, later re-erected as the *Crystal Palace*, Sydenham (1852–4).

Pei, **I(eoh) M(ing)** (1917–) Chinese–American, born Canton; *Mile High Center*, Denver (1954–9), *John Hancock Tower*, Boston (1973), *Glass Pyramids*, the Louvre, Paris (1983–9).

Perret, **Auguste** (1874–1954) French, born Brussels; *Théâtre des Champs Élysées*, Paris (1911–13), *Musée des travaux publics*, Paris (1936).

Piano, **Renzo** (1937–) Italian, born Genoa; *Centre George Pompidou*, Paris (with Richard Rogers) (1971), *Kansai International Air Terminal*, Osaka (1994), *Padre Pio Pilgrimage Church*, San Giovanni Rotondo, Italy (2004).

Piranesi, **Giambattista** (1720–78) Italian, born Venice; *Santa Maria Arentina*, Rome (1764–6).

Pisano, **Nicola** (c.1225–c.1284) Italian, born Tuscany; *Pisa Baptistry* (1260), façade renovation of *Pisa Cathedral* (1260–70).

Playfair, William Henry (1789–1857) Scottish, born London; *National Gallery of Scotland* (1850–7), *Royal Scottish Academy* (1832–5), *Surgeon's Hall* (1829–32), all Edinburgh.

Poelzig, Hans (1869–1936) German, born Berlin; *Exhibition Hall*, Posen (1910–11), *Salzburg Festival Theatre* (1920–2).

Pugin, Augustus Welby Northmore (1812–52) English, born London; drawings, decorations and sculpture for the *Houses of Parliament*, London (1836–7), *Birmingham Cathedral* (1839–41).

Renwick, James (1818–95) American, born New York; *Smithsonian Institution*, Washington (1844–55), *Grace Church*, New York (1846), *St Patrick's Cathedral*, New York (1858–79).

Rietveld, Gerrit Thomas (1888–1964) Dutch, born Utrecht; *Schröder House*, Utrecht (1924), *Van Gogh Museum*, Amsterdam (1963–4).

Rogers, Richard George Rogers, Baron (1933–) English, born Florence; *Pompidou Centre*, Paris (1971–9), *Lloyds*, London (1979–85), *Princeton Campus Centre*, New Jersey (1996–2000), *National Assembly for Wales* (1998–2005), *Madrid Barajas Airport*, Madrid (1997–2005).

Saarinen, Eero (1910–61) Finnish–American, born Kirkknonummi; *Jefferson Memorial Arch*, St Louis (1948–64), *American Embassy*, London (1955–60).

Sanmichele, Michele (c.1484–1559) Italian, born Verona; *Capella Pelegrini*, Verona (1527–57), *Palazzo Grimani*, Venice (1551–9).

Sansovino, Jacopo (originally Jacopo Tatti) (1486–1570) Italian, born Florence; *Library* (1537–60) and *Mint* (1537–45), Venice.

Schinkel, Karl Friederich (1781–1841) German, born Neurippen, Brandenburg; *War Memorial on the Kreuzberg* (1818), *Old Museum*, Berlin (1823–30).

Scott, Sir George Gilbert (1811–78) English, born Gawcott, Buckinghamshire; *Albert Memorial*, London (1862–3), *St Pancras station and hotel*, London (1865), *Glasgow University* (1865).

Serlio, Sebastiano (1475–1554) Italian, born Bologna; *Grand Ferrare*, Fontainebleau (1541–8), *Château*, Ancy-le-Franc, Tonnerre (from 1546).

Shaw, (Richard) Norman (1831–1912) English, born Edinburgh; *Old Swan House*, Chelsea (1876), *New Scotland Yard*, London (1888).

Smirke, Sir Robert (1781–1867) English, born London; *Covent Garden Theatre*, London (1809), *British Museum*, London (1823–47).

Smythson, Robert (c.1535–1614) English, place of birth unknown; *Wollaton Hall*, Nottingham (1580–8), *Hardwick Hall*, Derbyshire (1591–7).

Soane, Sir John (1753–1837) English, born near Reading; altered interior of *Bank of England* (1788–1833), *Dulwich College Art Gallery* (1811–14).

Soufflot, Jacques Germain (1713–80) French, born Irancy; *Hôtel Dieu*, Lyons (1741), *St Geneviève* (Panthéon), Paris (begun 1757).

Spence, Sir Basil Urwin (1907–76) Scottish, born India; Pavilions for *Festival of Britain* (1951), *Coventry Cathedral* (1951–62).

Stirling, Sir James (1926–92) Scottish, born Glasgow; *Department of Engineering*, Leicester University (1959–63) (with James Gowan), *History Faculty*, Cambridge (1965–8), *Florey Building*, Queen's College, Oxford (1966), *Neue Staatsgalerie*, Stuttgart (1980–4).

Street, George Edmund (1824–81) English, born Woodford, Essex; *London Law Courts* (1870–81).

Sullivan, Louis Henry (1856–1924) American, born Boston, Massachusetts; *Wainwright Building*, St Louis (1890), *Carson, Pirie and Scott Store*, Chicago (1899–1904).

Tange, Kenzo (1913–2005) Japanese, born Tokyo; *Hiroshima Peace Centre* (1949–55), *Shizoka Press and Broadcasting Centre*, Tokyo (1966–7).

Utzon, Jørn (1918–) Danish, born Copenhagen; *Sydney Opera House* (1956–68), *Kuwait House of Parliament* (1972–8).

Vanbrugh, Sir John (1664–1726) English, born London; *Castle Howard* (1699–1726), *Blenheim Palace* (1705–20).

Velde, Henri Clemens van de (1863–1957) Belgian, born Antwerp; *Werkbund Theatre*, Cologne (1914), *Museum Kröller-Muller*, Otterloo (1937–54).

Venturi, Robert Charles (1925–) American, born Philadelphia, Pennsylvania; *Brant-Johnson House*, Vail, Colorado (1976), *Sainsbury Wing* of the National Gallery, London (1986–91).

Vignola, Giacomo Barozzi da (1507–73) Italian, born Vignola; *Villa di Papa Giulio* (1550–5), *Church of The Gesu*, Rome (1586–73).

Viollet-le-Duc, Eugène Emmanuel (1814–79) French, born Paris; restored cathedral of *Notre Dame*, Paris (1845–64), *Château de Pierrefonds* (1858–70).

Vitruvius (in full **Marcus Vitruvius Pollio**) (1cBC) Roman; wrote the ten-volume *De Architectura* (35BC), the only extant Roman treatise on architecture.

Voysey, Charles Francis Annesley (1857–1941) English, born London; *Grove Town Houses*, Kensington (1891–2), *Sanderson's Wallpaper Factory*, Chiswick (1902).

Wagner, Otto (1841–1918) Austrian, born Penzing, near Vienna; stations for *Vienna Stadtbahn* (1894–7), *Post Office Savings Bank*, Vienna (1904–6).

Waterhouse, Alfred (1830–1905) English, born Liverpool; *Manchester Town Hall* (1867–77), *Natural History Museum*, South Kensington, London (1873–81).

Webb, Sir Aston (1849–1930) English, born London; *Admiralty Arch* (1903–10), *Imperial College of Science* (1906), eastern façade of *Buckingham Palace* (1912), all London.

Webb, Philip (1831–1915) English, born Oxford; *Red House*, Bexley (1859), *Clouds*, Wiltshire (1881–6), *Standen*, East Grinstead (1892).

Wood, John (the Elder) (1704–54) English. *Queen Square*, Bath (1729–36).

Wood, John (the Younger) (1728–82) English. *Royal Crescent*, Bath (1767–75), *Assembly Rooms*, Bath (1769–71).

Wren, Sir Christopher (1632–1723) English, born East Knoyle, Wiltshire; *Pembroke College Chapel*, Cambridge (1663–5), *The Sheldonian Theatre*, Oxford (1664), *Royal Greenwich Observatory* (1675–6), *St Paul's*, London (1675–1710), *Greenwich Hospital* (1696).

Wright, Frank Lloyd (1869–1959) American, born Richland Center, Wisconsin; *Larkin Building*, Buffalo (1904), *Robie House*, Chicago (1908), *Johnson Wax Factory*, Racine, Wisconsin (1936–9), *Falling Water*, Mill Run, Pennsylvania (1936), *Guggenheim Museum*, New York (begun 1942).

Wyatt, James (1746–1813) English, born Staffordshire; *London Pantheon* (1772), *Gothic Revival Country House*, Fonthill Abbey, Wiltshire (1796–1813).

Nobel Prizes 1986–2006

Nobel Prizes for Peace and Literature were first awarded in 1901.

Year	Peace	Literature	Economic Science
1986	Elie Wiesel	Wole Soyinka	James Buchanan, Jr
1987	Oscar Arias Sánchez	Joseph Brodsky	Robert Solow
1988	UN Peacekeeping Forces	Naguib Mahfouz	Maurice Allais
1989	Tenzin Gyatso (Dalai Lama)	Camilo José Cela	Trygve Haavelmo
1990	Mikhail Gorbachev	Octavio Paz	Harry Markowitz, Merton Miller, William Sharpe
1991	Aung San Suu Kyi	Nadine Gordimer	Ronald Coase
1992	Rigoberta Menchú Tum	Derek Walcott	Gary Becker
1993	Nelson Mandela, F W de Klerk	Toni Morrison	Robert Fogel, Douglass North
1994	Yasser Arafat, Shimon Peres, Yitzhak Rabin	Kenzaburo Ōe	John Harsanyi, John Nash, Reinhard Selten
1995	Joseph Rotblat and the Pugwash Conferences on Science and World Affairs	Seamus Heaney	Robert Lucas, Jr
1996	Carlos Filipe Ximenes Belo, José Ramos-Horta	Wislawa Szymborska	James Mirrlees, William Vickrey
1997	Jody Williams and the International Campaign to Ban Landmines	Dario Fo	Robert Merton, Myron Scholes
1998	John Hume, David Trimble	José Saramago	Amartya Sen
1999	Medécins Sans Frontières	Günter Grass	Robert Mundell
2000	Kim Dae Jung	Gao Xingjian	James Heckman, Daniel McFadden
2001	United Nations, Kofi Annan	V S Naipaul	George A Akerlof, A Michael Spence, Joseph E Stiglitz
2002	Jimmy Carter	Imre Kertész	Daniel Kahneman, Vernon L Smith
2003	Shirin Ebadi	J M Coetzee	Robert F Engle III, Clive W J Granger
2004	Wangari Maathai	Elfriede Jelenek	Finn E Kydland, Edward C Prescot

Year	Peace	Literature	Economic Science
2005	Mohamed ElBaradei and the International Atomic Energy Authority	Harold Pinter	Robert J Aumann, Thomas C Schelling
2006	Muhammad Yunus	Orhan Pamuk	Edmund S Phelps

THOUGHT AND BELIEF

Gods of Greek mythology

Adonis	God of vegetation and rebirth	Hebe	Goddess of youth
Aeolus	God of the winds	Hecate	Goddess of the moon
Alphito	Barley goddess of Argos	Helios	God of the sun
Aphrodite	Goddess of love and beauty	Hephaestus	God of fire
Apollo	God of prophecy, music, youth, archery and healing	Hera	Goddess of marriage and childbirth; queen of heaven
Ares	God of war	Hermes	Messenger of the gods
Arethusa	Goddess of springs and fountains	Hestia	Goddess of the hearth
		Hypnos	God of sleep
Artemis	Goddess of fertility, chastity and hunting	Iris	Goddess of the rainbow
		Morpheus	God of dreams
Asclepius	God of healing	Nemesis	God of destiny
Athene	Goddess of prudence and wise council; protectress of Athens	Nereus	God of the sea
		Nike	Goddess of victory
		Oceanus	God of the river Oceanus
Atlas	A Titan who bears up the earth	Pan	God of male sexuality and of herds
Attis	God of vegetation	Persephone	Goddess of the underworld and of corn
Boreas	God of the north wind		
Cronus	Father of Zeus	Poseidon	God of the sea
Cybele	Goddess of the earth	Rhea	The original mother goddess; wife of Cronus
Demeter	Goddess of the harvest		
Dionysus	God of wine, vegetation and ecstasy		
		Selene	Goddess of the moon
Eos	Goddess of the dawn	Thanatos	God of death
Eros	God of love	Zeus	Overlord of the Olympian gods and goddesses; god of the sky and all its properties
Gaia	Goddess of the earth		
Ganymede	God of rain		
Hades / Pluto	God of the underworld		

Principal Greek Gods

Rhea x Cronus
(Titans)

| Poseidon* | | | | | Demeter* (x Zeus) | | Hera* (x Zeus) |

ZEUS *   1. Metis†   2. Leto†   3. Maia†   4. Semele†   5. Dione†   Persephone

Athene*   Hermes*   Dionysus*   Aphrodite*

Apollo*   Artemis*   Ares*   Hebe   Eileithyia   Hephaestus*

* one of the 12 Olympians in the 'central group' of gods on the Parthenon frieze
† a consort of Zeus

Gods of Roman mythology

Apollo	God of the sun	Luna	Goddess of the moon
Bacchus	God of wine and ecstasy	Maia	Goddess of fertility
Bellona	Goddess of war	Mars	God of war
Ceres	Goddess of corn	Mercury	Messenger of the gods; also god of merchants
Consus	God of seed sowing		
Cupid	God of love	Minerva	Goddess of war, craftsmen, education and the arts
Diana	Goddess of fertility and hunting		
Egreria	Goddess of fountains and childbirth	Mithras	The sun god; god of regeneration
Epona	Goddess of horses	Neptune	God of the sea
Fauna	Goddess of fertility	Ops	Goddess of the harvest
Faunus	God of crops and herbs	Orcus	God of death
Feronia	Goddess of spring flowers	Pales	Goddess of flocks
		Penates	Gods of food and drink
Fides	God of honesty	Picus	God of woods
Flora	Goddess of fruitfulness and flowers	Pluto/Dis	God of the underworld
		Pomona	Goddess of fruit trees
Fortuna	Goddess of chance and fate	Portunus	God of husbands
		Proserpina	Goddess of the underworld
Genius	Protective god of individuals, groups and the state		
		Rumina	Goddess of nursing mothers
Janus	God of entrances, travel, the dawn		
		Saturn	God of fertility and agriculture
Juno	Goddess of marriage, childbirth, light		
		Silvanus	God of trees and forests
Jupiter	God of the sky and its attributes (sun, moon, thunder, rain, etc)	Venus	Goddess of spring, gardens and love
		Vertumnus	God of fertility
		Vesta	Goddess of the hearth
Lares	Gods of the house	Victoria	Goddess of victory
Liber Pater	God of agricultural and human fertility	Vulcan	God of fire
Libitina	Goddess of funeral rites		

Principal Roman gods

The twelve major gods of Olympus are shown in **bold** type.
* In some accounts, Vesta is supplanted by Bacchus.

Gods of Norse mythology

Aegir	God of the sea
Aesir	Race of warlike gods, including Odin, Thor, Tyr
Alcis	Twin gods of the sky
Balder	Son of Odin and favourite of the gods
Bor	Father of Odin
Bragi	God of poetry
Fafnir	Dragon god
Fjorgynn	Mother of Thor
Frey	God of fertility
Freyja	Goddess of libido
Frigg	Goddess of fertility; wife of Odin
Gefion	Goddess who received virgins after death
Heimdall	Guardian of the bridge Bifrost
Hel	Goddess of death; Queen of Niflheim, the land of mists
Hermod	Son of Odin
Hoder	Blind god who killed Balder
Hoenir	Companion to Odin and Loki
Idunn	Guardian goddess of the golden apples of youth; wife of Bragi
Kvasir	God of wise utterances
Logi	Fire god
Loki	God of mischief
Mimir	God of wisdom
Nanna	Goddess wife of Balder
Nehallenia	Goddess of plenty
Nerthus	Goddess of earth
Njord	God of ships and the sea
Norns	Goddesses of destiny
Odin (Woden, Wotan)	Chief of the Aesir family of gods, the 'father' god; the god of battle, death, inspiration
Otr	Otter god
Ran	Goddess of the sea
Sif	Goddess wife of Thor
Sigyn	Goddess wife of Loki
Thor (Donar)	God of thunder and sky; good crops
Tyr	God of battle
Ull	Stepson of Thor, an enchanter
Valkyries	Female helpers of the gods of war
Vanir	Race of benevolent gods, including Njord, Frey, Freyja
Vidar	Slayer of the wolf, Fenrir
Weland (Volundr, Wayland, Weiland)	Craftsman god

Gods of Egyptian mythology

Amun-Re	Universal god	Khonsou	Son of Amun-Re
Anubis	God of funerals	Maat	Goddess of order
Apis	God of fertility	Nephthys	Goddess of funerals
Aten	Unique god	Nut	God of the sky
Geb	God of the earth	Osiris	God of vegetation
Hathor	Goddess of love	Ptah	God of creation
Horus	God of light	Sekhmet	Goddess of might
Isis	Goddess of magic	Seth	God of evil
Khnum	Goddess of creation	Thoth	Supreme scribe

Baha'i

Founded   1863 in Persia.

Founder   Mirza Husayn Ali (1817–92), known as Baha'u'llah (Glory of God). He declared himself the prophet foretold by Mirza ali Mohammed (1819–50), a direct descendant of Muhammad, who proclaimed himself to be the Bab ('gate' or 'door').

Sacred texts   Most Holy Book, The Seven Valleys, The Hidden Words and The Bayan.

Beliefs   Baha'i teaches the oneness of God, the unity of all faiths, the inevitable unification of humankind, the harmony of all people, universal education, and obedience to government. It does not predict an end to this world or any intervention by God but believes there will be a change within man and society.

Organization   There is a network of elected local and national level bodies, and an elected international governing body. Although there is little formal ritual (most assemblies are simply gatherings of the claimed faithful), there are ceremonies for marriages and funerals, and there are shrines and temples.

Buddhism

Founded   c.500 BC in India.

Founder   Prince Siddhartha Gautama (c.560–c.480 BC) who became Buddha ('the enlightened one') through meditation.

Sacred texts   The Pali Canon or Tripitaka made up of the Vinaya Pitaka (monastic discipline), Sutta Pitaka (discourses of the Buddha) and the Abhidhamma Pitaka (analysis of doctrines). Other texts: the Mahayana Sutras, the Milindapanha (Questions of Milinda) and the Bardo Thodol (Tibetan Book of the Dead).

Beliefs   Buddha's teaching is summarized in the Four Noble Truths; suffering is always present in life; desire is the cause of suffering; freedom from suffering can be achieved by Nirvana (perfect peace and bliss); the Eightfold Path leads to Nirvana. Karma, by which good and evil deeds result in appropriate reward or punishment, and the cycle of rebirth can be broken by taking the Eightfold Path. All Buddhas are revered but particularly Gautama.

Organization   There is a monastic system which aims to create favourable conditions for spiritual development. This involves meditation, personal discipline and spiritual exercises in the hope of liberation from self. Buddhism has proved very flexible in adapting its organization, ceremony and pattern of belief to different cultural and social conditions. There are numerous festivals and ceremonies, and pilgrimage is of great spiritual value.

Divisions   There are two main traditions in Buddhism. Theravada Buddhism adheres to the teachings of the earliest Buddhist writings; salvation can be attained only by the few who accept the severe discipline and effort necessary to achieve it. Mahayana Buddhism developed later and is more flexible and creative, embracing popular piety. It teaches that salvation is possible for everyone and introduced the doctrine of the bodhisattva (one who attains enlightenment but out of compassion forestalls passing into Nirvana to help others achieve enlightenment). As Buddhism spread, other schools sprang up including Zen, Lamaism, Tendai, Nichiren and Soka Gakkai.

Major Buddhist Festivals

Weekly Uposatha Days, Buddha's Birth, Enlightenment, First Sermon and Death are observed in the different countries where Buddhism is practised but often on different dates. In some of these countries there are additional festivals in honour of Buddha.

Christianity

Founded 1c AD.

Founder Jesus Christ 'the Son of God' (c.4 BC–c.30 AD).

Sacred texts The Bible consisting of the Old and New Testaments. The New Testament written between AD 30 and AD 150 consists of the Gospels, the Acts of the Apostles, the Epistles and the Apocalypse.

Beliefs A monotheistic world religion, centred on the life and works of Jesus of Nazareth in Judaea, who proclaimed the most important rules of life to be love of God, followed by love of one's neighbour. Christians believe that Jesus was the Son of God who was put to death by crucifixion as a sacrifice in order to save humanity from the consequences of sin and death, and was raised from the dead; he makes forgiveness and reconciliation with God possible, and ensures eternal life for the repentant believer. The earliest followers of Jesus were Jews who believed him to be the Messiah or 'Saviour' promised by the prophets in the Old Testament. Christians believe he will come again to inaugurate the 'Kingdom of God'.

Organization Jesus Christ appointed twelve men to be his disciples:

1	Peter (brother of Andrew)
2	Andrew (brother of Peter)
3	James, son of Zebedee (brother of John)
4	John (brother of James)
5	Philip
6	Bartholomew
7	Thomas
8	Matthew
9	James of Alphaeus
10	Simon the Canaanite (in Matthew and Mark) or Simon 'the Zealot' (in Luke and the Acts)
11	Judas Iscariot

(Thaddeus in the book of Matthew and Mark is the twelfth disciple, while in Luke and the Acts the twelfth is Judas or James. Matthias succeeded to Judas's place.) Soon after the resurrection the disciples gathered for the festival of Pentecost and received special signs of the power of God, the Holy Spirit. The disciples became a defined new body, the Church. Through the witness of the Apostles and their successors, the Christian faith quickly spread and in AD 315 became the official religion of the Roman Empire. It survived the 'Dark Ages' to become the basis of civilization in the Middle Ages in Europe.

Divisions Major divisions – separated as a result of differences of doctrine and practice

– are the Orthodox or Eastern Church, the Roman Catholic Church, acknowledging the Bishop of Rome as head, and the Protestant Churches stemming from the split with the Roman Church in the 16c. All Christians recognize the authority of the Bible, read at public worship, which takes place at least every Sunday, to celebrate the resurrection of Jesus Christ. Most Churches recognize at least two sacraments (Baptism and the Eucharist, Mass, or Lord's Supper) as essential.

Major immovable Christian feasts

For Saints' Days ▶ page 315

1 Jan	Solemnity of Mary, Mother of God	15 Aug	Assumption of the Virgin Mary
6 Jan	Epiphany	22 Aug	Queenship of Mary
7 Jan	Christmas Day (*Eastern Orthodox*) [1]	8 Sep	Birthday of the Virgin Mary
		14 Sep	Exaltation of the Holy Cross
11 Jan	Baptism of Jesus	2 Oct	Guardian Angels
25 Jan	Conversion of Apostle Paul	1 Nov	All Saints
2 Feb	Presentation of Jesus (*Candlemas Day*)	2 Nov	All Souls
		9 Nov	Dedication of the Lateran Basilica
22 Feb	The Chair of Peter, Apostle	21 Nov	Presentation of the Virgin Mary
25 Mar	Annunciation of the Virgin Mary		
24 Jun	Birth of John the Baptist	8 Dec	Immaculate Conception
6 Aug	Transfiguration	25 Dec	Christmas Day
		28 Dec	Holy Innocents

[1] Fixed feasts in the Julian Calendar used by Eastern Orthodox churches fall 13 days later than the Gregorian Calendar date.

Movable Christian feasts 2006–2015

Year	Ash Wednesday	Easter	Ascension	Whit Sunday (Pentecost)	Trinity Sunday	Sundays after Trinity	Corpus Christi	Advent Sunday
2006	1 Mar	16 Apr	25 May	4 Jun	11 Jun	24	15 Jun	3 Dec
2007	21 Feb	8 Apr	17 May	27 May	3 Jun	25	7 Jun	2 Dec
2008	6 Feb	23 Mar	1 May	11 May	18 May	27	22 May	30 Nov
2009	25 Feb	12 Apr	21 May	31 May	7 Jun	24	11 Jun	29 Nov
2010	17 Feb	4 Apr	13 May	23 May	30 May	25	3 Jun	28 Nov
2011	9 Mar	24 Apr	2 Jun	12 Jun	19 Jun	22	23 Jun	27 Nov
2012	22 Feb	8 Apr	17 May	27 May	3 Jun	25	7 Jun	2 Dec
2013	13 Feb	31 Mar	9 May	19 May	26 May	26	30 May	1 Dec
2014	5 Mar	20 Apr	29 May	8 Jun	15 Jun	23	19 Jun	30 Nov
2015	18 Feb	5 Apr	14 May	24 May	31 May	25	4 Jun	29 Nov

Ash Wednesday, the first day of Lent, can fall at the earliest on 4 February and at the latest on 10 March.

Palm (Passion) Sunday is the Sunday before Easter; Good Friday is the Friday before Easter; Holy Saturday (often referred to as Easter Saturday) is the Saturday before Easter; Easter Saturday, in traditional usage, is the Saturday following Easter.

Easter Day can fall at the earliest on 22 March and at the latest on 25 April. Ascension Day can fall at the earliest on 30 April and at the latest on 3 June. Whit Sunday can fall at the earliest on 10 May and at the latest on 13 June. There are not fewer than 22 and not more than 27 Sundays after Trinity. Advent Sunday, or the first Sunday of Advent, is the Sunday nearest to 30 November.

Saints' days

Selected Saints' days are given below. The official recognition of Saints, and the choice of a Saint's Day, varies greatly between different branches of Christianity, calendars and localities. Only major variations are included below, using the following abbreviations:

C Coptic *E* Eastern *G* Greek *W* Western

■ **January**

1   Basil (*E*), Fulgentius, Telemachus
2   Basil and Gregory of Nazianzus
     (*W*), Macarius of Alexandria,
     Seraphim of Sarov
3   Geneviève
4   Angela of Foligno
5   Simeon Stylites (*W*)
7   Cedda, Lucian of Antioch (*W*),
     Raymond of Penyafort
8   Atticus (*E*), Gudule, Severinus
9   Hadrian the African
10   Agatho, Marcian
12   Ailred, Benedict Biscop
13   Hilary of Poitiers
14   Kentigern
15   Macarius of Egypt, Maurus, Paul
     of Thebes
16   Honoratus
17   Antony of Egypt
19   Wulfstan
20   Euthymius, Fabian, Sebastian
21   Agnes, Fructuosus, Maximus (*E*),
     Meinrad
22   Timothy (*G*), Vincent
23   Ildefonsus
24   Babylas (*W*), Francis de Sales
25   Gregory of Nazianzus (*E*)
26   Paula, Timothy and Titus,
     Xenophon (*E*)
27   Angela Merici
28   Ephraem Syrus (*E*), Paulinus of
     Nola, Thomas Aquinas
29   Gildas
31   John Bosco, Marcella

■ **February**

1   Brigid, Pionius
3   Anskar, Blaise (*W*), Werburga,
     Simeon (*E*)
4   Gilbert of Sempringham, Isidore
     of Pelusium, Phileas
5   Agatha, Avitus
6   Dorothy, Paul Miki and
     companions, Vedast
8   Theodore (*G*), Jerome Emiliani
9   Teilo
10   Scholastica
11   Benedict of Aniane, Blaise (*E*),
     Caedmon, Gregory II
12   Meletius
13   Agabus (*W*), Catherine dei Ricci,
     Priscilla (*E*)
14   Cyril and Methodius (*W*),
     Valentine (*W*)
16   Flavian (*E*), Pamphilus (*E*),
     Valentine (*E*)
18   Bernadette (*France*), Colman,
     Flavian (*W*), Leo I (*E*)
20   Wulfric
21   Peter Damian
23   Polycarp
25   Ethelbert, Tarasius, Walburga
26   Alexander (*W*), Porphyrius
27   Leander
28   Oswald of York

■ **March**

1   David
2   Chad, Simplicius
3   Ailred
4   Casimir
6   Chrodegang

7	Perpetua and Felicity
8	Felix, John of God, Pontius
9	Frances of Rome, Gregory of Nyssa, Pacian
10	John Ogilvie, Macarius of Jerusalem, Simplicius
11	Constantine, Oengus, Sophronius
12	Gregory (the Great)
13	Nicephorus
14	Benedict (E)
15	Clement Hofbauer
17	Gertrude, Joseph of Arimathea (W), Patrick
18	Anselm of Lucca, Cyril of Jerusalem, Edward
19	Joseph
20	Cuthbert, John of Parma, Martin of Braga
21	Serapion of Thmuis
22	Catherine of Sweden, Nicholas of Flüe
23	Turibius de Mongrovejo
30	John Climacus

■ April

1	Hugh of Grenoble, Mary of Egypt (E), Melito
2	Francis of Paola, Mary of Egypt (W)
3	Richard of Chichester
4	Isidore of Seville
5	Juliana of Liège, Vincent Ferrer
7	Hegesippus, John Baptist de la Salle
8	Agabus (E)
10	Fulbert
11	Gemma Galgani, Guthlac, Stanislaus
12	Julius I, Zeno
13	Martin I
15	Aristarchus, Pudus (E), Trophimus of Ephesus
17	Agapetus (E), Stephen Harding
18	Mme Acarie
19	Alphege, Leo IX
21	Anastasius (E), Anselm, Beuno, Januarius (E)
22	Alexander (C)

23	George
24	Egbert, Fidelis of Sigmaringen, Mellitus
25	Mark, Phaebadius
27	Zita
28	Peter Chanel, Vitalis and Valeria
29	Catherine of Siena, Hugh of Cluny, Peter Martyr, Robert
30	James (the Great) (E), Pius V

■ May

1	Asaph, Joseph the Worker, Walburga
2	Athanasius
3	Philip and James (the Less) (W)
4	Gotthard
5	Hilary of Arles
7	John of Beverley
8	John (E), Peter of Tarantaise
10	Antoninus, Comgall, John of Avila, Simon (E)
11	Cyril and Methodius (E), Mamertus
12	Epiphanius, Nereus and Achilleus, Pancras
14	Matthias (W)
16	Brendan, John of Nepomuk, Simon Stock
17	Robert Bellarmine, Paschal Baylon
18	John I
19	Dunstan, Ivo, Pudens (W), Pudentiana (W)
20	Bernardino of Siena
21	Helena (E)
22	Rita of Cascia
23	Ivo of Chartres
24	Vincent of Lérins
25	Aldhelm, Bede, Gregory VII, Mary Magdalene de Pazzi
26	Philip Neri, Quadratus
27	Augustine of Canterbury
30	Joan of Arc

■ June

1	Justin Martyr, Pamphilus
2	Erasmus, Marcellinus and Peter, Nicephorus (G), Pothinus

3   Charles Lwanga and companions, Clotilde, Kevin
4   Optatus, Petrock
5   Boniface
6   Martha (E), Norbert
7   Paul of Constantinople (W), Willibald
8   William of York
9   Columba, Cyril of Alexandria (E), Ephraem (W)
11   Barnabas, Bartholomew (E)
12   Leo III
13   Anthony of Padua
15   Orsisius, Vitus
17   Alban, Botulph
19   Gervasius and Protasius, Jude (E), Romuald
20   Alban
21   Alban of Mainz, Aloysius Gonzaga
22   John Fisher and Thomas More, Niceta, Pantaenus (C), Paulinus of Nola
23   Etheldreda
24   Birth of John the Baptist
25   Prosper of Aquitaine
27   Cyril of Alexandria (W), Ladislaus
28   Irenaeus
29   Peter and Paul
30   First Martyrs of the Church of Rome

■ July
1   Cosmas and Damian (E), Oliver Plunkett
3   Anatolius, Thomas
4   Andrew of Crete (E), Elizabeth of Portugal, Ulrich
5   Anthony Zaccaria
6   Maria Goretti
7   Palladius, Pantaenus
8   Kilian, Aquila and Prisca (W)
11   Benedict (W), Pius I
12   John Gualbert, Veronica
13   Henry II, Mildred, Silas
14   Camillus of Lellis, Deusdedit, Nicholas of the Holy Mountain (E)
15   Bonaventure, Jacob of Nisibis, Swithin, Vladimir

16   Eustathius, Our Lady of Mt Carmel
17   Ennodius, Leo IV, Marcellina, Margaret (E), Scillitan Martyrs
18   Arnulf, Philastrius
19   Macrina, Symmachus
20   Aurelius, Margaret (W)
21   Lawrence of Brindisi, Praxedes
22   Mary Magdalene
23   Apollinaris, Bridget of Sweden
25   Anne and Joachim (E), Christopher, James (the Great) (W)
26   Anne and Joachim (W)
27   Pantaleon
28   Innocent I, Samson, Victor I
29   Lupus, Martha (W), Olave
30   Peter Chrysologus, Silas (G)
31   Giovanni Colombini, Germanus, Joseph of Arimathea (E), Ignatius of Loyola

■ August
1   Alphonsus Liguori, Ethelwold
2   Eusebius of Vercelli, Stephen I
4   Jean-Baptiste Vianney
6   Hormisdas
7   Cajetan, Sixtus II and companions
8   Dominic
9   Matthias (G)
10   Laurence, Oswald of Northumbria
11   Clare, Susanna
13   Maximus (W), Pontian and Hippolytus, Radegunde
14   Maximilian Kolbe
15   Arnulf, Tarsicius
16   Roch, Simplicianus, Stephen of Hungary
17   Hyacinth
19   John Eudes, Sebaldus
20   Bernard, Oswin, Philibert
21   Jane Frances de Chantal, Pius X
23   Rose of Lima, Sidonius Apollinaris
24   Bartholomew (W), Ouen
25   Joseph Calasanctius, Louis IX, Menas of Constantinople
26   Blessed Dominic of the Mother of God, Zephyrinus
27   Caesarius, Monica

28   Augustine of Hippo

29   Beheading of John the Baptist, Sabina

30   Pammachius

31   Aidan, Paulinus of Trier

■ September

1   Giles, Simeon Stylites (E)

2   John the Faster (E)

3   Gregory (the Great)

4   Babylas (E), Boniface I

5   Zacharias (E)

9   Peter Claver, Sergius of Antioch

10   Finnian, Nicholas of Tolentino, Pulcheria

11   Deiniol, Ethelburga, Paphnutius

13   John Chrysostom (W)

15   Catherine of Genoa, Our Lady of Sorrows

16   Cornelius, Cyprian of Carthage, Euphemia, Ninian

17   Robert Bellarmine, Hildegard, Lambert, Satyrus

19   Januarius (W), Theodore of Tarsus

20   Agapetus or Eustace (W)

21   Matthew (W)

23   Adamnan, Linus

25   Sergius of Rostov

26   Cosmas and Damian (W), Cyprian of Antioch, John (E)

27   Frumentius (W), Vincent de Paul

28   Exuperius, Wenceslaus

29   Michael (*Michaelmas Day*), Gabriel and Raphael

30   Jerome, Otto

■ October

1   Remigius, Romanos, Teresa of the Child Jesus

2   Leodegar (Leger)

3   Teresa of Lisieux, Thomas de Cantilupe

4   Ammon, Francis of Assisi, Petronius

6   Bruno, Thomas (G)

9   Demetrius (W), Denis and companions, Dionysius of Paris, James (the Less) (E), John Leonardi

10   Francis Borgia, Paulinus of York

11   Atticus (E), Bruno, Nectarius

12   Wilfrid

13   Edward the Confessor

14   Callistus I, Cosmas Melodus (E)

15   Lucian of Antioch (E), Teresa of Avila

16   Gall, Hedwig, Lullus, Margaret Mary Alacoque

17   Ignatius of Antioch, Victor

18   Luke

19   John de Bréboeuf and Isaac Jogues and companions, Paul of the Cross, Peter of Alcantara

21   Hilarion, Ursula

22   Abercius

23   John of Capistrano

24   Anthony Claret

25   Crispin and Crispinian, Forty Martyrs of England and Wales, Gaudentius

26   Demetrius (E)

28   Firmilian (E), Simon and Jude

30   Serapion of Antioch

31   Wolfgang

■ November

1   All Saints, Cosmas and Damian (E)

2   Eustace (E), Victorinus

3   Hubert, Malachy, Martin de Porres, Pirminius, Winifred

4   Charles Borromeo, Vitalis and Agricola

5   Elizabeth (W)

6   Illtyd, Leonard, Paul of Constantinople (E)

7   Willibrord

8   Elizabeth (E), Willehad

9   Simeon Metaphrastes (E)

10   Justus, Leo I (W)

11   Martin of Tours (W), Menas of Egypt, Theodore of Studios

12   Josaphat, Martin of Tours (E), Nilus the Ascetic

13   Abbo, John Chrysostom (E), Nicholas I

14   Dubricius, Gregory Palamas (E)

15   Albert the Great, Machutus

16 Edmund of Abingdon, Eucherius, Gertrude (the Great), Margaret of Scotland, Matthew (E)
17 Elizabeth of Hungary, Gregory Thaumaturgus, Gregory of Tours, Hugh of Lincoln
18 Odo, Romanus
19 Mechthild, Nerses
20 Edmund the Martyr
21 Gelasius
22 Cecilia
23 Amphilochius, Clement I (W), Columban, Felicity, Gregory of Agrigentum
25 Clement I (E), Mercurius, Mesrob
26 Siricius
27 Barlam and Josaphat
28 Simeon Metaphrastes
29 Cuthbert Mayne
30 Andrew, Frumentius (G)

■ December
1 Eligius
2 Chromatius
3 Francis Xavier
4 Barbara, John Damascene, Osmund
5 Clement of Alexandria, Sabas
6 Nicholas
7 Ambrose
10 Miltiades
11 Damasus, Daniel
12 Jane Frances de Chantal, Spyridon (E), Vicelin
13 Lucy, Odilia
14 John of the Cross, Spyridon (W)
16 Eusebius
18 Frumentius (C)
20 Ignatius of Antioch (G)
21 Peter Canisius, Thomas
22 Anastasia (E), Chrysogonus (E)
23 John of Kanty
26 Stephen (W)
27 John (W), Fabiola, Stephen (E)
29 Thomas à Becket, Trophimus of Arles
31 Sylvester

Patron saints of occupations

Accountants	Matthew
Actors	Genesius, Vitus
Advertisers	Bernardino of Siena
Architects	Thomas (Apostle)
Artists	Luke, Angelico
Astronauts	Joseph (Cupertino)
Astronomers	Dominic
Athletes	Sebastian
Authors	Francis de Sales
Aviators	Our Lady of Loreto
Bakers	Honoratus
Bankers	Bernardino (Feltre)
Barbers	Cosmas and Damian
Blacksmiths	Eligius
Bookkeepers	Matthew
Book trade	John of God
Brewers	Amand, Wenceslaus
Builders	Barbara, Thomas (Apostle)
Butchers	Luke
Carpenters	Joseph
Chemists	Cosmas and Damian
Comedians	Vitus
Cooks	Lawrence, Martha
Dancers	Vitus
Dentists	Apollonia
Doctors	Cosmas and Damian, Luke
Editors	Francis de Sales
Farmers	Isidore
Firemen	Florian
Fishermen	Andrew, Peter
Florists	Dorothy, Teresa of Lisieux
Gardeners	Adam, Fiacre
Glassworkers	Luke, Lucy
Gravediggers	Joseph of Arimathea
Grocers	Michael
Hotelkeepers	Amand, Julian the Hospitaler
Housewives	Martha
Jewellers	Eligius

Journalists	Francis de Sales	Scholars	Thomas Aquinas
Labourers	James, John Bosco	Scientists	Albert the Great
Lawyers	Ivo, Thomas More	Sculptors	Luke, Louis
Librarians	Jerome, Catherine of Alexandria	Secretaries	Genesius
		Servants	Martha, Zita
Merchants	Francis of Assisi	Shoemakers	Crispin, Crispinian
Messengers	Gabriel	Singers	Cecilia, Gregory
Metalworkers	Eligius	Soldiers	George, Joan of Arc, Martin of Tours, Sebastian
Midwives	Raymond Nonnatus		
Miners	Anne, Barbara		
Motorists	Christopher	Students	Thomas Aquinas
Musicians	Cecilia, Gregory the Great	Surgeons	Luke, Cosmas and Damian
Nurses	Camillus de Lellis, John of God	Tailors	Homobonus
Philosophers	Thomas Aquinas, Catherine of Alexandria	Tax collectors	Matthew
		Taxi drivers	Fiacre
Poets	Cecilia, David	Teachers	Gregory the Great, John Baptiste de la Salle
Police	Michael		
Politicians	Thomas More	Theologians	Augustine, Alphonsus Liguori, Thomas Aquinas
Postal workers	Gabriel		
		Television workers	Gabriel
Priests	Jean-Baptiste Vianney		
Printers	John of God	Undertakers	Dismas, Joseph of Arimathea
Prisoners	Leonard		
Radio workers	Gabriel	Waiters	Martha
		Writers	Lucy
Sailors	Christopher, Erasmus, Francis of Paola		

Confucianism

Founded 6c BC in China.

Founder K'ung Fu-tse (Confucius) (c.551–479 BC).

Sacred texts Shih Ching, Li Ching, Shu Ching, Chu'un Ch'iu, I Ching.

Beliefs The oldest school of Chinese thought, Confucianism did not begin as a religion. Confucius was concerned with the best way to behave and live in this world and was not concerned with the afterlife. He emerges as a great moral teacher who tried to replace the old religious observances with moral values as the basis of social and political order. He laid particular emphasis on the family as the basic unit in society and the foundation of the whole community. He believed that government was a matter of moral responsibility, not just manipulation of power.

Organization Confucianism is not an institution and has no church or clergy. However, ancestor-worship and veneration of the sky have their sources in Confucian texts. Weddings and funerals follow a tradition handed down by Confucian scholars. Social life is ritualized and colour and patterns of clothes have a sacred meaning.

Divisions There are two ethical strands in Confucianism. One, associated with Confucius and Hsun Tzu (c.298–238 BC), is conventionalistic: we ought to follow the traditional codes of behaviour for their own sake. The other, associated with Mencius (c.371–289 BC) and medieval neo-Confucians, is intuitionistic: we ought to do as our moral natures dictate.

Major Chinese festivals

January/February	Chinese New Year
February/March	Lantern Festival
March/April	Festival of Pure Brightness
May/June	Dragon Boat Festival
July/August	Herd Boy and Weaving Maid Festival
August	All Souls' Festival
September	Mid-Autumn Festival
September/October	Double Ninth Festival
November/December	Winter Solstice

Hinduism

Founded c.1500 BC by Aryan invaders of India with their Vedic religion.

Sacred texts The Vedas ('knowledge'), including the Upanishads which contain much that is esoteric and mystical. Also included are the epic poems the Ramayana and the Mahabharata. Best known of all is the Bhagavad Gita, part of the Mahabharata.

Beliefs Hinduism emphasizes the right way of living (dharma) and embraces many diverse religious beliefs and practices rather than a set of doctrines. It acknowledges many gods who are seen as manifestations of an underlying reality. Devout Hindus aim to become one with the 'absolute reality' or Brahman. Only after a completely pure life will the soul be released from the cycle of rebirth. Until then the soul will be repeatedly reborn. Samsara refers to the cycle of birth and rebirth. Karma is the law by which consequences of actions within one life are carried over into the next.

Organization There is very little formal structure. Hinduism is concerned with the realization of religious values in every part of life, yet there is a great emphasis on the performance of complex demanding rituals under the supervision of a Brahman priest and teacher. There are three categories of worship: temple, domestic and congregational. The most common ceremony is prayer (puja). Many pilgrimages take place and there is an annual cycle of festivals.

Divisions As there is no concept of orthodoxy in Hinduism, there are many different sects worshipping different gods. The three most important gods are Brahman, the primeval god, Vishnu, the preserver, and Shiva, both destroyer and creator of life. The three major living traditions are those devoted to Vishnu, Shiva and the goddess Shakti. Folk beliefs and practices exist together with sophisticated philosophical schools.

Major Hindu festivals

Chaitra S 9	Ramanavami (Birthday of Lord Rama)
Asadha S 2	Rathayatra (Pilgrimage of the Jagannatha Chariot at Puri)
Sravana S 11–15	Jhulanayatra (Swinging the Lord Krishna)
Sravana S 15	Rakshabandhana (Tying on Lucky Threads)
Bhadrapada K 8	Janamashtami (Birthday of Lord Krishna)
Asvina S 7–10	Durga-puja (Homage to Goddess Durga) (*Bengal*)
Asvina S 1–10	Navaratri (Festival of Nine Nights)
Asvina S 15	Lakshmi-puja (Homage to Goddess Lakshmi)

Asvina K 15	Diwali, Dipavali (String of Lights)
Kartikka S 15	Guru Nanak Jananti (Birthday of Guru Nanak)
Magha K 5	Sarasvati-puja (Homage to Goddess Sarasvati)
Magha K 13	Maha-sivaratri (Great Night of Lord Shiva)
Phalguna S 14	Holi (Festival of Fire)
Phalguna S 15	Dolayatra (Swing Festival) (*Bengal*)

S = Sukla ('waxing fortnight') K = Krishna ('waning fortnight')

Islam

Founded 7C AD.

Founder Muhammad (c.570–c.632).

Sacred texts The Koran, the word of God as revealed to Muhammad, and the Hadith, a collection of the prophet's sayings.

Beliefs A monotheistic religion: God is the creator of all things and holds absolute power over man. All persons should devote themselves to lives of grateful and praise-giving obedience to God as they will be judged on the Day of Resurrection. It is acknowledged that Satan often misleads humankind but those who have obeyed God or have repented of their sins will dwell in paradise. Those sinners who are unrepentant will go to hell. Muslims accept the Old Testament and acknowledge Jesus Christ as an important prophet, but they believe the perfect word of God was revealed to Muhammad. Islam imposes five pillars of faith on its followers: belief in one God and his prophet, Muhammad; salat, formal prayer preceded by ritual cleansing five times a day, facing Mecca; saum, fasting during the month of Ramadan; Hajj, pilgrimage to Mecca at least once; zakat, a religious tax on the rich to provide for the poor.

Organization There is no organized priesthood but great respect is accorded to descendants of Muhammad and holy men, scholars and teachers such as mullahs and ayatollahs. The Shari'a is the Islamic law and applies to all aspects of life, not just religious practices.

Divisions There are two main groups within Islam. The Sunni are the majority and the more orthodox. They recognize the succession from Muhammad to Abu Bakr, his father-in-law, and to the next three caliphs. The Shiites are followers of Ali, Muhammad's cousin and son-in-law. They believe in twelve imams, perfect teachers, who still guide the faithful from paradise. Shi'ah practice tends towards the ecstatic. There are many other subsects including the Sufis, the Ismailis and the Wahhabis.

Major Islamic festivals

1 Muharram	New Year's Day; starts on the day which celebrates Muhammad's departure from Mecca to Medina in AD 622.
12 Rabi I	Birthday of Muhammad (Mawlid al-Nabi) AD 572; celebrated throughout month of Rabi I.
27 Rajab	'Night of Ascent' (Laylat al-Miraj) of Muhammad to Heaven.
1 Ramadan	Beginning of month of fasting during daylight hours.
27 Ramadan	'Night of Power' (Laylat al-Qadr); sending down of the Koran to Muhammad.
1 Shawwal	'Feast of Breaking the Fast' (Id al-Fitr); marks the end of Ramadan.
8–13 Dhu-l-Hijja	Annual pilgrimage ceremonies at and around Mecca; month during which the great pilgrimage (Hajj) should be made.
10 Dhu-l-Hijja	Feast of the Sacrifice (Id al-Adha).

Jainism

Founded 6c BC in India.

Founder Vardhamana Mahavira (c.540–468 BC).

Sacred texts Svetambara canon of scripture and Digambara texts.

Beliefs Jainism is derived from the ancient jinas ('those who overcome'). They believe that salvation consists in conquering material existence through adhering to a strict ascetic discipline, thus freeing the 'soul' from the working of karma for eternal, all-knowing bliss. Liberation requires detachment from worldly existence, an essential part of which is Ahimsa, non-injury to living beings. Jains are also strict vegetarians.

Organization Like Buddhists, the Jains are dedicated to the quest for liberation and the life of the ascetic. However, rather than congregating in monastic centres, Jain monks and nuns have developed a strong relationship with lay people. There are temple rituals resembling Hindu puja. There is also a series of lesser vows and specific religious practices that give the lay person an identifiable religious career.

Divisions There are two categories of religious and philosophical literature. The Svetambara have a canon of scripture consisting of 45 texts, including a group of 11 texts in which the sermons and dialogues of Mahavira himself are collected. The Digambara hold that the original teachings of Mahavira have been lost but that their texts preserve accurately the substance of the original message. This disagreement over scriptures has not led to fundamental doctrinal differences.

Judaism

Founded c.2000 BC.

Founder Abraham (c.2000–1650 BC), with whom God made a covenant, and Moses (15c–13c BC), who gave the Israelites the law.

Sacred texts The Hebrew Bible, consisting of 24 books, the most important of which are the Torah or Pentateuch – the first five books. Also the Talmud made up of the Mishna, the oral law, and the Gemara, an extensive commentary.

Beliefs A monotheistic religion: God is the creator of the world, delivered the Israelites out of bondage in Egypt, revealed his law to them, and chose them to be a light to all humankind. However varied their communities, Jews see themselves as members of a community whose origins lie in the patriarchal period. Ritual is very important and the family is the basic unit of ritual.

Organization Originally a theocracy, the basic institution is now the synagogue, operated by the congregation and led by a rabbi of their choice. The chief rabbis in France and Britain have authority over those who accept it; in Israel the two chief rabbis have civil authority in family law. The synagogue is the centre for community worship and study. Its main feature is the 'ark' (a cupboard) containing the handwritten scrolls of the Pentateuch. Daily life is governed by a number of practices and observances: male children are circumcised, the Sabbath is observed, and food has to be correctly prepared. The most important festival is the Passover, which celebrates the liberation of the Israelites from Egypt.

Divisions Today most Jews are descendants of either the Ashkenazim or the Sephardim, each with marked cultural differences. There are also several religious branches of Judaism from ultra-liberal to ultra-conservative, reflecting different points of view regarding the binding character of the prohibitions and duties prescribed for Jews.

Major Jewish festivals

1–2 Tishri	Rosh Hashana (New Year)
3 Tishri	Tzom Gedaliahu (Fast of Gedaliah)
10 Tishri	Yom Kippur (Day of Atonement)
15–21 Tishri	Sukkot (Feast of Tabernacles)
22 Tishri	Shemini Atzeret (8th Day of the Solemn Assembly)
23 Tishri	Simchat Torah (Rejoicing of the Law)
25 Kislev to 2–3 Tevet	Hanukkah (Feast of Dedication)
10 Tevet	Asara be-Tevet (Fast of 10th Tevet)
13 Adar	Taanit Esther (Fast of Esther)
14–15 Adar	Purim (Feast of Lots)
15–22 Nisan	Pesach (Passover)
5 Iyar	Israel Independence Day
6–7 Sivan	Shavuot (Feast of Weeks)
17 Tammuz	Shiva Asar be-Tammuz (Fast of 17th Tammuz)
9 Av	Tisha be-Av (Fast of 9th Av)

Shintoism

Founded 8c AD in Japan.

Sacred texts Kojiki and Nihon Shoki.

Beliefs Shinto 'the teaching' or 'way of the gods', came into existence independently from Buddhism which was coming to the mainland of Japan at that time. It subsequently incorporated many features of Buddhism. Founded on the nature-worship of Japanese folk religions, it is made up of many elements; animism, veneration of nature and ancestor-worship. Its gods are known as kami and there are many ceremonies appealing to these kami for benevolent treatment and protection. Great stress is laid on the harmony between humans, their kami and nature. Moral and physical purity is a basic law. Death and other pollutions are to be avoided. Shinto is primarily concerned with life and this world and the good of the group. Followers must show devotion and sincerity but aberrations can be erased by purification procedures.

Organization As a set of prehistoric agricultural ceremonies, Shinto was never supported by a body of philosophical or moralistic literature. Shamans originally performed the ceremonies and tended the shrines, then gradually a particular tribe took over the ceremonies. In the 8c Shinto became political when the imperial family were ascribed divine origins and state Shintoism was established.

Divisions In the 19c Shinto was divided into Shrine (jinga) Shinto and Sectarian (kyoko) Shinto. Jinga became a state cult and it remained the national religion until 1945.

Major Japanese festivals

1–3 Jan	Oshogatsu (New Year)
3 Mar	Ohinamatsuri (Doll's or Girls' Festival)
5 May	Tango no Sekku (Boys' Festival)
7 Jul	Hoshi matsuri or Tanabata (Star Festival)
13–31 Jul	Obon (Buddhist All Souls)

Sikhism

Founded 15c in India.

Founder Guru Nanak (1469–1539).

Sacred text Adi Granth.

Beliefs Nanak preached tolerance and devotion to one God before whom everyone is equal. Sikh is the Sanskrit word for disciple. Nanak's doctrine sought a fusion of Brahmanism and Islam on the grounds that both were monotheistic. God is the true Guru and his divine word has come to humanity through the ten historical gurus. The line ended in 1708, since when the Sikh community has been called guru.

Organization There is no priestly caste and all Sikhs are empowered to perform rituals connected with births, marriages and deaths. Sikhs worship in their own temples but they evolved distinct features like the langar, 'kitchen', a communal meal where people of any religion or caste could eat. Rest houses for travellers were also provided. The tenth guru instituted an initiation ceremony, the Khalsa. Initiates wear the Five Ks (uncut hair, steel bangle, comb, shorts, ceremonial sword) and a turban. Members of the Khalsa add the name Singh (lion) to their name and have to lead pure lives and follow a code of discipline. Sikhs generally rise before dawn, bathe and recite the japji, a morning prayer. Hindu festivals from northern India are observed.

Divisions There are several religious orders of Sikhs based either on disputes over the succession of gurus or points of ritual and tradition. The most important current issue is the number of Khalsa Sikhs cutting off their hair and beards and relapsing into Hinduism.

Taoism

Founded 600 BC in China.

Founder Lao-tzu (6c BC).

Sacred texts Chuang-tzu, Lao-tzu (Tao-te-ching).

Beliefs Taoism is Chinese for 'the school of the tao' and the 'Taoist religion'. Tao ('the way') is central in both Confucianism and Taoism. The former stresses the tao of humanity, the latter the tao of nature, harmony with which ensures appropriate conduct. Taoist religion developed later and was probably influenced by Buddhist beliefs. The doctrine emphasizes that good and evil action decide the fate of the soul. The Taoists believe that the sky, the earth and water are deities; that Lao-tzu is supreme master; that the disciple masters his body and puts evil spirits to flight with charms; that body and spirit are purified through meditation and by taking the pill of immortality to gain eternal life; and that the way is handed down from master to disciple. Religious Taoism incorporated ideas and images from philosophical Taoist texts, especially the Tao-te-ching but also the theory of Yin-Yang, the quest for immortality, mental and physical discipline, interior hygiene, internal alchemy, healing and exorcism, a pantheon of gods and spirits, and ideals of theocratic states. The Immortals are meant to live in the mountains far from the tumult of the world.

Organization This is similar to Buddhism in the matter of clergy and temple. The jiao is a ceremony to purify the ground. Zhon-gyual is the only important religious festival, when the hungry dead appear to the living and Taoist priests free the souls of the dead from suffering.

Divisions Religious Taoism emerged from many sects. These sects proliferated between 618 and 1126 AD and were described collectively as Spirit Cloud Taoists. They form the majority of Taoist priests in Taiwan, where they are called 'Masters of Methods' or Red-headed Taoists. The more orthodox priests are called 'Tao Masters' or Black-headed Taoists.

Sacred texts of world religions

Baha'i Most Holy Book, The Seven Valleys, The Hidden Words, The Bayan

Buddhism Tripitaka, Mahayana Sutras, Milindapanha, Bardo Thodol

Christianity Old Testament: Genesis, Exodus, Leviticus, Numbers, Deuteronomy, Joshua, Judges, Ruth, 1 Samuel, 2 Samuel, 1 Kings, 2 Kings, 1 Chronicles, 2 Chronicles, Ezra, Nehemiah, Esther, Job, Psalms, Proverbs, Ecclesiastes, Song of Solomon, Isaiah, Jeremiah, Lamentations, Ezekiel, Daniel, Hosea, Joel, Amos, Obadiah, Jonah, Micah, Nahum, Habakkuk, Zephaniah, Haggai, Zechariah, Malachi. New Testament: Matthew, Mark, Luke, John, Acts of the Apostles, Romans, 1 Corinthians, 2 Corinthians, Galatians, Ephesians, Philippians, Colossians, 1 Thessalonians, 2 Thessalonians, 1 Timothy, 2 Timothy, Titus, Philemon, Hebrews, James, 1 Peter, 2 Peter, 1 John, 2 John, 3 John, Jude, Revelation. Apocrypha (Revised Standard Version 1957): 1 Esdras, 2 Esdras, Tobit, Judith, Additions to Esther, Wisdom of Solomon, Ecclesiasticus, Epistle of Jeremiah, Baruch, Prayer of Azariah and the Song of the Three Young Men, (History of) Susanna, Bel and the Dragon, Prayer of Manasseh, 1 Maccabees, 2 Maccabees. (The Authorized version incorporates Jeremiah into Baruch; the prayer of Azariah is simply called the Song of the Three Holy Children. The Roman Catholic Church includes Tobit, Judith, all of Esther, Maccabees 1 and 2, Wisdom of Solomon, Ecclesiasticus and Baruch in its canon.)

Confucianism Shih ching, Li ching, Shu ching, Chu'un Ch'iu, I Ching

Hinduism The Vedas (including the Upanishads), Ramayana, Mahabharata and the Bhagavad Gita

Islam The Koran, the Hadith

Jainism Svetambara canon, Digambara texts

Judaism The Hebrew Bible: Torah (Pentateuch): Genesis, Exodus, Leviticus, Numbers, Deuteronomy. Also the books of the Prophets, Psalms, Chronicles and Proverbs. The Talmud including the Mishna and Gemara. The Zohar (Book of Splendour) is a famous Cabalistic book.

Shintoism Kojiki, Nihon Shoki

Sikhism Adi Granth

Taoism Chuang-tzu, Lao-tzu (Tao-te-ching)

Religious symbols

The Trinity

Equilateral triangle   Triangle in circle   Circle within triangle

Father   **God Son**   **Holy Spirit**

All-seeing eye   Fish   Sevenfold flame

Seven branch candlestick
The Menorah   Abraham   Pentateuch (The Law)   Doorposts and lintel (Passover)   Twelve tribes of Israel   Star of David

Crosses

Barbée   Trefly   Canterbury   Celtic   Cercelée   Cross crosslet

Crux ansata   Globical   Graded (Calvary)   Greek   Iona   Jerusalem

Latin   Maltese   Millvine   Papal   Patée   Patée formée   Patriarchal (or Lorraine)

Potent   Raguly or Ragulée   Russian Orthodox   St Andrews (Saltire)   St Peters   Tau (St Anthony's)

Ankh (Egyptian)   Yin-yang (Taoism; symbol of harmony)   torii (shinto)   Om (Hinduism, Buddhism, Jainism; sacred syllable)   Ik-onkar (Sikhism; symbol of God)   Swastika (traditional; symbol of wellbeing)   Yantra: Sri Cakra (wheel of fortune)

Signs of the zodiac

Fire signs	Earth signs	Air signs	Water signs
Aries	Capricorn	Libra	Cancer
21 Mar–19 Apr	*22 Dec–19 Jan*	*23 Sep–23 Oct*	*22 Jun–22 Jul*
Leo	Taurus	Aquarius	Scorpio
23 Jul–22 Aug	*20 Apr–20 May*	*20 Jan–18 Feb*	*24 Oct–21 Nov*
Sagittarius	Virgo	Gemini	Pisces
22 Nov–21 Dec	*23 Aug–22 Sep*	*21 May–21 Jun*	*19 Feb–20 Mar*

SPORTS AND GAMES

Olympic Games

First Modern Olympic Games took place in 1896, founded by Frenchman Baron de Coubertin (1863–1937); held every four years; women first competed in 1900; first separate Winter Games celebrations in 1924.

Venues

■ Summer Games

1896	Athens, Greece	1960	Rome, Italy
1900	Paris, France	1964	Tokyo, Japan
1904	St Louis, USA	1968	Mexico City, Mexico
1908	London, UK	1972	Munich, W Germany
1912	Stockholm, Sweden	1976	Montreal, Canada
1920	Antwerp, Belgium	1980	Moscow, USSR
1924	Paris, France	1984	Los Angeles, USA
1928	Amsterdam, Netherlands	1988	Seoul, South Korea
1932	Los Angeles, USA	1992	Barcelona, Spain
1936	Berlin, Germany	1996	Atlanta, USA
1948	London, UK	2000	Sydney, Australia
1952	Helsinki, Finland	2004	Athens, Greece
1956	Melbourne, Australia	2008	Beijing, China
		2012	London, UK

■ Winter Games

1924	Chamonix, France	1972	Sapporo, Japan
1928	St Moritz, Switzerland	1976	Innsbruck, Austria
1932	Lake Placid, New York, USA	1980	Lake Placid, New York, USA
1936	Garmisch-Partenkirchen, Germany	1984	Sarajevo, Yugoslavia
1948	St Moritz, Switzerland	1988	Calgary, Canada
1952	Oslo, Norway	1992	Albertville, France
1956	Cortina, Italy	1994	Lillehammer, Norway
1960	Squaw Valley, California, USA	1998	Nagano, Japan
1964	Innsbruck, Austria	2002	Salt Lake City, USA
1968	Grenoble, France	2006	Turin, Italy
		2010	Vancouver, Canada

Olympic Games were also held in 1906 in Athens, Greece, to commemorate the tenth anniversary of the birth of the modern Games. The 1956 equestrian events were held at Stockholm, Sweden, owing to quarantine laws in Australia. In 1994, the Winter Games celebrations were readjusted to take place every four years between the Summer Games years.

Leading medal winners

Summer Games (to 2004)					Winter Games (to 2006)				
Nation	G	S	B	Total	Nation	G	S	B	Total
1 USA	897	691	605	2193	1 Russia[1]	121	89	86	296
2 Russia[1]	526	437	410	1373	2 Norway	96	100	84	280
3 Germany[2]	231	274	304	809	3 Germany[2]	79	80	58	217
4 Great Britain	189	242	234	665	4 USA	78	81	58	217
5 France	183	191	213	587	5 Austria	51	64	71	186
6 Italy	182	147	164	493	6 Finland	41	58	52	151
7 Sweden	141	155	173	469	7 Canada	37	38	44	119
8 Hungary	156	136	156	448	8 Sweden	43	32	43	118
9 E Germany	153	129	127	409	9 Switzerland	38	37	43	118
10 Australia	120	126	152	398	10 E Germany	39	36	35	110

G=Gold; S=Silver; B=Bronze
[1] Includes medals won by the former USSR team, and by the Unified Team (Armenia, Azerbaijan, Belarus, Georgia, Kazakhstan, Kyrgyzstan, Moldova, Russia, Tajikistan, Turkmenistan, Ukraine and Uzbekistan) in 1992.
[2] Includes medals won as West Germany 1968–88.

Paralympic Games

Summer Games first held in Stoke Mandeville, England, in 1952 (solely for competitors from the UK and the Netherlands), then once every four years from 1960; Winter Games first held in Örnsköldsvik, Sweden, in 1976, then once every four years until 1992, after which they were held once every four years from 1994, to coincide with the Winter Olympic Games. Winter and Summer Games now always take place in the same venue as the corresponding Olympic Games.

Leading medal winners

Summer Games (to 2004)					Winter Games (to 2006)				
Nation	G	S	B	Total	Nation	G	S	B	Total
1 USA	408	374	403	1185	1 Germany	97	85	83	265
2 Great Britain	319	335	321	975	2 Austria	95	80	83	258
3 Germany	293	315	299	907	3 USA	92	93	64	249
4 Canada	255	210	222	687	4 Norway	103	75	65	243
5 France	235	235	217	687	5 Russia[1]	52	52	34	138
6 Australia	225	229	220	674	6 Switzerland	35	54	48	137
7 Spain	171	140	164	475	7 France	43	41	43	127
8 Sweden	153	130	86	369	8 Finland	54	31	39	124
9 Poland	115	129	101	345	9 Canada	24	33	38	95
10 China	143	117	83	343	10 Japan	14	24	25	63

G=Gold; S=Silver; B=Bronze
[1] Includes medals won by the former USSR team, and by the Unified Team (Armenia, Azerbaijan, Belarus, Georgia, Kazakhstan, Kyrgyzstan, Moldova, Russia, Tajikistan, Turkmenistan, Ukraine and Uzbekistan) in 1992.

Commonwealth Games

First held as the British Empire Games in 1930; became the British Empire and Commonwealth Games in 1954; current title adopted in 1970; take place every four years, between Olympic summer games.

Venues

1930	Hamilton, Canada	1978	Edmonton, Canada
1934	London, England	1982	Brisbane, Australia
1938	Sydney, Australia	1986	Edinburgh, Scotland
1950	Auckland, New Zealand	1990	Auckland, New Zealand
1954	Vancouver, Canada	1994	Victoria, Canada
1958	Cardiff, Wales	1998	Kuala Lumpur, Malaysia
1962	Perth, Australia	2002	Manchester, England
1966	Kingston, Jamaica	2006	Melbourne, Australia
1970	Edinburgh, Scotland	2010	New Delhi, India
1974	Christchurch, New Zealand		

Leading medal winners (to 2006)

Nation	Gold	Silver	Bronze	Total
1 Australia	732	619	555	1906
2 England	578	553	564	1695
3 Canada	414	445	459	1318
4 New Zealand	124	168	237	529
5 Scotland	82	94	154	330
6 South Africa	92	92	97	281
7 India	102	97	73	272
8 Wales	49	69	96	214
9 Kenya	59	47	56	162
10 Nigeria	39	47	57	143

Champions 1996–2006

For 1992 Summer Olympic events the designation (UT) is given for members of the Unified Team (Armenia, Azerbaijan, Belarus, Georgia, Kazakhstan, Kyrgyzstan, Moldova, Russia, Tajikistan, Turkmenistan, Ukraine and Uzbekistan).

American football

■ Super Bowl

First held in 1967; takes place each January; an end-of-season meeting between the champions of the two major US leagues, the National Football Conference (NFC) and the American Football Conference (AFC).

1996	Dallas Cowboys (NFC)
1997	Green Bay Packers (NFC)
1998	Denver Broncos (AFC)
1999	Denver Broncos (AFC)
2000	St Louis Rams (NFC)
2001	Baltimore Ravens (AFC)
2002	New England Patriots (AFC)
2003	Tampa Bay Buccaneers (NFC)
2004	New England Patriots (AFC)
2005	New England Patriots (AFC)
2006	Pittsburgh Steelers (AFC)

Athletics

■ World Championships

First held in Helsinki, Finland in 1983, then in Rome, Italy in 1987; since 1995 every two years.

Event (Men)	Winners
1997	
100m	Maurice Greene (USA)
200m	Ato Boldon (Trinidad)
400m	Michael Johnson (USA)
800m	Wilson Kipketer (Denmark)
1500m	Hicham El Guerrouj (Morocco)
5000m	Daniel Komen (Kenya)
10000m	Haile Gebrselassie (Ethiopia)
Marathon	Abel Antón (Spain)
3000m steeplechase	Wilson Kipketer (Denmark)
110m hurdles	Allen Johnson (USA)
400m hurdles	Stephane Diagana (France)
20km walk	Daniel Garcia (Mexico)
50km walk	Robert Korzeniowski (Poland)
4×100m relay	Canada
4×400m relay	USA
High jump	Javier Sotomayor (Cuba)
Long jump	Iván Pedroso (Cuba)
Triple jump	Yoelvis Quesada (Cuba)
Pole vault	Sergei Bubka (Ukraine)
Shot	Aleksandr Bagach[1] (Ukraine)
Discus	Lars Riedel (Germany)
Hammer	Heinz Weis (Germany)
Javelin	Marius Corbett (South Africa)
Decathlon	Tómas Dvorák (Czech Republic)
1999	
100m	Maurice Greene (USA)
200m	Maurice Greene (USA)
400m	Michael Johnson (USA)
800m	Wilson Kipketer (Denmark)
1500m	Hicham El Guerrouj (Morocco)
5000m	Salah Hissou (Morocco)
10000m	Haile Gebrselassie (Ethiopia)
Marathon	Abel Antón (Spain)
3000m steeplechase	Christopher Koskei (Kenya)
110m hurdles	Colin Jackson (Great Britain)
400m hurdles	Fabrizio Mori (Italy)
20km walk	Ilya Markov (Russia)
50km walk	German Skurygin (Russia)
4×100m relay	USA
4×400m relay	USA
High jump	Vyacheslav Voronin (Russia)
Long jump	Ivan Pedroso (Cuba)
Triple jump	Charles Michael Friedek (Germany)
Pole vault	Maksim Tarasov (Russia)
Shot	C J Hunter (USA)
Discus	Anthony Washington (USA)
Hammer	Karsten Kobs (Germany)
Javelin	Aki Parviainen (Finland)
Decathlon	Tomás Dvorák (Czech Republic)
2001	
100m	Maurice Greene (USA)
200m	Konstantinos Kederis (Greece)
400m	Avard Moncur (Bahamas)
800m	André Bucher (Switzerland)
1500m	Hicham El Guerrouj (Morocco)
5000m	Richard Limo (Kenya)
10000m	Charles Kamathi (Kenya)
Marathon	Gezahegne Abera (Ethiopia)
3000m steeplechase	Reuben Kosgei (Kenya)

110m hurdles	Allen Johnson (USA)
400m hurdles	Felix Sanchez (Dominican Republic)
20km walk	Roman Rasskazov (Russia)
50km walk	Robert Korzeniowski (Poland)
4 × 100m relay	USA
4 × 400m relay	Jamaica
High jump	Buss Martin (Germany)
Long jump	Ivan Pedroso (Cuba)
Triple jump	Jonathan Edwards (Great Britain)
Pole vault	Dmitry Markov (Russia)
Shot	John Godina (USA)
Discus	Lars Riedel (Germany)
Hammer	Szymon Ziólkowski (Poland)
Javelin	Jan Zelezný (Czech Republic)
Decathlon	Tomás Dvorák (Czech Republic)

2003

100m	Kim Collins (Saint Kitts and Nevis)
200m	John Capel (USA)
400m	Jerome Young (USA)
800m	Djabir Saïd-Guerni (Algeria)
1500m	Hicham El Guerrouj (Morocco)
5000m	Eliud Kipchoge (Kenya)
10000m	Kenenisa Bekele (Ethiopia)
Marathon	Jaoud Gharib (Morocco)
3000m steeplechase	Saif Shaheen (Qatar)
110m hurdles	Allen Johnson (USA)
400m hurdles	Felix Sanchez (Dominican Republic)
20km walk	Jefferson Pérez (Ecuador)
50km walk	Robert Korzeniowski (Poland)
4 × 100m relay	USA
4 × 400m relay	USA

High jump	Jacques Freitag (South Africa)
Long jump	Dwight Phillips (USA)
Triple jump	Christian Olsson (Sweden)
Pole vault	Giuseppe Gibilisco (Italy)
Shot	Andrei Mikhnevich (Belarus)
Discus	Virgilijus Alekna (Lithuania)
Hammer	Ivan Tikhon (Belarus)
Javelin	Sergei Makarov (Russia)
Decathlon	Tom Pappas (USA)

2005

100m	Justin Gatlin (USA)
200m	Justin Gatlin (USA)
400m	Jeremy Wariner (USA)
800m	Rashid Ramzi (Bahrain)
1500m	Rashid Ramzi (Bahrain)
5000m	Benjamin Limo (Kenya)
10000m	Kenenisa Bekele (Ethiopia)
Marathon	Jaoud Gharib (Morocco)
3000m steeplechase	Saif Shaheen (Qatar)
110m hurdles	Ladji Doucoure (France)
400m hurdles	Bershawn Jackson (USA)
20km walk	Jefferson Pérez (Ecuador)
50km walk	Sergey Kirdyapkin (Russia)
4 × 100m relay	France
4 × 400m relay	USA
High jump	Yuriy Kyrmarenko (Ukraine)
Long jump	Dwight Phillips (USA)
Triple jump	Walter Davis (USA)
Pole vault	Rens Blom (Netherlands)
Shot	Adam Nelson (USA)
Discus	Virgilijus Alekna (Lithuania)
Hammer	Ivan Tikhon (Belarus)
Javelin	Andrus Varnik (Estonia)
Decathlon	Bryan Clay (USA)

Event (Women)	Winners
1997	
100m	Marion Jones (USA)
200m	Zhanna Pintussevich (Ukraine)
400m	Cathy Freeman (Australia)
800m	Ana Fidelia Quirot (Cuba)
1500m	Carla Sacramento (Portugal)
5000m	Gabriela Szabo (Romania)
10000m	Sally Barsosio (Kenya)
Marathon	Hiromi Suzuki (Japan)
100m hurdles	Ludmila Engquist (Sweden)
400m hurdles	Nezha Bidouane (Morocco)
10km walk	Annarita Sidoti (Italy)
4 × 100m relay	USA
4 × 400m relay	Germany
High jump	Hanne Haugland (Norway)
Long jump	Lyudmila Galkina (Russia)
Triple jump	Sarka Kasparkova (Czech Republic)
Shot	Astrid Kumbernuss (Germany)
Discus	Beatrice Faumuina (New Zealand)
Javelin	Trine Hattestad (Norway)
Heptathlon	Sabine Braun (Germany)
1999	
100m	Marion Jones (USA)
200m	Inger Miller (USA)
400m	Cathy Freeman (Australia)
800m	Ludmilla Formanova (Czech Republic)
1500m	Svetlana Masterkova (Russia)
5000m	Gabriela Szabo (Romania)
10000m	Gete Wami (Ethiopia)

Marathon	Jong Song-Ok (North Korea)
100m hurdles	Gail Devers (USA)
400m hurdles	Daimi Pernia (Cuba)
20km walk	Liu Hongyu (China)
4 × 100m relay	Bahamas
4 × 400m relay	Russia
High jump	Inga Babakova (Ukraine)
Long jump	Niurka Montalvo (Spain)
Triple jump	Paraskevi Tsiamita (Greece)
Pole vault	Stacy Dragila (USA)
Shot	Astrid Kumbernuss (Germany)
Discus	Franka Dietzsch (Germany)
Hammer	Michaela Melinte (Romania)
Javelin	Mirela Manjani-Tzelili (Greece)
Heptathlon	Eunice Barber (France)
2001	
100m	Zhanna Pintusevich-Block (Ukraine)
200m	Marion Jones (USA)
400m	Amy Mbacke Thiam (Senegal)
800m	Maria Mutola (Mozambique)
1500m	Gabriela Szabo (Romania)
5000m	Olga Yegorova (Russia)
10000m	Derartu Tulu (Ethiopia)
Marathon	Lidia Simon (Romania)
100m hurdles	Anjanette Kirkland (USA)
400m hurdles	Nezha Bidouane (Morocco)
20km walk	Olimpiada Ivanova (Russia)
4 × 100m relay	USA
4 × 400m relay	USA
High jump	Hestrie Cloete (South Africa)
Long jump	Fiona May (Italy)

Triple jump	Tatyana Lebedeva (Russia)
Shot	Yanina Korolchik (Belarus)
Discus	Natalya Sadova (Russia)
Javelin	Osleidys Menéndez (Cuba)
Pole vault	Stacy Dragila (USA)
Hammer	Yipsi Moreno (Cuba)
Heptathlon	Yelena Prokhorova (Russia)

2003

100m	Torri Edwards (USA)
200m	Anastasiya Kapachinskaya (Russia)
400m	Ana Guevara (Mexico)
800m	Maria Mutola (Mozambique)
1500m	Tatyana Tomashova (Russia)
5000m	Tirunesh Dibaba (Ethiopia)
10000m	Berhane Adere (Ethiopia)
Marathon	Catherine Ndereba (Kenya)
100m hurdles	Perdita Felicien (Canada)
400m hurdles	Jana Pittman (Australia)
4×100m relay	France
4×400m relay	USA
20km walk	Yelena Nikolayeva (Russia)
High jump	Hestrie Cloete (South Africa)
Long jump	Eunice Barber (Italy)
Triple jump	Tatyana Lebedeva (Russia)
Pole vault	Svetlana Feofanova (Russia)
Shot	Svetlana Krivelyova (Russia)
Discus	Irina Yatchenko (Belarus)
Hammer	Yipsi Moreno (Cuba)
Javelin	Mirela Manjani-Tzelili (Greece)

Heptathlon	Carolina Kluft (Sweden)

2005

100m	Lauryn Williams (USA)
200m	Allyson Felix (USA)
400m	Tonique Williams Darling (Bahamas)
800m	Zulia Calatayud (Cuba)
1500m	Tatyana Tomashova (Russia)
5000m	Tirunesh Dibaba (Ethiopia)
10000m	Tirunesh Dibaba (Ethiopia)
Marathon	Paula Radcliffe (UK)
3000m steeplechase	Docus Inzikuru (Uganda)
100m hurdles	Michelle Perry (USA)
400m hurdles	Yuliya Pechonkina (Russia)
4×100m relay	USA
4×400m relay	Russia
20km walk	Olimpiada Ivanova (Russia)
High jump	Kajsa Bergqvist (Sweden)
Long jump	Tianna Madison (USA)
Triple jump	Trecia Smith (Jamaica)
Pole vault	Yelena Isinbayeva (Russia)
Shot	Nadezhda Ostapchuk (Belarus)
Discus	Franka Dietzsch (Germany)
Hammer	Olga Kuzenkova (Russia)
Javelin	Osleidys Menendez (Cuba)
Heptathlon	Carolina Kluft (Sweden)

[1] Stripped of gold medal following positive drugs test; medal awarded to John Godina (USA).

Australian rules football

■ **Australian Football League**
First held in 1897 as the Victoria Football League (1897–1989); inaugural winners were Essendon.

1996	North Melbourne
1997	Adelaide
1998	Adelaide
1999	North Melbourne
2000	Essendon
2001	Brisbane
2002	Brisbane
2003	Brisbane
2004	Adelaide
2005	Sydney
2006	West Coast

Baseball

■ **World Series**
First held in 1903; takes place each October, the best of seven matches; professional baseball's leading event, the end-of-season meeting between the winners of the two major baseball leagues in North America, the National League (NL) and American League (AL).

1996	New York Yankees (AL)
1997	Florida Marlins (NL)
1998	New York Yankees (AL)
1999	New York Yankees (AL)
2000	New York Yankees (AL)
2001	Arizona Diamondbacks (NL)
2002	Anaheim Angels (AL)
2003	Florida Marlins (NL)
2004	Boston Red Sox (AL)
2005	Chicago White Sox (AL)
2006	St Louis Cardinals (NL)

Basketball

■ **World Championship**
First held 1950 for men, 1953 for women; takes place approximately every four years.

Men
1998	Yugoslavia
2002	Yugoslavia
2006	Spain

Women
1998	USA
2002	USA
2006	Australia

■ **National Basketball Association Championship**
First held in 1947; the major competition in professional basketball in North America, end-of-season play-off involving the champion teams from the Eastern Conference (EC) and Western Conference (WC).

1996	Chicago Bulls (EC)
1997	Chicago Bulls (EC)
1998	Chicago Bulls (EC)
1999	San Antonio Spurs (WC)
2000	Los Angeles Lakers (WC)
2001	Los Angeles Lakers (WC)
2002	Los Angeles Lakers (WC)
2003	San Antonio Spurs (WC)
2004	Detroit Pistons (EC)
2005	San Antonio Spurs (WC)
2006	Miami Heat (EC)

Boxing

■ **World Heavyweight Champions**
The first world heavyweight champion under Queensbury Rules with gloves was James J Corbett in 1892.

		Recognizing Body
1995–6	Riddick Bowe (USA)	WBO
1995–6	Bruce Seldon (USA)	WBA
1995–6	Frank Bruno (UK)	WBC
1995–6	Frans Botha (South Africa)[1]	IBF
1996	Mike Tyson (USA)[2]	WBA/WBC
1996–7	Henry Akinwande (UK)	WBO

1996–7	Michael Moorer (USA)	IBF
1996–7	Evander Holyfield (USA)	WBA
1997–9	Evander Holyfield (USA)	WBA/IBF
1997–9	Lennox Lewis (UK)	WBC
1997–9	Herbie Hide (UK)	WBO
1999–2000	Vitali Klitschko (Ukraine)	WBO
1999–2000	Lennox Lewis (UK)[3]	UND (WBA/WBC/IBF)
2000	Chris Byrd (USA)	WBO
2000–1	Evander Holyfield (USA)	WBA
2000–1	Lennox Lewis (UK)	WBC/IBF
2001–3	John Ruiz (USA)	WBA
2000–3	Vladimir Klitschko (Ukraine)	WBO
2001	Hasim Rahman (USA)	WBC/IBF
2001–2	Lennox Lewis (UK)[4]	WBC/IBF
2002–4	Lennox Lewis (UK)	WBC
2002–6	Chris Byrd (USA)	IBF
2003	Corrie Sanders (South Africa)	WBO
2003–4	Roy Jones, Jr (USA)	WBA
2004–6	Lamon Brewster (USA)	WBO
2004–5	John Ruiz (USA)	WBA
2004–5	Vitali Klitschko (Ukraine)	WBC
2005	James Toney (USA)[5]	WBA
2005	John Ruiz (USA)	WBA
2005–6	Hasim Rahman (USA)	WBC
2005–	Nikolay Valuev (Russia)	WBA
2006	Sergei Liakhovich (Belarus)	WBO
2006–	Vladimir Klitschko (Ukraine)	IBF
2006–	Oleg Maskaev (Kazakhstan)	WBC
2006–	Shannon Briggs (USA)	WBO

[1] Stripped of IBF title in 1996
[2] Gave up WBC title in 1996
[3] Stripped of WBA title in 2000
[4] Gave up IBF title in 2002
[5] Stripped of title in 2005
UND = Undisputed Champion
WBC = World Boxing Council
WBA = World Boxing Association
IBF = International Boxing Federation
WBO = World Boxing Organization

Chess

■ **World Champions (FIDE)**
World Champions have been recognized since 1886. The first international tournament was held in London in 1851, and won by Adolf Anderssen (Germany); first women's champion recognized in 1927.

Men
1993–8	Anatoly Karpov (Russia)
1999–2000	Alexander Khalifman (Russia)
2000	Vishwanathan Anand (India)
2001–2	Ruslan Ponomariov (Ukraine)
2003	Yuri Shabanov (Russia)
2004	Rustam Kasimdzhanov (Uzbekistan)
2005	Vesalin Topolov (Bulgaria)
2006	Vladimir Kramnik (Russia)

Women
1991–6	Xie Jun (China)
1996–8	Zsuzsa Polgar (Hungary)
1999–2000	Xie Jun (China)
2001–2	Zhu Chen (China)
2003	Tamara Khmiadashvili (Georgia)

2004–5	Antoaneta Stefanova (Bulgaria)
2006	Xu Yuhua (China)

Cricket

■ **World Cup**

First played in England in 1975; usually held every four years; the 1987 competition, held in India and Pakistan, was the first to be played outside England.

1996	Sri Lanka
1999	Australia
2003	Australia

■ **County Championship**

The oldest cricket competition in the world; first won by Sussex in 1827; not officially recognized until 1890, when a proper points system was introduced.

1996	Leicestershire
1997	Glamorgan
1998	Leicestershire
1999	Surrey
2000	Surrey
2001	Yorkshire
2002	Surrey
2003	Sussex
2004	Warwickshire
2005	Nottinghamshire
2006	Sussex

■ **Pro 40 League**

First held in 1969; known as the John Player League until 1987, the Refuge Assurance League until 1991, the Axa Equity and Law League until 1999, the CGU League until 2000, the Norwich Union National Cricket League until 2003, and the Totesport National Cricket League until 2005.

1996	Surrey
1997	Warwickshire
1998	Lancashire
1999	Lancashire
2000	Gloucestershire
2001	Kent

2002	Glamorgan
2003	Surrey
2004	Glamorgan
2005	Essex
2006	Essex

■ **Cheltenham & Gloucester Trophy**

First held in 1963; known as the Gillette Cup until 1981 and the NatWest Bank Trophy until 2000.

1996	Lancashire
1997	Essex
1998	Lancashire
1999	Gloucestershire
2000	Gloucestershire
2001	Somerset
2002	Yorkshire
2003	Gloucestershire
2004	Gloucestershire
2005	Hampshire
2006	Sussex

■ **Pura Milk Cup**

Australia's leading domestic competition; contested inter-state since 1891–2; known as the Sheffield Shield until 1999.

1996	South Australia
1997	Queensland
1998	Western Australia
1999	Western Australia
2000	Queensland
2001	Queensland
2002	Queensland
2003	New South Wales
2004	Victoria
2005	New South Wales
2006	Queensland

Cycling

■ **Tour de France**

World's premier cycling event; first held in 1903.

1996	Bjarne Riis (Denmark)
1997	Jan Ullrich (Germany)
1998	Marco Pantani (Italy)
1999	Lance Armstrong (USA)
2000	Lance Armstrong (USA)

2001	Lance Armstrong (USA)
2002	Lance Armstrong (USA)
2003	Lance Armstrong (USA)
2004	Lance Armstrong (USA)
2005	Lance Armstrong (USA)
2006	Floyd Landis (USA)[1]

[1] Subject to findings of doping investigation.

■ World Road Race Championships

Men's race first held in 1927; first women's race in 1958; takes place annually.

Professional Men

1996	Johan Museeuw (Belgium)
1997	Laurent Brochard (France)
1998	Oskar Camenzind (Switzerland)
1999	Oscar Freire Gomez (Spain)
2000	Romans Vainsteins (Latvia)
2001	Oscar Freire Gomez (Spain)
2002	Mario Cipollini (Italy)
2003	Igor Astorloa (Spain)
2004	Oscar Freire Gomez (Spain)
2005	Tom Boonen (Belgium)
2006	Paolo Bettini (Italy)

Women

1996	Barbara Heeb (Switzerland)
1997	Alessandra Cappellotto (Italy)
1998	Diana Ziliute (Lithuania)
1999	Edita Pucinskaite (Lithuania)
2000	Zinaida Stahurskaia (Belarus)
2001	Rosa Polikeviciute (Lithuania)
2002	Susanne Ljungskog (Sweden)
2003	Susanne Ljungskog (Sweden)
2004	Judith Arndt (Germany)
2005	Regina Schleicher (Germany)
2006	Marianne Vos (Netherlands)

Football (Association)

■ FIFA World Cup

Association Football's premier event; first contested for the Jules Rimet Trophy in 1930; Brazil won it outright after winning for the third time in 1970; since then teams have competed for the FIFA (*Fédération Internationale de Football Association*) World Cup; held every four years.

Post-war winners

1950	Uruguay
1954	West Germany
1958	Brazil
1962	Brazil
1966	England
1970	Brazil
1974	West Germany
1978	Argentina
1982	Italy
1986	Argentina
1990	West Germany
1994	Brazil
1998	France
2002	Brazil
2006	Italy

■ European Championship

Held every four years since 1960; qualifying group matches held over the two years preceding the final.

All winners

1960	USSR
1964	Spain
1968	Italy
1972	West Germany
1976	Czechoslovakia
1980	West Germany
1984	France
1988	Netherlands
1992	Denmark
1996	Germany
2000	France
2004	Greece

■ South American Championship

Known as Copa América; first held in 1916, for South American national sides; there were two tournaments in 1959, won by Argentina and Uruguay; discontinued in 1967, but revived eight years later.

1997	Brazil
1999	Brazil
2001	Colombia
2004	Brazil

■ **European Champions Cup**

The leading club competition in Europe; open to the league champions of countries affiliated to UEFA (Union of European Football Associations); commonly known as the 'European Cup'; inaugurated in the 1955–6 season; played annually.

1996	Juventus (Italy)
1997	Borussia Dortmund (Germany)
1998	Real Madrid (Spain)
1999	Manchester United (England)
2000	Real Madrid (Spain)
2001	Bayern Munich (Germany)
2002	Real Madrid (Spain)
2003	AC Milan (Italy)
2004	Porto (Portugal)
2005	Liverpool (England)
2006	Barcelona (Spain)
2007	AC Milan (Italy)

■ **Football Association Challenge Cup (FA Cup)**

The world's oldest club knockout competition (the 'FA cup'), held annually; first contested in the 1871–2 season; first final at the Kennington Oval on 16 March 1872; first winners were The Wanderers.

1996	Manchester United
1997	Chelsea
1998	Arsenal
1999	Manchester United
2000	Chelsea
2001	Liverpool
2002	Arsenal
2003	Arsenal
2004	Manchester United
2005	Arsenal
2006	Liverpool
2007	Chelsea

■ **Football League (Premier League)**

The oldest league in the world, and regarded as the toughest; founded in 1888; consists of four divisions; the current complement of 92 teams achieved in 1950.

1995–6	Manchester United
1996–7	Manchester United
1997–8	Arsenal
1998–9	Manchester United
1999–2000	Manchester United
2000–1	Manchester United
2001–2	Arsenal
2002–3	Manchester United
2003–4	Arsenal
2004–5	Chelsea
2005–6	Chelsea
2006–7	Manchester United

Golf

■ **The Open**

First held at Prestwick in 1860, and won by Willie Park; takes place annually; regarded as the world's leading golf tournament.

1996	Tom Lehman (USA)
1997	Justin Leonard (USA)
1998	Mark O'Meara (USA)
1999	Paul Lawrie (Great Britain)
2000	Tiger Woods (USA)
2001	David Duval (USA)
2002	Ernie Els (South Africa)
2003	Ben Curtis (USA)
2004	Todd Hamilton (USA)
2005	Tiger Woods (USA)
2006	Tiger Woods (USA)

■ **United States Open**

First held at Newport, Rhode Island, in 1895, and won by Horace Rawlins; takes place annually.

1996	Steve Jones (USA)
1997	Ernie Els (South Africa)
1998	Lee Janzen (USA)
1999	Payne Stewart (USA)
2000	Tiger Woods (USA)
2001	Retief Goosen (South Africa)
2002	Tiger Woods (USA)
2003	Jim Furyk (USA)
2004	Retief Goosen (South Africa)
2005	Michael Campbell (New Zealand)
2006	Geoff Ogilvy (Australia)

■ US Masters
First held in 1934; takes place at the Augusta National course in Georgia every April.

1996	Nick Faldo (Great Britain)
1997	Tiger Woods (USA)
1998	Mark O'Meara (USA)
1999	José-María Olazábal (Spain)
2000	Vijay Singh (Fiji)
2001	Tiger Woods (USA)
2002	Tiger Woods (USA)
2003	Mike Weir (Canada)
2004	Phil Mickelson (USA)
2005	Tiger Woods (USA)
2006	Phil Mickelson (USA)

■ United States PGA Championship
The last of the season's four 'Majors'; first held in 1916, and a matchplay event until 1958; takes place annually.

1996	Mark Brooks (USA)
1997	Davis Love III (USA)
1998	Vijay Singh (Fiji)
1999	Tiger Woods (USA)
2000	Tiger Woods (USA)
2001	David Toms (USA)
2002	Rich Beem (USA)
2003	Shaun Micheel (USA)
2004	Vijay Singh (Fiji)
2005	Phil Mickelson (USA)
2006	Tiger Woods (USA)

■ Ryder Cup
The leading international team tournament; first held at Worcester, Massachusetts in 1927; takes place every two years between teams from the USA and Europe (Great Britain 1927–71; Great Britain and Ireland 1973–7).

1997	Europe	$14\frac{1}{2}$–$13\frac{1}{2}$
1999	USA	$14\frac{1}{2}$–$13\frac{1}{2}$
2002	Europe	$15\frac{1}{2}$–$12\frac{1}{2}$
2004	Europe	$18\frac{1}{2}$–$9\frac{1}{2}$
2006	Europe	$18\frac{1}{2}$–$9\frac{1}{2}$

Gymnastics

■ World Championships
First held in 1903.

Individual (Men)

1997	Ivan Ivankov (Belarus)
1999	Nikolay Krukov (Russia)
2001	Feng Jing (China)
2003	Paul Hamm (USA)
2005	Hiroyuki Tomita (Japan)
2006	Yang Wei (China)

Team (Men)

1997	China
1999	China
2001	Belarus
2003	China
2006	China

Individual (Women)

1997	Svetlana Khorkina (Russia)
1999	Maria Olaru (Romania)
2001	Svetlana Khorkina (Russia)
2003	Svetlana Khorkina (Russia)
2005	Chellsie Memmel (USA)
2006	Vanessa Ferrari (Italy)

Team (Women)

1997	Romania
1999	Romania
2001	Romania
2003	USA
2006	China

Hockey

■ World Cup
Men's tournament first held in 1971, and every four years since 1978; women's tournament first held in 1974, and now takes place every three or four years.

Men

1998	Netherlands
2002	Germany
2006	Germany

Women

1998	Australia
2002	Argentina
2006	Netherlands

■ Olympic Games

Regarded as hockey's leading competition; first held in 1908; included at every celebration since 1928; women's competition first held in 1980.

Men

1996	Netherlands
2000	Netherlands
2004	Australia

Women

1996	Australia
2000	Australia
2004	Germany

Horse-racing

■ The Derby

The 'Blue Riband' of the Turf; run at Epsom over $1\frac{1}{2}$ miles; first run in 1780.

	Horse (Jockey)
1996	Shaamit (Michael Hills)
1997	Benny the Dip (Willie Ryan)
1998	High Rise (Olivier Peslier)
1999	Oath (Kieren Fallon)
2000	Sinndar (Johnny Murtagh)
2001	Galileo (Michael Kinane)
2002	High Chaparral (Johnny Murtagh)
2003	Kris Kin (Kieren Fallon)
2004	North Light (Kieren Fallon)
2005	Motivator (Johnny Murtagh)
2006	Sir Percy (Martin Dwyer)

■ The Oaks

Raced at Epsom over $1\frac{1}{2}$ miles; for fillies only; first run in 1779.

	Horse (Jockey)
1996	Lady Carla (Pat Eddery)
1997	Reams of Verse (Kieren Fallon)
1998	Shahtoush (Michael Kinane)
1999	Ramruma (Kieren Fallon)
2000	Love Divine (Richard Quinn)
2001	Imagine (Michael Kinane)
2002	Kazzia (Frankie Dettori)
2003	Casual Look (Martin Dwyer)
2004	Ouija Board (Kieren Fallon)
2005	Eswarah (Richard Hills)

2006	Alexandrova (Kieren Fallon)

■ One Thousand Guineas

Run over 1 mile at Newmarket; for fillies only; first run in 1814.

	Horse (Jockey)
1996	Bosra Sham (Pat Eddery)
1997	Sleeptime (Kieren Fallon)
1998	Cape Verdi (Frankie Dettori)
1999	Wince (Kieren Fallon)
2000	Lahan (Richard Hills)
2001	Ameerat (Philip Robinson)
2002	Kazzia (Frankie Dettori)
2003	Russian Rhythm (Kieren Fallon)
2004	Attraction (Kevin Darley)
2005	Virginia Waters (Kieren Fallon)
2006	Speciosa (Michael Fenton)

■ Two Thousand Guineas

Run at Newmarket over 1 mile; first run in 1809.

	Horse (Jockey)
1996	Mark of Esteem (Frankie Dettori)
1997	Entrepreneur (Michael Kinane)
1998	King of Kings (Michael Kinane)
1999	Island Sands (Frankie Dettori)
2000	King's Best (Kieren Fallon)
2001	Golan (Kieren Fallon)
2002	Rock of Gibraltar (Johnny Murtagh)
2003	Refuse to Bend (Pat Smullen)
2004	Haafhd (Richard Hills)
2005	Footstepsinthesand (Kieren Fallon)
2006	George Washington (Kieren Fallon)

■ St Leger

The oldest of the five English classics; first run in 1776; raced at Doncaster annually over 1 mile 6 furlongs 127 yards.

	Horse (Jockey)
1996	Shantou (Frankie Dettori)

1997	Silver Patriarch (Pat Eddery)
1998	Nedawi (John Reid)
1999	Mutafaweq (Richard Hills)
2000	Millenary (Richard Quinn)
2001	Milan (Michael Kinane)
2002	Bollin Eric (Kevin Darley)
2003	Brian Boru (Jamie Spencer)
2004	Rule of Law (Kerrin McEvoy)
2005	Scorpion (Frankie Dettori)
2006	Sixties Icon (Frankie Dettori)

■ **Grand National**
Steeplechasing's most famous race; first run at Maghull in 1836; at Aintree since 1839; wartime races at Gatwick 1916–18.

	Horse (Jockey)
1996	Rough Quest (Mick Fitzgerald)
1997	Lord Gyllene (Tony Dobbin)
1998	Earth Summit (Carl Llewellyn)
1999	Bobbyjo (Paul Carberry)
2000	Papillon (Ruby Walsh)
2001	Red Marauder (Richard Guest)
2002	Bindaree (Jim Culloty)
2003	Monty's Pass (Barry Geraghty)
2004	Amberleigh House (Graham Lee)
2005	Hedgehunter (Ruby Walsh)
2006	Numbersixvalverde (Niall Madden)

■ **Prix de l'Arc de Triomphe**
The leading end-of-season race in Europe; raced over 2,400 metres at Longchamp; first run in 1920.

	Horse (Jockey)
1996	Helissio (Olivier Peslier)
1997	Peintre Celebre (Olivier Peslier)
1998	Sagamix (Olivier Peslier)
1999	Montjeu (Michael Kinane)
2000	Sinndar (Johnny Murtagh)
2001	Sakhee (Frankie Dettori)
2002	Marienbard (Frankie Dettori)
2003	Dalakhani (Christoph Soumillon)
2004	Bago (Thierry Gillet)
2005	Hurricane Run (Kieren Fallon)
2006	Rail Link (Stephane Pasquier)

Ice hockey

■ **World Championship**
First held in 1930; takes place annually (except 1980); up to 1968 Olympic champions also regarded as world champions.

1996	Czech Republic
1997	Canada
1998	Sweden
1999	Czech Republic
2000	Czech Republic
2001	Czech Republic
2002	Slovakia
2003	Canada
2004	Canada
2005	Czech Republic
2006	Sweden

■ **Stanley Cup**
The most sought-after trophy at club level; the end-of-season meeting between the winners of the two conferences in the National Hockey League in the USA and Canada.

1996	Colorado Avalanche
1997	Detroit Red Wings
1998	Detroit Red Wings
1999	Dallas Stars
2000	New Jersey Devils
2001	Colorado Avalanche
2002	Detroit Red Wings
2003	New Jersey Devils
2004	Tampa Bay Lightning
2005	*Cancelled over salary dispute*
2006	Carolina Hurricanes

Ice skating

■ **World Championships**
First men's championships in 1896; first women's event in 1906; pairs first contested in 1908; Ice Dance officially recognized in 1952.

Men
1996	Todd Eldredge (USA)
1997	Elvis Stojko (Canada)
1998	Alexei Yagudin (Russia)

1999	Alexei Yagudin (Russia)
2000	Alexei Yagudin (Russia)
2001	Yevgeny Plushenko (Russia)
2002	Alexei Yagudin (Russia)
2003	Yevgeny Plushenko (Russia)
2004	Yevgeny Plushenko (Russia)
2005	Stephane Lambiel (Switzerland)
2006	Stephane Lambiel (Switzerland)

Women

1996	Michelle Kwan (USA)
1997	Tara Lipinski (USA)
1998	Michelle Kwan (USA)
1999	Maria Butyrskaya (Russia)
2000	Michelle Kwan (USA)
2001	Michelle Kwan (USA)
2002	Irina Slutskaya (Russia)
2003	Michelle Kwan (USA)
2004	Shizuka Arakawa (Japan)
2005	Irina Slutskaya (Russia)
2006	Kimmie Meissner (USA)

Pairs

1996	Andrei Bushkov/Marina Eltsova (Russia)
1997	Ingo Steuer/Mandy Woetzel (Germany)
1998	Anton Sikharulidze/Elena Berezhnaya (Russia)
1999	Anton Sikharulidze/Elena Berezhnaya (Russia)
2000	Alexei Tikhonov/Maria Petrova (Russia)
2001	David Pelletier/Jamie Sale (Canada)
2002	Xue Shen/Zhao Hongbo (China)
2003	Xue Shen/Zhao Hongbo (China)
2004	Maxim Marinin/Tatiana Totmianina (Russia)
2005	Maxim Marinin/Tatiana Totmianina (Russia)
2006	Tong Jian/Pang Qing (China)

Ice Dance

1996	Yevgeni Platov/Oksana Gritschuk (Russia)
1997	Yevgeni Platov/Oksana Gritschuk (Russia)
1998	Oleg Ovsyannikov/Anjelika Krylova (Russia)
1999	Oleg Ovsyannikov/Anjelika Krylova (Russia)
2000	Gwendal Peizerat/Marina Anissina (France)
2001	Maurizio Margaglio/Barbara Fusar-Poli (Italy)
2002	Ilia Averbukh/Irina Lobacheva (Russia)
2003	Victor Kraatz/Shae-Lynn Bourne (Canada)
2004	Roman Kostomarov/Tatiana Navka (Russia)
2005	Roman Kostomarov/Tatiana Navka (Russia)
2006	Maxim Staviski/Albena Denkova (Bulgaria)

Motor racing

■ **World Championship**

A Formula One drivers' world championship instituted in 1950; constructors' championship instituted in 1958.

1996	Damon Hill (Great Britain)	*Williams*
1997	Jacques Villeneuve (Canada)	*Williams*
1998	Mika Hakkinen (Finland)	*McLaren*
1999	Mika Hakkinen (Finland)	*McLaren*
2000	Michael Schumacher (Germany)	*Ferrari*
2001	Michael Schumacher (Germany)	*Ferrari*
2002	Michael Schumacher (Germany)	*Ferrari*
2003	Michael Schumacher (Germany)	*Ferrari*
2004	Michael Schumacher (Germany)	*Ferrari*
2005	Fernando Alonso (Spain)	*Renault*
2006	Fernando Alonso (Spain)	*Renault*

■ Le Mans 24-Hour Race
The greatest of all endurance races; first
held in 1923.

1996	Manuel Reuter (Germany)
	Davy Jones (USA)
	Alexander Wurz (Austria)
1997	Michele Alboreto (Italy)
	Stefan Johansson (Sweden)
	Tom Kristensen (Denmark)
1998	Allan McNish (UK)
	Laurent Aiello (France)
	Stephane Ortelli (France)
1999	Pierluigi Martini (Italy)
	Joachim Winkelhock (Germany)
	Yannick Dalmas (France)
2000	Frank Biela (Germany)
	Tom Kristensen (Denmark)
	Emanuele Pirro (Italy)
2001	Frank Biela (Germany)
	Tom Kristensen (Denmark)
	Emanuele Pirro (Italy)
2002	Frank Biela (Germany)
	Tom Kristensen (Denmark)
	Emanuele Pirro (Italy)
2003	Tom Kristensen (Denmark)
	Rinaldo Capello (Italy)
	Guy Smith (UK)
2004	Tom Kristensen (Denmark)
	Rinaldo Capello (Italy)
	Seiji Ara (Japan)
2005	J J Lehto (Finland)
	Tom Kristensen (Denmark)
	Marco Werner (Germany)
2006	Frank Biela (Germany)
	Emanuele Pirro (Italy)
	Marco Werner (Germany)

■ Indianapolis 500
First held in 1911; raced over the
Indianapolis Raceway as part of the
Memorial Day celebrations at the end of
May each year.

1996	Buddy Lazier (USA)
1997	Arie Luyendyk (Netherlands)
1998	Eddie Cheever (USA)
1999	Kenny Brack (Sweden)
2000	Juan Montoya (Colombia)
2001	Helio Castroneves (Brazil)

2002	Helio Castroneves (Brazil)
2003	Gil de Ferran (Brazil)
2004	Buddy Rice (USA)
2005	Dan Wheldon (UK)
2006	Sam Hornish (USA)

■ Monte Carlo Rally
The world's leading rally; first held in
1911.

1996	Patrick Bernardini (France)
	Bernard Occelli (France)
1997	Piero Liatti (Italy)
	Fabrizia Pons (Italy)
1998	Carlos Sainz (Spain)
	Luis Moya (Spain)
1999	Tommi Mäkinen (Finland)
	Risto Mannisenmäki (Finland)
2000	Tommi Mäkinen (Finland)
	Risto Mannisenmäki (Finland)
2001	Tommi Mäkinen (Finland)
	Risto Mannisenmäki (Finland)
2002	Tommi Mäkinen (Finland)
	Kaj Lindstrom (Finland)
2003	Sebastien Loeb (France)
	Daniel Elena (Monaco)
2004	Sebastien Loeb (France)
	Daniel Elena (Monaco)
2005	Sebastien Loeb (France)
	Daniel Elena (Monaco)
2006	Marcus Grönholm (Finland)
	Timo Rautiainen (Finland)

Rowing

■ World Championships
First held for men in 1962 and for women
in 1974; Olympic champions assume the
role of world champion in Olympic years;
principal event is the single sculls.

Single Sculls (Men)

1996	Xeno Müller (Switzerland)
1997	Jamie Koven (USA)
1998	Rob Waddell (New Zealand)
1999	Rob Waddell (New Zealand)
2000	Rob Waddell (New Zealand)
2001	Olaf Tufte (Norway)
2002	Marcel Hacker (Germany)
2003	Olaf Tufte (Norway)

2004	Olaf Tufte (Norway)
2005	Mahe Drysdale (New Zealand)
2006	Mahe Drysdale (New Zealand)

Single Sculls (Women)

1996	Ekaterina Karsten-Khodotovich (Belarus)
1997	Ekaterina Karsten-Khodotovich (Belarus)
1998	Irina Fedotova (Russia)
1999	Ekaterina Karsten-Khodotovich (Belarus)
2000	Ekaterina Karsten-Khodotovich (Belarus)
2001	Katrin Rutschow-Stomporowski (Germany)
2002	Rumyana Neykova (Bulgaria)
2003	Rumyana Neykova (Bulgaria)
2004	Katrin Rutschow-Stromporowski (Germany)
2005	Ekaterina Karsten-Khodotovitch (Belarus)
2006	Ekaterina Karsten-Khodotovitch (Belarus)

■ The Boat Race

An annual contest between the crews from the Oxford and Cambridge University rowing clubs; first contested in 1829; the current course is from Putney to Mortlake.

1996	Cambridge
1997	Cambridge
1998	Cambridge
1999	Cambridge
2000	Oxford
2001	Cambridge
2002	Oxford
2003	Oxford
2004	Cambridge
2005	Oxford
2006	Oxford

■ Diamond Sculls

Highlight of Henley Royal Regatta held every July; first contested in 1884.

1996	Merlin Vervoorn (Netherlands)
1997	Greg Searle (Great Britain)

1998	Jamie Koven (USA)
1999	Marcel Hacker (Germany)
2000	Aquil Abdullah (USA)
2001	Duncan Free (Australia)
2002	Peter Wells (Great Britain)
2003	Alan Campbell (Great Britain)
2004	Marcel Hacker (Germany)
2005	Wyatt Allen (USA)
2006	Mahe Drysdale (New Zealand)

Rugby League

■ World Cup

First held in 1954 between Great Britain, France, Australia and New Zealand; played intermittently since and now with the inclusion of other countries. In 1957, 1960 and 1975 (when it was renamed the World Championship) it was played on a league basis. The 1975 tournament stretched over eight months, whereas the winners in 1988 and 1992 lifted the trophy after rounds of games played over three years.

All winners

1954	Great Britain
1957	Australia
1960	Great Britain
1968	Australia
1970	Australia
1972	Great Britain
1975	Australia
1977	Australia
1988	Australia
1992	Australia
1995	Australia
2000	Australia

■ Challenge Cup Final

First contested in 1897 and won by Batley; first final at Wembley Stadium in 1929.

1996	St Helens
1997	St Helens
1998	Sheffield Eagles
1999	Leeds Rhinos
2000	Bradford Bulls
2001	St Helens
2002	Wigan Warriors

2003	Bradford Bulls
2004	St Helens
2005	Hull
2006	St Helens

■ **Premiership Trophy**
End-of-season knockout competition involving the top eight teams in the first division; first contested at the end of the 1974–5 season; discontinued in 1997.

1990	Widnes
1991	Hull
1992	Wigan
1993	St Helens
1994	Wigan
1995	Wigan
1996	Wigan
1997	Wigan

■ **Tetley's Super League**
First held in 1996. The top five teams in the league at the end of the season play off for the title; known as the JJB Super League from 1996 to 1999.

1996	St Helens
1997	Bradford Bulls
1998	Wigan Warriors
1999	St Helens
2000	St Helens
2001	Bradford Bulls
2002	St Helens
2003	Bradford Bulls
2004	Leeds Rhinos
2005	Bradford Bulls
2006	St Helens

Rugby Union

■ **World Cup**
The first Rugby Union World Cup was staged in 1987 and won by New Zealand; takes place every four years.

All winners

1987	New Zealand
1991	Australia
1995	South Africa
1999	Australia
2003	England

■ **Six Nations' Championship**
A round robin competition involving England, Ireland, Scotland, Wales, France and, from 2000, Italy; first contested in 1884.

* = Grand Slam

1996	England
1997	France*
1998	France*
1999	Scotland
2000	England
2001	England
2002	France*
2003	England*
2004	France*
2005	Wales*
2006	France

■ **Powergen Cup**
An annual knockout competition for English Club sides; first held in the 1971–2 season; known as the John Player Special Cup until 1988, the Pilkington Cup until 1997, and the Tetley's Bitter Cup until 2000; Welsh clubs introduced in 2006.

1996	Bath
1997	Leicester
1998	Saracens
1999	Wasps
2000	Wasps
2001	Newcastle Falcons
2002	London Irish
2003	Gloucester
2004	Newcastle Falcons
2005	Leeds
2006	Wasps

■ **Welsh Rugby Union Challenge Cup (Konica Minolta Cup)**
The knockout tournament for Welsh clubs; first held in 1971–2; formerly known as the Schweppes Welsh Cup, the Swalec Cup and the Principality Cup.

1996	Pontypridd
1997	Cardiff
1998	Llanelli
1999	Swansea

2000	Llanelli
2001	Newport
2002	Pontypridd
2003	Llanelli
2004	Neath
2005	Llanelli
2006	Pontypridd

■ **Heineken European Cup**

Established in 1996 as a cup competition for major European clubs and provincial teams. English clubs did not take part in 1996 or 1999.

1996	Stade Toulousain
1997	Brive
1998	Bath
1999	Ulster
2000	Northampton
2001	Leicester
2002	Leicester
2003	Stade Toulousain
2004	Wasps
2005	Stade Toulousain
2006	Munster

Skiing

■ **World Cup**

A season-long competition first organized in 1967; champions are declared in downhill, slalom, giant slalom and super-giant slalom, as well as the overall champion; points are obtained for performances in each category.

Overall winners

Men

1996	Lasse Kjus (Norway)
1997	Luc Alphand (France)
1998	Hermann Maier (Austria)
1999	Lasse Kjus (Norway)
2000	Hermann Maier (Austria)
2001	Hermann Maier (Austria)
2002	Stephan Eberharter (Austria)
2003	Stephan Eberharter (Austria)
2004	Hermann Maier (Austria)
2005	Bode Miller (USA)
2006	Benjamin Raich (Austria)

Women

1996	Katja Seizinger (Germany)
1997	Pernilla Wiberg (Sweden)
1998	Katja Seizinger (Germany)
1999	Alexandra Meissnitzer (Austria)
2000	Renate Götschl (Austria)
2001	Janica Kostelic (Croatia)
2002	Michaela Dorfmeister (Austria)
2003	Janica Kostelic (Croatia)
2004	Anja Paerson (Sweden)
2005	Anja Paerson (Sweden)
2006	Janica Kostelic (Croatia)

Snooker

■ **World Professional Championship**

Instituted in the 1926–7 season; a knockout competition open to professional players who are members of the World Professional Billiards and Snooker Association; played at the Crucible Theatre, Sheffield.

1996	Stephen Hendry (Scotland)
1997	Ken Doherty (Ireland)
1998	John Higgins (Scotland)
1999	Stephen Hendry (Scotland)
2000	Mark Williams (Wales)
2001	Ronnie O'Sullivan (England)
2002	Peter Ebdon (England)
2003	Mark Williams (Wales)
2004	Ronnie O'Sullivan (England)
2005	Shaun Murphy (England)
2006	Graeme Dott (Scotland)

■ **The Masters**

The Masters is an individual non-ranking tournament but is regarded as one of the game's majors. It has been played at the Wembley Conference Centre since 1979 and was sponsored between 1975 and 2003 by Benson & Hedges.

1996	Stephen Hendry (Scotland)
1997	Steve Davis (England)
1998	Mark Williams (Wales)
1999	John Higgins (Scotland)
2000	Matthew Stevens (Wales)
2001	Paul Hunter (England)
2002	Paul Hunter (England)
2003	Mark Williams (Wales)

2004	Paul Hunter (England)
2005	Ronnie O'Sullivan (England)
2006	John Higgins (Scotland)

■ **World Amateur Championship**
First held in 1963; originally took place every two years, but annual since 1984.

1996	Stuart Bingham (England)
1997	Marco Fu (China/Hong Kong)
1998	Luke Simmonds (England)
1999	Ian Preece (Wales)
2000	Stephen Maguire (Scotland)
2001	*not held*
2002	Steve Mifsud (Australia)
2003	Pankaj Advani (India)
2004	Mark Allen (Northern Ireland)
2005	*not held*
2006	Kurt Maflin (Norway)

Softball

■ **World Championships**
First held for women in 1965 and for men the following year; now held every four years.

Men

1996	New Zealand
2000	New Zealand
2004	New Zealand

Women

1998	USA
2002	USA
2006	USA

Squash

■ **World Open Championship**
First held in 1976; takes place annually for men and women; every two years for women 1976–89.

Men

1996	Jansher Khan (Pakistan)
1997	Rodney Eyles (Australia)
1998	Jonathon Power (Canada)
1999	Peter Nicol (Scotland)
2000	*not held*
2001	*not held*
2002	David Palmer (Australia)

2003	Amr Shabana (Egypt)
2004	Thierry Lincou (France)
2005	Amr Shabana (Egypt)
2006	David Palmer (Australia)

Women

1996	Sarah Fitz-Gerald (Australia)
1997	Sarah Fitz-Gerald (Australia)
1998	Sarah Fitz-Gerald (Australia)
1999	Cassie Campion (Great Britain)
2000	Carol Owens (Australia)
2001	Sarah Fitz-Gerald (Australia)
2002	Sarah Fitz-Gerald (Australia)
2003	Carol Owens (Australia)
2004	Vanessa Atkinson (Netherlands)
2005	Nicol David (Malaysia)
2006	Nicol David (Malaysia)

Surfing

■ **World Professional Championship**
A season-long series of Grand Prix events; first held in 1970.

Men

1996	Kelly Slater (USA)
1997	Kelly Slater (USA)
1998	Kelly Slater (USA)
1999	Mark Occhilupo (Australia)
2000	Sunny Garcia (Hawaii)
2001	CJ Hobgood (USA)
2002	Andy Irons (Hawaii)
2003	Andy Irons (Hawaii)
2004	Andy Irons (Hawaii)
2005	Kelly Slater (USA)
2006	Kelly Slater (USA)

Women

1996	Lisa Andersen (USA)
1997	Lisa Andersen (USA)
1998	Layne Beachley (Australia)
1999	Layne Beachley (Australia)
2000	Layne Beachley (Australia)
2001	Layne Beachley (Australia)
2002	Layne Beachley (Australia)
2003	Layne Beachley (Australia)
2004	Sofia Mulanovich (Peru)
2005	Chelsea Georgeson (Australia)
2006	Layne Beachley (Australia)

Swimming and diving

■ Olympic Games

In 1904 the first 50m freestyle event for men was held (won by Zoltán Halmaj of Hungary), but was then discontinued until 1988. The women's 50m was introduced at the Seoul Games of 1988. The complete list of 2004 Olympic champions is given below.

Men

50m freestyle	Gary Hall (USA)
100m freestyle	Pieter van den Hoogenband (Netherlands)
200m freestyle	Ian Thorpe (Australia)
400m freestyle	Ian Thorpe (Australia)
1500m freestyle	Grant Hackett (Australia)
100m backstroke	Aaron Peirsol (USA)
200m backstroke	Aaron Peirsol (USA)
100m breaststroke	Kosuke Kitajima (Japan)
200m breaststroke	Kosuke Kitajima (Japan)
100m butterfly	Michael Phelps (USA)
200m butterfly	Michael Phelps (USA)
200m individual medley	Michael Phelps (USA)
400m individual medley	Michael Phelps (USA)
4 × 100m freestyle relay	South Africa
4 × 200m freestyle relay	USA
4 × 100m medley relay	USA
3m springboard diving	Peng Bo (China)
10m platform diving	Hu Jia (China)
Synchronized springboard diving	Nikolaos Sirandis/Thomas Bimis (Greece)
Synchronized platform diving	Tian Liang/Yang Jinghui (China)

Women

50m freestyle	Inge de Bruijn (Netherlands)
100m freestyle	Jodie Henry (Australia)
200m freestyle	Camelia Potec (Romania)
400m freestyle	Laure Manaudou (France)
800m freestyle	Ai Shibata (Japan)
100m backstroke	Natalie Coughlin (USA)
200m backstroke	Kirsty Coventry (Zimbabwe)
100m breaststroke	Luo Xuejuan (China)
200m breaststroke	Amanda Beard (USA)
100m butterfly	Petria Thomas (Australia)
200m butterfly	Otylia Jedrzejczak (Poland)
200m individual medley	Yana Klochova (Ukraine)
400m individual medley	Yana Klochova (Ukraine)
4 × 100m freestyle relay	Australia
4 × 200m freestyle relay	USA
4 × 100m medley relay	Australia
3m springboard diving	Guo Jingjing (China)
10m platform diving	Chantelle Newbery (Australia)
Synchronized springboard diving	Wu Minxia/Guo Jingjing (China)

Synchronized platform diving	Lao Lishi/Li Ting (China)
Synchronized swimming duet	Anastasia Davydova/Anastasia Ermakova (Russia)
Team	Russia

Table tennis

■ World Championships
First held in 1926 and every two years since 1957, with the exception of 1999.

Swaythling Cup (Men's Team)
1997	China
1999	*not held*
2000	Sweden
2001	China
2004	China
2006	China

Corbillon Cup (Women's Team)
1997	China
1999	*not held*
2000	China
2001	China
2004	China
2006	China

Men's Singles
1997	Jan-Ove Waldner (Sweden)
1999	Liu Guoliang (China)
2001	Wang Liqin (China)
2003	Werner Schlager (Austria)
2005	Wang Liqin (China)

Women's Singles
1997	Deng Yaping (China)
1999	Wang Nan (China)
2001	Wang Nan (China)
2003	Wang Nan (China)
2005	Zhang Yining (China)

Men's Doubles
1997	Liu Guoliang/Kong Linghui (China)
1999	Liu Guoliang/Kong Linghui (China)
2001	Wang Liqin/Yan Sen (China)
2003	Wang Liqin/Yan Sen (China)

2005	Wang Hao/Kong Linghui (China)

Women's Doubles
1997	Li Ju/Wang Nan (China)
1999	Wang Nan/Li Ju (China)
2001	Li Ju/Wang Nan (China)
2003	Wang Nan/Zhang Yining (China)
2005	Wang Nan/Zhang Yining (China)

Mixed Doubles
1997	Kong Linghui/Deng Yaping (China)
1999	Zhang Yingying/Ma Lin (China)
2001	Qin Zhijian/Yang Yin (China)
2003	Wang Nan/Ma Lin (China)
2005	Guo Yue/Wang Liqin (China)

Tennis (lawn)

■ All-England Championships at Wimbledon
The All-England Championships at Wimbledon are lawn tennis's most prestigious championships; first held in 1877.

Men's Singles
1996	Richard Krajicek (Netherlands)
1997	Pete Sampras (USA)
1998	Pete Sampras (USA)
1999	Pete Sampras (USA)
2000	Pete Sampras (USA)
2001	Goran Ivanisevic (Croatia)
2002	Lleyton Hewitt (Australia)
2003	Roger Federer (Switzerland)
2004	Roger Federer (Switzerland)
2005	Roger Federer (Switzerland)
2006	Roger Federer (Switzerland)

Women's Singles
1996	Steffi Graf (Germany)
1997	Martina Hingis (Switzerland)
1998	Jana Novotna (Czech Republic)
1999	Lindsay Davenport (USA)
2000	Venus Williams (USA)
2001	Venus Williams (USA)
2002	Serena Williams (USA)

2003	Serena Williams (USA)
2004	Maria Sharapova (Russia)
2005	Venus Williams (USA)
2006	Amelie Mauresmo (France)

Men's Doubles

1996	Todd Woodbridge/Mark Woodforde (Australia)
1997	Todd Woodbridge/Mark Woodforde (Australia)
1998	Jacco Eltingh/Paul Haarhuis (Netherlands)
1999	Mahesh Bhupathi/Leander Paes (India)
2000	Todd Woodbridge/Mark Woodforde (Australia)
2001	Donald Johnson/Jared Palmer (USA)
2002	Todd Woodbridge (Australia)/Jonas Bjorkman (Sweden)
2003	Todd Woodbridge (Australia)/Jonas Bjorkman (Sweden)
2004	Todd Woodbridge (Australia)/Jonas Bjorkman (Sweden)
2005	Stephen Huss (Australia)/Wesley Moodie (South Africa)
2006	Bob Bryan/Mike Bryan (USA)

Women's Doubles

1996	Helena Sukova (Czech Republic)/Martina Hingis (Switzerland)
1997	Gigi Fernandez (USA)/Natalya Zvereva (Belarus)
1998	Jana Novotna (Czech Republic)/Martina Hingis (Switzerland)
1999	Lindsay Davenport/Corina Morariu (USA)
2000	Serena Williams/Venus Williams (USA)
2001	Lisa Raymond (USA)/Rennae Stubbs (Australia)
2002	Serena Williams/Venus Williams (USA)
2003	Kim Clijsters (Belgium)/Ai Sugiyama (Japan)
2004	Cara Black (Zimbabwe)/Rennae Stubbs (Australia)
2005	Cara Black (Zimbabwe)/Liezel Huber (South Africa)

| 2006 | Zi Yan/Jie Zheng (China) |

Mixed Doubles

1996	Helena Sukova/Cyril Suk (Czech Republic)
1997	Helena Sukova/Cyril Suk (Czech Republic)
1998	Serena Williams (USA)/Max Mirnyi (Belarus)
1999	Lisa Raymond (USA)/Leander Paes (India)
2000	Kimberly Po/Donald Johnson (USA)
2001	Daniela Hantuchova (Slovakia)/Leos Friedl (Czech Republic)
2002	Elena Likhovtseva (Russia)/Mahesh Bhupathi (India)
2003	Martina Navratilova (USA)/Leander Paes (India)
2004	Cara Black/Wayne Black (Zimbabwe)
2005	Mary Pierce (France)/Mahesh Bhupathi (India)
2006	Vera Zvonereva (Russia)/Andy Ram (Israel)

■ United States Open
First held in 1891 as the United States Championship; became the United States Open in 1968.

Men's Singles

1996	Pete Sampras (USA)
1997	Pat Rafter (Australia)
1998	Pat Rafter (Australia)
1999	Andre Agassi (USA)
2000	Marat Safin (Russia)
2001	Lleyton Hewitt (Australia)
2002	Pete Sampras (USA)
2003	Andy Roddick (USA)
2004	Roger Federer (Switzerland)
2005	Roger Federer (Switzerland)
2006	Roger Federer (Switzerland)

Women's Singles

1996	Steffi Graf (Germany)
1997	Martina Hingis (Switzerland)
1998	Lindsay Davenport (USA)
1999	Serena Williams (USA)
2000	Venus Williams (USA)

2001	Venus Williams (USA)
2002	Serena Williams (USA)
2003	Justine Henin-Hardenne (Belgium)
2004	Svetlana Kuznetsova (Russia)
2005	Kim Clijsters (Belgium)
2006	Maria Sharapova (Russia)

■ Davis Cup

International team competition organized on a knockout basis; first held in 1900; contested on a challenge basis until 1972.

1996	France
1997	Sweden
1998	Sweden
1999	Australia
2000	Spain
2001	France
2002	Russia
2003	Australia
2004	Spain
2005	Croatia
2006	Russia

Weightlifting

■ World Championships

First held in 1898; 11 weight divisions; the most prestigious is the 105kg-plus category (formerly known as Super Heavy-weight, then 110kg-plus; in 1993 changed to 108kg-plus; in 1998 reduced to current weight); Olympic champions are automatically world champions in Olympic years.

105kg-plus

1996	Andrey Chemerkin (Russia)
1997	Andrey Chemerkin (Russia)
1998	Andrey Chemerkin (Russia)
1999	Andrey Chemerkin (Russia)
2000	Hossein Reza Zadeh (Iran)
2001	Saeed Salem Jaber (Qatar)
2002	Hossein Reza Zadeh (Iran)
2003	Hossein Reza Zadeh (Iran)

2004	Hossein Reza Zadeh (Iran)
2005	Dmitry Klokov (Russia)
2006	Marcin Dolega (Poland)

Wrestling

■ World Championships

Graeco-Roman world championships first held in 1921; first freestyle championships in 1951; each style contests ten weight divisions, the heaviest being the 120kg (formerly over 100kg, and until December 2001 130kg) category; Olympic champions become world champions in Olympic years.

Super-heavyweight / 120kg
Freestyle

1996	Mahmut Demir (Turkey)
1997	Zekeriya Güglü (Turkey)
1998	Alexis Rodriguez (Cuba)
1999	Stephen Neal (USA)
2000	David Moussoulbes (Russia)
2001	David Moussoulbes (Russia)
2002	David Moussoulbes (Russia)
2003	Artur Taymazov (Uzbekistan)
2004	Artur Taymazov (Uzbekistan)
2005	Aydin Polatci (Turkey)
2006	Artur Taymazov (Uzbekistan)

Graeco-Roman

1996	Aleksandr Karelin (Russia)
1997	Aleksandr Karelin (Russia)
1998	Aleksandr Karelin (Russia)
1999	Aleksandr Karelin (Russia)
2000	Rulon Gardner (USA)
2001	Rulon Gardner (USA)
2002	Dremiel Byers (USA)
2003	Khasan Baroev (Russia)
2004	Khasan Baroev (Russia)
2005	Mijain Lopez Nunez (Cuba)
2006	Khasan Baroev (Russia)

Yachting

■ America's Cup

One of sport's famous trophies; first won by the schooner *Magic* in 1870; now held approximately every four years, when challengers compete in a series of races to find which of them races against the holder; all 25 winners up to 1983 were from the USA.

Winning yacht and Skipper

2000	Black Magic (New Zealand; Russell Coutts)
2003	Alinghi (Switzerland; Russell Coutts)

■ Admiral's Cup

A two-yearly series of races, originally held in the English Channel, around Fastnet rock and at Cowes; originally four national teams of three boats per team, now nine teams of three boats per team (except for the 2003 race, when two-boat teams represented clubs); first held in 1957.

1999	Netherlands
2001	*not held*
2003	Australia
2005	*not held*

TIME

Year equivalents

Jewish[1] (AM)

5756	(25 Sep 1995–13 Sep 1996)
5757	(14 Sep 1996–1 Oct 1997)
5758	(2 Oct 1997–20 Sep 1998)
5759	(21 Sep 1998–10 Sep 1999)
5760	(11 Sep 1999–29 Sep 2000)
5761	(30 Sep 2000–17 Sep 2001)
5762	(18 Sep 2001–6 Sep 2002)
5763	(7 Sep 2002–26 Sep 2003)
5764	(27 Sep 2003–15 Sep 2004)
5765	(16 Sep 2004–3 Oct 2005)
5766	(4 Oct 2005–22 Sep 2006)
5767	(23 Sep 2006–12 Sep 2007)
5768	(13 Sep 2007–29 Sep 2008)

Jewish[1] (AM)

5769	(30 Sep 2008–18 Sep 2009)
5770	(19 Sep 2009–8 Sep 2010)
5771	(9 Sep 2010–28 Sep 2011)
5772	(29 Sep 2011–16 Sep 2012)
5773	(17 Sep 2012–4 Sep 2013)
5774	(5 Sep 2013–24 Sep 2014)
5775	(25 Sep 2014–13 Sep 2015)
5776	(14 Sep 2015–2 Oct 2016)
5777	(3 Oct 2016–20 Sep 2017)
5778	(21 Sep 2017–9 Sep 2018)
5779	(10 Sep 2018–29 Sep 2019)
5780	(30 Sep 2019–18 Sep 2020)

Islamic[2] (H)

1416	(31 May 1995–18 May 1996)
1417	(19 May 1996–8 May 1997)
1418	(9 May 1997–27 Apr 1998)
1419	(28 Apr 1998–16 Apr 1999)
1420	(17 Apr 1999–5 Apr 2000)
1421	(6 Apr 2000–25 Mar 2001)
1422	(26 Mar 2001–14 Mar 2002)
1423	(15 Mar 2002–3 Mar 2003)
1424	(4 Mar 2003–21 Feb 2004)
1425	(22 Feb 2004–9 Feb 2005)
1426	(10 Feb 2005–30 Jan 2006)
1427	(31 Jan 2006–20 Jan 2007)
1428	(21 Jan 2007–9 Jan 2008)

Islamic[2] (H)

1429	(10 Jan 2008–28 Dec 2008)
1430	(29 Dec 2008–17 Dec 2009)
1431	(18 Dec 2009–6 Dec 2010)
1432	(7 Dec 2010–26 Nov 2011)
1433	(27 Nov 2011–14 Nov 2012)
1434	(15 Nov 2012–4 Nov 2013)
1435	(5 Nov 2013–24 Oct 2014)
1436	(25 Oct 2014–13 Oct 2015)
1437	(14 Oct 2015–1 Oct 2016)
1438	(2 Oct 2016–21 Sep 2017)
1439	(22 Sep 2017–10 Sep 2018)
1440	(11 Sep 2018–31 Aug 2019)
1441	(1 Sep 2019–19 Aug 2020)

Hindu [3] (SE)		Hindu [3] (SE)	
1917	(22 Mar 1995–20 Mar 1996)	1930	(21 Mar 2008–21 Mar 2009)
1918	(21 Mar 1996–21 Mar 1997)	1931	(22 Mar 2009–21 Mar 2010)
1919	(22 Mar 1997–21 Mar 1998)	1932	(22 Mar 2010–21 Mar 2011)
1920	(22 Mar 1998–21 Mar 1999)	1933	(22 Mar 2011–20 Mar 2012)
1921	(22 Mar 1999–20 Mar 2000)	1934	(21 Mar 2012–21 Mar 2013)
1922	(21 Mar 2000–21 Mar 2001)	1935	(22 Mar 2013–21 Mar 2014)
1923	(22 Mar 2001–21 Mar 2002)	1936	(22 Mar 2014–21 Mar 2015)
1924	(22 Mar 2002–21 Mar 2003)	1937	(22 Mar 2015–20 Mar 2016)
1925	(22 Mar 2003–20 Mar 2004)	1938	(21 Mar 2016–21 Mar 2017)
1926	(21 Mar 2004–21 Mar 2005)	1939	(22 Mar 2017–21 Mar 2018)
1927	(22 Mar 2005–21 Mar 2006)	1940	(22 Mar 2018–21 Mar 2019)
1928	(22 Mar 2006–21 Mar 2007)	1941	(22 Mar 2019–20 Mar 2020)
1929	(22 Mar 2007–20 Mar 2008)		

Gregorian equivalents are given in parentheses and are AD (= Anno Domini, also called CE, Common Era).

[1] Calculated from 3761 BC, said to be the year of the creation of the world. AM = Anno Mundi.

[2] Calculated from AD 622, the year in which the Prophet went from Mecca to Medina.
 H = Hegira.

[3] Calculated from AD 78, the beginning of the Saka era (SE), used alongside Gregorian dates in Government of India publications since 22 Mar 1957.

Chinese animal years and times 1984–2019

Chinese	English	Years			Time of day (hours)
Shu	Rat	1984	1996	2008	2300–0100
Niu	Ox	1985	1997	2009	0100–0300
Hu	Tiger	1986	1998	2010	0300–0500
Tu	Hare	1987	1999	2011	0500–0700
Long	Dragon	1988	2000	2012	0700–0900
She	Serpent	1989	2001	2013	0900–1100
Ma	Horse	1990	2002	2014	1100–1300
Yang	Sheep	1991	2003	2015	1300–1500
Hou	Monkey	1992	2004	2016	1500–1700
Ji	Cock	1993	2005	2017	1700–1900
Gou	Dog	1994	2006	2018	1900–2100
Zhu	Boar	1995	2007	2019	2100–2300

The seasons

N Hemisphere	Duration
Spring	From vernal equinox (c.21 Mar) to summer solstice (c.21 Jun)
Summer	From summer solstice (c.21 Jun) to autumnal equinox (c.23 Sep)
Autumn	From autumnal equinox (c.23 Sep) to winter solstice (c.22 Dec)
Winter	From winter solstice (c.22 Dec) to vernal equinox (c.21 Mar)

S Hemisphere	Duration
Autumn	From autumnal equinox (c.21 Mar) to winter solstice (c.21 Jun)
Winter	From winter solstice (c.21 Jun) to spring equinox (c.23 Sep)
Spring	From spring equinox (c.23 Sep) to summer solstice (c.22 Dec)
Summer	From summer solstice (c.22 Dec) to autumnal equinox (c.21 Mar)

Months (Associations with gems and flowers)

In many Western countries, the months are traditionally associated with gemstones and flowers. There is considerable variation between countries. The following combinations are widely recognized in North America and the UK.

Month	Gemstone	Flower
January	Garnet	Carnation, Snowdrop
February	Amethyst	Primrose, Violet
March	Aquamarine, Bloodstone	Jonquil, Violet
April	Diamond	Daisy, Sweet Pea
May	Emerald	Hawthorn, Lily of the Valley
June	Alexandrite, Moonstone, Pearl	Honeysuckle, Rose
July	Ruby	Larkspur, Water Lily
August	Peridot, Sardonyx	Gladiolus, Poppy
September	Sapphire	Aster, Morning Glory
October	Opal, Tourmaline	Calendula, Cosmos
November	Topaz	Chrysanthemum
December	Turquoise, Zircon	Holly, Narcissus, Poinsettia

International time differences

The time zones of the world are conventionally measured from longitude 0° at Greenwich Observatory (Greenwich Mean Time, GMT).

Each 15° of longitude east of this point is one hour ahead of GMT (eg when it is 2pm in London it is 3pm or later in time zones to the east). Hours ahead of GMT are shown by a plus sign, eg +3, +4/8.

Each 15° west of this point is one hour behind GMT (eg 2pm in London would be 1pm or earlier in time zones to the west). Hours behind GMT are shown by a minus sign, eg −3, −4/8.

Some countries adopt time zones that vary from standard time. Also, during the summer, several countries adopt Daylight Saving Time (or Summer Time), which is one hour ahead of the times shown overleaf.

Afghanistan	$+4\frac{1}{2}$	Comoros	+3	Honduras	−6
Albania	+1	Congo	+1	Hong Kong	+8
Algeria	+1	Congo, DR	+1/2	Hungary	+1
Andorra	+1	Costa Rica	−6	Iceland	0
Angola	+1	Côte d'Ivoire	0	India	$+5\frac{1}{2}$
Antigua and Barbuda	−4	Croatia	+1	Indonesia	+7/9
Argentina	−3	Cuba	−5	Iran	$+3\frac{1}{2}$
Armenia	+4	Cyprus	+2	Iraq	+3
Australia	+8/10	Czech Republic	+1	Ireland	0
Austria	+1	Denmark	+1	Israel	+2
Azerbaijan	+4	Djibouti	+3	Italy	+1
Bahamas	−5	Dominica	−4	Jamaica	−5
Bahrain	+3	Dominican Republic	−4	Japan	+9
Bangladesh	+6			Jordan	+2
Barbados	−4	East Timor	+8	Kazakhstan	+4/6
Belarus	+2	Ecuador	−5	Kenya	+3
Belgium	+1	Egypt	+2	Kiribati	+12/14
Belize	−6	El Salvador	−6	Korea, North	+9
Benin	+1	Equatorial Guinea	+1	Korea, South	+9
Bermuda	−4	Eritrea	+3	Kuwait	+3
Bhutan	+6	Estonia	+2	Kyrgyzstan	+6
Bolivia	−4	Ethiopia	+3	Laos	+7
Bosnia and Herzegovina	+1	Falkland Is	−4	Latvia	+2
Botswana	+2	Fiji	+12	Lebanon	+2
Brazil	−2/5	Finland	+2	Lesotho	+2
Brunei	+8	France	+1	Liberia	0
Bulgaria	+2	Gabon	+1	Libya	+2
Burkina Faso	0	Gambia	0	Liechtenstein	+1
Burundi	+2	Georgia	+4	Lithuania	+2
Cambodia	+7	Germany	+1	Luxembourg	+1
Cameroon	+1	Ghana	0	Macedonia	+1
Canada	$-3\frac{1}{2}/8$	Gibraltar	+1	Madagascar	+3
Cape Verde	−1	Greece	+2	Malawi	+2
Central African Republic	+1	Greenland	−3	Malaysia	+8
		Grenada	−4	Maldives	+5
Chad	+1	Guatemala	−6	Mali	0
Chile	−4	Guinea	0	Malta	+1
China	+8	Guinea-Bissau	0	Marshall Is	+12
Colombia	−5	Guyana	−4	Mauritania	0
		Haiti	−5	Mauritius	+4

Mexico	-6/8	Portugal	0	Switzerland	+1
Micronesia, Federated States of	+10/11	Qatar	+3	Syria	+2
		Romania	+2	Taiwan	+8
Moldova	+2	Russia	+2/12	Tajikistan	+5
Monaco	+1	Rwanda	+2	Tanzania	+3
Mongolia	+7/8	St Kitts and Nevis	-4	Thailand	+7
Montenegro	+1			Togo	0
Morocco	0	St Lucia	-4	Tonga	+13
Mozambique	+2	St Vincent and the Grenadines	-4	Trinidad and Tobago	-4
Myanmar (Burma)	$+6\frac{1}{2}$	Samoa	-11	Tunisia	+1
Namibia	+1	San Marino	+1	Turkey	+2
Nauru	+12	São Tomé and Príncipe	0	Turkmenistan	+5
Nepal	$+5\frac{3}{4}$			Tuvalu	+12
Netherlands	+1	Saudi Arabia	+3	Uganda	+3
New Zealand	+12	Senegal	0	Ukraine	+2
Nicaragua	-6	Serbia	+1	United Arab Emirates	+4
Niger	+1	Seychelles	+4		
Nigeria	+1	Sierra Leone	0	United Kingdom	0
Norway	+1	Singapore	+8	United States of America	-5/10
Oman	+4	Slovakia	+1		
Pakistan	+5	Slovenia	+1	Uruguay	-3
Palau	+9	Solomon Is	+11	Uzbekistan	+5
Panama	-5	Somalia	+3	Vanuatu	+11
Papua New Guinea	+10	South Africa	+2	Vatican	+1
		Spain	+1	Venezuela	-4
Paraguay	-4	Sri Lanka	$+5\frac{1}{2}$	Vietnam	+7
Peru	-5	Sudan	+3	Yemen	+3
Philippines	+8	Suriname	-3	Zambia	+2
Poland	+1	Swaziland	+2	Zimbabwe	+2
		Sweden	+1		

International time zones

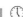
National holidays

The first part of each country's listing gives the holidays that occur on fixed dates (although these might vary occasionally). Most dates are accompanied by an indication of the purpose of the day, eg Independence = Independence Day; dates which have no gloss are either fixed dates within a religious or civil calendar (for which see below) or bank holidays.

The second part of the listing gives holidays whose dates vary, usually depending on religious factors. The most common of these are given in abbreviated form (see list below).

A number in brackets such as (Independence) (2) refers to the number of days devoted to the holiday. The listings do not include holidays that affect only certain parts of a country, half-day holidays or Sundays.

National holidays are subject to change.

The following abbreviations are used for variable religious feast-days:

A	Ascension Thursday
Ad	Id-ul-Adha (also found with other spellings — especially Eid-ul-Adha; various names relating to this occasion are used in different countries, such as Tabaski, Id el-Kebir, Hari Raja Haji)
Ar	Arafa
As	Ashora (found with various spellings)
C	Carnival (immediately before Christian Lent, unless otherwise specified)
CC	Corpus Christi
D	Diwali, Deepavali
EM	Easter Monday
ER	End of Ramadan (known generally as Id/Eid-ul-Fitr, but various names relating to this occasion are used in different countries, such as Karite, Hari Raja Puasa)
ES	Easter Sunday
GF	Good Friday
HS	Holy Saturday
HT	Holy Thursday
NY	New Year
PB	Prophet's Birthday (known generally as Maul-id-al-Nabi in various forms and spellings)
R	First day of Ramadan
WM	Whit Monday

The following fixed dates are shown without gloss:

Jan 1	New Year's Day
Jan 6	Epiphany
Mar 21	Novrus (Persian New Year; various spellings)
May 1	Labour Day (often known by a different name, such as Workers' Day)
Aug 15	Assumption of Our Lady
Nov 1	All Saints' Day
Nov 2	All Souls' Day
Dec 8	Immaculate Conception
Dec 24	Christmas Eve

Dec 25	Christmas Day
Dec 26	Boxing Day/St Stephen's Day
Dec 31	New Year's Eve

Afghanistan Mar 21, Apr 18 (Liberation), 28 (Revolution), May 1, Aug 19 (Independence); Ad (3), Ar, As, ER (3), NY (Hindu), PB, R

Albania Jan 1, 2, Mar 14 (Summer), 22 (Nevrus), May 1, Oct 19 (Mother Teresa), Nov 28 (Independence), 29 (Liberation), Dec 25; Ad, ER, ES, NY (Albanian), Orthodox Easter (Apr/May)

Algeria Jan 1, May 1, Jun 19, Jul 5 (Independence), Nov 1 (Revolution); Ad (2), As, ER (2), NY (Muslim), PB

Andorra Jan 1, 6, Mar 14 (Constitution), May 1, 25, Jun 24 (St John), Aug 15, Sep 8 (National), Nov 1, 4 (St Charles), Dec 8, 24, 25, 26, 31; EM, GF, WM

Angola Jan 1, 4 (Martyrs of the Colonial Repression), 25 (Luanda City), Feb 4 (Beginning of the Armed Struggle), Mar 8 (Women), April 4 (Peace), May 1, 25 (Africa), Jun 1 (Children), Sep 17 (Nation's Founder/National Hero), Nov 2, 11 (Independence), Dec 25

Antigua and Barbuda Jan 1, Jul 4 (Caricom), Nov 1 (Independence), Dec 9 (National Heroes), Dec 25, 26; C (2), EM, GF, WM, Labour (1st Mon in May), Emancipation (1st Mon in Aug) (2)

Argentina Jan 1, May 1, 25 (Independence), Jun 12 (Malvinas), 19 (Flag), Jul 9 (National), Aug 17 (San Martín), Oct 12 (Columbus), Dec 8, 25; GF, HT

Armenia Jan 1, 2, 6 (Armenian Orthodox Christmas), Mar 8 (Women's), Apr 7 (Motherhood and Beauty), 24 (Genocide Memorial), May 9 (Victory and Peace), 28 (Declaration of the First Republic, 1918), Jul 5 (Constitution), Sep 21 (Independence), Dec 7 (Earthquake Memorial), Dec 31; EM, ES, GF, HS

Australia Jan 1, 26 (Australia), Apr 25 (Anzac), Dec 25, 26 (Boxing/Proclamation); Queen's Birthday (Jun, *except Western Australia*, Sept/Oct); EM, GF, HS; *additional days vary between states*

Austria Jan 1, 6, May 1, Aug 15, Oct 26 (National), Nov 1, Dec 8, 25, 26; A, CC, EM, WM

Azerbaijan Jan 1, 20 (Martyrs), 8 Mar (Women), May 9 (Victory), 28 (Republic), June 15 (National Salvation), 26 (Army and Navy), Oct 18 (Independence), Nov 12 (Constitution), 17 (National Revival), Dec 31 (World Azeri Solidarity); Ad, ER, NY (Muslim) (2)

Bahamas, The Jan 1, Jul 10 (Independence), Oct 12 (National Heroes), Dec 25, 26; EM, GF, WM; Labour (1st Mon in Jun), Emancipation (1st Fri in Aug)

Bahrain Jan 1, Dec 16 (National); Ad (3), As, ER (3), NY (Muslim), PB

Bangladesh Feb 21 (International Mother Language), Mar 26 (Independence), May 1, Nov 7 (National Revolution), Dec 25, 26 (Victory); Ad (3), As, Buddha Purnima (Apr/May), Durga Puja (Dashami), ER (3), Jamatul Wida, Janmashtami, NY (Bengali), NY (Muslim), PB, Shab-e-Barat, Shab-e-Qadr

Barbados Jan 1, 21 (Errol Barrow), Apr 28 (National Heroes), May 1, Aug 7 (Emancipation/Kadooment), Nov 30 (Independence), Dec 25, 26; EM, GF, WM

Belarus Jan 1, 7 (Orthodox Christmas), Mar 8 (Women), 15 (Constitution), May 1, 6 (Memorial/Radounitsa), 9 (Victory), Jul 3 (Independence), Nov 2 (Dzyady), 7 (October Revolution), Dec 25; GF, HS, ES, EM, Orthodox Easter

Belgium Jan 1, May 1, Jul 21 (Independence), Aug 15, Nov 1, 11 (Armistice), 15 (King's Birthday), Dec 25, 26; A, EM, ES, WM; *also community holidays* (Jul 11 Flemish, Sep 27 French, Nov 15 German)

Belize Jan 1, Mar 9 (Baron Bliss), May 1, 24 (Commonwealth), Sep 10 (St George's Caye), 21 (Independence), Oct 12 (Columbus), Nov 19 (Garifuna Settlement), Dec 25, 26; EM, GF, HS

Benin Jan 1, 10 (Traditional religions), May 1, Aug 1 (Independence), 15, Oct 26 (Armed Forces), Nov 1, 30 (National), Dec 25, 31 (Tabaski); A, Ad, EM, ER, PB, WM

Bhutan Aug 8 (Independence), Nov 11–13 (Birthday of HM Jigme Singye Wangchuk), Dec 17 (National); *all traditional Buddhist holidays*

Bolivia Jan 1, May 1, Jul 17 (La Paz), Aug 7 (National), Nov 2, Dec 25; C, CC, GF

Bosnia and Herzegovina Jan 27 (St Sava's Day), Feb 2 (Kurban Bajram), Mar 1 (Independence), May 1, Aug 15; Orthodox Christmas (2), Orthodox New Year (2); *much local variation*

Botswana Jan 1, May 1, Jul 1 (Sir Seretse Khama), Sep 30 (Botswana), Dec 25, 26; A, EM, GF, HS, President's Day (Jul) (2); Jul, Oct Public Holidays

Brazil Jan 1, Apr 21 (Tiradentes), May 1, Sep 7 (Independence), Oct 12 (Our Lady of Aparecida), Nov 2, 15 (Republic), Dec 25; C (5), CC, GF; *much local variation*

Brunei Jan 1, 29 (Feast of the Sacrifice), Feb 23 (National), May 31 (Royal Brunei Malay Regiment), Jul 15 (Sultan's Birthday), Dec 25; Ad, ER (2), Isra' Me'raj, NY (Chinese), NY (Muslim), PB, R, Revelation of the Koran

Bulgaria Jan 1, Mar 3 (National), May 1, 6 (Bulgarian Army), 24 (Culture and Literacy), Sep 6 (Unification), 22 (Independence), Dec 1 (Revival), 24, 25, 26; Orthodox Easter (Apr/May)

Burkina Faso Jan 1, 3 (1966 Revolution), Mar 8 (Women), May 1, Aug 4 (Revolution), 5 (Independence), 15, Oct 15 (1987 Coup), Nov 1, Dec 11 (National), 25, 31; A, Ad, EM, ER, NY (Muslim), PB

Burma ▶ Myanmar

Burundi Jan 1, Feb 5 (Unity), Mar 12 (Labour), Jul 1 (Independence), Aug 15, Oct 13 (Rwagasore Assassination), Oct 21 (Ndadaye Assassination), Nov 1, Dec 25; A

Cambodia Jan 1, 7 (Victory over Genocide), Mar 8 (Women), Apr 3 (Culture), May 1, Jun 1 (Children), 18 (Queen's Birthday), Sep 24 (Constitution and Coronation), Oct 23 (Paris Peace Agreement), 30 (Former King Sihanouk's Birthday) (3), Nov 9 (Independence), Dec 10 (Human Rights); Cambodian New Year (Apr) (3), Meak Bochea (Feb), Pchum Ben (Sep) (3), Royal Ploughing Ceremony (May), Visakha Bochea (May), Water/Moon Festival (Nov) (3)

Cameroon Jan 1, Feb 11 (Youth), May 1, 20 (National), Aug 15, Dec 25; A, Ad, ER, GF, ES, EM, HS, PB

Canada Jan 1, Jul 1 (Canada), Nov 11 (Remembrance), Dec 25, 26; EM, GF; Labour (1st Mon in Sep), Thanksgiving (2nd Mon in Oct), Victoria (Mon preceding May 25)

Cape Verde Jan 1, 20 (National Heroes), May 1, Jul 5 (Independence), Aug 15, Sep 12 (National), Nov 1, Dec 25; ES, GF, Ash Wednesday

Central African Republic Jan 1, Mar 29 (Death of President Boganda), May 1, Jun 1 (Mothers), Aug 13 (Independence), 15, Nov 1, Dec 1 (National), 25; A, EM

Chad Jan 1, Apr 13 (National), May 1, 25 (OAU Foundation), Aug 11 (Independence), Nov 1, 28 (Republic), Dec 1 (Liberty and Democracy), 25; Ad, EM, ES, ER

Chile Jan 1, May 1, Jun 29 (Sts Peter and Paul), Aug 15, Sep 18 (National), 19 (Army), Oct 9 (Americas), Dec 8, 25, 26; CC, GF, EM; Aug public holiday, May public holiday

China Jan 1, Mar 8 (Women), May 1, 4 (Youth), Oct 1 (National) (2); Spring Festival (4) (Jan/Feb), NY (Chinese)

Colombia Jan 1, 6, Mar 19 (St Joseph), May 1, Jun 29 (Sts Peter and Paul), Jul 20 (Independence), Aug 7 (Battle of Boyacá), 15, Oct 12 (Columbus), Nov 1, 11 (Independence of Cartagena), Dec 8, 25; A, CC, GF, HT, Sacred Heart (Jun)

Comoros Mar 18 (Death of President Cheikh), May 25 (African Unity), Jul 6 (Independence), Nov 26 (President Abdallah's Assassination), 28 (Leilat al-Meiraj/Ascension of the Prophet); Ad, As, ER, NY (Muslim), PB, R

Congo Jan 1, Mar 18 (Day of the Supreme Sacrifice), May 1, Jul 31 (Revolution), Aug 13–15 (The Three Glorious Days), Nov 1 (Day of the Dead), Dec 25 (Children), 31 (Foundation of the Party and People's Republic)

Congo, Democratic Republic of the Jan 1, 4 (Martyrs of Independence), 17 (National Heroes), May 1, 17 (National Liberation), Aug 1 (Parents), Oct 14 (Youth), Nov 17 (Army), Dec 25

Costa Rica Jan 1, May 1, Jul 25 (Annexation of Guanacaste), Aug 2 (Virgin de Los Angeles), 15 (Mothers), Sep 15 (Independence), Oct 12 (Columbus), Nov 2, Dec 24, 25, 31; Holy Week

Côte d'Ivoire Jan 1, May 1, Aug 7 (Republic), 15, Nov 1, 15 (Peace), Dec, 25; A, Ad, EM, ER, GF, WM

Croatia Jan 1, May 1, 30 (National), Jun 22 (Antifascist Resistance), Aug 5 (National Thanksgiving), 15, Oct 8 (Independence), Nov 1, Dec 25, 26; EM, GF

Cuba Jan 1 (Liberation), May 1, Jul 25 (National Rebellion) (2), Oct 10 (Beginning of the Independence Wars)

Cyprus Jan 1, 6, Apr 1 (Greek Cypriot National), May 1, Jun 25 (Greek National), Aug 15, Oct 1 (Independence), 28 (Greek National Ochi), Dec 24, 25, 26; ES, Green Monday, Kataklysmos, Orthodox Easter (Apr/May) (3)

Czech Republic Jan 1, May 1, 8 (Liberation), Jul 5 (Sts Cyril and Methodius), 6 (Martyrdom of Jan Hus), Oct 28 (Independence), Nov 17 (Velvet Revolution), Dec 24, 25, 26; EM

Denmark Jan 1, May 12, 25, Jun 5 (Constitution), Dec 25, 26; A, EM, GF, HT, WM, General Prayer (Apr/May)

Djibouti Jan 1, May 1, Jun 27 (Independence) (2), Dec 25; Ad (2), ER (2), NY (Muslim), PB, Al-Isra Wal-Mira'age (Mar/Apr)

Dominica Jan 1 (2), May 1, Nov 3 (Independence), 4 (Community Service), Dec 25, 26; C (2), EM, GF, WM, August Monday

Dominican Republic Jan 1, 6, 21 (Our Lady of Altagracia), 26 (Duarte), Feb 27 (Independence), May 1, Aug 16 (Restoration of the Republic), Sep 24 (Our Lady of Mercy), Nov 6 (Constitution), Dec 25; CC, GF

East Timor Jan 1, May 1, 20 (Independence), 30 (Constitution), Sep 20 (Liberation), Nov 1, 12 (Santa Cruz), Dec 8, 25; A, GF

Ecuador Jan 1, Feb 12 (Amazon and Galapagos), 27 (Civicism and National Unity), May 1, 24 (Battle of Pichincha), Aug 10 (Independence), Oct 9 (Independence of Guayaquil), Nov 2, 3 (Independence of Cuenca), Dec 6 (Quito), 25, 31; C (2), GF, EM

Egypt May 1, Jun 18 (Liberation), Jul 23 (Revolution), Aug 15 (Flooding of Nile), Oct 6 (Armed Forces), 24 (Suez Victory), Dec 31 (Victory); Ad (2), Ar, ER (2), NY (Muslim), PB, Sham El Nassim (Coptic Easter) (Apr/May); *Coptic Christmas and New Year celebrated in some parts*

Eire ▶ Ireland, Republic of

El Salvador Jan 1, May 1, Aug 4 (Transfiguration), 6 (El Salvador del Mundo) (2), Sep 15 (Independence), Oct 9 (Columbus), Nov 2, 5 (Cry of Independence), Dec 24, 25, 31; ES, GF, HS, HT; *some local variation; public and private sector holidays may differ*

England and Wales Jan 1, Dec 25, 26; EM, GF; Early May (1st Mon), Spring (last Mon in May) and Summer (last Mon in Aug) Bank Holidays

Equatorial Guinea Jan 1, Mar 8 (Women), May 1, 25 (Africa), Jun 5 (President's Birthday), Aug 3 (Armed Forces), Oct 12 (Independence), Dec 10 (Human Rights), 25; CC, GF; Constitution (Aug)

Eritrea Jan 1, 6, Mar 8 (Women), May 24 (Independence), Jun 20 (Martyrs), Sep 1 (Start of the Armed Struggle), Dec 25; Ad, ER, PB; *Coptic Christmas, Epiphany (Jan), Easter, New Year (Sep) also observed*

Estonia Jan 1, Feb 24 (Independence), May 1 (Spring), Jun 23 (Victory), 24 (St John/Midsummer), Aug 20 (Restoration of Independence), Dec 25, 26; GF, ES, Whit Sunday

Ethiopia Jan 7 (Ethiopian Christmas), 19 (Ethiopian Epiphany), Mar 2 (Victory of Adwa), May 1, 28 (Downfall of the Dergue), Sep 26 (Finding of the True Cross); Ad, ER, NY (Ethiopian) (Sep), PB, Ethiopian Good Friday and Easter Sunday

Fiji Jan 1, Dec 25, 26; D, EM, GF, HS, PB, Queen's Birthday (Jun), National Youth (Apr/May), Ratu Sir Lala Sukuna (1st Mon in Jun), Fiji (Oct)

Finland Jan 1, 6, May 1, Nov 1, Dec 6 (Independence), 24, 25, 26; A, EM, ES, GF; Midsummer Day (Jun), Whitsun (May/Jun)

France Jan 1, May 1, 8 (Victory), Jul 14 (Bastille), Aug 15, Nov 1, 11 (Armistice), Dec 25; A, EM, WM

Gabon Jan 1, Mar 12 (Renovation), May 1, 6 (Martyrs), Aug 15, 16 (Independence) (2), Nov 1, Dec 25; Ad, EM, ER, WM

Gambia, The Jan 1, Feb 18 (Independence), May 1, Dec 25; A, Ad, As, EM, ER (2), GF, PB

Georgia Jan 1, 7 (Orthodox Christmas), 19 (Orthodox Epiphany), Mar 3 (Mothers), Apr 9 (National), May 9 (National), 26 (Independence), Oct 14 (Svetitskhovloba), Nov 23 (St George); A, ES, EM

Germany Jan 1, May 1, Oct 3 (Unity), Dec 25, 26; A, EM, ES, GF, WM; *much regional variation*

Ghana Jan 1, Mar 6 (Independence), May 1, Jul 1 (Republic), Dec 2 (National Farmers), 25, 26; EM, GF

Greece Jan 1, 6, Mar 25 (Independence), May 1, Aug 15, Oct 28 (Ochi), Dec 25, 26; GF, EM, ES, WM, Whit Sunday, Orthodox Shrove Monday

Grenada Jan 1, Feb 7 (Independence), May 1, Aug 3 (Emancipation) (2), Oct 25 (Thanksgiving), Dec 25, 26; C, CC, EM, GF, WM

Guatemala Jan 1, May 1, Jun 30 (Army), Sep 15 (Independence), Oct 20 (Revolution), Nov 1, Dec 25, 31; GF, HT, Assumption (*date varies locally*)

Guinea Jan 1, May 1, Aug 15, 27 (Women's Revolt Anniversary), Oct 2 (Republic), Dec 25; A, Ad, EM, ER, PB

Guinea-Bissau Jan 1, 20 (Death of Amilcar Cabral), Mar 8 (Women), May 1, Aug 3 (Martyrs of Colonialism), Sep 24 (National), Nov 4 (Readjustment), Dec 25, 31; ER

Guyana Jan 1, Feb 23 (Republic), Apr 15 (You-Man-Nabi), May 1, 5 (Arrival Day), 26 (Independence), Jul 3 (Caricom), Aug 7 (Freedom), Dec 25, 26; Ad, D, EM, GF, PB, Phagwah (Mar), Caribbean (Jul)

Haiti Jan 1 (Independence), 2 (Ancestors), Apr 14 (Americas), May 1, 18 (Flag/University), Aug 15, Oct 17 (Death of Dessalines), 24 (United Nations), Nov 1, 2, 18 (Battle of Vertières), Dec 25; A, C, CC, GF

Honduras Jan 1, Apr 14 (Americas), May 1, Sep 15 (Independence), Oct 3 (Soldiers), 12 (Americas), 21 (Armed Forces), Dec 25; GF, ES, HT

Hong Kong Jan 1, May 1, May 5 (Buddha's Birthday), Jul 1 (Establishment), Oct 1 (National), Dec 25, 26; Chung Yeung (Oct), Tuen Ng (May/Jun)

Hungary Jan 1, Mar 15 (Independence), May 1, Aug 20 (National/St Stephen), Oct 23 (Revolution), Nov 1, Dec 25, 26; EM, WM

Iceland Jan 1, May 1, Jun 17 (National), Aug 7 (Commerce), Dec 25, 26; A, EM, ES, GF, HT, WM, Whit Sunday; First Day of Summer (Apr), August Holiday Monday

India Jan 1 (*some states*), 26 (Republic), May 1 (*some states*), Jun 30, Aug 15 (Independence), Oct 2 (Mahatma Ghandi's Birthday), Dec 25, 31; NY (Parsi, Aug, *some states*)

Indonesia Jan 1, Mar 19 (Nyepi), Aug 17 (Independence), Dec 25; A, Ad, ER (2), GF, NY (Balinese Hindu), NY (Chinese), NY (Muslim), PB, Ascension of the Prophet, Waisak (May)

Iran Feb 11 (Islamic Revolution), Mar 19 (Nationalization of Oil), 21, 31 (Islamic Republic), Apr 2 (13th Day of New Year), Jun 3 (Death of Imam Khomeini), 4 (Uprising), Aug 22 (Prophet's call to mission), Sep 9 (Birthday of the 12th living Imam), Nov 18 (Martyrdom of Imam Sadegh); Ad, As, ER, PB, Eid Ghadir Khom, Tasooah, Arbaeen, Death of the Prophet, Martyrdom of Imam Reza, Birthday of Imam Ali, Ascension of the Prophet, Birthday of Imam Hussein, Martyrdom of Imam Ali, Death of Hadrath Zahra

Iraq Jan 1, 6 (Army), Feb 8 (8th February Revolution), Mar 21, 17 (Liberation), May 1, Jul 14 (14th July Revolution), 17 (National), Aug 8 (Ceasefire); Ad (4), As, ER (3), NY (Muslim), PB

Ireland, Republic of Jan 1, Mar 17 (St Patrick), Dec 25, 26; EM, 1st Mon in May, 1st Mon in Jun, 1st Mon in Aug, last Mon in Oct public holidays

Ireland, Northern ► Northern Ireland

Israel Jan 18 (Tu B'Shvat), Apr 29 (Martyrs and Heroes of the Holocaust), May 6 (Memorial for the Fallen in Wars), 7 (Independence), 20 (Lag Ba'omer), 30 (Jerusalem); NY (Jewish) (Sep/Oct) (2), Purim (Mar), Passover (Apr), Pentecost (Jun), Tisha B'Av (Aug), Yom Kippur (Oct), Feast of Tabernacles (Oct), Chanuka (Dec)

Italy Jan 1, 6, Apr 25 (Liberation), May 1, Jun 2 (National), 29 (Sts Peter and Paul), Aug 15, Nov 1, Dec 8, 25, 26; EM; *much local variation*

Jamaica Jan 1, May 23 (Labour), Aug 1 (Emancipation), 6 (Independence), Oct 15 (National Heroes), Dec 25, 26; Ash Wednesday, EM, GF

Japan Jan 1, Feb 11 (National Foundation), Apr 29 (Greenery), May 3 (Constitution Memorial), May 4 (Citizen), 5 (Children), Sep 18 (Respect for the Aged), Oct 9 (Physical Fitness), Nov 3 (Culture), 23 (Labour Thanksgiving), Dec 22 (Emperor's Birthday); Dec 31, Autumnal Equinox, Coming-of-Age (2nd Mon in Jan), Marine Day (Jul), Sports (2nd Mon in Oct), Vernal Equinox

Jordan Jan 1, May 1, 25 (Independence), Jun 9 (Accession of King Abdullah),10 (Army), Nov 14 (King Hussein Remembrance); Ad (4), R, ER (3), NY (Muslim), PB, Al-Isra' wal mi'raj, Birth of the Prophet

Kazakhstan Jan 1, 2, Mar 8 (Women), 21, May 1 (Unity), 9 (Victory), Aug 30 (Constitution), Oct 25 (Republic), Dec 16 (Independence), 31; NY (Central Asian)

Kenya Jan 1, May 1, Jun 1 (Madaraka), Oct 10 (Moi), 20 (Kenyatta) (2), Dec 12 (Jamhuri), 25, 26; EM, ER, GF

Kiribati Jan 1, Mar 8 (Women), Apr 17 (National Health), Jul 11 (Gospel), 12 (Independence) (3), Aug 6 (Youth), Dec 10 (Human Rights), 25, 26; GF, HS, EM, ES; *length of holidays varies locally*

Korea, Democratic People's Republic of (North Korea) Jan 1, Feb 16 (Kim Jong Il's Birthday), Mar 8 (Women), Apr 15 (Kim Il Sung's Birthday), Apr 25 (Army Foundation), May 1, Jul 8 (Kim Il–Sung Anniversary), 27 (Fatherland Liberation War Victory), Aug 15 (Liberation), Sep 9 (Foundation of the Republic), Oct 10 (Foundation of the Workers' Party), Dec 27 (Constitution)

Korea, Republic of (South Korea) Jan 1–3, Mar 1 (Independence Movement), 10 (Labour), Apr 5 (Arbor), May 5 (Children), Jun 6 (Memorial), Jul 17 (Constitution), Aug 15 (Liberation), Oct 1 (Armed Forces), 3 (National Foundation), 9 (Korean Alphabet), Dec 25; NY (Chinese, Jan/Feb), Lord Buddha's Birthday (May), Moon Festival (Sep/Oct)

Kuwait Jan 1, Feb 25 (National), 26 (Liberation); Ad (4), ER (3), NY (Muslim), PB, Ascension of the Prophet

Kyrgyzstan Jan 1, 7 (Russian Orthodox Christmas), Mar 8 (Women), 21 (Kyrgyz New Year), May 1, 5 (Constitution), 9 (Victory), Aug 31 (Independence); Ad, ER

Laos Jan 1, 6 (Pathet Lao), 20 (Army's Foundation), Mar 8 (Women), 22 (Party's Foundation), May 1, Jun 1 (Children), Aug 23 (Declaration of Power), Oct 7 (Teachers), 12 (Independence), Dec 2 (National); New Year/Water Festival (3) (Apr), Boat Racing Festival (Oct), That Luang Festival (Nov), Makhabouxa (Feb), Visakhabouxa (May), Hokhaopadabdine (Aug), Hokhaosalak (Sep), Buddhist days (2)

Latvia Jan 1, May 1, 4 (Independence), Jun 23 (Ligo), 24 (Janis/Summer Solstice), Nov 18 (Proclamation of the Republic), Dec 25, 26, 31; EM, ES, GF; Mothers (2nd Sun in May)

Lebanon Jan 1, 6 (Armenian Christmas), Feb 9 (St Maron), May 1, 6 (Martyrs), 25 (Resistance and Liberation), Aug 15, Nov 1, 22 (Independence), Dec 25; Ad (3), As, EM, GF, ER (3), NY (Muslim); PB

Lesotho Jan 1, Mar 11 (Moshoeshoe), Apr 4 (Heroes), May 1, Jul 17 (King's Birthday), Oct 4 (Independence), Dec 25, 26; A, EM, GF

Liberia Jan 1, Feb 11 (Armed Forces), Mar 15 (J J Roberts), Apr 12 (Redemption), May 6 (Samuel K Doe), 14 (National Unification), 25 (Africa), Jul 26 (Independence), Aug 24 (National Flag), Nov 29 (President Tubman's Birthday), Dec 25; Decoration (Mar), National Fast and Prayer (Apr), Thanksgiving (Nov)

Libya Mar 2 (Declaration of Establishment of Authority of People), 8 (National), 28 (Evacuation of British Troops), Jun 11 (Evacuation of US Troops), Jul 23 (Revolution), Sep 1 (National), Oct 7 (Evacuation of Italian Fascists); Ad (4), As, ER (3), PB

Liechtenstein Jan 1, 2 (Berchtold), 6, Feb 2 (Candlemas), Mar 19 (St Joseph), May 1, Aug 15, Sep 8 (Nativity of Our Lady), Nov 1, Dec 8, 24, 25, 26, 31; A, C, CC, EM, ES, GF, WM, Whit Sunday

Lithuania Jan 1, Feb 16 (Independence), Mar 11 (Restoration of Statehood), May 1, Jul 6 (Coronation of Mindaugas/Statehood), Aug 15, Nov 1, Dec 25, 26; EM, ES; Mother's Day (1st Sun in May)

Luxembourg Jan 1, May 1, Jun 23 (National), Aug 15, Nov 1, Dec 24, 25, 26; A, C, ES, EM, WM, Shrove Monday

Macedonia Jan 1, 6 (Orthodox Christmas) (2), Mar 8 (Women), May 1, 24 (Sts Cyril and Methodius), Aug 2 (Ilinden), Sep 8 (Independence)

Madagascar Jan 1, Mar 29 (Memorial), May 1, Jun 26 (Independence), Aug 15, Sep 27 (St Vincent de Paul), Nov 1, Dec 25, 30 (National); A, EM, GF

Malawi Jan 1, 15 (Chilembwe), Mar 3 (Martyrs), May 1, Jun 14 (Freedom), Jul 6 (Independence), Dec 11 (Arbor), 25, 26; EM, ER, GF; Mothers (2nd Mon in Oct)

Malaysia May 1, Jun 3 (Birthday of Yang Di Pertuan Agong), Aug 31 (National), Dec 25; Ad (2), D (*most states*), ER (2), Hari Raya Qurban (3), NY (Chinese) (Jan/Feb), NY (Muslim), PB, Wesak; *several local festivals*

Maldives Jan 1, May 3 (National), Jul 26 (Independence) (2), Nov 3 (Victory), 11 (Republic) (2); Ad (4), Ar, ER (3), NY (Muslim), PB, R, Day the Maldives Embraced Islam, Martyrs' Day (Sep)

Mali Jan 1, 20 (Armed Forces), Mar 26 (Democracy), May 1, 25 (African Unity), Sep 22 (Independence), Dec 25; Ad, EM, ER, PB, R

Malta Jan 1, Feb 10 (St Paul's Shipwreck), Mar 19 (St Joseph), 31 (Freedom), May 1, Jun 7 (Sette Giugno), 29 (Sts Peter and Paul), Aug 15, Sep 8 (Our Lady of the Victories), 21 (Independence), Dec 8, 13 (Republic), 25; GF

Marshall Islands Jan 1, Mar 1 (Nuclear Victims), May 1 (Constitution), Oct 21 (Compact), Nov 17 (President), Dec 25; Fishermen (1st Fri in Jul), Workers (1st Fri in Sep), Customs (last Fri in Sep), Thanksgiving (3rd Thur in Nov), Gospel (1st Fri in Dec)

Mauritania Jan 1, May 1, 25 (Celebration of the African Union), Jul 10 (Armed Forces), Nov 28 (National); Ad, ER, NY (Muslim), PB

Mauritius Jan 1, 2, Feb 1 (Abolition of Slavery), Mar 12 (National), May 1, Aug 15, Nov 1, 2 (Arrival of Indentured Labourers), Dec 25; Ad, Chinese Spring Festival (Jan/Feb), D, ER, Ganesh Chathurti (Aug/Sep), Maha Shivaratree (Feb/Mar), NY (Chinese), Ougadi (Mar/Apr), Thaipoosam Cavadee (Jan/Feb)

Mexico Jan 1, Feb 5 (Constitution), Mar 21 (Birthday of Benito Juárez), May 1, 16 (Independence), Nov 2, 20 (Mexican Revolution), Dec 1 (Presidential Inauguration), 24, 25; HT, GF, EM

Micronesia, Federated States of Jan 1, May 10 (Proclamation of the Federated States of Micronesia), Oct 24 (United Nations), Nov 4 (National Day), Dec 25; GF; *additional days vary between states*

Moldova Jan 1, 7 (Orthodox Christmas) (2), Mar 8 (Women), Apr 18 (Memorial), May 1, 9 (Victory), Aug 27 (Independence), 31 (National Language), Oct 13 (Wine) (2); EM (Orthodox), ES

Monaco Jan 1, 27 (St Devote), May 1, Aug 15, Nov 1, 19 (National), Dec 8, 25; A, CC, EM, WM

Mongolia Jan 1, Jun 1 (Mothers and Children), Jul 10 (People's Revolution) (3), Nov 26 (Independence); NY (lunar)

Montenegro Jan 1, 7 (Orthodox Christmas), May 1 (2), 9 (Victory), Jul 13 (National), Nov 29 (Republic); Orthodox Easter (Apr/May)

Morocco Jan 1, 11 (Independence Manifesto), Mar 3 (Throne Day), May 1, 23 (National), Jul 9 (King's Birthday), Aug 14 (Qued-ed-Dahab Allegiance), Aug 20 (King and People), Nov 6 (Green March), 18 (Independence); Ad, ER, NY (Muslim), PB

Mozambique Jan 1, Feb 3 (Heroes), Apr 7 (Mozambican Women), May 1, Jun 25 (Independence), Sep 7 (Victory), 26 (Armed Forces), Oct 4 (Peace and Reconciliation), Nov 10 (Maputo), Dec 25 (Christmas/Family)

Myanmar (Burma) Jan 4 (Independence), Feb 12 (Union), Mar 2 (Peasants'), 27 (Armed Forces), May 1, Jul 19 (Martyrs'), Dec 25; Ad, D, 4 Full Moon days, National (Nov), NY (Burmese), NY (Kayin), Tazaungdaing Festival (Nov), Thingyan (Apr) (5)

Namibia Jan 1, Mar 21 (Independence), May 1, 4 (Cassinga), Aug 26 (Heroes), Dec 10 (Human Rights), Dec 25, 26 (Family/Goodwill); A, GF, EM

Nauru Jan 1, 31 (Independence), May 17 (Constitution), Oct 26 (Angam), Dec 25, 26; GF, EM

Nepal Jan 11 (National Unity), 29 (Martyrs), Feb 19 (Democracy), Mar 8 (Women), Jul 8 (King's Birthday), Nov 8 (Constitution); D, NY (Nepalese) (Apr), Shivaratri (Feb), Vasant Panchami (Feb), Vijaya Dashami (Oct), Bhai Tika (Nov)

Netherlands Jan 1, Apr 30 (Queen's Birthday), May 5 (Liberation), 25, Dec 25, 26; A, EM, ES, WM

New Zealand Jan 1, 2, Feb 6 (Waitangi), Apr 25 (Anzac), Dec 25, 26; EM, ES, GF, Queen's Birthday (Jun), Labour (Oct)

Nicaragua Jan 1, May 1, 30 (Mothers), Jul 19 (Sandinista Revolution), Sep 14 (Battle of San Jacinto), 15 (Independence), Dec 2 (Memorial), 8, 25; GF, HT

Niger Jan 1, Apr 24 (Concord), May 1, Aug 3 (Independence), Dec 18 (Republic), 25; Ad, EM, ER, PB, Leilat-ul-kadr

Nigeria Jan 1, May 1, Oct 1 (National), Dec 25, 26; Ad, EM, ER, ES, GF, PB

Northern Ireland Jan 1, Mar 17 (St Patrick), Dec 25, 26; GF, EM; Early May, Spring (May) Bank Holiday, Battle of the Boyne/Orangemen (Jul), Summer Bank Holiday (Aug)

Norway May 1, 17 (Constitution), Dec 25, 26; A, EM, GF, HT, WM

Oman Jan 1, Nov 18 (National) (2), Dec 31; Ad (5), ER (4), NY (Muslim), PB, Lailat al-Miraj (Mar/Apr)

Pakistan Mar 23 (Pakistan), Aug 14 (Independence), Nov 9 (Iqbal), Dec 25 (Christmas/Birthday of Quaid-e-Azam); Ad (2), As (2), ER (3), PB, R; *additional religious optional holidays*

Palau Jan 1, Mar 15 (Youth), May 5 (Senior Citizens), Jun 1 (President), Jul 9 (Constitution), Oct 1 (Independence), 24 (United Nations), Dec 25; Labour Day (1st Mon in Sep), Thanksgiving (last Thurs in Nov)

Panama Jan 1, 9 (Martyrs), May 1, Nov 3 (Independence), 4 (Flag), 10 (First Call of Independence), 28 (Independence from Spain), Dec 8 (Mothers), 24, 25; C, GF; *some local variation*

Papua New Guinea Jan 2, Apr 25 (Remembrance), Sep 16 (Independence), Dec 25, 26; EM, ES, GF, HS; Queen's Birthday (Jun)

Paraguay Jan 1, Mar 1 (Heroes), May 1, 15 (Independence), Jun 12 (Chaco Peace), Aug 15 (Foundation of Asuncion), Sep 29 (Battle of Boqueron), Dec 8, 25; EM, GF, HT

Peru Jan 1, May 1, Jun 29 (Sts Peter and Paul), Jul 28 (Independence), Aug 30 (St Rosa de Lima), Nov 1, 8, Dec 25; GF, HT

Philippines Jan 1, Apr 9 (Bataan), May 1, Jun 12 (Independence), Aug 30 (National Heroes), Nov 1, 30 (Bonifacio), Dec 25, 30 (Rizal), 31; EM, ER, GF, HT

Poland Jan 1, May 1, 3 (National), Aug 15, Nov 1, 11 (Independence), Dec 25, 26; CC, EM, ES

Portugal Jan 1, 6, Mar 19 (St Joseph), Apr 25 (Liberty), May 1, Jun 13 (St Anthony), Aug 15, Oct 5 (Republic), Nov 1, Dec 1 (Independence), Dec 6 (Constitution), 8, 25, 26; C, CC, EM, ES, GF, HT

Qatar Sep 3 (Independence); Ad (4), ER (4)

Romania Jan 1, 2, 6, May 1, Dec 1 (National), 25, 26; Orthodox Easter (Apr/May) (2); *other major religions each have 2 days for festivals*

Russia Jan 1, 2, 7 (Russian Orthodox Christmas), Feb 24 (Soldiers), Mar 8 (Women), May 1 (Spring and Labour) (2), 9 (Victory), Jun 12 (Independence), Nov 7 (Accord and Conciliation), Dec 12 (Constitution), 25, 26; Russian Orthodox Easter (Apr/May)

Rwanda Jan 1, 28 (Democracy), Apr 7 (Genocide Memorial), May 1, Jul 1 (Independence), 5 (Peace), Aug 1 (Harvest), 15, Sep 8 (Culture), 25 (Republic), Dec 25, 26; A, EM, WM

St Kitts and Nevis Jan 1, 2, May 1, Jun 12 (Queen's Birthday), Sep 19 (Independence), Dec 25, 26; EM, GF, WM, Labour (May), August Monday

St Lucia Jan 1, 2, Feb 22 (Independence), May 1, Oct 2 (Thanksgiving), Dec 13 (National), Dec 25, 26; CC, GF, EM, WM; Emancipation (Aug)

St Vincent and the Grenadines Jan 1, Mar 14 (National Heroes), May 1, Oct 27 (Independence), Dec 25, 26; C (Jul) (2), EM, GF, WM; Caricom (Jul), Emancipation (Aug)

Samoa Jan 1, 2, Apr 25, Mar 14 (Mothers) (2), Jun 1 (Independence), Aug 4 (Labour), Oct 12 (White Sunday) (2), Nov 7 (Arbor), Dec 25, 26; EM, GF

San Marino Jan 1, 6, Feb 5 (Liberation and St Agatha), Mar 25 (Arengo), Apr 1 (Captains Regents' Ceremony), May 1, Jul 28 (Fall of Fascism), Aug 15, Sep 3 (San Marino and Republic), Oct 1 (Investiture of the New Captains Regent), Nov 1, 2 (Commemoration of the Dead), Dec 8, 24, 25, 26, 31; CC

São Tomé and Príncipe Jan 1, Feb 3 (Liberty Heroes), May 1, Jul 12 (National Independence), Sep 6 (Armed Forces), 30 (Agricultural Reform), Dec 21 (Power of the People), 25 (Family)

Saudi Arabia Sep 23 (National); Ad (4), ER (3)

Scotland Jan 1, 2, Dec 25, 26; GF; Early May, Spring (May) and Summer (Aug) Bank Holidays

Senegal Jan 1, Feb 10 (Tabaski), Apr 4 (National), May 1, Aug 15, Nov 1, Dec 25; Ad, EM, ER, NY (Muslim), WM

Serbia Jan 1, 7 (Orthodox Christmas), Apr 27 (Statehood), May 1 (2), 9 (Victory), Nov 29 (Republic); Orthodox Easter (Apr/May) (4)

Seychelles Jan 1, 2, May 1, Jun 5 (Liberation), 18 (National), 29 (Independence), Aug 15, Nov 1, Dec 8, 25; CC, EM, GF, HS

Sierra Leone Jan 1, Apr 19 (Republic), Apr 27 (Independence), Dec 25, 26; Ad, EM, ER, GF, PB

Singapore Jan 1, May 1, Aug 9 (National), Dec 25; Ad, D, ER, GF, NY (Chinese, Jan/Feb) (2), Vesak

Slovakia Jan 1 (New Year/Establishment of Republic), 6, May 1, 8 (Triumph over Fascism), Jul 5 (Sts Cyril and Methodius), Aug 29 (Slovak National Uprising), Sep 1 (Constitution), 15 (Our Lady of the Seven Sorrows), Nov 1, 17 (Velvet Revolution), Dec 24, 25, 26; GF, EM

Slovenia Jan 1, 2, Feb 8 (Culture), Apr 27 (National Resistance), May 1 (2), Jun 25 (National), Aug 15, Oct 31 (Reformation), Nov 1, Dec 25, 26 (Independence); EM

Solomon Islands Jan 1, Jul 7 (Independence), Dec 25, 26; EM, ES, GF, HS, WM, Queen's Birthday (Jun)

Somalia Jan 1, May 1, Jun 26 (Independence), Jul 1 (Republic); Ad (2), As, ER (2), PB

South Africa Jan 1, Mar 21 (Human Rights), Apr 27 (Freedom Day), May 1, Jun 16 (Youth), Aug 9 (Women), Sep 24 (Heritage), Dec 16 (Reconciliation), 25, 26; GF, ES, EM (Family)

Spain Jan 1, 6, Mar 19 (St Joseph) (2), May 1, Aug 15, Oct 12 (National), Nov 1, Dec 6 (Constitution), 8, 25, 26; ES, GF, HT (*most areas*); *much regional variation*

Sri Lanka Jan 14 (Tamil Thai Pongal), Feb 4 (National), May 1, Dec 25; Ad, D, ER, GF, NY

(Sinhala/Tamil) (Apr) (2), PB, Mahasivarathri (Feb/Mar), Full Moon (*monthly*), day following Vesak Full Moon (May)

Sudan Jan 1 (Independence), Mar 3 (Unity), Apr 6 (Uprising), May 25 (Revolution), Dec 25; Ad (5), ER (5), NY (Muslim), PB, Sham al-Naseem (Apr/May)

Suriname Jan 1, May 1, Jul 1 (Freedom), Nov 25 (Independence), Dec 25, 26; EM, ER, GF, Holi Phagwa (Mar)

Swaziland Jan 1, Apr 19 (King's Birthday), 25 (National Flag), May 1, Jul 22 (Birthday of King Sobhuza), Sep 6 (Independence), Dec 25, 26; A, EM, GF; Incwala (Dec/Jan), Umhlanga/Reed Dance (Aug/Sep), July public holiday

Sweden Jan 1, 6, May 1, 25, Jun 6 (National), Nov 1, Dec 25, 26; A, EM, GF, WM; Midsummer (Jun)

Switzerland Jan 1, 2 (Berchtold), Aug 1 (National), Dec 25, 26; A, EM, GF, WM; *other canton and local holidays*

Syria Jan 1, Mar 18 (Revolution), 21 (Mothers), Apr 17 (Evacuation), May 1, 6 (Martyrs), Oct 6 (Liberation), Dec 25; Ad (3), ER (4), ES, NY (Muslim), PB

Taiwan Jan 1 (Foundation of the Republic of China), Feb 28 (Peace Memorial), Apr 5 (National Tomb Sweeping), May 1, Oct 10 (National); NY (Chinese) (Jan/Feb) (3), Dragon Boat Festival (Jun), Moon Festival (Sep/Oct)

Tajikistan Jan 1, Mar 8 (Women), 21, May 1, 9 (Victory), Sep 9 (Independence) Nov 6 (Constitution); Ad, ER, NY (Muslim)

Tanzania Jan 1, 12 (Zanzibar Revolution), Apr 26 (Union), May 1, Jul 7 (Industrial), Aug 8 (Farmers), Oct 14 (Nyerere Day), Dec 9 (Independence/Republic), 25, 26; Ad, EM, ER (2), GF, NY (Muslim), PB

Thailand Jan 1, Apr 6 (Chakri), 13 (Songkran) (3), May 1, 5 (Coronation), Jul 1, 11 (Asahala Bucha), Aug 12 (Queen's Birthday), Oct 23 (Chulalongkorn Memorial), Dec 5 (King's Birthday), 10 (Constitution), 31; Buddhist Lent (Jul), Makha Bucha (Feb), Visakha Bucha (May)

Togo Jan 1, 13 (Liberation), Apr 11 (Buddha's Birthday), 27 (Independence), May 1, Jun 21 (Martyrs), Aug 15, 24 (Anniversary of Failed Attack on Lomé), Nov 1, Dec 25; A, Ad, EM, ER, GF, WM

Tonga Jan 1, Apr 25 (Anzac), May 4 (Birthday of Crown Prince Tupouto'a), Jun 4 (Emancipation), Jul 4 (King's Birthday), Nov 4 (Constitution), Dec 4 (King Tupou I), 25, 26; EM, GF

Trinidad and Tobago Jan 1, Mar 30 (Spiritual Baptist Liberation Shouter), May 30 (Indian Arrival), Jun 19 (Labour), Aug 1 (Emancipation), 31 (Independence), Sept 24 (Republic), Dec 25, 26; C, CC, D, EM, ER, GF

Tunisia Jan 1, 18 (Revolution), Mar 20 (Independence), 21 (Youth), Apr 9 (Martyrs), May 1, Jun 1 (Victory), Jul 25 (Republic), Aug 13 (Women), Nov 7 (Commemoration); Ad (2), ER (2), NY (Muslim), PB

Turkey Jan 1, Apr 23 (National Sovereignty and Children), May 19 (Atatürk Commemoration/Youth and Sports), Aug 30 (Victory), Oct 29 (Republic); Ad (4), ER (3), Kurban Bayrami (Dec/Jan) (3)

Turkmenistan Jan 1, 12 (Remembrance/Anniversary of the Battle of Geok-Tepe), Feb 19 (President's Birthday), Mar 8 (Women), 21, May 9 (Victory), 18 (Constitution), Jun 21 (Election of First President), Oct 6 (Remembrance), Dec 12 (Neutrality); Ad, Day of Revival and Unity (May), ER, Independence (Oct), NY (Turkmen)

Tuvalu Jan 1, Aug 5 (Children), Oct 1 (Independence) (2), Nov 11 (Prince of Wales's Birthday), Dec 25, 26; EM, GF; Commonwealth Day (2nd Mon in Mar), Queen's Birthday (Jun)

Uganda Jan 1, 19, 26 (Liberation), Mar 2 (Adwa Victory), 8 (Women), May 1, Jun 3 (Martyrs), 9 (Heroes), Oct 9 (Independence), Dec 25, 26; Ad, EM, ER, GF

UK ► England and Wales; Northern Ireland; Scotland

Ukraine Jan 1, 7 (Eastern Orthodox Christmas), Mar 8 (Women), May 1 (2), 9 (Victory), Jun 28 (Constitution), Aug 24 (Independence); Nov 7 (October Revolution) (2), Orthodox Easter (Apr/May) (2)

United Arab Emirates Jan 1, Aug 6 (Accession of Ruler), Dec 2 (National) (2), 25; Ad (4), Ascension of the Prophet, ER (3), NY (Muslim), Waqfa (Jan), PB, R

Uruguay Jan 1, 6, May 1, 18 (Battle of Las Piedras), Jun 19 (Artigas's Birthday), Jul 18 (Constitution), Aug 25 (Independence), Oct 12 (Americas), Nov 1, Dec 25; C (2), GF, HT

USA Jan 1, Jul 4 (Independence), Nov 11 (Veterans), Dec 25; Martin Luther King's Birthday (3rd Mon in Jan), Washington's Birthday (3rd Mon in Feb), Memorial (last Mon in May), Labor (1st Mon in Sep), Columbus (2nd Mon in Oct), Thanksgiving (4th Thurs in Nov); *additional days vary between states*

Uzbekistan Jan 1, Mar 8 (Women), 21, May 1, 9 (Memory and Respect), Sep 1 (Independence), Nov 18 (Flag), Dec 8 (Constitution); Ad, ER, PB

Vanuatu Jan 1, Feb 21 (Father Lini), Mar 5 (Custom Chiefs), May 1, Jul 24 (Children), 30 (Independence), Aug 15, Oct 5 (Constitution), Nov 29 (Unity), Dec 25, 26; A, EM, ES, GF

Venezuela Jan 1, Apr 19 (Independence), May 1, Jun 24 (Battle of Carabobo), Jul 5 (National), 24 (Bolívar's Birthday), Oct 12 (Discovery), Dec 17 (Liberator's Death), 25; C (2), EM, GF

Vietnam Jan 1, Apr 30 (Saigon Liberation), May 1, 19 (Ho Chi Minh's Birthday), Sep 2 (National); NY (Vietnamese) (4)

Western Samoa ► Samoa

Yemen Jan 1, May 1, 22 (National), Sep 26 (Revolution), Oct 14 (Revolution), Nov 30 (Independence); Ad (5), ER (5), NY (Muslim), PB

Yugoslavia ► Montenegro; Serbia

Zaire ► Congo, Democratic Republic of

Zambia Jan 1, May 1, 25 (African Freedom), Oct 24 (Independence), Dec 25; EM, GF, HS; Youth (2nd Mon in Mar), Heroes (1st Mon in Jul), Unity (1st Tues in Jul), Farmers (1st Mon in Aug)

Zimbabwe Jan 1, Apr 18 (Independence), May 1, 25 (Africa), Aug 11 (Heroes), 12 (Defence Forces), Dec 22 (Unity), 25, 26; EM, ES, GF, HS

COMMUNICATION

Language families

Estimates of the numbers of speakers in the main language families of the world in the early 1980s. The list includes Japanese and Korean, which are not clearly related to any other languages.

Main language families

Indo-European	2 000 000 000
Sino-Tibetan	1 040 000 000
Niger-Congo	260 000 000
Afro-Asiatic	230 000 000
Austronesian	200 000 000
Dravidian	140 000 000
Japanese	120 000 000
Altaic	90 000 000
Austro-Asiatic	60 000 000
Korean	60 000 000
Tai	50 000 000

Main language families

Nilo-Saharan	30 000 000
Amerindian (North, Central, South America)	25 000 000
Uralic	23 000 000
Miao-Yao	7 000 000
Caucasian	6 000 000
Indo-Pacific	3 000 000
Khoisan	50 000
Australian aborigine	50 000
Palaeosiberian	25 000

Specific languages

The first column gives estimates for mother-tongue speakers of the 20 most widely used languages. The second column gives estimates of the total population of all countries where the language has official or semi-official status; these totals are often overestimates, as only a minority of people in countries where a second language is recognized may actually be fluent in it.

Mother-tongue speakers

Chinese	1 000 000 000
English	350 000 000
Spanish	250 000 000
Hindi	200 000 000
Arabic	150 000 000
Bengali	150 000 000
Russian	150 000 000
Portuguese	135 000 000
Japanese	120 000 000
German	100 000 000

Mother-tongue speakers

French	70 000 000
Panjabi	70 000 000
Bihari	65 000 000
Javanese	65 000 000
Italian	60 000 000
Korean	60 000 000
Tamil	55 000 000
Telugu	55 000 000
Marathi	50 000 000
Vietnamese	50 000 000

Official language populations		Official language populations	
English	1 400 000 000	Japanese	120 000 000
Chinese	1 000 000 000	German	100 000 000
Hindi	700 000 000	Urdu	85 000 000
Spanish	280 000 000	Italian	60 000 000
Russian	270 000 000	Korean	60 000 000
French	220 000 000	Vietnamese	60 000 000
Arabic	170 000 000	Persian	55 000 000
Malay	160 000 000	Tagalog	50 000 000
Portuguese	160 000 000	Thai	50 000 000
Bengali	150 000 000	Turkish	50 000 000

Speakers of English

The first column gives figures for countries where English is used as a mother tongue or first language; for countries where no figure is given, English is not the first language of a significant number of people. (A question mark indicates that no agreed estimates are available.) The second column gives total population figures (mainly 1996 estimates) for countries where English has official or semi-official status as a medium of communication. These totals are likely to bear little correlation with the real use of English in the area.

Country	First language speakers of English	Country population
Anguilla		1 650
Antigua and Barbuda	61 400	64 400
Australia	17 700 000	18 287 000
The Bahamas	230 000	280 000
Bangladesh	3 200 000	123 100 000
Barbados	265 000	265 000
Belize	111 000	219 000
Bermuda	61 000	61 400
Bhutan	?	1 622 000
Botswana	590 000	1 478 000
Brunei	10 000	290 000
Cameroon	2 720 000	13 609 000
Canada	18 112 000	29 784 000
Dominica	?	73 800
Fiji	160 000	802 000
Ghana	?	16 904 000
Gibraltar	24 000	27 100
Grenada	97 900	97 900
Guyana	700 000+	825 000
India	330 000	952 969 000
Ireland	3 599 000	3 599 000
Jamaica	2 505 000	2 505 000
Kenya		29 137 000
Kiribati		81 800
Lesotho		2 017 000
Liberia	570 000	2 110 000

Country	First language speakers of English	Country population
Malawi	540 000	9 453 000
Malaysia	100 000	20 359 000
Malta	8 000	373 000
Mauritius	2 000	1 141 000
Montserrat	12 000	12 000
Namibia	13 000	1 709 000
Nauru	800	10 600
Nepal	?	20 892 000
New Zealand	3 290 000	3 619 000
Nigeria	?	103 912 000
Pakistan	?	133 500 000
Papua New Guinea	70 000	4 400 000
Philippines		71 750 000
St Kitts and Nevis	39 400	39 400
St Lucia	29 000	144 000
St Vincent and the Grenadines	100 000+	113 000
Samoa	1 000	214 000
Seychelles	2 000	76 100
Sierra Leone	700 000	4 617 000
Singapore	1 139 000	3 045 000
Solomon Islands		396 000
South Africa	3 800 000	41 734 000
Sri Lanka	10 000	18 318 000
Suriname		436 000
Swaziland		934 000
Tanzania	900 000	29 165 000
Tonga		101 000
Trinidad and Tobago	1 262 000	1 262 000
Tuvalu		9 500
Uganda	190 000	20 158 000
UK	57 190 000	58 784 000
USA	228 700 000	265 455 000
US territories in Pacific	?	196 300
Vanuatu	60 000	172 000
Zambia	300 000	9 715 000
Zimbabwe	260 000	11 515 000
Other British territories	?	106 167
TOTALS	349 764 500	2 038 046 117

Foreign words and phrases

à bon marché (Fr) 'good market'; at a good bargain, cheap.

a cappella (Ital) 'in the style of the chapel'; sung without instrumental accompaniment.

Achtung (Ger) 'Look out! Take care!'.

addendum *plural* **addenda** (Lat) 'that which is to be added'; supplementary material

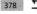

for a book.

à deux (Fr) 'for two'; often denotes a dinner or conversation of a romantic nature.

ad hoc (Lat) 'towards this'; for this special purpose.

ad hominem (Lat) 'to the man'; appealing not to logic or reason but to personal preferences or feelings.

ad infinitum (Lat) 'to infinity'; denotes endless repetition.

ad nauseam (Lat) 'to the point of sickness'; disgustingly endless or repetitive.

ad referendum (Lat) 'for reference'; to be further considered.

affaire (Fr) liaison, intrigue; an incident arousing speculation and scandal.

aficionado (Span) 'amateur'; an ardent follower; a 'fan'.

a fortiori (Lat) 'from the stronger' (argument); denotes the validity and stronger reason of a proposition.

agent provocateur (Fr) 'provocative agent'; someone who incites others, by pretended sympathy, to commit crimes.

aggiornamento (Ital) 'modernization'; reform (often political).

aide-de-camp (Fr) 'assistant on the field'; an officer who acts as a confidential personal assistant for an officer of higher rank.

aide-mémoire (Fr) 'help-memory'; a reminder; memorandum-book; a written summary of a diplomatic agreement.

à la carte (Fr) 'from the menu'; each dish individually priced.

à la mode (Fr) 'in fashion, fashionable'; also a culinary term.

al fresco (Ital) 'fresh'; painting on fresh or moist plaster; in the fresh, cool or open air.

alma mater (Lat) 'bountiful mother'; one's former school, college, or university; official college or university song (American English).

aloha (Hawaiian) 'love'; a salutation, 'hello' or 'goodbye'.

alumnus *plural* **alumni** (Lat) 'pupil' or 'foster son'; a former pupil or student.

ambiance (Fr) surroundings, atmosphere.

amende honorable (Fr) a public apology satisfying the honour of the injured party.

amour-propre (Fr) 'own love, self-love'; legitimate self-esteem, sometimes exaggerated; vanity, conceit.

ancien régime (Fr) 'old regime'; a superseded and outdated political system or ruling élite.

angst (Ger) 'anxiety'; an unsettling feeling produced by awareness of the uncertainties and paradoxes inherent in the state of being human.

anno Domini (Lat) 'in the year of the Lord'; used in giving dates of the Christian era, counting forward from the year of Christ's birth.

annus mirabilis (Lat) 'year of wonders'; a remarkably successful or auspicious year.

Anschluss (Ger) 'joining together'; union, especially the political union of Germany and Austria in 1938.

antebellum (Lat) 'before the war'; denotes a period before a specific war, especially the American Civil War.

ante meridiem (Lat) 'before midday'; between midnight and noon, abbreviated to am.

a posteriori (Lat) 'from the later'; applied to reasoning from experience, from effect to cause; inductive reasoning.

apparatchik (Russ) a Communist spy or agent; (humorous) any bureaucratic hack.

appellation contrôlée (Fr) 'certified name'; used in the labelling of French wines, a guarantee of specified conditions of origin, strength, etc.

après-ski (Fr) 'after-ski'; pertaining to the evening's amusements after skiing.

a priori (Lat) 'from the previous'; denotes argument from the cause to the effect; deductive reasoning.

atelier (Fr) a workshop; an artist's studio.

au contraire (Fr) 'on the contrary'.

au fait (Fr) 'to the point'; highly skilled; knowledgeable or familiar with something.

au fond (Fr) 'at the bottom'; fundamentally.

au naturel (Fr) 'in the natural state'; naked; also a culinary term.

au pair (Fr) 'on an equal basis'; originally an arrangement of mutual service without payment; now used of a girl (usually foreign) who performs domestic duties for board, lodging and pocket money.

auto-da-fé (Port) 'act of the faith'; the public declaration or carrying out of a sentence imposed on heretics in Spain and Portugal by the Inquisition, eg burning at the stake.

avant-garde (Fr) 'front guard'; applied to those in the forefront of an artistic movement.

ave atque vale (Lat) hail and farewell.

babushka (Russ) 'grandmother'; granny; a triangular headscarf worn under the chin.

banzai (Jap) a Japanese battle cry, salute to the emperor, or exclamation of joy.

barrio (Span) 'district, suburb'; a community (usually poor) of Spanish-speaking immigrants (esp American English).

batik (Javanese) 'painted'; method of producing patterns on fabric by drawing with wax before dyeing.

beau geste (Fr) 'beautiful gesture'; a magnanimous action.

belle époque (Fr) 'fine period'; the time of gracious living for the well-to-do immediately preceding World War I.

bête noire (Fr) 'black beast'; a bugbear; something one especially dislikes.

Bildungsroman (Ger) 'educational novel'; a novel concerning its hero's early spiritual and emotional development and education.

blasé (Fr) 'cloyed'; dulled to enjoyment.

blitzkrieg (Ger) 'lightning war'; a sudden overwhelming attack by ground and air forces; a burst of intense activity.

bodega (Span) a wine shop that usually sells food as well; a building for wine storage.

bona fides (Lat) 'good faith'; genuineness.

bonsai (Jap) art of growing miniature trees in pots; a dwarf tree grown by this method.

bon vivant (Fr) 'good living (person)'; one who lives well, particularly enjoying good food and wine; a jovial companion.

bon voyage (Fr) have a safe and pleasant journey.

bourgeois (Fr) 'citizen'; a member of the middle class; a merchant; conventional, conservative.

camera obscura (Lat) 'dark room'; a light-free chamber in which an image of outside objects is thrown upon a screen.

canard (Fr) 'duck'; a false rumour; a second wing fitted as a horizontal stabilizer near the nose of an aircraft.

carpe diem (Lat) 'seize the day'; enjoy the pleasures of the present moment while they last.

carte blanche (Fr) 'blank sheet of paper'; freedom of action.

casus belli (Lat) 'occasion of war'; whatever sparks off or justifies a war or quarrel.

cause célèbre (Fr) a very notable or famous trial; a notorious controversy.

caveat emptor (Lat) 'let the buyer beware'; warns the buyer to examine carefully the article about to be purchased.

c'est la vie (Fr) 'that's life'; denotes fatalistic resignation.

chacun à son goût (Fr) 'each to his own taste'; implies surprise at another's choice.

chambré (Fr) 'put into a room'; (of red wine) at room temperature.

chargé-d'affaires (Fr) a diplomatic agent of lesser rank; an ambassador's deputy.

chef d'oeuvre (Fr) a masterpiece; the best piece of work by a particular artist, writer, etc.

chicano (Span) *mejicano* 'Mexican'; or an American of Mexican descent.

chutzpah (Yiddish) 'effrontery'; nerve to do or say outrageous things.

cinéma vérité (Fr) 'cinema truth'; realism in films usually sought by photographic scenes of real life.

circa (Lat) 'surrounding'; of dates and numbers: approximately.

cliché (Fr) 'stereotype printing block'; the impression made by a die in any soft metal; a hackneyed phrase or concept.

coitus interruptus (Lat) 'interrupted intercourse'; coitus intentionally interrupted by withdrawal before semen is ejaculated; anticlimax when something ends prematurely.

comme il faut (Fr) 'as it is necessary'; correct; genteel.

compos mentis (Lat) 'having control of one's mind'; sane.

contra mundum (Lat) 'against the world'; denotes defiant perseverance despite universal criticism.

cordon bleu (Fr) 'blue ribbon'; denotes food cooked to a very high standard.

coup de foudre (Fr) 'flash of lightning'; a sudden and astonishing happening; love at first sight.

coup de grâce (Fr) 'blow of mercy'; a finishing blow to end pain; a decisive action which ends a troubled enterprise.

coup d'état (Fr) 'blow of state'; a violent overthrow of a government or subversive stroke of state policy.

coupé (Fr) 'cut'; (usually) two-door motor-car with sloping roof.

crème de la crème (Fr) 'cream of the cream'; the very best.

cuisine minceur (Fr) 'slenderness cooking'; a style of cooking characterized by imaginative use of light, simple, low-fat ingredients.

cul-de-sac (Fr) 'bottom of the bag'; a road closed at one end.

curriculum vitae (Lat) 'course of life'; denotes a summary of someone's educational qualifications and work experience for presenting to a prospective employer.

décolleté (Fr) 'with bared neck and shoulders'; with neck uncovered; (of dress) low-cut.

de facto (Lat) 'from the fact'; in fact; actually; irrespective of what is legally recognized.

de gustibus non est disputandum (Lat) (often in English shortened for convenience to *de gustibus*) 'there is no disputing about tastes'; there is no sense in challenging people's preferences.

déjà vu (Fr) 'already seen'; in any of the arts: unoriginal material; an illusion of having experienced something before; something seen so often it has become tedious.

de jure (Lat) 'according to law'; denotes the legal or theoretical position, which may not correspond with reality.

delirium tremens (Lat) 'trembling delirium'; psychotic condition caused by alcoholism, involving anxiety, shaking, hallucinations, etc.

Deo volente (Lat) 'God willing'; a sort of good-luck talisman.

de rigueur (Fr) 'of strictness'; compulsory; required by strict etiquette.

derrière (Fr) 'behind'; the buttocks.

déshabillé (Fr) 'undressed'; state of being only partially dressed, or of being casually dressed.

de trop (Fr) 'of too much'; superfluous; in the way.

deus ex machina (Lat) 'a god from a machine'; a contrived solution to a difficulty in a plot.

distingué (Fr) 'distinguished'; having an aristocratic or refined demeanour; striking.

dolce far niente (Ital) 'sweet doing nothing'; denotes the pleasure of idleness.

doppelgänger (Ger) 'double goer'; a ghostly duplicate of a living person; a wraith; someone who looks exactly like someone else.

double entendre (Fr) 'double meaning'; ambiguity (normally with indecent connotations).

doyen (Fr) 'dean'; most distinguished member or representative by virtue of seniority, experience, and often also excellence.

droit du seigneur (Fr) 'the lord's right'; originally the alleged right of a feudal superior to take the virginity of a vassal's bride; any excessive claim imposed on a subordinate.

Dummkopf (Ger) 'dumb-head'; blockhead; idiot.

élan (Fr) 'dash, rush, bound'; flair; flamboyance.

El Dorado (Span) 'the gilded man'; the golden land (or city) imagined by the Spanish conquerors of America; any place which offers the opportunity of acquiring fabulous wealth.

embarras de richesse (Fr) 'embarrassment of wealth'; a perplexing amount of wealth or an abundance of any kind.

embonpoint (Fr) *en bon point* 'in fine form'; well-fed; stout; plump.

emeritus (Lat) 'having served one's time'; eg of a retired professor, honourably discharged from a public duty; holding a position on an honorary basis only.

éminence grise (Fr) 'grey eminence'; someone exerting power through their influence over a superior.

enfant terrible (Fr) 'terrible child'; a precocious child whose sayings embarrass its parents; a person whose behaviour is indiscreet, embarrassing to his associates.

ennui (Fr) 'boredom'; world-weary listlessness.

en passant (Fr) 'in passing'; by the way; incidentally; applied in chess to the taking of a pawn that has just moved two squares as if it had moved only one.

en route (Fr) 'on the way, on the road'; let us go.

entente (Fr) 'understanding'; a friendly agreement between nations.

erratum *plural* **errata** (Lat) an error in writing or printing.

ersatz (Ger) 'replacement, substitute'; connotes a second-rate substitute; a supplementary reserve from which waste can be made good.

et al (Lat) *et alii* 'and other things'; used to avoid giving a complete and possibly over-lengthy list of all items eg of authors.

eureka (Gr) *heureka* 'I have found!'; cry of triumph at a discovery.

ex cathedra (Lat) 'from the seat'; from the chair of office; authoritatively; judicially.

ex gratia (Lat) 'from favour'; of a payment; one that is made as a favour, without any legal obligation and without admitting legal liability.

ex officio (Lat) 'from office, by virtue of office'; used as a reason for membership of a body.

ex parte (Lat) 'from (one) part, from (one) side'; on behalf of one side only in legal proceedings; partial; prejudiced.

fait accompli (Fr) 'accomplished fact'; already done or settled, and therefore irreversible.

fata Morgana (Ital) a striking kind of mirage, attributed to witchcraft.

fatwa (Arabic) 'the statement of a formal legal opinion'; a formal legal opinion delivered by an Islamic religious leader.

faute de mieux (Fr) 'for lack of anything better'.

faux pas (Fr) 'false step'; a social blunder.

femme fatale (Fr) 'fatal woman'; an irresistibly attractive woman who brings difficulties or disasters on men; a siren.

film noir (Fr) 'black film'; a bleak and pessimistic film.

fin de siècle (Fr) 'end of the century'; of the end of the 19c in Western culture or of an era; decadent.

floruit (Lat) 'he or she flourished'; denotes a period during which a person lived.

force de frappe (Fr) 'strike force'; equivalent of the 'independent nuclear deterrent'.

force majeure (Fr) 'superior force'; an unforeseeable or uncontrollable course of events, excusing one from fulfilling a contract; a legal term.

Führer (Ger) 'leader, guide'; an insulting term for anyone bossily asserting authority.

Gastarbeiter (Ger) 'guest-worker'; an immigrant worker, especially one who does menial work.

Gauleiter (Ger) 'district leader'; a chief official of a district under the Nazi regime; an overbearing wielder of petty authority.

gemütlich (Ger) amiable; comfortable; cosy.

gestalt (Ger) 'form, shape'; original whole or unit, more than the sum of its parts.

Gesundheit (Ger) 'health', 'your health'; said to someone who has just sneezed.

glasnost (Russ) 'publicity'; the policy of openness and forthrightness followed by the Soviet government, initiated by Mikhail Gorbachev.

Götterdämmerung (Ger) 'twilight of the gods'; the downfall of any once powerful system.

grand mal (Fr) 'large illness'; a violently convulsive form of epilepsy.

grand prix (Fr) 'great prize'; any of several international motor races; any competition of similar importance in other sports.

gran turismo (Ital) 'great touring, touring on a grand scale'; a motor car designed for high speed touring in luxury (abbreviation GT).

gratis (Lat) *gratiis* 'kindness, favour'; free of charge.

gravitas (Lat) 'weight'; seriousness; weight of demeanour; avoidance of unseemly frivolity.

gringo (Mexican Spanish) 'foreigner'.

guru (Hindi) a spiritual leader; a revered instructor or mentor.

habeas corpus (Lat) 'you should have the body'; a writ to a jailer to produce a prisoner in person, and to state the reasons for detention; maintains the right of the subject to protection from unlawful imprisonment.

haiku (Jap) 'amusement poem'; a Japanese poem consisting of only three lines, containing respectively five, seven and five syllables.

hajj (Arabic) 'pilgrimage'; the Muslim pilgrimage to Mecca.

haka (Maori) a Maori ceremonial war dance; a similar dance performed by New Zealanders eg before a rugby game.

halal (Arabic) 'lawful'; meat from an animal killed in strict accordance with Islamic law.

haute couture (Fr) 'higher tailoring'; fashionable, expensive dress designing and tailoring.

haut monde (Fr) 'high world'; high society; fashionable society; composed of the aristocracy and the wealthy.

hoi polloi (Gr) 'the many'; the rabble; the vulgar.

hombre (Span) 'man'.

hors concours (Fr) 'out of the competition'; not entered for a contest; unequalled.

ibidem (Lat) 'in the same place'; used in footnotes to indicate that the same book (or chapter) has been cited previously. Often used in its abbreviated form **ibid**.

id (Lat) 'it'; the sum total of the primitive instinctive forces in an individual.

idée fixe (Fr) 'a fixed idea'; an obsession.

idem (Lat) 'the same'.

ikebana (Jap) 'living flowers'; the Japanese art of flower arrangement.

in absentia (Lat) 'in absence'; used for occasions, such as the receiving of a degree award, when the recipient would normally be present.

in camera (Lat) 'in the room'; in a private room; in secret.

incommunicado (Span) 'unable to communicate'; deprived of the right to communicate with others.

in extremis (Lat) 'in the last'; at the point of death; in desperate circumstances.

in flagrante delicto (Lat) 'with the crime blazing'; in the very act of committing the crime.

infra dig (Lat) 'below dignity'; below one's dignity.

in loco parentis (Lat) 'in place of a parent'.

in Shallah (Arabic) 'if God wills'; ▶ Deo volente

inter alia (Lat) 'among other things'; used to show that a few examples have been chosen from many possibilities.

in vitro (Lat) 'in glass'; in the test tube.

ipso facto (Lat) 'by the fact itself'; thereby.

je ne sais quoi (Fr) 'I do not know what'; an indefinable something.

jihad (Arabic) 'struggle'; a holy war undertaken by Muslims against unbelievers.

kamikaze (Jap) 'divine wind'; Japanese pilots making a suicide attack; any reckless, potentially self-destructive act.

karaoke (Jap) 'empty orchestra'; in bars, clubs, etc members of the public sing a solo to a recorded backing.

karma (Sanskrit) 'act'; the concept that the actions in a life determine the future condition of an individual.

kibbutz (Hebrew) a Jewish communal agricultural settlement in Israel.

kitsch (Ger) 'rubbish'; work in any of the arts that is pretentious and inferior or in bad taste.

la dolce vita (Ital) 'the sweet life'; the name of a film made by Federico Fellini in 1960 showing a life of wealth, pleasure and self-indulgence.

laissez-faire (Fr) 'let do'; a general principle of non-interference.

Lebensraum (Ger) 'life space'; room to live; used by Hitler to justify his acquisition of land for Germany.

leitmotiv (Ger) 'leading motive'; a recurrent theme.

lèse-majesté (Fr) 'injured majesty'; offence against the sovereign power; treason.

lingua franca (Ital) 'Frankish language'; originally a mixed Italian trading language used in the Levant, subsequently any language chosen as a means of communication among speakers of different languages.

macho (Mexican Spanish) 'male'; originally a positive term denoting masculinity or virility, it has come in English to describe an ostentatious virility.

magnum opus (Lat) 'great work'; a person's greatest achievement, especially a literary work.

maharishi (Sanskrit) a Hindu sage or spiritual leader; a guru.

mañana (Span) 'tomorrow'; an unspecified time in the future.

mea culpa (Lat) 'through my fault'; originally part of the Latin mass; an admission of fault and an expression of repentance.

ménage à trois (Fr) 'household of three'; a household comprising a husband and wife and the lover of one of them.

mens sana in corpore sano (Lat) 'a sound mind in a sound body' (Juvenal *Satires* X, 356); the guiding rule of the 19c English educational system.

modus operandi (Lat) 'mode of working'; the characteristic methods employed by a particular criminal.

mot juste (Fr) 'exact word'; the word which fits the context exactly.

mutatis mutandis (Lat) 'with the necessary changes made'.

négociant (Fr) 'merchant, trader'; often used for *négociant en vins*: 'wine merchant'.

ne plus ultra (Lat) 'not more beyond'; extreme perfection.

netsuke (Jap) a small Japanese carved ornament used to fasten small objects, eg a purse, tobacco pouch, or medicine box, to the sash of a kimono. They are now collectors' pieces.

noblesse oblige (Fr) 'nobility obliges'; rank imposes obligations.

non sequitur (Lat) 'it does not follow'; a conclusion that does not follow logically from the premise; a remark that has no relation to what has gone before.

nostalgie de la boue (Fr) 'hankering for mud'; a craving for a debased physical life without civilized refinements.

nota bene (Lat) 'observe well, note well'; often abbreviated NB.

nouveau riche (Fr) 'new rich'; one who has only lately acquired wealth (without acquiring good taste).

nouvelle cuisine (Fr) 'new cooking'; a style of simple French cookery that aims to produce dishes that are light and healthy, utilizing fresh fruit and vegetables, and avoiding butter and cream.

nouvelle vague (Fr) 'new wave'; a movement in the French cinema aiming at imaginative quality films.

origami (Jap) 'paper-folding'; Japanese art of folding paper to make shapes suggesting birds, boats, etc.

outré (Fr) 'gone to excess'; beyond what is customary or proper; eccentric.

passim (Lat) 'everywhere, throughout'; dispersed through a book.

per capita (Lat) 'by heads'; per head of the population in statistical contexts.

perestroika (Russ) 'reconstruction'; restructuring of an organization.

persona non grata (Lat) one who is not welcome or favoured (originally a term in diplomacy).

pied-à-terre (Fr) 'foot to the ground'; a flat, small house etc kept for temporary or occasional accommodation.

plus ça change (Fr) abbreviated form of **plus ça change, plus c'est la même chose**

'the more things change, the more they stay the same'; a comment on the unchanging nature of the world.

post meridiem (Lat) 'after midday, after noon'; abbreviated to pm.

post mortem (Lat) 'after death'; an examination of a body in order to determine the cause of death; an after-the-event discussion.

poule de luxe (Fr) 'luxurious hen'; a sexually attractive promiscuous young woman; a prostitute.

pour encourager les autres (Fr) 'to encourage the others' (Voltaire *Candide*, on the execution of Admiral Byng); exemplary punishment.

premier cru (Fr) 'first growth'; wine of the highest quality in a system of classification.

prêt-à-porter (Fr) 'ready to wear'; refers to 'designer' clothes that are made in standard sizes as opposed to made-to-measure clothes.

prima donna (Ital) 'first lady'; leading female singer in an opera; a person who is temperamental and hard to please.

prima facie (Lat) 'at first sight'; a legal term for evidence that is assumed to be true unless disproved by other evidence.

primus inter pares (Lat) 'first among equals'.

prix fixe (Fr) 'fixed price'; used of a meal in a restaurant offered at a set price for a restricted choice. Compare table d'hôte.

pro bono publico (Lat) 'for the public good'; something done for no fee.

quid pro quo (Lat) 'something for something'; something given or taken as equivalent to another, often as retaliation.

quod erat demonstrandum (Lat) 'which was to be shown'; often used in its abbreviated form QED.

raison d'être (Fr) 'reason for existence'.

realpolitik (Ger) 'politics of realism'; practical politics based on the realities and necessities of life, rather than moral or ethical ideas.

recherché (Fr) 'sought out'; carefully chosen; particularly choice; rare or exotic.

reductio ad absurdum (Lat) 'reduction to absurdity'; originally used in logic to mean the proof of a proposition by proving the falsity of its contradictory; the application of a principle so strictly that it is carried to absurd lengths.

répondez, s'il vous plaît (Fr) 'reply, please'; in English mainly in its abbreviated form, RSVP, on invitations.

revenons à nos moutons (Fr) 'let us return to our sheep'; let us get back to our subject.

risqué (Fr) 'risky, hazardous'; audaciously bordering on the unseemly.

rus in urbe (Lat) 'The country in the town' (Martial *Epigrams* XII, 57); the idea of country charm in the centre of a city.

salus populi suprema est lex (Lat) 'Let the welfare of the people be the chief law' (Cicero *De Legibus* III, 3).

samizdat (Russ) 'self-publisher'; the secret printing and distribution of banned literature in the former USSR and other Eastern European countries previously under Communist rule.

sangfroid (Fr) 'cold blood'; self-possession; coolness under stress.

savoir faire (Fr) 'knowing what to do'; knowing what to do and how to do it in any situation.

schadenfreude (Ger) 'hurt joy'; pleasure in others' misfortunes.

schlimazel (Yiddish) 'bad luck'; a persistently unlucky person.

schlock (Yiddish) 'broken or damaged goods'; inferior; shoddy.

schmaltz (Yiddish) 'melted fat, grease'; showy sentimentality, particularly in writing, music, art, etc.

schmuck (Yiddish) 'penis'; a (male) stupid person.

shogun (Jap) 'leader of the army'; ruler of feudal Japan.

sic (Lat) 'so, thus'; used in brackets within printed matter to show that the original is faithfully reproduced even if incorrect.

sine qua non (Lat) 'without which not'; an indispensable condition.

sotto voce (Ital) 'below the voice'; in an undertone; aside.

status quo (Lat) 'the state in which'; the existing condition.

sub judice (Lat) 'under a judge'; under consideration by a judge or a court of law.

subpoena (Lat) 'under penalty'; a writ commanding attendance in court.

sub rosa (Lat) 'under the rose'; in secret; privately.

succès de scandale (Fr) 'success of scandal'; the success of a book, film, etc due not to merit but to its connection with, or reference to, a scandal.

summa cum laude (Lat) 'with the highest praise'; with great distinction; the highest class of degree award that can be gained by a US college student.

summum bonum (Lat) 'the chief good'.

table d'hôte (Fr) 'host's table'; a set meal at a fixed price. Compare **prix fixe**.

tabula rasa (Lat) 'scraped table'; a cleaned tablet; a mind not yet influenced by outside impressions and experience.

t'ai chi (Chin) 'great art of boxing'; a system of exercise and self-defence in which good use of balance and co-ordination allows effort to be minimized.

tempus fugit (Lat) 'time flies'; delay cannot be tolerated.

touché (Fr) 'touched'; claiming or acknowledging a hit made in fencing; claiming or acknowledging a point scored in an argument.

tour de force (Fr) 'turning movement'; feat of strength or skill.

trompe l'oeil (Fr) 'deceives the eye'; an appearance of reality achieved by the use of perspective and detail in painting, architecture, etc.

tsunami (Jap) 'wave in harbour'; a wave generated by movement of the earth's surface underwater; commonly (and erroneously) called a 'tidal wave'.

Übermensch (Ger) 'over-person'; superman.

ultra vires (Lat) 'beyond strength, beyond powers'; beyond one's power or authority.

urbi et orbi (Lat) 'to the city and the world'; used of the Pope's pronouncements; to everyone.

vade-mecum (Lat) 'go with me'; a handbook; pocket companion.

vin du pays (Fr) 'wine of the country'; a locally produced wine for everyday consumption.

vis-à-vis (Fr) 'face to face'; one who faces or is opposite another; in relation to.

viva voce (Lat) 'with the living voice'; in speech, orally; an oral examination, particularly at a university (commonly 'viva' alone).

volte-face (Fr) 'turn-face'; a sudden and complete change in opinion or in views expressed.

vox populi (Lat) 'voice of the people'; public or popular opinion. Often used in its abbreviated form **vox pop**.

Weltschmerz (Ger) 'world pain'; sympathy with universal misery; thoroughgoing pessimism.

wunderkind (Ger) 'wonder-child'; a 'child prodigy'; one who shows great talent and/or achieves great success at an early (or comparatively early) age.

zeitgeist (Ger) 'time-spirit'; the spirit of the age.

First name meanings in the UK and USA

The meanings of the most popular first names in the UK and USA are given below, along with a few other well-known names.

Name	Original meaning	Name	Original meaning
Aaron	high mountain (*Hebrew*)	Barry	spear, javelin (*Celtic*)
Abigail	father rejoices (*Hebrew*)	Beatrice	bringer of joy (*Latin*)
Adam	redness (*Hebrew*)	Benjamin	son of my right hand (*Hebrew*)
Ahmed	more commendable (*Arabic*)		
Alan	harmony (*Celtic*)	Bernard	bear + brave (*Germanic*)
Albert	nobly bright (*Germanic*)	Beth	*pet form of Elizabeth*
Alexander	defender of men (*Greek*)	Bethany	*Biblical place name*
		Betty	*pet form of Elizabeth*
Alexandra	*female form of* Alexander	Bill/Billy	*pet form of* William
		Bob	*pet form of* Robert
Alexis	helper (*Greek*)	Brandon	place name; broom-covered hill (*Germanic*)
Alfred	elf counsel (*Germanic*)		
Alice	of noble kind (*Germanic*)	Brian	?hill (?*Celtic*)
Alison	*French diminutive* of Alice	Cal(l)um	*Gaelic form of* Columba; dove (*Latin*)
Amanda	fit to be loved (*Latin*)	Carl	man, husbandman (*Germanic*)
Amelia	struggling, labour (*Germanic*)		
		Carol(e)	*forms of Caroline*
Amy	loved (*French*)	Caroline	*Italian female form of* Charles
Andrea	*female form of* Andrew		
		Catherine	pure (*Greek*)
Andrew	manly (*Greek*)	Chandra	moon (*Sanskrit*)
Angela	messenger, angel (*Greek*)	Charles	man, husbandman (*Germanic*)
		Charlotte	*French female form* of Charles
Ann(e)	*English forms of* Hannah		
Anthony	*Roman family name*	Chloe	green shoot, verdure (*Greek*)
Antonia	*female form of* Anthony	Christian	follower of Christ
		Christine	*French form of* Christina, *ultimately from* Christian
Arthur	?bear, stone (*Celtic*)		
Ashley	*Germanic place name*; ashwood	Christopher	carrier of Christ (*Greek*)
Austin	*English form of* Augustus; venerated	Claire	bright, shining (*Latin*)
		Colin	*form of* Nicholas
Barbara	strange, foreign (*Greek*)	Craig	rock (*Celtic*)

Name	Original meaning	Name	Original meaning
Daniel	God is my judge (Hebrew)	Fatima	chaste, motherly (Arabic)
Danielle	female form of Daniel	Francis/ Frances	Frenchman/-woman
Darren	Irish surname		
Darryl	surname; uncertain origin	Frank	pet form of Francis
David	beloved, friend (Hebrew)	Frederick	peaceful ruler (Germanic)
Dean	surname; valley or leader	Gail	pet form of Abigail
		Gareth	gentle (Welsh)
Deborah	bee (Hebrew)	Gary	US place name
Dennis	of Dionysus (Greek), the god of wine	Gavin	Scottish form of Gawain; hawk + white (Welsh)
Derek	form of Theodoric; ruler of the people (Germanic)		
		Gemma	gem (Italian)
Diane	French form of Diana; divine (Latin)	Geoffrey	?peace (Germanic)
		George	husbandman, farmer (Greek)
Dipak	little lamp (Sanskrit)		
Donald	world mighty (Gaelic)	Georgia	female form of George
Donna	lady (Latin)	Grace	grace (French)
Doreen	from Dora, a short form of Dorothy	Graham	Germanic place name
		Hannah	grace, favour (Hebrew)
Doris	woman from Doris (Greek)		
		Harold	army power/ruler (Germanic)
Dorothy	gift of God (Greek)		
Edward	property guardian (Germanic)	Harry	pet form of Henry
		Has(s)an	good, handsome (Arabic)
Eileen	Irish form of ?Helen		
Elizabeth	oath/perfection of God (Hebrew)	Hayley	English place name; hay-meadow
Ella	diminutive of Ellen or Eleanor, from Helen, or of Isabella	Heather	plant name
		Helen	bright/shining one (Greek)
Ellie	diminutive of Ellen or Eleanor, from Helen	Henry	home ruler (Germanic)
		Holly	plant name
Emily	Roman family name (Aemilius)	Hussein	diminutive of Has(s)an
		Ian/Iain	modern Scottish form of John
Emma	all-embracing (Germanic)		
		Imran	prosperity (Arabic)
Eric	ruler of all (Norse)	Indira	beauty (Sanskrit)
Erica	female form of Eric	Irene	peace (Greek)
Ethan	strong one, enduring (Hebrew)	Jacob	he seized the heel (Hebrew)
Eugene	well-born (Greek)	Jacqueline	French female form of Jacques (James)
Eugenie	French female form of Eugene	James	Latin form of Jacob
		Jane	from Latin Johanna, female form of John

Name	Original meaning	Name	Original meaning
Janet	*diminutive form of Jane*	Kevin	handsome at birth (*Irish*)
Jasmine	*flower name (Persian)*	Kimberly	South African place name
Jason	*form of Joshua*		
Jeffrey	*alternative spelling of Geoffrey*	Lakisha	La +?Aisha; woman (*Arabic*)
Jean	*French form of Johanna, from John*	Latoya	La + form of Tonya (Antonia)
Jennifer	fair/white + yielding/smooth (*Celtic*)	Laura	bay, laurel (*Latin*)
		Lauren	*diminutive of Laura*
Jeremy	*English form of Jeremiah; Jehovah exalts (Hebrew)*	Lee	Germanic place name; wood, clearing
Jessica	he beholds (*Hebrew*)	Leslie	*Scottish place name*
Joan	contracted form of Johanna, from John	Lewis	famous warrior (*Germanic*)
Joanne	*French form of Johanna, from John*	Lilian	lily (*Italian*)
		Lily	*plant name*
John	Jehovah has been gracious (*Hebrew*)	Linda	serpent (symbol of wisdom) (*Germanic*)
Jonathan	Jehovah's gift (*Hebrew*)	Lindsay/ Lindsey	*Scottish place name*
Jordan	flowing down (*Hebrew*)	Lisa	*pet form of Elizabeth*
Joseph	Jehovah adds (*Hebrew*)	Lucy	*English form of Lucia, from Lucius; light (Latin)*
Joshua	Jehovah is salvation (*Hebrew*)	Luke	of Lucania, in Italy (*Latin*)
Joyce	?joyful (?*Latin*)	Margaret	pearl (*Greek*)
Julie	*French female form of Latin Julius; descended from Jove*	Marjorie	from Marguerite, French form of Margaret
Karen	Danish form of Katarina (Catherine)	Mark	*English form of Marcus, from Mars, god of war (Latin)*
Katherine	*alternative spelling of Catherine*	Martin	from Mars, god of war (*Latin*)
Kathleen	*English form of Irish Caitlin (from Catherine)*	Mary	Greek form of Miriam (*Hebrew*)
Katie	*pet form of Catherine*	Matthew	gift of the Lord (*Hebrew*)
Kelly	*Irish surname; warlike one*	Megan	*pet form of Margaret*
		Melissa	bee (*Greek*)
Kenneth	*English form of Gaelic; fair one or fire-sprung*	Mia	Scandinavian diminutive of Maria (Mary)
Kerry	*Irish place name*	Michael	like the Lord (*Hebrew*)

Name	Original meaning
Michelle	*English spelling of French* Michèle, *from* Michael
Millicent	hard-working, industrious (*Germanic*)
Millie	*diminutive of* Amelia, Emily *or* Millicent
Miriam	*meaning unknown* (*Hebrew*)
Mohammed	*form of* Muhammad
Molly	*diminutive of* Mary
Morgan	?sea + ?circle (*Welsh*)
Muhammad	commendable (*Arabic*)
Nancy	*pet form of* Ann
Natalie	birthday of the Lord (*Latin*)
Neil	champion (*Irish*)
Nicholas	victory people (*Greek*)
Nicola	*Italian female form of* Nicholas
Nicole	*French female form of* Nicholas
Oliver	olive-tree, *or alteration of* Olaf (*French*)
Olivia	olive (*Latin*)
Omar	flourishing (*Arabic*)
Pamela	?all honey (*Greek*)
Patricia	noble (*Latin*)
Paul	small (*Latin*)
Pauline	*French female form of* Paul
Peter	stone, rock (*Greek*)
Philip	fond of horses (*Greek*)
Rachel	ewe (*Hebrew*)
Rebecca	?noose (*Hebrew*)
Richard	strong ruler (*Germanic*)
Robert	fame bright (*Germanic*)
Ronald	counsel + power (*Germanic*)
Ruby	*name of gemstone*
Ruth	?vision of beauty (*Hebrew*)
Ryan	*Irish surname*
Sally	*pet form of* Sarah
Samantha	*female form of* Samuel

Name	Original meaning
Samuel	heard/name of God (*Hebrew*)
Sandra	*pet form of* Alexandra
Sarah	princess (*Hebrew*)
Scott	*surname; from* Scotland
Sean	*Irish form of* John
Sharon	the plain (*Hebrew*)
Shaun	*English spelling of Irish* Sean
Shirley	bright clearing (*Germanic*)
Simon	*form of* Simeon; listening attentively (*Hebrew*)
Sophie/ Sophia	wisdom (*Greek*)
Stephanie	*French female form of* Stephen
Stephen	crown (*Greek*)
Stuart	steward (*Germanic*)
Susan	*short form of* Susannah; lily (*Hebrew*)
T(h)eresa	woman of Theresia (*Greek*)
Thomas	twin (*Hebrew*)
Tiffany	manifestation of God (*Greek*)
Timothy	honouring God (*Greek*)
Trac(e)y	?pet form of T(h)eresa
Vera	faith (*Slavic*)
Victoria	victory (*Latin*)
Vincent	conquer (*Latin*)
Virginia	maiden (*Latin*)
Walter	ruling people (*Germanic*)
Wayne	*surname; wagon-maker*
William	will + helmet (*Germanic*)
Zachary	Jehovah has remembered (*Hebrew*)
Zaynab	?name of fragrant plant (*Arabic*)
Zoë	life (*Greek*)

National newspapers – UK

Name	Location	Circulation[1]	Date founded
The Business (s)	London	18 600	1997
Daily Express	London	782 700	1900
Daily Mail	London	2 157 600	1896
Daily Mirror	London	1 494 400	1903
Daily Record	Glasgow	416 200	1895
Daily Star	London	667 000	1978
Daily Star Sunday (s)	London	319 500	2002
Daily Telegraph	London	848 000	1855
Financial Times	London	134 300	1880
The Guardian	London	330 500	1821
The Independent	London	201 000	1986
The Independent on Sunday (s)	London	176 300	1990
The Mail on Sunday (s)	London	2 165 900	1982
News of the World (s)	London	3 212 000	1843
Observer (s)	London	414 700	1791
The People (s)	London	740 400	1881
Scotland on Sunday (s)	Edinburgh	711 800	1988
The Scotsman	Edinburgh	60 700	1817
The Sun	London	2 949 700	1964
The Sunday Express (s)	London	760 000	1918
Sunday Mail (s)	Glasgow	504 000	1914
The Sunday Mirror (s)	London	1 311 600	1963
Sunday Sport (s)	Manchester	114 600	1986
The Sunday Telegraph (s)	London	611 000	1961
The Sunday Times (s)	London	1 132 100	1822
The Times	London	612 998	1785

(s) published on Sundays only
[1] June 2006 figures (rounded to nearest 100).

National newspapers – Europe

Name	Location	Circulation[1]	Date founded
ABC	Madrid	251 000	1905
AD	Rotterdam	549 000	2005
Aftenposten	Oslo	252 800	n/a
Aujourd'hui en France	Paris	484 000	n/a
B.T.	Copenhagen	93 900	1916
Berlingske Tidende	Copenhagen	126 200	1749
Bild	Hamburg	9 560 000	1952
Blick	Zürich	262 100	1959
Correio do Manha	Lisbon	112 600	1979
Corriere della Sera	Milan	619 900	1876
Dagbladet	Oslo	162 000	1869
Dagens Nyheter	Stockholm	907 000	n/a
De Standaard	Brussels	331 400	n/a
De Telegraaf	Amsterdam	704 000	1893

Name	Location	Circulation[1]	Date founded
De Volkskrant	Amsterdam	291 200	1919
Die Welt	Hamburg	710 000	1946
Ekstra Bladet	Copenhagen	105 300	1904
El Mundo	Madrid	301 000	n/a
El Pais	Madrid	365 000	1976
El Periodico	Barcelona	157 000	1978
Evening Herald	Dublin	87 600	1891
France-Soir	Paris	344 000	1944
Frankfurter Allgemeine Sonntagzeitung(s)	Frankfurt	1 210 000	1990
Frankfurter Allgemeine Zeitung	Frankfurt	860 000	1949
Gazet Van Antwerpen	Antwerp	442 000	1891
Helsingin Sanomat	Helsinki	1 058 000	1889
Het Laatste Nieuws	Brussels	1 060 100	1888
Het Nieuwsblad/De Gentenaar	Brussels	779 000	n/a
Il Giornale	Milan	204 000	1974
Il Sole 24 Ore	Milan	328 000	1865
Irish Independent	Dublin	163 000	1905
Irish Times	Dublin	118 000	1859
Jornal de Noticias	Porto	95 000	n/a
Journal du Dimanche (s)	Paris	1 151 000	n/a
Kronen-Zeitung	Vienna	847 000	n/a
La Dernière Heure	Brussels	496 000	1906
La Libre Belgique	Brussels	198 000	1884
La Repubblica	Rome	587 300	1976
La Stampa	Turin	307 000	1867
La Vanguardia	Barcelona	194 000	1881
Le Figaro	Paris	1 225 000	1828
Le Monde	Paris	1 889 000	1944
Le Parisien	Paris	1 771 000	1944
Les Echos	Paris	553 000	1908
Le Soir	Brussels	546 000	1887
L'Humanité	Paris	393 000	1904
Libération	Paris	879 000	1973
MF Dnes	Prague	1 227 000	n/a
Novy Cas	Bratislava	189 000	n/a
NRC Handelsblad	Rotterdam	243 700	1970
Politiken	Copenhagen	129 300	1884
Süddeutsche Zeitung	Munich	1 540 000	1945
Sud Presse	Liège	641 000	n/a
Sunday Independent (s)	Dublin	287 600	1905
Sunday World (s)	Dublin	204 000	1973
Tages-Anzeiger	Zurich	231 000	n/a
VG-Verdens Gang	Oslo	343 700	n/a
Welt am Sonntag (s)	Hamburg	1 080 000	n/a

(s) published on Sundays only
[1] 2005/06 figures (rounded to nearest 100).

Major newspapers – USA

Includes national newspapers and local newspapers having a circulation of 250,000 or more. Figures represent the highest circulation of the week, which is often that of the Sunday edition.

Name	Location	Circulation[1]	Date founded
Arizona Republic	Phoenix, AZ	556 500	1890
Atlanta Journal-Constitution	Atlanta, GA	561 400	1868
Baltimore Sun	Baltimore, MD	402 000	1837
Boston Globe	Boston, MA	604 100	1872
Chicago Tribune	Chicago, IL	957 200	1847
Columbus Dispatch	Columbus, OH	352 500	1871
Dallas Morning News	Dallas, TX	649 700	1885
Denver Post/Rocky Mountain News	Denver, CO	704 800	1859
Detroit News/Free Press	Detroit, MI	669 300	1831
Houston Chronicle	Houston, TX	692 600	1901
Indianapolis Star	Indianapolis, IN	347 200	1903
Kansas City Star	Kansas City, MO	367 800	1880
Long Island Newsday	Long Island, NY	488 900	1940
Los Angeles Times	Los Angeles, CA	1 231 300	1881
Miami Herald	Miami, FL	390 200	1910
Milwaukee Journal Sentinel	Milwaukee, WI	405 400	1995
Minneapolis Star/Tribune	Minneapolis, MN	606 700	1867
New York Post	New York, NY	691 400	1801
New York Daily News	New York, NY	745 200	1919
New York Times[2]	New York, NY	1 683 900	1851
Newark Star-Ledger	Newark, NJ	599 600	1832
Orange County Register	Santa Ana, CA	354 700	1905
Philadelphia Inquirer	Washington, DC	706 000	1829
Plain Dealer	Cleveland, OH	450 900	1842
Portland Oregonian	Portland, OR	384 800	1850
St Louis Post-Dispatch	St Louis, MO	423 300	1878
St Petersburg Times	St Petersburg, FL	422 400	1884
San Antonio Express-News	San Antonio, TX	342 800	1865
San Diego Union-Tribune	San Diego, CA	408 400	1868
San Francisco Chronicle	San Francisco, CA	451 500	1865
Seattle Times	Seattle, WA	435 600	1891
USA Today[2]	Arlington, VA	2 528 400	1982
Wall Street Journal[2]	New York, NY	2 058 300	1889
Washington Post	Washington, DC	960 700	1877

[1] March 2006 (rounded to the nearest 100).

[2] National newspapers

Symbols in general use

&,	ampersand (*and*)
&c.	et cetera
@	at; per (in costs)
×	by (measuring dimensions, eg 3 x 4)
£	pound
€	euro
$	dollar (also peso, escudo, etc in certain countries)
¢	cent (also centavo etc in certain countries)
©	copyright
®	registered trademark
¶	new paragraph
§	new section
"	ditto
*	born (in genealogy)
†	died
*	hypothetical or unacceptable form (in linguistics)
☠	poison; danger
♂, □	male
♀, ○	female
⌖	bishop's name follows
☎	telephone number follows

	this way
✂ ✂⋯	cut here
♲	recyclable

In astronomy

●	new moon
☽	moon, first quarter
○	full moon
☾	moon, last quarter

In meteorology

▲▲▲	cold front
●●●	warm front
▲●▲●	stationary front
▲●▲●	occluded front

In cards

♥	hearts
♦	diamonds
♠	spades
♣	clubs

Clothes care symbols

Do not iron

Can be ironed with *cool* iron (up to 110°C)

Can be ironed with *warm* iron (up to 150°C)

Can be ironed with *hot* iron (up to 200°C)

Hand wash only

Can be washed in a washing machine
The number shows the most effective
washing temperature (in °C)

Reduced (medium) washing conditions

Much reduced (minimum) washing
conditions (for wool products)

Do not wash

Can be tumble dried (one dot within the
circle means a low temperature setting; two
dots for higher temperatures)

Do not tumble dry

Do not dry clean

Dry cleanable (letter indicates which
solvents can be used)

A: all solvents

F: white spirit and solvent 11 can be used

P: perchloroethylene (tetrachloroethylene),
white spirit, solvent 113 and solvent 11 can
be used

Dry cleanable, if special care taken

Chlorine bleach may be used with care

Do not use chlorine bleach

Car index marks – International

A	Austria	EAU	Uganda*	LV	Latvia
AFG	Afghanistan	EC	Ecuador	M	Malta*
AL	Albania	ES	El Salvador	MA	Morocco
AM	Armenia	EST	Estonia	MAL	Malaysia*
AN	Angola	ET	Egypt	MC	Monaco
AND	Andorra	ETH	Ethiopia	MD	Moldova
AUS	Australia*	F	France	MNE	Montenegro
AX	Åland	FIN	Finland	MEX	Mexico
AZ	Azerbaijan	FJI	Fiji*	MGL	Mongolia
B	Belgium	FL	Liechtenstein	MK	Macedonia
BD	Bangladesh*	FO	Faroe Is	MNE	Montenegro
BDS	Barbados*	G	Gabon	MOC	Mozambique*
BF	Burkina Faso	GB	UK*	MS	Mauritius*
BG	Bulgaria	GBA	Alderney*	MW	Malawi*
BIH	Bosnia and	GBG	Guernsey*	N	Norway
	Herzegovina	GBJ	Jersey*	NA	Netherlands
BOL	Bolivia	GBM	Isle of Man*		Antilles
BR	Brazil	GBZ	Gibraltar	NAM	Namibia*
BRN	Bahrain	GCA	Guatemala	NAU	Nauru*
BRU	Brunei*	GE	Georgia	NEP	Nepal*
BS	The Bahamas*	GH	Ghana	NGR	Nigeria
BUR	Myanmar	GR	Greece	NIC	Nicaragua
BVI	British Virgin	GUY	Guyana*	NL	Netherlands
	Islands*	H	Hungary	NZ	New Zealand*
BW	Botswana*	HK	Hong Kong*	P	Portugal
BY	Belarus	HKJ	Jordan	PA	Panama
BZ	Belize	HR	Croatia	PE	Peru
C	Cuba	I	Italy	PK	Pakistan*
CAM	Cameroon	IL	Israel	PL	Poland
CDN	Canada	IND	India*	PNG	Papua New
CH	Switzerland	IR	Iran		Guinea*
CI	Côte d'Ivoire	IRL	Ireland*	PY	Paraguay
CL	Sri Lanka*	IRQ	Iraq	Q	Qatar
CO	Colombia	IS	Iceland	RA	Argentina
CR	Costa Rica	J	Japan*	RB	Benin
CY	Cyprus*	JA	Jamaica*	RC	Taiwan
CZ	Czech Republic	K	Cambodia	RCA	Central African
D	Germany	KS	Kyrgyzstan		Republic
DK	Denmark	KWT	Kuwait	RCB	Congo
DOM	Dominican	KZ	Kazakhstan	RCH	Chile
	Republic	L	Luxembourg	RG	Guinea
DY	Benin	LAO	Laos	RGB	Guinea-Bissau
DZ	Algeria	LAR	Libya	RH	Haiti
E	Spain	LB	Liberia	RI	Indonesia*
EAK	Kenya*	LS	Lesotho*	RIM	Mauritania
EAT	Tanzania*	LT	Lithuania	RL	Lebanon

RM	Madagascar	SN	Senegal	V	Vatican City
RMM	Mali	SO	Somalia	VN	Vietnam
RN	Niger	SRB	Serbia	WAG	The Gambia
RO	Romania	SUD	Sudan	WAL	Sierra Leone
ROK	Korea, Republic of	SY	Seychelles*	WD	Dominica*
ROU	Uruguay	SYR	Syria	WG	Grenada*
RP	Philippines	T	Thailand*	WL	St Lucia*
RSM	San Marino	TCH	Chad	WS	Samoa
RU	Burundi	TG	Togo	WV	St Vincent and
RUS	Russia	TJ	Tajikistan		the Grenadines*
RWA	Rwanda	TM	Turkmenistan	YAR	Yemen
S	Sweden	TN	Tunisia	YV	Venezuela
SA	Saudi Arabia	TR	Turkey	Z	Zambia*
SD	Swaziland*	TT	Trinidad and	ZA	South Africa*
SGP	Singapore*		Tobago*	ZRE	Congo,
SK	Slovakia	UA	Ukraine		Democratic
SLO	Slovenia	USA	USA		Republic of
SME	Suriname*	UZ	Uzbekistan	ZW	Zimbabwe*

* In countries so marked, the rule of the road is to drive on the left; in others, vehicles drive on the right.

UK road distances

Road distances between British centres are given in statute miles, using routes recommended by the Automobile Association based on the quickest travelling time. To convert to kilometres, multiply number given by 1.6093.

	Aberdeen	Birmingham	Bristol	Cambridge	Cardiff	Dover	Edinburgh	Exeter	Glasgow	Holyhead	Hull	Leeds	Liverpool	Manchester	Newcastle	Norwich	Nottingham	Oxford	Penzance	Plymouth	Shrewsbury	Southampton	Stranraer	York
Birmingham	430																							
Bristol	511	85																						
Cambridge	468	101	156																					
Cardiff	532	107	45	198																				
Dover	591	202	198	121	234																			
Edinburgh	130	293	373	337	395	457																		
Exeter	584	157	81	233	119	248	446																	
Glasgow	149	291	372	349	393	490	45	457																
Holyhead	457	151	232	246	209	347	325	278	305															
Hull	361	136	216	157	246	265	229	288	229	209														
Leeds	336	115	195	143	200	283	205	265	205	143	62													
Liverpool	361	98	178	195	153	295	218	250	216	104	123	72												
Manchester	354	88	167	153	188	283	215	260	214	123	97	43	34											
Newcastle	239	198	291	224	311	348	107	361	160	220	104	91	173	141										
Norwich	501	161	217	62	252	167	365	295	379	309	153	173	232	183	258									
Nottingham	402	59	151	82	170	202	268	222	281	174	92	73	107	71	156	123								
Oxford	497	63	74	82	109	118	361	152	354	218	188	171	164	153	253	144	104							
Penzance	696	272	195	346	232	362	561	112	559	419	341	328	366	355	410	336	265	193						
Plymouth	624	199	125	275	164	290	488	45	486	347	253	235	294	281	407	205	85	113	78					
Shrewsbury	571	48	75	123	110	243	276	201	114	88	190	142	75	62	192	205	67	171	315	155				
Southampton	412	128	75	128	130	155	437	130	436	361	241	234	226	210	337	195	174	66	242	160	150			
Stranraer	241	307	386	361	406	503	130	457	88	332	259	196	210	199	164	393	295	371	572	502	287	447		
York	325	128	221	153	241	274	191	307	291	241	38	24	100	71	83	185	86	185	406	340	144	226	228	
London	543	118	119	60	155	77	405	170	402	263	215	196	210	199	280	115	128	56	283	215	162	76	419	209

UK airports

'International' is abbreviated to 'Int'.

Aberdeen (Dyce)	Aberdeen
Alderney	Channel Is
Barra	Hebrides
Belfast City (George Best)	N Ireland
Belfast Int	N Ireland
Benbecula	Hebrides
Birmingham Int	West Midlands
Blackpool Int	Lancashire
Bournemouth	Dorset
Bristol Int	Avon
Cambridge	Cambridgeshire
Campbeltown	Argyll and Bute
Cardiff Int	Wales
City of Derry (Eglinton)	N Ireland
Coventry	West Midlands
Doncaster Sheffield (Robin Hood)	South Yorkshire
Dundee	Dundee
Durham Tees Valley	Cleveland
East Midlands	Leicestershire
Edinburgh (Turnhouse)	Edinburgh
Exeter Int	Devon
Glasgow Int	Glasgow
Glasgow Prestwick Int	Ayrshire
Guernsey	Channel Is
Hawarden	Wales
Humberside	
Inverness	Highland
Islay	Hebrides
Isle of Man	
Jersey	Channel Is
Kent Int	
Kirkwall	Orkney
Lands End (St Just)	Cornwall
Leeds Bradford	West Yorkshire
Lerwick/Tingwall	Shetlands
Liverpool (John Lennon)	Merseyside
London City	London
London Gatwick	West Sussex
London Heathrow	Middlesex
London Luton	Bedfordshire
London Stansted	Essex
Lydd	Kent
Manchester	Lancashire
Newcastle	Northumbria
Newquay Cornwall Int	
Norwich	Norfolk
Penzance Heliport	Cornwall
Plymouth City	Devon
St Mary's	Isles of Scilly
Scatsa	Shetlands
Shoreham	West Sussex
Southampton	Hampshire
Southend	Essex
Stornoway	Hebrides
Sumburgh	Shetlands
Swansea	Wales
Tiree	Hebrides
Tresco	Isles of Scilly
Wick	Caithness

SOCIAL STRUCTURE

Nations of the World

Population figures are estimates for 2006 unless otherwise stated; dates without 'e' indicate the year of census.

English name	Capital	Official language(s)	Population
Afghanistan	Kabul	Dari, Pashto	31 057 000
Albania	Tirana	Albanian	3 582 000
Algeria	Algiers	Arabic	32 930 000
Andorra	Andorra la Vella	Catalan	71 201
Angola	Luanda	Portuguese	12 127 000
Antigua and Barbuda	St John's	English	69 100
Argentina	Buenos Aires	Spanish	39 922 000
Armenia	Yerevan	Armenian	2 976 000
Australia	Canberra	English	20 264 000
Austria	Vienna	German	8 193 000
Azerbaijan	Baku	Azeri	7 962 000
The Bahamas	Nassau	English	304 000
Bahrain	Manama	Arabic	699 000
Bangladesh	Dhaka	Bengali	147 365 000
Barbados	Bridgetown	English	280 000
Belarus	Minsk	Belarusian, Russian	10 293 000
Belgium	Brussels	Flemish, French, German	10 379 000
Belize	Belmopan	English	288 000
Benin	Porto Novo	French	7 863 000
Bhutan	Thimphu	Dzongkha	2 280 000
Bolivia	La Paz/Sucre	Spanish, Quechua, Ayamará	8 989 046
Bosnia and Herzegovina	Sarajevo	Bosnian, Serbian, Croatian	4 499 000
Botswana	Gaborone	English, Setswana	1 640 000
Brazil	Brasilia	Portuguese	188 078 000
Brunei	Bandar Seri Begawan	Malay	379 000
Bulgaria	Sofia	Bulgarian	7 385 000
Burkina Faso	Ouagadougou	French	13 903 000
Burma ▶ Myanmar			
Burundi	Bujumbura	French, Kirundi	8 090 000
Cambodia	Phnom Penh	Khmer	13 881 000
Cameroon	Yaoundé	French, English	17 341 000

NATIONS OF THE WORLD

English name	Capital	Official language(s)	Population
Canada	Ottawa	English, French	33 099 000
Cape Verde	Praia	Portuguese	421 000
Central African Republic	Bangui	French, Sango	4 303 000
Chad	N'Djamena	French, Arabic	9 944 000
Chile	Santiago	Spanish	16 134 000
China	Beijing	Mandarin Chinese	1 313 974 000
Colombia	Bogotá	Spanish	43 953 000
Comoros	Moroni	French, Arabic	691 000
Congo	Brazzaville	French	3 702 000
Congo, Democratic Republic of the	Kinshasa	French	62 660 000
Costa Rica	San José	Spanish	4 075 000
Côte d'Ivoire	Yamoussoukro	French	17 655 000
Croatia	Zagreb	Croatian	4 495 000
Cuba	La Habana (Havana)	Spanish	11 383 000
Cyprus	Nicosia	Greek, Turkish	784 000
Czech Republic	Prague	Czech	10 235 000
Denmark	Copenhagen	Danish	5 451 000
Djibouti	Djibouti	Arabic, French	486 000
Dominica	Roseau	English	69 000
Dominican Republic	Santo Domingo	Spanish	9 184 000
East Timor	Dili	Portuguese, Tetum	1 063 000
Ecuador	Quito	Spanish	13 547 000
Egypt	Cairo	Arabic	78 887 000
El Salvador	San Salvador	Spanish	6 822 000
Equatorial Guinea	Malabo	Spanish, French	540 000
Eritrea	Asmara	Arabic, Tigrinya	4 787 000
Estonia	Tallinn	Estonian	1 324 000
Ethiopia	Addis Ababa	Amharic	74 778 000
Federated States of Micronesia ▶ Micronesia			
Fiji	Suva	Fijian, English, Hindi	846 000
Finland	Helsinki	Finnish, Swedish	5 231 000
France	Paris	French	60 876 000
Gabon	Libreville	French	1 425 000
The Gambia	Banjul	English	1 641 000
Georgia	T'bilisi	Georgian	4 661 000
Germany	Berlin	German	82 422 000
Ghana	Accra	English	22 410 000
Greece	Athens	Greek	10 688 000
Grenada	St George's	English	89 700
Guatemala	Guatemala City	Spanish	12 293 000
Guinea	Conakry	French	9 690 000
Guinea-Bissau	Bissau	Portuguese	1 442 000
Guyana	Georgetown	English	767 200

English name	Capital	Official language(s)	Population
Haiti	Port-au-Prince	French, Creole	8 308 000
Holland ▶ Netherlands, The			
Honduras	Tegucigalpa	Spanish	7 326 000
Hungary	Budapest	Hungarian	9 981 000
Iceland	Reykjavík	Icelandic	299 388
India	New Delhi	Hindi, English	1 095 352 000
Indonesia	Jakarta	Bahasa Indonesia	245 453 000 (2003e)
Iran	Tehran	Farsi	68 688 000
Iraq	Baghdad	Arabic	26 783 000
Ireland	Dublin	Irish, English	4 062 000
Israel	Tel Aviv-Jaffa	Hebrew, Arabic	6 352 000
Italy	Rome	Italian	58 133 000
Ivory Coast ▶ Côte d'Ivoire			
Jamaica	Kingston	English	2 758 000
Japan	Tokyo	Japanese	127 464 000
Jordan	Amman	Arabic	5 907 000
Kazakhstan	Astana	Kazakh, Russian	15 233 000
Kenya	Nairobi	English, Swahili	34 708 000
Kiribati	Tawara	English, I-Kiribati	105 400
Korea, North	Pyongyang	Korean	23 113 000
Korea, South	Seoul	Korean	48 847 000
Kuwait	Kuwait City	Arabic	2 418 000
Kyrgyzstan	Bishkek	Kyrgyz, Russian	5 214 000
Laos	Vientiane	Lao	6 368 000
Latvia	Riga	Latvian	2 290 000
Lebanon	Beirut	Arabic, French	3 874 000
Lesotho	Maseru	Sesotho, English	2 022 000
Liberia	Monrovia	English	3 042 000
Libya	Tripoli	Arabic	5 901 000
Liechtenstein	Vaduz	German	34 000
Lithuania	Vilnius	Lithuanian	3 586 000
Luxembourg	Luxembourg	French, German, Lëtzebuergesch	459 500
Macedonia	Skopje	Macedonian	2 050 000
Madagascar	Antananarivo	Malagasy, French	18 595 000
Malawi	Lilongwe	English, Chichewa	13 014 000
Malaysia	Kuala Lumpur	Malay	24 386 000
Maldives	Malé	Dhivehi	359 000
Mali	Bamako	French	11 717 000
Malta	Valletta	English, Maltese	400 200
Marshall Islands	Majuro	Marshallese, English	60 600
Mauritania	Nouakchott	Hasanya Arabic	3 177 000
Mauritius	Port Louis	English	1 241 000
Mexico	Mexico City	Spanish	107 449 00

English name	Capital	Official language(s)	Population
Micronesia	Palikir (on Pohnpei)	English	108 000
Moldova	Chisinau	Moldovan	4 467 000
Monaco	Monaco	French	32 500
Mongolia	Ulan Bator	Khalkha Mongolian	2 832 000
Montenegro	Podgorica	Serbian [1]	620 000
Morocco	Rabat	Arabic	33 241 000
Mozambique	Maputo	Portuguese	19 889 000
Myanmar (Burma)	Rangoon	Burmese	52 000 000
Namibia	Windhoek	English	2 044 000
Nauru	Yaren District	Nauruan, English	13 300
Nepal	Kathmandu	Nepali	28 287 000
The Netherlands	Amsterdam (official); The Hague (seat of government)	Dutch	16 491 000
New Zealand	Wellington	English, Maori	4 076 000
Nicaragua	Managua	Spanish	5 570 000
Niger	Niamey	French	12 525 000
Nigeria	Abuja	English	140 000 000 (2005)
Norway	Oslo	Norwegian	4 611 000
Oman	Muscat	Arabic	3 102 000
Pakistan	Islamabad	Urdu, English	165 803 000
Palau	Melekeok	Palauan, English	20 600
Panama	Panama City	Spanish	3 191 000
Papua New Guinea	Port Moresby	Hiri Motu, Tok Pisin, English	5 670 000
Paraguay	Asunción	Spanish, Guaraní	6 506 000
Peru	Lima	Spanish	28 303 000
Philippines	Manila	Filipino, English	89 469 000
Poland	Warsaw	Polish	38 537 000
Portugal	Lisbon	Portuguese	10 606 000
Qatar	Doha	Arabic	885 300
Romania	Bucharest	Romanian	22 303 000
Russia	Moscow	Russian	142 893 000
Rwanda	Kigali	English, French, Kinyarwanda	8 648 000
St Kitts and Nevis	Basseterre	English	39 100
St Lucia	Castries	English	168 000
St Vincent and the Grenadines	Kingstown	English	118 000
Samoa	Apia	Samoan, English	177 000
San Marino	San Marino	Italian	29 000
São Tomé and Príncipe	São Tomé	Portuguese	193 000
Saudi Arabia	Riyadh	Arabic	27 020 000
Senegal	Dakar	French, Wolof	11 987 000

English name	Capital	Official language(s)	Population
Serbia	Belgrade	Serbian	9 396 000
Seychelles	Victoria	English, French, Creole	81 500
Sierra Leone	Freetown	English	6 005 000
Singapore	Singapore City	Mandarin Chinese, English, Malay, Tamil	4 492 000
Slovakia	Bratislava	Slovak	5 439 000
Slovenia	Ljubljana	Slovene	2 010 000
Solomon Islands	Honiara	English	552 400
Somalia	Mogadishu	Somali, Arabic	10 312 000
South Africa	Pretoria/Cape Town	Afrikaans, Ndebele, Northern Sotho, Southern Sotho, Swati, Tsonga, Tswana, Venda, Xhosa, Zulu, English	44 188 000
Spain	Madrid	Spanish	40 398 000
Sri Lanka	Colombo	Sinhala, Tamil	20 222 000
Sudan	Khartoum	Arabic	41 236 000
Suriname	Paramaribo	Dutch	439 000
Swaziland	Mbabane	English, Siswati	1 136 000
Sweden	Stockholm	Swedish	9 016 000
Switzerland	Berne	German, French, Italian, Romansch	7 524 000
Syria	Damascus	Arabic	18 881 000
Taiwan	Taipei	Mandarin Chinese	23 036 000
Tajikistan	Dushanbe	Tajik	7 321 000
Tanzania	Dodoma	Swahili, English	37 445 000
Thailand	Bangkok	Thai	64 631 000
Togo	Lomé	French	5 549 000
Tonga	Nuku'alofa	English, Tongan	114 700
Trinidad and Tobago	Port of Spain	English	1 100 000
Tunisia	Tunis	Arabic	10 175 000
Turkey	Ankara	Turkish	70 414 000
Turkmenistan	Ashgabat	Turkmen	5 043 000
Tuvalu	Funafuti	Tuvaluan, English	11 800
Uganda	Kampala	English	28 196 000
Ukraine	Kiev	Ukrainian, Russian	47 425 000
United Arab Emirates	Abu Dhabi	Arabic	2 603 000
United Kingdom	London	English	60 209 500 (2005e)
United States of America	Washington, DC	English	298 444 000
Uruguay	Montevideo	Spanish	3 432 000
Uzbekistan	Tashkent	Uzbek	27 307 000
Vanuatu	Port Vila	Bislama, English, French	209 000
Vatican City	Vatican City	Latin	932

English name	Capital	Official language(s)	Population
Venezuela	Caracas	Spanish	25 730 000
Vietnam	Hanoi	Vietnamese	84 403 000
Western Samoa ▶ Samoa			
Yemen	Sana'a	Arabic	21 456 000
Zaire ▶ Congo, Democratic Republic of			
Zambia	Lusaka	English	11 502 000
Zimbabwe	Harare	English	12 237 000

[1] The name and precise nature of the official language(s) is under review

United Nations (UN) membership

Member countries are grouped by year of entry. Where membership has transferred owing to a name change or division of a country, the new name and date of transfer are indicated in brackets.

1945	Argentina, Australia, Belgium, Byelorussian SSR (Belarus, 1991), Bolivia, Brazil, Canada, Chile, China (Taiwan to 1971), Colombia, Costa Rica, Cuba, Czechoslovakia (to 1993), Denmark, Dominican Republic, Ecuador, Egypt, El Salvador, Ethiopia, France, Greece, Guatemala, Haiti, Honduras, India, Iran, Iraq, Lebanon, Liberia, Luxembourg, Mexico, Netherlands, New Zealand, Nicaragua, Norway, Panama, Paraguay, Peru, Philippines, Poland, Saudi Arabia, South Africa, Syria, Turkey, Ukrainian SSR (Ukraine, 1991), USSR (Russia, 1991), UK, USA, Uruguay, Venezuela, Yugoslavia (to 1992)
1946	Afghanistan, Iceland, Sweden, Thailand
1947	Pakistan, Yemen (N, to 1990)
1948	Burma (Myanmar, 1989)
1949	Israel
1950	Indonesia
1955	Albania, Austria, Bulgaria, Kampuchea (Cambodia, 1989), Ceylon (Sri Lanka, 1970), Finland, Hungary, Ireland, Italy, Jordan, Laos, Libya, Nepal, Portugal, Romania, Spain
1956	Japan, Morocco, The Sudan, Tunisia
1957	Ghana, Malaya (Malaysia, 1963)
1958	Guinea
1960	Cameroon, Central African Republic, Chad, Congo, Côte d'Ivoire (Ivory Coast), Cyprus, Dahomey (Benin, 1975), Gabon, Madagascar, Mali, Niger, Nigeria, Senegal, Somalia, Togo, Upper Volta (Burkina Faso, 1984), Zaire (Democratic Republic of the Congo, 1997)
1961	Mauritania, Mongolia, Sierra Leone, Tanganyika (within Tanzania, 1964)
1962	Algeria, Burundi, Jamaica, Rwanda, Trinidad and Tobago, Uganda
1963	Kenya, Kuwait, Zanzibar (within Tanzania, 1964)
1964	Malawi, Malta, Zambia, Tanzania
1965	The Gambia, Maldives, Singapore
1966	Barbados, Botswana, Guyana, Lesotho
1967	Yemen (S, to 1990)
1968	Equatorial Guinea, Mauritius, Swaziland
1970	Fiji

1971	Bahrain, Bhutan, China (People's Republic), Oman, Qatar, United Arab Emirates
1973	The Bahamas, German Democratic Republic (within GFR 1990), German Federal Republic
1974	Bangladesh, Grenada, Guinea-Bissau
1975	Cape Verde, Comoros, Mozambique, Papua New Guinea, São Tomé and Príncipe, Suriname
1976	Angola, Seychelles, Western Samoa (Samoa, 1997)
1977	Djibouti, Vietnam
1978	Dominica, Solomon Islands
1979	St Lucia
1980	St Vincent and the Grenadines, Zimbabwe
1981	Antigua and Barbuda, Belize, Vanuatu
1983	St Kitts and Nevis
1984	Brunei
1990	Liechtenstein, Namibia, Yemen (formerly N Yemen and S Yemen)
1991	Estonia, Federated States of Micronesia, Latvia, Lithuania, Marshall Islands, N Korea, S Korea
1992	Armenia, Azerbaijan, Bosnia-Herzegovina, Croatia, Georgia, Kazakhstan, Kyrgyzstan, Moldova, San Marino, Slovenia, Tajikistan, Turkmenistan, Uzbekistan
1993	Andorra, Czech Republic, Eritrea, Former Yugoslav Republic of Macedonia, Monaco, Slovakia
1994	Palau
1999	Kiribati, Nauru, Tonga
2000	Tuvalu, Yugoslavia (Serbia, 2006)
2002	Switzerland, East Timor
2006	Montenegro

United Nations (UN) specialized agencies

Abbreviated form	Full title	Area of concern
FAO	Food and Agriculture Organization	Improvement of the production and distribution of agricultural products
IAEA	International Atomic Energy Agency	Promotes safe, secure and peaceful nuclear technologies
IBRD[1]	International Bank for Reconstruction and Development	Aid of development through investment
ICAO	International Civil Aviation Organization	Encouragement of safety measures in international flight
ICSID[1]	International Centre for Settlement of Investment Disputes	Settlement of investment disputes between governments and foreign investors
IDA[1]	International Development Association	Credit on special terms to provide assistance for less developed countries

Abbreviated form	Full title	Area of concern
IFAD	International Fund for Agricultural Development	Increase of food production in developing countries by the generation of grants or loans
IFC[1]	International Finance Corporation	Promotion of the international flow of private capital
ILO	International Labour Organization	Social justice
IMF	International Monetary Fund	Promotion of international monetary co-operation
IMO	International Maritime Organization	Co-ordination of safety at sea
ITU	International Telecommunication Union	Allocation of frequencies and regulation of procedures
MIGA[1]	Multilateral Investment Guarantee Agency	Promotion of foreign investment in economies of developing countries
UNESCO	United Nations Educational, Scientific and Cultural Organization	Stimulation of popular education and the spread of culture
UNIDO	United Nations Industrial Development Organization	Assists developing countries in improving their economies and growth
UPU	Universal Postal Union	Uniting members within a single postal territory
WHO	World Health Organization	Promotion of the highest standards of health for all people
WMO	World Meteorological Organization	Standardization and utilization of meteorological observations
WIPO	World Intellectual Property Organization	Protection of copyright, designs, inventions, etc

[1] These institutions are part of the World Bank Group.

Commonwealth membership

Member countries are grouped by year of entry.

1931	Australia, Canada, New Zealand, United Kingdom[1], South Africa (left 1961, rejoined 1994)
1947	India, Pakistan (left 1972, rejoined 1989; suspended 1999, readmitted 2004)
1948	Sri Lanka
1957	Ghana, Malaysia
1960	Nigeria (suspended 1995, readmitted 1999)
1961	Cyprus, Sierra Leone, Tanzania
1962	Jamaica, Trinidad and Tobago, Uganda
1963	Kenya
1964	Malawi, Malta, Zambia
1965	The Gambia, Singapore
1966	Barbados, Botswana, Guyana, Lesotho

1968	Mauritius, Nauru[2], Swaziland
1970	Tonga, Samoa (formerly Western Samoa), Fiji (left 1987, rejoined 1997; suspended 2000, readmitted 2001, suspended 2006)
1972	Bangladesh
1973	The Bahamas
1974	Grenada
1975	Papua New Guinea
1976	Seychelles
1978	Dominica, Solomon Islands, Tuvalu[2]
1979	Kiribati, St Lucia, St Vincent and the Grenadines
1980	Vanuatu, Zimbabwe (suspended 2002, left 2003)
1981	Antigua and Barbuda, Belize
1982	Maldives
1983	St Kitts and Nevis
1984	Brunei
1990	Namibia
1995	Cameroon, Mozambique

[1] The Republic of Ireland ceased to be a member in 1949.

[2] Nauru is a special member; Tuvalu joined as a special member and became a full member in 2000.

European Union (EU) membership

Member countries are grouped by year of entry.

1958	Belgium, France, Germany, Italy, Luxembourg, The Netherlands
1973	Denmark, Republic of Ireland, United Kingdom
1981	Greece
1986	Portugal, Spain
1995	Austria, Finland, Sweden
2004	Cyprus, Czech Republic, Estonia, Hungary, Latvia, Lithuania, Malta, Poland, Slovakia, Slovenia
2007	Bulgaria, Romania

Candidate countries: Croatia, Macedonia, Turkey.

European Union (EU) institutions

Title	Task
Council of the European Union	represents the member states
Court of Auditors	checks the financing of the EU
European Court of Justice	upholds European law
European Central Bank	responsible for EU monetary policy
European Commission	upholds the interests of the EU
European Investment Bank	finances EU investment projects
European Parliament	represents the EU citizens

County and unitary councils of England

		Area		
	Abbreviation[1]	sq km	sq mi	Population[2]
Non-metropolitan counties				
Bedfordshire	Beds	1 192	460	397 700
Buckinghamshire	Bucks	1 568	605	481 500
Cambridgeshire	Cambs	3 056	1 180	588 900
Cheshire	Ches	2 081	803	679 900
Cornwall and Isles of Scilly	none	3 559	1 374	519 400
Cumbria	[Cumb]	6 824	2 635	498 900
Derbyshire	Derby	2 551	985	747 500
Devon	[Dev]	6 562	2 534	731 900
Dorset	[Dors]	2 542	981	401 100
Durham	Dur	2 232	862	499 800
East Sussex	[E Suss]	1 713	661	497 900
Essex	[Ess]	3 469	1 339	1 340 000
Gloucestershire	Glos	2 653	1 024	575 200
Hampshire	Hants	3 689	1 424	1 259 000
Hertfordshire	Herts	1 639	633	1 048 200
Kent	none	3 543	1 368	1 369 900
Lancashire	Lancs	2 897	1 119	1 156 000
Leicestershire	Leics	2 084	805	627 800
Lincolnshire	Lincs	5 921	2 286	678 700
London[3]	none	1 579	610	7 517 700
Norfolk	[Norf]	5 372	2 074	824 200
Northamptonshire	Northants	2 367	914	651 800
Northumberland	Northumb	5 026	1 941	311 300
North Yorkshire	N Yorks	8 038	3 103	582 000
Nottinghamshire	Notts	2 085	805	762 700
Oxfordshire	Oxon	2 606	1 006	626 900
Shropshire	[Shrops]	3 197	1 234	289 000
Somerset	Som	3 452	1 333	515 600
Staffordshire	Staffs	2 623	1 013	816 700
Suffolk	[Suff]	3 798	1 466	692 100
Surrey	[Sur]	1 677	647	1 075 500
Warwickshire	War	1 979	764	533 900
West Sussex	[W Suss]	1 988	768	764 400
Wiltshire	Wilts	3 246	1 253	446 600
Worcestershire	Worcs	1 761	680	555 800
Metropolitan boroughs				
Barnsley	none	329	127	222 100
Birmingham	none	268	103	1 001 200
Bolton	none	140	54	265 400
Bradford	none	366	141	485 000
Bury	none	99	38	183 500

	Abbreviation[1]	Area		Population[2]
		sq km	sq mi	
Calderdale	none	364	141	195 300
Coventry	none	99	38	304 200
Doncaster	none	568	219	289 600
Dudley	none	98	38	305 600
Gateshead	none	142	55	191 500
Kirklees	none	409	158	394 600
Knowsley	none	86	33	149 400
Leeds	none	552	213	723 100
Liverpool	none	112	43	447 500
Manchester	none	116	45	441 200
Newcastle upon Tyne	none	113	44	276 400
North Tyneside	none	82	32	192 300
Oldham	none	142	55	219 200
Rochdale	none	158	61	206 400
Rotherham	none	286	110	253 200
St Helens	none	136	53	176 300
Salford	none	97	37	216 400
Sandwell	none	86	33	286 300
Sefton	none	153	59	280 900
Sheffield	none	368	142	520 700
Solihull	none	178	69	200 900
South Tyneside	none	64	25	151 300
Stockport	none	126	47	281 600
Sunderland	none	137	53	283 700
Tameside	none	103	40	214 100
Trafford	none	106	41	213 200
Wakefield	none	339	131	320 600
Walsall	none	104	40	253 500
Wigan	none	188	73	306 700
Wirral	none	157	61	313 100
Wolverhampton	none	69	27	239 600

Unitary authorities

Bath and North East Somerset	none	351	136	173 700
Blackburn with Darwen	none	137	53	140 200
Blackpool	none	35	14	142 900
Bournemouth	none	46	18	163 600
Bracknell Forest	none	109	42	111 200
Brighton and Hove	none	82	32	255 000
Bristol, City of	none	110	42	398 300
Darlington	none	197	76	99 200
Derby	none	78	30	233 700
East Riding of Yorkshire	none	2415	932	327 400
Halton	none	74	29	118 800

	Abbreviation[1]	Area sq km	Area sq mi	Population[2]
Hartlepool	none	94	36	90 000
Herefordshire, County of	[Herefs]	2162	835	178 800
Isle of Wight	IOW	380	147	140 000
Kingston upon Hull, City of	none	71	27	249 100
Leicester	none	73	28	288 000
Luton	none	43	17	184 900
Medway	none	192	74	251 100
Middlesbrough	none	54	21	137 600
Milton Keynes	none	309	119	218 500
North East Lincolnshire	none	192	74	157 500
North Lincolnshire	none	833	322	157 100
North Somerset	N Som	373	144	195 100
Nottingham	none	75	29	278 700
Peterborough	none	344	133	159 700
Plymouth	none	80	31	246 100
Poole	none	65	25	137 100
Portsmouth	none	40	15	189 600
Reading	none	40	15	145 100
Redcar and Cleveland	none	245	95	138 600
Rutland	none	394	152	37 300
Slough	none	27	10	117 500
Southampton	none	50	19	222 000
South Gloucestershire	S Glos	497	192	248 100
Southend-on-Sea	none	42	16	159 300
Stockton-on-Tees	none	204	79	186 700
Stoke-on-Trent	none	93	36	238 300
Swindon	none	230	89	184 000
Telford and Wrekin	none	290	112	161 600
Thurrock	none	164	63	146 600
Torbay	none	63	24	132 800
Warrington	none	176	68	194 700
West Berkshire	W Berks	704	272	146 300
Windsor and Maidenhead	none	198	76	135 300
Wokingham	none	179	69	153 600
York	none	271	105	186 800

[1] Square brackets denote that the abbreviation is not generally regarded as established. Those without are generally accepted abbreviations.

[2] Mid-2005 population estimates.

[3] Greater London comprises 32 boroughs (divided into Inner London and Outer London boroughs) and the City of London.

Note: Figures do not add up exactly because of rounding.

Total area includes inland, but not tidal, water.

Population data source: ONS, © Crown copyright 2006.

Council areas of Scotland

Unitary authority[1]	Admin centre	Area sq km	sq mi	Population[2]
Aberdeen City	Aberdeen	186	72	202370
Aberdeenshire	Aberdeen	6318	2439	235440
Angus	Forfar	2181	842	109170
Argyll and Bute	Lochgilphead	6930	2676	90870
Clackmannanshire	Alloa	157	61	48630
Dumfries and Galloway	Dumfries	6439	2486	148340
Dundee City	Dundee	65	25	142170
East Ayrshire	Kilmarnock	1252	483	119400
East Dunbartonshire	Kirkintilloch	172	66	105960
East Lothian	Haddington	679	262	91800
East Renfrewshire	Giffnock	173	67	89600
Edinburgh, City of	Edinburgh	262	101	457830
Eilean Siar[3]	Stornoway	3134	1210	26370
Falkirk	Falkirk	299	115	149150
Fife	Glenrothes	1323	511	356740
Glasgow City	Glasgow	175	68	578790
Highland	Inverness	25784	9955	213590
Inverclyde	Greenock	162	63	82130
Midlothian	Dalkeith	356	137	79190
Moray	Elgin	2238	864	88120
North Ayrshire	Irvine	884	341	135830
North Lanarkshire	Motherwell	474	183	323420
Orkney Islands	Kirkwall	992	383	19590
Perth and Kinross	Perth	5311	2051	138400
Renfrewshire	Paisley	261	101	170000
Scottish Borders	Newton St Boswells	4734	1828	109730
Shetland Islands	Lerwick	1438	555	22000
South Ayrshire	Ayr	1202	464	111780
South Lanarkshire	Hamilton	1771	684	306280
Stirling	Stirling	2196	848	86930
West Dunbartonshire	Dumbarton	162	63	91400
West Lothian	Livingston	425	164	163780

[1] The counties of Scotland were replaced by 9 regional and 53 district councils in 1975; these in turn became 29 Unitary Authorities or Council Areas on 1 April 1996, the 3 island councils remaining as before.

[2] 2005 mid-year population estimates published 27 Jul 2006.

[3] Formerly known as Western Isles.

Note: Figures may not add up exactly because of rounding.
      Total area includes inland, but not tidal, water.
      Data obtained from the General Register Office for Scotland, © Crown copyright 2006.

Council areas of Wales

Unitary authority	Admin centre	Area sq km	sq mi	Population[1]
Blaenau Gwent	Ebbw Vale	109	42	68 413
Bridgend	Bridgend	246	95	130 772
Caerphilly	Hengoed	279	108	170 238
Cardiff	Cardiff	139	54	319 702
Carmarthenshire	Carmarthen	2 398	926	178 119
Ceredigion	Aberaeron	1 797	694	77 258
Conwy	Conwy	1 130	436	111 521
Denbighshire	Ruthin	844	326	94 991
Flintshire	Mold	437	169	150 230
Gwynedd	Caernarfon	2 548	984	117 985
Merthyr Tydfil	Merthyr Tydfil	111	43	54 868
Monmouthshire	Cwmbran	851	328	87 704
Neath Port Talbot	Port Talbot	442	171	135 586
Newport	Newport	191	74	139 573
Pembrokeshire	Haverfordwest	1 590	614	117 490
Powys	Llandrindod Wells	5 204	2 009	131 498
Rhondda, Cynon, Taff	Clydach Vale	424	164	231 622
Swansea	Swansea	378	146	226 369
Torfaen	Pontypool	126	49	90 303
Vale of Glamorgan	Barry	337	130	122 932
Wrexham	Wrexham	499	193	130 482
Ynys Mon (Isle of Anglesey)	Llangefni	719	277	68 934

[1] 2005 mid-year population estimates published 2006.
Note: Figures may not add up exactly because of rounding.
Population data source: ONS, © Crown copyright 2006.

Districts of Northern Ireland

District	Admin centre	Area sq km	sq mi	Population[1]
Antrim	Antrim	563	217	50 530
Ards	Newtownards	369	142	75 279
Armagh	Armagh	672	259	55 755
Ballymena	Ballymena	638	246	60 738
Ballymoney	Ballymoney	419	162	28 730
Banbridge	Banbridge	444	171	44 778
Belfast	—	140	54	267 999
Carrickfergus	Carrickfergus	87	34	39 175
Castlereagh	Belfast	85	33	65 665
Coleraine	Coleraine	485	187	56 565
Cookstown	Cookstown	623	240	34 102
Craigavon	Craigavon	382	147	84 679
Derry	—	382	147	107 296

District	Admin centre	Area sq km	sq mi	Population[1]
Down	Downpatrick	646	249	67 436
Dungannon	Dungannon	779	301	50 747
Fermanagh	Enniskillen	1 876	715	59 712
Larne	Larne	338	131	31 067
Limavady	Limavady	587	227	34 147
Lisburn	Lisburn	444	171	111 521
Magherafelt	Magherafelt	573	221	41 819
Moyle	Ballycastle	495	191	16 515
Newry and Mourne	Newry	895	346	91 572
Newtownabbey	Newtownabbey	152	59	80 834
North Down	Bangor	73	28	78 272
Omagh	Omagh	1 129	436	50 730
Strabane	Strabane	870	336	38 745

[1] 2005 mid-year population estimates.
Note: Figures may not add up exactly due to rounding.
Population data source: Northern Ireland Statistics and Research Agency, © Crown Copyright 2006.

British islands

Unitary authority	Admin centre	Area[1] sq km	sq mi	Population[2]
Isle of Man	Douglas	572	221	75 441
Jersey	St Helier	116	45	91 084
Guernsey	St Peter Port	63	24	65 409
Alderney (dependency of Guernsey)	St Anne's	8	3	2 400
Sark	—	4	2	620[3]

[1] Data obtained from: States of Guernsey, Advisory and Finance Committee, © States of Guernsey 2002; Economic Affairs Division, Isle of Man Government Treasury, © Isle of Man Government 2002; Statistics Unit, States of Jersey Policy and Resources Department.
[2] 2006 estimated figures.
[3] 2000 figure.

Counties of Ireland

County	Admin centre	Area sq km	sq mi	Population[1]
Carlow	Carlow	896	346	46 014
Cavan	Cavan	1 891	730	56 546
Clare	Ennis	3 188	1 231	103 277
Cork	Cork	7 459	2 880	447 829
Donegal	Lifford	4 830	1 865	137 575
Dublin	Dublin	922	356	1 122 821
Galway	Galway	5 939	2 293	209 077
Kerry	Tralee	4 701	1 815	132 527
Kildare	Naas	1 694	654	163 944

County	Admin centre	Area sq km	Area sq mi	Population[1]
Kilkenny	Kilkenny	2062	796	80339
Laoighis (Leix)	Portlaoise	1720	664	58774
Leitrim	Carrick	1526	589	25799
Limerick	Limerick	2686	1037	175304
Longford	Longford	1044	403	31068
Louth	Dundalk	821	317	101821
Mayo	Castlebar	5398	2084	117446
Meath	Trim	2339	903	134005
Monaghan	Monaghan	1290	498	52593
Offaly	Tullamore	1997	771	63663
Roscommon	Roscommon	2463	951	53774
Sligo	Sligo	1795	693	58200
Tipperary	Clonmel	4254	1642	140131
Waterford	Waterford	1839	710	101546
Westmeath	Mullingar	1764	681	71858
Wexford	Wexford	2352	908	116596
Wicklow	Wicklow	2025	782	114676

[1] Figures from 2002 population census.
Population data source: Central Statistics Office, Dublin, © 2003.

States of the USA

Population figures are Census Bureau population estimates for 1 July 2004. Abbreviations are given after each state name: the first is the most common abbreviation, the second is the ZIP (postal) code.

Alabama (Ala; AL)
 Entry to Union 1819 (22nd)
 Population 4530000
 Area 131443 sq km/50750 sq mi
 Capital Montgomery
 Inhabitant Alabamian
 Nickname Yellowhammer State, Heart of Dixie
Alaska (Alaska; AK)
 Entry to Union 1959 (49th)
 Population 655000
 Area 1477268 sq km/570373 sq mi
 Capital Juneau
 Inhabitant Alaskan
 Nickname Mainland State, The Last Frontier
Arizona (Ariz; AZ)
 Entry to Union 1912 (48th)
 Population 5744000
 Area 295276 sq km/114006 sq mi
 Capital Phoenix

Inhabitant Arizonan
 Nickname Apache State, Grand Canyon State
Arkansas (Ark; AR)
 Entry to Union 1836 (25th)
 Population 2753000
 Area 137754 sq km/53187 sq mi
 Capital Little Rock
 Inhabitant Arkansan
 Nickname Natural State, Land of Opportunity
California (Calif; CA)
 Entry to Union 1850 (31st)
 Population 35894000
 Area 403971 sq km/155973 sq mi
 Capital Sacramento
 Inhabitant Californian
 Nickname Golden State
Colorado (Colo; CO)
 Entry to Union 1876 (38th)
 Population 4601000

Area 268 658 sq km/103 729 sq mi
Capital Denver
Inhabitant Coloradan
Nickname Centennial State

Connecticut (Conn; CT)
Entry to Union 1788 (5th)
Population 3 504 000
Area 12 547 sq km/4844 sq mi
Capital Hartford
Inhabitant Nutmegger
Nickname Nutmeg State, Constitution State

Delaware (Del; DE)
Entry to Union 1787 (1st)
Population 830 000
Area 5133 sq km/1985 sq mi
Capital Dover
Inhabitant Delawarean
Nickname Diamond State, First State

District of Columbia (DC; DC)
Population 554 000
Area 159 sq km/61 sq mi
Capital Washington
Inhabitant Washingtonian

Florida (Fla; FL)
Entry to Union 1845 (27th)
Population 17 397 000
Area 139 697 sq km/53 937 sq mi
Capital Tallahassee
Inhabitant Floridian
Nickname Everglade State, Sunshine State

Georgia (Ga; GA)
Entry to Union 1788 (4th)
Population 8 829 000
Area 152 571 sq km/58 908 sq mi
Capital Atlanta
Inhabitant Georgian
Nickname Empire State of the South, Peach State

Hawaii (Hawaii; HI)
Entry to Union 1959 (50th)
Population 1 263 000
Area 16 636 sq km/6423 sq mi
Capital Honolulu
Inhabitant Hawaiian
Nickname Aloha State

Idaho (Idaho; ID)
Entry to Union 1890 (43rd)
Population 1 393 000

Area 214 325 sq km/82 751 sq mi
Capital Boise
Inhabitant Idahoan
Nickname Gem State

Illinois (Ill; IL)
Entry to Union 1818 (21st)
Population 12 714 000
Area 144 123 sq km/55 646 sq mi
Capital Springfield
Inhabitant Illinoisan
Nickname Prairie State, Land of Lincoln

Indiana (Ind; IN)
Entry to Union 1816 (19th)
Population 6 238 000
Area 92 903 sq km/35 870 sq mi
Capital Indianapolis
Inhabitant Hoosier
Nickname Hoosier State

Iowa (Iowa; IA)
Entry to Union 1846 (29th)
Population 2 954 000
Area 144 716 sq km/55 875 sq mi
Capital Des Moines
Inhabitant Iowan
Nickname Hawkeye State, Corn State

Kansas (Kans; KS)
Entry to Union 1861 (34th)
Population 2 736 000
Area 211 922 sq km/81 823 sq mi
Capital Topeka
Inhabitant Kansan
Nickname Sunflower State, Jayhawker State

Kentucky (Ky; KY)
Entry to Union 1792 (15th)
Population 4 146 000
Area 102 907 sq km/39 732 sq mi
Capital Frankfort
Inhabitant Kentuckian
Nickname Bluegrass State

Louisiana (La; LA)
Entry to Union 1812 (18th)
Population 4 516 000
Area 112 836 sq km/43 566 sq mi
Capital Baton Rouge
Inhabitant Louisianian
Nickname Pelican State, Sugar State, Creole State

Maine (Maine, ME)
Entry to Union 1820 (23rd)

Population 1 317 000
Area 79 931 sq km/30 861 sq mi
Capital Augusta
Inhabitant Downeaster
Nickname Pine Tree State

Maryland (Md; MD)
Entry to Union 1788 (7th)
Population 5 558 000
Area 25 316 sq km/9775 sq mi
Capital Annapolis
Inhabitant Marylander
Nickname Old Line State, Free State

Massachusetts (Mass; MA)
Entry to Union 1788 (6th)
Population 6 417 000
Area 20 300 sq km/7838 sq mi
Capital Boston
Inhabitant Bay Stater
Nickname Bay State, Old Colony

Michigan (Mich; MI)
Entry to Union 1837 (26th)
Population 10 113 000
Area 150 544 sq km/58 125 sq mi
Capital Lansing
Inhabitant Michigander
Nickname Wolverine State, Great Lake State

Minnesota (Minn; MN)
Entry to Union 1858 (32nd)
Population 5 101 000
Area 206 207 sq km/79 617 sq mi
Capital St Paul
Inhabitant Minnesotan
Nickname Gopher State, North Star State

Mississippi (Miss; MS)
Entry to Union 1817 (20th)
Population 2 903 000
Area 123 510 sq km/47 687 sq mi
Capital Jackson
Inhabitant Mississippian
Nickname Magnolia State

Missouri (Mo; MO)
Entry to Union 1821 (24th)
Population 5 755 000
Area 178 446 sq km/68 898 sq mi
Capital Jefferson City
Inhabitant Missourian
Nickname Bullion State, Show Me State

Montana (Mont; MT)
Entry to Union 1889 (41st)
Population 927 000
Area 376 991 sq km/145 556 sq mi
Capital Helena
Inhabitant Montanan
Nickname Treasure State, Big Sky Country

Nebraska (Nebr; NE)
Entry to Union 1867 (37th)
Population 1 747 000
Area 199 113 sq km/76 878 sq mi
Capital Lincoln
Inhabitant Nebraskan
Nickname Cornhusker State, Beef State

Nevada (Nev; NV)
Entry to Union 1864 (36th)
Population 2 335 000
Area 273 349 sq km/105 540 sq mi
Capital Carson City
Inhabitant Nevadan
Nickname Silver State, Sagebrush State

New Hampshire (NH; NH)
Entry to Union 1788 (9th)
Population 1 300 000
Area 23 292 sq km/8993 sq mi
Capital Concord
Inhabitant New Hampshirite
Nickname Granite State

New Jersey (NJ; NJ)
Entry to Union 1787 (3rd)
Population 8 699 000
Area 19 210 sq km/7417 sq mi
Capital Trenton
Inhabitant New Jerseyite
Nickname Garden State

New Mexico (N Mex; NM)
Entry to Union 1912 (47th)
Population 1 903 000
Area 314 334 sq km/121 364 sq mi
Capital Santa Fe
Inhabitant New Mexican
Nickname Sunshine State, Land of Enchantment

New York (NY; NY)
Entry to Union 1788 (11th)
Population 19 227 000
Area 122 310 sq km/47 224 sq mi
Capital Albany
Inhabitant New Yorker
Nickname Empire State

North Carolina (NC; NC)
Entry to Union 1789 (12th)
Population 8 541 000

Area 126 180 sq km/48 718 sq mi
Capital Raleigh
Inhabitant North Carolinian
Nickname Old North State, Tar Heel State

North Dakota (N Dak; ND)
Entry to Union 1889 (39th)
Population 634 000
Area 178 695 sq km/68 994 sq mi
Capital Bismarck
Inhabitant North Dakotan
Nickname Flickertail State, Sioux State, Peace Garden State

Ohio (Ohio; OH)
Entry to Union 1803 (17th)
Population 11 459 000
Area 106 067 sq km/40 952 sq mi
Capital Columbus
Inhabitant Ohioan
Nickname Buckeye State

Oklahoma (Okla; OK)
Entry to Union 1907 (46th)
Population 3 524 000
Area 177 877 sq km/68 678 sq mi
Capital Oklahoma City
Inhabitant Oklahoman
Nickname Sooner State

Oregon (Oreg; OR)
Entry to Union 1859 (33rd)
Population 3 595 000
Area 251 385 sq km/97 060 sq mi
Capital Salem
Inhabitant Oregonian
Nickname Sunset State, Beaver State

Pennsylvania (Pa; PA)
Entry to Union 1787 (2nd)
Population 12 406 000
Area 116 083 sq km/44 820 sq mi
Capital Harrisburg
Inhabitant Pennsylvanian
Nickname Keystone State

Rhode Island (RI; RI)
Entry to Union 1790 (13th)
Population 1 081 000
Area 2707 sq km/1045 sq mi
Capital Providence
Inhabitant Rhode Islander
Nickname Ocean State, Plantation State

South Carolina (SC; SC)
Entry to Union 1788 (8th)
Population 4 198 000

Area 77 988 sq km/30 111 sq mi
Capital Columbia
Inhabitant South Carolinian
Nickname Palmetto State

South Dakota (S Dak; SD)
Entry to Union 1889 (40th)
Population 771 000
Area 196 576 sq km/75 898 sq mi
Capital Pierre
Inhabitant South Dakotan
Nickname Mount Rushmore State, Coyote State

Tennessee (Tenn; TN)
Entry to Union 1796 (16th)
Population 5 901 000
Area 106 759 sq km/41 220 sq mi
Capital Nashville
Inhabitant Tennessean
Nickname Volunteer State

Texas (Tex; TX)
Entry to Union 1845 (28th)
Population 22 490 000
Area 678 358 sq km/261 914 sq mi
Capital Austin
Inhabitant Texan
Nickname Lone Star State

Utah (Utah; UT)
Entry to Union 1896 (45th)
Population 2 389 000
Area 212 816 sq km/82 168 sq mi
Capital Salt Lake City
Inhabitant Utahn
Nickname Mormon State, Beehive State

Vermont (Vt; VT)
Entry to Union 1791 (14th)
Population 621 000
Area 23 955 sq km/9249 sq mi
Capital Montpelier
Inhabitant Vermonter
Nickname Green Mountain State

Virginia (Va; VA)
Entry to Union 1788 (10th)
Population 7 460 000
Area 102 558 sq km/39 598 sq mi
Capital Richmond
Inhabitant Virginian
Nickname Old Dominion State, Mother of Presidents

Washington (Wash; WA)
Entry to Union 1889 (42nd)

Population 6 204 000
Area 172 447 sq km/66 582 sq mi
Capital Olympia
Inhabitant Washingtonian
Nickname Evergreen State, Chinook State
West Virginia (W Va; WV)
Entry to Union 1863 (35th)
Population 1 815 000
Area 62 758 sq km/24 231 sq mi
Capital Charleston
Inhabitant West Virginian
Nickname Panhandle State, Mountain
State
Wisconsin (Wis; WI)

Entry to Union 1848 (30th)
Population 5 509 000
Area 145 431 sq km/56 151 sq mi
Capital Madison
Inhabitant Wisconsinite
Nickname Badger State, America's
Dairyland
Wyoming (Wyo; WY)
Entry to Union 1890 (44th)
Population 507 000
Area 251 501 sq km/97 105 sq mi
Capital Cheyenne
Inhabitant Wyomingite
Nickname Equality State, Cowboy State

Australian states and territories

Name	State capital	Area sq km	Area sq mi	Population (2006e)
Australian Capital Territory	Canberra	2432	939	328 800
New South Wales	Sydney	801 427	309 431	6 827 700
Northern Territory	Darwin	1 346 200	519 768	206 700
Queensland	Brisbane	1 732 700	668 995	4 053 400
South Australia	Adelaide	984 376	380 070	1 554 724
Tasmania	Hobart	68 331	26 383	488 900
Victoria	Melbourne	227 600	87 876	5 091 700
Western Australia	Perth	2 525 500	975 096	2 050 900

Canadian provinces

Name	Provincial capital	Area sq km	Area sq mi	Population (2006e)
Alberta	Edmonton	661 848	255 472	3 375 800
British Columbia	Victoria	944 735	364 667	4 310 500
Manitoba	Winnipeg	647 797	250 050	1 177 800
New Brunswick	Fredericton	72 908	28 142	749 200
Newfoundland and Labrador	St John's	405 212	156 412	509 700
Northwest Territories	Yellowknife	1 346 106	519 597	41 900
Nova Scotia	Halifax	55 284	21 340	934 400
Nunavut	Iqaluit	2 093 190	807 971	30 800
Ontario	Toronto	1 076 395	415 488	12 687 000
Prince Edward Island	Charlottetown	5660	2185	138 500
Quebec	Quebec City	1 542 056	595 234	7 651 500
Saskatchewan	Regina	651 036	251 300	985 400
Yukon Territory	Whitehorse	482 443	186 223	31 200

FIC
ADA

Adams, Douglas

The Restaurant at the End of the
3-8-94
Universe

	DATE DUE	
MAY 1 2 1994		
MAY 1 7 1994		
OCT 1 4 1994		
NOV 0 3 1994		
MAY 1 0 1996		

"So, Ladies and Gentlemen," He Breathed, "The Candles Are Lit,

the band plays softly and as the force-shielded dome above us fades into transparency, revealing a dark and sullen sky hung heavy with the ancient light of livid swollen stars, I can see we're all in for a fabulous evening's apocalypse!"

A monstrous, grisly light poured in on them. . . .

The Universe was coming to an end. . . .

"Thank you, ladies and gentlemen," cried Max, "I'll be back with you again in just a moment, and meanwhile I leave you in the very capable hands of Mr. Reg Nullify and his Cataclysmic Combo!"

"The Hitchhiker's Trilogy is irreverent and satiric, wacky and whimsical, loony and zany, off-the-wall and bizarre."
—*Los Angeles Herald Examiner*

Books by Douglas Adams

The Hitchhiker's Guide to the Galaxy
The Restaurant at the End of the Universe
Life, the Universe and Everything
So Long, and Thanks for All the Fish
Dirk Gently's Holistic Detective Agency
The Long Dark Tea-Time of the Soul

Published by POCKET BOOKS

The Restaurant at the end of the Universe

Douglas Adams

POCKET BOOKS

New York   London   Toronto   Sydney   Tokyo   Singapore

This book is a work of fiction. Names, characters, places and
incidents are either products of the author's imagination or are used
fictitiously. Any resemblance to actual events or locales or persons,
living or dead, is entirely coincidental.

POCKET BOOKS, a division of Simon & Schuster Inc.
1230 Avenue of the Americas, New York, NY 10020

Published by arrangement with Crown Publishers, Inc.

ISBN: 0-671-70160-6

First Pocket Books printing October 1982

30 29 28 27 26 25 24 23 22

POCKET and colophon are registered trademarks of
Simon & Schuster Inc.

Printed in the U.S.A.

To Jane and James

with many thanks
   to Geoffrey Perkins for achieving the Improbable
   to Paddy Kingsland, Lisa Braun and Alick Hale
Munro for helping him
   to John Lloyd for his help with the original
Milliways script
   to Simon Brett for starting the whole thing off

to the Paul Simon album *One Trick Pony* which I
played incessantly while writing this book. Five years
is far too long

And with very special thanks to Jacqui Graham for
infinite patience, kindness and food in adversity

There is a theory which states that if ever anyone discovers exactly what the Universe is for and why it is here, it will instantly disappear and be replaced by something even more bizarre and inexplicable.

There is another which states that this has already happened.

T

he story so far:

In the beginning the Universe was created. This has made a lot of people very angry and been widely regarded as a bad move.

Many races believe that it was created by some sort of god, though the Jatravartid people of Viltvodle VI believe that the entire Universe was in fact sneezed out of the nose of a being called the Great Green Arkleseizure.

The Jatravartids, who live in perpetual fear of the time they call the Coming of the Great White Handkerchief, are small blue creatures with more than fifty arms each, who are therefore unique in being the only race in history to have invented the aerosol deodorant before the wheel.

However, the Great Green Arkleseizure Theory is not widely accepted outside Viltvodle VI and so, the Universe being the puzzling place it is, other explanations are constantly being sought.

For instance, a race of hyperintelligent pan-dimensional beings once built themselves a gigantic supercomputer called Deep Thought to calculate once and for all the Answer to the Ultimate Question of Life, the Universe and Everything.

For seven and a half million years, Deep Thought computed and calculated, and in the end announced that the answer was in fact Forty-two—and so another, even bigger, computer had to be built to find out what the actual question was.

And this computer, which was called the Earth, was so large that it was frequently mistaken for a planet—especially by the strange apelike beings who roamed its surface, totally unaware that they were simply part of a gigantic computer program.

And this is very odd, because without that fairly simple and obvious piece of knowledge, nothing that ever happened on the Earth could possibly make the slightest bit of sense.

Sadly, however, just before the critical moment of read-out, the Earth was unexpectedly demolished by the Vogons to make way—so they claimed—for a new hyperspace bypass, and so all hope of discovering a meaning for life was lost for ever.

Or so it would seem.

Two of these strange, apelike creatures survived.

Arthur Dent escaped at the very last moment because an old friend of his, Ford Prefect, suddenly turned out to be from a small planet somewhere in the vicinity of Betelgeuse and not from Guildford as he had hitherto claimed; and, more to the point, he knew how to hitch rides on flying saucers.

Tricia McMillan—or Trillian—had skipped the planet six months earlier with Zaphod Beeblebrox, the then President of the Galaxy.

Two survivors.

They are all that remains of the greatest experiment ever conducted—to find the Ultimate Question and the Ultimate Answer of Life, the Universe and Everything.

And, less than half a million miles from where their starship is drifting lazily through the inky blackness of space, a Vogon ship is moving slowly toward them.

ike all Vogon ships it looked as if it had been not so much designed as congealed. The unpleasant yellow lumps and edifices which protruded from it at unsightly angles would have disfigured the looks of most ships, but in this case that was sadly impossible. Uglier things have been spotted in the skies, but not by reliable witnesses.

In fact to see anything much uglier than a Vogon ship you would have to go inside it and look at a Vogon. If you are wise, however, this is precisely what you will avoid doing because the average Vogon will not think twice before doing something so pointlessly hideous to you that you will wish you had never been born—or (if you are a clearer minded thinker) that the Vogon had never been born.

In fact, the average Vogon probably wouldn't even think once. They are simple-minded, thick-willed, slug-brained creatures, and thinking is not really something they are cut out for. Anatomical analysis of the Vogon reveals that its brain was originally a badly deformed, misplaced and dyspeptic liver. The fairest thing you can say about them, then, is that they know what they like, and what they like generally involves hurting people and, wherever possible, getting very angry.

One thing they don't like is leaving a job unfinished—particularly this Vogon, and particularly—for various reasons—this job.

This Vogon was Captain Prostetnic Vogon Jeltz of the Galactic Hyperspace Planning Council, and he it was who had had the job of demolishing the so-called "planet" Earth.

He heaved his monumentally vile body round in his ill-fitting, slimy seat and stared at the monitor screen on which the starship *Heart of Gold* was being systematically scanned.

It mattered little to him that the *Heart of Gold*, with its Infinite Improbability Drive, was the most beautiful and revolutionary ship ever built. Aesthetics and technology were closed books to him and, had he had his way, burned and buried books as well.

It mattered even less to him that Zaphod Beeblebrox was aboard. Zaphod Beeblebrox was now the ex-President of the Galaxy, and though every police force in the Galaxy was currently pursuing both him and this ship he had stolen, the Vogon was not interested.

He had other fish to fry.

It has been said that Vogons are not above a little bribery and corruption in the same way that the sea is not above the clouds, and this was certainly true in his case. When he heard the words *integrity* or *moral rectitude* he reached for his dictionary, and when he heard the chink of ready money in large quantities he reached for the rule book and threw it away.

In seeking so implacably the destruction of the Earth and all that therein lay he was moving somewhat above and beyond the call of his professional duty. There was even some doubt as to whether the said bypass was actually going to be built, but the matter had been glossed over.

He grunted a repellent grunt of satisfaction.

"Computer," he croaked, "get me my brain care specialist on the line."

Within a few seconds the face of Gag Halfrunt appeared on the screen, smiling the smile of a man who knew he was ten light-years away from the Vogon face he was looking at. Mixed up somewhere in the smile was a glint of irony too. Though the Vogon persistently referred to him as "my private brain care specialist" there was not a lot of brain to take care of, and it was in fact Halfrunt who was employing the Vogon. He was paying him an awful lot of money to do some very dirty work. As one of the Galaxy's most prominent and successful psychiatrists, he and a consortium of his colleagues were quite prepared to spend an awful lot of money when it seemed that the entire future of psychiatry might be at stake.

"Well," he said, "hello my Captain of Vogons Prostetnic, and how are we feeling today?"

The Vogon Captain told him that in the last few hours he had wiped out nearly half his crew in a disciplinary exercise.

Halfrunt's smile did not flicker for an instant.

"Well," he said, "I think this is perfectly normal

behavior for a Vogon, you know? The natural and healthy channeling of the aggressive instincts into acts of senseless violence."

"That," rumbled the Vogon, "is what you always say."

"Well again," said Halfrunt, "I think that this is perfectly normal behavior for a psychiatrist. Good. We are clearly both very well adjusted in our mental attitudes today. Now tell me, what news of the mission?"

"We have located the ship."

"Wonderful," said Halfrunt, "wonderful! And the occupants?"

"The Earthman is there."

"Excellent! And...?"

"A female from the same planet. They are the last."

"Good, good," beamed Halfrunt. "Who else?"

"The man Prefect."

"Yes?"

"And Zaphod Beeblebrox."

For an instant Halfrunt's smile flickered.

"Ah, yes," he said, "I had been expecting this. It is most regrettable."

"A personal friend?" inquired the Vogon, who had heard the expression somewhere once and decided to try it out.

"Ah, no," said Halfrunt, "in my profession you know, we do not make personal friends."

"Ah," grunted the Vogon, "professional detachment."

"No," said Halfrunt cheerfully, "we just don't have the knack."

He paused. His mouth continued to smile, but his eyes frowned slightly.

"But Beeblebrox, you know," he said, "he is one of my most profitable clients. He has personality problems beyond the dreams of analysts."

He toyed with this thought a little before reluctantly dismissing it.

"Still," he said, "you are ready for your task?"

"Yes."

"Good. Destroy the ship immediately."

"What about Beeblebrox?"

"Well," said Halfrunt brightly, "Zaphod's just this guy, you know?"

He vanished from the screen.

The Vogon Captain pressed a communicator button which connected him with the remains of his crew.

"Attack," he said.

At that precise moment Zaphod Beeblebrox was in his cabin swearing very loudly. Two hours ago, he had said that they would go for a quick bite at the Restaurant at the End of the Universe, whereupon he had had a blazing row with the ship's computer and stormed off to his cabin shouting that he would work out the Improbability factors with a pencil.

The *Heart of Gold*'s Improbability Drive made it the most powerful and unpredictable ship in existence. There was nothing it couldn't do, provided you knew exactly how improbable it was that the thing you wanted it to do would even happen.

He had stolen it when, as President, he was meant to

be launching it. He didn't know exactly why he had stolen it, except that he liked it.

He didn't know why he had become President of the Galaxy, except that it seemed a fun thing to be.

He did know that there were better reasons than these, but that they were buried in a dark, locked off section of his two brains. He wished the dark, locked off section of his two brains would go away because they occasionally surfaced momentarily and put strange thoughts into the light, fun sections of his mind and tried to deflect him from what he saw as being the basic business of his life, which was to have a wonderfully good time.

At the moment he was not having a wonderfully good time. He had run out of patience and pencils and was feeling very hungry.

"Starpox!" he shouted.

At that same precise moment, Ford Prefect was in midair. This was not because of anything wrong with the ship's artificial gravity field, but because he was leaping down the stairwell which led to the ship's personal cabins. It was a very high jump to do in one bound and he landed awkwardly, stumbled, recovered, raced down the corridor sending a couple of miniature service robots flying, skidded around the corner, burst into Zaphod's door and explained what was on his mind.

"Vogons," he said.

A short while before this, Arthur Dent had set out from his cabin in search of a cup of tea. It was not a quest he embarked upon with a great deal of optimism, because he knew that the only source of hot drinks on the entire ship was a benighted piece of equipment produced by the Sirius Cybernetics Corporation. It was called a Nutri-Matic Drinks Synthesizer, and he had encountered it before.

It claimed to produce the widest possible range of drinks personally matched to the tastes and metabolism of whoever cared to use it. When put to the test, however, it invariably produced a plastic cup filled with a liquid which was almost, but not quite, entirely unlike tea.

He attempted to reason with the thing.

"Tea," he said.

"Share and Enjoy," the machine replied and provided him with yet another cup of the sickly liquid.

He threw it away.

"Share and Enjoy," the machine repeated and produced another one.

"Share and Enjoy" is the company motto of the hugely successful Sirius Cybernetics Corporation Complaints Division, which now covers the major land masses of three medium-size planets and is the only part of the Corporation to have shown a consistent profit in recent years.

The motto stands—or rather stood—in three mile high illuminated letters near the Complaints Department spaceport on Eadrax. Unfortunately its weight was such that shortly after it was erected, the ground beneath the letters caved in and they dropped for nearly half their length through the offices of many talented young Complaints executives—now deceased.

The protruding upper halves of the letters now

appear, in the local language, to read "Go stick your head in a pig," and are no longer illuminated, except at times of special celebration.

Arthur threw away a sixth cup of the liquid.

"Listen, you machine," he said, "you claim you can synthesize any drink in existence, so why do you keep giving me the same undrinkable stuff?"

"Nutrition and pleasurable sense data," burbled the machine. "Share and Enjoy."

"It tastes filthy!"

"If you have enjoyed the experience of this drink," continued the machine, "why not share it with your friends?"

"Because," said Arthur tartly, "I want to keep them. Will you try to comprehend what I'm telling you? That drink..."

"That drink," said the machine sweetly, "was individually tailored to meet your personal requirements for nutrition and pleasure."

"Ah," said Arthur, "so I'm a masochist on a diet am I?"

"Share and Enjoy."

"Oh, shut up."

"Will that be all?"

Arthur decided to give up.

"Yes," he said.

Then he decided he'd be damned if he'd give up.

"No," he said, "look, it's very, very simple...all I want...is a cup of tea. You are going to make one for me. Keep quiet and listen."

And he sat. He told the Nutri-Matic about India, he told it about China, he told it about Ceylon. He told it about broad leaves drying in the sun. He told it about silver teapots. He told it about summer afternoons on the lawn. He told it about putting in the milk before the tea so it wouldn't get scalded. He even told it (briefly) about the history of the East India Company.

"So that's it, is it?" said the Nutri-Matic when he had finished.

"Yes," said Arthur, "that is what I want."

"You want the taste of dried leaves boiled in water?"

"Er, yes. With milk."

"Squirted out of a cow?"

"Well, in a manner of speaking I suppose…"

"I'm going to need some help with this one," said the machine tersely. All the cheerful burbling had dropped out of its voice and it now meant business.

"Well, anything I can do," said Arthur.

"You've done quite enough," the Nutri-Matic informed him.

It summoned up the ship's computer.

"Hi there!" said the ship's computer.

The Nutri-Matic explained about tea to the ship's computer. The computer boggled, linked logic circuits with the Nutri-Matic and together they lapsed into a grim silence.

Arthur watched and waited for a while, but nothing further happened.

He thumped it, but still nothing happened.

Eventually he gave up and wandered up to the bridge.

"If you're upset about something..." said Arthur.

"Vogons!" snapped Ford. "We're under attack!"

Arthur gibbered.

"Well, what are you doing? Let's get out of here!"

"Can't. Computer's jammed."

"Jammed?"

"It says all its circuits are occupied. There's no power anywhere in the ship."

Ford moved away from the computer terminal, wiped a sleeve across his forehead and slumped back against the wall.

"Nothing we can do," he said. He glared at nothing and bit his lip.

When Arthur had been a boy at school, long before the Earth had been demolished, he had used to play football. He had not been at all good at it, and his particular speciality had been scoring own goals in important matches. Whenever this happened he used to experience a peculiar tingling round the back of his neck that would slowly creep up across his cheeks and heat his brow. The image of mud and grass and lots of little jeering boys flinging it at him suddenly came vividly to his mind at this moment.

A peculiar tingling sensation at the back of his neck was creeping up across his cheeks and heating his brow.

He started to speak, and stopped.

He started to speak again and stopped again.

Finally he managed to speak.

"Er," he said. He cleared his throat.

"Tell me," he continued, and said it so nervously that

the others all turned to stare at him. He glanced at the approaching yellow blob on the vision screen.

"Tell me," he said again, "did the computer say what was occupying it? I just ask out of interest...."

Their eyes were riveted on him.

"And, er...well, that's it really, just asking."

Zaphod put out a hand and held Arthur by the scruff of the neck.

"What have you done to it, Monkeyman?" he breathed.

"Well," said Arthur, "nothing in fact. It's just that I think a short while ago it was trying to work out how to..."

"Yes?"

"Make some tea."

"That's right, guys," the computer sang out suddenly, "just coping with that problem right now, and wow, it's a biggy. Be with you in a while." It lapsed back into a silence that was only matched for sheer intensity by the silence of the three people staring at Arthur Dent.

As if to relieve the tension, the Vogons chose that moment to start firing.

The ship shook, the ship thundered. Outside, the inch thick force shield around it blistered, crackled and spat under the barrage of a dozen 30-Megahurt Definit-Kil Photrazon Cannon, and looked as if it wouldn't be around for long. Four minutes is how long Ford Prefect gave it.

"Three minutes and fifty seconds," he said a short while later.

"Forty-five seconds," he added at the appropriate time. He flicked idly at some useless switches, then gave Arthur an unfriendly look.

"Dying for a cup of tea, eh?" he said. "Three minutes and forty seconds."

"Will you stop counting!" snarled Zaphod.

"Yes," said Ford Prefect, "in three minutes and thirty-five seconds."

Aboard the Vogon ship, Prostetnic Vogon Jeltz was puzzled. He had expected a chase, he had expected an exciting grapple with tractor beams, he had expected to have to use the specially installed Sub-Cyclic Normality Assert-i-Tron to counter the *Heart of Gold*'s Infinite Improbability Drive; but the Sub-Cyclic Normality Assert-i-Tron lay idle as the *Heart of Gold* just sat there and took it.

A dozen 30-Megahurt Definit-Kil Photrazon Cannon continued to blaze away at the *Heart of Gold*, and still it just sat there and took it.

He tested every sensor at his disposal to see if there was any subtle trickery afoot, but no subtle trickery was to be found.

He didn't know about the tea of course.

Nor did he know exactly how the occupants of the *Heart of Gold* were spending the last three minutes and thirty seconds of life they had left to spend.

Quite how Zaphod Beeblebrox arrived at the idea of holding a seance at this point is something he was never quite clear on.

Obviously the subject of death was in the air, but more as something to be avoided than harped upon.

Possibly the horror that Zaphod experienced at the prospect of being reunited with his deceased relatives led on to the thought that they might just feel the same way about him and, what's more, be able to do something about helping to postpone this reunion.

Or again it might just have been one of the strange promptings that occasionally surfaced from that dark area of his mind that he had inexplicably locked off prior to becoming President of the Galaxy.

"You want to talk to your great-grandfather?" boggled Ford.

"Yeah."

"Does it have to be *now?*"

The ship continued to shake and thunder. The temperature was rising. The light was getting dimmer—all the energy the computer didn't require for thinking about tea was being pumped into the rapidly fading force field.

"Yeah!" insisted Zaphod. "Listen, Ford, I think he may be able to help us."

"Are you sure you mean *think?* Pick your words with care."

"Suggest something else we can do."

"Er, well..."

"Okay, round the central console. Now. Come on! Trillian, Monkeyman, move."

They clustered round the central console in confusion, sat down and, feeling exceptionally foolish, held hands. With his third hand Zaphod turned off the lights.

Darkness gripped the ship.

Outside, the thunderous roar of the Definit-Kil Cannon continued to rip at the force field.

"Concentrate," hissed Zaphod, "on his name."

"What is it?" asked Arthur.

"Zaphod Beeblebrox the Fourth."

"What?"

"Zaphod Beeblebrox the Fourth. Concentrate!"

"The Fourth?"

"Yeah. Listen, I'm Zaphod Beeblebrox, my father was Zaphod Beeblebrox the Second, my grandfather Zaphod Beeblebrox the Third..."

"What?"

"There was an accident with a contraceptive and a time machine. Now concentrate!"

"Three minutes," said Ford Prefect.

"Why," said Arthur Dent, "are we doing this?"

"Shut up," suggested Zaphod Beeblebrox.

Trillian said nothing. What, she thought, was there to say?

The only light on the bridge came from two dim red triangles in a far corner where Marvin the Paranoid Android sat slumped, ignoring all and ignored by all, in a private and rather unpleasant world of his own.

Round the central console four figures hunched in tight concentration trying to blot from their minds the terrifying shuddering of the ship and the fearful roar that echoed through it.

They concentrated.

Still they concentrated.

And still they concentrated.

The seconds ticked by.

On Zaphod's brows stood beads of sweat, first of concentration, then of frustration and finally of embarrassment.

At last he let out a cry of anger, snatched back his hands from Trillian and Ford and stabbed at the light switch.

"Ah, I was beginning to think you'd never turn the lights on," said a voice. "No, not too bright please, my eyes aren't what they once were."

Four figures jolted upright in their seats. Slowly they turned their heads to look, though their scalps showed a distinct propensity to try and stay in the same place.

"Now. Who disturbs me at this time?" said the small, bent, gaunt figure standing by the sprays of fern at the far end of the bridge. His two small wispy-haired heads looked so ancient that it seemed they might hold dim memories of the birth of the galaxies themselves. One lolled in sleep, the other squinted sharply at them. If his eyes weren't what they once were, they must once have been diamond cutters.

Zaphod stuttered nervously for a moment. He gave the intricate little double nod which is the traditional Betelgeusian gesture of familial respect.

"Oh...er, hi Great-granddad...." he breathed.

The little old figure moved closer toward them. He peered through the dim light. He thrust out a bony finger at his great grandson.

20

"Ah," he snapped, "Zaphod Beeblebrox. The last of our great line. Zaphod Beeblebrox the Nothingth."

"The First."

"The Nothingth," spat the figure. Zaphod hated his voice. It always seemed to him to screech like fingernails across the blackboard of what he liked to think of as his soul.

He shifted awkwardly in his seat.

"Er, yeah," he muttered. "Er, look, I'm really sorry about the flowers, I meant to send them along, but you know, the shop was fresh out of wreaths and..."

"You forgot!" snapped Zaphod Beeblebrox the Fourth.

"Well..."

"Too busy. Never think of other people. The living are all the same."

"Two minutes, Zaphod," whispered Ford in an awed whisper.

Zaphod fidgeted nervously.

"Yeah, but I did mean to send them," he said. "And I'll write to my great-grandmother as well, just as soon as we get out of this...."

"Your great-grandmother," mused the gaunt little figure to himself.

"Yeah," said Zaphod, "er, how is she? Tell you what, I'll go and see her. But first we've just got to..."

"Your *late* great-grandmother and I are very well," rasped Zaphod Beeblebrox the Fourth.

"Ah. Oh."

"But very disappointed in you, young Zaphod...."

"Yeah, well..." Zaphod felt strangely powerless to

take charge of this conversation, and Ford's heavy breathing at his side told him that the seconds were ticking away fast. The noise and the shaking had reached terrifying proportions. He saw Trillian's and Arthur's faces white and unblinking in the gloom.

"Er, Great-grandfather..."

"We've been following your progress with considerable despondency..."

"Yeah, look, just at the moment you see..."

"Not to say contempt!"

"Could you sort of listen for a moment...?"

"I mean what exactly are you doing with your life?"

"I'm being attacked by a Vogon fleet!" cried Zaphod. It was an exaggeration, but it was his only opportunity so far of getting the basic point of the exercise across.

"Doesn't surprise me in the least," said the little old figure with a shrug.

"Only it's happening right now, you see," insisted Zaphod feverishly.

The spectral ancestor nodded, picked up the cup Arthur Dent had brought in and looked at it with interest.

"Er... Great-granddad—"

"Did you know," interrupted the ghostly figure, fixing Zaphod with a stern look, "that Betelgeuse Five has now developed a very slight eccentricity in its orbit?"

Zaphod didn't and found the information hard to concentrate on what with all the noise and the imminence of death and so on.

"Er, no... look," he said.

"Me spinning in my grave!" barked the ancestor. He slammed the cup down and pointed a quivering, stick-like see-through finger at Zaphod.

"Your fault!" he screeched.

"One minute thirty," muttered Ford, his head in his hands.

"Yeah, look Great-granddad, can you actually help because..."

"Help?" exclaimed the old man as if he'd been asked for a weasel.

"Yeah, help, and like, now, because otherwise..."

"Help!" repeated the old man as if he'd been asked for a lightly grilled weasel in a bun with French fries. He stood amazed.

"You go swanning your way round the Galaxy with your"—the ancestor waved a contemptuous hand—"with your disreputable friends, too busy to put flowers on my grave, plastic ones would have done, would have been quite appropriate from you, but no. Too busy. Too modern. Too skeptical—till you suddenly find yourself in a bit of a fix and come over suddenly all astrally minded!"

He shook his head—carefully, so as not to disturb the slumber of the other one, which was already becoming restive.

"Well, I don't know, young Zaphod," he continued, "I think I'll have to think about this one."

"One minute ten," said Ford hollowly.

Zaphod Beeblebrox the Fourth peered at him curiously.

"Why does that man keep talking in numbers?" he said.

"Those numbers," said Zaphod tersely, "are the time we've got left to live."

"Oh," said his great-grandfather. He grunted to himself. "Doesn't apply to me, of course," he said and moved off to a dimmer recess of the bridge in search of something else to poke around at.

Zaphod felt he was teetering on the edge of madness and wondered if he shouldn't just jump over and have done with it.

"Great-grandfather," he said, "it applies to us! We are still alive, and we are about to lose our lives."

"Good job too.'

"What?"

"What use is your life to anyone? When I think of what you've made of it the phrase 'pig's ear' comes irresistibly to mind."

"But I was President of the Galaxy, man!"

"Huh," muttered his ancestor. "And what kind of a job is that for a Beeblebrox?"

"Hey, what? Only President you know! Of the whole Galaxy!"

"Conceited little megapuppy."

Zaphod blinked in bewilderment.

"Hey—er, what are you at, man? I mean Great-grandfather."

The hunched up little figure stalked up to his great-grandson and tapped him sternly on the knee. This had the effect of reminding Zaphod that he was talking to a ghost because he didn't feel a thing.

"You know and I know what being President means, young Zaphod. You know because you've been it, and I know because I'm dead and it gives one such a wonderfully uncluttered perspective. We have a saying up here. 'Life is wasted on the living.'"

"Yeah," said Zaphod bitterly, "very good. Very deep. Right now I need aphorisms like I need holes in my heads."

"Fifty seconds," grunted Ford Prefect.

"Where was I?" said Zaphod Beeblebrox the Fourth.

"Pontificating," said Zaphod Beeblebrox.

"Oh yes."

"Can this guy," muttered Ford quietly to Zaphod, "actually in fact help us?"

"Nobody else can," whispered Zaphod.

Ford nodded despondently.

"Zaphod!" the ghost was saying, "you became President of the Galaxy for a reason. Have you forgotten?"

"Could we go into this later?"

"Have you forgotten?" insisted the ghost.

"Yeah! Of course I forgot! I had to forget. They screen your brain when you get the job, you know. If they'd found my head full of tricksy ideas I'd have been right out on the streets again with nothing but a fat pension, secretarial staff, a fleet of ships and a couple of slit throats."

"Ah," nodded the ghost in satisfaction, "then you do remember!"

He paused for a moment.

"Good," he said and the noise stopped.

"Forty-eight seconds," said Ford. He looked again at

his watch and tapped it. He looked up.

"Hey, the noise has stopped," he said.

A mischievous twinkle gleamed in the ghost's hard little eyes.

"I've slowed down time for a moment," he said, "just for a moment you understand. I would hate you to miss all I have to say."

"No, you listen to me, you see-through old bat," said Zaphod leaping out of his chair, "A—Thanks for stopping time and all that, great, terrific, wonderful, but B—no thanks for the homily, right? I don't know what this great thing I'm meant to be doing is, and it looks to me as if I was supposed not to know. And I resent that, right?

"The old me knew. The old me cared. Fine, so far so good. Except that the old me cared so much that he actually got inside his own brain—my own brain—and locked off the bits that knew and cared, because if I knew and cared I wouldn't be able to do it. I wouldn't be able to go and be President, and I wouldn't be able to steal this ship, which must be the important thing.

"But this former self of mine killed himself off, didn't he, by changing my brain? Okay, that was his choice. This new me has its own choices to make, and by a strange coincidence those choices involve not knowing and not caring about this big number, whatever it is. That's what he wanted, that's what he got.

"Except this old self of mine tried to leave himself in control, leaving orders for me in the bit of my brain he locked off. Well, I don't want to know, and I don't want to hear them. That's my choice. I'm not going to be anybody's puppet, particularly not my own."

Zaphod banged on the console in fury, oblivious of the dumbfounded looks he was attracting.

"The old me is dead!" he raved. "Killed himself! The dead shouldn't hang about trying to interfere with the living!"

"And yet you summon me up to help you out of a scrape," said the ghost.

"Ah," said Zaphod, sitting down again, "well that's different, isn't it?"

He grinned at Trillian weakly.

"Zaphod," rasped the apparition, "I think the only reason I waste my breath on you is that being dead I don't have any other use for it."

"Okay," said Zaphod, "why don't you tell me what the big secret is. Try me."

"Zaphod, you knew when you were President of the Galaxy, as did Yooden Vranx before you, that the President is nothing. A cipher. Somewhere in the shadows behind is another man, being, something, with ultimate power. That man, or being, or something, you must find—the man who controls this Galaxy, and—we suspect—others. Possibly the entire Universe."

"Why?"

"Why?" exclaimed an astonished ghost. "Why? Look around you, lad, does it look to you as if it's in very good hands?"

"It's all right."

The old ghost glowered at him.

"I will not argue with you. You will simply take this ship, this Improbability Drive ship, to where it is needed. You will do it. Don't think you can escape your purpose. The Improbability Field controls you, you are in its grip. What's this?"

He was standing tapping at one of the terminals of Eddie the Shipboard Computer. Zaphod told him.

"What's it doing?"

"It is trying," said Zaphod with wonderful restraint, "to make tea."

"Good," said his great-grandfather, "I approve of that. Now Zaphod," he said, turning and wagging a finger at him, "I don't know if you are really capable of succeeding in your job. I think you will not be able to avoid it. However, I am too long dead and too tired to care as much as I did. The principal reason I am helping you now is that I couldn't bear the thought of you and your modern friends slouching about up here. Understood?"

"Yeah, thanks a bundle."

"Oh, and Zaphod?"

"Er, yeah?"

"If you ever find you need help again, you know, if you're in trouble, need a hand out of a tight corner..."

"Yeah?"

"Please don't hesitate to get lost."

Within the space of one second, a bolt of light flashed from the wizened old ghost's hands to the computer, the ghost vanished, the bridge filled with billowing smoke and the *Heart of Gold* leaped an unknown distance through the dimensions of time and space.

Ten light-years away, Gag Halfrunt jacked up his smile by several notches. As he watched the picture on his vision screen, relayed across the sub-ether from the bridge of the Vogon ship, he saw the final shreds of the *Heart of Gold*'s force shield ripped away, and the ship itself vanish in a puff of smoke.

Good, he thought.

The end of the last stray survivors of the demolition he had ordered on the planet Earth, he thought.

The final end of this dangerous (to the psychiatric profession) and subversive (also to the psychiatric profession) experiment to find the Question to the Ultimate Question of Life, the Universe and Everything, he thought.

There would be some celebration with his fellows tonight, and in the morning they would meet again their unhappy, bewildered and highly profitable patients, secure in the knowledge that the Meaning of Life would not now be, once and for all, well and truly sorted out, he thought.

"Family's always embarrassing isn't it?" said Ford to Zaphod as the smoke began to clear.

He paused, he looked about.

"Where's Zaphod?" he said.

Arthur and Trillian looked about blankly. They were pale and shaken and didn't know where Zaphod was.

"Marvin?" said Ford, "where's Zaphod?"

A moment later he said:

"Where's Marvin?"

The robot's corner was empty.

The ship was utterly silent. It lay in thick black space. Occasionally it rocked and swayed. Every instrument was dead, every vision screen was dead. They consulted the computer. It said:

"I regret I have been temporarily closed to all communication. Meanwhile, here is some light music."

They turned off the light music.

They searched every corner of the ship in increasing bewilderment and alarm. Everywhere was dead and silent. Nowhere was there any trace of Zaphod or of Marvin.

One of the last areas they checked was the small bay in which the Nutri-Matic machine was located.

On the delivery plate of the Nutri-Matic Drink Synthesizer was a small tray, on which sat three bone china cups and saucers, a bone china jug of milk, a silver teapot full of the best tea Arthur had ever tasted and a small printed note saying "Wait."

Ursa Minor Beta is, some say, one of the most appalling places in the known Universe.

Although it is excruciatingly rich, horrifyingly sunny and more full of wonderfully exciting people than a pomegranate is of pips, it can hardly be insignificant that when a recent edition of *Playbeing* magazine headlined an article with the words "When you are tired of Ursa Minor Beta you are tired of life," the suicide rate there quadrupled overnight.

Not that there are any nights on Ursa Minor Beta. It is a West zone planet which by an inexplicable and somewhat suspicious freak of topography consists almost entirely of subtropical coastline. By an equally suspicious freak of temporal relastatics, it is nearly always Saturday afternoon just before the beach bars close.

No adequate explanation for this has been forthcoming from the dominant life forms on Ursa Minor Beta, who spend most of their time attempting to achieve spiritual enlightenment by running round swimming pools, and inviting Investigation Officials from the Galactic Geo-Temporal Control Board to "have a nice diurnal anomaly."

There is only one city on Ursa Minor Beta, and that is

only called a city because the swimming pools are slightly thicker on the ground there than elsewhere.

If you approach Light City by air—and there is no other way of approaching it, no roads, no port facilities —if you don't fly they don't want to see you in Light City—you will see why it has this name. Here the sun shines brightest of all, glittering on the swimming pools, shimmering on the white, palm-lined boulevards, glistening on the healthy bronzed specks moving up and down them, gleaming off the villas, the hazy airpads, the beach bars and so on.

Most particularly it shines on a building, a tall, beautiful building consisting of two thirty-story white towers connected by a bridge halfway up their length.

The building is the home of a book, and was built here on the proceeds of an extraordinary copyright lawsuit fought between the book's editors and a breakfast cereal company.

The book is a guide book, a travel book.

It is one of the most remarkable, certainly the most successful, books ever to come out of the great publishing corporations of Ursa Minor—more popular than *Life Begins at Five Hundred and Fifty*, better selling than *The Big Bang Theory—A Personal View* by Eccentrica Gallumbits (the tripled-breasted whore of Eroticon Six) and more controversial then Oolon Colluphid's latest blockbusting title *Everything You Never Wanted to Know About Sex but Have Been Forced to Find Out*.

(And in many of the more relaxed civilizations on the Outer Eastern Rim of the Galaxy, it has long supplanted the great *Encyclopedia Galactica* as the standard repository of all knowledge and wisdom, for though it has many omissions and contains much that is apocryphal, or at least wildly inaccurate, it scores over the older more pedestrian work in two important respects. First, it is slightly cheaper, and secondly it has the words DON'T PANIC printed in large friendly letters on its cover.)

It is of course that invaluable companion for all those who want to see the marvels of the known Universe for less than thirty Altairian dollars a day—*The Hitchhiker's Guide to the Galaxy.*

If you stood with your back to the main entrance lobby of the *Guide* offices (assuming you had landed by now and freshened up with a quick dip and shower) and then walked east, you would pass along the leafy shade of Life Boulevard, be amazed by the pale golden color of the beaches stretching away to your left, astounded by the mind-surfers floating carelessly along two feet above the waves as if this was nothing special, surprised and eventually slightly irritated by the giant palm trees that hum tuneless nothings throughout the daylight hours, in other words continuously.

If you then walked to the end of Life Boulevard you would enter the Lalamatine district of shops, bolonut trees and pavement cafés where the UM-Betans come to relax after a hard afternoon's relaxation on the beach. The Lalamatine district is one of those very few areas which doesn't enjoy a perpetual Saturday afternoon—it enjoys instead the cool of a perpetual early Saturday evening. Behind it lie the nightclubs.

If, on this particular day, afternoon, stretch of eve-ningtime—call it what you will—you had approached the second pavement café on the right, you would have seen the usual crowd of UM-Betans chatting, drinking, looking very relaxed and casually glancing at each other's watches to see how expensive they were.

You would also have seen a couple of rather dishev-eled-looking hitchhikers from Algol who had recently arrived on an Arcturan Megafreighter aboard which they had been roughing it for a few days. They were angry and bewildered to discover that here, within sight of the *Hitchhiker's Guide* building itself, a simple glass of fruit juice cost the equivalent of over sixty Altairian dollars.

"Sell out," one of them said, bitterly.

If at that moment you had then looked at the next table you would have seen Zaphod Beeblebrox sitting and looking very startled and confused.

The reason for his confusion was that five seconds earlier he had been sitting on the bridge of the starship *Heart of Gold*.

"Absolute sell out," said the voice again.

Zaphod looked nervously out of the corners of his eyes at the two disheveled hitchhikers at the next table. Where the hell was he? How had he got there? Where was his ship? His hand felt the arm of the chair on which he was sitting, and then the table in front of him. They seemed solid enough. He sat very still.

"How can they sit and write a guide for hitchhikers in a place like this?" continued the voice. "I mean look at it. Look at it!"

Zaphod was looking at it. Nice place, he thought. But where? And why?

He fished in his pocket for his two pairs of sunglasses. In the same pocket he felt a hard, smooth, unidentified lump of very heavy metal. He pulled it out and looked at it. He blinked at it in surprise. Where had he got that? He returned it to his pocket and put on the sunglasses, annoyed to discover that the metal object had scratched one of the lenses. Nevertheless, he felt much more comfortable with them on. They were a double pair of Joo Janta 200 Super-Chromatic Peril Sensitive Sunglasses, which had been specially designed to help people develop a relaxed attitude to danger. At the first hint of trouble they turn totally black and thus prevent you from seeing anything that might alarm you.

Apart from the scratch the lenses were clear. He relaxed, but only a little bit.

The angry hitchhiker continued to glare at his monstrously expensive fruit juice.

"Worse thing that ever happened to the *Guide*, moving to Ursa Minor Beta," he grumbled; "they've all gone soft. You know, I've even heard that they've created a whole electronically synthesized Universe in one of their offices so they can go and research stories during the day and still go to parties in the evening. Not that day and evening mean much in this place."

Ursa Minor Beta, thought Zaphod. At least he knew where he was now. He assumed that this must be his great-grandfather's doing, but why?

Much to his annoyance, a thought popped into his mind. It was very clear and very distinct, and he had now come to recognize these thoughts for what they were. His instinct was to resist them. They were the preordained promptings from the dark and locked off parts of his mind.

He sat still and ignored the thought furiously. It nagged at him. He ignored it. It nagged at him. He ignored it. It nagged at him. He gave in to it.

What the hell, he thought, go with the flow. He was too tired, confused and hungry to resist. He didn't even know what the thought meant.

Chapter 6

Hello? Yes? Megadodo Publications, home of the *Hitchhiker's Guide to the Galaxy,* the most totally remarkable book in the whole of the known Universe, can I help you?" said the large pink-winged insect into one of the seventy phones lined up along the vast chrome expanse of the reception desk in the foyer of the *Hitchhiker's Guide to the Galaxy* offices. It fluttered its wings and rolled its eyes. It glared at all the grubby people cluttering up the foyer, soiling the carpets and leaving dirty handmarks on the upholstery. It adored working for the *Hitchhiker's Guide to the Galaxy,* it just wished there was some way of keeping all the hitchhikers away. Weren't they meant to be hanging around dirty spaceports or something? It was certain that it had read something somewhere in the book about the importance of hanging around dirty spaceports. Unfortunately most of them seemed to come and hang around in this nice clean shiny foyer immediately after hanging around in extremely dirty spaceports. And all they ever did was complain. It shivered its wings.

"What?" it said into the phone. "Yes, I passed on your message to Mr. Zarniwoop, but I'm afraid he's too cool to see you right now. He's on an intergalactic cruise."

It waved a petulant tentacle at one of the grubby people who was angrily trying to engage its attention. The petulant tentacle directed the angry person to look at the notice on the wall to its left and not to interrupt an important phone call.

"Yes," said the insect, "he is in his office, but he's on an intergalactic cruise. Thank you so much for calling." It slammed down the phone.

"Read the notice," it said to the angry man who was trying to complain about one of the more ludicrous and dangerous pieces of misinformation contained in the book.

The Hitchhiker's Guide to the Galaxy is an indispensable companion to all those who are keen to make sense of life in an infinitely complex and confusing Universe, for though it cannot hope to be useful or informative on all matters, it does at least make the reassuring claim, that where it is inaccurate it is at least *definitively* inaccurate. In cases of major discrepancy it's always reality that's got it wrong.

This was the gist of the notice. It said "The *Guide* is definitive. Reality is frequently inaccurate."

This has led to some interesting consequences. For instance, when the editors of the *Guide* were sued by the families of those who had died as a result of taking the entry on the planet Traal literally (it said "Ravenous Bugblatter Beasts often make a very good meal for visiting tourists" instead of "Ravenous Bugblatter Beasts often make a very good meal *of* visiting tourists"), they claimed that the first version of the sentence was the more aesthetically pleasing, summoned a qualified poet to testify under oath that beauty was truth, truth beauty and hoped thereby to prove that the guilty party in this case was Life itself for failing to be either beautiful or true. The judges concurred, and in a moving speech held that Life itself was in contempt of court, and duly confiscated it from all those there present before going off to enjoy a pleasant evening's ultragolf.

Zaphod Beeblebrox entered the foyer. He strode up to the insect receptionist.

"Okay," he said, "where's Zarniwoop? Get me Zarniwoop."

"Excuse me, sir?" said the insect icily. It did not care to be addressed in this manner.

"Zarniwoop. Get him, right? Get him now."

"Well, sir," snapped the fragile little creature, "if you could be a little cool about it...."

"Look," said Zaphod, "I'm up to here with cool, okay? I am so amazingly cool you could keep a side of meat in me for a month. I am so hip I have difficulty seeing over my pelvis. Now will you move before I blow it?"

"Well, if you'd let me explain, *sir*," said the insect, tapping the most petulant of all the tentacles at its disposal, "I'm afraid that isn't possible right now as Mr. Zarniwoop is on an intergalactic cruise."

Hell, thought Zaphod.

"When's he going to be back?" he said.

"Back, sir? He's in his office."

Zaphod paused while he tried to sort this particular

thought out in his mind. He didn't succeed.

"This cat's on an intergalactic cruise... in his *office?*" He leaned forward and gripped the tapping tentacle.

"Listen, three eyes," he said, "don't you try to outweird me, I get stranger things than you free with my breakfast cereal."

"Well, just who do you think you are, honey?" flounced the insect, quivering its wings in rage. "Zaphod Beeblebrox or something?"

"Count the heads," said Zaphod in a low rasp.

The insect blinked at him. It blinked at him again.

"You *are* Zaphod Beeblebrox?" it squeaked.

"Yeah," said Zaphod, "but don't shout it out or they'll all want one."

"*The* Zaphod Beeblebrox?"

"No, just *a* Zaphod Beeblebrox; didn't you hear I come in six packs?"

The insect rattled its tentacles together in agitation.

"But, sir," it squealed, "I just heard on the sub-ether radio report. It said you were dead...."

"Yeah, that's right," said Zaphod, "I just haven't stopped moving yet. Now. Where do I find Zarniwoop?"

"Well, sir, his office is on the fifteenth floor, but—"

"But he's on an intergalactic cruise, yeah, yeah, how do I get to him?"

"The newly installed Sirius Cybernetics Corporation Happy Vertical People Transporters are in the far corner, sir. But, sir..."

Zaphod was turning to go. He turned back.

"Yeah?" he said.

"Can I ask you why you want to see Mr. Zarni-woop?"

"Yeah," said Zaphod, who was unclear on this point himself, "I told myself I had to."

"Come again, sir?"

Zaphod leaned forward, conspiratorially.

"I just materialized out of thin air in one of your cafés," he said, "as a result of an argument with the ghost of my great-grandfather. No sooner had I got there than my former self, the one that operated on my brain, popped into my head and said 'Go see Zarni-woop.' I have never heard of the cat. That is all I know. That and the fact that I've got to find the man who rules the Universe."

He winked.

"Mr. Beeblebrox, sir," said the insect in awed wonder, "you're so weird you should be in movies."

"Yeah," said Zaphod patting the thing on a glittering pink wing, "and you, baby, should be in real life."

The insect paused for a moment to recover from its agitation and then reached out a tentacle to answer a ringing phone.

A metal hand restrained it.

"Excuse me," said the owner of the metal hand in a voice that would have made an insect of a more sentimental disposition collapse in tears.

This was not such an insect, and it couldn't stand robots.

"Yes, *sir*," it snapped, "can I help you?"

"I doubt it," said Marvin.

"Well, in that case, if you'll just excuse me...." Six of the phones were now ringing. A million things awaited the insect's attention.

"No one can help me," intoned Marvin.

"Yes, sir, well..."

"Not that anyone's tried of course." The restraining metal hand fell limply by Marvin's side. His head hung forward very slightly.

"Is that so," the insect said tartly.

"Hardly worth anyone's while to help a menial robot, is it?"

"I'm sorry, sir, if..."

"I mean, where's the percentage in being kind or helpful to a robot if it doesn't have any gratitude circuits?"

"And you don't have any?" said the insect, who didn't seem to be able to drag itself out of this conversation.

"I've never had occasion to find out," Marvin informed it.

"Listen, you miserable heap of maladjusted metal..."

"Aren't you going to ask me what I want?"

The insect paused. Its long thin tongue darted out and licked its eyes and darted back again.

"Is it *worth* it?" it asked.

"Is anything?" said Marvin immediately.

"*What...do...you...want?*"

"I'm looking for someone."

"Who?" hissed the insect.

"Zaphod Beeblebrox," said Marvin, "he's over there."

The insect shook with rage. It could hardly speak.

"Then why did you ask *me?*" it screamed.

"I just wanted something to talk to," said Marvin.

"What!"

"Pathetic, isn't it?"

With a grinding of gears Marvin turned and trundled off. He caught up with Zaphod approaching the elevators. Zaphod spun around in astonishment.

"Hey...Marvin?" he said. "Marvin! How did you get here?"

Marvin was forced to say something which came very hard to him.

"I don't know," he said.

"But—"

"One moment I was sitting in your ship feeling very depressed, and the next moment I was standing here feeling utterly miserable. An Improbability Field I expect."

"Yeah," said Zaphod, "I expect my great-grandfather sent you along to keep me company.

"Thanks a bundle, Granddad," he added to himself under his breath.

"So, how are you?" he said aloud.

"Oh, fine," said Marvin, "if you happen to like being me, which personally I don't."

"Yeah, yeah," said Zaphod as the elevator doors opened.

"Hello," said the elevator sweetly, "I am to be your elevator for this trip to the floor of your choice. I have been designed by the Sirius Cybernetics Corporation to take you, the visitor to the *Hitchhiker's Guide to the Galaxy*, into these their offices. If you enjoy your ride, which will be swift and pleasurable, then you may care to experience some of the other elevators which have recently been installed in the offices of the Galactic tax department, Boobiloo Baby Foods and the Sirian State Mental Hospital, where many ex-Sirius Cybernetics Corporation executives will be delighted to welcome your visits, sympathy and happy tales of the outside world."

"Yeah," said Zaphod, stepping into it, "what else do you do besides talk?"

"I go up," said the elevator, "or down."

"Good," said Zaphod, "we're going up."

"Or down," the elevator reminded him.

"Yeah, okay, up please."

There was a moment of silence.

"Down's very nice," suggested the elevator hopefully.

"Oh yeah?"

"Super."

"Good," said Zaphod, "now will you take us up?"

"May I ask you," inquired the elevator in its sweetest, most reasonable voice, "if you've considered all the possibilities that down might offer you?"

Zaphod knocked one of his heads against the inside wall. He didn't need this, he thought to himself, this of all things he had no need of. He hadn't asked to be here. If he was asked at this moment where he would like to be he would probably have said he would like to be lying on the beach with at least fifty beautiful women and a small team of experts working out new ways they could be nice to him, which was his usual reply. To this he would probably have added something passionate on the subject of food.

One thing he didn't want to be doing was chasing after the man who ruled the Universe, who was only doing a job which he might as well keep at, because if it wasn't him it would only be someone else. Most of all he didn't want to be standing in an office block arguing with an elevator.

"Like what other possibilities?" he said wearily.

"Well," the voice trickled on like honey on biscuits, "there's the basement, the microfiles, the heating system ...er..."

It paused.

"Nothing particularly exciting," it admitted, "but they are alternatives."

"Holy Zarquon," muttered Zaphod, "did I *ask* for an existential elevator?" He beat his fists against the wall.

"What's the matter with the thing?" he spat.

"It doesn't want to go up," said Marvin simply. "I think it's afraid."

"Afraid?" cried Zaphod. "Of what? Heights? An elevator that's afraid of heights?"

"No," said the elevator miserably, "of the future...."

"The *future*?" exclaimed Zaphod. "What does the wretched thing want, a pension plan?"

At that moment a commotion broke out in the

reception hall behind them. From the walls around them came the sound of suddenly active machinery.

"We can all see into the future," whispered the elevator in what sounded like terror, "it's part of our programming."

Zaphod looked out of the elevator—an agitated crowd had gathered round the elevator area, pointing and shouting.

Every elevator in the building was coming down, very fast.

He ducked back in.

"Marvin," he said, "just get this elevator to go up, will you? We've got to get to Zarniwoop."

"Why?" asked Marvin dolefully.

"I don't know," said Zaphod, "but when I find him, he'd better have a very good reason for me wanting to see him."

Modern elevators are strange and complex entities. The ancient electric winch and "maximum-capacity-eight-persons" jobs bear as much relation to a Sirius Cybernetics Corporation Happy Vertical People Transporter as a packet of mixed nuts does to the entire west wing of the Sirian State Mental Hospital.

This is because they operate on the curious principle of "defocused temporal perception." In other words they have the capacity to see dimly into the immediate future, which enables the elevator to be on the right floor to pick you up even before you knew you wanted it, thus eliminating all the tedious chatting, relaxing and making friends that people were previously forced to do while waiting for elevators.

Not unnaturally, many elevators imbued with intelligence and precognition became terribly frustrated with the mindless business of going up and down, up and down, experimented briefly with the notion of going sideways, as a sort of existential protest, demanded participation in the decision-making process and finally took to squatting in basements sulking.

An impoverished hitchhiker visiting any planets in the Sirius star system these days can pick up easy money working as a counselor for neurotic elevators.

At the fifteenth floor the elevator doors snapped open quickly.

"Fifteenth," said the elevator, "and remember, I'm only doing this because I like your robot."

Zaphod and Marvin bundled out of the elevator which instantly snapped its doors shut and dropped as fast as its mechanism would take it.

Zaphod looked around warily. The corridor was deserted and silent and gave no clue as to where Zarniwoop might be found. All the doors that let off the corridor were closed and unmarked.

They were standing close to the bridge which led across from one tower of the building to the other. Through a large window the brilliant sun of Ursa Minor Beta threw blocks of light in which danced small specks of dust. A shadow flitted past momentarily.

"Left in the lurch by a lift," muttered Zaphod, who was feeling at his least jaunty.

They both stood and looked in both directions.

"You know something?" said Zaphod to Marvin.

"More than you can possibly imagine."

"I'm dead certain this building shouldn't be shaking," Zaphod said.

It was just a light tremor through the soles of his feet—and another one. In the sunbeams the flecks of dust danced more vigorously. Another shadow flitted past.

Zaphod looked at the floor.

"Either," he said, not very confidently, "they've got some vibro system for toning up your muscles while you work, or..."

He walked across to the window and suddenly stumbled because at that moment his Joo Janta 200 Super-Chromatic Peril Sensitive Sunglasses had turned utterly black. A large shadow flitted past the window with a sharp buzz.

Zaphod ripped off his sunglasses, and as he did so the building shook with a thunderous roar. He leaped to the window.

"Or," he said, "this building's being bombed!"

Another roar cracked through the building.

"Who in the Galaxy would want to bomb a publishing company?" asked Zaphod, but never heard Marvin's reply because at that moment the building shook with another bomb attack. He tried to stagger back to the elevator—a pointless maneuver he realized, but the only one he could think of.

Suddenly, at the end of a corridor leading at right angles from this one, he caught sight of a figure as it lunged into view, a man. The man saw him.

"Beeblebrox, over here!" he shouted.

Zaphod eyed him with distrust as another bomb blast rocked the building.

"No," called Zaphod. "Beeblebrox over here! Who are you?"

"A friend!" shouted back the man. He ran toward Zaphod.

"Oh yeah?" said Zaphod. "Anyone's friend in particular, or just generally well-disposed to people?"

The man raced along the corridor, the floor bucking beneath his feet like an excited blanket. He was short, stocky and weatherbeaten and his clothes looked as if they'd been twice around the Galaxy and back with him in them.

"Do you know," Zaphod shouted in his ear when he arrived, "your building's being bombed?"

The man indicated his awareness.

It suddenly stopped being light. Glancing round at the window to see why, Zaphod gaped as a huge slug-like, gunmetal-green spacecraft crept through the air past the building. Two more followed it.

"The government you deserted is out to get you, Zaphod," hissed the man. "They've sent a squadron of Frogstar Fighters."

"Frogstar Fighters!" muttered Zaphod. "Zarquon!"

"You get the picture?"

"What are Frogstar Fighters?" Zaphod was sure he'd heard someone talk about them when he was President, but he never paid much attention to official matters.

The man was pulling him back through a door. He went with him. With a searing whine a small black spiderlike object shot through the air and disappeared down the corridor.

"What was that?" hissed Zaphod.

"Frogstar Scout robot class A out looking for you," said the man.

"Hey, yeah?"

"Get down!"

From the opposite direction came a larger black spiderlike object. It zapped past them.

"And that was...?"

"A Frogstar Scout robot class B out looking for you."

"And that?" said Zaphod, as a third one seared through the air.

"A Frogstar Scout robot class C out looking for you."

"Hey," chuckled Zaphod to himself, "pretty stupid robots, eh?"

From over the bridge came a massive rumbling hum. A gigantic black shape was moving over it from the opposite tower, the size and shape of a tank.

"Holy photon, what's that?" breathed Zaphod.

"A tank," said the man. "Frogstar Scout robot class D come to get you."

"Should we leave?"

"I think we should."

"Marvin!" called Zaphod.

"What do you want?"

Marvin rose from a pile of rubble farther down the corridor and looked at them.

"You see that robot coming toward us?"

Marvin looked at the gigantic black shape edging forward toward them over the bridge. He looked down at his own small metal body. He looked back up at the tank.

"I suppose you want me to stop it," he said.

"Yeah."

"While you save your skins."

"Yeah," said Zaphod, "get in there!"

"Just so long," said Marvin, "as I know where I stand."

The man tugged at Zaphod's arm, and Zaphod followed him off down the corridor.

A point occurred to him about this.

"Where are we going?" he said.

"Zarniwoop's office."

"Is this any time to keep an appointment?"

"Come on."

Marvin stood at the end of the bridge corridor. He was not in fact a particularly small robot. His silver body gleamed in the dusty sunbeams and shook with the continual barrage which the building was still undergoing.

He did, however, look pitifully small as the gigantic black tank rolled to a halt in front of him. The tank examined him with a probe. The probe withdrew.

Marvin stood there.

"Out of my way little robot," growled the tank.

"I'm afraid," said Marvin, "that I've been left here to stop you."

The probe extended again for a quick recheck. It withdrew again.

"You? Stop me?" roared the tank. "Go on!"

"No, really I have," said Marvin simply.

"What are you armed with?" roared the tank in disbelief.

"Guess," said Marvin.

The tank's engines rumbled, its gears ground. Molecule-size electronic relays deep in its microbrain flipped backward and forward in consternation.

"Guess?" said the tank.

Zaphod and the as yet unnamed man lurched up one corridor, down a second and along a third. The building continued to rock and shudder and this puzzled Zaphod. If they wanted to blow the bulding up, why was it taking so long?

With difficulty they reached one of a number of totally anonymous unmarked doors and heaved at it. With a sudden jolt it opened and they fell inside.

All this way, thought Zaphod, all this trouble, all this not-lying-on-the-beach-having-a-wonderful-time, and for what? A single chair, a single desk and a single dirty ashtray in an undecorated office. The desk, apart from a bit of dancing dust and single, revolutionary new form of paper clip, was empty.

"Where," said Zaphod, "is Zarniwoop?" feeling that his already tenuous grasp of the point of this whole exercise was beginning to slip.

"He's on an intergalactic cruise," said the man.

Zaphod tried to size the man up. Earnest type, he thought, not a barrel of laughs. He probably apportioned a fair whack of his time to running up and down heaving corridors, breaking down doors and making cryptic remarks in empty offices.

"Let me introduce myself," the man said. "My name is Roosta, and this is my towel."

"Hello Roosta," said Zaphod.

"Hello, towel," he added as Roosta held out to him a rather nasty old flowery towel. Not knowing what to do with it, he shook it by the corner.

Outside the window, one of the huge sluglike, gun-metal-green spaceships growled past.

"Yes, go on," said Marvin to the huge battle machine, "you'll never guess."

"Errrmmm..." said the machine, vibrating with unaccustomed thought, "laser beams?"

Marvin shook his head solemnly.

"No," muttered the machine in its deep guttural rumble. "Too obvious. Antimatter ray?" it hazarded.

"Far too obvious," admonished Marvin.

"Yes," grumbled the machine, somewhat abashed. "Er...how about an electron ram?"

This was new to Marvin.

"What's that?" he said.

"One of these," said the machine with enthusiasm.

From its turret emerged a sharp prong which spat a single lethal blaze of light. Behind Marvin a wall roared and collapsed as a heap of dust. The dust billowed briefly, then settled.

"No," said Marvin, "not one of those."

"Good though, isn't it?"

"Very good," agreed Marvin.

"I know," said the Frogstar battle machine, after another moment's consideration, "you must have one of those new Xanthic Restructron Destabilized Zenon Emitters!"

"Nice, aren't they?" said Marvin.

"That's what you've got?" said the machine in considerable awe.

"No," said Marvin.

"Oh," said the machine, disappointed, "then it must be..."

"You're thinking along the wrong lines," said Marvin. "You're failing to take into account something fairly basic in the relationship between men and robots."

"Er, I know," said the battle machine, "is it . . . ?" it trailed off into thought again.

"Just think," urged Marvin, "they left me, an ordinary, menial robot, to stop you, a gigantic heavy-duty battle machine, while they ran off to save themselves. What do you think they would leave me with?"

"Oooh, er," muttered the machine in alarm, "something pretty damn devastating I should expect."

"Expect!" said Marvin. "Oh yes, expect. I'll tell you what they gave me to protect myself with, shall I?"

"Yes, all right," said the battle machine, bracing itself.

"Nothing," said Marvin.

There was a dangerous pause.

"*Nothing?*" roared the battle machine.

"Nothing at all," intoned Marvin dismally, "not an electronic sausage."

The machine heaved about with fury.

"Well, doesn't that just take the biscuit!" it roared. "Nothing, eh? Just don't think, do they?"

"And me," said Marvin in a soft low voice, "with this terrible pain in all the diodes down my left side."

"Makes you spit, doesn't it?"

"Yes," agreed Marvin with feeling.

"Hell, that makes me angry," bellowed the machine. "Think I'll smash that wall down!"

The electron ram stabbed out another searing blaze of light and took out the wall next to the machine.

"How do you think I feel?" said Marvin bitterly.

"Just ran off and left you, did they?" the machine thundered.

"Yes," said Marvin.

"I think I'll shoot down their bloody ceiling as well!" raged the tank.

It took out the ceiling of the bridge.

"That's very impressive," murmured Marvin.

"You ain't seen nothing yet," promised the machine. "I can take out this floor too, no trouble!"

It took out the floor too.

"Hell's bells!" the machine roared as it plummeted fifteen stories and smashed itself to bits on the ground below.

"What a depressingly stupid machine," said Marvin and trudged away.

So, do we just sit here, or what?" said Zaphod angrily; "what do these guys out here want?"

"You, Beeblebrox," said Roosta. "They're going to take you to the Frogstar—the most totally evil world in the Galaxy."

"Oh yeah?" said Zaphod. "They'll have to come and get me first."

"They have come and got you," said Roosta. "Look out the window."

Zaphod looked, and gaped.

"The ground's going away!" he gasped. "Where are they taking the ground?"

"They're taking the building," said Roosta. "We're airborne."

Clouds streaked past the office window.

Out in the open air again Zaphod could see the ring of dark green Frogstar Fighters around the uprooted tower of the building. A network of force beams radiated in from them and held the tower in a firm grip.

Zaphod shook his head in perplexity.

"What have I done to deserve this?" he said. "I walk into a building, they take it away."

"It's not what you've done they're worried about,"

said Roosta, "it's what you're going to do."

"Well, don't I get a say in that?"

"You did, years ago. You'd better hold on, we're in for a fast and bumpy journey."

"If I ever meet myself," said Zaphod, "I'll hit myself so hard I won't know what's hit me."

Marvin trudged in through the door, looked at Zaphod accusingly, slumped in a corner and switched himself off.

On the bridge of the *Heart of Gold*, all was silent. Arthur stared at the rack in front of him and thought. He caught Trillian's eyes as she looked at him inquiringly. He looked back at the rack.

Finally he saw it.

He picked up five small plastic squares and laid them on the board that lay just in front of the rack.

The five squares had on them the five letters *E, X, Q, U* and *I*. He laid them next to the letters *S, I, T, E.*

"Exquisite," he said, "on a triple word score. Scores rather a lot I'm afraid."

The ship bumped and scattered some of the letters for the nth time.

Trillian sighed and started to sort them out again.

Up and down the silent corridors echoed Ford Prefect's feet as he stalked the ship thumping dead instruments.

Why did the ship keep shaking? he thought.

Why did it rock and sway?

Why could he not find out where they were?

Where, basically, were they?

The left-hand tower of the *Hitchhiker's Guide to the Galaxy* offices streaked through interstellar space at a speed never equaled either before or since by any other office block in the Universe.

In a room halfway up it, Zaphod Beeblebrox strode angrily.

Roosta sat on the edge of the desk doing some routine towel maintenance.

"Hey, where did you say this building was flying to?" demanded Zaphod.

"The Frogstar," said Roosta, "the most totally evil place in the Universe."

"Do they have food there?" said Zaphod.

"Food? You're going to the Frogstar and you're worried about whether they've got food?"

"Without food I may not make it to the Frogstar."

Out of the window, they could see nothing but the flickering light of the force beams, and vague green streaks which were presumably the distorted shapes of the Frogstar Fighters. At this speed, space itself was invisible, and indeed unreal.

"Here, suck this," said Roosta, offering Zaphod his towel.

Zaphod stared at him as if he expected a cuckoo to leap out of his forehead on a small spring.

"It's soaked in nutrients," explained Roosta.

"What are you, a messy eater or something?" said Zaphod.

"The yellow stripes are high in protein, the green ones have vitamin B and C complexes, the little pink flowers contain wheatgerm extract."

Zaphod took and looked at it in amazement.

"What are the brown stains?" he asked.

"Bar-B-Q sauce," said Roosta, "for when I get sick of wheatgerm."

Zaphod sniffed it doubtfully.

Even more doubtfully, he sucked a corner. He spat it out again.

"Ugh," he stated.

"Yes," said Roosta, "when I've had to suck that end I usually need to suck the other end a bit too."

"Why," asked Zaphod suspiciously, "what's in that?"

"Antidepressants," said Roosta.

"I've gone right off this towel, you know," said Zaphod handing it back.

Roosta took it back from him, swung himself off the desk, walked around it, sat in the chair and put his feet up.

"Beeblebrox," he said, sticking his hands behind his head, "have you any idea what's going to happen to you on the Frogstar?"

"They're going to feed me?" hazarded Zaphod hopefully.

"They're going to feed you," said Roosta, "into the Total Perspective Vortex!"

Zaphod had never heard of this. He believed that he had heard of all the fun things in the Galaxy, so he assumed that the Total Perspective Vortex was not fun. He asked Roosta what it was.

"Only," said Roosta, "the most savage psychic torture a sentient being can undergo."

Zaphod nodded a resigned nod.

"So," he said, "no food, huh?"

"Listen!" said Roosta urgently. "You can kill a man, destroy his body, break his spirit, but only the Total Perspective Vortex can annihilate a man's soul! The treatment lasts seconds, but the effects last the rest of your life!"

"You ever had a Pan Galactic Gargle Blaster?" asked Zaphod sharply.

"This is worse."

"Phreeow!" admitted Zaphod, much impressed.

"Any idea why these guys might want to do this to me?" he added a moment later.

"They believe it will be the best way of destroying you for ever. They know what you're after."

"Could they drop me a note and let me know as well?"

"You know," said Roosta, "you know, Beeblebrox. You want to meet the man who rules the Universe."

"Can he cook?" said Zaphod. On reflection he added:

"I doubt if he can. If he could cook a good meal he wouldn't worry about the rest of the Universe. I want to meet a cook."

Roosta sighed heavily.

"What are you doing here anyway?" demanded Zaphod. "What's all this got to do with you?"

"I'm just one of those who planned this thing, along with Zarniwoop, along with Yooden Vranx, along with your great-grandfather, along with you, Beeblebrox."

"Me?"

"Yes, you. I was told you had changed, I didn't realize how much."

"But..."

"I am here to do one job. I will do it before I leave you."

"What job, man? What are you talking about?"

"I will do it before I leave you."

Roosta lapsed into an impenetrable silence.

Zaphod was terribly glad.

The air around the second planet of the Frog-star system was stale and unwholesome.

The dank winds that swept continually over its surface swept over salt flats, dried up marshland, tangled and rotting vegetation and the crumbling remains of ruined cities. No life moved across its surface. The ground, like that of many planets in this part of the Galaxy, had long been deserted.

The howl of the wind was desolate enough as it gusted through the old decaying houses of the cities; it was more desolate as it whipped about the bottoms of the tall black towers that swayed uneasily here and there about the surface of this world. At the top of these towers lived colonies of large, scraggy, evil-smelling birds, the sole survivors of the civilization that once lived here.

The howl of the wind was at its most desolate, however, when it passed over a pimple of a place set in the middle of a wide gray plain on the outskirts of the largest of the abandoned cities.

This pimple of a place was the thing that had earned this world the reputation of being the most totally evil place in the Galaxy. From without it was simply a steel dome about thirty feet across. From within it was something more monstrous than the mind can comprehend.

About a hundred yards or so away, and separated from it by a pockmarked and blasted stretch of the most barren land imaginable was what would probably have to be described as a landing pad of sorts. That is to say that scattered over a largish area were the ungainly hulks of two or three dozen crash-landed buildings.

Flitting over and around these buildings was a mind, a mind that was waiting for something.

The mind directed its attention into the air, and before very long a distant speck appeared, surrounded by a ring of smaller specks.

The larger speck was the left-hand tower of the *Hitchhiker's Guide to the Galaxy* office building, descending through the stratosphere of Frogstar World B.

As it descended, Roosta suddenly broke the long uncomfortable silence that had grown up between the two men.

He stood up and gathered his towel into a bag. He said:

"Beeblebrox, I will now do the job I was sent here to do."

Zaphod looked up at him from where he was sitting in a corner sharing unspoken thoughts with Marvin.

"Yeah?" he said.

"The building will shortly be landing. When you leave the building, do not go out of the door," said Roosta, "go out of the window.

"Good luck," he added, and walked out of the door, disappearing from Zaphod's life as mysteriously as he had entered it.

Zaphod leaped up and tried the door, but Roosta had already locked it. He shrugged and returned to the corner.

Two minutes later, the building crash-landed amongst the other wreckage. Its escort of Frogstar Fighters deactivated their force beams and soared off into the air again, bound for Frogstar World A, an altogether more congenial spot. They never landed on Frogstar World B. No one did. No one ever walked on its surface other than the intended victims of the Total Perspective Vortex.

Zaphod was badly shaken by the crash. He lay for a while in the silent dusty rubble to which most of the room had been reduced. He felt that he was at the lowest ebb he had ever reached in his life. He felt bewildered, he felt lonely, he felt unloved. Eventually he felt he ought to get whatever it was over with.

He looked around the cracked and broken room. The wall had split round the door frame, and the door hung open. The window, by some miracle, was closed and unbroken. For a while he hesitated, then he thought that if his strange and recent companion had been through all that he had been through just to tell him what he had told him, then there must be a good reason for it. With Marvin's help he got the window open. Outside it, the cloud of dust aroused by the crash, and the hulks of the other buildings with which this one was surrounded, effectively prevented Zaphod from seeing anything of the world outside.

Not that this concerned him unduly. His main concern was what he saw when he looked down. Zarniwoop's office was on the fifteenth floor. The building had landed at a tilt of about forty-five degrees, but still the descent looked heart-stopping.

Eventually, stung by the continuous series of contemptuous looks that Marvin appeared to be giving him, he took a deep breath and clambered out on to the steeply inclined side of the building. Marvin followed him, and together they began to crawl slowly and painfully down the fifteen floors that separated them from the ground.

As he crawled, the dank air and dust choked his lungs, his eyes smarted and the terrific distance down made his heads spin.

The occasional remark from Marvin of the order of "This is the sort of thing you life forms enjoy, is it? I ask merely for information," did little to improve his state of mind.

About halfway down the side of the shattered building they stopped to rest. It seemed to Zaphod as he lay there panting with fear and exhaustion that Marvin seemed a mite more cheerful than usual. Eventually he realized this wasn't so. The robot just seemed cheerful in comparison with his own mood.

A large, scraggy black bird came flapping through the slowly settling clouds of dust and, stretching down its scrawny legs, landed on an inclined window ledge a couple of yards from Zaphod. It folded its ungainly wings and teetered awkwardly on its perch.

Its wingspan must have been something like six feet, and its head and neck seemed curiously large for a bird. Its face was flat, the beak underdeveloped, and halfway along the underside of its wings the vestiges of something handlike could be clearly seen.

In fact, it looked almost human.

It turned its heavy eyes on Zaphod and clicked its beak in a desultory fashion.

"Go away," said Zaphod.

"Okay," muttered the bird morosely and flapped off into the dust again.

Zaphod watched its departure in bewilderment.

"Did that bird just talk to me?" he asked Marvin nervously. He was quite prepared to believe the alternative explanation, that he was in fact hallucinating.

"Yes," confirmed Marvin.

"Poor souls," said a deep, ethereal voice in Zaphod's ear.

Twisting around violently to find the source of the voice nearly caused Zaphod to fall off the building. He grabbed savagely at a protruding window fitting and cut his hand on it. He hung on, breathing heavily.

The voice had no visible source whatsoever—there was no one there. Nevertheless, it spoke again.

"A tragic history behind them, you know. A terrible blight."

Zaphod looked wildly about. The voice was deep and quiet. In other circumstances it would even be described as soothing. There is, however, nothing soothing about being addressed by a disembodied voice out of nowhere, particularly when you are, like Zaphod Beeblebrox, not at your best and hanging from a ledge eight stories up a crashed building.

"Hey, er..." he stammered.

"Shall I tell you their story?" inquired the voice quietly.

"Hey, who are you?" panted Zaphod. "Where are you?"

"Later then, perhaps," murmured the voice. "I am Gargravarr. I am the Custodian of the Total Perspective Vortex."

"Why can't I see...?"

"You will find your progress down the building greatly facilitated," the voice lifted, "if you move about two yards to your left. Why don't you try it?"

Zaphod looked and saw a series of short horizontal grooves leading all the way down the side of the building. Gratefully he shifted himself across to them.

"Why don't I see you again at the bottom?" said the voice in his ear, and as it spoke it faded.

"Hey," called out Zaphod, "where are you...?"

"It'll only take you a couple of minutes...." said the voice very faintly.

"Marvin," said Zaphod earnestly to the robot squatting dejectedly next to him, "did a...did a voice just...?"

"Yes," Marvin replied tersely.

Zaphod nodded. He took out his Peril Sensitive Sunglasses again. They were completely black, and by now quite badly scratched by the unexpected metal object in his pocket. He put them on. He would find his way down the building more comfortably if he didn't actually have to look at what he was doing.

Minutes later he clambered over the ripped and mangled foundations of the building and, once more removing his sunglasses, he dropped to the ground.

Marvin joined him a moment or so later and lay face down in the dust and rubble, from which position he seemed disinclined to move.

"Ah, there you are," said the voice suddenly in Zaphod's ear. "Excuse me leaving you like that; it's just that I have a terrible head for heights. At least," it added wistfully, "I did have a terrible head for heights."

Zaphod looked around slowly and carefully, just to see if he had missed something which might be the source of the voice. All he saw, however, was the dust, the rubble and the towering hulks of the encircling buildings.

"Hey, er, why can't I see you?" he said. "Why aren't you here?"

"*I* am here," said the voice slowly. "My body wanted to come but it's a bit busy at the moment. Things to do, people to see." After what seemed like a sort of ethereal sigh it added, "You know how it is with bodies."

Zaphod wasn't sure about this.

"I thought I did," he said.

"I only hope it's gone in for a rest cure," continued the voice; "the way it's been living recently it must be on its last elbows."

"Elbows?" said Zaphod. "Don't you mean last legs?"

The voice said nothing for a while. Zaphod looked around uneasily. He didn't know if it had gone or was still there or what it was doing. Then the voice spoke again.

"So, you are to be put into the Vortex, yes?"

"Er, well," said Zaphod with a very poor attempt at nonchalance, "this cat's in no hurry, you know. I can just slouch about and take in a look at the local scenery, you know?"

"Have you seen the local scenery?" asked the voice of Gargravarr.

"Er, no."

Zaphod clambered over the rubble, and rounded the corner of one of the wrecked buildings that was obscuring his view.

He looked out at the landscape of Frogstar World B.

"Ah, okay," he said, "I'll just sort of slouch about then."

"No," said Gargravarr, "the Vortex is ready for you now. You must come. Follow me."

"Er, yeah?" said Zaphod. "And how am I meant to do that?"

"I'll hum for you," said Gargravarr. "Follow the humming."

A soft keening sound drifted through the air, a pale, sad sound that seemed to be without any kind of focus. It was only by listening very carefully that Zaphod was able to detect the direction from which it was coming. Slowly, dazedly, he stumbled off in its wake. What else was there to do?

The Universe, as has been observed before, is an unsettlingly big place, a fact which for the sake of a quiet life most people tend to ignore. Many would happily move to somewhere rather smaller of their own devising, and this is what most beings in fact do.

For instance, in one corner of the Eastern Galactic Arm lies the large forest planet Oglaroon, the entire "intelligent" population of which lives permanently in one fairly small and crowded nut tree. In which tree they are born, live, fall in love, carve tiny speculative articles in the bark on the meaning of life, the futility of death and the importance of birth control, fight a few extremely minor wars and eventually die strapped to the underside of some of the less accessible outer branches.

In fact the only Oglaroonians who ever leave their tree are those who are hurled out of it for the heinous crime of wondering whether any of the other trees might be capable of supporting life at all, or indeed whether the other trees are anything other than illusions brought on by eating too many Oglanuts.

Exotic though this behavior may seem, there is no life form in the galaxy which is not in some way guilty of the same thing, which is why the Total Perspective Vortex is as horrific as it is.

For when you are put into the Vortex you are given just one momentary glimpse of the entire unimaginable infinity of creation, and somewhere in it a tiny little marker, a microscopic dot on a microscopic dot, which says "You are here."

The gray plain stretched before Zaphod, a ruined, shattered plain. The wind whipped wildly over it.

Visible in the middle was the steel pimple of the dome. This, gathered Zaphod, was where he was going. This was the Total Perspective Vortex.

As he stood and gazed bleakly at it, a sudden inhuman wail of terror emanated from it as of a man having his soul burned from his body. It screamed above the wind and died away.

Zaphod started with fear and his blood seemed to turn to liquid helium.

"Hey, what was that?" he muttered voicelessly.

"A recording," said Gargravarr, "of the last man who was put in the Vortex. It is always played to the next victim. A sort of prelude."

"Hey, it really sounds bad...." stammered Zaphod. "Couldn't we maybe slope off to a party or something for a while, think it over?"

"For all I know," said Gargravarr's ethereal voice, "I'm probably at one. My body that is. It goes to a lot of parties without me. Says I only get in the way. Hey ho."

"What is all this with your body?" said Zaphod, anxious to delay whatever it was that was going to happen to him.

"Well, it's...it's busy you know," said Gargravarr hesitantly.

"You mean it's got a mind of its own?" said Zaphod.

There was a long and slightly chilly pause before Gargravarr spoke again.

"I have to say," he replied eventually, "that I find that remark in rather poor taste."

Zaphod muttered a bewildered and embarrassed apology.

"No matter," said Gargravarr, "you weren't to know."

The voice fluttered unhappily.

"The truth is," it continued in tones which suggested he was trying very hard to keep it under control, "the truth is that we are currently undergoing a period of legal trial separation. I suspect it will end in divorce."

The voice was still again, leaving Zaphod with no idea of what to say. He mumbled uncertainly.

"I think we were probably not very well-suited," said Gargravarr again at length; "we never seemed to be happy doing the same things. We always had the greatest arguments over sex and fishing. Eventually we tried to combine the two, but that only led to disaster, as you can probably imagine. And now my body refuses to let me in. It won't even see me...."

He paused again, tragically. The wind whipped across the plain.

"It says I only inhibit it. I pointed out that in fact I was meant to inhabit it, and it said that that was exactly the sort of smart alec remark that got right up a body's left nostril, and so we left it. It will probably get custody of my forename."

"Oh...?" said Zaphod faintly. "And what's that?"

"Pizpot," said the voice. "My name is Pizpot Gargravarr. Says it all really, doesn't it?"

"Errr..." said Zaphod sympathetically.

"And that is why I, as a disembodied mind, have this job, Custodian of the Total Perspective Vortex. No one will ever walk on the ground of this planet. Except the victims of the Vortex—they don't really count I'm afraid."

"Ah..."

"I'll tell you the story. Would you like to hear it?"

"Er..."

"Many years ago this was a thriving, happy planet—people, cities, shops, a normal world. Except that on the high streets of these cities there were slightly more shoe shops than one might have thought necessary. And slowly, insidiously, the numbers of these shoe shops were increasing. It's a well-known economic phenomenon but tragic to see it in operation, for the more shoe shops there were, the more shoes they had to make and the worse and more unwearable they became. And the worse they were to wear, the more people had to buy to keep themselves shod, and the more the shops proliferated, until the whole economy of the place passed what I believe is termed the Shoe Event Horizon, and it became no longer economically possible to build anything other than shoe shops. Result—collapse, ruin and famine. Most of the population died out. Those few who had the right kind of genetic instability mutated into birds—you've seen one of them—who cursed their feet, cursed the ground and vowed that none should walk on it again. Unhappy lot. Come, I must take you to the Vortex."

Zaphod shook his head in bemusement and stumbled forward across the plain.

"And you," he said, "you come from this hellhole pit, do you?"

"No no," said Gargravarr, taken aback, "I come from the Frogstar World C. Beautiful place. Wonderful fishing. I flit back there in the evenings. Though all I can do now is watch. The Total Perspective Vortex is the only thing on this planet with any function. It was built here because no one else wanted it on their doorstep."

At that moment another dismal scream rent the air and Zaphod shuddered.

"What can do that to a guy?" he breathed.

"The Universe," said Gargravarr simply, "the whole infinite Universe. The infinite suns, the infinite distances between them and yourself an invisible dot on an invisible dot, infinitely small."

"Hey, I'm Zaphod Beeblebrox, man, you know," muttered Zaphod trying to flap the last remnants of his ego.

Gargravarr made no reply, but merely resumed his mournful humming till they reached the tarnished steel dome in the middle of the plain.

As they reached it, a door hummed open in the side,

revealing a small darkened chamber within.

"Enter," said Gargravarr.

Zaphod started with fear.

"Hey, what, now?" he said.

"Now."

Zaphod peered nervously inside. The chamber was very small. It was steel-lined and there was hardly space in it for more than one man.

"It...er...it doesn't look like any kind of Vortex to me," said Zaphod.

"It isn't," said Gargravarr, "it's just the elevator. Enter."

With infinite trepidation Zaphod stepped into it. He was aware of Gargravarr being in the elevator with him, though the disembodied man was not for the moment speaking.

The elevator began its descent.

"I must get myself into the right frame of mind for this," muttered Zaphod.

"There is no right frame of mind," said Gargravarr sternly.

"You really know how to make a guy feel inadequate."

"I don't. The Vortex does."

At the bottom of the shaft, the rear of the elevator opened up and Zaphod stumbled out into a smallish, functional, steel-lined chamber.

At the far side of it stood a single upright steel box, just large enough for a man to stand in.

It was that simple.

It connected to a small pile of components and instruments via a single thick wire.

"Is that it?" said Zaphod in surprise.

"That is it."

Didn't look too bad, thought Zaphod.

"And I get in there, do I?" said Zaphod.

"You get in there," said Gargravarr, "and I'm afraid you must do it now."

"Okay, okay," said Zaphod.

He opened the door of the box and stepped in.

Inside the box he waited.

After five seconds there was a click, and the entire Universe was there in the box with him.

The Total Perspective Vortex derives its picture of the whole Universe on the principle of extrapolated matter analyses.

To explain—since every piece of matter in the Universe is in some way affected by every other piece of matter in the Universe, it is in theory possible to extrapolate the whole of creation—every sun, every planet, their orbits, their composition and their economic and social history from, say, one small piece of fairy cake.

The man who invented the Total Perspective Vortex did so basically in order to annoy his wife.

Trin Tragula—for that was his name—was a dreamer, a thinker, a speculative philosopher or, as his wife would have it, an idiot.

And she would nag him incessantly about the utterly inordinate amount of time he spent staring out into space, or mulling over the mechanics of safety pins, or doing spectrographic analyses of pieces of fairy cake.

"Have some sense of proportion!" she would say, sometimes as often as thirty-eight times in a single day.

And so he built the Total Perspective Vortex—just to show her.

And into one end he plugged the whole of reality as

A short while later he was running across the plain in the direction of the ruined city.

The dank air wheezed heavily in his lungs and he frequently stumbled with the exhaustion he was still feeling. Night was beginning to fall too, and the rough ground was treacherous.

The elation of his recent experience was still with him though. The whole Universe. He had seen the whole Universe stretching to infinity around him—everything. And with it had come the clear and extraordinary knowledge that he was the most important thing in it. Having a conceited ego is one thing. Actually being told by a machine is another.

He didn't have time to reflect on this matter.

Gargravarr had told him that he would have to alert his masters as to what had happened, but that he was prepared to leave a decent interval before doing so. Enough time for Zaphod to make a break and find somewhere to hide.

What he was going to do he didn't know, but feeling that he was the most important person in the Universe gave him the confidence to believe that something would turn up.

Nothing else on this blighted planet could give him much grounds for optimism.

He ran on, and soon reached the outskirts of the abandoned city.

He walked along cracked and gaping roads riddled with scrawny weeds, the holes filled with rotting shoes. The buildings he passed were so crumbled and decrepit he thought it unsafe to enter any of them. Where could he hide? He hurried on.

After a while the remains of a wide sweeping road led off from the one down which he was walking, and at its end lay a vast low building, surrounded with sundry smaller ones, the whole surrounded by the remains of a perimeter barrier. The large main building still seemed reasonably solid, and Zaphod turned off to see if it might provide him with... well with anything.

He approached the building. Along one side of it—the front it would seem since it faced a wide concreted apron area—were three gigantic doors, maybe sixty feet high. The far one of these was open, and toward this, Zaphod ran.

Inside, all was gloom, dust and confusion. Giant cobwebs lay over everything. Part of the infrastructure of the building had collapsed, part of the rear wall had caved in and a thick choking dust lay inches over the floor.

Through the heavy gloom huge shapes loomed, covered with debris.

The shapes were sometimes cylindrical, sometimes bulbous, sometimes like eggs, or rather cracked eggs. Most of them were split open or falling apart, some were mere skeletons.

They were all spacecraft, all derelict.

Zaphod wandered in frustration among the hulks. There was nothing here that remotely approached the serviceable. Even the mere vibration of his footsteps caused one precarious wreck to collapse further into itself.

Toward the rear of the building lay one old ship, slightly larger than the others, and buried beneath even deeper piles of dust and cobwebs. Its outline, however, seemed unbroken. Zaphod approched it with interest, and as he did so, he tripped over an old feedline.

He tried to toss the feedline aside, and to his surprise discovered that it was still connected to the ship.

To his utter astonishment he realized that the feedline was also humming slightly.

He stared at the ship in disbelief, and then back down at the feedline in his hands.

He tore off his jacket and threw it aside. Crawling along on his hands and knees he followed the feedline to the point where it connected with the ship. The connection was sound, and the slight humming vibration was more distinct.

His heart was beating fast. He wiped away some grime and laid an ear against the ship's side. He could hear only a faint, indeterminate noise.

He rummaged feverishly among the debris lying on the floor all about him and found a short length of tubing and a nonbiodegradable plastic cup. Out of this he fashioned a crude stethoscope and placed it against the side of the ship.

What he heard made his brains turn somersaults.

The voice said:

"Transtellar Cruise Lines would like to apologize to passengers for the continuing delay to this flight. We are currently awaiting the loading of our complement of small lemon-soaked paper napkins for your comfort, refreshment and hygiene during the journey. Meanwhile we thank you for your patience. The cabin crew will shortly be serving coffee and biscuits again."

Zaphod staggered backward, staring wildly at the ship.

He walked around for a few moments in a daze. In so doing he suddenly caught sight of a giant departure board still hanging, but by only one support, from the ceiling above him. It was covered with grime, but some of the figures were still discernible.

Zaphod's eyes searched among the figures, then made some brief calculations. His eyes widened.

"Nine hundred years..." he breathed to himself. That was how late the ship was.

Two minutes later he was on board.

As he stepped out of the airlock, the air that greeted him was cool and fresh—the air conditioning was still working.

The lights were still on.

He moved out of the small entrance chamber into a short narrow corridor and stepped nervously down it.

Suddenly a door opened and a figure stepped out in front of him.

"Please return to your seat, sir," said the android

stewardess and, turning her back on him, she walked on down the corridor in front of him.

When his heart had started beating again he followed her. She opened the door at the end of the corridor and walked through.

He followed her through the door.

They were now in the passenger compartment and Zaphod's heart stopped still again for a moment.

In every seat sat a passenger, strapped into his or her seat.

The passengers' hair was long and unkempt, their fingernails were long, the men wore beards.

All of them were quite clearly alive—but sleeping.

Zaphod had the creeping horrors.

He walked slowly down the aisle as in a dream. By the time he was halfway down the aisle, the stewardess had reached the other end. She turned and spoke.

"Good afternoon ladies and gentlemen," she said sweetly. "Thank you for bearing with us during this slight delay. We will be taking off as soon as we possibly can. If you would like to wake up now I will serve you coffee and biscuits."

There was a slight hum.

At that moment, all the passengers awoke.

They awoke screaming and clawing at the straps and life support systems that held them tightly in their seats. They screamed and bawled and hollered till Zaphod thought his ears would shatter.

They struggled and writhed as the stewardess patiently moved up the aisle placing a small cup of coffee and a packet of biscuits in front of each one of them.

Then one of them rose from his seat.

He turned and looked at Zaphod.

Zaphod's skin was crawling all over his body as if it was trying to get off. He turned and ran from the bedlam.

He plunged through the door and back into the corridor.

The man pursued him.

He raced in a frenzy to the end of the corridor, through the entrance chamber and beyond. He arrived on the flight deck, slammed and bolted the door behind him. He leaned back against the door breathing hard.

Within seconds, a hand started beating on the door.

From somewhere on the flight deck a metallic voice addressed him.

"Passengers are not allowed on the flight deck. Please return to your seat, and wait for the ship to take off. Coffee and biscuits are being served. This is your autopilot speaking. Please return to your seat."

Zaphod said nothing. He breathed hard; behind him the hand continued to knock on the door.

"Please return to your seat," repeated the autopilot. "Passengers are not allowed on the flight deck."

"I'm not a passenger," panted Zaphod.

"Please return to your seat."

"I am not a passenger!" shouted Zaphod again.

"Please return to your seat."

"I am not a...hello, can you hear me?"

"Please return to your seat."

"You're the autopilot?" said Zaphod.

"Yes," said the voice from the flight console.

"You're in charge of this ship?"

"Yes," said the voice again, "there has been a delay. Passengers are to be kept temporarily in suspended animation, for their comfort and convenience. Coffee and biscuits are served every year, after which passengers are returned to suspended animation for their continued comfort and convenience. Departure will take place when the flight stores are complete. We apologize for the delay."

Zaphod moved away from the door, on which the pounding now ceased. He approached the flight console.

"Delay?" he cried. "Have you seen the world outside this ship? It's a wasteland, a desert. Civilization's been and gone, man. There are no lemon-soaked paper napkins on the way from anywhere!"

"The statistical likelihood," continued the autopilot primly, "is that other civilizations will arise. There will one day be lemon-soaked paper napkins. Till then there will be a short delay. Please return to your seat."

"But..."

But at that moment the door opened. Zaphod spun around to see the man who had pursued him standing there. He carried a large briefcase. He was smartly dressed, and his hair was short. He had no beard and no long fingernails.

"Zaphod Beeblebrox," he said, "my name is Zarniwoop. I believe you wanted to see me."

Zaphod Beeblebrox withered. His mouths said foolish

things. He dropped into a chair.

"Oh man, oh man, where did you spring from?" he said.

"I have been waiting here for you," he said in a businesslike tone.

He put the briefcase down and sat in another chair.

"I am glad you followed instructions," he said. "I was a bit nervous that you might have left my office by the door rather than the window. Then you would have been in trouble."

Zaphod shook his heads at him and burbled.

"When you entered the door of my office, you entered my electronically synthesized Universe," he explained. "If you had left by the door you would have been back in the real one. The artificial one works from here."

He patted his briefcase smugly.

Zaphod glared at him with resentment and loathing.

"What's the difference?" he muttered.

"Nothing," said Zarniwoop, "they are identical. Oh —except that I think the Frogstar Fighters are gray in the real Universe."

"What's going on?" spat Zaphod.

"Simple," said Zarniwoop. His self-assurance and smugness made Zaphod seethe.

"Very simple," repeated Zarniwoop. "I discovered the coordinates at which this man could be found—the man who rules the Universe, and discovered that his world was protected by an Unprobability Field. To protect my secret—and myself—I retreated to the safety of this totally artificial Universe and hid myself away in a forgotten cruise liner. I was secure. Meanwhile, you and I..."

"You and *I?*" said Zaphod angrily. "You mean I knew you?"

"Yes," said Zarniwoop, "we knew each other well."

"I had no taste," said Zaphod and resumed a sullen silence.

"Meanwhile, you and I arranged that you would steal the Improbability Drive ship—the only one which could reach the ruler's world—and bring it to me here. This you have now done I trust, and I congratulate you." He smiled a tight little smile which Zaphod wanted to hit with a brick.

"Oh, and in case you were wondering," added Zarniwoop, "this Universe was created specifically for you to come to. You are therefore the most important person in this Universe. You would never," he said with an even more brickable smile, "have survived the Total Perspective Vortex in the real one. Shall we go?"

"Where?" said Zaphod sullenly. He felt collapsed.

"To your ship. The *Heart of Gold.* You did bring it, I trust?"

"No."

"Where is your jacket?"

Zaphod looked at him in mystification.

"My jacket? I took it off. It's outside."

"Good, we will go and find it."

Zarniwoop stood up and gestured to Zaphod to follow him.

Out in the entrance chamber again, they could hear the screams of the passengers being fed coffee and biscuits.

"It has not been a pleasant experience waiting for you," said Zarniwoop.

"Not pleasant for *you!*" bawled Zaphod. "How do you think...?"

Zarniwoop held up a silencing finger as the hatchway swung open. A few feet away from them they could see Zaphod's jacket lying in the debris.

"A very remarkable and very powerful ship," said Zarniwoop. "Watch."

As they watched, the pocket on the jacket suddenly bulged. It split, it ripped. The small metal model of the *Heart of Gold* that Zaphod had been bewildered to discover in his pocket was growing.

It grew, it continued to grow. It reached, after two minutes, its full size.

"At an Improbability Level," said Zarniwoop, "of... oh I don't know, but something very large."

Zaphod swayed.

"You mean I had it with me all the time?"

Zarniwoop smiled. He lifted up his briefcase and opened it.

He twisted a single switch inside it.

"Goodbye artificial Universe," he said; "hello real one!"

The scene before them shimmered briefly—and reappeared exactly as before.

"You see?" said Zarniwoop. "Exactly the same."

"You mean," repeated Zaphod tautly, "that I had it with me all the time?"

"Oh yes," said Zarniwoop, "of course. That was the whole point."

"That's it," said Zaphod. "You can count me out, from here on in you can count me out. I've had all I want of this. You play your own games."

"I'm afraid you cannot leave," said Zarniwoop, "you are entwined in the Improbability Field. You cannot escape."

He smiled the smile that Zaphod had wanted to hit and this time Zaphod hit it.

Ford Prefect bounded up to the bridge of the *Heart of Gold.*

"Trillian! Arthur!" he shouted. "It's working! The ship's reactivated!"

Trillian and Arthur were asleep on the floor.

"Come on, you guys, we're going, we're off," he said kicking them awake.

"Hi there, guys!" twittered the computer. "It's really great to be back with you again, I can tell you, and I just want to say that..."

"Shut up," said Ford. "Tell us where the hell we are."

"Frogstar World B, and man it's a dump," said Zaphod running onto the bridge. "Hi, guys, you must be so amazingly glad to see me you can't even find words to tell me what a cool frood I am."

"What a what?" said Arthur blearily, picking himself up from the floor and not taking any of this in.

"I know how you feel," said Zaphod. "I'm so great even I get tongue-tied talking to myself. Hey it's good to see you Trillian, Ford, Monkeyman. Hey, er, computer..."

"Hi there, Mr. Beeblebrox, sir, sure is a great honor to..."

"Shut up and get us out of here, fast fast fast."

"Sure thing, fella, where do you want to go?"

"Anywhere, doesn't matter," shouted Zaphod. "Yes it does!" he said again. "We want to go to the nearest place to eat!"

"Sure thing," said the computer happily and a massive explosion rocked the bridge.

When Zarniwoop entered a minute or so later with a black eye, he regarded the four wisps of smoke with interest.

our inert bodies sank through spinning blackness. Consciousness had died, cold oblivion pulled the bodies down and down into the pit of unbeing. The roar of silence echoed dismally around them and they sank at last into a dark and bitter sea of heaving red that slowly engulfed them, seemingly for ever.

After what seemed an eternity the sea receded and left them lying on a cold hard shore, the flotsam and jetsam of the stream of Life, the Universe and Everything.

Cold spasms shook them, lights danced sickeningly around them. The cold hard shore tipped and spun and then stood still. It shone darkly—it was a very highly polished cold hard shore.

A green blur watched them disapprovingly.

It coughed.

"Good evening, madam, gentlemen," it said. "Do you have a reservation?"

Ford Prefect's consciousness snapped back like elastic, making his brain smart. He looked up woozily at the green blur.

"Reservation?" he said weakly.

"Yes, sir," said the green blur.

"Do you need a reservation for the afterlife?"

In so far as it is possible for a green blur to arch its eyebrows disdainfully, this is what the green blur now did.

"Afterlife, sir?" it said.

Arthur Dent was grappling with his consciousness the way one grapples with a lost bar of soap in the bath.

"Is this the afterlife?" he stammered.

"Well, I assume so," said Ford Prefect trying to work out which way was up. He tested the theory that it must lie in the opposite direction from the cold hard shore on which he was lying, and staggered to what he hoped were his feet.

"I mean," he said, swaying gently, "there's no way we could have survived that blast is there?"

"No," muttered Arthur. He had raised himself on to his elbows but it didn't seem to improve things. He slumped down again.

"No," said Trillian, standing up, "no way at all."

A dull hoarse gurgling sound came from the floor. It was Zaphod Beeblebrox attempting to speak.

"I certainly didn't survive," he gurgled. "I was a total goner. Wham bang and that was it."

"Yeah, thanks to you," said Ford, "we didn't stand a chance. We must have been blown to bits. Arms, legs everywhere."

"Yeah," said Zaphod struggling noisily to his feet.

"If the lady and gentlemen would care to order drinks..." said the green blur, hovering impatiently beside them.

"Kerpow, splat," continued Zaphod, "instantaneously zonked into our component molecules. Hey, Ford," he said, identifying one of the slowly solidifying blurs around him, "did you get that thing of your whole life flashing before you?"

"You got that too?" said Ford. "Your whole life?"

"Yeah," said Zaphod, "at least I assume it was mine. I spend a lot of time out of my skulls you know."

He looked around him at the various shapes that were at last becoming proper shapes instead of vague and wobbling shapeless shapes.

"So..." he said.

"So what?" said Ford.

"So here we are," said Zaphod hesitantly, "lying dead..."

"Standing," Trillian corrected him.

"Er, standing dead," continued Zaphod, "in this desolate..."

"Restaurant," said Arthur Dent who had got to his feet and could now, much to his surprise, see clearly. That is to say, the thing that surprised him was not that he could see, but what he could see.

"Here we are," continued Zaphod doggedly, "standing dead in this desolate..."

"Five star," said Trillian.

"Restaurant," concluded Zaphod.

"Odd, isn't it?" said Ford.

"Er, yeah."

"Nice chandeliers though," said Trillian.

They looked about themselves in bemusement.

"It's not so much an afterlife," said Arthur, "more a sort of *après vie*."

The chandeliers were in fact a little on the flashy side and the low vaulted ceiling from which they hung would not, in an ideal Universe, have been painted in that particular shade of deep turquoise, and even if it had been it wouldn't have been highlighted by concealed moodlighting. This is not, however, an ideal Universe, as was further evidenced by the eye-crossing patterns of the inlaid marble floor, and the way in which the fronting for the eighty-yard-long marble-topped bar had been made. The fronting for the eighty-yard-long marble-topped bar had been made by stitching together nearly twenty thousand Antarean Mosaic Lizard skins, despite the fact that the twenty thousand lizards concerned had needed them to keep their insides in.

A few smartly dressed creatures were lounging casually at the bar or relaxing in the richly colored body-hugging seats that were deployed here and there about the bar area. A young Vl'Hurg officer and his green steaming young lady passed through the large smoked glass doors at the far end of the bar into the dazzling light of the main body of the Restaurant beyond.

Behind Arthur was a large curtained bay window. He pulled aside the corner of the curtain and looked out at a bleak and dreary landscape, gray, pockmarked and dismal, a landscape which under normal circumstances would have given Arthur the creeping horrors. These were not, however, normal circumstances, for the thing that froze his blood and made his skin try to crawl up his back and off the top of his head was the sky. The sky was...

An attendant flunky politely drew the curtain back into place.

"All in good time, sir," he said.

Zaphod's eyes flashed.

"Hey, wait a minute, you dead guys," he said. "I think we're missing some ultraimportant thing here, you know. Something somebody said and we missed it."

Arthur was profoundly relieved to turn his attention from what he had just seen.

He said, "I said it was a sort of *après*..."

"Yeah, and don't you wish you hadn't?" said Zaphod, "Ford?"

"I said it was odd."

"Yeah, shrewd but dull, perhaps it was—"

"Perhaps," interrupted the green blur who had by this time resolved into the shape of a small wizened dark-suited green waiter, "perhaps you would care to discuss the matter over drinks...."

"Drinks!" cried Zaphod. "That was it! See what you miss if you don't stay alert."

"Indeed, sir," said the waiter patiently. "If the lady and gentlemen would care to take drinks before dinner..."

"Dinner!" Zaphod exclaimed with passion. "Listen, little green person, my stomach could take you home and cuddle you all night for the mere idea."

"...and the Universe," continued the waiter, determined not to be deflected on his home stretch, "will explode later for your pleasure."

Ford's head swiveled slowly toward him. He spoke with feeling.

"Wow," he said, "what sort of drinks do you serve in this place?"

The waiter laughed a polite little waiter's laugh.

"Ah," he said, "I think sir has perhaps misunderstood me."

"Oh, I hope not," breathed Ford.

The waiter coughed a polite little waiter's cough.

"It is not unusual for our customers to be a little disorientated by the time journey," he said, "so if I might suggest—"

"Time journey?" said Zaphod.

"Time journey?" said Ford.

"Time journey?" said Trillian.

"You mean this isn't the afterlife?" said Arthur.

The waiter smiled a polite little waiter's smile. He had almost exhausted his polite little waiter repertoire and would soon be slipping into his role of a rather tight-lipped and sarcastic little waiter.

"Afterlife, sir?" he said. "No, sir."

"And we're not dead?" said Arthur.

The waiter tightened his lips.

"Aha, ha," he said. "Sir is most evidently alive, otherwise I would not attempt to serve sir."

In an extraordinary gesture which it is pointless attempting to describe, Zaphod Beeblebrox slapped both his foreheads with two of his arms and one of his thighs with the other.

"Hey, guys," he said, "this is crazy. We did it. We

finally got to where we were going. This is Milliways!"

"Milliways!" said Ford.

"Yes, sir," said the waiter, laying on the patience with a trowel, "this is Milliways—the Restaurant at the End of the Universe."

"End of what?" said Arthur.

"The Universe," repeated the waiter, very clearly and unnecessarily distinctly.

"When did that end?" said Arthur.

"In just a few minutes, sir," said the waiter. He took a deep breath. He didn't need to do this since his body was supplied with the peculiar assortment of gases it required for survival from a small intravenous device strapped to his leg. There are times, however, when whatever your metabolism you have to take a deep breath.

"Now, if you would care to order your drinks at last," he said, "I will then show you to your table."

Zaphod grinned two manic grins, sauntered over to the bar and bought most of it.

The Restaurant at the End of the Universe is one of the most extraordinary ventures in the entire history of catering. It has been built on the fragmented reamins of...it *will* be built on the fragmented...that is to say it will have been built by this time, and indeed has been—

One of the major problems encountered in time travel is not that of accidentally becoming your own father or mother. There is no problem involved in becoming your own father or mother that a broad-minded and well-adjusted family can't cope with. There is no problem about changing the course of history—the course of history does not change because it all fits together like a jigsaw. All the important changes have happened before the things they were supposed to change and it all sorts itself out in the end.

The major problem is quite simply one of grammar, and the main work to consult in this matter is Dr. Dan Streetmentioner's *Time Traveler's Handbook of 1001 Tense Formations*. It will tell you, for instance, how to describe something that was about to happen to you in the past before you avoided it by time-jumping forward two days in order to avoid it. The event will be described differently according to whether you are talking about it from the standpoint of your own natural time, from a time in the further future, or a time in the further past and is further complicated by the possibility of conducting conversations while you are actually traveling from one time to another with the intention of becoming your own mother or father.

Most readers get as far as the Future Semiconditionally Modified Subinverted Plagal Past Subjunctive Intentional before giving up; and in fact in later editions of the book all the pages beyond this point have been left blank to save on printing costs.

The Hitchhiker's Guide to the Galaxy skips lightly over this tangle of academic abstraction, pausing only to note that the term "Future Perfect" has been abandoned since it was discovered not to be.

To resume:

The Restaurant at the End of the Universe is one of the most extraordinary ventures in the entire history of catering.

It is built on the fragmented remains of an eventually ruined planet which is (wioll haven be) enclosed in a vast time bubble and projected forward in time to the precise moment of the End of the Universe.

This is, many would say, impossible.

In it, guests take (willan on-take) their places at table and eat (willan on-eat) sumptuous meals while watching (willing watchen) the whole of creation explode around them.

This, many would say, is equally impossible.

You can arrive (mayan arrivan on-when) for any

sitting you like without prior (late fore-when) reservation because you can book retrospectively, as it were when you return to your own time (you can have on-book haventa forewhen presooning returningwenta retrohome).

This is, many would now insist, absolutely impossible.

At the Restaurant you can meet and dine with (mayan meetan con with dinan on when) a fascinating cross-section of the entire population of space and time.

This, it can be explained patiently, is also impossible.

You can visit it as many times as you like (mayan onvisit re-onvisiling...and so on—for further tense correction consult Dr. Streetmentioner's book) and be sure of never meeting yourself, because of the embarrassment this usually causes.

This, even if the rest were true, which it isn't, is patently impossible, say the doubters.

All you have to do is deposit one penny in a savings account in your own era, and when you arrive at the End of Time the operation of compound interest means that the fabulous cost of your meal has been paid for.

This, many claim, is not merely impossible but clearly insane, which is why the advertising executives of the star system of Bastablon came up with this slogan: "If you've done six impossible things this morning, why not round it off with breakfast at Milliways, the Restaurant at the End of the Universe?"

At the bar, Zaphod was rapidly becoming as tired as a newt. His heads knocked together and his smiles were coming out of sync. He was miserably happy.

"Zaphod," said Ford, "while you're still capable of speech, would you care to tell me what the photon happened? Where have you been? Where have we been? Small matter, but I'd like it cleared up."

Zaphod's left head sobered up, leaving his right to sink further into the obscurity of drink.

"Yeah," he said, "I've been around. They want me to find the man who rules the Universe, but I don't care to meet him. I believe the man can't cook."

His left head watched his right head saying this and then nodded.

"True," it said, "have another drink."

Ford had another Pan Galactic Gargle Blaster, the drink which has been described as the alcoholic equivalent of a mugging—expensive and bad for the head. Whatever had happened, Ford decided, he didn't really care too much.

"Listen, Ford," said Zaphod, "everything's cool and froody."

"You mean everything's under control."

"No," said Zaphod, "I do not mean everything's under control. That would not be cool and froody. If you want to know what happened let's just say I had the whole situation in my pocket. Okay?"

Ford shrugged.

Zaphod giggled into his drink. It frothed up over the side of the glass and started to eat its way into the marble bar top.

A wild-skinned sky-gypsy approached them and played electric violin at them until Zaphod gave him a lot of money and he agreed to go away again.

The gypsy approached Arthur and Trillian sitting in another part of the bar.

"I don't know what this place is," said Arthur, "but I think it gives me the creeps."

"Have another drink," said Trillian. "Enjoy yourself."

"Which?" said Arthur. "The two are mutually exclusive."

"Poor Arthur, you're not really cut out for this life are you?"

"You call this life?"

"You're beginning to sound like Marvin."

"Marvin's the clearest thinker I know. How do you think we make this violinist go away?"

The waiter approached.

"Your table is ready," he said.

Seen from the outside, which it never is, the Restaurant resembles a giant glittering starfish beached on a forgotten rock. Each of its arms house the bars, the kitchens, the force-field generators which protect the entire structure and the decayed hunk of planet on which it sits, and the Time Turbines which slowly rock the whole affair backward and forward across the crucial moment.

In the center sits the gigantic golden dome, almost a complete globe, and it was into this area that Zaphod, Ford, Arthur and Trillian now passed.

At least five tons of glitter alone had gone into it before them, and covered every available surface. The other surfaces were not available because they were already encrusted with jewels, precious seashells from Santraginus, gold leaf, mosaic tiles, lizard skins and a million unidentifiable embellishments and decorations. Glass glittered, silver shone, gold gleamed, Arthur Dent goggled.

"Wowee," said Zaphod. "Zappo."

"Incredible!" breathed Arthur. "The people...! The things...!"

"The things," said Ford Prefect quietly, "are also people."

"The people..." resumed Arthur, "the... other people..."

"The lights...!" said Trillian.

"The tables..." said Arthur.

"The clothes...!" said Trillian.

The waiter thought they sounded like a couple of bailiffs.

"The End of the Universe is very popular," said Zaphod threading his way unsteadily through the throng of tables, some made of marble, some of rich ultramahogany, some even of platinum, and at each a party of exotic creatures chatting among themselves and studying menus.

"People like to dress up for it," continued Zaphod. "Gives it a sense of occasion."

The tables were fanned out in a large circle around a central stage area where a small band were playing light music, at least a thousand tables was Arthur's guess, and interspersed among them were swaying palms, hissing fountains, grotesque statuary, in short, all the paraphernalia common to all restaurants where little expense has been spared to give the impression that no expense has been spared. Arthur glanced round, half expecting to see someone making an American Express commercial.

Zaphod lurched into Ford, who lurched back into Zaphod.

"Wowee," said Zaphod.

"Zappo," said Ford.

"My great-granddaddy must have really screwed up the computer's works, you know," said Zaphod. "I told it to take us to the nearest place to eat and it sends us to the End of the Universe. Remind me to be nice to it one day."

He paused.

"Hey, everybody's here you know. Everybody who was anybody."

"Was?" said Arthur.

"At the End of the Universe you have to use the past tense a lot," said Zaphod, "'cause everything's been done, you know. Hi, guys," he called out to a nearby party of giant iguana lifeforms. "How did you do?"

"Is that Zaphod Beeblebrox?" asked one iguana of another iguana.

"I think so," replied the second iguana.

"Well, doesn't that just take the biscuit," said the first iguana.

"Funny old thing, life," said the second iguana.

"It's what you make it," said the first and they lapsed back into silence. They were waiting for the greatest show in the Universe.

"Hey, Zaphod," said Ford, grabbing for his arm and, on account of the third Pan Galactic Gargle Blaster, missing. He pointed a swaying finger.

"There's an old mate of mine," he said. "Hotblack Desiato! See the man at the platinum table with the platinum suit on?"

Zaphod tried to follow Ford's finger with his eyes but it made him feel dizzy. Finally he saw.

"Oh yeah," he said, then recognition came a moment later. "Hey," he said, "did that guy ever make it megabig! Wow, bigger than the biggest thing ever. Other than me."

"Who's he supposed to be?" asked Trillian.

"Hotblack Desiato?" said Zaphod in astonishment. "You don't know? You never heard of Disaster Area?"

"No," said Trillian, who hadn't.

"The biggest," said Ford, "loudest..."

"Richest..." suggested Zaphod.

"...rock band in the history of..." he searched for the word.

"...history itself," said Zaphod.

"No," said Trillian.

"Zowee," said Zaphod, "here we are at the End of the Universe and you haven't even lived yet. Did you miss out."

He led her off to where the waiter had been waiting all this time at the table. Arthur followed them feeling very lost and alone.

Ford waded off through the throng to renew an old acquaintance.

"Hey, er, Hotblack," he called out, "how you doing? Great to see you big boy, how's the noise? You're looking great, really very, very fat and unwell. Amazing." He slapped the man on the back and was mildly surprised that it seemed to elicit no response. The Pan Galactic Gargle Blasters swilling around inside him told him to plunge on regardless.

"Remember the old days?" he said. "We used to hang out, right? The Bistro Illegal, remember? Slim's Throat Emporium? The Evildrome Boozarama, great days, eh?"

Hotblack Desiato offered no opinion as to whether they were great days or not. Ford was not perturbed.

"And when we were hungry we'd pose as public health inspectors, you remember that? And go around confiscating meals and drinks, right? Till we got food poisoning. Oh, and then there were the long nights of talking and drinking in those smelly rooms above the Café Lou in Gretchen Town, New Betel, and you were always in the next room trying to write songs on your ajuitar and we all hated them. And you said you didn't care, and we said we did because we hated them so much." Ford's eyes were beginning to mist over.

"And you said you didn't want to be a star," he continued, wallowing in nostalgia, "because you despised the star system. And we said—Hadra and Sulijoo and me—that we didn't think you had the option. And what do you do now? You *buy* star systems!"

He turned and solicited the attention of those at nearby tables.

"Here," he said, "is a man who *buys* star systems!"

Hotblack Desiato made no attempt either to confirm or deny this fact, and the attention of the temporary audience waned rapidly.

"I think someone's drunk," muttered a purple bush-like being into his wineglass.

Ford staggered slightly, and sat down heavily on the chair facing Hotblack Desiato.

"What's that number you do?" he said, unwisely grabbing at a bottle for support and tipping it over—into a nearby glass as it happened. Not to waste a happy accident, he drained the glass.

"That really huge number," he continued, "how does it go? 'Bwarm! Bwarm! Baderr!!' something, and in the stage act you do it ends with this ship crashing right into the sun, and you actually *do* it!"

Ford crashed his fist into his other hand to illustrate this feat graphically. He knocked the bottle over again.

"Ship! Sun! Wham bang!" he cried. "I mean forget lasers and stuff, you guys are into solar flares and *real* sunburn! Oh, and terrible songs."

His eyes followed the stream of liquid glugging out of the bottle onto the table. Something ought to be done about it, he thought.

"Hey, you want a drink?" he said. It began to sink into his squelching mind that something was missing from this reunion, and that the missing something was in some way connected with the fact that the fat man sitting opposite him in the platinum suit and the silvery hat had not yet said "Hi, Ford" or "Great to see you after all this time," or in fact anything at all. More to the point he had not yet even moved.

"Hotblack?" said Ford.

A large meaty hand landed on his shoulder from behind and pushed him aside. He slid gracelessly off his seat and peered upward to see if he could spot the owner of this discourteous hand. The owner was not hard to spot, on account of his being something of the order of seven feet tall and not slightly built with it. In fact he was built the way one builds leather sofas, shiny, lumpy and with lots of solid stuffing. The suit into which the man's body had been stuffed looked as if its only purpose in life was to demonstrate how difficult it was to get this sort of body into a suit. The face had the texture of an orange and the color of an apple, but there the resemblance to anything sweet ended.

"Kid..." said a voice which emerged from the man's mouth as if it had been having a really rough time down in his chest.

"Er, yeah?" said Ford conversationally. He staggered back to his feet again and was disappointed that the top of his head didn't come further up the man's body.

"Beat it," said the man.

"Oh yeah?" said Ford, wondering how wise he was being, "and who are you?"

The man considered this for a moment. He wasn't used to being asked this sort of question. Nevertheless, after a while he came up with an answer.

"I'm the guy who's telling you to beat it," he said, "before you get it beaten for you."

"Now listen," said Ford nervously—he wished his head would stop spinning, settle down and get to grips with the situation—"Now listen," he continued, "I am one of Hotblack's oldest friends and..."

He glanced at Hotblack Desiato, who still hadn't moved so much as an eyelash.

"...and..." said Ford again, wondering what would be a good word to say after "and."

The large man came up with a whole sentence to go after "and." He said it.

"And I am Mr. Desiato's bodyguard," it went, "and I am responsible for his body, and I am not responsible for yours, so take it away before it gets damaged."

"Now wait a minute," said Ford.

"No minutes!" boomed the bodyguard, "no waiting! Mr. Desiato speaks to no one!"

"Well, perhaps you'd let him say what he thinks about the matter himself," said Ford.

"He speaks to no one!" bellowed the bodyguard.

Ford glanced anxiously at Hotblack again and was forced to admit to himself that the bodyguard seemed to have the facts on his side. There was still not the slightest sign of movement, let alone keen interest in Ford's welfare.

"Why?" said Ford. "What's the matter with him?"

The bodyguard told him.

The *Hitchhiker's Guide to the Galaxy* notes that Disaster Area, a plutonium rock band from the Gagrakacka Mind Zones, are generally held to be not only the loudest rock band in the Galaxy, but in fact the loudest noise of any kind at all. Regular concert goers judge that the best sound balance is usually to be heard from within large concrete bunkers some thirty-seven miles from the stage, while the musicians themselves play their instruments by remote control from within a heavily insulated spaceship which stays in orbit around the planet—or more frequently around a completely different planet.

Their songs are on the whole very simple and mostly follow the familiar theme of boy-being meets girl-being beneath a silvery moon, which then explodes for no adequately explored reason.

Many worlds have now banned their act altogether, sometimes for artistic reasons, but most commonly because the band's public address system contravenes local strategic arms limitations treaties.

This has not, however, stopped their earnings from pushing back the boundaries of pure hypermathematics, and their chief research accountant has recently been appointed Professor of Neomathematics at the University of Maximegalon, in recognition of both his General and his Special Theories of Disaster Area Tax Returns, in which he proves that the whole fabric of the space-time continuum is not merely curved, it is in fact totally bent.

Ford staggered back to the table where Zaphod, Arthur and Trillian were sitting waiting for the fun to begin.

"Gotta have some food," said Ford.

"Hi, Ford," said Zaphod. "You speak to the big noise boy?"

Ford waggled his head noncommitally.

"Hotblack? I sort of spoke to him, yeah."

"What'd he say?"

"Well, not a lot really. He's...er..."

"Yeah?"

"He's spending a year dead for tax reasons. I've got to sit down."

He sat down.

The waiter approached.

"Would you like to see the menu?" he said. "Or would you like to meet the Dish of the Day?"

"Huh?" said Ford.

"Huh?" said Arthur.

"Huh?" said Trillian.

"That's cool," said Zaphod. "We'll meet the meat."

In a small room in one of the arms of the Restaurant complex a tall, thin, gangling figure pulled aside a curtain and oblivion looked him in the face.

It was not a pretty face, perhaps because oblivion had looked him in it so many times. It was too long for a start, the eyes too sunken and hooded, the cheeks too hollow, his lips were too thin and too long, and when they parted his teeth looked too much like a recently polished bay window. The hands that held the curtain were long and thin too: they were also cold. They lay lightly along the folds of the curtain and gave the impression that if he didn't watch them like a hawk they would crawl away of their own accord and do something unspeakable in a corner.

He let the curtain drop and the terrible light that had played on his features went off to play somewhere more healthy. He prowled around his small chamber like a mantis contemplating an evening's preying, finally settling on a rickety chair by a trestle table, where he leafed through a few sheets of jokes.

A bell rang.

He pushed the thin sheaf of papers aside and stood up. His hands brushed limply over some of the one million rainbow-colored sequins with which his jacket was festooned, and he was gone through the door.

In the Restaurant the lights dimmed, the band quickened its pace, a single spotlight stabbed down into the darkness of the stairway that led up to the center of the stage.

Up the stairs bounded a tall brilliantly colored figure. He burst onto the stage, tripped lightly up to the microphone, removed it from its stand with one swoop of his long thin hand and stood for a moment bowing left and right to the audience, acknowledging their applause and displaying to them his bay window. He waved to his particular friends in the audience even though there weren't any there, and waited for the applause to die down.

He held up his hand and smiled a smile that stretched not merely from ear to ear, but seemed to extend some way beyond the mere confines of his face.

"Thank you, ladies and gentlemen!" he cried. "Thank you very much. Thank you so much."

He eyed them with a twinkling eye.

"Ladies and gentlemen," he said, "the Universe as we know it has now been in existence for over one hundred and seventy thousand million billion years and will be ending in a little over half an hour. So, welcome one and all to Milliways, the Restaurant at the End of the Universe!"

With a gesture he deftly conjured another round of spontaneous applause. With another gesture he cut it.

"I am your host for tonight," he said. "My name is Max Quordlepleen..." (Everybody knew this, his act was famous throughout the known Galaxy, but he said it for the fresh applause it generated, which he acknowledged with a disclaiming smile and wave.) "...and I've just come straight from the very very other End of Time, where I've been hosting a show at the Big Bang Burger Bar—where I can tell you we had a very exciting evening, ladies and gentlemen—and I will be with you right through this historic occasion, the End of History itself!"

Another burst of applause died away quickly as the lights dimmed down further. On every table candles ignited themselves spontaneously, eliciting a slight gasp from all the diners and wreathing them in a thousand tiny flickering lights and a million intimate shadows. A tremor of excitement thrilled through the darkened Restaurant as the vast golden dome above them began very very slowly to dim, to darken, to fade.

Max's voice was hushed as he continued.

"So, ladies and gentlemen," he breathed, "the candles are lit, the band plays softly and as the force-shielded dome above us fades into transparency, revealing a dark and sullen sky hung heavy with the ancient light of livid swollen stars, I can see we're all in for a fabulous evening's apocalypse!"

Even the soft tootling of the band faded away as stunned shock descended on all those who had not seen this sight before.

A monstrous, grisly light poured in on them
—a hideous light
—a boiling, pestilential light
—a light that would have disfigured hell.

The Universe was coming to an end.

For a few interminable seconds the Restaurant spun silently through the raging void. Then Max spoke again.

"For those of you who ever hoped to see the light at the end of the tunnel," he said, "this is it."

The band struck up again.

"Thank you, ladies and gentlemen," cried Max, "I'll

be back with you again in just a moment, and meanwhile I leave you in the very capable hands of Mr. Reg Nullify and his Cataclysmic Combo. Big hand please, ladies and gentlemen, for Reg and the boys!"

The baleful turmoil of the skies continued.

Hesitantly the audience began to clap and after a moment or so normal conversation resumed. Max began his round of the tables, swapping jokes, shouting with laughter, earning his living.

A large dairy animal approached Zaphod Beeblebrox's table, a large fat meaty quadruped of the bovine type with large watery eyes, small horns and what might almost have been an ingratiating smile on its lips.

"Good evening," it lowed and sat back heavily on its haunches, "I am the main Dish of the Day. May I interest you in parts of my body?" It harrumphed and gurgled a bit, wriggled its hind quarters into a more comfortable position and gazed peacefully at them.

Its gaze was met by looks of startled bewilderment from Arthur and Trillian, a resigned shrug from Ford Prefect and naked hunger from Zaphod Beeblebrox.

"Something off the shoulder perhaps?" suggested the animal. "Braised in a white wine sauce?"

"Er, *your* shoulder?" said Arthur in a horrified whisper.

"But naturally my shoulder, sir," mooed the animal contentedly, "nobody else's is mine to offer."

Zaphod leapt to his feet and started prodding and feeling the animal's shoulder appreciatively.

"Or the rump is very good," murmured the animal.

"I've been exercising it and eating plenty of grain, so there's a lot of good meat there." It gave a mellow grunt, gurgled again and started to chew the cud. It swallowed the cud again.

"Or a casserole of me perhaps?" it added.

"You mean this animal actually wants us to eat it?" whispered Trillian to Ford.

"Me?" said Ford, with a glazed look in his eyes. "I don't mean anything."

"That's absolutely horrible," exclaimed Arthur, "the most revolting thing I've ever heard."

"What's the problem, Earthman?" said Zaphod, now transferring his attention to the animal's enormous rump.

"I just don't want to eat an animal that's standing there inviting me to," said Arthur. "It's heartless."

"Better than eating an animal that doesn't want to be eaten," said Zaphod.

"That's not the point," Arthur protested. Then he thought about it for a moment. "All right," he said, "maybe it is the point. I don't care, I'm not going to think about it now. I'll just...er..."

The Universe raged about him in its death throes.

"I think I'll just have a green salad," he muttered.

"May I urge you to consider my liver?" asked the animal, "it must be very rich and tender by now, I've been force-feeding myself for months."

"A green salad," said Arthur emphatically.

"A green salad?" said the animal, rolling his eyes disapprovingly at Arthur.

"Are you going to tell me," said Arthur, "that I shouldn't have green salad?"

"Well," said the animal, "I know many vegetables that are very clear on that point. Which is why it was eventually decided to cut through the whole tangled problem and breed an animal that actually wanted to be eaten and was capable of saying so clearly and distinctly. And here I am."

It managed a very slight bow.

"Glass of water please," said Arthur.

"Look," said Zaphod, "we want to eat, we don't want to make a meal of the issues. Four rare steaks please, and hurry. We haven't eaten in five hundred and seventy-six thousand million years."

The animal staggered to its feet. It gave a mellow gurgle.

"A very wise choice, sir, if I may say so. Very good," it said. "I'll just nip off and shoot myself."

He turned and gave a friendly wink to Arthur.

"Don't worry, sir," he said, "I'll be very humane."

It waddled unhurriedly off to the kitchen.

A matter of minutes later the waiter arrived with four huge steaming steaks. Zaphod and Ford wolfed straight into them without a second's hesitation. Trillian paused, then shrugged and started into hers.

Arthur stared at his feeling slightly ill.

"Hey, Earthman," said Zaphod with a malicious grin on the face that wasn't stuffing itself, "what's eating you?"

And the band played on.

All around the Restaurant people and things relaxed and chatted. The air was filled with talk of this and that, and with the mingled scents of exotic plants, extravagant foods and insidious wines. For an infinite number of miles in every direction the universal cataclysm was gathering to a stupefying climax. Glancing at his watch, Max returned to the stage with a flourish.

"And now, ladies and gentlemen," he beamed, "is everyone having one last wonderful time?"

"Yes," called out the sort of people who call out "yes" when comedians ask them if they're having a wonderful time.

"That's wonderful," enthused Max, "absolutely wonderful. And as the photon storms gather in swirling crowds around us, preparing to tear apart the last of the red hot suns, I know you're all going to settle back and enjoy with me what I know we will all find an immensely exciting and terminal experience."

He paused. He caught the audience with a glittering eye.

"Believe me, ladies and gentlemen," he said, "there is nothing penultimate about this one."

He paused again. Tonight his timing was immaculate. Time after time he had done this show, night after night. Not that the word *night* had any meaning here at the extremity of time. All there was was the endless repetition of the final moment, as the Restaurant rocked slowly forward over the brink of time's farthest edge— and back again. This "night" was good though, the audience was writhing in the palm of his sickly hand. His voice dropped. They had to strain to hear him.

"This," he said, "really is the absolute end, the final chilling desolation, in which the whole majestic sweep of creation becomes extinct. This ladies and gentlemen is the proverbial 'it.'"

He dropped his voice still lower. In the stillness, a fly would not have dared clear its throat.

"After this," he said, "there is nothing. Void. Emptiness. Oblivion. Absolute nothing...."

His eyes glittered again—or did they twinkle?

"Nothing...except, of course, for the desserts and a fine selection of Aldebaran liqueurs!"

The band gave him a music sting. He wished they wouldn't, he didn't need it, not an artist of his caliber. He could play the audience like his own musical instrument. They were laughing with relief. He followed on.

"And for once," he cried cheerily, "you don't need to worry about having a hangover in the morning—because there won't *be* any more mornings!"

He beamed at his happy, laughing audience. He glanced up at the sky, going through the same death routine every night, but his glance was only for a fraction of a second. He trusted it to do its job, as one professional trusts another.

"And now," he said, strutting about the stage, "at the risk of putting a damper on the wonderful sense of doom and futility here this evening, I would like to welcome a few parties."

He pulled a card from his pocket.

"Do we have"—he put up a hand to hold back the cheers—"Do we have a party here from the Zansellquasure Flamarion Bridge Club from beyond the Vortvoid of Qvarne? Are they here?"

A rousing cheer came from the back, but he pretended not to hear. He peered around trying to find them.

"Are they here?" he asked again, to elicit a louder cheer.

He got it, as he always did.

"Ah, there they are. Well, last bids, lads—and no cheating, remember this is a very solemn moment."

He lapped up the laughter.

"And do we also have, do we have...a party of minor deities from the Halls of Asgard?"

Away to his right came a rumble of thunder. Lightning arced across the stage. A small group of hairy men with helmets sat looking very pleased with themselves, and raised their glasses to him.

Has-beens, he thought to himself.

"Careful with that hammer, sir," he said.

They did their trick with the lightning again. Max gave them a very thin-lipped smile.

"And thirdly," he said, "thirdly a party of Young Conservatives from Sirius B, are they here?"

A party of smartly dressed young dogs stopped throwing rolls at each other and started throwing rolls at the stage. They yapped and barked unintelligibly.

"Yes," said Max, "well, this is all your fault, you realize that?

"And finally," said Max, quieting the audience down and putting on his solemn face, "finally I believe we have with us here tonight, a party of believers, very devout believers, from the Church of the Second Coming of the Great Prophet Zarquon."

There were about twenty of them, sitting right out on the edge of the floor, ascetically dressed, sipping mineral water nervously and staying apart from the festivities. They blinked resentfully as the spotlight was turned on them.

"There they are," said Max, "sitting there, patiently. He said he'd come again, and he's kept you waiting a long time, so let's hope he's hurrying fellas, because he's only got eight minutes left!"

The party of Zarquon's followers sat rigid, refusing to be buffeted by the waves of uncharitable laughter which swept over them.

Max restrained his audience.

"No, but seriously though, folks, seriously though, no offense meant. No, I know we shouldn't make fun of deeply held beliefs, so I think a big hand please for the Great Prophet Zarquon..."

The audience clapped respectfully.

"...wherever he's gone to!"

He blew a kiss to the stony-faced party and returned to the center of the stage.

He grabbed a tall stool and sat on it.

"It's marvelous though," he rattled on, "to see so many of you here tonight—no, isn't it though? Yes, absolutely marvelous. Because I know that so many of you come here time and time again, which I think is really wonderful, to come and watch this final end of everything, and then return home to your own eras... and raise families, strive for new and better societies, fight terrible wars for what you know to be right.... It really gives one hope for the future of all lifekind. Except of course"—he waved at the blitzing turmoil above and around them—"that we know it hasn't got one...."

Arthur turned to Ford—he hadn't quite got this place worked out in his mind.

"Look, surely," he said, "if the Universe is about to end...don't we go with it?"

Ford gave him a three-Pan-Galactic-Gargle-Blaster look, in other words a rather unsteady one.

"No," he said, "look," he said, "as soon as you come into this dive you get held in this sort of amazing force-shielded temporal warp thing. I think."

"Oh," said Arthur. He turned his attention back to a bowl of soup he'd managed to get from the waiter to replace his steak.

"Look," said Ford. "I'll show you."

He grabbed at a napkin off the table and fumbled hopelessly with it.

"Look," he said again, "imagine this napkin, right, as the temporal Universe, right? And this spoon as a transductional mode in the matter curve..."

It took him a while to say this last part, and Arthur hated to interrupt him.

"That's the spoon I was eating with," he said.

"All right," said Ford, "imagine *this* spoon"—he found a small wooden spoon on a tray of relishes—"this spoon"—but found it rather tricky to pick up—"no, better still this fork...."

"Hey, would you let go of my fork?" snapped Zaphod.

"All right," said Ford, "all right, all right. Why don't we say... why don't we say that this wineglass is the temporal Universe...."

"What, the one you've just knocked on the floor?"

"Did I do that?"

"Yes."

"All right," said Ford, "forget that. I mean... I mean, look, do you know—do you know how the Universe actually began for a kick off?"

"Probably not," said Arthur, who wished he'd never embarked on any of this.

"All right," said Ford, "imagine this. Right. You get this bath. Right. A large round bath. And it's made of ebony."

"Where from?" said Arthur. "Harrods was destroyed by the Vogons."

"Doesn't matter."

"So you keep saying."

"Listen."

'All right."

"You get this bath, see? Imagine you've got this bath. And it's ebony. And it's conical."

"Conical?" said Arthur. "What sort of..."

"Shhh!" said Ford. "It's conical. So what you do is, you see, you fill it with fine white sand, all right? Or sugar. Fine white sand, and/or sugar. Anything. Doesn't matter. Sugar's fine. And when it's full, you pull the plug out... are you listening?"

"I'm listening."

"You pull the plug out, and it all just twirls away, twirls away you see, out of the plughole."

"I see."

"You don't see. You don't see at all. I haven't got to the clever bit yet. You want to hear the clever bit?"

"Tell me the clever bit."

"I'll tell you the clever bit."

Ford thought for a moment, trying to remember what the clever bit was.

"The clever bit," he said, "is this. You film it happening."

"Clever," agreed Arthur.

"You get a movie camera, and you film it happening."

"Clever."

"That's not the clever bit. This is the clever bit, I remember now that this is the clever bit. The clever bit is that you then thread the film in the projector...backward!"

"Backward?"

"Yes. Threading it backward is definitely the clever bit. So then, you just sit and watch it, and everything just appears to spiral upward out of the plughole and fill the bath. See?"

"And that's how the Universe began, is it?" said Arthur.

"No," said Ford, "but it's a marvelous way to relax."

He reached for his wineglass.

"Where's my wineglass?" he said.

"It's on the floor."

"Ah."

Tipping back his chair to look for it, Ford collided with the small green waiter who was approaching the table carrying a portable telephone.

Ford excused himself to the waiter explaining that it was because he was exremely drunk.

The waiter said that that was quite all right and that he perfectly understood.

Ford thanked the waiter for his kind indulgence, attempted to tug his forelock, missed by six inches and slid under the table.

"Mr. Zaphod Beeblebrox?" inquired the waiter.

"Er, yeah?" said Zaphod, glancing up from his third steak.

"There is a phone call for you."

"Hey, what?"

"A phone call, sir."

"For me? Here? Hey, but who knows where I am?"

One of his minds raced. The other dawdled lovingly over the food it was still shoveling in.

"Excuse me if I carry on, won't you?" said his eating head and carried on.

There were now so many people after him he'd lost count. He shouldn't have made such a conspicuous entrance. Hell, why not though, he thought. How do you know you're having fun if there's no one watching you have it?

"Maybe somebody here tipped off the Galactic Police," said Trillian. "Everyone saw you come in."

"You mean they want to arrest me over the phone?" said Zaphod. "Could be. I'm a pretty dangerous dude when I'm cornered."

"Yeah," said a voice from under the table, "you go to pieces so fast people get hit by the shrapnel."

"Hey, what is this, Judgment Day?" snapped Zaphod.

"Do we get to see that as well?" asked Arthur nervously.

"I'm in no hurry," muttered Zaphod, "Okay, so who's the cat on the phone?" He kicked Ford. "Hey, get up there, kid," he said to him. "I may need you."

"I am not," said the waiter, "personally acquainted with the metal gentleman in question, sir...."

"Metal?"

"Yes, sir."

"Did you say metal?"

"Yes, sir. I said that I am not personally acquainted with the metal gentleman in question...."

"Okay, carry on."

"But I am informed that he has been awaiting your return for a considerable number of millennia. It seems you left here somewhat precipitately."

"*Left* here?" said Zaphod. "Are you being strange? We only just arrived here."

"Indeed, sir," persisted the waiter doggedly, "but before you arrived here, sir, I understand that you left here."

Zaphod tried this in one brain, then in the other.

"You're saying," he said, "that before we arrived here, we left here?"

This is going to be a long night, thought the waiter.

"Precisely, sir," he said.

"Put your analyst on danger money, baby," advised Zaphod.

"No, wait a minute," said Ford, emerging above table level again, "where exactly is here?"

"To be absolutely exact, sir, it is Frogstar

"But we just *left* there," protested Zaphod. "We left there and came to the Restaurant at the End of the Universe."

"Yes, sir," said the waiter, feeling that he was now into the home stretch and running well, "the one was constructed on the ruins of the other."

"Oh," said Arthur brightly, "you mean we've traveled in time but not in space."

"Listen, you semievolved simian," cut in Zaphod, "go climb a tree will you?"

Arthur bristled.

"Go bang your heads together four-eyes," he advised Zaphod.

"No, no," the waiter said to Zaphod, "your monkey has got it right, sir."

Arthur stuttered in fury and said nothing apposite, or indeed coherent.

"You jumped forward...I believe five hundred and seventy-six thousand million years while staying in exactly the same place," explained the waiter. He smiled. He had a wonderful feeling that he had finally won through against what had seemed to be insuperable odds.

"That's it!" said Zaphod. "I got it. I told the computer to send us to the nearest place to eat, that's exactly what it did. Give or take five hundred and seventy-six thousand million years or whatever, we never moved. Neat."

They all agreed this was very neat.

"But who," said Zaphod, "is the cat on the phone?"

"Whatever happened to Marvin?" said Trillian.

Zaphod clapped his hands to his heads.

"The Paranoid Android! I left him moping about on Frogstar World B."

"When was this?"

"Well, er, five hundred and seventy-six thousand million years ago I suppose," said Zaphod. "Hey, er, hand me the raprod, Plate Captain."

The little waiter's eyebrows wandered about his forehead in confusion.

"I beg your pardon, sir?" he said.

"The phone, waiter," said Zaphod, grabbing it off him. "Shee, you guys are so unhip it's a wonder your bums don't fall off."

"Indeed, sir."

"Hey, Marvin, is that you?" said Zaphod into the phone, "How you doing, kid?"

There was a long pause before a thin low voice came up the line.

"I think you ought to know I'm feeling very depressed," it said.

Zaphod cupped his hand over the phone.

"It's Marvin," he said.

"Hey, Marvin," he said into the phone again, "we're having a great time. Food, wine, a little personal abuse and the Universe going foom. Where can we find you?"

Again the pause.

"You don't have to pretend to be interested in me you know," said Marvin at last. "I know perfectly well I'm only a menial robot."

"Okay, okay," said Zaphod, "but where are you?"

"'Reverse primary thrust, Marvin,' that's what they

say to me, 'open airlock number three, Marvin. Marvin, can you pick up that piece of paper?' Can I pick up that piece of paper! Here I am, brain the size of a planet and they ask me to..."

"Yeah, yeah," sympathized Zaphod hardly at all.

"But I'm quite used to being humiliated," droned Marvin, "I can even go and stick my head in a bucket of water if you like. Would you like me to go and stick my head in a bucket of water? I've got one ready. Wait a minute."

"Er, hey, Marvin..." interrupted Zaphod, but it was too late. Sad little clunks and gurgles came up the line.

"What's he saying?" asked Trillian.

"Nothing," said Zaphod, "he just phoned to wash his head at us."

"There," said Marvin, coming back on the line and bubbling a bit, "I hope that gave satisfaction...."

"Yeah, yeah," said Zaphod, "now will you please tell us where you are?"

"I'm in the parking lot," said Marvin.

"The parking lot?" said Zaphod. "What are you doing there?"

"Parking cars, what else does one do in a parking lot?"

"Okay, hang in there, we'll be right down."

In one movement Zaphod leaped to his feet, threw down the phone and wrote "Hotblack Desiato" on the bill.

"Come on, guys," he said, "Marvin's in the parking lot. Let's get on down."

"What's he doing in the parking lot?" asked Arthur.

"Parking cars, what else? Dum dum."

"But what about the End of the Universe? We'll miss the big moment."

"I've seen it. It's rubbish," said Zaphod, "nothing but a gnab gib."

"A what?"

"Opposite of a big bang. Come on, let's get zappy."

Few of the other diners paid them any attention as they weaved their way through the Restaurant to the exit. Their eyes were riveted on the horror of the skies.

"An interesting effect to watch for," Max was telling them, "is in the upper left-hand quadrant of the sky, where if you look very carefully you can see the star system Hastromil boiling away into the ultraviolet. Anyone here from Hastromil?"

There were one or two slightly hesitant cheers from somewhere at the back.

"Well," said Max beaming cheerfully at them, "it's too late to worry about whether you left the gas on now."

The main reception foyer was almost empty but Ford nevertheless weaved his way through it.

Zaphod grasped him firmly by the arm and maneuvered him into a cubicle standing to one side of the entrance hall.

"What are you doing to him?" asked Arthur.

"Sobering him up," said Zaphod and pushed a coin into a slot. Lights flashed, gases swirled.

"Hi," said Ford stepping out a moment later, "where are we going?"

"Down to the parking lot, come on."

"What about the personnel Time Teleports?" said Ford. "Get us straight back to the *Heart of Gold*."

"Yeah, but I've cooled on that ship. Zarniwoop can have it. I don't want to play his games. Let's see what we can find."

A Sirius Cybernetics Corporation Happy Vertical People Transporter took them down deep into the substrata beneath the Restaurant. They were glad to see it had been vandalized and didn't try to make them happy as well as take them down.

At the bottom of the shaft the elevator doors opened and a blast of cold stale air hit them.

The first thing they saw on leaving the elevator was a long concrete wall with over fifty doors in it offering lavatory facilities for all of fifty major life forms. Nevertheless, like every parking lot in the Galaxy throughout the entire history of parking lots, this parking lot smelled predominantly of impatience.

They turned a corner and found themselves on a moving catwalk that traversed a vast cavernous space that stretched off into the dim distance.

It was divided off into bays each of which contained a spaceship belonging to one of the diners upstairs, some smallish and utilitarian mass production models, others vast shining limoships, the playthings of the very rich.

Zaphod's eyes sparkled with something that may or may not have been avarice as he passed over them. In fact it's best to be clear on this point—avarice is definitely what it was.

"There he is," said Trillian. "Marvin, down there."

They looked where she was pointing. Dimly they could see a small metal figure listlessly rubbing a small rag on one remote corner of a giant silver suncruiser.

At short intervals along the moving catwalk, wide transparent tubes led down to floor level. Zaphod stepped off the catwalk into one of these and floated gently downward. The others followed. Thinking back to this later, Arthur Dent thought it was the single most enjoyable experience of his travels in the Galaxy.

"Hey, Marvin," said Zaphod, striding over toward to him. "Hey, kid, are we pleased to see you."

Marvin turned, and insofar as it is possible for a

totally inert metal face to look reproachful, this is what it did.

"No you're not," he said, "no one ever is."

"Suit yourself," said Zaphod and turned away to ogle the ships. Ford went with him.

Only Trillian and Arthur actually went up to Marvin.

"No, really we are," said Trillian and patted him in a way that he disliked intensely, "hanging around waiting for us all this time."

"Five hundred and seventy-six thousand million, three thousand five hundred and seventy-nine years," said Marvin. "I counted them."

"Well, here we are now," said Trillian, feeling—quite correctly in Marvin's view—that it was a slightly foolish thing to say.

"The first ten million years were the worst," said Marvin, "and the second ten million years, they were the worst too. The third ten million I didn't enjoy at all. After that I went into a bit of a decline."

He paused just long enough to make them feel they ought to say something, and then interrupted.

"It's the people you meet in this job that really get you down," he said and paused again.

Trillian cleared her throat.

"Is that . . .

"The best conversation I had was over forty million years ago," continued Marvin.

Again the pause.

"Oh d—"

"And that was with a coffee machine."

He waited.

"That's a—"

"You don't like talking to me, do you?" said Marvin in a low desolate tone.

Trillian talked to Arthur instead.

Farther down the chamber Ford Prefect had found something of which he very much liked the look, several such things in fact.

"Zaphod," he said in a quiet voice, "just look at some of these little star trolleys...."

Zaphod looked and liked.

The craft they were looking at was in fact pretty small but extraordinary, and very much a rich kid's toy. It was not much to look at. It resembled nothing so much as a paper dart about twenty feet long made of thin but tough metal foil. At the rear end was a small horizontal two-man cockpit. It had a tiny charm-drive engine, which was not capable of moving it at any great speed. The thing it did have, however, was a heat-sink.

The heat-sink had a mass of some two thousand billion tons and was contained within a black hole mounted in an electromagnetic field situated halfway along the length of the ship, and this heat-sink enabled the craft to be maneuvered to within a few miles of a yellow sun, there to catch and ride the solar flares that burst out from its surface.

Flare riding is one of the most exotic and exhilarating sports in existence, and those who can dare and afford to do it are among the most lionized men in the Galaxy.

It is also of course stupefyingly dangerous—those who don't die riding invariably die of sexual exhaustion at one of the Daedalus Club's Après-Flare parties.

Ford and Zaphod looked and passed on.

"And this baby," said Ford, "the tangerine star buggy with the black sunbusters..."

Again, the star buggy was a small ship—a totally misnamed one in fact, because the one thing it couldn't manage was interstellar distances. Basically it was a sporty planet hopper dolled up to look like something it wasn't. Nice lines though. They passed on.

The next one was a big one and thirty yards long—a coach-limoship and obviously designed with one aim in mind, that of making the beholder sick with envy. The paintwork and accessory detail clearly said, "Not only am I rich enough to afford this ship, I am also rich enough not to take it seriously." It was wonderfully hideous.

"Just look at it," said Zaphod, "multicluster quark drive, perspulex running boards. Got to be a Lazlar Lyricon custom job."

He examined every inch.

"Yes," he said, "look, the infrapink lizard emblem on the neutrino cowling. Lazlar's trademark. The man has no shame."

"I was passed by one of these mothers once, out by the Axel Nebula," said Ford. "I was going flat out and this thing just strolled past me, star drive hardly ticking over. Just incredible."

Zaphod whistled appreciatively.

"Ten seconds later," said Ford, "it smashed straight into the third moon of Jaglan Beta."

"Yeah, right?"

"Amazing-looking ship though. Looks like a fish, moves like a fish, steers like a cow."

Ford looked round the other side.

"Hey, come see," he called out, "there's a big mural painted on this side. A bursting sun—Disaster Area's trademark. This must be Hotblack's ship. Lucky old bugger. They do this terrible song you know which ends with a stuntship crashing into the sun. Meant to be an amazing spectacle. Expensive in stuntships though."

Zaphod's attention however was elsewhere. His attention was riveted on the ship standing next to Hotblack Desiato's limo. His mouths hung open.

"That," he said, "that ... is really bad for the eyes...."

Ford looked. He too stood astonished.

It was a ship of classic, simple design, like a flattened salmon, twenty yards long, very clean, very sleek. There was just one remarkable thing about it.

"It's so ... *black*!" said Ford Prefect. "You can hardly make out its shape ... light just seems to fall into it!"

Zaphod said nothing. He had simply fallen in love.

The blackness of it was so extreme that it was almost impossible to tell how close you were standing to it.

"Your eyes just slide off it...." said Ford in wonder. It was an emotional moment. He bit his lip.

Zaphod moved forward to it, slowly, like a man possessed—or more accurately like a man who wanted to possess. His hand reached out to stroke it. His hand stopped. His hand reached out to stroke it again. His hand stopped again.

"Come and feel this surface," he said in a hushed voice.

Ford put his hand out to feel it. His hand stopped.

"You ... you can't...." he said.

"See?" said Zaphod. "It's just totally frictionless. This must be one mother of a mover...."

He turned to look at Ford seriously. At least, one of his heads did—the other stayed gazing in awe at the ship.

"What do you reckon, Ford?" he said.

"You mean ... er"—Ford looked over his shoulder—"you mean stroll off with it? You think we should?"

"No."

"Nor do I."

"But we're going to, aren't we?"

"How can we not?"

They gazed a little longer, till Zaphod suddenly pulled himself together.

"We better shift soon," he said. "In a moment or so the Universe will have ended and all the Captain Creeps will be pouring down here to find their bourge-mobiles."

"Zaphod," said Ford.

"Yeah?"

"How do we do it?"

"Simple," said Zaphod. He turned. "Marvin!" he called.

Slowly, laboriously and with a million little clanking and creaking noises that he had learned to simulate,

Marvin turned round to answer the summons.

"Come on over here," said Zaphod. "We've got a job for you."

Marvin trudged toward them.

"I won't enjoy it," he said.

"Yes, you will," enthused Zaphod, "there's a whole new life stretching out ahead of you."

"Oh, not another one," groaned Marvin.

"Will you shut up and listen!" hissed Zaphod. "This time there's going to be excitement and adventure and really wild things."

"Sounds awful," Marvin said.

"Marvin! All I'm trying to ask you..."

"I suppose you want me to open this spaceship for you?"

"What? Er...yes. Yeah, that's right," said Zaphod jumpily. He was keeping at least three eyes on the entrance. Time was short.

"Well, I wish you'd just tell me rather than try to engage my enthusiasm," said Marvin, "because I haven't got one."

He walked on up to the ship, touched it, and a hatchway swung open.

Ford and Zaphod stared at the opening.

"Don't mention it," said Marvin. "Oh, you didn't." He trudged away again.

Arthur and Trillian clustered around.

"What's happening?" asked Arthur.

"Look at this," said Ford. "Look at the interior of this ship."

"Weirder and weirder," breathed Zaphod.

"It's black," said Ford. "Everything in it is just totally black...."

In the Restaurant, things were fast approaching the moment after which there wouldn't be any more moments.

All eyes were fixed on the dome, other than those of Hotblack Desiato's bodyguard, which were looking intently at Hotblack Desiato, and those of Hotblack Desiato himself which the bodyguard had closed out of respect.

The bodyguard leaned forward over the table. Had Hotblack Desiato been alive, he probably would have deemed this a good moment to lean back, or even go for a short walk. His bodyguard was not a man who improved with proximity. On account of his unfortunate condition, however, Hotblack Desiato remained totally inert.

"Mr. Desiato, sir?" whispered the bodyguard. Whenever he spoke, it looked as if the muscles on either side of his mouth were clambering over each other to get out of the way.

"Mr. Desiato? Can you hear me?"

Hotblack Desiato, quite naturally, said nothing.

"Hotblack?" hissed the bodyguard.

Again, quite naturally, Hotblack Desiato did not reply. Supernaturally, however, he did.

On the table in front of him a wineglass rattled, and a fork rose an inch or so and tapped against the glass. It settled on the table again.

The bodyguard gave a satisfied grunt.

"It's time we were going, Mr. Desiato," muttered the bodyguard; "don't want to get caught in the rush, not in your condition. You want to get to the next gig nice and relaxed. There was a really big audience for it. One of the best. Kakrafoon. Five hundred and seventy-six thousand and two million years ago. Had you will have been looking forward to it?"

The fork rose again, paused, waggled in a noncommittal sort of way and dropped again.

"Ah, come on," said the bodyguard, "it's going to have been great. You knocked 'em cold." The bodyguard would have given Dr. Dan Streetmentioner an apoplectic attack.

"The black ship going into the sun always gets 'em, and the new one's a beauty. Be real sorry to see it go. If we get on down there, I'll set the black ship autopilot and we'll cruise off in the limo. Okay?"

The fork tapped once in agreement, and the glass of wine mysteriously emptied itself.

The bodyguard wheeled Hotblack Desiato's chair out of the Restaurant.

"And now," cried Max from the center of the stage, "the moment you've all been waiting for!" He flung his arms into the air. Behind him, the band went into a frenzy of percussion and rolling synthochords. Max had argued with them about this but they had claimed it was in their contract that that's what they would do. His agent would have to sort it out.

"The skies begin to boil!" he cried. "Nature collapses into the screaming void! In twenty seconds' time, the

Universe itself will be at an end! See where the light of infinity bursts in upon us!"

The hideous fury of destruction blazed about them—and at that moment a still small trumpet sounded as from an infinite distance. Max's eyes swiveled round to glare at the band. None of them seemed to be playing a trumpet. Suddenly a wisp of smoke was swirling and shimmering on the stage next to him. The trumpet was joined by more trumpets. Over five hundred times Max had done this show, and nothing like this had ever happened before. He drew back in alarm from the swirling smoke, and as he did so, a figure slowly materialized inside, the figure of an ancient man, bearded, robed and wreathed in light. In his eyes were stars and on his brow a golden crown.

"What's this?" whispered Max, wild-eyed. "What's happening?"

At the back of the Restaurant the stony-faced party from the Church of the Second Coming of the Great Prophet Zarquon leaped ecstatically to their feet chanting and crying.

Max blinked in amazement. He threw up his arms to the audience.

"A big hand please, ladies and gentlemen," he hollered, "for the Great Prophet Zarquon! He has come! Zarquon has come again!"

Thunderous applause broke out as Max strode across the stage and handed his microphone to the Prophet.

Zarquon coughed. He peered round at the assembled gathering. The stars in his eyes twinkled uneasily. He handled the microphone with confusion.

"Er..." he said, "hello. Er, look, I'm sorry I'm a bit late. I've had the most ghastly time, all sorts of things cropping up at the last moment."

He seemed nervous of the expectant awed hush. He cleared his throat.

"Er, how are we for time?" he said. "Have I just got a min—"

And so the Universe ended.

One of the major selling points of that wholly remarkable travel book, *The Hitchhiker's Guide to the Galaxy*, apart from its relative cheapness and the fact that it has the words DON'T PANIC written in large friendly letters on its cover, is its compendious and occasionally accurate glossary. The statistics relating to the geo-social nature of the Universe, for instance, are deftly set out between pages nine hundred and thirty-eight thousand three hundred and twenty-four and nine hundred and thirty-eight thousand three hundred and twenty-six; and the simplistic style in which they are written is partly explained by the fact that the editors, having to meet a publishing deadline, copied the information off the back of a packet of breakfast cereal, hastily embroidering it with a few footnotes in order to avoid prosecution under the incomprehensibly tortuous Galactic Copyright laws.

It is interesting to note that a later and wilier editor sent the book backward in time through a temporal warp, and then successfully sued the breakfast cereal company for infringement of the same laws.

Here is a sample:

The Universe—some information to help you live in it.

1 AREA: Infinite.

The Hitchhiker's Guide to the Galaxy *offers this definition of the word "Infinite."*

Infinite: *Bigger than the biggest thing ever and then some. Much bigger than that in fact, really amazingly immense, a totally stunning size, real "wow, that's big," time. Infinity is just so big that by comparison, bigness itself looks really titchy. Gigantic multiplied by colossal multiplied by staggeringly huge is the sort of concept we're trying to get across here.*

2 IMPORTS: None.

It is impossible to import things into an infinite area, there being no outside to import things in from.

3 EXPORTS: None.

See Imports.

4 POPULATION: None.

It is known that there are an infinite number of worlds, simply because there is an infinite amount of space for them to be in. However, not every one of them is inhabited. Therefore, there must be a finite number of inhabited worlds. Any finite number divided by infinity is as near to nothing as makes no odds, so the average population of all the planets in the Universe can be said to be zero. From this it follows that the population of the whole Universe is also zero, and that any people you may meet from time to time are merely the products of a deranged imagination.

5 MONETARY UNITS. None.

In fact there are three freely convertible currencies in the Galaxy, but none of them count. The Altairian Dollar has recently collapsed, the Flainian Pobble Bead is only exchangeable for other Flainian Pobble Beads, and the Triganic Pu has its own very special problems. Its exchange rate of eight Ningis to one Pu is simple enough, but since a Ningi is a triangular rubber coin six thousand eight hundred miles along each side, no one has ever collected enough to own one Pu. Ningis are not negotiable currency, because the Galactibanks refuse to deal in fiddling small change. From this basic premise it is very simple to prove that the Galactibanks are also the product of a deranged imagination.

6 ART: None.

The function of art is to hold the mirror up to nature, and there simply isn't a mirror big enough—see point one.

7 SEX: None.

Well, in fact there is an awful lot of this, largely because of the total lack of money, trade, banks, art or anything else that might keep all the nonexistent people of the Universe occupied.

However, it is not worth embarking on a long discussion of it now because it really is terribly complicated. For further information see Guide Chapters seven, nine, ten, eleven, fourteen, sixteen, seventeen, nineteen, twenty-one to eighty-four inclusive, and in fact most of the rest of the Guide.

The Restaurant continued existing, but everything else had stopped. Temporal relastatics held it and protected it in a nothingness that wasn't merely a vacuum, it was simply nothing—there was nothing in which a vacuum could be said to exist.

The force-shielded dome had once again been rendered opaque, the party was over, the diners were leaving, Zarquon had vanished along with the rest of the Universe, the Time Turbines were preparing to pull the Restaurant back across the brink of time in readiness for the lunch sitting, and Max Quordlepleen was back in his small curtained dressing room trying to raise his agent on the tempophone.

In the parking lot stood the black ship, closed and silent.

Into the parking lot came the late Mr. Hotblack Desiato, propelled along the moving catwalk by his bodyguard.

They descended one of the tubes. As they approached the limoship a hatchway swung down from its side, engaged the wheels of the wheelchair and drew it inside. The bodyguard followed, and having seen his boss safely connected up to his death-support system, moved up to the small cockpit. Here he operated the remote control system which activated the autopilot in the black ship lying next to the limo, thus causing great relief to Zaphod Beeblebrox who had been trying to start the thing for over ten minutes.

The black ship glided smoothly forward out of its bay, turned and moved down the central causeway swiftly and quietly. At the end it accelerated rapidly, flung itself into the temporal launch chamber and began the long journey back into the distant past.

The Milliways Lunch Menu quotes, by permission, a passage from *The Hitchhiker's Guide to the Galaxy*. The passage is this:

The History of every major Galactic Civilization tends to pass through three distinct and recognizable phases, those of Survival, Inquiry and Sophistication, otherwise known as the How, Why and Where phases.

For instance, the first phase is characterized by the question, "How can we eat?", the second by the question, "Why do we eat?" and the third by the question, "Where shall we have lunch?"

The Menu goes on to suggest that Milliways, the Restaurant at the End of the Universe, would be a very agreeable and sophisticated answer to that third question.

What it doesn't go on to say is that though it will usually take a large civilization many thousands of years to pass through the How, Why and Where phases, small social groupings under stressful conditions can pass through them with extreme rapidity.

"How are we doing?" said Arthur Dent.

"Badly," said Ford Prefect.

"Where are we going?" said Trillian.

"I don't know," said Zaphod Beeblebrox.

"Why not?" demanded Arthur Dent.

"Shut up," suggested Zaphod Beeblebrox and Ford Prefect.

"Basically, what you're trying to say," said Arthur Dent, ignoring this suggestion, "is that we're out of control."

The ship was rocking and swaying sickeningly as Ford and Zaphod tried to wrest control from the autopilot. The engines howled and whined like tired children in a supermarket.

"It's the wild color scheme that freaks me," said Zaphod whose love affair with this ship had lasted almost three minutes into the flight. "Every time you try to operate one of these weird black controls that are labeled in black on a black background, a little black light lights up black to let you know you've done it. What is this? Some kind of galactic hyperhearse?"

The walls of the swaying cabin were also black, the ceiling was black, the seats—which were rudimentary since the only important trip this ship was designed for was supposed to be unmanned—were black, the control panel was black, the instruments were black, the little screws that held them in place were black, the thin tufted nylon floor covering was black, and when they had lifted up a corner of it they had discovered that the foam underlay also was black.

"Perhaps whoever designed it had eyes that responded to different wavelengths," offered Trillian.

"Or didn't have much imagination," muttered Arthur.

"Perhaps," said Marvin, "he was feeling very depressed."

In fact, though they weren't to know it, the decor had been chosen in honor of its owner's sad, lamented and tax deductible condition.

The ship gave a particularly sickening lurch.

"Take it easy," pleaded Arthur, "you're making me space sick."

"Time sick," said Ford. "We're plummeting backward through time."

"Thank you," said Arthur, "now I think I really am going to be ill."

"Go ahead," said Zaphod, "we could do with a little color about the place."

"This is meant to be polite afterdinner conversation, is it?" snapped Arthur.

Zaphod left the controls to Ford to figure out, and lurched over to Arthur.

"Look, Earthman," he said angrily, "you've got a job to do, right? The Question to the Ultimate Answer, right?"

"What, that thing?" said Arthur. "I thought we'd forgotten about that."

"Not me, baby. Like the mice said, it's worth a lot of

money in the right quarters. And it's all locked up in that head thing of yours."

"Yes but—"

"But nothing! Think about it. The Meaning of Life! We get our fingers on that we can hold every shrink in the Galaxy up to ransom, and that's worth a bundle. I owe mine a mint."

Arthur took a deep breath without much enthusiasm.

"All right," he said, "but where do we start? How should I know? They say the Ultimate Answer or whatever is Forty-two, how am I supposed to know what the question is? It could be anything. I mean, what's six times seven?"

Zaphod looked at him hard for a moment. Then his eyes blazed with excitement.

"Forty-two!" he cried.

Arthur wiped his palm across his forehead.

"Yes," he said patiently, "I know that."

Zaphod's faces fell.

"I'm just saying the question could be anything at all," said Arthur, "and I don't see how I'm meant to know."

"Because," hissed Zaphod, "you were there when your planet did the big firework."

"We have a thing on Earth..." began Arthur.

"Had," corrected Zaphod.

"...called tact. Oh, never mind. Look, I just don't know."

A low voice echoed dully around the cabin.

"I know," said Marvin.

Ford called out from the controls he was still fighting a losing battle with.

"Stay out of this, Marvin," he said. "This is organism talk."

"It's printed in the Earthman's brainwave patterns," continued Marvin, "but I don't suppose you'll be very interested in knowing that."

"You mean," said Arthur, "you mean you can see into my mind?"

"Yes," said Marvin.

Arthur stared in astonishment.

"And...?" he said.

"It amazes me how you can manage to live in anything that small."

"Ah," said Arthur, "abuse."

"Yes," confirmed Marvin.

"Ah, ignore him," said Zaphod, "he's only making it up."

"Making it up?" said Marvin, swiveling his head in a parody of astonishment. "Why should I want to make anything up? Life's bad enough as it is without wanting to invent any more of it."

"Marvin," said Trillian in the gentle, kindly voice that only she was still capable of assuming in talking to this misbegotten creature, "if you knew all along, why then didn't you tell us?"

Marvin's head swiveled back to her.

"You didn't ask," he said simply.

"Well, we're asking you now, metal man," said Ford, turning round to look at him.

At that moment the ship suddenly stopped rocking and swaying, the engine pitch settled down to a gentle hum.

"Hey, Ford," said Zaphod, "that sounds good. Have you worked out the controls on this boat?"

"No," said Ford, "I just stopped fiddling with them. I reckon we just go to wherever this ship is going and get off it fast."

"Yeah, right," said Zaphod.

"I could tell you weren't really interested," murmured Marvin to himself and slumped into a corner and switched himself off.

"Trouble is," said Ford, "that the one instrument in this whole ship that is giving any reading is worrying me. If it is what I think it is, and if it's saying what I think it's saying, then we've already gone too far back into the past. Maybe as much as two million years before our own time."

Zaphod shrugged.

"Time is bunk," he said.

"I wonder who this ship belongs to anyway," said Arthur.

"Me," said Zaphod.

"No. Who it really belongs to."

"Really me," insisted Zaphod. "Look, property is theft, right? Therefore theft is property. Therefore this ship is mine, Okay?"

"Tell the ship that," said Arthur.

Zaphod strode over to the console.

"Ship," he said, banging on the panels, "this is your new owner speaking to..."

He got no further. Several things happened at once.

The ship dropped out of time travel mode and reemerged into real space.

All the controls on the console, which had been shut down for the time trip, now lit up.

A large vision screen above the console winked into life revealing a wide starscape and a single very large sun dead ahead of them.

None of these things, however, were responsible for the fact that Zaphod was at the same moment hurled bodily backward against the rear of the cabin, as were all the others.

They were hurled back by a single thunderous clap of noise that thudded out of the monitor speakers surrounding the vision screen.

own on the dry, red world of Kakrafoon, in the middle of the vast Rudlit Desert, the stage technicians were testing the sound system.

That is to say, the sound system was in the desert, not the technicians. They had retreated to the safety of Disaster Area's giant control ship which hung in orbit some four hundred miles above the surface of the planet, and they were testing the sound from there. Anyone within five miles of the speaker silos wouldn't have survived the tuning up.

If Arthur Dent had been within five miles of the speaker silos then his expiring thought would have been that in both size and shape the sound rig closely resembled Manhattan. Risen out of the silos, the neutron phase speaker stacks towered monstrously against the sky, obscuring the banks of plutonium reactors and seismic amps behind them.

Buried deep in concrete bunkers beneath the city of speakers lay the instruments that the musicians would control from their ship, the massive photon-ajuitar, the bass detonator and the Megabang drum complex.

It was going to be a noisy show.

Aboard the giant control ship, all was activity and bustle. Hotblack Desiato's limoship, a mere tadpole beside it, had arrived and docked, and the lamented gentleman was being transported down the high vaulted corridors to meet the medium who was going to interpret his psychic impulses onto the ajuitar keyboard.

A doctor, a logician and a marine biologist had also just arrived, flown in at phenomenal expense from Maximegalon to try to reason with the lead singer who had locked himself in the bathroom with a bottle of pills and was refusing to come out till it could be proved conclusively to him that he wasn't a fish. The bass player was busy machine-gunning his bedroom and the drummer was nowhere on board.

Frantic inquiries led to the discovery that he was standing on a beach on Santraginus V over a hundred light-years away where, he claimed, he had been happy for over half an hour now and had found a small stone that would be his friend.

The band's manager was profoundly relieved. It meant that for the seventeenth time on this tour the drums would be played by a robot and that therefore the timing of the cymbalistics would be right.

The sub-ether was buzzing with the communications of the stage technicians testing the speaker channels, and it was this that was being relayed to the interior of the black ship.

Its dazed occupants lay against the back wall of the cabin, and listened to the voices on the monitor speakers.

"Okay, channel nine on power," said a voice, "testing channel fifteen...."

Another thumping crack of noise walloped through the ship.

"Channel fifteen A-okay," said another voice.

A third voice cut in.

"The black stuntship is now in position," it said, "it's looking good. Gonna be a great sundive. Stage computer on line?"

A computer voice answered.

"On line," it said

"Take control of the black ship."

"Black ship locked into trajectory program, on standby."

"Testing channel twenty."

Zaphod leaped across the cabin and switched frequencies on the sub-ether receiver before the next mind-pulverizing noise hit them. He stood there quivering.

"What," said Trillian in a small quiet voice, "does sundive mean?"

"It means," said Marvin, "that the ship is going to dive into the sun. Sun.... Dive. It's very simple to understand. What do you expect if you steal Hotblack Desiato's stuntship?"

"How do you know," said Zaphod in a voice that would make a Vegan snow lizard feel chilly, "that this is Hotblack Desiato's stuntship?"

"Simple," said Marvin. "I parked it for him."

"Then why...didn't...you...tell us!"

"You said you wanted excitement and adventure and really wild things."

"This is awful," said Arthur unnecessarily in the pause which followed.

"That's what I said," confirmed Marvin.

On a different frequency, the sub-ether receiver had

picked up a public broadcast, which now echoed around the cabin.

"...fine weather for the concert here this afternoon. I'm standing here in front of the stage," the reporter lied, "in the middle of the Rudlit Desert, and with the aid of hyperbinoptic glasses I can just about make out the huge audience cowering there on the horizon all around me. Behind me the speaker stacks rise like a sheer cliff face, and high above me the sun is shining away and doesn't know what's going to hit it. The environmentalist lobby do know what's going to hit it, and they claim that the concert will cause earthquakes, tidal waves, hurricanes, irreparable damage to the atmosphere and all the usual things that environmentalists usually go on about.

"But I've just had a report that a representative of Disaster Area met with the environmentalists at lunchtime, and had them all shot, so nothing now lies in the way of..."

Zaphod switched it off. He turned to Ford.

"You know what I'm thinking?" he said.

"I think so," said Ford.

"Tell me what you think I'm thinking."

"I think you're thinking it's time we got off this ship."

"I think you're right," said Zaphod.

"I think you're right," said Ford.

"How?" said Arthur.

"Quiet," said Ford and Zaphod, "we're thinking."

"So this is it," said Arthur, "we're going to die."

"I wish you'd stop saying that," said Ford.

It is worth repeating at this point the theories that

Ford had come up with, on his first encounter with human beings, to account for their peculiar habit of continually stating and restating the very very obvious, as in "It's a nice day," or "You're very tall," or "So this is it, we're going to die."

His first theory was that if human beings didn't keep exercising their lips, their mouths probably shriveled up.

After a few months of observation he had come up with a second theory, which was this—"If human beings don't keep exercising their lips, their brains start working."

In fact, this second theory is more literally true of the Belcerebon people of Kakrafoon.

The Belcerebon people used to cause great resentment and insecurity among neighboring races by being one of the most enlightened, accomplished and, above all, quiet civilizations in the Galaxy.

As a punishment for this behavior, which was held to be offensively self-righteous and provocative, a Galactic Tribunal inflicted on them that most cruel of all social diseases, telepathy. Consequently, in order to prevent themselves broadcasting every slightest thought that crosses their minds to anyone within a five mile radius, they now have to talk very loudly and continuously about the weather, their little aches and pains, the match this afternoon and what a noisy place Kakrafoon has suddenly become.

Another method of temporarily blotting out their minds is to play host to a Disaster Area concert.

The timing of the concert was critical.

The ship had to begin its dive before the concert began in order to hit the sun six minutes and thirty-seven seconds before the climax of the song to which it related, so that the light of the solar flares had time to travel out to Kakrafoon.

The ship had already been diving for several minutes by the time that Ford Prefect had completed his search of the other compartments of the black ship. He burst back into the cabin.

The sun of Kakrafoon loomed terrifyingly large on the vision screen, its blazing white inferno of fusing hydrogen nuclei growing moment by moment as the ship plunged onward, unheeding the thumping and banging of Zaphod's hands on the control panel. Arthur and Trillian had the fixed expressions of rabbits on a night road who think that the best way of dealing with approaching headlights is to stare them out.

Zaphod spun around, wild-eyed.

"Ford," he said, "how many escape capsules are there?"

"None," said Ford.

Zaphod gibbered.

"Did you *count* them?" he yelled.

"Twice," said Ford. "Did you manage to raise the stage crew on the radio?"

"Yeah," said Zaphod bitterly, "I said there were a whole bunch of people on board, and they said to say 'hi' to everybody."

Ford goggled.

"Didn't you tell them who you were?"

"Oh yeah. They said it was a great honor. That and something about a restaurant bill and my executors."

Ford pushed Arthur aside roughly and leaned forward over the control console.

"Does *none* of this function?" he said savagely.

"All overridden."

"Smash the autopilot."

"Find it first. Nothing connects."

There was a moment's cold silence.

Arthur was stumbling around the back of the cabin. He stopped suddenly.

"Incidentally," he said, "what does teleport mean?"

Another moment passed.

Slowly, the others turned to face him.

"Probably the wrong moment to ask," said Arthur. "It's just I remember hearing you use the word a short while ago and I only bring it up because..."

"Where," said Ford Prefect quietly, "does it say teleport?"

"Well, just over here in fact," said Arthur, pointing at a dark control box in the rear of the cabin. "Just under the word *emergency*, above the word *system* and beside the sign saying *out of order*.

In the pandemonium that instantly followed, the only action to follow was that of Ford Prefect lunging across the cabin to the small black box that Arthur had indicated and stabbing repeatedly at the single small black button set into it.

A six-foot square panel slid open beside it revealing a compartment which resembled a multiple shower unit that had found a new function in life as an electrician's junk store. Half-finished wiring hung from the ceiling, a jumble of abandoned components lay strewn on the floor, and the programming panel lolled out of the cavity in the wall into which it should have been secured.

A junior Disaster Area accountant, visiting the ship-yard where this ship was being constructed, had demanded to know of the works foreman why the hell they were fitting an extremely expensive teleport into a ship which only had one important journey to make, and that unmanned. The foreman had explained that the teleport was available at a ten percent discount and the accountant had explained that this was immaterial; the foreman had explained that it was the finest, most powerful and sophisticated teleport that money could buy and the accountant had explained that the money did not wish to buy it; the foreman had explained that people would still need to enter and leave the ship and the accountant had explained that the ship sported a perfectly serviceable door; the foreman had explained that the accountant could go and boil his head and the accountant had explained to the foreman that the thing approaching him rapidly from his left was a knuckle sandwich. After the explanations had been concluded, work was discontinued on the teleport which subsequently passed unnoticed on the invoice as "Sund. explns." at five times the price.

"Hell's donkeys," muttered Zaphod as he and Ford attempted to sort through the tangle of wiring.

After a moment or so Ford told him to stand back. He tossed a coin into the teleport and jiggled a switch on the lolling control panel. With a crackle and spit of light, the coin vanished.

"That much of it works," said Ford, "however, there is no guidance system. A matter transference teleport with no guidance programming could put you ... well, anywhere."

The sun of Kakrafoon loomed huge on the screen.

"Who cares," said Zaphod; "we go where we go."

"And," said Ford, "there is no autosystem. We couldn't all go. Someone would have to stay and operate it."

A solemn moment shuffled past. The sun loomed larger and larger.

"Hey, Marvin kid," said Zaphod brightly, "how you doing?"

"Very badly I suspect," muttered Marvin.

A shortish while later, the concert on Kakrafoon reached an unexpected climax.

The black ship with its single morose occupant had plunged on schedule into the nuclear furnace of the sun. Massive solar flares licked out from it millions of miles into space, thrilling and in a few cases spilling the dozen or so flare riders who had been coasting close to the surface of the sun in anticipation of the moment.

Moments before the flare light reached Kakrafoon the pounding desert cracked along a deep faultline. A huge and hitherto undetected underground river lying far beneath the surface gushed to the surface to be followed seconds later by the eruption of millions of tons of boiling lava that flowed hundreds of feet into the air, instantaneously vaporizing the river both above and below the surface in an explosion that echoed to the far side of the world and back again.

Those—very few—who witnessed the event and survived swear that the whole hundred thousand square miles of the desert rose into the air like a mile-thick pancake, flipped itself over and fell back down. At that precise moment the solar radiation from the flares filtered through the clouds of vaporized water and struck the ground.

A year later, the hundred thousand square mile desert was thick with flowers. The structure of the atmosphere around the planet was subtly altered. The sun blazed less harshly in the summer, the cold bit less bitterly in the winter, pleasant rain fell more often and slowly the desert world of Kakrafoon became a paradise. Even the telepathic power with which the people of Kakrafoon had been cursed was permanently dispersed by the force of the explosion.

A spokesman for Disaster Area—the one who had had all the environmentalists shot—was later quoted as saying that it had been "a good gig."

Many people spoke movingly of the healing powers of music. A few skeptical scientists examined the records of the events more closely, and claimed that they had discovered faint vestiges of a vast artificially induced Improbability Field drifting in from a nearby region of space.

Arthur woke up and instantly regretted it. Hangovers he'd had, but never anything on this scale. This was it, this was the big one, this was the ultimate pits. Matter transference beams, he decided, were not as much fun as, say, a good solid kick in the head.

Being for the moment unwilling to move on account of a dull stomping throb he was experiencing, he lay a while and thought. The trouble with most forms of transport, he thought, is basically that not one of them is worth all the bother. On Earth—when there had been an Earth, before it was demolished to make way for a new hyperspace bypass—the problem had been with cars. The disadvantages involved in pulling lots of black sticky slime from out of the ground where it had been safely hidden out of harm's way, turning it into tar to cover the land with, smoke to fill the air with and pouring the rest into the sea, all seemed to outweigh the advantages of being able to get more quickly from one place to another—particularly when the place you arrived at had probably become, as a result of this, very similar to the place you had left, i.e., covered with tar, full of smoke and short of fish.

And what about matter transference beams? Any form of transport which involved tearing you apart atom by atom, flinging those atoms through the sub-ether, and then jamming them back together again just when they were getting their first taste of freedom for years had to be bad news.

Many people had thought exactly this before Arthur Dent and had even gone to the lengths of writing songs about it. Here is one that used regularly to be chanted by huge crowds outside the Sirius Cybernetics Corporation Teleport Systems factory on Happi-Werld III:

Aldebaran's great, okay,
Algol's pretty neat,
Betelgeuse's pretty girls
Will knock you off your feet.
They'll do anything you like
Real fast and then real slow,
But if you have to take me apart to get me there
Then I don't want to go.

Singing,
Take me apart, take me apart,
What a way to roam
And if you have to take me apart to get me there
I'd rather stay at home.

Sirius is paved with gold
So I've heard it said
By nuts who then go on to say
"See Tau before you're dead."
I'll gladly take the high road
Or even take the low,
But if you have to take me apart to get me there
Then I, for one, won't go.

Singing,
Take me apart, take me apart,
You must be off your head,
And if you try to take me apart to get me there
I'll stay right here in bed.

...and so on. Another favorite song was much shorter:

I teleported home one night
With Ron and Sid and Meg.
Ron stole Meggie's heart away
And I got Sidney's leg.

Arthur felt the waves of pain slowly receding, though he was still aware of a dull stomping throb. Slowly, carefully, he stood up.

"Can you hear a dull stomping throb?" said Ford Prefect.

Arthur spun around and wobbled uncertainly. Ford Prefect was approaching, looking red-eyed and pasty.

"Where are we?" gasped Arthur.

Ford looked around. They were standing in a long curving corridor which stretched out of sight in both directions. The outer steel wall—which was painted in that sickly shade of pale green which they use in schools, hospitals and mental asylums to keep the inmates subdued—curved over the tops of their heads to where it met the inner perpendicular wall which, oddly enough, was covered in dark brown hessian wall weave. The floor was of dark green ribbed rubber.

Ford moved over to a very thick dark transparent panel set in the outer wall. It was several layers deep, yet through it he could see pinpoints of distant stars.

"I think we're in a spaceship of some kind," he said.

Down the corridor came the sound of a dull stomping throb.

"Trillian?" called Arthur nervously. "Zaphod?"

Ford shrugged.

"Nowhere about," he said, "I've looked. They could be anywhere. An unprogrammed teleport can throw you light-years in any direction. Judging by the way I feel I should think we've traveled a very long way indeed."

"How do you feel?"

"Bad."

"Do you think they're..."

"Where they are, how they are, there's no way we can know and no way we can do anything about it. Do what I do."

"What?"

"Don't think about it."

Arthur turned this thought over in his mind, reluctantly saw the wisdom of it, tucked it up and put it away. He took a deep breath.

"Footsteps!" exclaimed Ford suddenly.

"Where?"

"That noise. That stomping throb. Pounding feet. Listen!"

Arthur listened. The noise echoed round the corridor at them from an indeterminate distance. It was the muffled sound of pounding footsteps, and it was noticeably louder.

"Let's move," said Ford sharply. They both moved —in opposite directions.

"Not that way," said Ford. "That's where they're coming from."

"No, it's not," said Arthur. "They're coming from that way."

"They're not, they're..."

They both stopped. They both turned. They both listened intently. They both agreed with each other. They both set off in opposite directions again.

Fear gripped them.

From both directions the noise was getting louder.

A few yards to their left another corridor ran at right angles to the inner wall. They ran to it and hurried along it. It was dark, immensely long and, as they passed down it, gave them the impression that it was getting colder and colder. Other corridors gave off it to the left and right, each very dark and each subjecting them to sharp blasts of icy air as they passed.

They stopped for a moment in alarm. The further down the corridor they went, the louder became the sound of pounding feet.

They pressed themselves back against the cold wall and listened furiously. The cold, the dark and the drumming of disembodied feet was getting to them badly. Ford shivered, partly with the cold, but partly with the memory of stories his favorite mother used to tell him when he was a mere slip of a Betelgeusian, ankle high to an Arcturan Megagrasshopper: stories of death ships, haunted hulks that roamed restlessly round the obscurer regions of deep space infested with demons or the ghosts of forgotten crews; stories too of incautious travelers who found and entered such ships; stories of—

Then Ford remembered the brown hessian wall weave in the first corridor and pulled himself together. However ghosts and demons may choose to decorate their death hulks, he thought to himself, he would lay any money you liked it wasn't with hessian wall weave. He grasped Arthur by the arm.

"Back the way we came," he said firmly and they started to retrace their steps.

A moment later they leaped like startled lizards down the nearest corridor junction as the owners of the drumming feet suddenly hove into view directly in front of them.

Hidden behind the corner they goggled in amazement as about two dozen overweight men and women pounded past them in track suits panting and wheezing in a manner that would make a heart surgeon gibber.

Ford Prefect stared after them.

"Joggers!" he hissed, as the sound of their feet echoed away up and down the network of corridors.

"Joggers?" whispered Arthur Dent.

"Joggers," said Ford Prefect with a shrug.

The corridor they were concealed in was not like the others. It was very short, and ended at a large steel door. Ford examined it, discovered the opening mechanism and pushed it wide.

The first thing that hit their eyes was what appeared to be a coffin.

And the next four thousand nine hundred and ninety-nine things that hit their eyes were also coffins.

Chapter 23

The vault was low ceilinged, dimly lit and gigantic. At the far end, about three hundred yards away, an archway let through to what appeared to be a similar chamber, similarly occupied.

Ford Prefect let out a low whistle as he stepped down on to the floor of the vault.

"Wild," he said.

"What's so great about dead people?" asked Arthur, nervously stepping down after him.

"Dunno," said Ford. "Let's find out, shall we?"

On closer inspection the coffins seemed to be more like sarcophagi. They stood about waist high and were constructed of what appeared to be white marble, which is almost certainly what it was—something that only appeared to be white marble. The tops were semitranslucent, and through them could dimly be perceived the features of their late and presumably lamented occupants. They were humanoid, and had clearly left the troubles of whatever world it was they came from far behind them, but beyond that little else could be discerned.

Rolling slowly round the floor between the sarcophagi was a heavy, oily white gas which Arthur at first thought might be there to give the place a little atmosphere until he discovered that it also froze his ankles. The sarcophagi too were intensely cold to the touch.

Ford suddenly crouched down beside one of them. He pulled a corner of his towel out of his satchel and started to rub furiously at something.

"Look, there's a plaque on this one," he explained to Arthur. "It's frosted over."

He rubbed the frost clear and examined the engraved characters. To Arthur they looked like the footprints of a spider that had had one too many of whatever it is that spiders have on a night out, but Ford instantly recognized an early form of Galactic Eezzeereed.

"It says 'Golgafrincham Ark Fleet, Ship B, Hold Seven, Telephone Sanitizer Second Class'—and a serial number."

"A telephone sanitizer?" said Arthur. "A dead telephone sanitizer?"

"Best kind."

"But what's he doing here?"

Ford peered through the top at the figure within.

"Not a lot," he said, and suddenly flashed one of those grins of his which always made people think he'd been overdoing things recently and should try to get some rest.

He scampered over to another sarcophagus. A moment's brisk towel work and he announced:

"This one's a dead hairdresser. Hoopy!"

The next sarcophagus revealed itself to be the last resting place of an advertising account executive; the one after that contained a secondhand car salesman, third class.

An inspection hatch let into the floor suddenly caught Ford's attention, and he squatted down to unfasten it, thrashing away at the clouds of freezing gas that threatened to envelope him.

A thought occurred to Arthur.

"If these are just coffins," he said, "why are they kept so cold?"

"Or, indeed, why are they kept anyway," said Ford tugging the hatchway open. The gas poured down through it. "Why in fact is anyone going to all the trouble and expense of carting five thousand dead bodies through space?"

"Ten thousand," said Arthur, pointing at the archway through which the next chamber was dimly visible.

Ford stuck his head down through the floor hatchway. He looked up again.

"Fifteen thousand," he said. "There's another lot down there."

"Fifteen million," said a voice.

"That's a lot," said Ford. "A lot a lot."

"Turn around slowly," barked the voice, "and put your hands up. Any other move and I blast you into tiny tiny bits."

"Hello?" said Ford, turning round slowly, putting his hands up and not making any other move.

"Why," said Arthur Dent, "isn't anyone ever pleased to see us?"

Standing silhouetted in the doorway through which they had entered the vault was the man who wasn't pleased to see them. His displeasure was communicated partly by the barking hectoring quality of his voice and partly by the viciousness with which he waved a long silver Kill-O-Zap gun at them. The designer of the gun had clearly not been instructed to beat about the bush.

"Make it evil," he'd been told. "Make it totally clear that this gun has a right end and a wrong end. Make it totally clear to anyone standing at the wrong end that things are going badly for them. If that means sticking all sort of spikes and prongs and blackened bits all over it then so be it. This is not a gun for hanging over the fireplace or sticking in the umbrella stand, it is a gun for going out and making people miserable with."

Ford and Arthur looked at the gun unhappily.

The man with the gun moved from the door and circled around them. As he came into the light they could see his black and gold uniform on which the buttons were so highly polished that they shone with an intensity that would have made an approaching motorist flash his lights in annoyance.

He gestured at the door.

"Out," he said. People who can supply that amount of firepower don't need to supply verbs as well. Ford and Arthur went out, closely followed by the wrong end of the Kill-O-Zap gun and the buttons.

Turning into the corridor they were jostled by twenty-four oncoming joggers, now showered and changed, who swept on past them into the vault. Arthur turned to watch them in confusion.

"Move!" screamed their captor.

Arthur moved.

Ford shrugged and moved.

In the vault the joggers went to twenty-four empty sarcophagi along the side wall, opened them, climbed in and fell into twenty-four dreamless sleeps.

Er, Captain..."

"Yes, Number One?"

"Just had a sort of report thingy from Number Two."

"Oh dear."

High up in the bridge of the ship, the Captain stared out into the infinite reaches of space with mild irritation. From where he reclined beneath a wide domed bubble he could see before and above him the vast panorama of stars through which they were moving—a panorama that had thinned out noticeably during the course of the voyage. Turning and looking backward, over the vast two-mile bulk of the ship he could see the far denser mass of stars behind them which seemed to form almost a solid band. This was the view through the Galactic center from which they were traveling, and indeed had been traveling for years, at a speed that he couldn't quite remember at the moment, but he knew it was terribly fast. It was something approaching the speed of something or other, or was it three times the speed of something else? Jolly impressive anyway. He peered into the bright distance behind the ship, looking for something. He did this every few minutes or so, but never found what he was looking for. He didn't let it worry him though. The scientist chaps had been very insistent that everything was going to be perfectly all right providing nobody panicked and everybody got on and did their bit in an orderly fashion.

He wasn't panicking. As far as he was concerned everything was going splendidly. He dabbed at his shoulder with a large frothy sponge. It crept back into his mind that he was feeling mildly irritated about something. Now what was all that about? A slight cough alerted him to the fact that the ship's first officer was still standing nearby.

Nice chap, Number One. Not of the very brightest, had the odd spot of difficulty tying his shoelaces, but jolly good officer material for all that. The Captain wasn't a man to kick a chap when he was bending over trying to do up his shoelaces, however long it took him. Not like that ghastly Number Two, strutting about all over the place, polishing his buttons, issuing reports every hour: "Ship's still moving, Captain." "Still on course, Captain." "Oxygen levels still being maintained, Captain." "Give it a miss," was the Captain's vote. Ah yes, that was the thing that had been irritating him. He peered down at Number One.

"Yes, Captain, he was shouting something or other about having found some prisoners...."

The Captain thought about this. Seemed pretty unlikely to him, but he wasn't one to stand in his officers' way.

"Well, perhaps that'll keep him happy for a bit," he said. "He's always wanted some."

Ford Prefect and Arthur Dent trudged onward up the ship's apparently endless corridors. Number Two marched behind them barking the occasional order about not making any false moves or trying any funny stuff. They seemed to have passed at least a mile of continuous brown hessian wall weave. Finally they reached a large steel door which slid open when Number Two shouted at it.

They entered.

To the eyes of Ford Prefect and Arthur Dent, the most remarkable thing about the ship's bridge was not the fifty-foot diameter hemispherical dome which covered it, and through which the dazzling display of stars shone down on them: to people who have eaten at the Restaurant at the End of the Universe, such wonders are commonplace. Nor was it the bewildering array of instruments that crowded the long circumferential wall around them. To Arthur this was exactly what spaceships were traditionally supposed to look like, and to Ford it looked thoroughly antiquated: it confirmed his suspicions that Disaster Area's stuntship had taken them back at least a million, if not two million, years before their own time.

No, the thing that really caught them off balance was the bathtub.

The bathtub stood on a six-foot pedestal of rough-hewn blue water crystal and was of a baroque monstrosity not often seen outside the Maximegalon Museum of Diseased Imaginings. An intestinal jumble of plumbing had been picked out in gold leaf rather than decently buried at midnight in an unmarked grave; the taps and shower attachment would have made a gargoyle jump.

As the dominant certerpiece of a starship bridge it was terribly wrong, and it was with the embittered air of a man who knew this that Number Two approached it.

"Captain, sir!" he shouted through clenched teeth—a difficult trick but he'd had years during which to perfect it.

A large genial face and genial foam-covered arm popped up above the rim of the monstrous bath.

"Ah, hello, Number Two," said the Captain, waving a cheery sponge, "having a nice day?"

Number Two snapped even further to attention than he already was.

"I have brought you the prisoners I located in freezer bay seven, sir!" he yapped.

Ford and Arthur coughed in confusion.

"Er...hello," they said.

The Captain beamed at them. So Number Two had really found some prisoners. Well, good for him, thought the Captain, nice to see a chap doing what he's best at.

"Oh, hello there," he said to them. "Excuse me not getting up, just having a quick bath. Well, jynnan tonnyx all round then. Look in the fridge Number One."

"Certainly, sir."

It is a curious fact, and one to which no one knows quite how much importance to attach, that something like 85 percent of all known worlds in the Galaxy, be they primitive or highly advanced, have invented a drink called jynnan tonnyx, or gee-N-N-T'N-ix, or jinond-o-nicks, or any one of a thousand or more variations on the same phonetic theme. The drinks themselves are not the same, and vary between the Sivolvian "chinanto/mnigs" which is ordinary water served at slightly above room temperature, and the Gagrakackan "tzjin-anthony-ks" which kills cows at a hundred paces; and in fact the one common factor between all of them, beyond that fact that the names sound the same, is that they were all invented and named *before* the worlds concerned made contact with any other worlds.

What can be made of this fact? It exists in total isolation. As far as any theory of structural linguistics is concerned it is right off the graph, and yet it persists. Old structural linguists get very angry when young structural linguists go on about it. Young structural linguists get deeply excited about it and stay up late at night convinced that they are very close to something of profound importance, and end up becoming old structural linguists before their time, getting very angry with the young ones. Structural linguistics is a bitterly divided and unhappy discipline, and a large number of its practitioners spend too many nights drowning their problems in Ouisghian Zodahs.

Number Two stood before the Captain's bathtub trembling with frustration.

"Don't you want to interrogate the prisoners, sir?" he squealed.

The Captain peered at him in bemusement.

"Why on Golgafrincham should I want to do that?" he asked.

"To get information out of them, sir! To find out why they came here!"

"Oh no, no, no," said the Captain. "I expect they just dropped in for a quick jynnan tonnyx, don't you?"

"But, sir, they're my prisoners! I must interrogate them!"

The Captain looked at them doubtfully.

"Oh all right," he said, "if you must. Ask them what they want to drink."

A hard cold gleam came into Number Two's eyes. He advanced slowly on Ford Prefect and Arthur Dent.

"All right, you scum," he growled, "you vermin..." He jabbed Ford with the Kill-O-Zap gun.

"Steady on, Number Two," admonished the Captain gently.

"*What do you want to drink?!!*" Number Two screamed.

"Well the jynnan tonnyx sounds very nice to me," said Ford. "What about you, Arthur?"

Arthur blinked.

"What? Oh, er, yes," he said.

"*With ice or without?!*" bellowed Number Two.

"Oh, with, please," said Ford.

"*Lemon??!!*"

"Yes, please," said Ford, "and do you have any of those little biscuits? You know, the cheesey ones?"

"*I'm asking the questions!!!!*" howled Number Two, his body quaking with apoplectic fury.

"Er, Number Two..." said the Captain softly.

"Sir?!"

"Shove off, would you, there's a good chap. I'm trying to have a relaxing bath."

Number Two's eyes narrowed and became what are known in the Shouting and Killing People trade as cold slits, the idea presumably being to give your opponent the impression that you have lost your glasses or are having difficulty keeping awake. Why this is frightening is an, as yet, unresolved problem.

He advanced on the Captain, his (Number Two's) mouth a thin hard line. Again, tricky to know why this is understood as fighting behavior. If, while wandering through the jungle of Traal, you were suddenly to come upon the fabled Ravenous Bugblatter Beast, you would have reason to be grateful if its mouth was a thin hard line rather than, as it usually is, a gaping mass of slavering fangs.

"May I remind you, sir," hissed Number Two at the Captain, "that you have now been in that bath for over *three years?!*" This final shot delivered, Number Two spun on his heel and stalked off to a corner to practice darting eye movements in the mirror.

The Captain squirmed in his bath. He gave Ford Prefect a lame smile.

"Well, you need to relax a lot in a job like mine," he said.

Ford slowly lowered his hands. It provoked no reaction. Arthur lowered his.

Treading very slowly and carefully, Ford moved over to the bath pedestal. He patted it.

"Nice," he lied.

He wondered if it was safe to grin. Very slowly and carefully, he grinned. It was safe.

"Er..." he said to the Captain.

"Yes?" said the Captain.

"I wonder," said Ford, "could I ask you actually what your job is in fact?"

A hand tapped him on the shoulder. He spun around. It was the first officer.

"Your drinks," he said.

"Ah, thank you," said Ford. He and Arthur took their jynnan tonnyx. Arthur sipped his, and was surprised to discover it tasted very like a whisky and soda.

"I mean, I couldn't help noticing," said Ford, also taking a sip, "the bodies. In the hold."

"Bodies?" said the Captain in surprise.

Ford paused and thought to himself. Never take anything for granted, he thought. Could it be that the Captain doesn't know he's got fifteen million dead bodies on his ship?

The Captain was nodding cheerfully at him. He also appeared to be playing with a rubber duck.

Ford looked around. Number Two was staring at him in the mirror, but only for an instant: his eyes were constantly on the move. The first officer was just standing there holding the drinks tray and smiling benignly.

"Bodies?" said the Captain again.

Ford licked his lips.

"Yes," he said, "all those dead telephone sanitizers.

and account executives, you know, down in the hold."

The Captain stared at him. Suddenly he threw back his head and laughed.

"Oh, they're not dead," he said. "Good Lord, no, no they're frozen. They're going to be revived."

Ford did something he very rarely did. He blinked.

Arthur seemed to come out of a trance.

"You mean you've got a hold full of frozen hairdressers?" he said.

"Oh yes," said the Captain. "Millions of them. Hairdressers, tired TV producers, insurance salesmen, personnel officers, security guards, public relations executives, management consultants, you name it. We're going to colonize another planet."

Ford wobbled very slightly.

"Exciting, isn't it?" said the Captain.

"What, with that lot?" said Arthur.

"Ah, now don't misunderstand me," said the Captain. "We're just one of the ships in the Ark Fleet. We're the 'B' Ark, you see. Sorry, could I just ask you to run a bit more hot water for me?"

Arthur obliged, and a cascade of pink frothy water swirled around the bath. The Captain let out a sigh of pleasure.

"Thank you so much, my dear fellow. Do help yourselves to more drinks of course."

Ford tossed down his drink, took the bottle from the first officer's tray and refilled his glass to the top.

"What," he said, "is a 'B' Ark?"

"This is," said the Captain, and swished the foamy

water around joyfully with the duck.

"Yes," said Ford, "but—"

"Well, what happened you see was," said the Captain, "our planet, the world from which we have come, was, so to speak, doomed."

"Doomed?"

"Oh yes. So what everyone thought was, let's pack the whole population into some giant spaceships and go and settle on another planet."

Having told this much of his story, he settled back with a satisfied grunt.

"You mean a less doomed one?" prompted Arthur.

"What did you say dear fellow?"

"A less doomed planet. You were going to settle on."

"Are going to settle on, yes. So it was decided to build three ships, you see, three Arks in Space, and . . . I'm not boring you, am I?"

"No, no," said Ford firmly, "it's fascinating."

"You know it's delightful," reflected the Captain, "to have someone else to talk to for a change."

Number Two's eyes darted feverishly about the room again and then settled back on the mirror, like a pair of flies briefly distracted from their favorite piece of month-old meat.

"Trouble with a long journey like this," continued the Captain, "is that you end up just talking to yourself a lot, which gets terribly boring because half the time you know what you're going to say next."

"Only half the time?" asked Arthur in surprise.

The Captain thought for a moment.

"Yes, about half, I'd say. Anyway—where's the soap?" He fished around and found it.

"Yes, so anyway," he resumed, "the idea was that into the first ship, the 'A' ship, would go all the brilliant leaders, the scientists, the great artists, you know, all the achievers; and then into the third, or 'C' ship, would go all the people who did the actual work, who made things and did things; and then into the 'B' ship—that's us—would go everyone else, the middlemen, you see."

He smiled happily at them.

"And we were sent off first," he concluded, and hummed a little bathing tune.

The little bathing tune, which had been composed for him by one of his world's most exciting and prolific jingle writers (who was currently asleep in hold thirty-six some nine hundred yards behind them) covered what would otherwise have been an awkward moment of silence. Ford and Arthur shuffled their feet and furiously avoided each other's eyes.

"Er..." said Arthur after a moment, "what exactly was it that was wrong with your planet then?"

"Oh, it was doomed, as I said," said the Captain. "Apparently it was going to crash into the sun or something. Or maybe it was that the moon was going to crash into us. Something of the kind. Absolutely terrifying prospect whatever it was."

"Oh," said the first officer suddenly, "I thought it was that the planet was going to be invaded by a gigantic swarm of twelve-foot piranha bees. Wasn't that it?"

Number Two spun around, eyes ablaze with a cold hard light that only comes with the amount of practice he was prepared to put in.

"That's not what I was told!" he hissed. "My commanding officer told me that the entire planet was in imminent danger of being eaten by an enormous mutant star goat!"

"Oh really..." said Ford Prefect.

"Yes! A monstrous creature from the pit of hell with scything teeth ten thousand miles long, breath that would boil oceans, claws that could tear continents from their roots, a thousand eyes that burned like the sun, slavering jaws a million miles across, a monster such as you have never...never...ever..."

"And they made sure they sent you lot off first, did they?" inquired Arthur.

"Oh yes," said the Captain, "well, everyone said, very nicely I thought, that it was very important for morale to feel that they would be arriving on a planet where they could be sure of a good haircut and where the phones were clean."

"Oh yes," agreed Ford, "I can see that would be very important. And the other ships, er... they followed on after you, did they?"

For a moment the Captain did not answer. He twisted round in his bath and gazed backward over the huge bulk of the ship toward the bright galactic center. He squinted into the inconceivable distance.

"Ah. Well, it's funny you should say that," he said and allowed himself a slight frown at Ford Prefect, "because curiously enough we haven't heard a peep out of them since we left five years ago.... But they must be behind us somewhere."

He peered off into the distance again.

Ford peered with him and gave a thoughtful frown.

"Unless of course," he said softly, "they were eaten by the goat...."

"Ah yes..." said the Captain with a slight hesitancy creeping into his voice, "the goat...." His eyes passed over the solid shapes of the instruments and computers that lined the bridge. They winked away innocently at him. He stared out at the stars, but none of them said a word. He glanced at his first and second officers, but they seemed lost in their own thoughts for a moment. He glanced at Ford Prefect who raised his eyebrows at him.

"It's a funny thing, you know," said the Captain at last, "but now that I actually come to tell the story to someone else...I mean does it strike you as odd, Number One?"

"Errrrrrrrrrrrr..." said Number One.

"Well," said Ford, "I can see that you've got a lot of things you're going to want to talk about, so, thanks for the drinks, and if you could sort of drop us off at the nearest convenient planet..."

"Ah, well that's a little difficult you see," said the Captain, "because our trajectory thingy was preset before we left Golgafrincham, I think partly because I'm not very good with figures...."

"You mean we're stuck here on this ship?" exclaimed

Ford, suddenly losing patience with the whole charade. "When are you meant to be reaching this planet you're meant to be colonizing?"

"Oh, we're nearly there I think," said the Captain, "any second now. It's probably time I was getting out of this bath in fact. Oh, I don't know though, why stop just when I'm enjoying it?"

"So we're actually going to land in a minute?" said Arthur.

"Well, not so much *land*, in fact, not actually land as such, no ... er—"

"What are you talking about?" asked Ford sharply.

"Well," said the Captain, picking his way through the words carefully, "I think as far as I can remember we were programmed to crash on it."

"Crash?" shouted Ford and Arthur.

"Er, yes," said the Captain, "yes, it's all part of the plan, I think. There was a terribly good reason for it which I can't quite remember at the moment. It was something to do with ... er ..."

Ford exploded.

"You're a load of useless bloody loonies!" he shouted.

"Ah yes, that was it," beamed the Captain, "that was the reason."

The *Hitchhiker's Guide to the Galaxy* has this to say about the planet of Golgafrincham: *it is a planet with an ancient and mysterious history, rich in legend, red, and occasionally green with the blood of those who sought in times gone by to conquer her; a land of parched and barren landscapes, of sweet and sultry air heady with the scent of the perfumed springs that trickle over its hot and dusty rocks and nourish the dark and musky lichens beneath; a land of fevered brows and intoxicated imaginings, particularly among those who taste the lichens; a land also of cool and shaded thoughts among those who have learned to forswear the lichens and find a tree to sit beneath; a land also of steel and blood and heroism; a land of the body and of the spirit. This was its history.*

And in all this ancient and mysterious history, the most mysterious figures of all were without doubt those of the Great Circling poets of Arium. These Circling Poets used to live in remote mountain passes where they would lie in wait for small bands of unwary travelers, circle around them, and throw rocks at them.

And when the travelers cried out, saying why didn't they go away and get on with writing some poems instead of pestering people with all this rock-throwing business, they *would suddenly stop, and then break into one of the seven hundred and ninety-four great Song Cycles of Vassillian. These songs were all of extraordinary beauty, and even more extraordinary length, and all fell into exactly the same pattern.*

The first part of each song would tell how there once went forth from the City of Vassillian a party of five sage princes with four horses. The princes, who are of course brave, noble and wise, travel widely in distant lands, fight giant ogres, pursue exotic philosophies, take tea with weird gods and rescue beautiful monsters from ravening princesses before finally announcing that they have achieved enlightenment and that their wanderings are therefore accomplished.

The second, and much longer, part of each song would then tell of all their bickerings about which one of them is going to have to walk back.

All this lay in the planet's remote past. It was, however, a descendant of one of these eccentric poets who invented the spurious tales of impending doom which enabled the people of Golgafrincham to rid themselves of an entire useless third of their population. The other two-thirds stayed firmly at home and lived full, rich and happy lives until they were all suddenly wiped out by a virulent disease contracted from a dirty telephone.

Chapter 26

That night the ship crash-landed onto an utterly insignificant little blue-green planet which circled a small unregarded yellow sun in the uncharted backwaters of the unfashionable end of the Western spiral arm of the Galaxy.

In the hours preceding the crash Ford Prefect had fought furiously but in vain to unlock the controls of the ship from their preordained flight path. It had quickly become apparent to him that the ship had been programmed to convey its payload safely, if uncomfortably, to its new home but to cripple itself beyond all hope of repair in the process.

Its screaming, blazing descent through the atmosphere had stripped away most of its superstructure and outer shielding, and its final inglorious bellyflop into a murky swamp had left its crew only a few hours of darkness during which to revive and offload its deep-frozen and unwanted cargo for the ship began to settle almost at once, slowly upending its gigantic bulk in the stagnant slime. Once or twice during the night it was starkly silhouetted against the sky as burning meteors—the detritus of its descent—flashed across the sky.

In the gray predawn light it let out an obscene roaring

gurgle and sank for ever into the stinking depths.

When the sun came up that morning it shed its thin watery light over a vast area heaving with wailing hairdressers, public relations executives, opinion pollsters and the rest, all clawing their way desperately to dry land.

A less strong-minded sun would probably have gone straight back down again, but it continued to climb its way through the sky and after a while the influence of its warming rays began to have some restoring effect on the feebly struggling creatures.

Countless numbers had, unsurprisingly, been lost to the swamp in the night, and millions more had been sucked down with the ship, but those who survived still numbered hundreds of thousands and as the day wore on they crawled out over the surrounding countryside, each looking for a few square feet of solid ground on which to collapse and recover from their nightmare ordeal.

Two figures moved farther afield.

From a nearby hillside Ford Prefect and Arthur Dent watched the horror of which they could not feel a part.

"Filthy dirty trick to pull," muttered Arthur.

Ford scraped a stick along the ground and shrugged.

"An imaginative solution to a problem I'd have thought," he said.

"Why can't people just learn to live together in peace and harmony?" said Arthur.

Ford gave a loud, very hollow laugh.

"Forty-two!" he said with a malicious grin. "No, doesn't work. Never mind."

Arthur looked at him as if he'd gone mad and, seeing nothing to indicate the contrary, realized that it would be perfectly reasonable to assume that this had in fact happened.

"What do you think will happen to them all?" he said after a while.

"In an infinite Universe anything can happen," said Ford. "Even survival. Strange but true."

A curious look came into his eyes as they passed over the landscape and then settled again on the scene of misery below them.

"I think they'll manage for a while," he said.

Arthur looked up sharply.

"Why do you say that?" he said.

Ford shrugged.

"Just a hunch," he said, and refused to be drawn on any further questions.

"Look," he said suddenly.

Arthur followed his pointing finger. Down among the sprawling masses a figure was moving—or perhaps lurching would be a more accurate description. He appeared to be carrying something on his shoulder. As he lurched from prostrate form to prostrate form he seemed to wave whatever the something was at them in a drunken fashion. After a while he gave up the struggle and collapsed in a heap.

Arthur had no idea what this was meant to mean to him.

"Movie camera," said Ford. "Recording the historic moment."

"Well, I don't know about you," said Ford again after a moment, "but I'm off."

He sat a while in silence.

After a while this seemed to require comment.

"Er, when you say you're off, what do you mean exactly?" said Arthur.

"Good question," said Ford. "I'm getting total silence."

Looking over his shoulder Arthur saw that he was twiddling with knobs on a small black box. Ford had already introduced this box to Arthur as a Sub-Etha Sens-O-Matic, but Arthur had merely nodded absently and not pursued the matter. In his mind the Universe still divided into two parts—the Earth, and everything else. The Earth having been demolished to make way for a hyperspace bypass meant that this view of things was a little lopsided, but Arthur tended to cling to that lopsidedness as being his last remaining contact with his home. Sub-Etha Sens-O-Matics belonged firmly in the "everything else" category.

"Not a sausage," said Ford, shaking the thing.

Sausage, thought Arthur to himself as he gazed listlessly at the primitive world about him, what I wouldn't give for a good Earth sausage.

"Would you believe," said Ford in exasperation, "that there are no transmissions of any kind within light-years of this benighted tip? Are you listening to me?"

"What?" said Arthur.

"We're in trouble," said Ford.

"Oh," said Arthur. This sounded like month-old news to him.

"Until we pick up anything on this machine," said Ford, "our chances of getting off this planet are zero. It may be some freak standing wave effect in the planet's magnetic field—in which case we just travel round and round till we find a clear reception area. Coming?"

He picked up his gear and strode off.

Arthur looked down the hill. The man with the movie camera had struggled back up to his feet just in time to film one of his colleagues collapsing.

Arthur picked a blade of grass and strode off after Ford.

Chapter 27

trust you had a pleasant meal?" said Zarniwoop to Zaphod and Trillian as they rematerialized on the bridge of the starship *Heart of Gold* and lay panting on the floor.

Zaphod opened some eyes and glowered at him.

"You," he spat. He staggered to his feet and stomped off to find a chair to slump into. He found one and slumped into it.

"I have programmed the computer with the Improbability Coordinates pertinent to our journey," said Zarniwoop. "We will arrive there very shortly. Meanwhile, why don't you relax and prepare yourself for the meeting?"

Zaphod said nothing. He got up again and marched over to a small cabinet from which he pulled a bottle of old Janx Spirit. He took a long pull at it.

"And when this is all done," said Zaphod savagely, "it's done, all right? I'm free to go and do what the hell I like and lie on beaches and stuff?"

"It depends what transpires from the meeting," said Zarniwoop.

"Zaphod, who is this man?" said Trillian shakily, wobbling to her feet. "What's he doing here? Why's he on our ship?"

"He's a very stupid man," said Zaphod, "who wants to meet the man who rules the Universe."

"Ah," said Trillian, taking the bottle from Zaphod and helping herself, "a social climber."

The major problem—*one* of the major problems, for there are several—one of the many major problems with governing people is that of whom you get to do it; or rather of who manages to get people to let them do it to them.

To summarize: it is a well-known fact that those people who must *want* to rule people are, ipso facto, those least suited to do it. To summarize the summary: anyone who is capable of getting themselves made President should on no account be allowed to do the job. To summarize the summary of the summary: people are a problem.

And so this is the situation we find: a succession of Galactic Presidents who so much enjoy the fun and palaver of being in power that they very rarely notice that they're not.

And somewhere in the shadows behind them—who?

Who can possibly rule if no one who wants to do it can be allowed to?

Chapter 29

On a small obscure world somewhere in the middle of nowhere in particular—nowhere, that is, that could ever be found, since it is protected by a vast field of Unprobability to which only six men in this Galaxy have a key—it was raining.

It was bucketing down, and had been for hours. It beat the top of the sea into a mist, it pounded the trees, it churned and slopped a stretch of scrubby land near the sea into a mudbath.

The rain pelted and danced on the corrugated iron roof of the small shack that stood in the middle of this patch of scrubby land. It obliterated the small rough pathway that led from the shack down to the seashore and smashed apart the neat piles of interesting shells which had been placed there.

The noise of the rain on the roof of the shack was deafening within, but went largely unnoticed by its occupant, whose attention was otherwise engaged.

He was a tall shambling man with rough straw-colored hair that was damp from the leaking roof. His clothes were shabby, his back was hunched, and his eyes, though open, seemed closed.

In his shack was an old beaten-up armchair, an old

scratched table, an old mattress, some cushions and a stove that was small but warm.

There was also an old and slightly weatherbeaten cat, and this was currently the focus of the man's attention. He bent his shambling form over it.

"Pussy, pussy, pussy," he said, "coochicoochicoochicoo...pussy want his fish? Nice piece of fish...pussy want it?"

The cat seemed undecided on the matter. It pawed rather condescendingly at the piece of fish the man was holding out, and then got distracted by a piece of dust on the floor.

"Pussy not eat his fish, pussy get thin and waste away, I think," said the man. Doubt crept into his voice.

"I imagine this is what will happen," he said, "but how can I tell?"

He proffered the fish again.

"Pussy think," he said, "eat fish or not eat fish. I think it is better if I don't get involved." He sighed.

"I think fish is nice, but then I think that rain is wet, so who am I to judge?"

He left the fish on the floor for the cat, and retired to his seat.

"Ah, I seem to see you eating it," he said at last, as the cat exhausted the entertainment possibilities of the speck of dust and pounced onto the fish.

"I like it when I see you eat fish," said the man, "because in my mind you will waste away if you don't."

He picked up from the table a piece of paper and the stub of a pencil. He held one in one hand and the other in the other, and experimented with the different ways of bringing them together. He tried holding the pencil under the paper, then over the paper, then next to the paper. He tried wrapping the paper round the pencil, he tried rubbing the stubby end of the pencil against the paper and then he tried rubbing the sharp end of the pencil against the paper. It made a mark, and he was delighted with the discovery, as he was every day. He picked up another piece of paper from the table. This had a crossword on it. He studied it briefly and filled in a couple of clues before losing interest.

He tried sitting on one of his hands and was intrigued by the feel of the bones of his hip.

"Fish come from far away," he said, "or so I'm told. Or so I imagine I'm told. When the men come, or when in my mind the men come in their six black shiny ships, do they come in your mind too? What do you see, pussy?"

He looked at the cat, which was more concerned with getting the fish down as rapidly as possible than it was with these speculations.

"And when I hear their questions, do you hear questions? What do their voices mean to you? Perhaps you just think they're singing songs to you." He reflected on this, and saw the flaw in the supposition.

"Perhaps they are singing songs to you," he said, "and I just think they're asking me questions."

He paused again. Sometimes he would pause for days, just to see what it was like.

"Do you think they came today?" he said. "I do.

There's mud on the floor, cigarettes and whisky on the table, fish on a plate for you and a memory of them in my mind. Hardly conclusive evidence I know, but then all evidence is circumstantial. And look what else they've left me."

He reached over to the table and pulled some things off it.

"Crosswords, dictionaries and a calculator."

He played with the calculator for an hour, while the cat went to sleep and the rain outside continued to pour. Eventually he put the calculator aside.

"I think I must be right in thinking they ask me questions," he said. "To come all that way and leave all these things just for the privilege of singing songs to you would be very strange behavior. Or so it seems to me. Who can tell, who can tell."

From the table he picked up a cigarette and lit it with a spill from the stove. He inhaled deeply and sat back.

"I think I saw another ship in the sky today," he said at last. "A big white one. I've never seen a big white one, just the six black ones. And the six green ones. And the others who say they come from so far away. Never a big white one. Perhaps six small black ones can look like one big white one at certain times. Perhaps I would like a glass of whisky. Yes, that seems more likely."

He stood up and found a glass that was lying on the floor by his mattress. He poured in a measure from his whisky bottle. He sat again.

"Perhaps some other people are coming to see me," he said.

A hundred yards away, pelted by the torrential rain, lay the *Heart of Gold*.

Its hatchway opened, and three figures emerged, huddling into themselves to keep the rain off their faces.

"In there?" shouted Trillian above the noise of the rain.

"Yes," said Zarniwoop.

"That shack?"

"Yes."

"Weird," said Zaphod.

"But it's in the middle of nowhere," said Trillian. "We must have come to the wrong place. You can't rule the Universe from a shack."

They hurried through the pouring rain, and arrived, wet through, at the door. They knocked. They shivered.

The door opened.

"Hello?" said the man.

"Ah, excuse me," said Zarniwoop, "I have reason to believe..."

"Do you rule the Universe?" said Zaphod.

The man smiled at him.

"I try not to," he said. "Are you wet?"

Zaphod looked at him in astonishment.

"Wet?" he cried. "Doesn't it look as if we're wet?"

"That's how it looks to me," said the man, "but how you feel about it might be an altogether different matter. If you find warmth makes you dry, you'd better come in."

They went in.

They looked around the tiny shack, Zarniwoop with

slight distaste, Trillian with interest, Zaphod with delight.

"Hey, er..."said Zaphod, "what's your name?"

The man looked at them doubtfully.

"I don't know. Why, do you think I should have one? It seems very odd to give a bundle of vague sensory perceptions a name."

He invited Trillian to sit in the chair. He sat on the edge of the chair, Zarniwoop leaned stiffly against the table and Zaphod lay on the mattress.

"Wowee!" said Zaphod. "The seat of power!" He tickled the cat.

"Listen," said Zarniwoop, "I must ask you some questions."

"All right," said the man kindly, "you can sing to my cat if you like."

"Would he like that?" asked Zaphod.

"You'd better ask him," said the man.

"Does he talk?" said Zaphod.

"I have no memory of him talking," said the man, "but I am very unreliable."

Zarniwoop pulled some notes out of a pocket.

"Now," he said, "you do rule the Universe, do you?"

"How can I tell?" said the man.

Zarniwoop ticked off a note on the paper.

"How long have you been doing this?"

"Ah," said the man, "this is a question about the past, is it?"

Zarniwoop looked at him in puzzlement. This wasn't exactly what he had been expecting.

"Yes," he said.

"How can I tell," said the man, "that the past isn't a fiction designed to account for the discrepancy between my immediate physical sensations and my state of mind?"

Zarniwoop stared at him. The steam began to rise from his sodden clothes.

"So you answer all questions like this?" he said.

The man answered quickly.

"I say what it occurs to me to say when I think I hear people say things. More I cannot say."

Zaphod laughed happily.

"I'll drink to that," he said and pulled out the bottle of Janx Spirit. He leaped up and handed the bottle to the ruler of the Universe, who took it with pleasure.

"Good on you, great ruler," he said, "tell it like it is."

"No, listen to me," said Zarniwoop, "people come to you, do they? In ships..."

"I think so," said the man. He handed the bottle to Trillian.

"And they ask you," said Zarniwoop, "to make decisions for them? About people's lives, about worlds, about economies, about wars, about everything going on out there in the Universe?"

"Out there?" said the man. "Out where?"

"Out there!" said Zarniwoop, pointing at the door.

"How can you tell there's anything out there?" said the man politely. "The door's closed."

The rain continued to pound the roof. Inside the shack it was warm.

"But you know there's a whole Universe out there!" cried Zarniwoop. "You can't dodge your responsibilities by saying they don't exist!"

The ruler of the Universe thought for a long while while Zarniwoop quivered with anger.

"You're very sure of your facts," he said at last. "I couldn't trust the thinking of a man who takes the Universe—if there is one—for granted."

Zarniwoop still quivered, but was silent.

"I only decide about my Universe," continued the man quietly. "My Universe is my eyes and my ears. Anything else is hearsay."

"But don't you believe in anything?"

The man shrugged and picked up his cat.

"I don't understand what you mean," he said.

"You don't understand that what you decide in this shack of yours affects the lives and fates of millions of people? This is all monstrously wrong!"

"I don't know. I've never met all these people you speak of. And neither, I suspect, have you. They only exist in words we hear. It is folly to say you know what is happening to other people. Only they know, if they exist. They have their own Universes of their eyes and ears."

Trillian said:

"I think I'm just popping outside for a moment."

She left and walked into the rain.

"Do you believe other people exist?" insisted Zarniwoop.

"I have no opinion. How can I say?"

"I'd better see what's up with Trillian," said Zaphod and slipped out.

Outside, he said to her:

"I think the Universe is in pretty good hands, yeah?"

"Very good," said Trillian. They walked off into the rain.

Inside, Zarniwoop continued.

"But don't you understand that people live or die on your word?"

The ruler of the Universe waited for as long as he could. When he heard the faint sound of the ship's engines starting, he spoke to cover it.

"It's nothing to do with me," he said. "I am not involved with people. The Lord knows I am not a cruel man."

"Ah!" barked Zarniwoop, "you say 'The Lord.' You believe in something!"

"My cat," said the man benignly, picking it up and stroking it. "I call him The Lord. I am kind to him."

"All right," said Zarniwoop, pressing home his point, "how do you know he exists? How do you know he knows you to be kind, or enjoys what he thinks of as your kindness?"

"I don't," said the man with a smile, "I have no idea. It merely pleases me to behave in a certain way to what appears to be a cat. Do you behave any differently? Please, I think I am tired."

Zarniwoop heaved a thoroughly dissatisfied sigh and looked about.

"Where are the other two?" he said suddenly.

"What other two?" said the ruler of the Universe, settling back into his chair and refilling his whisky glass.

"Beeblebrox and the girl! The two who were here!"

"I remember no one. The past is a fiction to account for..."

"Stuff it," snapped Zarniwoop and ran out into the rain. There was no ship. The rain continued to churn the mud. There was no sign to show where the ship had been. He hollered into the rain. He turned and ran back to the shack and found it locked.

The ruler of the Universe dozed lightly in his chair. After a while he played with the pencil and the paper again and was delighted when he discovered how to make a mark with the one on the other. Various noises continued outside, but he didn't know whether they were real or not. He then talked to his table for a week to see how it would react.

The stars came out that night, dazzling in their brilliance and clarity. Ford and Arthur had walked more miles than they had any means of judging and finally stopped to rest. The night was cool and balmy, the air pure, the Sub-Etha Sens-O-Matic totally silent.

A wonderful stillness hung over the world, a magical calm which combined with the soft fragrances of the woods, the quiet chatter of insects and the brilliant light of the stars to soothe their jangled spirits. Even Ford Prefect, who had seen more worlds than he could count on a long afternoon, was moved to wonder if this was the most beautiful he had ever seen. All that day they had passed through rolling green hills and valleys, richly covered with grasses, wild scented flowers and tall thickly leaved trees; the sun had warmed them, light breezes had kept them cool and Ford Prefect had checked his Sub-Etha Sens-O-Matic at less and less frequent intervals, and had exhibited less and less annoyance at its continued silence. He was beginning to think he liked it here.

Cool though the night air was they slept soundly and comfortably in the open and awoke a few hours later with the light dewfall, feeling refreshed but hungry.

Ford had stuffed some small rolls into his satchel at Milliways and they breakfasted on these before moving on.

So far they had wandered purely at random, but now they struck out firmly eastward, feeling that if they were going to explore this world they should have some clear idea of where they had come from and where they were going.

Shortly before noon they had their first indication that the world they had landed on was not an uninhabited one: a half-glimpsed face amongst the trees, watching them. It vanished at the moment they both saw it, but the image they were both left with was of a humanoid creature, curious to see them but not alarmed. Half an hour later they glimpsed another such face, and ten minutes after that another.

A minute later they stumbled into a wide clearing and stopped short.

Before them in the middle of the clearing stood a group of about two dozen men and women. They stood still and quiet facing Ford and Arthur. Around some of the women huddled some small children and behind the group was a ramshackle array of small dwellings made of mud and branches.

Ford and Arthur held their breath.

The tallest of the men stood little over five feet high, they all stooped forward slightly, had longish arms and lowish foreheads and clear bright eyes with which they stared intently at the strangers.

Seeing that they carried no weapons and made no

move toward them, Ford and Arthur relaxed slightly.

For a while the two groups simply stared at each other, neither side making any move. The natives seemed puzzled by the intruders, and while they showed no sign of aggression they were quite clearly not issuing any invitations.

Nothing happened.

For a full two minutes nothing continued to happen.

After two minutes Ford decided it was time something happened.

"Hello," he said.

The women drew their children slightly closer to them.

The men made hardly any discernible move and yet their whole disposition made it clear that the greeting was not welcome—it was not resented in any great degree, it was just not welcome.

One of the men, who had been standing slightly forward of the rest of the group and who might therefore have been their leader, stepped forward. His face was quiet and calm, almost serene.

"Ugghhhuuggghhhrrrr uh uh ruh uurgh," he said quietly.

This caught Arthur by surprise. He had grown so used to receiving an instantaneous and unconscious translation of everything he heard via the Babel fish lodged in his ear that he had ceased to be aware of it, and he was only reminded of its presence now by the fact that it didn't seem to be working. Vague shadows of meaning had flickered at the back of his mind, but there was nothing he could get any firm grasp on. He guessed, correctly as it happens, that these people had as yet evolved no more than the barest rudiments of language, and that the Babel fish was therefore powerless to help. He glanced at Ford, who was infinitely more experienced in these matters.

"I think," said Ford out of the corner of his mouth, "he's asking us if we'd mind walking on around the edge of the village."

A moment later, a gesture from the man-creature seemed to confirm this.

"Ruurgggghhhh urrgggh; urgh urgh (uh ruh) rruurruuh ug," continued the man-creature.

"The general gist," said Ford, "as far as I can make out, is that we are welcome to continue our journey in any way we like, but if we would walk around his village rather than through it it would make them all very happy."

"So what do we do?"

"I think we make them happy," said Ford.

Slowly and watchfully they walked around the perimeter of the clearing. This seemed to go down very well with the natives who bowed to them very slightly and then went about their business.

Ford and Arthur continued their journey through the wood. A few hundred yards past the clearing they suddenly came upon a small pile of fruit lying in their path—berries that looked remarkably like raspberries and strawberries, and pulpy, green-skinned fruit that looked remarkably like pears.

So far they had steered clear of the fruit and berries they had seen, though the trees and bushes were laden with them.

"Look at it this way," Ford Prefect had said, "fruit and berries on strange planets either make you live or make you die. Therefore the point at which to start toying with them is when you're going to die if you don't. That way you stay ahead. The secret of healthy hitchhiking is to eat junk food."

They looked at the pile that lay in their path with suspicion. It looked so good it made them almost dizzy with hunger.

"Look at it this way," said Ford, "er..."

"Yes?" said Arthur.

"I'm trying to think of a way of looking at it which means we get to eat it," said Ford.

The leaf-dappled sun gleamed on the plump skins of the things which looked like pears. The things which looked like raspberries and strawberries were fatter and riper than any Arthur had ever seen, even in ice cream commercials.

"Why don't we eat them and think about it afterward?" he said.

"Maybe that's what they want us to do."

"All right, look at it this way...."

"Sounds good so far."

"It's there for us to eat. Either it's good or it's bad, either they want to feed us or to poison us. If it's poisonous and we don't eat it they'll just attack us some other way. If we don't eat, we lose out either way."

"I like the way you're thinking," said Ford. "Now eat one."

Hesitantly, Arthur picked up one of the things that looked like pears.

"I always thought that about the Garden of Eden story," said Ford.

"Eh?"

"Garden of Eden. Tree. Apple. That bit, remember?"

"Yes, of course I do."

"Your God person puts an apple tree in the middle of a garden and says, do what you like guys, oh, but don't eat the apple. Surprise surprise, they eat it and he leaps out from behind a bush shouting 'Gotcha.' It wouldn't have made any difference if they hadn't eaten it."

"Why not?"

"Because if you're dealing with somebody who has the sort of mentality which likes leaving hats on the pavement with bricks under them you know perfectly well they won't give up. They'll get you in the end."

"What are you talking about?"

"Never mind, eat the fruit."

"You know, this place almost looks like the Garden of Eden."

"Eat the fruit."

"Sounds quite like it too."

Arthur took a bite from the thing which looked like a pear.

"It's a pear," he said.

A few moments later, when they had eaten the lot, Ford Prefect turned round and called out.

"Thank you. Thank you very much," he called, "you're very kind."

They went on their way.

For the next fifty miles of their journey eastward they kept on finding the occasional gift of fruit lying in their path, and though they once or twice had a quick glimpse of a native man-creature among the trees, they never again made direct contact. They decided they rather liked a race of people who made it clear that they were grateful simply to be left alone.

The fruit and berries stopped after fifty miles, because that was where the sea started.

Having no pressing calls on their time they built a raft and crossed the sea. It was relatively calm, only about sixty miles wide and they had a reasonably pleasant crossing, landing in a country that was at least as beautiful as the one they had left.

Life was, in short, ridiculously easy and for a while at least they were able to cope with the problems of aimlessness and isolation by deciding to ignore them. When the craving for company became too great they would know where to find it, but for the moment they were happy to feel that the Golgafrinchans were hundreds of miles behind them.

Nevertheless, Ford Prefect began to use his Sub-Etha Sens-O-Matic more often again. Only once did he pick up a signal, but that was so faint and from such enormous distance that it depressed him more than the silence that had otherwise continued unbroken.

On a whim they turned northward. After weeks of traveling they came to another sea, built another raft and crossed it. This time it was harder going, the climate was getting colder. Arthur suspected a streak of masochism in Ford Prefect—the increasing difficulty of the journey seemed to give him a sense of purpose that was otherwise lacking. He strode onward relentlessly.

Their journey northward brought them into steep mountainous terrain of breathtaking sweep and beauty. The vast, jagged, snow-covered peaks ravished their senses. The cold began to bite into their bones.

They wrapped themselves in animal skins and furs which Ford Prefect acquired by a technique he once learned from a couple of ex-Pralite monks running a mind-surfing resort in the Hills of Hunian.

The Galaxy is littered with ex-Pralite monks, all on the make, because the mental control techniques the Order have evolved as a form of devotional discipline are, frankly, sensational—and extraordinary numbers of monks leave the Order just after they have finished their devotional training and just before they take their final vows to stay locked in small metal boxes for the rest of their lives.

Ford's technique seemed to consist mainly of standing still for a while and smiling.

After a while an animal—a deer perhaps—would appear from out of the trees and watch him cautiously. Ford would continue to smile at it, his eyes would soften and shine, and he would seem to radiate a deep and universal love, a love which reached out to embrace all of creation. A wonderful quietness would descend on the surrounding countryside, peaceful and serene, emanating from this transfigured man. Slowly the deer would approach, step by step, until it was almost nuzzling him, whereupon Ford Prefect would reach out to it and break its neck.

"Pheromone control," he said it was. "You just have to know how to generate the right smell."

few days after landing in this mountainous land they hit a coastline which swept diagonally before them from the southwest to the northeast, a coastline of monumental grandeur: deep majestic ravines, soaring pinnacles of ice—fjords.

For two further days they scrambled and climbed over the rocks and glaciers, awestruck with beauty.

"Arthur!" yelled Ford suddenly.

It was the afternoon of the second day. Arthur was sitting on a high rock watching the thundering sea smashing itself against the craggy promontories.

"Arthur!" yelled Ford again.

Arthur looked to where Ford's voice had come from, carried faintly in the wind.

Ford had gone to examine a glacier, and Arthur found him there crouching by the solid wall of the blue ice. He was tense with excitement—his eyes darted up to meet Arthur's.

"Look," he said, "look!"

Arthur looked. He saw the solid wall of blue ice.

"Yes," he said, "it's a glacier. I've already seen it."

"No," said Ford, "you've looked at it, you haven't seen it. Look."

Ford was pointing deep into the heart of the ice.

Arthur peered—he saw nothing but vague shadows.

"Move back from it," insisted Ford, "look again."

Arthur moved back and looked again.

"No," he said, and shrugged. "What am I supposed to be looking for?"

And suddenly he saw it.

"You see it?"

He saw it.

His mouth started to speak, but his brain decided it hadn't got anything to say yet and shut it again. His brain then started to contend with the problem of what his eyes told it they were looking at, but in doing so relinquished control of the mouth which promptly fell open again. Once more gathering up the jaw, his brain lost control of his left hand which then wandered around in an aimless fashion. For a second or so the brain tried to catch the left hand without letting go of the mouth and simultaneously tried to think about what was buried in the ice, which is probably why the legs went and Arthur dropped restfully to the ground.

The thing that had been causing all this neural upset was a network of shadows in the ice, about eighteen inches beneath the surface. Looked at from the right angle they resolved into the solid shapes of letters from an alien alphabet, each about three feet high; and for those, like Arthur, who couldn't read Magrathean there was above the letters the outline of a face hanging in the ice.

It was an old face, thin and distinguished, careworn but not unkind.

It was the face of the man who had won an award for designing the coastline they now knew themselves to be standing on.

A thin whine filled the air. It whirled and howled through the trees, upsetting the squirrels. A few birds flew off in disgust. The noise danced and skittered round the clearing. It whooped, it rasped, it generally offended.

The Captain, however, regarded the lone bagpiper with an indulgent eye. Little could disturb his equanimity; indeed, once he had got over the loss of his gorgeous bath during that unpleasantness in the swamp all those months ago he had begun to find his new life remarkably congenial. A hollow had been scooped out of a large rock which stood in the middle of the clearing, and in this he would bask daily while attendants sloshed water over him. Not particularly warm water, it must be said, as they hadn't yet worked out a way of heating it. Never mind, that would come, and in the meantime search parties were scouring the countryside far and wide for a hot spring, preferably one in a nice leafy glade, and if it was near a soap mine—perfection. To those who said that they had a feeling soap wasn't found in mines, the Captain had ventured to suggest that perhaps that was because no one had looked hard enough, and this possibility had been reluctantly acknowledged.

No, life was very pleasant, and the great thing about it was that when the hot spring was found, complete with leafy glade *en suite,* and when in the fullness of time the cry came reverberating across the hills that the soap mine had been located and was producing five hundred cakes a day it would be more pleasant still. It was very important to have things to look forward to.

Wail, wail, screech, wail, howl, honk, squeak went the bagpipes, increasing the Captain's already considerable pleasure at the thought that any moment now they might stop. That was something he looked forward to as well.

What else was pleasant, he asked himself? Well, so many things: the red and gold of the trees, now that autumn was approaching; the peaceful chatter of scissors a few feet from his bath where a couple of hairdressers were exercising their skills on a dozing art director and his assistant; the sunlight gleaming off the six shiny telephones lined up along the edge of his rock-hewn bath. The only thing nicer than a phone that didn't ring all the time (or indeed at all) was six phones that didn't ring all the time (or indeed at all).

Nicest of all was the happy murmur of all the hundreds of people slowly assembling in the clearing around him to watch the afternoon committee meeting.

The Captain punched his rubber duck playfully on the beak. The afternoon committee meetings were his favorite.

Other eyes watched the assembling crowds. High in a tree on the edge of the clearing squatted Ford Prefect, lately returned from foreign climes. After his six-month journey he was lean and healthy, his eyes gleamed, he wore a reindeer-skin coat; his beard was as thick and his face as bronzed as a country-rock singer's.

He and Arthur Dent had been watching the Golgafrinchans for almost a week now, and Ford had decided it was time to stir things up a bit.

The clearing was now full. Hundreds of men and women lounged around, chatting, eating fruit, playing cards and generally having a fairly relaxed time of it. Their track suits were now all dirty and even torn, but they all had immaculately styled hair. Ford was puzzled to see that many of them had stuffed their track suits full of leaves and wondered if this was meant to be some form of insulation against the coming winter. Ford's eyes narrowed. They couldn't be interested in botany all of a sudden could they?

In the middle of these speculations the Captain's voice rose above the hubbub.

"All right," he said, "I'd like to call this meeting to some sort of order, if that's at all possible. Is that all right with everybody?" He smiled genially. "In a minute. When you're all ready."

The talking gradually died away and the clearing fell silent, except for the bagpiper who seemed to be in some wild and uninhabitable musical world of his own. A few of those in his immediate vicinity threw some leaves to him. If there was any reason for this then it escaped Ford Prefect for the moment.

A small group of people had clustered round the Captain and one of them was clearly preparing to speak.

He did this by standing up, clearing his throat and then gazing off into the distance as if to signify to the crowd that he would be with them in a minute.

The crowd of course were riveted and all turned their eyes on him.

A moment of silence followed, which Ford judged to be the right dramatic moment to make his entry. The man turned to speak.

Ford dropped down out of the tree.

"Hi there," he said.

The crowd swiveled round.

"Ah, my dear fellow," called out the Captain, "got any matches on you? Or a lighter? Anything like that?"

"No," said Ford, sounding a little deflated. It wasn't what he'd prepared. He decided he'd better be a little stronger on the subject.

"No, I haven't," he continued. "No matches. Instead I bring you news..."

"Pity," said the Captain. "We've all run out you see. Haven't had a hot bath in weeks."

Ford refused to be headed off.

"I bring you news," he said, "of a discovery that might interest you."

"Is it on the agenda?" snapped the man whom Ford had interrupted.

Ford smiled a broad country-rock singer smile.

"Now, come on," he said.

"Well, I'm sorry," said the man huffily, "but speaking as a management consultant of many years' standing, I must insist on the importance of observing the committee structure."

Ford looked around the crowd.

"He's mad, you know," he said, "this is a prehistoric planet."

"Address the chair!" snapped the management consultant.

"There isn't a chair," explained Ford, "there's only a rock."

The management consultant decided that testiness was what the situation now called for.

"Well, call it a chair," he said testily.

"Why not call it a rock?" asked Ford.

"You obviously have no conception," said the management consultant, now abandoning testiness in favor of good old-fashioned hauteur, "of modern business methods."

"And you have no conception of where you are," said Ford.

A girl with a strident voice leaped to her feet and used it.

"Shut up, you two," she said, "I want to table a motion."

"You mean boulder a motion," tittered a hairdresser.

"Order, order!" yapped the management consultant.

"All right," said Ford, "let's see how you're doing." He plunked himself down on the ground to see how long he could keep his temper.

The Captain made a sort of conciliatory harrumphing noise.

"I would like to call to order," he said pleasantly, "the

five hundred and seventy-third meeting of the colonization committee of Fintlewoodlewix...."

Ten seconds, thought Ford, as he leaped to his feet again.

"This is futile," he exclaimed. "Five hundred and seventy-three committee meetings and you haven't even discovered fire yet!"

"If you would care," said the girl with the strident voice, "to examine the agenda sheet—"

"Agenda rock," trilled the hairdresser happily.

"Thank you, I've made that point," muttered Ford.

"...you...will...see..." continued the girl firmly, "that we are having a report from the hairdressers' Fire Development Subcommittee today."

"Oh...ah—" said the hairdresser with a sheepish look, which is recognized the whole Galaxy over as meaning "Er, will next Tuesday do?"

"All right," said Ford, rounding on him, "What have you done? What are you going to do? What are your thoughts on fire development?"

"Well, I don't know," said the hairdresser. "All they gave me was a couple of sticks...."

"So what have you done with them?"

Nervously, the hairdresser fished in his track suit top and handed over the fruits of his labor to Ford.

Ford held them up for all to see.

"Curling tongs," he said.

The crowd applauded.

"Never mind," said Ford. "Rome wasn't burned in a day."

The crowd hadn't the faintest idea what he was talking about, but they loved it nevertheless. They applauded.

"Well, you're obviously being totally naive of course," said the girl. "When you've been in marketing as long as I have you'll know that before any new product can be developed it has to be properly researched. We've got to find out what people want from fire, how they relate to it, what sort of image it has for them."

The crowd were tense. They were expecting something wonderful from Ford.

"Stick it up your nose," he said.

"Which is precisely the sort of thing we need to know," insisted the girl. "Do people want fire that can be fitted nasally?"

"Do you?" Ford asked the crowd.

"Yes!" shouted some.

"No!" shouted others happily.

They didn't know, they just thought it was great.

"And the wheel," said the Captain, "what about this wheel thingy? It sounds a terribly interesting project."

"Ah," said the marketing girl, "well, we're having a little difficulty there."

"Difficulty?" exclaimed Ford. "Difficulty? What do you mean, difficulty? It's the single simplest machine in the entire Universe!"

The marketing girl soured him with a look.

"All right, Mr. Wiseguy," she said, "you're so clever, you tell us what color it should be."

The crowd went wild. One up to the home team, they thought. Ford shrugged his shoulders and sat down again.

"Almighty Zarquon," he said, "have none of you done anything?"

As if in answer to his question there was a sudden clamor of noise from the entrance to the clearing. The crowd couldn't believe the amount of entertainment they were getting this afternoon: in marched a squad of about a dozen men dressed in the remnants of their Golgafrinchan 3rd Regiment dress uniforms. About half of them still carried Kill-O-Zap guns, the rest now carried spears which they struck together as they marched. They looked bronzed, healthy and utterly exhausted and bedraggled. They clattered to a halt and banged to attention. One of them fell over and never moved again.

"Captain, sir!" cried Number Two—for he was their leader—"Permission to report, sir!"

"Yes, Number Two, welcome back and all that. Find any hot springs?" said the Captain despondently.

"No, sir!"

"Thought you wouldn't."

Number Two strode through the crowd and presented arms before the bath.

"We have discovered another continent!"

"When was this?"

"It lies across the sea . . ." said Number Two, narrowing his eyes significantly, "to the east!"

"Ah."

Number Two turned to face the crowd. He raised his gun above his head. This is going to be great, thought the crowd.

"We have declared war on it!"

Wild abandoned cheering broke out in all corners of the clearing—this was beyond all expectation.

"Wait a minute," shouted Ford Prefect. "Wait a minute!"

He leaped to his feet and demanded silence. After a while he got it, or at least the best silence he could hope for under the circumstances: the circumstances were that the bagpiper was spontaneously composing a national anthem.

"Do we have to have the piper?" demanded Ford.

"Oh yes," said the Captain, "we've given him a grant."

Ford considered opening this idea up for debate but quickly decided that that way madness lay. Instead he slung a well judged rock at the piper and turned to face Number Two.

"War?" he said.

"Yes!" Number Two gazed contemptuously at Ford Prefect.

"On the next continent?"

"Yes! Total warfare! The war to end all wars!"

"But there's no one even living there yet!"

Ah, interesting, thought the crowd, nice point.

Number Two's gaze hovered undisturbed. In this respect his eyes were like a couple of mosquitoes that hover purposefully three inches from your nose and refuse to be deflected by arm thrashes, fly swats or rolled newspapers.

"I know that," he said, "but there will be one day! So we have left an open-ended ultimatum."

"What?"

"And blown up a few military installations."

The Captain leaned forward out of his bath.

"Military installations, Number Two?" he said.

For a moment the eyes wavered.

"Yes, sir, well potential military installations. All right ... trees."

The moment of uncertainty passed—his eyes flicked like whips over his audience.

"And," he roared, "we interrogated a gazelle!"

He flipped his Kill-O-Zap smartly under his arm and marched off through the pandemonium that had now erupted throughout the ecstatic crowd. A few steps was all he managed before he was caught up and carried shoulder high for a lap of honor around the clearing.

Ford sat and idly tapped a couple of stones together.

"So what else have you done?" he inquired after the celebrations had died down.

"We have started a culture," said the marketing girl.

"Oh yes?" said Ford.

"Yes. One of our film producers is already making a fascinating documentary about the indigenous cavemen of the area."

"They're not cavemen."

"They look like cavemen."

"Do they live in caves?"

"Well..."

"They live in huts."

"Perhaps they're having their caves redecorated," called out a wag from the crowd.

Ford rounded on him angrily.

"Very funny," he said, "but have you noticed that they're dying out?"

On their journey back, Ford and Arthur had come across two derelict villages and the bodies of many natives in the woods, where they had crept away to die. Those that still lived seemed stricken and listless, as if they were suffering from some disease of the spirit rather than the body. They moved sluggishly and with an infinite sadness. Their future had been taken away from them.

"Dying out!" repeated Ford. "Do you know what that means?"

"Er...we shouldn't sell them any life insurance?" called out the wag again.

Ford ignored him, and appealed to the whole crowd.

"Can you try and understand," he said, "that it's just since we've arrived here that they've started dying out!"

"In fact that comes over terribly well in this film," said the marketing girl, "and just gives it that poignant twist which is the hallmark of the really great documentary. The producer's very committed."

"He should be," muttered Ford.

"I gather," said the girl, turning to address the Captain who was beginning to nod off, "that he wants to make one about you next, Captain."

"Oh really?" he said, coming to with a start. "That's awfully nice."

"He's got a very strong angle on it, you know, the burden of responsibility, the loneliness of command...."

The Captain hummed and hahed about this for a moment.

"Well, I wouldn't overstress that angle, you know," he said finally. "One's never alone with a rubber duck."

He held the duck aloft and it got an appreciative round from the crowd.

All this while, the management consultant had been sitting in stony silence, his fingertips pressed to his temples to indicate that he was waiting and would wait all day if it was necessary.

At this point he decided he would not wait all day after all, he would merely pretend that the last half hour hadn't happened.

He rose to his feet.

"If," he said tersely, "we could for a moment move on to the subject of fiscal policy..."

"Fiscal policy!" whooped Ford Prefect. "Fiscal policy!"

The management consultant gave him a look that only a lungfish could have copied.

"Fiscal policy..." he repeated, "that is what I said."

"How can you have money," demanded Ford, "if none of you actually produces anything? It doesn't grow on trees you know."

"If you would allow me to continue..."

Ford nodded dejectedly.

"Thank you. Since we decided a few weeks ago to adopt the leaf as legal tender, we have, of course, all become immensely rich."

Ford stared in disbelief at the crowd who were murmuring appreciatively at this and greedily fingering the wads of leaves with which their track suits were stuffed.

"But we have also," continued the management consultant, "run into a small inflation problem on account of the high level of leaf availability, which means that, I gather, the current going rate has something like three deciduous forests buying one ship's peanut."

Murmurs of alarm came from the crowd. The management consultant waved them down.

"So in order to obviate this problem," he continued, "and effectively revalue the leaf, we are about to embark on a massive defoliation campaign, and . . . er, burn down all the forests. I think you'll all agree that's a sensible move under the circumstances."

The crowd seemed a little uncertain about this for a second or two until someone pointed out how much this would increase the value of the leaves in their pockets whereupon they let out whoops of delight and gave the management consultant a standing ovation. The accountants among them looked forward to a profitable autumn.

"You're all mad," explained Ford Prefect.

"You're absolutely barmy," he suggested.

"You're a bunch of raving nutters," he opined.

The tide of opinion was beginning to turn against

him. What had started out as excellent entertainment had now, in the crowd's view, deteriorated into mere abuse, and since this abuse was in the main directed at them they wearied of it.

Sensing this shift in the wind, the marketing girl turned on him.

"Is it perhaps in order," she demanded, "to inquire what you've been doing all these months then? You and that other interloper have been missing since the day we arrived."

"We've been on a journey," said Ford. "We went to try and find out something about this planet."

"Oh," said the girl archly, "doesn't sound very productive to me."

"No? Well, have I got news for you, my love. We have discovered this planet's future."

Ford waited for this statement to have its effect. It didn't have any. They didn't know what he was talking about.

He continued.

"It doesn't matter a pair of fetid dingo's kidneys what you all choose to do from now on. Burn down the forests, anything, it won't make a scrap of difference. Your future history has already happened. Two million years you've got and that's it. At the end of that time your race will be dead, gone and good riddance to you. Remember that, two million years!"

The crowd muttered to itself in annoyance. People as rich as they had suddenly become shouldn't be obliged to listen to this sort of gibberish. Perhaps they could tip the fellow a leaf or two and he would go away.

They didn't need to bother. Ford was already stalking out of the clearing, pausing only to shake his head at Number Two who was already firing his Kill-O-Zap into some neighboring trees.

He turned back once.

"Two million years!" he said and laughed.

"Well," said the Captain with a soothing smile, "still time for a few more baths. Could someone pass me the sponge? I just dropped it over the side."

A mile or so away through the wood, Arthur Dent was too busily engrossed with what he was doing to hear Ford Prefect approach.

What he was doing was rather curious, and this is what it was: on a wide flat piece of rock he had scratched out the shape of a large square, subdivided into one hundred and sixty-nine smaller squares, thirteen to a side.

Furthermore he had collected together a pile of smallish flattish stones and scratched the shape of a letter on to each. Sitting morosely around the rock were a couple of the surviving local native men to whom Arthur Dent was trying to introduce the curious concept embodied in these stones.

So far they had not done well. They had attempted to eat some of them, bury others and throw the rest of them away. Arthur had finally encouraged one of them to lay a couple of stones on the board he had scratched out, which was not even as far as he'd managed to get the day before. Along with the rapid deterioration in the morale of these creatures, there seemed to be a corresponding deterioration in their actual intelligence.

In an attempt to egg them along, Arthur set out a number of letters on the board himself, and then tried to encourage the natives to add some more themselves.

It was not going well.

Ford watched quietly from beside a nearby tree.

"No," said Arthur to one of the natives who had just shuffled some of the letters round in a fit of abysmal dejection, "*Q* scores ten you see, and it's on a triple word score, so...look, I've explained the rules to you...no, no, look please, put down that jawbone... All right, we'll start again. And try to concentrate this time."

Ford leaned his elbow against the tree and his hand against his head.

"What are you doing, Arthur?" he asked quietly.

Arthur looked up with a start. He suddenly had a feeling that all this might look slightly foolish. All he knew was that it had worked like a dream on him when he was a child. But things were different then, or rather would be.

"I'm trying to teach the cavemen to play Scrabble," he said.

"They're not cavemen," said Ford.

"They look like cavemen."

Ford let it pass.

"I see," he said.

"It's uphill work," said Arthur wearily. "The only word they know is *grunt* and they can't spell it."

He sighed and sat back.

"What's that supposed to achieve?" asked Ford.

"We've got to encourage them to evolve! To develop!" Arthur burst out angrily. He hoped that the weary sigh and then the anger might do something to counteract the overriding feeling of foolishness from which he was currently suffering. It didn't. He jumped to his feet.

"Can you imagine what a world would be like descended from those ... cretins we arrived with?" he said.

"Imagine?" said Ford, raising his eyebrows. "We don't have to imagine. We've seen it."

"But ..." Arthur waved his arms about hopelessly.

"We've seen it," said Ford, "there's no escape."

Arthur kicked at a stone.

"Did you tell them what we'd discovered?" he asked.

"Hmmmm?" said Ford, not really concentrating.

"Norway," said Arthur. "Slartibartfast's signature in the glacier. Did you tell them?"

"What's the point?" said Ford. "What would it mean to them?"

"Mean?" said Arthur. "Mean? You know perfectly well what it means, It means that this planet is the Earth! It's my home! It's where I was born!"

"Was?" said Ford.

"All right, will be."

"Yes, in two million years' time. Why don't you tell them that? Go and say to them, 'Excuse me, I'd just like to point out that in two million years' time I will be born just a few miles from here.' See what they say. They'll chase you up a tree and set fire to it."

Arthur absorbed this unhappily.

"Face it," said Ford, "those zeebs over there are your ancestors, not these poor creatures here."

He went over to where the apemen creatures were rummaging listlessly with the stone letters. He shook his head.

"Put the Scrabble away, Arthur," he said, "it won't save the human race, because this lot aren't going to be the human race. The human race is currently sitting around a rock on the other side of this hill making documentaries about themselves."

Arthur winced.

"There must be something we can do," he said. A terrible sense of desolation thrilled through his body that he should be here, on the Earth, the Earth which had lost its future in a horrifying arbitrary catastrophe and which now seemed set to lose its past as well.

"No," said Ford, "there's nothing we can do. This doesn't change the history of the Earth, you see, this *is* the history of the Earth. Like it or leave it, the Golgafrinchans are the people you are descended from. In two million years they get destroyed by the Vogons. History is never altered you see, it just fits together like a jigsaw. Funny old thing, life, isn't it?"

He picked up the letter *Q* and hurled it into a distant privet bush where it hit a young rabbit. The rabbit hurtled off in terror and didn't stop till it was set upon and eaten by a fox which choked on one of its bones and died on the bank of a stream which subsequently washed it away.

During the following weeks Ford Prefect swallowed his pride and struck up a relationship with a girl who had been a personnel officer on Golgafrincham, and he was terribly upset when she suddenly passed away as a result of drinking water from a pool that had been polluted by the body of a dead fox. The only moral it is possible to draw from this story is that one should never throw the letter *Q* into a privet bush, but unfortunately there are times when it is unavoidable.

Like most of the really crucial things in life, this chain of events was completely invisible to Ford Prefect and Arthur Dent. They were looking sadly at one of the natives morosely pushing the other letters around.

"Poor bloody caveman," said Arthur.

"They're not..."

"What?"

"Oh, never mind," said Ford.

The wretched creature let out a pathetic howling noise and banged on the rock.

"It's all been a bit of a waste of time for them, hasn't it?" said Arthur.

"Uh uh urghhhhh," muttered the native and banged on the rock again.

"They've been outevolved by telephone sanitizers."

"Urgh, grr grr, gruh!" insisted the native, continuing to bang on the rock.

"Why does he keep banging on the rock?" said Arthur.

"I think he probably wants you to Scrabble with him again," said Ford. "He's pointing at the letters."

"Probably spelled *crzjgrdwldiwdc* again, poor bastard. I keep on telling him there's only one g in *crzjgrdwldiwdc*."

The native banged on the rock again.

They looked over his shoulder.

Their eyes popped.

There among the jumble of letters were eight that had been laid out in a clear straight line.

They spelled two words.

The words were these:

"*Forty-Two.*"

"Grrrurgh guh guh," explained the native. He swept the letters angrily away and went and mooched under a nearby tree with his colleague.

Ford and Arthur stared at him. Then they stared at each other.

"Did that say what I thought it said?" they both said to each other.

"Yes," they both said.

"Forty-two," said Arthur.

"Forty-two," said Ford.

Arthur ran over to the two natives.

"What are you trying to tell us?" he shouted. "What's it supposed to mean?"

One of them rolled over on the ground, kicked his legs up in the air, rolled over again and went to sleep.

The other bounded up the tree and threw horse chestnuts at Ford Prefect. Whatever it was they had to say, they had already said it.

"You know what this means," said Ford.

"Not entirely."

"Forty-two is the number Deep Thought gave as being the Ultimate Answer."

"Yes."

"And the Earth is the computer Deep Thought designed and built to calculate the Question to the Ultimate Answer."

"So we are led to believe."

"And organic life was part of the computer matrix."

"If you say so."

"I do say so. That means that these natives, these apemen are an integral part of the computer program, and that we and the Golgafrinchans are *not*."

"But the cavemen are dying out and the Golgafrinchans are obviously set to replace them."

"Exactly. So you do see what this means."

"What?"

"Cock up," said Ford Prefect.

Arthur looked around him.

"This planet is having a pretty bloody time of it," he said.

Ford puzzled for a moment.

"Still, something must have come out of it," he said at last, "because Marvin said he could see the Question printed in your brain wave patterns."

"But . . ."

"Probably the wrong one, or a distortion of the right one. It might give us a clue though if we could find it. I don't see how we can though."

They moped about for a bit. Arthur sat on the ground and started pulling up bits of grass, but found that it wasn't an occupation he could get deeply engrossed in. It wasn't grass he could believe in, the trees seemed pointless, the rolling hills seemed to be rolling to nowhere and the future seemed just a tunnel to be crawled through.

Ford fiddled with his Sub-Etha Sens-O-Matic. It was silent. He sighed and put it away.

Arthur picked up one of the letter stones from his homemade Scrabble set. It was a *T*. He sighed and put it down again. The letter he put it down next to was an *I*. That spelled *IT*. He tossed another couple of letters next to them. They were an *S* and an *H* as it happened. By a curious coincidence the resulting word perfectly expressed the way Arthur was feeling about things just then. He stared at it for a moment. He hadn't done it deliberately, it was just a random chance. His brain got slowly into first gear.

"Ford," he said suddenly, "look, if that Question is printed in my brain wave patterns but I'm not consciously aware of it it must be somewhere in my unconscious."

"Yes, I suppose so."

"There might be a way of bringing that unconscious pattern forward."

"Oh yes?"

"Yes, by introducing some random element that can be shaped by that pattern."

"Like how?"

"Like by pulling Scrabble letters out of a bag blindfolded."

Ford leaped to his feet.

"Brilliant!" he said. He tugged his towel out of his satchel and with a few deft knots transformed it into a bag.

"Totally mad," he said, "utter nonsense. But we'll do it because it's brilliant nonsense. Come on, come on."

The sun passed respectfully behind a cloud. A few small sad raindrops fell.

They piled together all the remaining letters and dropped them into the bag. They shook them up.

"Right," said Ford, "close your eyes. Pull them out. Come on, come on, come on."

Arthur closed his eyes and plunged his hand into the

towel full of stones. He jiggled them about, pulled out four and handed them to Ford. Ford laid them along the ground in the order he got them.

"*W*," said Ford, "*H, A, T* ... What!"

He blinked.

"I think it's working!" he said.

Arthur pushed three more at him.

"*D, O, Y* ... Doy. Oh, perhaps it isn't working," said Ford.

"Here's the next three."

"*O, U, G* ... Doyoug.... It's not making sense I'm afraid."

Arthur pulled another two from the bag. Ford put them in place.

"*E, T*, doyouget.... Do you get!" shouted Ford. "It is working! This is amazing, it really is working!"

"More here." Arthur was throwing them out feverishly as fast as he could go.

"*I, F*," said Ford, "*Y, O, U*, ...*M, U, L, T, I, P, L, Y* ... What do you get if you multiply ...*S, I, X* ... six ...*B, Y*, by, six by ... what do you get if you multiply six by ...*N, I, N, E* ... six by nine..." He paused. "Come on, where's the next one?"

"Er, that's the lot," said Arthur, "that's all there were."

He sat back, nonplussed.

He rooted around again in the knotted up towel but there were no more letters.

"You mean that's it?" said Ford.

"That's it."

"Six by nine. Forty-two."

"That's it. That's all there is."

Chapter 34

The sun came out and beamed cheerfully at them. A bird sang. A warm breeze wafted through the trees and lifted the heads of the flowers, carrying their scent away through the woods. An insect droned past on its way to do whatever it is that insects do in the late afternoon. The sound of voices lilted through the trees followed a moment later by two girls who stopped in surprise at the sight of Ford Prefect and Arthur Dent apparently lying on the ground in agony, but in fact rocking with noiseless laughter.

"No, don't go," called Ford Prefect between gasps, "we'll be with you in just a moment."

"What's the matter?" asked one of the girls. She was the taller and slimmer of the two. On Golgafrincham she had been a junior personnel officer, but hadn't liked it much.

Ford pulled himself together.

"Excuse me," he said, "hello. My friend and I were just contemplating the meaning of life. Frivolous exercise."

"Oh, it's you," said the girl, "you made a bit of a spectacle of yourself this afternoon. You were quite funny to begin with but you did bang on a bit."

"Did I? Oh yes."

"Yes, what was all that for?" asked the other girl, a shorter, round-faced girl who had been an art director for a small advertising company on Golgafrincham. Whatever the privations of this world were, she went to sleep every night profoundly grateful for the fact that whatever she had to face in the morning it wouldn't be a hundred almost identical photographs of moodily lit tubes of toothpaste.

"For? For nothing. Nothing's *for* anything," said Ford Prefect happily. "Come and join us, I'm Ford, this is Arthur. We were just about to do nothing at all for a while but it can wait."

The girls looked at them doubtfully.

"I'm Agda," said the tall one, "this is Mella."

"Hello, Agda, hello, Mella," said Ford.

"Do you talk at all?" said Mella to Arthur.

"Oh, eventually," said Arthur with a smile, "but not as much as Ford."

"Good."

There was a slight pause.

"What did you mean," asked Agda, "about only having two million years? I couldn't make sense of what you were saying."

"Oh that," said Ford. "It doesn't matter."

"It's just that the world gets demolished to make way for a hyperspace bypass," said Arthur with a shrug. "But that's two million years away, and anyway it's just Vogons doing what Vogons do."

"Vogons?" said Mella.

"Yes, you wouldn't know them."

"Where'd you get this idea from?"

"It really doesn't matter. It's just like a dream from the past, or the future." Arthur smiled and looked away.

"Does it worry you that you don't talk any kind of sense?" asked Agda.

"Listen, forget it," said Ford, "forget all of it. Nothing matters. Look, it's a beautiful day, enjoy it. The sun, the green of hills, the river down in the valley, the burning trees."

"Even if it's only a dream, it's a pretty horrible idea," said Mella, "destroying a world just to make a bypass."

"Oh, I've heard of worse," said Ford. "I read of one planet off in the seventh dimension that got used as a ball in a game of intergalactic bar billiards. Got potted straight into a black hole. Killed ten billion people."

"That's mad," said Mella.

"Yes, only scored thirty points too."

Agda and Mella exchanged glances.

"Look," said Agda, "there's a party after the committee meeting tonight. You can come along if you like."

"Yeah, okay," said Ford.

"I'd like to," said Arthur.

Many hours later Arthur and Mella sat and watched the moon rise over the dull red glow of the trees.

"That story about the world being destroyed..." began Mella.

"In two million years, yes."

"You say it as if you really think it's true."

"Yes, I think it is. I think I was there."

She shook her head in puzzlement.

"You're very strange," she said.

"No, I'm very ordinary," said Arthur, "but some very strange things have happened to me. You could say I'm more differed from than differing."

"And that other world your friend talked about, the one that got pushed into a black hole."

"Ah, that I don't know about. It sounds like something from the book."

"What book?"

Arthur paused.

"*The Hitchhiker's Guide to the Galaxy,*" he said at last.

"What's that?"

"Oh, just something I threw into the river this evening. I don't think I'll be wanting it any more," said Arthur Dent.